The S. J. Clarke Publishing Company

The Biographical Record of Ogle County, Illinois

The S. J. Clarke Publishing Company

The Biographical Record of Ogle County, Illinois

ISBN/EAN: 9783337075088

Printed in Europe, USA, Canada, Australia, Japan

Cover: Foto ©ninafisch / pixelio.de

More available books at **www.hansebooks.com**

BIOGRAPHICAL RECORD

OF

OGLE COUNTY,

ILLINOIS.

ILLUSTRATED

"Biography is the only true history." Emerson.

PREFACE.

HE greatest of English historians, MACAULAY, and one of the most brilliant writers of the present century, has said: "The history of a country is best told in a record of the lives of its people." In conformity with this idea, the BIOGRAPHICAL RECORD has been prepared. Instead of going to musty records, and taking therefrom dry statistical matter that can be appreciated by but few, our corps of writers have gone to the people, the men and women who have, by their enterprise and industry, brought this county to a rank second to none among those comprising this great and noble State, and from their lips have the story of their life struggles. No more interesting or instructive matter could be presented to an intelligent public. In this volume will be found a record of many whose lives are worthy the imitation of coming generations. It tells how some, commencing life in poverty, by industry and economy have accumulated wealth. It tells how others, with limited advantages for securing an education, have become learned men and women, with an influence extending throughout the length and breadth of the land. It tells of men who have risen from the lower walks of life to eminence as statesmen, and whose names have become famous. It tells of those in every walk in life who have striven to succeed, and records how that success has usually crowned their efforts. It tells also of many, very many, who, not seeking the applause of the world, have pursued the "even tenor of their way," content to have it said of them, as Christ said of the woman performing a deed of mercy—"They have done what they could." It tells how many, in the pride and strength of young manhood, left the plow and the anvil, the lawyer's office and the counting-room, left every trade and profession, and at their country's call went forth valiantly "to do or die," and how through their efforts the Union was restored and peace once more reigned in the land. In the life of every man and of every woman is a lesson that should not be lost upon those who follow after.

Coming generations will appreciate this volume and preserve it as a sacred treasure, from the fact that it contains so much that would never find its way into public records, and which would otherwise be inaccessible. Great care has been taken in the compilation of the work, and every opportunity possible given to those represented to insure correctness in what has been written; and the publishers flatter themselves that they give to their readers a work with few errors of consequence. In addition to biographical sketches, portraits of a number of representative citizens are given.

The faces of some, and biographical sketches of many, will be missed in this volume. For this the publishers are not to blame. Not having a proper conception of the work, some refused to give the information necessary to compile a sketch, while others were indifferent. Occasionally some member of the family would oppose the enterprise, and on account of such opposition the support of the interested one would be withheld. In a few instances men never could be found, though repeated calls were made at their residence or place of business.

May, 1899.   THE S. J. CLARKE PUBLISHING CO.

BIOGRAPHICAL.

HON. ROBERT R. HITT, who has so ably represented his district as a member of congress, since 1882, is without doubt the most distinguished of the citizens of Ogle county. It is not an easy matter to briefly write the record of such a man, especially for perusal by his old friends and acquaintances, many of whom have known him from early childhood, and to whom his record is like an open book. For him they have the greatest admiration, and to them no honors bestowed upon him could be thought undeserved. He belongs to them, and while they know him he also knows them, and few there be of the old settlers of Ogle county that he cannot call by name.

Robert Roberts Hitt was born in Urbana, Champaign county, Ohio, January 16, 1834, and is the second son of Rev. Thomas S. Hitt, who drove across the country from his Ohio home in 1837 and made himself and family a home in Ogle county, where the remainder of his life was spent. He located in Maryland colony, so called because of the number of settlers from that state who had migrated to northern Illinois, led by Samuel Merritt Hitt, an elder brother of Rev. Thomas, and a man of remarkable mental attainments and strong personality. One of the pioneers of Ogle county, he brought with him from Maryland a well-filled purse in addition to a fine college education, two attributes that commanded the deepest respect in that struggling community, where ready cash in particular was all too scarce. By entry and purchase Squire Hitt secured thousands of acres of the best farming lands for his brothers and sisters, who hastened westward to occupy the choice sites thus selected, so that in a short time the "tribe of Hittites," as an old circuit-rider jokingly dubbed the colony, was a powerful factor in that new country.

Some of the old settlers who have not forgotten the characteristics of the Hitt tribe say the family was noted for its fine physical appearance, whose six feet of manhood and womanhood did full credit to its Kentucky origin. Rev. Thomas Smith Hitt, who was born in Bourbon county, Kentucky, at the close of the last century, was a trifle over six feet tall, and, like his father before him, was a pronounced anti-slavery man. It was this predilection which led old Martin Hitt, grandfather of the present congressman, to move across to Ohio in 1816, where his first act was to free his slaves. Twenty-one years later his son Thomas, with his young family, moved to Illinois, attracted thither by the glowing accounts of the country as reported by Squire Hitt, who left Maryland for Illinois in 1836, one year in advance of his relations.

A warm adherent of the Methodist church, of which he was an ordained minister, as was also his father, Rev. Martin Hitt, Rev. Thomas S. Hitt was well fitted by education and temperament to promote the interests of Methodism in the newly settled country to which he had migrated, and when the name of Mt. Morris, in honor of the Methodist bishop, was given to the Maryland colony, Rev. Thomas Hitt was one of the first to suggest the founding of a seminary by the conference. Through his efforts, ably seconded by his brother, Squire Hitt, Rock River Seminary was called into existence, in whose historical walls many of the most illustrious sons of Illinois—men famous in the forum and on the battlefield —received their education.

Here young Robert Hitt early went to school, and here, too, contemporary with him, only in older classes, were Senator Cullom, Governor Beveridge, State Senator Beveridge, John Rawlins, secretary of war under Grant; Judge Cothran, of the supreme court of Wisconsin; Congressman Magoon, and many other students who later rose to eminence in their respective professions. Of a genial disposition and remarkably proficient in his studies, Robert Hitt, although much younger than the majority of the lads with whom he associated, was a great favorite with all, and when he left Mt. Morris to complete his education at Asbury University, in Greencastle, Indiana, no one in the circle was missed more than he.

The fact that he outstripped his companions in the race for college honors and graduated while but a youth attests his love for knowledge and early discipline of mind and determined application to which he owes his success in life. While but a lad he developed a fondness for phonography, and giving to the art all his leisure hours became an expert, and upon the completion of his education went forth into the world well equipped to enter what was then a comparatively new field of usefulness, and today he is one of the most remarkable men in the public life of America of this generation.

The commencement of his public career is contemporaneous with the agitation of the question of the perpetuation or overthrow of the institution of slavery in the United States. He was the pioneer newspaper reporter of the west and through the instrumentality of his skill, tact, quick intelligence and a capacity that lay in many directions, coupled with a breadth of mind capable of comprehending and appreciating all the phases of that humane and magnificent enterprise in which his great party had its birth, the world was given the merits of the memorable Lincoln and Douglas debate of 1858, upon which the glorious battle of liberty was fought and won.

In one of his published reminiscences, Albert Woodcock, an old citizen of the state, speaks of the debate at Freeport, and the part taken in it by Mr. Hitt:

"A stand was erected in the field adjacent to the city. Thousands of people gathered about the platform. The speakers were ready. The throng was impatient. The tall form of Lincoln arose. He looked anxiously over the crowd. He called out 'Where's Hitt? Is Hitt present?' Hitt, from the extreme outskirts of the living mass, answered, 'Here I am, but I cannot get to the platform.' The good-natured people understood the situation. They seized the slender youth and passed him over their heads to the stand."

The story became current that Lincoln was always asking, "Where is Bob Hitt?" And "Bob" found himself famous. He happened in this connection to do an important historical service. All civilized people know now how excellent was Lincoln's command of language, and how admirable his literary form. He was a master of speech; but during the Lincoln-Douglas campaign the Douglas party assailed him as illiterate, and charged that Hitt touched up all his speeches so as to make them presentable. This Mr. Hitt always denied, stating that frequently his phonographic notes were written out by an assistant, and he did not see the transcription from his notes until it was printed.

During the legislative sessions of the assembly of Illinois, in 1858, '59 and '60, Mr. Hitt was the official reporter employed by the state. In 1860, when the trouble arose in the department of the Missouri, under General Fremont, calling for immediate examination, Mr. Lincoln sent the Holt-Davis commission to St. Louis, and Mr. Hitt was there laboriously engaged for many months as its secretary in that memorable investigation. This duty called for the exercise of abilities of no common order, and the work was one of immediate importance and historical value. Its voluminous reports, which detailed the disorders of the unfortunate Fremont *regime* in Missouri, led to many and important changes and improvements in the efficiency of that department.

Judge Holt, ex-secretary of war, in the account of their labors, which he submitted to the president, paid a high tribute to the value of Mr. Hitt's services. The severity of the labors attendant upon this duty brought on a long illness, and after his recovery he reported in person to Secretary Stanton, who requested him to remain at the war department for important confidential work and duties in the department of military justice. In 1863 he was engaged in the senate of the United States as secretary of a committee examining into the naval expeditions of Burnside and Banks. In 1865 he accompanied a board of treaty commissioners to the northwest, ascending the Missouri river a distance of one thousand five hundred miles, for the purpose of negotiating with the Indian tribes in what was then a wilderness, which he described in letters to the Chicago Tribune as the "abomination of desolation," a lonely desert, scourged by ferocious savages. It has now thousands of homesteads scattered over it and is increasing every month in population. He returned home in the fall of the same year. Most of the following year he passed at Washington and at Raleigh, North Carolina, as recorder of military courts, spending the summer months at home.

In 1867-8 he visited Scotland, Switzerland, Greece, Egypt, and Palestine, spending five weeks in Jerusalem. He visited the famous plain of Marathon, though warned against robbers, and told he certainly would be taken by bandits and probably killed. He dressed in a wretched old suit borrowed from a peasant, mounted the worst horse to be had, and took a Greek history and a wallet with a few coppers. He had hardly opened his book on the ancient battle-field when robbers came sure enough and seized him. He begged for food, and they gave him black bread, which he ate with avidity, though it was a horror, and gave each of them a copper. That was too much, and they let him go.

In 1871 he went to Santo Domingo, with the three commissioners—Senator Ben Wade, of Ohio; President White, of Cornell University, and Dr. Samuel G. Howe, the Boston philanthropist, who were sent to that island by President Grant to inquire into its resources and affairs, with a view to its annexation to the United States. Mr. Hitt prepared their report, an interesting and valuable work, of which fifty thousand copies were printed.

In the latter part of this year and in 1872 he was busily engaged as reporter of the noted Kuklux committee of the two houses, and wrote a large portion of their enormously extensive report, in thirteen volumes, exhibiting in great detail the political condition of the southern states, nearly every one of which he visited with the committee. For some time after this he acted as private secretary of Senator O. P. Morton, who was one of the great leaders of the Republican party.

In 1873 the Rock River Seminary had become so embarrassed that the school stopped and the creditors sold it out. Mr. Hitt, not forgetful of the deep interest taken in it long ago by his father, bought it, put it in repair, and it was started again with a corps of excellent teachers. It became again a good school, though it brought no money profit to repay his liberality. After six years he transferred it to the Brethren, or Dunkards, who are carrying it on with continuous efficiency.

On the 28th of October, 1874, Mr. Hitt was united in marriage with Miss Sallie Reynolds, of Lafayette, Indiana, of whom it has been beautifully and truly said, "Gifted and highly educated, she is a charming and sweet-spirited woman, and her heart is in the work of her husband." Immediately after their marriage, they sailed for Europe, and while on their wedding tour, in December, 1874, Mr. Hitt was appointed by President Grant secretary of the legation at Paris, in which position he was continued under President Hayes. During their official residence of six years in Paris the home of the secretary of the legation and his charming wife was the center of a distinguished coterie of Americans and foreigners who were no less captivated by the intellect, courtliness and tact of Secretary Hitt than by his wife's brilliant conversational powers and her talents as a most entertaining hostess.

Two sons were born during their residence abroad, Robert Reynolds and William Floyd.

Returning to this country, in 1880, and while at his home in Mount Morris, Mr. Hitt one day received an urgent telegram from Mr. Blaine, secretary of state under President Garfield, asking him to come to Washington immediately. Supposing the secretary wished to consult him regarding French affairs, the late secretary of legation hastened to the capital, and to his great surprise was there asked to fill the post of assistant secretary of state. After a brief consideration Mr. Hitt accepted the honor, and it is noteworthy that from that time until the hour of his death the brilliant secretary and his able assistant remained on terms of intimate relationship with each other. When Blaine resigned the state portfolio after President Garfield's death, Mr. Hitt went out with his chief the same day. President Arthur had a high opinion of Assistant Secretary Hitt, and would gladly have given him a responsible mission abroad, but, wisely enough, the proffered honor was declined, Mr. Hitt believing he had been away from home too long already.

The sudden death of Congressman Hawk, of the sixth Illinois district, June 29, 1882, two days before the convention to nominate a candidate, upset all preconceived plans, and a committee asked Mr. Hitt if it might present his name. The convention approved the choice and Mr. Hitt was nominated, elected, and has since been continued in congress. Writing of Mr. Hitt's personality in a recent number of Harper's Weekly, the veteran Washington correspondent, Murat Halstead, after commenting on Mr. Hitt's useful career in congress, where his habits of industry and his information, knowledge of men and nations, history and languages and the varied phases of public life at home and abroad have given him high distinction, continuing, says:

"His congressional work has been chiefly done in the committee on foreign relations. He is a positive and systematic protectionist, was an early advocate of removing the duty on sugar and strongly against reducing the tax on whisky. He has attempted to regulate the jurisdiction of consuls, as he well knew their deficiencies, and he strongly urged, when he had little company, the observance of treaty stipulations with the Chinese. The vigilance and experience of Mr. Hitt on the committee on foreign relations have been of general and marked value. In the Cutting case he saved congress from making a mistaken menace against Mexico. On the Hawaiian intervention he delivered a speech of extraordinary energy and acumen and thoroughness. Perhaps the strongest of all his speeches was on 'Commercial Union with Canada.' Mr. Hitt wears well and is a satisfactory example of the value of the training of journalism for public life."

From 1883 until 1890 his party were in minority in congress, but Mr. Hitt advanced in grade, step by step, till he became the leading member of the Republican minority in the committee on foreign affairs and its representative on the floor of the house, which gave opportunity for important services to the country. For example, in 1888, when a measure was brought in by the administration authorizing an immediate threatening demand upon Mexico for the instant liberation of Cutting, which the committee on the previous day had endorsed, and the whole house was about to adopt, Mr. Hitt, having in the interval made sure of the real facts, that Cutting was not held oppressively and that the Mexican government was most anxious to do anything we requested, and that the inflamed state of feeling in Mexico would be fanned into an attack upon Mexico and another disgraceful Mexican war, if such a resolution were passed, in a short, clean speech, reversed opinion in the house, defeated the resolution and prevented infinite mischief, or war.

He was an advocate of wider commerce with our neighbors on the south and north. He introduced and secured the unanimous adoption by the house in March, 1889, of a resolution contemplating complete commercial union with Canada, which, once in operation, would ultimately result in peaceful annexation. His speech on this measure, Murat Halstead said, "was a thorough and logical presentation of a great, far-reaching proposition."

In the previous session, in September, 1888, when President Cleveland's Canadian retaliation message came suddenly in, right in the midst of the presidential campaign, he exposed the mischievous character of this electioneering device to catch Irish votes, and discussed the whole question searchingly. A long debate ensued. Hon. Bourke Cockran replied to the argument, but saying of his opponent

"Mr. Speaker: The distinguishing address on the other side, the one that has furnished the key-note to this discussion, was the very able and eloquent speech of the gentleman from Illinois (Mr. Hitt), to whom, and to whom alone, is due the credit of lifting the debate to a high plane of parliamentary procedure. But I regret to say that while the speech was eloquent, it lacked those elements of candor and fairness that would have made it the greatest speech of the session."

In 1887 and afterwards he supported the interstate commerce law, taking exception only to the long-and-short-haul clause as injurious to his constituents.

In 1890, when the Republicans came into power and the memorable struggle of the Reed congress began, he was at last made chairman of the committee on foreign affairs, and has since held that position whenever his party was in power, and when they were in minority leading the minority on questions of foreign policy.

He has been an active member of congress on all current legislation. He efficiently supported the oleomargarine bill to protect genuine butter from bogus butter being sold under the same name, the bill to check counterfeiting lard and other meat products, and to promote and facilitate their exportation on favorable terms. He urged the law passed to foil the subtle attack on the moral sense of the people by the liquor interest sheltering itself under a provision of the interstate commerce act as construed by a decision of the supreme court. The original package law abrogated that decision, and left the state free to regulate the sale of liquors, whether imported into the state in original packages or not. He attacked the Louisiana lottery swindle, which was using the postal system until a bill was passed prohibiting the United States mails from being made the instrument of their nefarious business.

When in 1890, provision was to be made for a World's fair in 1893, he supported the claims of Chicago as the best site; and he and Mr. Springer were appointed the two Illinois members of the special committee to which the subject was entrusted. He had charge of the bill when it came before the house; and as the result of long, hard labor, Chicago was victorious. His speech in advocacy of Chicago, February 20, 1890, presented the claims of that city in the strongest light. On the seventh vote, Chicago received one hundred and fifty-seven votes—exactly a majority.

He was during the eighties returned in "off years" by about three thousand five hundred majority, in presidential years by about six thousand five hundred majority, until 1890, when, in the tempest of dissatisfaction after the passage of the McKinley bill, just before election, he was well nigh defeated, receiving only five hundred and eleven majority. In subsequent elections, with the great popularity of the same measure after it had been in operation, the old time majorities were renewed. After the Wilson tariff bill passed in 1894, his majority rose to twelve thousand, and in 1896, with increased dissatisfaction over the results of that bill, his majority was nearly eighteen thousand; and again in 1898 it was over fifteen thousand, though it was an "off year."

By watching and urging local interests in his own district, Mr. Hitt obtained an appropriation of one hundred thousand dollars for the improvement of Galena river, one hundred thousand dollars for a public building at Rockford, and in 1899, seventy-five thousand dollars for a public building at Freeport.

He has advocated and secured the passage of various measures to promote reciprocity and increase trade with the other American republics; and each year has watched that liberal provision be made for this cause and for the Bureau of American Republics in the consular and diplomatic appropriation bill, of which the chairman of foreign affairs has charge in its framing and in its passage through the house and through the conference committee with the senate.

In 1890 he brought in a resolution recognizing the Republic of Brazil, which was soon unanimously passed. His conservative counsel and course contributed to the prompt and peaceful settlement of the difficulties with Chili in 1892.

In the same year, when a proposition was made by the majority to reduce our mission to Venezuela in grade, he seized the opportunity, in opposing it, to call public attention to the encroachment of England upon that feeble republic, in violation of our Monroe doctrine. When, in December, 1895, President Cleveland sent in his Venezuelan message demanding a just settlement of this question between Great Britain and the helpless republic, which was being gradually swallowed, Mr. Hitt immediately prepared and offered a bill providing for a commission to investigate and report the true divisional line, which he urged in such a patriotic spirit upon all parties that it was at once unanimously adopted; by thus referring the question to a calm tribunal, the public alarm was quieted. The unanimity of the American congress led Lord Salisbury to yield to investigation and arbitration, which the British government had twice before refused.

Mr. Hitt has labored to improve the efficiency of our consular service. He delivered an address on the subject before the Boston Merchants' Association in 1893. In a speech in the house April 17, 1894, he discussed the general subject and mercilessly exposed the recent scandals in the sale of public office and the degradation of the service. He has been for many years an agent of the Smithsonian institution. In 1895 he was appointed by Speaker Crisp, one of the delegates to the expected international monetary conference.

He endeavored, successfully, in 1893 to secure the passage of a bill to check the abuses and violations of the interstate commerce act by Canadian railways. He moved an amendment to the Wilson tariff bill, January 20, 1894, to secure reciprocity with Canada in coal, instead of granting the free admission of Canadian coal without compensation. He again tried to amend the Wilson tariff act, January 29, 1895, by striking out the extra duty on refined sugar, which was there solely to protect the sugar trust.

Several times he has advocated and urged the construction of a cable to Hawaii, in 1890, and again in 1895, when he discussed the matter at length and thoroughly.

In 1894 he arraigned in a strenuous speech the policy of President Cleveland in trying to overthrow the republican government in Hawaii and restore the ex-queen; and in 1898 he brought in the measure for the annexation of the Hawaiian islands, which passed the house June 5. Very soon afterwards he was appointed by the President one of the commissioners to visit the islands, examine the government and recommend necessary legislation to congress. With Senators Cullom and Morgan, he went to the islands, and when congress met in troduced in the house a bill, the result of their labors, to organize the territory of Hawaii.

In 1896 when the struggle in Cuba seemed to be regarded by President Cleveland with indifference, he brought in and advocated a resolution expressing the opinion of the house that a state of war existed, the parties to which were entitled to belligerent rights. It passed, but no heed was paid to it.

President McKinley desired to appoint Mr. Hitt minister to Spain when the gravest questions were pending, but he did not accept.

In the spring of 1898, when, with the the change of administration, there was expectation of change in events, and great impatience for some immediate action by the house, he made a speech or statement which, by its conservative tone and assurances, did much to satisfy opinion and prevent hasty action upon a resolution which the senate had passed, recognizing the Cuban republic, and which would have brought embarrassing complications in the war.

In 1895 Mr. Hitt suffered a long and severe illness, from which he did not recover full health for nearly two years. In January, 1897, when the election of United States senator was impending, Mr. Hitt was supported in an animated and agreeable contest by the members of the legislature from his part of the state, but was not elected. He is a member of the fifty-sixth congress, which meets December 4, 1899.

In his own district Mr. Hitt is very popular. There is an entire absence of the dictator in his political composition. He never meddles with the local campaigns, has no desire to "boss" any town or county convention and is proud of the fact that no "machine" prevails in his district. In Ogle county, for example, there are often five or six different candidates running for the same office, and the people usually have the voice and vote to say which is their choice. In all his campaigns his personality counts much. He is the same "Bob" Hitt to-day that he was a score of years ago, with a kindly word for all his constituents, and ready to give his advice and the benefit of his experience to Republican or Democrat alike.

On the platform he maintains the fair ground of debate, never makes the Democrats angry by innuendos or vituperation, but tries to score his points by a clear, incisive presentation of his case that is well calculated to carry conviction to the hearts and minds of his hearers. Animated in tone, he assumes a conversational style of address, and is never dull. He pronounces distinctly, leaves no doubt about the meaning he intends to convey, and has a vocabulary that is large and particularly well chosen. He has a most retentive memory, and it is said of him that he knows the personal history of every family living in his district, most of the voters of which he can call by their given names.

It is an entertainment in itself to watch Mr. Hitt on the platform just prior to a political gathering or an old settlers' meeting where he is to deliver an address. Easy and natural in manner, he is at once the master of ceremonies as well as the distinguished guest.

"Now, Uncle Daniel," he will say, "you can't see anything over there; just step forward and take this seat," at the same time placing a chair in a convenient spot where the old gentleman addressed may best see and hear everything. In this way Mr. Hitt gets close to the people, chats with them about their personal affairs and dropping politics folds his hands and discusses those simple, every-day occurrences that, after all, are nearest the heart. The Dunkards, of which denomination there is a strong following in his district, and who, allied to no particular party, vote according to the dictates of conscience, have an abiding respect for Mr. Hitt, whom they greatly admire for his squareness and high purpose. That they stand by him in every election is proof "strong as holy writ" of the sterling character of the man whom the sixth district delights to honor.

As already intimated, Mr. Hitt is a modest man and is rarely heard on the platform outside his district. He has repeatedly been invited to deliver addresses in Chicago and elsewhere before social and semi-political bodies, but has invariably asked to be excused, although, it is safe to say, fewer public speakers are better qualified by nature to interest an audience than he. An omnivorous reader, his entire house at Mount Morris might be termed a library, for every room teems with "man's best gift to man." Notwithstanding his strong practical sense, there is a fine undercurrent of sentiment in his composition which softens and at the same time elevates the man. The death of his beloved mother on his return from Paris in 1880 was a severe blow to one who fairly idolized the woman who bore him, and to whom for years he had carried every confidence and with whom he had discussed every move of his life. His father having died many years before, the bond between the mother and son was more strongly cemented, although for the memory of his father Mr. Hitt has the most tender regard. It is his wish that his two sons may forever keep intact the homestead farm which their grandfather received from the government in 1837, and which, curious to relate, is the only landed property held by the Hitts in Ogle county, where once their forefathers were possessed of thousands of acres.

Mr. Hitt is just as popular in Washington as he is at home, and some of the best and brainiest people of the country are proud to claim his friendship, as he is theirs. The late James G. Blaine, William Walter Phelps and James Russell Lowell were among his warmest friends, and between him and big brainy Tom Reed, of Maine, there is a deep and long-standing attachment. Mrs. Hitt is justly regarded as one of the best entertainers at Washington, and during the season their beautiful home is in a constant state of receptivity. Vivacious, beautiful, full of tact and graciousness, she is an ideal wife of a public man, and both in his official and home life the able congressman is rarely blessed in this respect. Murat Halstead, in an interesting article in Harper's Weekly, says: "Mr. Hitt's knowledge of Europe enhances his estimation of America. He has known two generations of our foremost men of affairs, from Lincoln and Douglas to Blaine, Harrison and Cleveland; and in the rare scope of his recollections and the invaluable education of his personal services he has retained and refined, and holds with unaffected dignity, the simple modesty of his laborious early manhood; and there is no more attractive household than in the happy, hospitable homes his wife and sons grace and enliven at Mt. Morris and in Washington."

PETER B. WRAGG, whose farm lies in sections 5 and 6, Grand Detour township, is a native of Ogle county, born December 22, 1852, and is the son of Peter and Nancy Jane (Thompson) Wragg, the former a native of England, born October 4, 1814, and the latter of Washington county, Maryland, born April 23, 1825. They were the parents of the following named children: William H., born February 13, 1846; Sarah, October 3, 1847, and who is now the wife of William Hoffman; Ann E., January 17, 1850; Mary I., August 10, 1851; Peter B., December 22, 1852; Daniel S., April 18, 1854; Edward F., June 3, 1857, and who died April 6, 1860; John M., April 7, 1861; and Martha E., wife of John Nettz, April 11, 1863.

Peter Wragg was the son of Peter F. and Hannah (Smith) Wragg, also natives of England. Being put out to service on a farm, at which he was displeased, at the age of fourteen he ran away, and joined his brother, Thomas, who came to America a short time previously. The two brothers engaged at work in a saw and planing mill in Troy for about six years, and then determined to come west, having heard of the great opportunities afforded the poor man in what was known as the Prairie state. On coming to Ogle county, Peter Wragg found employment in a sawmill at Grand Detour, where he remained two years, saving his earnings and investing the same in government land. He later engaged in breaking prairie and freighting to and from Chicago, to Peoria and the Galena lead mines. He was married June 17, 1845, to Miss Nancy Jane Thompson, daughter of James and Judith (Funck) Thompson, and soon after located on a farm on section 32, Pine Creek township, which was his home for about eighteen months, when he moved to the farm in Grand Detour township now owned by our subject. Commencing life in this country with a capital of two shillings, which he had on landing, by his industry and good management, assisted by his faithful wife, he succeeded in accumulating much property, having at the time of his death, in January, 1892, some fifteen hundred acres of good land, besides his personal property. Politically he was a Democrat. While he could neither read nor write, he was a man of great natural ability, and a good business man.

Peter B. Wragg was reared on the old home farm on which he still resides. He was early learned to know the meaning of hard work, and when quite young was expected to do his full share of farm labor. He never shirked his duty and toiled early and late, assisting in the cultivation of the farm. On the 12th of January, 1875, he was united in marriage with Miss Margaret Ellen Nettz, who was born March 8, 1856, in Pine Creek township, and a daughter of Jacob and Ruann (Drenner) Netts, both of whom were natives of Washington county, Maryland, and who came to Ogle county in 1855. The former was born May 24, 1813, and the latter September 17, 1819. They were the parents of twelve children, four of whom died in infancy or early childhood. The living are: Mary E., born December 28, 1836; Joseph H., December 10, 1840; Amanda Caroline, September 17, 1847; Jacob F., January 18, 1854; Margaret Ellen, March 8, 1856; Lyida A., February 8, 1858; Alice Amelia, July 14, 1862, and Clara, March 30, 1850. By trade Jacob Nettz was a blacksmith, but on coming to Ogle county he followed farming in connection with his trade. He died November 18, 1898. To Mr. and Mrs. Wragg one child has been born, Lura May, born July 3, 1885, and who is now attending the district school.

The subject of this sketch has made his home on the farm where he now resides with the exception of three years. In addition to the cultivation of his farm he has been raising red and black polled Angus cattle, Morgan and Norman horses, and Poland-China hogs. He is meeting with success in his chosen calling and has the confidence of the community in which he resides. In politics he is a Democrat, and for nine years has served as school director. Religiously, he and his wife are members of the Christian church.

MICHAEL MILLER, now living a retired life in the village of Haldane, was for years numbered among the active farmers and business men of Ogle county. He is a native of Germany, born in Hessen Darmstadt, February 10, 1831, and is a son of John and Amelia Carlotte Miller, both of whom were natives of the same country. In early life the father engaged in farming, and in later life was in the hotel business. He died in his native land in 1840. His wife survived him about ten years. Our subject is the youngest of their family of thirteen children who grew to mature years. He and his brother Nicholas, now residing in Adair county, Missouri, are the only survivors.

Michael Miller grew to manhood in his native land and received a good education in the German and French languages. His knowledge of English was acquired after his removal to this country. In his youth he learned the blacksmith trade, at which he became quite proficient before his emigration to the United States. His native land afforded little inducements to the poor man to acquire either wealth or position, and so he determined to come to a country where an equal chance was given to all alike. Accordingly he set sail for New York, by way of Rotterdam and London. His vessel was a slow sailing one and he was thirty-five days on the Atlantic ocean, a voyage which can now be made in six days. While on the voyage they encountered but one severe storm.

Mr. Miller arrived in New York the week before Christmas in 1853, and at once set out for Chambersburg, Pennsylvania, where he went to work at his trade, and continued there nearly two years. He then came to Illinois and located at Freeport. The first Sunday at that place he saw what to him was a strange sight, a wagon loaded with people coming into church, the wagon being drawn by oxen. For about one year he remained at Freeport, working at his trade, and then moved to Mt. Morris, where he continued at his trade for a year and a half. He then returned to Pennsylvania, and was married at Chambersburg, August 16, 1857, to Miss Margaret Florig, a native of Hessen Darmstadt, Germany, but reared in Baden. Her father, Leonholt Florig, also a native of Germany, was a miller and baker by trade. In 1852 he removed with his family to the United States and settled in Chambersburg, Pennsylvania, and there spent the remainder of his life. Mrs. Miller is the oldest of a family of eight children, of whom three only survive, the others being Mrs. Catherine Bowers and Mrs. Eva Burket, both residing in Chambersburg, Pennsylvania.

After marriage, Miller returned with his bride to Illinois and located at Polo, where he worked at his trade about nine months, and March 12, 1858, removed to Haldane, where he built a shop and began working at his trade, at which he continued to work for thirty-five years. For many years he had the only shop in the place, and in connection had a wagon repair shop. In 1861 he built a residence and located on the lots where he now resides. He also bought a a tract of sixty-two acres near the village, which later his sons began to cultivate. He also bought eight acres adjoining the village which he had platted as an addition to the village. He still owns the farm, which lies about one mile west of the village, and which is a well improved place.

Mr. and Mrs. Miller are the parents of nine children, all of whom have reached maturity. Benjamin F., a farmer, is married, and resides in Wright county, Iowa. Anna is the wife of Frank Forney, a farmer of Ogle county. John resides in Logan, Montana, where he is engaged in the hotel business. Kate married Lewis Garman, a farmer of Wright county, Iowa, where they now live. Emma is the wife of A. Hedwick, of Haldane. Mary now makes her home in Polo. William, Ida and Charles yet reside at home.

Politically Mr. Miller is a Republican, and during the war was the only Republican and stanch supporter of the administration in Haldane. He cast his first presidential vote for Abraham Lincoln, in 1860, and has never missed casting his vote for the nominee of the Republican party for president from that time to the present. The only official position that he has ever held was that of school director, an office that he held for nine years. He and his wife are members of the Evangelical church and assisted in the organization of the church and in the erection of the church building. He was for years one of the official board of the church, and also superintendent of the Sunday-school.

Mr. Miller has been a resident of Ogle county for more than forty-three years, and one of the two of the original settlers of Haldane that are now left. He is well known, and by whom known is held in the highest respect. He has been an industrious man, and all that he possesses has been secured by hard work, his good wife rendering that assistance which the true wife always gives.

GEORGE DREXLER, a retired farmer living in the village of Creston, came to Ogle county in 1869, and in the thirty years of his residence here has become a well-known citizen, one in whom the community has implicit confidence. He was born in Wildenberg, Bavaria, Germany, April 5, 1834, and is the son of Nicholas and Catherine (Himler) Drexler, both of whom were natives of Germany, where their entire lives were spent. The father, who was a farmer by occupation, died in 1864, his wife surviving him many years, dying in 1887.

The subject of this sketch remained in his native country until he was in his eighteenth year. He received a good education in the schools of Bavaria, and in the meantime assisted his father in the cultivation of the farm. Friends of his youth had already emigrated to the United States, and the desire came into his heart to also go to that favored land, where even the lowliest had the opportunity of making a name and acquiring wealth. With his sister, Anna, he set sail for the new world in a slow sailing vessel, and after a long and tedious voyage of twenty-eight days they landed in New York in March, 1852. They located at Palatine, New York, where his sister later married Henry Wagner. Mr. and Mrs. Wagner, who yet remain in Palatine, where he owns a valuable and well improved farm, have a family of five living children, one of whom is married.

On his arrival in Palatine, Mr. Drexler hired to a farmer for the sum of forty dollars per year and a pair of boots. After some seven months had passed, he was convinced that the farmer was about to beat him out of the forty dollars promised. He settled with him, however, for twenty-eight dollars for the seven months and quit his service. The next year he worked for sixty dollars per year, and continued to be thus employed at a slight advance until the beginning of the war, receiving thirteen dollars per month in 1860. In the fall of 1861 he returned to his native land and there remained until 1866, assisting his parents on the home farm. Returning to Palatine, New York, he went to work on a farm for twenty-five dollars per month, and continued there until 1869.

Mr. Drexler was married in Schenectady, New York, December 8, 1868, to Miss Eliza Bauder, a native of the town of Palatine, New York, and a daughter of Christopher and Lana (Nellis) Bauder, early settlers of the Mohawk valley, of German parentage. Mrs. Bauder died in 1854, but he lived until 1898, and died at the ripe old age of eighty-seven years. They had a family of nine children, all of whom are yet living, as follows: Simon P., of Amsterdam, New York; Rufus, of Palatine, New York; Ervin, of Sterling, Illinois; Henry, of Malta, Illinois; George, of Montgomery county, New York; Eliza C., wife of our subject; Ella, wife of Josiah Nestle, of Palatine, New York; Mrs. Amanda Miller, of Palatine, New York; Lana, wife of Jeremiah Van Wie, of Palatine, New York.

In March, 1869, Mr. Drexler came with his bride to Ogle county, where for one year he worked by the month. In January, 1870, he purchased eighty acres of partially improved land in Lynnville township, and commenced life in earnest. Industrious as the day was long, and with a wife who was likewise industrious, one who believed the interests of her husband was that of her own, he went to work with a determination to more than make an ordinary living. In 1875 he purchased eighty acres of land adjoining his farm, erected a new barn, and made many other improvements. In 1888 he purchased one hundred and sixty acres, giving him a half-section of good land, all of which was well improved.

Mr. and Mrs. Drexler have two children living. Libbie J. is now the wife of David Deily, whose parents reside in the same township, and they have one child, Alla Blanche. They reside in the township of Malta, DeKalb county, Illinois. Ervin married Mary Kempson, in 1896, and is now successfully carrying on the home farm. His wife's parents reside in Creston.

Mr. Drexler came to Ogle county with little else than a stout heart and willing hands. He had always before worked for wages, and of course could not lay by very much of this world's goods. He knew how to work and was a practical farmer. Day in and day out he toiled on and the result is shown by his fine farm and large quantity of personal property. He had no special fad in farming, but in addition to the crops annually raised on the farm, he was also engaged in stock raising, feeding a large number of head of cattle and hogs for the general markets. He was successful in all that he did, and his success has come from industry, economy, wise management, assisted in part by his good wife.

Politically Mr. Drexler is a Republican, his first presidential ballot having been cast for General Grant. From that time to the present he has voted the party ticket, but has never wanted or cared for public office. However he was elected, finally qualified, and served as road commissioner. Interested in the cause of education, he served for fifteen years on the school board. Mr. and Mrs. Drexler have on several occasions visited the home of her parents in New York state. They were reared in the Lutheran faith, and while now they are members of no church, they attend the Methodist Episcopal church at Creston.

WILLIAM BIRD, deceased, was a representative of the sturdy English race that have done so much in the civilization of the world, and whose influence will be felt in all time to come. He was born in the parish of Chawleigh, Devonshire, England, February 11, 1806, and in his native land grew to manhood. In his youth he learned the trade of wool comber, which he followed in Devonshire. After his removal to the United States he learned the trade of harnessmaker, which he followed for a number of years. His educational advantages were not of the best, but by reading and observation he became a well informed man.

The countries of Europe, with their pride of aristocracy, give but little opportunity to the poor man to advance in life, and for that reason many are compelled to sunder home ties and emigrate to a land where all are equal in the eyes of the law, and all have the opportunity to seek and secure a higher position in life. Because of this fact William Bird left his native land in 1834, and after a long and tedious voyage in the slow sailing vessels of that time finally landed in this country and located in Ohio, which was his home for twenty-three years and where he made a fairly good start in life. Still farther west the opportunities were even greater, and in 1857 he came with his family to Ogle county and located in Lynnville township, which continued to be his home until his death.

Mr. Bird was married in Norwalk, Ohio, in 1835, to Miss Elizabeth Ford, also a native of Devonshire, England. Her father, Rev. James Ford, was born near Cornwall, Devonshire, England, in 1787. He was a well educated man, and was a distinguished minister of the Non-Conformists. He married Mary Webber, of his native shire, and to them were born eight children, five daughters and three sons—Elizabeth, Ann, Mary, Susanna, Betsy, James, John W. and George. They came to the United States in 1833, and also located in Ohio, where the father died shortly after their arrival. The mother survived him many years, dying in 1866.

To William Bird and wife six children were born, five sons and one daughter. James F. married Jeannette Payne, and they have one daughter, Nellie. They reside in Rochelle, where he is in the produce business. John W. was twice married, first to Martha Nashold, who died, and he later married Martha Reasoner, by whom he has two children, F. Ernest and Clara E. They reside in Iowa, where he has attained considerable prominence as a stock raiser and a politician, having served two terms in the legislature of that state. W. Reed died of an accident in a runaway, December 26, 1896, at the age of fifty-six years. Clara E. married John A. McCrea, now of Creston, and they have two daughters, Ella B. and Florence. (See sketch elsewhere in this work.) George E. married Margaret Starrett, of Jasper county, Iowa, and they have one daughter, Mary L. They reside in Rockford, Iowa, where he is engaged in the farm implement business. Frank F. is managing the home farm for his mother. He received a good education in the schools of Rochelle, and later attended one year in the normal school at Valparaiso, Indiana. He has taught several terms in the public schools of Ogle county, and has given good satisfaction as a teacher.

William Bird departed this life February 23, 1875. He was a believer in the Christian religion, and died in the full assurance of faith in a glorious resurrection. Mrs. Bird, who still survives him, is a member of the Methodist Episcopal church, and is a firm believer in the religion of Christ. She is well known in the township in which she has made her home for more than forty-two years, and wherever known she is greatly esteemed.

HOMER W. MULNIX, who resides on section 30, Buffalo township, is a worthy representative of the younger generation of farmers and stock raisers of Ogle county. He is a native of the county, and was born in Eagle Point township, September 2, 1858. His father, John Mulnix, was born in Delaware county, New York, in 1897, and there grew to manhood. He was twice married, first in his native county, and with his wife and family came to Illinois in 1850, locating in Lee county, where his first wife died, leaving a family of six children, three sons and three daughters. He later married Mrs. Lydia Sanford, née Sweet, also a native of Delaware county, New York. After the death of his first wife and his second marriage he removed to Eagle Point township, where he spent the remainder of his life. He was a successful farmer and acquired a comfortable competence. His death occurred in February, 1891. His wife survived him, and passed away in 1897. They were the parents of three children: Louisa, who died a young lady; Homer W., our subject, and Corydon, a farmer of Ogle county.

Homer W. Mulnix spent his boyhood and youth on his father's farm, and received his education in the home school and in the Polo high school. He continued on the home farm, and assisted his father in the management of the farm until the latter's death. He was married in Cedar county, Iowa, March 18, 1885, to Miss Nellie E. Williams, a native of Ohio, who was reared and educated in Cedar county, Iowa, and daughter of James Williams, a well known citizen of that county. After his marriage he rented one season and then moved to his place of residence, having succeeded to sixty acres of his father's estate. He later bought an adjoining eighty acres, giving him one hundred and forty acres in the home farm. Subsequently he bought another farm of one hundred and forty-six acres in the same neighborhood, and is now cultivating both farms. For some years he made a specialty raising, buying and selling horses, but of late he has turned his attention more especially to breeding, raising and dealing in cattle, and is counted among the successful stock raisers and farmers of Ogle county. To Mr. and Mrs. Mulnix have been born two sons: Forest Robert and John T., the former a student of the home school.

Mr. Mulnix cast his first presidential vote for James A. Garfield, in 1880, since which time he has been an earnest advocate of the principles of the Republican party. He has never sought or wanted public office, but having at heart the interest of the public schools, he has served on the school board for nine years, and is now township trustee of schools. Fraternally he is a member of the Independent Order of Odd Fellows, of Polo, and also of the Knights of the Globe. It is as a farmer and stock raiser that he is best known throughout Ogle and adjoining counties. He has shown himself well qualified for the business, and is a thoroughly practical man. A man of strict integrity of character he makes friends and ever retains that friendship.

CHARLES M. HALLER, an old and highly-esteemed citizen of Forreston, traces his ancestry back to colonial days. His maternal grandfather, Captain Meach, who was in command of a vessel, took part in the Revolutionary war. His daughter, Abigail Meach, married Robert Hewitt, who was of English and French ancestry, and who also took part in the Revolutionary war, having many narrow escapes in several engagements. Robert Hewitt was a native of Connecticut, but with his wife and family he emigrated to Maryland in 1815. They were the parents of twelve children, of whom the mother of our subject was fifth in order of birth. He died in 1830, and his remains were buried at Middlebury, Franklin county, Pennsylvania. His wife survived him many years, and came with her family to Illinois in 1840. She lived to a ripe old age, dying in November, 1855, in her ninety-fourth year, having been born August 10, 1761. Her remains were interred in the Hewitt cemetery, at Forreston. She used to cook for the Indians, and had many interesting stories to relate of her Revolutionary experiences.

The mother of our subject, Abigail (Hewitt) Haller, was the daughter of Robert and Abigail (Meach) Hewitt. She was born in 1800, at Tolland, Windham county, Connecticut. She was married in January, 1819, to Charles A. Haller, who, by his first wife, Catherine Bruner, daughter of John Bruner, a farmer of Frederick county, Maryland, had four children: John, a farmer, who lived and died in Attica, Indiana; Henry, a wagonmaker, who also died at Attica, Indiana; Katherine, wife of Jacob Dovenbarger, of Washington county, Maryland, but who came to Ogle county, and lived near Adeline; and Samuel, who lived and died at Attica, Indiana. To Charles A. and wife seven children were born. Charles M. is the subject of this sketch. Jane Abigail married Francis Hamilton, of Maryland, who removed to Ogle county, Illinois, where he engaged in farming. He later removed to Keokuk, Iowa. Sarah Ann is the widow of Jacob Flaut. She resides in Lanark, Illinois. James Robert died when about eleven months old. Louis lived to be twenty-two years old, and died in Pine Creek township, and was buried at Mt. Morris. George William, who had been a successful school teacher and insurance agent, died at Decatur, Illinois. Joseph is a physician engaged in practice at Lanark, Illinois. The mother of these children died at the home of her daughter,

CHARLES M. HALLER.

Sarah, at Lanark, Illinois, in 1882, and was buried in the cemetery at that place.

Charles Haller, the grandfather of our subject, came to America from Germany in colonial days, paying for his passage by his labor. He landed in Baltimore, and from there went to Washington, and later to Loudoun county, Virginia, where Charles A. Haller, the father of our subject, was born. By occupation he was a farmer. He died and was buried at New Market, Maryland. When a young man, Charles A. Haller moved with his parents to Frederick county, Maryland, where he learned the wagon-maker's trade and conducted a shop. Later he moved to Boonesborough, Maryland, on the National road. With his wife and four children, in May, 1846, he came to Ogle county, Illinois, and settled five and a half miles south of Mt. Morris, on the Grand Detour road, where he purchased one hundred and twenty acres of land. He lived there, however, only six months, and died December 7, 1848, at the age of seventy years.

The subject of this sketch was born in Boonesborough, Washington county, Maryland, November 15, 1819, and there received his education in the subscription schools, in the meantime assisting his father in the cultivation of the thirty-three-acre tract of land which he owned, and in the manufacture of brick, in which he was engaged. After attaining his majority, he aided his old school-master, James Brown, in the management of his school, which had an attendance of one hundred scholars, and engaged in their instruction.

In April, 1846, when twenty-seven years old, he was united in marriage with Miss Elizabeth Nikirk, daughter of Samuel Nikirk, a carpet weaver in the town of Boonesborough, Maryland, where she was born, educated, and grew to womanhood. The month after his marriage, in company with his parents and brothers and sisters, he brought his young bride to Ogle county. They left Boonesborough May 21, 1846, their household goods in a two-horse wagon, and a light wagon with accommodation for six persons, the younger children finding place in the wagon with the furniture. Their trip overland took just six weeks, and they arrived near Mt. Morris, their destination, July 3, 1846, and immediately set about erecting a house of four rooms, two stories high, the lumber for the construction of which our subject had to get in Chicago. He set out on Monday morning for Chicago and arrived home the following Monday. Those were the days of "ox team transportation," when the traveler cooked for himself along the roadside, slept in his wagon, and whistled a song along the lonesome roads to keep himself company.

Their little home erected, young Haller helped his mother and brothers the next year, but the years 1847 and 1848 he took charge of a school at Phelps' Grove, and in 1848-9 taught the school on the Grand Detour road, near Mt. Morris. In the fall of 1850 he moved to West Grove and settled on eighty acres of land given him by his uncle, George W. Hewitt. He built a frame house and set about improving the place, dividing his time, however, between school teaching and farming. He remained on that place until 1859, when he went to Forreston and engaged in general merchandising. Later he purchased a stock of drugs from Frank Barker, now of Rochelle, and a former resident of Forreston, and still conducts the establishment under the management of his son, E. E. Haller.

To Mr. and Mrs. Haller seven children were born. Samuel Henry died when seven years old. Susan married John Mullen, but is now deceased. Charles Louis died at the age of three years. Theodore F. is the editor and proprietor of the Forreston Herald. George Louis is now deceased. Charles M. is now living at Portland, Oregon. Edward Everett is in the drug business at Forreston. The mother of these children died December 23, 1893, at the age of sixty-five years, and her remains were interred in the Hewitt cemetery at Forreston.

Mr. Haller sawed the log and split the stakes used in laying out the town of Forreston in 1855, the town being laid out on the land of his uncle, George W. Hewitt, who had located a claim of eight hundred acres. The first house built in the place was a rude frame structure built by the railroad company for a boarding house. Dr. Kingsbury was the first physician in Forreston. The first school teacher was Thomas J. Hewitt. Mr. Haller was selected as the first teacher, but having so much to do on his farm at the time, he secured the place for his cousin, Mr. Hewitt. The latter married Miss Fannie Rockwood, who was his assistant in the school. The first school building was just west of where the present school building now stands. It was a large frame structure and built under the supervision of George W. Hewitt at a cost of about two thousand dollars.

Mr. Haller cast his first vote at a special election in his native state, and his first presidential vote was cast in 1848 for Zachary Taylor, the Whig candidate. With the Whig party he continued to act until the organization of the Republican party, since which time he has given his support to the men and measures of that party. Religiously he is a Lutheran, and assisted in organizing the Lutheran church in Forreston in 1858, and has since been an elder in the same. He aided and supervised the building of the church which was dedicated July 10, 1864. By the county court Mr. Haller was appointed justice of the peace, was then elected and served one year. He was later appointed notary public by the governor and filled the position twenty years. He was also township school treasurer six years. All in all, Mr. Haller has led an active life. He is well known throughout the county, and all who know him esteem him for his many excellent qualities of head and heart.

ZIBA A. LANDERS, senior editor and proprietor of the Ogle County Republican, Oregon, Illinois, was born March 21, 1857, at Waukegan, Illinois, and is the son of Hezekiah M. and Permelia (Ketchum) Landers, the former being a native of Canada, but who came to the United States in the 'forties, locating in Lake county, Illinois, where he engaged in farming. In 1858 he removed to Dade county, Missouri, where he likewise engaged in agricultural pursuits. He remained in Missouri until 1864, when he was driven out by the Confederates, entailing on him a great loss of property. Leaving Missouri, he returned to Illinois in June, 1865, and located in Ogle county, in the town of Dement.

The subject of this sketch was about eight years old when his parents left Missouri and he has a vivid recollection of that time and the conditions which compelled the family to leave. In the district schools of Ogle county he obtained his education, attending the same until he was fourteen years old, when he went out to earn his own living. Choosing the printer's trade, he commenced to learn the business with an Oregon mechanic, and after completing the trade he worked as a journeyman, in all a period of twelve years, when he engaged in merchandising, at which he continued for eight years, when he sold out and purchased the Creston Observer. This was in 1891, and he continued the publication of the paper until July, 1894, when he sold the establishment, and January 1, 1895, he purchased the Ogle County Republican, in connection with E. L. Reed, which partnership continued until October, 1898, when Mr. Reed retired from the business and Mr. Frank C. Sorrel was duly installed in his position upon the Republican.

Mr. Landers was married November 30, 1881, to Miss Harriet P. Spickerman, daughter of William and Sarah (Sherman) Spickerman, both of whom were natives of Wayne county, New York, where Mrs. Landers was also born. Her parents came to Ogle county in 1870, her father engaging in farming. By this union four children have been born—Ernest D., Chester, Clifford and Sherman. Clifford died when one year old.

Mr. and Mrs. Landers are members of the Methodist Episcopal church. Fraternally, he is a member of Creston Lodge, No. 320, A. F. & A. M., and Rock River Chapter, No. 151, R. A. M. In politics he is a Republican, with which party he has been identified since attaining his majority, and served in the forty-first general assembly as sergeant-at-arms of the senate in a very creditable manner. He is at present a member of the Republican town committee of Oregon, and aids with voice and pen in promulgating the principles of his party.

While residing at Creston he served as a member of the school board, and also held other official positions.

The Ogle County Republican was founded in 1888 by Bemis & Wagoner, and is now conducted by Landers & Sorrel, who are first-class newspaper men, good writers and men of unimpeachable integrity. The paper is a six-column quarto, and in politics is uncompromisingly Republican.

MILTON BURRIGHT, a retired farmer residing in Oregon, is one of the oldest living settlers in Ogle county, having taken up his residence here shortly after he attained his majority. He was born near Schenectady, New York, December 25, 1815, and is the son of Cornelius Burright, and the grandson of John Burright, of whom little is known. Cornelius Burright was born in the Mohawk Valley, New York, and was by occupation a farmer, a calling that he pursued during his entire life. He married Olive Messenger, also a native of New York. She died in Licking county, Ohio, in 1827, when about forty-five years old. Her father and mother lived to be one hundred and one hundred and three years, respectively. Some years after the death of his wife Cornelius Burright came to Ogle county and for twenty-five years prior to his death made his home with our subject. He died in August, 1875, at the age of ninety-eight years and seven months.

While he was yet an infant our subject's parents moved to Cuyahoga county, Ohio, and about 1823 moved to Licking county, in the same state. He was but twelve years old when his mother died, and the following year his father remarried, and from that time he had to make his own way in the world. For one season he worked on the Ohio canal, driving an ox team at twenty-five cents per day. For three seasons he worked in a brick yard in Franklin county, Ohio, and during the winter cut cord wood for use in the brick yard in the summer. He saved his money and in 1836 he walked one hundred miles to Van Wert county, Ohio, and entered eighty acres of timber land, which he held until after he came to Illinois. About this time he spent two winters in Mississippi and Louisiana, cutting wood for steamboats. He was an unusually good chopper, and on one occasion, with the assistance of three companions, cut twelve cords of wood in one day. On a wager, alone, he cut four and a half cords in a half day, a record which has probably never been beaten. His first summer in Illinois was spent in Grand Detour, and his second one in Dixon.

In April, 1838, Mr. Burright bought a claim to three quarter-sections of land in Pine Rock township, and after remaining on the claim until the following August he went to Missouri to spend the winter, fearing the cold of northern Illinois. He went on south to Natchez, Mississippi, and later to Louisiana. In the spring of 1839 he returned to Ogle county, and has never felt the necessity of again leaving it. His farm he at once began to improve and from time to time he added to his original purchase until he once owned over one thousand acres of choice land. Much of this he disposed of to his children, retaining only two hundred and fifty-four acres. After living upon the farm for nearly a half century, he purchased a house and lot in Oregon and has since lived a retired life.

Since coming to Ogle county, Mr. Burright has never lived under any but his own roof. The first log house built upon his claim was a very rude affair. No stove was ever used, all cooking being done in the fireplace. The chimney was made of sticks, and his bedstead was of his own construction and had but one leg. It was built in the corner of the cabin, two sides being fastened into the logs, one post or leg holding up the other sides. Its springs were slats or "shakes" split out of oak logs, and were thin and elastic, taking the place of the modern woven wire springs. He later built a more commodious log house, and finally a fine brick house, which is the farm residence to-day. It was one of the first of its kind between St. Charles, Kane county, and Dixon, Lee county.

With but little schooling in early life, Mr. Burright has made up for lost time by being an extensive reader. After marriage, his wife, who had a good education for that day, taught him, and his own natural ability and perseverance did the rest. His first two crops of grain he hauled to Chicago with ox teams, being several days on the road. Produce was then very low and provisions very high.

Mr. Burright was first married October 24, 1839, in Lafayette township, Ogle county, to Miss Susanna Drummond, born in Allegheny county, Pennsylvania, December 18, 1819, and a daughter of Andrew and Elizabeth (Loutzenheiser) Drummond. The latter, who attained the age of seventy-three years, was a daughter of Henry Loutzenheiser, whose parents emigrated to the United States when he was but two years old. He married Judith Merchant, whose brother, Dr. David Merchant, was a surgeon in the Revolutionary war. Two other brothers were also surgeons, but were not in the Continental service. Andrew Drummond was born in New York state, and came west in the fall of 1838. He was by occupation a farmer, and was quite prominent in the early days of the county. He was instrumental in organizing every school district between Ashton, Lee county, and Polo. Being a man of superior education, he was of great service in that connection. For some years he served as postmaster of Ashton. His death occurred at the age of eighty-seven years. Of the eleven children born to Andrew and Elizabeth Drummond, four are yet living in Ogle county. Levi and Lewis are living in Pine Rock township; Jackson resides in Lafayette township; and the present Mrs. Burright in Oregon.

To our subject and his first wife nine children were born, two of whom died in infancy. Thomas Sheldon married Margaret Bailey, and they now reside in Dixon, Illinois, with their family of seven children. Sarah Olive married Jacob Acker, and with their five children they live in Pine Rock township. John married Emma Ashbaugh, by whom he has had thirteen children. They reside in Iowa. Thornton lives in Chana. He first married Christine Dugdale, by whom he had four children. His second wife was Miss Addie Lee, by whom he has one child. Albert lives in Pine Rock township, near the old home farm. He first married Armista Thurber, by whom he has two sons. He next married Mrs. Julia Grimes, née Haymaker. Jeannette married Oscar Dugdale, and with their four children they live in Pine Rock township, adjoining the village of Chana. Mary married Charles Dailey, and they reside in Pine Rock township. They have had five children, three of whom are living. The mother of these children died August 24, 1873.

Mr. Burright's second marriage was solemnized February 10, 1875, when he wedded Mrs. Judith Rinker, a sister of his first wife, who was born in Licking county, Ohio. She was the widow of Alhanen Rinker, a native of Louisville, Kentucky, and who died near Oregon, October 2, 1855, at the age of thirty years. He was the father of four children who lived to maturity. Wallace E. married Margaret Sutter, by whom he had seven children. He served in the Union army, during the Civil war, but was drowned in a river in Kansas in 1878. Ellen married Robert Garrison, of Portland, Oregon, and they have four children. Frank married Annie Wicks, who died leaving three children. He lives in Clearfield, Iowa. Loretta A. married Henry Yates, who is engaged in the grocery trade at Chana, Illinois. They have one child.

In politics Mr. Burright is a Republican. He has not been an office seeker, but has held several local offices, including school director, road commissioner, and township trustee. Fraternally he is a Mason, and religiously he is identified with the Christian church, but there being no service held by that church in Oregon he attends the Methodist Episcopal church. His wife has been a church member since the age of fifteen years, and is one of the only two original members of the first church organized in Pine Rock township. She has been an efficient teacher in the Sunday-school for many years. At the age of sixteen she taught school at Lafayette Grove. She has now a bed of violets, the sprouts of which grew at the door of the first school which she attended when a girl.

Mr. Burright has not only reared his own children in comfort, giving them good educations, but has reared several of his kindred who were left homeless, and is now educating his wife's grandson, a son of Frank Rinker. He is a man highly esteemed for his works' sake.

WILLIAM C. BUNN.—In this enlightened age when men of energy, industry and merit are rapidly pushing their way to the front, those who, by their own individual efforts, have won favor and fortune may properly claim recognition. Years ago, when the west was entering upon an era of growth and Ogle county was laying its foundation for future prosperity, there came thither from all parts of the country men poor but honest, and with sturdy independence and a determination to succeed that justly entitled them to representation in the history of the great west. Among this now is Mr. Bunn, who has met with remarkable success in his business undertakings, and is now practically living retired in Byron.

He was born on the 10th of February, 1837, in Hunterdon county, New Jersey, of which county his father, John E. Bunn, was also a native. On attaining to man's estate the latter married Sarah Conover, who was born in New Jersey, in 1817. He continued to successfully engage in farming in his native county until 1855, when he brought his family to Illinois, where he joined some New Jersey friends. For a few years he resided in Byron township, Ogle county, and then purchased land in Winnebago county, where he developed a fine farm of two hundred and thirty acres, operating the same for many years. He finally sold and in 1882 returned to Byron township, Ogle county, where he died in 1892, at the ripe old age of eighty-two years. His wife had passed away in 1872 and both were laid to rest in the Stillman Valley cemetery. In the family of this worthy couple were thirteen children, four sons and nine daughters, all of whom reached years of maturity. William C., of this review, is the oldest; Mary wedded Wesley Yard and is now deceased; A. M. resides on a farm in Byron township; Mrs. Sarah Powell is a widow; Anna is deceased; Henry died at the age of eighteen; Mrs. Lucinda Wells resides in Rockford, Illinois; Hannah is the wife of William Van Valzy, of Ogle county; Caroline is the wife of Benjamin Anderson, who owns and occupies the old Bunn homestead; Jane married but is now deceased; Garrett is a farmer of Winnebago county; and Martha is the wife of Henry Liggett, of Marcus, Iowa.

William C. Bunn was reared in New Jersey and educated in its common schools. He came with the family to this state and assisted his father in opening up the farm, remaining with him until twenty-five years of age. In 1861 he was married, in Ogle county, to Miss Julia Jarver, a native of New York, who was brought to the county at the age of twelve years by her father, Anthony Jarver, a worthy pioneer of Byron township, where he reared his family. Four children have been born of their union: John, who is married and conducts the elevator and buys grain in Byron; Alma, wife of Homer Long, a business man of Mt. Carroll, Carroll county, Illinois; Arthur, a business man of Myrtle, Ogle county; and George, who is employed in the Farmers & Merchants Bank, of Byron.

For eight years after his marriage Mr. Bunn engaged in farming on rented land, but two years before the close of that period he purchased a half interest in a farm of two hundred acres, which he operated in connection with the rented farm. In the spring of 1870 he located upon his place, but sold his interest in the same two years later and again became a renter. In 1872 he bought an improved farm of two hundred acres in Marion township, to the further development and cultivation of which he devoted his energies for four years. He remodeled the house, enlarged the barn and made many other improvements which added to its value and attractive appearance. On account of impaired health he removed to Byron in the spring of 1876, but three years later returned to the farm and continued to follow agricultural pursuits until 1886, when he rented his place and purchased residence property in the village where he still resides. He became interested in the grain business, and four years later bought the elevator at Byron. He also began buying and shipping cattle and hogs on an extensive scale, and became a large dealer in flour, feed, salt, coal, etc. At one time Mr. Bunn was one of the heaviest depositors in the Byron Bank, but owing to a change of ownership and management he became dissatisfied and decided to establish a bank of his own. Later the bank closed and a number of the depositors lost heavily. Since then the present Byron Bank has been started. Withdrawing from the former institution Mr. Bunn established, in 1891, the Farmers & Merchants Bank, which has since done a large and profitable business, and is one of the solid financial institutions of the county. Although our subject started out in life for himself in limited circumstances he is now one of the most successful business men of the community, and is the owner of much valuable real estate besides his business property, all of which has been acquired through his own well-directed efforts. At all times he supports the principles of the Republican party by his ballot, and though he served as collector of Marion township at one time, he has never cared for political preferment. He is public-spirited and enterprising, giving a liberal support to all measures which he believes calculated to advance the moral, intellectual or material welfare of his own town or county.

F. W. HOWE, an enterprising business man and postmaster of Monroe Center, was born in Cherry Valley, Winnebago county, Illinois, November 28, 1865, and is the son of Maynard and Susan (Foster) Howe, both of whom were natives of New York state, but who came west in an early day and settled in Cherry Valley, where the father engaged in the grain business, having a large elevator, and building up an extensive trade, there spent the remainder of his life. He was also engaged in the hardware trade for a time. His death occurred at Cherry Valley some years since, and his widow later married T. M. Lee, a lumber merchant of Cherry Valley. Maynard and Susan (Foster) Howe were the parents of two children,—Fannie, residing in Cherry Valley, and our subject.

In his native village our subject grew to manhood and attended the district school until sixteen years of age, when he found employment in the lumber-yard of his stepfather, continuing with him for three years. While thus employed he learned telegraphy, and later secured a position with the Chicago & Northwestern railway, where he was employed about six months. He then purchased an interest in the lumber-yard with his stepfather, at Monroe Center, and later they purchased the hardware store of Hildebrand & Eychaner, since which time they have continued both lines of trade. In addition to his mercantile interests, Mr. Howe has an interest in a farm of two hundred acres near Cherry Valley, and has also considerable town property in Monroe Center.

On the 12th of March, 1889, Mr. Howe was united in marriage with Miss Cora Alexander, of Monroe Center, and daughter of J. Alexander, and by this union two children have been born,—Maynard A. and Vera May.

In politics Mr. Howe has always been a Republican and an earnest advocate of the principles of the party. For three years he served as town clerk of Monroe, and in 1896 and 1897 was assessor of the township. In April, 1897, he received his appointment as postmaster of Monroe, which position he fills in a most satisfactory manner. Fraternally, he is a Mason, and also a member of the Modern Woodmen of America. In his local camp he has served as clerk for three years. He is also a member of the Home Forum and Knights of Pythias. Always interested in the public schools, he has given of his time to advance their interests, serving three years as a school director. Religiously, Mrs. Howe is a member of the Methodist Episcopal church, in the work of which she is deeply interested. As a business man Mr. Howe is thoroughly progressive and always up with the times.

NOAH SPEAKER. One of the busiest, most energetic and most enterprising citizens of Ogle county is Noah Speaker the founder of Egan City. It was through his influence and determination that a station was established at that time and the people of the community owe to him a debt of gratitude which can never be repaid for it has proved of inestimable value to neighboring farmers. For over half a century he has taken a most prominent and active part in the development and upbuilding of the county, and has advanced its interests in every possible way.

Mr. Speaker was born in Washington county, Maryland, December 24, 1820, and on the paternal side is of German extraction. His father, Samuel Speaker, was born about 1791, in Ohio, where the grandfather resided for a few years prior to locating in Pennsylvania, but later in life he became a resident of Washington county, Maryland. Samuel Speaker was reared in Pennsylvania, and there married Miss Margaret Kretsinger. He was a carpenter and joiner by trade and followed contracting and building throughout his active life. He was a soldier of the war of 1812 and received a land warrant for his services. In 1855 he joined his children in Ogle county, Illinois, and here spent his last years, dying in 1864. The death of his wife occurred in 1862. Their family, consisting of four sons and two daughters, were reared in Maryland. William, the eldest, came west in 1855 and settled in Stephenson county, Illinois, where he died. Noah is the next in order of birth. Washington also came to Illinois in 1855, but afterward settled in Ohio, where his death occurred, but his remains were interred in Egan cemetery, this county. Isaiah, a carpenter and joiner, resides in Toledo, Iowa. Eliza remained in Maryland, where she married and reared a family, but is now deceased. Mary

Ann, also deceased, married and settled in Mt. Morris, Illinois.

Noah Speaker is wholly a self-educated man as he had no school advantages. In May, 1844, he came to Ogle county, driving a team across the country for Samuel Rinehart, who settled in Adeline. Here our subject worked by the month for William Hopwood for four years on his farm near Oregon, and in 1849 returned to his native county, where he was united in marriage with Miss Catherine Ann Garvin. The following year he again came to Ogle county and made a permanent location. He had previously entered a tract of forty acres, where he now resides and after his marriage rented a little house near his land. While breaking and improving his property he worked at anything by which he could earn a livelihood and in this way secured a start in life. In 1853 he built a house upon his place, and afterwards bought an adjoining forty acres. He now has a large, neat and substantial residence, good outbuildings, and, in fact, all of the conveniences and accessories of a model farm of the nineteenth century. Two years after the railroad was laid out he made an effort to get a station established, and, after a hard struggle, succeeded. It was located near the northeast corner of his place by J. M. Egan, a railroad official, and was named in honor of that gentleman. Mr. Speaker laid out the town and has since sold many lots and has succeeded in founding a thriving little village which is a credit to him.

He has been called upon to mourn the loss of his estimable wife, who died April 6, 1895, and was laid to rest in Egan cemetery. To them were born four children, namely: William, a successful physician of Manson, Iowa; Alice, wife of John Harmon, of Haldane, Illinois; Rosa, wife of W. W. Williams, of Des Moines, Iowa; and Marian, deceased wife of Newton Harmon.

In his political affiliations Mr. Speaker has been a life-long Democrat, casting his first presidential vote for Martin Van Buren in 1836. For sixteen years he was an efficient member of the school board of Egan, but has never sought nor desired official honors, preferring to give his entire attention to his business interests. As a public-spirited, enterprising citizen, he certainly deserves honorable mention in a work of this kind, and his many friends in Ogle county will read with interest this brief sketch of his life.

SAMUEL S. McGUFFIN.—Among the prominent and enterprising men who are identified with Ogle county and its advancement, belongs the subject of this review. His birth occurred in Canada on the 23d of December, 1832, where he lived until his tenth year. He is a son of John and Margaret (Howard) McGuffin, who came to Illinois in 1843 and purchased one hundred and sixty acres in Ogle county. They were the parents of seven children, five of whom are living. Andrew is the second oldest. The second son, John, is a Methodist minister in Chicago. Annie is the wife of Benjamin Canfield, a farmer in Ogle county. Sarah married Solomon Whitaker, also a farmer in Ogle county. Katie is the wife of Joseph Mossit and resides in Canada. The sixth child is the subject of this sketch.

Samuel S. McGuffin worked for his father until 1860, when he accepted a contract to clear and break a tract of farm land in Rockvale township, and received in payment one hundred and sixty acres on section 21, where he now resides, and the present fine residence, outbuildings, orchards, fences, ornamental trees and general thrifty appearance, all bespeak the owner's enterprise and energy. In 1865 Mr. McGuffin married Frances Elizabeth Griswold, who was born February 3, 1845, in Rockvale township, which place has always been her home. Nine children have blessed this union and are here named in order of birth: Ida married Isaac Price, who is in the employ of one of the Chicago railroad companies. Maud is living at home. May is the wife of R. L. Thomas, a farmer of Ogle county. Nellie, the fourth child, died in infancy. Maggie is the wife of Martin Ashbaugh, of Oregon. Blanch married George Crowell, of Pocahontas county, Iowa. Catherine is deceased. Talbot is at home aiding in the management of the home farm, and Edith Frances, the youngest, is also living at home.

Mrs. McGuffin is a daughter of George and Hannah (Jackson) Griswold, who came to Ogle county, in 1838, and settled in Oregon. Her father is an Englishman and her mother a native of Boston. She is one of six chidren, namely: William, now deceased; Henry, a well-to-do banker of Manson, Iowa, now deceased; Mary, who died in infancy; Harvey, a farmer and stock-dealer of Rockvale township; Alice, the wife of A. W. Price, a dental surgeon and a large property-owner of Pine Creek township. Mrs. McGuffin's brother enlisted with the Seventy-fourth Illinois Volunteer Infantry and was wounded in the battle of of Shiloh. Her uncle, Charles H. Jackson, served with distinction throughout the Civil war.

Mr. McGuffin cast his first vote for Abraham Lincoln, but is an independent voter rather than a party man, voting his convictions without reference to the politics of the candidate. He has at all times been an advocate of good roads, and his ideas, which he put into practice during his term of township trustee, did not receive the endorsement of his fellow citizens. The wisdom of his opinions in this particular is now everywhere apparent, and his ideas and suggestions, while in "advance of his time," are now being rapidly carried out. Mr. and Mrs. McGuffin are surrounded by a bright and intelligent family, each member of which has displayed marked taste for educational pursuits, all the girls adopting the profession of school teaching. They are active members of the Methodist church, and the high esteem in which they have always been held, is the reward for uprightness, integrity and sociability in their relations to all.

DENNIS SULLIVAN, the agreeable, accommodating and efficient agent and telegraph operator for the Milwaukee & St. Paul railroad at Harper, is a native son of Illinois, born in Winnebago county, December 31, 1857, a son of Dennis Sullivan, Sr., who died just prior to the birth of our subject. The mother later removed to Mt. Carroll, Illinois, where her son grew to manhood, and completed his education in the Mt. Carroll high school. He then worked on a farm for a short time, and subsequently entered the service of the Milwaukee & St. Paul railroad as brakeman for a few months. He next entered the Mt. Carroll office, where he assisted the agent and learned telegraphy, remaining there about three years, during which time he became an expert operator. On the 1st of August, 1887, he was given the position of night operator at Harper, and after three years and three months spent here, he went to Galewood, where he was agent and operator for two years. On the 28th of July, 1892, he was again transferred to Harper, where he has since served as operator and agent to the entire satisfaction of the company and the general public.

At Freeport, Illinois, July 2, 1889, was celebrated the marriage of Mr. Sullivan and Miss Catherine Lang, who was born, reared and educated in Forreston, and they have become the parents of three children, namely: Daniel H., Floyd D. and Helen S. Since attaining his majority, Mr. Sullivan has been an ardent supporter of the Republican party, having cast his first presidential vote for James A. Garfield, but he has never been an aspirant for office. He is a wide-awake, energetic business man and since coming to Harper has bought lots and erected two neat and substantial residences thereon. In social as well as business circles he stands deservedly high, as he is pleasant, genial and affable and makes friends readily.

JOHN WATERBURY CLINTON, editor and proprietor of the Ogle County Press, Polo, was born in Andes, Delaware county, New York, and is the son of George N. and Jane A. (Gibbs) Clinton. On his father's side he traces his ancestry to Joseph Clinton, his great-grandfather, of New Canaan, Connecticut, who married Phœbe Benedict. Their son, Joseph Benedict Clinton, married Abigail Camp, and they were the parents of George Nelson Clinton, the father of our subject. On his mother's side he goes back to his grandfather, Phineas Gibbs, of Andes, New York, who was a native of Massachusetts, and who married Anna Thompson, daughter of John Thompson, of Andes, New York, who was in religion, a Quaker. Joseph Benedict Clinton was a soldier in the Revolutionary war, in the First Connecticut Line, under Colonel Webb. He died in 1828.

George N. Clinton was a shoemaker by trade, but in his native city engaged in the general mercantile trade, having a small general store. He was for a time postmaster of the place. In the winter of 1839-40, he came to Ogle county and purchased a settlers' claim of one hundred and sixty acres of prairie land and forty acres of timber, then returned east, with a view of returning and making the claim his permanent home. On account of the failing health of his wife, he abandoned the idea, losing the amount paid for the claim. In 1870, he came once more to the county, but only on a visit to his son. The changes wrought in the country in the thirty years he could scarcely realize. His death occurred in his home at Andes, New York, in June, 1883. His good wife preceded him many years, dying in 1847.

The subject of this sketch received an academic education in his native state, where he engaged in teaching until October, 1857, when he came to Polo. During the ensuing winter he taught the school in Buffalo Grove, and the next summer taught a select school in the old seminary. He was afterward employed as a teacher in the Buffalo, Forreston and Polo schools until 1865, when he became editor and proprietor of the Polo Press, of which he is sole proprietor. He was also publisher and proprietor of the Poultry Argus, and the Forreston Journal, the predecessor of the Herald, of the former during 1875-6, and the latter 1871-4. He has held the position of town clerk and assistant supervisor of Buffalo township, and was postmaster at Polo for eight years, from 1875 to 1883.

Mr. Clinton is known throughout the state as a newspaper man, and has been connected with the Illinois Press Association since 1869. He has been one of its active members, serving it as treasurer from 1873 to 1875, and from 1876 to 1881. In February, 1883, he was elected president of the Association and served one year. He has been elected several times a delegate from the Illinois Press Association to the National Association.

On the 24th of January, 1861, Mr. Clinton was united in marriage with Miss Carrie A. Perkins, a native of Delhi, Delaware county, New York, and a daughter of Deacon Timothy and Sarah (Veghte) Perkins. Timothy Perkins was the son of Rufus, and grandson of Timothy Perkins, who were natives of Massachusetts. Timothy Perkins, the father of Mrs. Clinton, served in the war of 1812, in Colonel Farrington's regiment, light infantry, and with his regiment was stationed near Fort Gainesworth. He married Sarah Veghte, daughter of John Veghte, of Johnstown, New York. In 1840 he came to Ogle county, where they spent the remainder of their lives, the mother dying in the spring of 1876, when about seventy-five years of age. The father died November 23, 1884, aged ninety years.

To Mr. and Mrs. Clinton seven children were born, of whom five are yet living Evangeline, George P., John D., Edgar M. and Anna Lucile; Georgiana, the eldest, and Bertie F. died in infancy. The living children are all graduates of the Polo high school. George P. and John D. are graduates of the University of Illinois, the former now serving as assistant botanist in the Illinois Experiment Station connected with the University of Illinois. Edgar M. is a student in Stanford University, California.

In politics Mr. Clinton is a Republican, the Press being an advocate of Republican principles. He was initiated in the I. O. O. F., April 26, 1858.

MARTIN L. ETTINGER, retired, is a gentleman who has retained a personal association with the affairs of Rochelle and Oregon for almost half a century. His life has been one of honest endeavor, and due success has not been denied him. A man of unswerving integrity and honor, who has a perfect appreciation of the higher ethics of life, he has gained the respect of his associates, and is distinctively one of the leading citizens of Rochelle. He is a native of Pennsylvania, having been born in the village of Dover, York county, on the 23rd of December, 1832, where he was reared and educated, attending the common schools until his seventeenth year. After leaving school he worked at his trade, that of carpenter, for three years and in 1854 left the parental roof for the west, going direct to Oregon, Illinois, where he worked at his trade for four years. At this time he was appointed to a clerkship in the recorder's office, where he soon made himself at the necessary official, so much so, that at the breaking out of the Civil war, it was a most earnest request of the recorder that he refrained from enlisting, which he had fully intended doing. He served as deputy clerk of the Circuit court until 1864, when he was elected county treasurer, serving four years. At the expiration of this term he opened a music store dealing in pianos, organs, etc. Two years later he was appointed accountant at Chicago, for the Chicago & Iowa Railroad Company, and in 1877 he was appointed general ticket agent and auditor at Rochelle. He filled these two positions with great credit to himself, until 1887, since which time he has lived a retired life.

Mr. Ettinger is the second of six children, three of whom are living. His father was Daniel M. Ettinger, who was born in Rossville, York county, Pennsylvania, and attained the age of eighty-five years. Mr. Ettinger, Sr., taught school for thirty-five years, a record few could equal, and during that time acted as local surveyor and engineer. In 1852 he came to Chicago and had charge of the engineering department of the Wisconsin division of the Chicago & Northwestern railroad. The following year he returned to York county, Pennsylvania, where he made his home until his death. In politics he was a Whig, and during the war was in charge of one of the underground railroads. He attended the Methodist Episcopal church, where he was a highly respected member. The mother of our subject was Lavina (Toomy) Ettinger, a daughter of Peter Toomy, a resident of Perry county, Pennsylvania, formerly of York county.

In March, 1855, there occurred in Freeport, Illinois, the marriage of our subject to Miss Eleanor Creger, of New Jersey, and they are the parents of seven children, three of whom are living: Frank, an engineer on the Chicago, Burlington & Quincy railroad, is married, and has three children: Carrie, Charles and Blanche. The second child Blanche, is the wife of B. W. Fraser, a merchant of Polo, Illinois. Carrie, the youngest living child, is attending school at Rochelle. The paternal grandparents of our subject were Adam and Abbie (Miller) Ettinger. The former was born in York county, Pennsylvania, dying at the age of ninety-six, and was a minister of a denomination known as the Albrights.

Martin L. Ettinger is an independent Democrat, and is serving as chairman of the county central committee. For a number of years he was a justice of the peace. He was for two years a member of the city council of Rochelle and is a member of the Masonic fraternity. When the Ogle & Carroll county railroad was projected he was instrumental in aiding the enterprise through, and was a stockholder and secretary of said company until it was absorbed by the Chicago, Burlington & Quincy Railroad Company. Most of his mature years have been spent in active railroad life, and he has that genial bearing common to railroad officials. He has served as president of the Rochelle Whist club, and is voted by his friends as an all around good fellow.

JOHN SMALL, a retired farmer living on section 20, Lincoln township, came to Ogle county in March, 1864, when in his eighteenth year. He was born in Washington county, Maryland, July 28, 1846, and is the son of John and Elizabeth (Wenrick) Small, the former a native of Maryland and the latter of Pennsylvania. The parents never came west, but both passed to their reward in Maryland, the father dying in 1853, the mother surviving him a number of years, rearing and caring for their children. They were the parents of three sons and four daughters, who grew to mature years, but of the number our subject and his sister, Sarah J., wife of Henry A. Long, of Scott county, Kansas, are the only survivors.

In his native county John Small remained until in his eighteenth year. His educational advantages were very limited, but he has made use of the opportunities he has had in mingling with the world until to-day he is a well-informed man. He came to Ogle county and here joined his sister, Mrs. Long, who, with her husband, had settled here some time previously. On his arrival he commenced farm work by the month and continued to be thus employed during the summer and fall of 1864. The war for the Union had now been in progress for nearly four years, and although not eighteen years old he determined to offer his services to his country. He enlisted March 8, 1865, "for one year or during the war," becoming a member of Company K, Fifteenth Illinois Volunteer Infantry, and joined his regiment, which was then at Raleigh, North Carolina. With his regiment he was engaged in doing guard duty along the railroads, and continued to be thus actively employed until near the close of the war. He was later taken sick and was in Harewood hospital, at Washington City, for about three weeks. He received an honorable discharge July 13, 1865.

Being within a few miles of his old home when discharged he concluded to visit relatives and friends in Maryland and Pennsylvania, and so spent delightfully a couple of weeks. He then returned to Ogle county and the following season worked by the month. He then purchased a threshing machine and for several years engaged in threshing grain, a business which was then fairly remunerative. On the 13th of January, 1876, he was united in marriage with Miss Susanna Tschopp, who was born and reared in Ogle county, and daughter of Philip Tschopp, a native of Northumberland county, Pennsylvania, who there grew to manhood and married Susanna Heckart, also a native of Pennsylvania. They had a family of five daughters and one son who grew to mature years: Helen, who married John Rebuck, and died about 1881; Mrs. Catherine Weaver, of Mt. Morris township; Anna, wife of John Fagan, of Lincoln township; Charles Henry, who resides at Haldane, Ogle county; Sarah, wife of Fred Martz, of Lincoln township; and Susanna, wife of our subject. Mr. Tschopp came with his family to Ogle county in 1854, and settled in Leaf River township and afterward moved to Mt. Morris township, that part which is now Lincoln township, and here spent the remainder of his life, dying in the fall of 1891. His wife survives him and is now living in Forreston.

After his marriage Mr. Small rented a farm in Mt. Morris township, and continued to rent for several years. In 1883 he purchased a farm of one hundred and twenty acres in Lincoln township, to which he removed with his family, and on which they lived for nine years, in the meantime putting some substantial improvements upon the place. Selling that farm, he bought the place on which they now reside, which lies about three-fourths of a mile west of Haldane, and where he has since lived retired.

Politically Mr. Small is a Republican, although he was reared a Democrat. He never, however, voted the Democratic ticket, but cast his first presidential ballot for General Grant in 1868. He has taken quite an active part in local politics and has been a delegate to various conventions of his party. He is at present a member of the Lincoln township central committee of his party, and of the county central committee. For seven consecutive years he served as assessor of his township, and for nine years was a member of the school board, and president of the same for years. In all local affairs he has been quite active. Since 1890 he has been secretary of the Lincoln Township Insurance Company. He is also secretary and treasurer of the Ogle County Farmers' Institute, and was a delegate to the Farmers' National Congress, which met at Fort Worth, Texas, December 6, 1898. While gone he visited Galveston, Houston, Waco, San Antonio, and a number of other important points in the "Lone Star state." Fraternally he is a member of the G. A. R., of Mt. Morris. In the thirty-five years he has been a resident of Ogle county he has made many friends, who esteem him as one worthy of their confidence.

GEORGE H. ANDREW, one of the leading citizens of Ogle county, was born in Paine's Point, Pine Rock township, Ogle county, July 16, 1855. He is a son of Nicholas and Margaret (Eychaner) Andrew, who were married in 1840. Nicholas Andrew was born in 1818, on the Mohawk river, New York, where he was reared and educated, and followed the occupation of farming. Mrs. Andrew was born in 1824, in the state of New York, and is the daughter of Conrad Eychaner, a farmer of New York state. Mr. Eychaner took an active part in the Mexican war, and served with much distinction. Shortly after his marriage he came to Illinois and was among the first settlers of the county. Mr. and Mrs. Andrew had five children. Daniel, the eldest and a prominent farmer of Ogle county, was born in 1845 and died in 1898. Franklin, born in March, 1847, is at present road commissioner of Pine Rock township. Nathan, born in 1850, is a prominent merchant in the town of Oregon. Amanda was born in 1852 and died in 1863. Mr. Andrew died in 1856, in the prime of life, being only thirty-eight years of age. His wife is still living at Paine's Point, and enjoys a comfortable old age.

The gentleman whose name heads this review, received his education in the common school, and after completing his education took up the pursuit of farming, which he followed until 1879, when he removed to Chana. On the nineteenth of September, 1878, he was united in marriage to Ida M. Eddy, a daughter of Horace and Jane (Woodward) Eddy, natives of De Kalb county, where Mr. Eddy is a prominent farmer. To Mr. and Mrs. Andrew two children have been born: Eddy Glenn, attending school at Oregon; and Edith Lyle at home with her parents. At various times Mr. Andrew's popularity has been evinced by his election to office in township and county. He has for thirteen years fulfilled the office of township assessor, and in December, 1894, he was appointed deputy sheriff. In this capacity he served with great distinction, which led up to his election, in 1898, to the office of sheriff of Ogle county. After election he removed to Oregon, where he now resides. Mr. Andrew is a prominent member of the Masonic fraternity, Oregon Lodge, No. 420, Knights of Pythias, and the Modern Woodmen of America. He attained his majority in 1876 and cast his first vote for Rutherford B. Hayes, and each succeeding election, town, county, state or national he has given his support and ballot to the principles of the Republican platform.

BENJAMIN T. HEDRICK, deceased, who was numbered among the early settlers of Ogle county, was a true representative of that class of men who enter into a new country, where hardships must be experienced, and by the sweat of their face, prepare the way, rendering the paths smooth for those who shall come after them. He was a native of Washington county, Maryland, and was born November 1, 1812, in Sharpsburg. His father, George Hedrick, was a native of Pennsylvania, and was born February 3, 1779, while his mother was born in Washington county, Maryland, April 12, 1785. George Hedrick was a mechanic, but on going to Maryland engaged in agricultural pursuits on a large scale, owning several slaves. During the war of 1812 he served as a recruiting officer. He never came west, but died in Washington county, Maryland, April 21, 1831, his wife surviving him some eighteen years, dying January 10, 1859. They had a large family.

The subject of this sketch grew to manhood in his native county, and after passing through the common schools, entered Williamstown College, Virginia. On the 10th of October, 1841, he was united in marriage with Miss Anna Shryock, who was born October 21, 1808, in Hagerstown, Maryland. She was the daughter of George Shryock, born February 24, 1783, and Elizabeth (Lewis) Shryock, born August 5, 1784. He was an officer, with the rank of captain, in the war of 1812, under General Ringold. He was the son of John Shryock, a representative of one of the old Maryland families. Elizabeth Lewis was the daughter of Captain William Lewis, who served in the Revolutionary war, under General Wayne. Anna Shryock was the oldest of a family of eight children born to George and Elizabeth Shryock. John Shryock was the son of Leonard Shryock, one of two brothers who emigrated to the colonies from one of the German states, probably about the year 1720, settling in York county, Pennsylvania.

To B. T. and Anna Hedrick five children were born, one of whom died in infancy. George M. is married, and is engaged in farming in Lincoln township, Ogle county. He has five children. Lucy T. resides in Polo, where she is well known and universally esteemed. She is a member and an active worker in the Lutheran church. Walter K. is married and has four children. He also lives in Lincoln township, where he is engaged in farming. Allen M. is married and has had five children. He is now living in Santa Paula, California.

In 1845 Mr. Hedrick came with his family to Ogle county and settled on a tract of land consisting of one hundred and twenty acres, in Mt. Morris township, which he had previously purchased. He at once commenced its improvement, and in due time had a farm of which he had just reason to be proud. After living upon that farm for thirty-one years, and there rearing his children, he went to California for a stay of one year, and in 1879 moved to Polo, in order that he might live a retired life. He was quite a traveller, and thoroughly enjoyed visiting various parts of his native land and associating with people of whom he had heard but had not seen. Success had crowned his efforts and he felt that he could take some enjoyment in life. At the time of his death he was the owner of several farms in Ogle county, and was considered one of the county's best and most prosperous citizens.

B. T. HEDRICK.

In politics Mr. Hedrick was a Republican, after the organization of the party. His experience with slavery made him a warm advocate of Republican principles, and he did not hesitate to express his convictions. During the Civil war he was a strong Union man, and on one occasion when a draft was imminent, in company with Prof. Williamson, of Mt. Morris College, and the pastor of the Methodist Episcopal church at Mt. Morris, went to Dixon and secured enough men to save the township from a draft. He was a very capable and influential man and served the county well during that trying period. His death occurred July 19, 1886, his faithful wife having preceded him to their heavenly home some thirty years, having died July 27, 1866. They were both devoted members of the Lutheran church, and died in the faith of a blessed resurrection. He was well known in every part of the county, and those knowing him had for him the greatest respect. He served his township as a member of the county board of supervisors, and in various local positions, and in whatever position he was asked to fill, he was ever faithful.

EZRA H. EVANS.—In the respect that is accorded to men who have fought their own way to success through unfavorable environments we find an unconscious recognition of the intrinsic worth of a character which can not only endure so rough a test, but gain new strength through the discipline. The following history sets forth briefly the steps by which our subject, now one of the substantial citizens of Byron, overcame the disadvantages of his early life.

This worthy pioneer of Ogle county, was born in Oneida county, New York, November 22, 1829, and is a representative of an old New York family of Welsh descent. His father, Ozias Evans, and his grandfather, Hugh Evans, were both natives of Oneida county. The former wedded Miss Mary Jeffords, who was born in Herkimer county, New York and was left an orphan in childhood. In Oneida county they reared their family, but finally removed to New Milford, Illinois, where they spent their last years. The father died, however, in Wisconsin, while on a visit, but was laid to rest by the side of his wife in Byron cemetery, her death having occurred several years previously. To them were born six children, two sons and six daughters, of whom all are still living with the exception of the eldest, Mary, wife of Thomas Cook, and Sally and Sally 2d; Ezra H., of this sketch; Mrs. Nancy Soper is a widow living in California; Caroline is the wife of Robert Andrews, of Rockford, Illinois; Mrs. Martha Fisher is a widow living at Black River Falls, Wisconsin, and Erastus C. is living retired in Denver, Colorado.

Ezra H. Evans was reared on a farm and received a good common-school education which well fitted him for the practical duties of life. He was eighteen years of age on coming to Ogle county in the fall of 1848, but the following year was spent on a farm in Wisconsin. Returning to this county in 1849, he secured one hundred and sixty acres of land in Marion township with a land warrant. He located in New Milford and engaged in teaming for five years, hauling flour to Rockford.

In August, 1850, Mr. Evans was married in Winnebago county, Illinois, to Miss Phebe Ann Osborn, a native of Northamptonshire, England, and a daughter of George Osborn, who was born in the same shire and emigrated to the new world about 1831, locating at Hudson, New York, where he spent four or five years. At the end of that time he bought a farm in Oneida county, where he made his home for eleven years, and on coming west, in 1846, settled in Winnebago county, Illinois, ten miles west of Rockford, where he purchased a partially improved farm and there spent his remaining days in agricultural pursuits. In his native land he married Hannah Webster, who died in Oneida county, New York, and he subsequently married again. Mrs. Evans was the only daughter by the first marriage, but there were three sons, all of whom were born in England and are now deceased. All married and lived for a time in Illinois, but Joseph died in Texas, and William died in Ogle county, Illinois, and George died in California. Mrs. Evans was principally reared and educated in Oneida county, New York, being a young lady when the family removed to this state. By her marriage to our subject she has become the mother of three children: Fransula M., wife of David Creager, a farmer of Byron township, Ogle county; Arthur A. died at the age of nineteen months; and Earnest E., who has been in the drug business in Los Gatos, California, for the last three years. For about ten years he was engaged in Byron, Illinois, in drug business. In 1885 he married Miss Elizabeth Spalding, daughter of Phineas Spalding, of Beloit, Wisconsin.

Mr. and Mrs. Evans spent the first year of their married life with her father, our subject assisting in the operation of the farm, and then removed to New Milford, where he engaged in teaming for five years. In 1857 they located on the land he had purchased in Marion township, moving down the river in a ferry boat in the spring of that year, when the streams were very high and the roads almost impassable. Mr. Evans built a frame house, fenced his land and began the development of his farm, which he successfully operated for about twelve years. He then sold the place and bought a residence in Byron, where he still resides. Three years after locating here he purchased a farm of fifty-five acres in Byron township, adjoining the village, and has since added to it a thirty-acre tract, all of which he operates. He also owns a well-improved and valuable farm of eighty acres on the northern line of the county in Byron township, and is to-day one of the most prosperous and successful citizens of the community, the result of his own industry, enterprise and good management.

Politically Mr. Evans has been a supporter of the men and measures of the Republican party since casting his first vote for John C. Fremont in 1856, but he has never sought or cared for official honors, though he served as commissioner of highways in Byron township and as township trustee. Religiously his wife is a faithful member of the Congregational church of Byron, and socially he is one of the oldest members of the Masonic lodge at that place, in which he has served as senior warden and also belongs to Rockford chapter, R. A. M. Mr. and Mrs. Evans spent the winter of 1896-97 on the Pacific slope, visiting their son and other relatives, including Mrs. Evans' brother's wife and family, and an uncle of Mr. Evans. They thoroughly enjoyed the trip and returned home by way of the Southern Pacific route, stopping in Texas for a time. They brought home with them a fine collection of mosses, shells, pebbles and other curios gathered on the beach of the Pacific. In 1876 they spent four months in visiting the Centennial exposition at Philadelphia, and old friends in New York. They receive and merit the high regard of the entire community in which they live and have a host of warm friends throughout Ogle county, who will read with interest this short sketch of so worthy a couple.

TIMOTHY W. ALDEN. There are few men more worthy of representation in a work of this character than the subject of this sketch, who is now passing his declining years in retirement from active labor on his farm on section 8, Leaf River township. His has been a long and busy career, rich with experience, and in which he has established himself in the esteem and confidence of all who know him. Since 1837 he has been a resident of the county, and has taken an active part in its growth and development.

This worthy pioneer was born in Bradford county, Pennsylvania, March 13, 1821, and is of the eighth generation from John Alden, clerk of Captain Miles Standish. The family is of English origin, and its first representative in this country was brought to our shores by the Mayflower. Timothy Alden, our subject's grandfather, was a native of Massachusetts, and in 1801 removed with his family to Bradford county, Pennsylvania, becoming one of its first settlers. The father of our subject, Adonijah Alden, was then about two years old, his birth having occurred in Massachusetts, in 1799, and in Bradford county he grew to manhood. He married Vesta York, a native of Pennsylvania, and a daughter of Rev. Minor York, one of its pioneers. She was living in Wyoming at the time of the massacre and was a child of twelve years. Her father was away with the army, and her mother, with her children, got into a canoe and succeeded in slipping down the river unseen by the Indians. Mr. Alden settled at Durell, on the Susquehanna river, and continued to engage in farming in Bradford county for a number of years, but in 1837 came by team to Ogle county, Illinois, and took up a claim in Marion township, two miles below Byron. He did not long enjoy his new home, however, for he died in the prime of life, in 1839, at the age of forty-eight years. His wife had passed away a few months previous, and a son and two daughters died the same year, all between March and August, of 1839. The other seven children all reached years of maturity, and remained together on the farm for a few years.

In his native state Timothy W. Alden had received fair school advantages. He aided in the development of the new farm in Ogle county, pre-empted the land and devoted his time to its cultivation and improvement for five years. He then sold the claim and engaged in teaming and threshing, having purchased a thresher, which he operated in season for ten years. At the end of that time he bought eighty acres of raw land in Leaf River township, and during the six years he resided thereon he placed it under cultivation and made many improvements. On selling the place in 1856 he bought another tract of eighty acres of unimproved land, on which he has since made his home. To the original purchase he added one hundred and sixty acres, but has since sold forty acres, so that he now has two hundred acres, which he has placed under excellent cultivation, but now leaves the active management of the farm to younger hands. His first home here he has enlarged and improved and there is spending his declining days in ease and quiet.

In Byron township, Ogle county, in 1852, Mr. Alden married Miss Orpha Coolbaugh, also a native of Bradford county, Pennsylvania, and a daughter of Moses Coolbaugh, who was born in the same state. She came to this state with her parents when a young girl and died July 9, 1891, and was laid to rest in Byron cemetery. Thirteen children were born of this union and eleven are still living, namely: Professor Martin M., principal of the Kirkland, Illinois, schools; C. A., editor and proprietor of a paper published in Fulton, Illinois; Vista, wife of Frank Lindley, a farmer of Winnebago county, Illinois; Rev. David, minister of the Congregational church at Prophetstown, Illinois; Fred Grant, a resident of Winnebago county; James, a farmer of Leaf River township; Nancy E., wife of Joseph Curtis, of Winnebago county; John and Emmett, both farmers of that county; and Lilly M., who is attending the nurses training school in Chicago.

Mr. Alden cast his first presidential vote for the Whig candidate in 1844, and continued to support that party until 1856, when he joined the ranks of the Republican party, voting for John C. Fremont, and has since fought under its banner. He has always taken an active and commendable interest in politics, but has never been a politician in the sense of office-seeking. When the Great Western railroad was built through the county, he took stock and helped to establish the elevator at Egan City, and at all times has been prominently identified with those interests calculated to promote the general welfare of the community. In 1841 he united with the Congregational church at Byron, and assisted in building the house of worship, getting out the timber and hauling it to Byron. He has since transferred his membership to the church at Seward. The wonderful changes which have taken place in this region since his arrival here can scarcely be realized, the country at that time was wild and unimproved, but now are seen on every hand churches, schoolhouses, fine farms, thriving villages and cities, while the county is crossed and re-crossed by railroads and telegraphs.

GEORGE W. GARNHART, who is living a retired life on his farm about two miles from Polo, on section 14, Buffalo township, is a well-known citizen of Ogle county, of which he has been a resident since 1849. He was born in Northumberland county, Pennsylvania, December 13, 1839, and is the son of John Garnhart, and a brother of Charles W. Garnhart, of Ogle county, whose family sketch appears elsewhere in this work.

From his native county in Pennsylvania, Mr. Garnhart accompanied his parents to Ogle county, Illinois, the father locating in Marion township. In the public schools of Marion and White Rock townships, Ogle county, he received his primary education. Later he attended Franklin College, in Indiana, where he spent one year and a half in obtaining a higher education. Subsequently he attended Parson Bros. Commercial College, at LaPorte, Indiana, for one year. In his youth he learned the carpenter's trade, which he followed some three or four years in LaPorte, but the greater part of his life has been spent in teaching in the public schools and in farming. While in Indiana, he spent some three years as a teacher in the schools of that state. Returning to Illinois, he here engaged in teaching in the public schools, and as a professional teacher continued to be employed for some years. He then purchased an improved farm in White Rock township, Ogle county, and there engaged in farming for a few years, then sold out and purchased the farm where he now resides in Buffalo township. This farm was also improved, but on coming into possession he made further improvements to the place, and has it now under a high state of cultivation. The house was remodeled by him, good barns and outbuildings were erected, shade and ornamental trees set out, and the whole place transformed.

Mr. Garnhart was married about 1863, and is the father of three children, two sons and a daughter, Walter W., Alwilda E. and Dewitt C. (deceased). Walter W. is a well educated young man, a graduate of Brown University, while the latter is also well educated, and is a teacher of music.

Mr. Garnhart has been an earnest advocate of the principles of the Republican party since its organization. His first presidential vote was cast for our first martyr president, Abraham Lincoln, and he has since voted for every presidential nominee of the party, including William McKinley. He has never asked or desired public office, having no inclinations in that respect. His interest in the cause of education has always been great, and some eighteen or twenty years of his life were passed as a teacher in the public schools, and about the same length of time as a member of the school board, and clerk of the school district. For a half century he has been a resident of the county and he has always been interested in its advancement. As a professional teacher, as a farmer, and as a citizen, he has contributed his share to make the county one of the best in the great prairie state. He is well known as a man of sterling character, and has the confidence and esteem of a large circle of friends.

JACOB STEFFA is one of the old and honored citizens of Ogle county who has aided so materially in the development of this region from pioneer days. He is the owner of a fine farm of one hundred and twenty acres on section 8, Rockvale township, on which he has successfully engaged in agricultural pursuits for many years.

Mr. Steffa is a native of Maryland, born in Washington county, February 21, 1818, and a son of William and Elizabeth (Otoalt) Steffa, the former born in Washington county, and the latter in Hagerstown, Maryland. The father was a farmer by occupation. In their family were ten children, of whom our subject is the eldest, the others being John, a resident of Pomona, California; Joseph, of Mt. Morris, Illinois; David, who is living with his son, William Steffa, in Rockvale township, Ogle county; Solomon; William; Elizabeth, Matilda and Mary, deceased; and Hannah, who is now living in Iowa.

During his boyhood and youth Jacob Steffa attended the district schools during the winter months, while during the summer season he assisted his father in the labors of the farm until eighteen years of age, when he left school and began working for Christly Hershe, with whom he remained for two years. The following two years were spent on a farm near Sharpsburg, Maryland, on the Potomac river, at the end of which time he came west by team, arriving in Ogle county, October 6, 1844, after being a month upon the road. His brother had located here the spring previous and was then working for John Phelps. When our subject and his father arrived, they rented the Phelps farm of three hundred and twenty acres, which they operated for three years and then the son leased the Washington Phelps farm of one hundred and sixty acres for two years. At the end of that time he made his first purchase, consisting of eighty acres, but subsequently sold that place and bought his present farm of one hundred and twenty acres in Rockvale township, upon which he has made many valuable and useful improvements which add greatly to its value and attractive appearance. As a citizen he has the respect and confidence of all who know him, and his friends are many throughout the commontiy in which he makes his home.

On the 31st of January, 1831, occurred the marriage of Mr. Steffa and Miss Mary Houze, who was born in Maryland, September 28, 1822, a daughter of Edward and Lydia (Funk) Houze, also natives of that state. The children born of this union are as follows: Daniel, born March 31, 1841, was one of the boys in blue during the Civil war, a member of the Thirty-fourth Illinois Volunteer Infantry, and is now living in Colorado. He married first Elizabeth Randall, and for his second wife wedded Mrs. Browning, by whom he has three children. Sarah Margaret, born March 11, 1843, married Jacob Bolembaugh, who was killed during the Civil war, and she later married a Mr. Morse, by whom she has two children. She is also living in Colorado. Samuel, born January 7, 1845, enlisted in the Thirty-fourth Illinois Volunteer Infantry during the Rebellion and served until hostilities ceased, taking part in many important battles and the celebrated march to the sea. He married Charlotte McDonald, by whom he has two children, and they live at Rockford, Illinois. Reuben Jonathan, born March 25, 1847, married Mrs. Thema Myers, by whom he has one child, and they live in Redwing, Minnesota. Ann Celesta, born September 28, 1850, married Thomas Mallory and lives in Chicago. William Arthur, born July 8, 1852, married Lorina Waite, by whom he has two children, and they live in Oregon, Ogle county. Mary Alice, born August 31, 1854, married Jacob Hemmer. She has two children: Harry Wilbur, born July 12, 1882; and Wilfred, born October 27, 1884.

In his political views Mr. Steffa is a Republican, and he has ever taken an active and commendable interest in political affairs, serving as school director several terms and as road commissioner for one term of three years, to the entire satisfaction of all concerned.

DANIEL H. TOBIAS, who resides on section 2, Lincoln township, has been a resident of Ogle county almost a third of a century, coming here in March, 1866. The farm which he owns and operates contains two hundred and eighty acres of well improved land and is one of the best in Lincoln township. He is a native of Dauphin county, Pennsylvania, about thirty-four miles from Harrisburg, and was born April 30, 1843, and is a son of John Tobias, a native of the same county and state, and the grandson of Daniel Tobias.

John Tobias grew to manhood in his native county and in his youth learned the stone mason's trade, and followed that occupation, in connection with mining during his entire life. He was twice married, his first wife being Miss Nancy Rowe, also a native of Dauphin county, Pennsylvania, and daughter of Wendell Rowe, of the same county. She became the mother of five sons, four of whom grew to manhood, and three now living: Daniel H., our subject; Henry, residing in Schuylkill county, Pennsylvania; and John, a resident of Northumberland county, in the same state. A few years after his marriage, John Tobias removed with his family to Schuylkill county, Pennsylvania, where he engaged at his trade and also at mining. His first wife, the mother of the children named, died in 1850, but he survived her many years, dying in 1896 when about seventy-five years old.

In his native county our subject spent his boyhood and youth, and in its common schools obtained his education, attending usually in the winter months and farming in the summer. He attained his majority during the trying period of the Civil war, and on the 19th of September, 1864, at Harrisburg, he enlisted in Company H, Two Hundred and Tenth Pennsylvania Volunteer Infantry, and served until the close of the war, his regiment forming a part of the Fifth Corps, army of the Potomac. He participated in the two battles at Hatches Run, Gravelly Run, Five Forks, Appomattox Court House, and was present at the time of Lee's surrender, April 9, 1865. In addition to the engagements mentioned he was in several minor ones, and participated in the grand review at Washington at the close of the war. The regiment went out with nine hundred and sixty men and returned with four hundred and ninety-three. Of the remainder, some were killed in battle, and some wounded or otherwise disabled. Mr. Tobias received several shots through his clothing, but was never wounded.

On receiving his discharge, Mr. Tobias returned to his old home and engaged in teaming until the spring of 1866, when he came to Ogle county in company with Aaron Meyers, who is a substantial farmer of Lincoln township. After coming here, for two years he worked by the month for various persons. He was married in Lincoln township, Ogle county, December 26, 1867, to Margaret Meyers, daughter of Jacob M. Meyers, who was an Ogle county pioneer, coming here, in 1837, from Boonsborough, Maryland. He was, however, a native of Berks county, Pennsylvania, born in 1799, but reared in Dauphin county, going to Maryland a young man of nineteen. He was a stonemason by trade, an occupation that he followed while residing in Maryland. He married Elizabeth Gloss, a native of Washington county, Maryland, and daughter of Lewis Gloss, a German ancestry. On coming to Ogle county, Jacob Meyers located in that part of Mt. Morris township which has since been organized under the name of Lincoln, where he bought a claim of eight hundred acres, entered the land when it came into market, and became one of the most substantial farmers of the county. He died in Lincoln township August 26, 1877, at the age of seventy-eight years. His wife passed away April 6, of the same year. Their remains were interred in the West Grove cemetery. They were the parents of eleven children, of whom one son and six daughters grew to mature years, though but three are now living. Sarah, wife of Daniel Fager, of Forreston; Ellen, wife of John Mace, a farmer of Lincoln township; and Margaret, wife of our subject. Jacob S. Meyers, the son, who grew to manhood, enlisted in the One Hundred and Forty-second Illinois Volunteer Infantry, was taken sick while in the service, brought home and died October 4, 1864.

After their marriage Mr. and Mrs. Tobias commenced life on the old Myers homestead, where Mrs. Myers was born and reared. They lived on that farm until the spring of 1897, when Mr. Tobias purchased his present farm to which they at once removed. They are the parents of three daughters. Emma Luella is the wife of Samuel W. Hamilton, a farmer of Lincoln township. Ella Viola, who was well educated in the schools of Forreston and Oregon, is now a successful teacher in the schools of Ogle county for about four years. Edna Agnes is a student in the home school. Politically, Mr. Tobias is a stanch Republican, and has voted for ten presidential candidates of that party. He has never cared for public office, but for the reason that he has always taken a deep interest in the public schools, he has served on the school board for eighteen years, a portion of which time he has been president of the board. He has also served as district clerk and one term as road commissioner. He and his wife are members of the Reformed church at West Grove, and take a lively interest in the work of the church. Both are highly esteemed wherever known. Mrs. Tobias has been a life-long resident of the township, while Mr. Tobias has given some thirty-three years of his life to the building up and development of his adopted county. Fraternally, he is a member of the G. A. R. Post, No. 116, of Oregon, and of White Oak Camp, No. 667, M. W. A., of Forreston.

ASAPH M. TRUMBULL.—The subject of this review is one whose history touches the pioneer epoch in the annals of the state of Illinois and whose days have been an integral part of that indissoluble chain which links the early formative period with that of later-day progress and prosperity. Not alone is there particular interest attaching to his career as one of the pioneers of Ogle county, but in reviewing his genealogical record we find his lineage tracing back to the colonial history of the nation and to that period which marked the inception of the grandest republic the world has ever known.

Mr. Trumbull was born near Hartford, Connecticut, September 13, 1813, and is a worthy representative of an old and honored New England family, which was founded in this country by three brothers of English birth. One of these, Governor Jonathan Trumbull, of Connecticut, was a great friend of General Washington, who always made his home headquarters when in that region, and it is believed that the term "Brother Jonathan" originated from this friendship. Four generations of the family, including our subject, were born in the same house on the old Trumbull homestead in Connecticut. Among these was the grandfather, David Trumbull, and the father, James Trumbull, who spent their entire life there engaged in agricultural pursuits. He served as a sergeant in the war of 1812, and died at the age of forty-two years, honored and respected by all who knew him. In early life he married Jane Watson also a native of the Nutmeg state, who survived him a number of years and died on the old homestead. To them were born nine children, but only two are now living: Mrs. Fanny Weller, a widow, now ninety-three years of age, who resides in Waterbury, Connecticut; and Asaph M., our subject.

Until he attained his majority Asaph M. Trumbull remained with his mother and aided in the operation of the home farm. His educational advantages were good for those days, as he attended both the common schools and academies, and for two winter terms he engaged in teaching. When a young man he went to Milton, Union county, Pennsylvania, where he engaged in the manufacture of brooms for two years. While there he was married in 1838 to Miss Sarah Gotshall, a native of Milton. The following year he purchased a team and wagon, which he loaded with his effects, and in May started for Illinois, being four weeks in making the journey. He joined two brothers, David and Joseph, who had settled in Ogle county early that spring, and he secured a claim of one hundred and forty acres near Byron. He spent the first winter in a log cabin on the banks of a creek, but in the spring that stream overflowed its banks, and as they were threatened with drowning they were forced to leave, moving out of their little home in a boat. Mr. Trumbull then erected a house and barn on higher ground and proceeded to break his land preparatory to planting crops. Two years later he traded that place for a farm in Marion township, of one hundred and ninety acres, which were slightly improved. He planted an orchard, erected a comfortable residence and good outbuildings, and for forty years devoted his energies to the cultivation of his land, making it one of the best and most desirable farms of the township. In 1881 he rented the place and moved to Stillman Valley, where he built a good home and has since lived retired from active labor, though he still looks after his farm and other interests. He has given his support to a number of business enterprises that have done much for the development and prosperity of this part of the county.

Soon after coming to Illinois Mr. Trumbull's first wife died, and he subsequently wedded Mary Patrick, who was a native of Massachusetts, and when young came west with her father, Samuel Patrick, an early settler of Ogle county. She died on the farm in Marion township, and of the three children born to them one died at the age of eleven years and one at the age of two. The only one now living, George Trumbull, a farmer of Marion township, is married and has two children. On the 6th of August, 1861, in Camden, Oneida county, New York, Mr. Trumbull was united in marriage with Miss Honor Preston, who was born, reared and educated at that place, and is a daughter of Rossiter and Orril (Curtis) Preston, both natives of Connecticut. They later lived for a number of years in Camden, New York, finally removing to Rockford, Illinois.

Politically Mr. Trumbull was an old-line Whig and cast his first presidential ballot for Martin Van Buren, but on the organization of the Republican party he joined its ranks, voting for John C. Fremont in 1856, and has never failed to support each presidential candidate of that party since then. He has ever used his influence toward securing good schools and for a number of years was a most efficient member of the school board. He has also served his fellow citizens in a most creditable and satisfactory manner as supervisor, township clerk and assessor for a few years each. In early life he joined the Presbyterian church, but after coming to this county he united with the Congregational church at Byron.

On his removal to Stillman Valley he became connected with the Congregational church at that place, has taken an active part in church and Sabbath school work, and for thirty years has been a member of the official board, being a deacon at the present time. His life is exemplary in many respects and he has ever supported those interests which are calculated to uplift and benefit humanity, while his own high moral worth is deserving of the highest commendation.

GEORGE W. SHAFER, who resides on section 10, Buffalo township, has been a resident of Ogle county since October, 1867. He was born in Delaware county, New York, September 2, 1843, and is of German ancestry, the family being early settlers, however, of Duchess county, New York, from which county the grandfather of our subject removed to Delaware county, in the same state, becoming one of the pioneers of that county. Strange as it may seem to those who think of the east as old settled country, when Henry Shafer moved to Delaware county they were compelled to go to Kingston, a distance of sixty miles, on horseback, to get their milling done.

Henry S. Shafer, the son of Henry Shafer and the father of our subject, was born in Delaware county, March 19, 1814, and on his father's farm grew to manhood and there married Deborah Shafer, daughter of Adam Shafer, also a pioneer of that county. They were the parents of three sons and four daughters, as follows: Adam H., of Binghamton, New York; George W., of this review; Juliana, wife of Daniel Waterbury, of Polo; Ransom, a business man of Chicago; Eliff, wife of Henry C. Wood, of Binghamton, New York; Elizabeth, wife of D. Kelley, of Walton, New York; and Celia, who died in 1876. Both parents are now deceased, the mother dying in May, 1896, and the father in March, 1897.

George W. Shafer grew to manhood in Delaware county, New York, and was educated in the common schools of his native county. He remained at home, assisting in the cultivation of the home farm until after he attained his majority, but with that desire to better himself in life, he came to Ogle county in 1867, where he joined his sister, Mrs. Waterbury, who had preceded him. Soon after his arrival he purchased the farm where he now resides, a place which was fairly well improved. Taking possession of the place he put in a crop in the spring of 1868 and attended to its cultivation. He came here, however, alone, and believing the scriptural statement "that it was not good for man to be alone," he returned to his old home, and on the 21st of September, 1868, was united in marriage with Miss Sarah Shafer, also a native of Delaware county, New York, and daughter of Townsend and Adeline (Van Gaasbeek) Shafer, the former a native of Delaware county and the latter of Ulster county, New York, of Holland ancestry. Townsend Shafer spent his entire life in his native state, where his death occurred, March 18, 1873. His wife survived him many years, and for about twenty years prior to her death made her home with our subject, dying, however, in Middletown, Orange county, New York, April 20, 1896, while on a visit to that city. Mrs. Shafer was one of two daughters born to her parents, her sister, Josephine, now being the wife of J. A. Frasier, of California. In the common schools of her native county, and in Delphi

Academy, Mrs. Shafer was educated, and for a time prior to her marriage engaged in teaching in the public schools.

Immediately after his marriage Mr. Shafer returned to Ogle county and took care of his crop, subsequently joining his wife in Delaware county, where they remained until February, 1868, when they came to their new home near Polo, where he resumed farming, and where they have since continued to reside. Soon after taking possession of his farm, Mr. Shafer erected a small frame house, and four years later built an addition to, and there they lived until 1882, when he built a larger and more pretentious dwelling. From time to time he has made improvements on his place, setting out shade and ornamental trees, tilling the land, and erecting the necessary outbuildings. His farm is very conveniently located, being within one mile of the corporate limits of the city of Polo.

In 1864 Mr. Shafer attained his majority, and in November following he cast his first presidential vote for Abraham Lincoln, since which time he has continued to support the candidates of the Republican party. He and his wife are members of the Baptist church of Polo, and he is one of its official board. In the work of the church they are both greatly interested, and do what they can to advance the Master's kingdom. They believe in enjoying life and to that end have made a number of visits back to their old home in Delaware county, New York, and in November, 1896, went to California, where they remained until February, 1897, during which time they visited San Francisco, Sacramento, and other noted places on the Pacific slope. Their trip was a most enjoyable one. Both are well known in Polo and vicinity and their friends are many throughout the western part of the county. As a farmer, he thoroughly understands his business.

DAVID THOMSON.—Quite a number of the leading and prominent citizens of Ogle county are of alien birth, and have transported to this land of fertility and plenty the thrifty habits of their native country. Among these there is none that is better known or more widely respected than the gentleman whose name introduces this sketch. He now owns and operates a valuable farm of about two hundred and fifty acres on section 5, Leaf River township.

Mr. Thomson is a native of Scotland, born in Renfrewshire, January 8, 1829, and is a son of James and Eughemia (St. Clare) Thomson, also natives of that country. The father, who was born in Ayrshire, was a baker by trade, and in 1810 embarked in that business at Johnstown, Scotland, where he carried on operations until his death in 1841. His wife survived him twenty years, departing this life in 1861. In the family were twelve children, eight sons and four daughters, of whom eleven reached years of maturity, but only three are now living, namely: Mrs. Jane Caldwell, who was born in 1807, and now resides near Glasgow, Scotland; Nesbit, who was born in 1811, and is also living in that country; and David, our subject.

In early life David Thomson learned the baker's trade with his father, and continued to work at the same until coming to the new world in 1848. He first located in Troy, New York, where he had two sisters living, Mrs. Euphemia Turner and Mrs. Mary Ann Craig, who later became residents of Ogle county, Illinois. Each had but one child. In Troy, Mr. Thomson worked at his trade for about three years, and the following year was spent in a bakery in Newark, New Jersey. He went to California in 1852, taking passage on a steamer at New York City. He crossed the Isthmus and proceeded up the Pacific to San Francisco, where he worked in a bakery for two months. He then went to the mines and spent about ten years in search for the yellow metal. In 1862 he returned to New York and shortly afterward came to Ogle county, Illinois, where his sisters had located in the meantime. The same year he purchased seventy-five acres of prairie land and ten acres of timber land, and at once turned his attention to the improvement and cultivation of his place. He bought more land from time to time and now has about two hundred and fifty acres, which he has placed under a high state of cultivation, and improved with good and substantial buildings. Although this was his first experience in farming, he met with success almost from the start, and is now numbered among the most successful farmers and stock raisers of Leaf River township.

On the 20th of February, 1863, in Ogle county, Mr. Thomson was united in marriage with Miss Mary Ballaugh, who was born in Albany, New York, and reared in that state. Her father, John Ballaugh, was a molder and foundryman, and was engaged in business in Williamsburg, New York, for some years. There were thirteen children born to Mr. and Mrs. Thomson and all are living with the exception of two, one of whom died in infancy, and the other, Mary, at the age of ten years. William is a farmer of Washington county, Illinois; Jane is the wife of William McCartney, a farmer of Winnebago county, Illinois; Euphemia is the wife of Chris Kilker, a farmer of Leaf River township, Ogle county; John is a farmer of Jackson county, Minnesota; Dr. Stewart is a physician of Washington county, Illinois. The above are all married, while the others are still single, namely: David A., who is clerking in a grocery store in Steward, Illinois; Mattie, who is teaching in Winnebago county; Nesbit, who assists in the farm work; and Edward, Robert and George, all at home.

Mr. Thomson cast his first presidential vote for Abraham Lincoln in 1864, and has since been an ardent supporter of the Republican party. He has ever used his influence for the good of the public schools, and for a number of years was a member of the school board. He was also clerk of his district for several years and township trustee for three years. He and his wife are leading members of the Middle Creek Presbyterian church, and their sterling worth and many excellencies of character have endeared them to all with whom they have come in contact.

JAMES C. WOODBURN has for a quarter of a century been prominently identified with the business and political interests of Byron and is distinctively a man of affairs, one who wields a wide influence. He is actively engaged in the practice of law and is also interested in the real-estate and insurance business. His intellectual energy, professional integrity, prudent business methods, and reliable sagacity have all combined to make him one of the ablest business men of the community.

A native of Ogle county, Mr. Woodburn

JAMES C. WOODBURN.

was born on the old homestead in Byron township, October 13, 1846, and belongs to a family of English extraction, whose representatives were among the first settlers of Connecticut. His grandfather, John Woodburn, was born in that state, and was among the pioneers of Bradford county, Pennsylvania, where the father, Allen Woodburn, first opened his eyes to the light in 1810, and where he grew to manhood. The year 1836 witnessed his arrival in Ogle county, Illinois, and in Byron township, near the present village of Byron, he took a claim of one hundred and sixty acres, on which he erected a log house and raised three or four small crops. Returning to his native county, he was there married, in 1840, to Miss Mary A. Whitney, who was born in Luzerne county, Pennsylvania, and was a daughter of William Whitney, Esq., a representative of an old Pennsylvanian family. Mr. Woodburn brought his bride to the home he had prepared for her in Ogle county and resumed his farming operations here. He was one of the most active, enterprising and successful farmers of this region and soon had his land under excellent cultivation. His little pioneer home was replaced by a large, neat and substantial residence, good outbuildings were erected, and fruit, forest and ornamental trees set out. From time to time he purchased more land until he owned one thousand acres, all in one body, on which were three sets of farm buildings besides those on his own homestead, it being one of the improved and most highly cultivated places in the county. Mr. Woodburn was quite prominent and influential and was elected to a number of local offices of trust and honor. He was also one of the foremost to aid by his influence or support any object which he believed calculated to promote the upbuilding or advancement of Ogle county. He died at his home December 22, 1887, at the ripe old age of seventy-eight years, and his wife passed away in 1879. Both were laid to rest in the Byron cemetery, where has been erected to their memory a neat and substantial monument. They were the parents of three children: Fred C., the eldest, is now living retired in Rockford, Illinois; James C. is next in order of birth; and Carrie E. is the wife of Charles H. Patrick, of Rockford.

James C. Woodburn completed his literary education in Wheaton College, and later entered the law department of the Michigan University at Ann Arbor, graduating at that noted institution with the class of 1870. He then successfully engaged in teaching in Ogle county for two years, and at the end of that time opened an office in Byron for the practice of law. Being an able lawyer, and a man of sound judgment, he manages his cases with masterly skill and tact, and practices in all of the courts. As a business man he has also met with marked success and still carries on a large real estate and insurance business. In 1882 he became interested in banking, in which he also succeeded, but at the end of five years he sold out.

On the 10th of November, 1880, in Ogle county, was celebrated the marriage of Mr. Woodburn and Miss Ada M. Patrick, a daughter of George T. Patrick, one of the first settlers of the county. She was born, reared and educated here, and for some years prior to her marriage successfully engaged in teaching. Four children bless this union: Mary A., Roy M., Adelbert and Grace E.

Politically Mr. Woodburn is a life-long Republican, having cast his first presidential ballot for U. S. Grant in 1868. He has ever taken an active and prominent part in local politics and campaign work, has been a delegate to many county, congressional and state conventions, and has rendered his party efficient service. He was elected and served as the only temperance mayor of Byron, was a leading member of the town board for several years, treasurer of Byron township twenty years, and for twenty-four years has been justice of the peace in the township, a position he is still most creditably and satisfactorily filling. He is also notary public, and in whatever position he has been called upon to fill he has proved a most faithful trustworthy official. Socially he is a Master Mason, and has served as secretary of Byron lodge for the past fifteen years. He was largely instrumental in organizing the Eastern Star at that place, of which he and his wife are charter members, and Mrs. Woodburn is now worthy matron of the order. Both hold membership in the Congregational church, and in social circles occupy an enviable position.

HON. ALBERT F. BROWN.—More than sixty years have passed since this gentleman arrived in Ogle county, and he is justly numbered among her honored pioneers and leading citizens. As an agriculturist he has been prominently identified with her business interests and in early life took quite an influential part in the political affairs of this section. His is an honorable record of a conscientious man, who by his upright life has won the confidence of all with whom he has come in contact.

Mr. Brown was born September 4, 1819, in Brimfield, Hampden county, Massachusetts, near Springfield, and belongs to an old and distinguished family of that state. The first to come to America was Jonathan Brown, a native of England, who settled in Massachusetts in 1736 and received a grant of land from King George. His homestead remained in the family for several generations. He not only aided the colonies in their struggle for independence during the Revolution, but also bore an active part in the early Indian wars. At a meeting of the citizens of the colony he was appointed to visit each house to ascertain whether the inmates were using imported tea and if so to report the same that such families might be ostracised, this being just prior to the famous Boston tea party. His son, Bartholomew Brown, our subject's grandfather, was born in Brimfield, Massachusetts, and spent his entire life there, his remains being interred in the village cemetery. He was a farmer by occupation and served with distinction as a lieutenant in the Continental army during the Revolutionary war.

Colonel Dauphin Brown, father of our subject, was also a native of Brimfield, born November 9, 1792, and was reared on his father's farm. He was married December 1, 1814, to Miss Sila Patrick, who was born in Brimfield, February 9, 1792, a daughter of Samuel and Persis (Smith) Patrick. The Patrick family is also of English origin and was founded in Massachusetts in 1716. The Colonel and his wife lived on the old Brown homestead until April, 1837, when, accompanied by their sons, Albert F., Samuel Patrick and J. M. Clayton, he started for Illinois, taking the route via Hartford, New York city, Philadelphia and Pittsburg, thence down the Ohio and up the Mississippi and Illinois rivers to Peoria, where they procured teams and drove to Dixon. There they rented land about a mile and a half from the village for one summer. Colonel Brown and Mr. Patrick visited Ogle county and the former purchased eighty acres at Black Walnut Grove, on section 9, Marion township. In the fall of that year, 1887, in company with Jared and J. F. Sanford, he built a sawmill on Mill creek, in what is now Byron township, and in December returned to Massachusetts. The following spring he sold his farm at Brimfield, settled up all business claims, and shipped his goods from Boston by way of New Orleans, to Savanna, Carroll county, Illinois, while his family came west by the the same route that he had previously taken, with the exception that they landed at Savanna instead of Peoria, and from there came to Ogle county. Colonel Brown bought a claim of eighty acres in the immediate vicinity of Byron and built a frame house in the village, where the family resided for seven years while he opened up and developed his farm. As soon as the land came into market, he entered his claim on section 9, Marion township, and also purchased the southeast quarter of section 35, townships 25 and 11, on which he erected a residence that was ever afterward his home. There his death occurred November 15, 1871. His first wife had passed away in 1840, and in 1854 he wedded Miss Lucia Homer, who was also born in Brimfield, Massachusetts, in May, 1793, and died in 1881. He was commissioned colonel in the Massachusetts state militia by Governor Levi Lincoln, but entered the service as a private. He was also one of the most prominent men in the early settlement of Ogle county, was one of the first commissioners elected and was serving in that office at the time of the erection of the first court house. In 1849 he ably represented his district in the Sixteenth General Assembly of Illinois. With his first wife he joined the Congregational church at Brimfield in early life, and after coming to this state was an active and prominent member of that denomination, assisting in the organization of the churches at Byron and Stillman Valley and serving as deacon for many years.

To Colonel Dauphin and Sila (Patrick) Brown were born eight children, who in order of birth are as follows: Persis P. married Dr. Arnold E. Hurd, a pioneer and prominent citizen of Ogle county, and both are now deceased, Mrs. Hurd departing this life at Stillman Valley in August, 1861. Lucy A. married Hon. Joshua White, a leading citizen of Ogle county, now deceased, who served for sixteen years as a member of the county board and also served in the Twenty-first General Assembly of Illinois, and she died October 13, 1885. Albert F., our subject, is the next in the family. Henry F. died at Byron, July 30, 1839, at the age of eighteen years. Sarah S. is the wife of Frank A. Smith and resides near Byron. Harriet L. married William J. Mix and died November 24, 1849. George F. died at Stillman Valley, November 24, 1850. Julia A. married Hon. James G. White, a prominent man of Ogle county, now deceased, and she is now living in Stillman Valley.

Albert F. Brown was sixteen years of age when he accompanied his father on his first trip to Illinois and amid pioneer scenes in Ogle county he grew to manhood, early becoming familiar with the arduous task of transforming the wild land into rich and productive fields. His education was principally obtained in the common schools, supplemented by one year's attendance at

Wesleyan Academy, in Massachusetts. For a few years he operated a ferry at Byron, but throughout life has given the greater part of his attention to agricultural pursuits. In 1845 he and his brother-in-law, Dr. Hurd, came to Stillman Valley and entered between eight and nine hundred acres of land and each opened up a fine farm. Mr. Brown owned five hundred acres, and of this he placed three hundred acres under the plow. For two years after his marriage he continued to reside in Byron and then removed to Stillman Valley, owning the first frame house in that place. Later he built a more commodious and substantial residence, and is still successfully engaged in farming upon one of the best improved and most valuable farms in the county.

On the 8th of December, 1842, at Byron, Mr. Brown was united in marriage with Miss Eunice Cordelia Cothren, who was born in Cayuga county, New York, May 8, 1823, a daughter of Nathaniel Cothren, also a pioneer of Ogle county. She was called to her final rest November 10, 1892. The children born of this union were as follows: Henrietta C., at home; Charles F., a farmer of Marion township; George H., a prominent business man of Stillman Valley, and a stanch Republican, who is president of the village school board and supervisor of Marion township; Esther J., wife of Harvey Rood, of Chicago; Cora C., wife of William F. Hannum, of Stillman Valley; A. Chester, a stockholder and cashier of the Stillman Valley Bank; Sila Persis, wife of Joseph G. Pratt, an attorney of Hilo, Hawaiian Islands; and Edwin, who died in infancy.

Originally Mr. Brown was an old-line Whig in politics, and cast his first ballot in 1840 for Tippecanoe and Tyler, too; but in 1859 he joined the newly organized Republican party, and has since fought under its banner. He assisted in the formation of the party in his congressional district, and has since been an active and influential worker in its ranks. He has been called upon to fill many local offices of honor and trust, such as assessor and supervisor, and was chairman of the board a number of terms. In 1878 he was elected to the thirty-second general assembly of Illinois, and so acceptably did he fill the office that he was twice re-elected, proving a most popular and capable official. He was a member of several important committees, and was chairman of the committees on county and township organizations and on roads, and state buildings. Since his retirement from that office he has declined all political honors. For thirty-eight years he has been an active member of the Congregational church, and has served as its trustee for forty years. As a citizen he stands ready to discharge every duty devolving upon him; over his life record there falls no shadow of wrong; his public service was most exemplary, and his private life has been marked by the utmost fidelity to duty.

J F. SNYDER, M. D., who resides at Monroe Center, Illinois, where he is engaged in the practice of his profession with gratifying success, is a native of Schoharie county, New York, and was born May 26, 1860. He is the son of Nelson and Henrietta (Hale) Snyder, both of whom were natives of New York, the father being a farmer by occupation and following that vocation during his entire life. The paternal grandfather, Daniel Snyder, married Mary Eckerson, both being New York people, and both living and dying in that state. For many years he engaged in hotel keeping in Middleburg, New York, at the same time engaging in agricultural pursuits.

In the family of Nelson and Henrietta Snyder were six children, four sons and two daughters, all of whom are yet living. Daniel is married and is now a prosperous farmer residing in Stillman Valley. Charles S. married Mary Bly, and is also a substantial farmer living at Stillman Valley. Henry H., a portrait artist, is married and makes his home in Rockford, Illinois. J. F. is the subject of this sketch. Julia married J. Huff, and they live at Byron, where he is employed at his trade, that of a carpenter. Helen married A. J. Woodcock, M. D., and they reside in Byron, where he is engaged in active practice. In his native state, Nelson Snyder owned and operated a farm of one hundred and sixty acres, which he sold in 1868, and coming to Ogle county, purchased a farm of one hundred and sixty acres in Marion township, where he yet resides. Many improvements have been made upon the place since it came into his possession, the farm being well tilled, with good barns and other outbuildings which show that it is owned by one who thoroughly understands his business. The good wife and mother passed to her reward May 26, 1896, leaving not only the family, but many friends to mourn her loss.

The subject of this sketch was but eight years old when he accompanied his parents to Ogle county. His education, which was begun in the common schools of his native state, was continued in the schools of Ogle county. He was an apt scholar, and at the early age of sixteen years passed an examination and commenced teaching in the public schools of his adopted county. Teaching in the winter months, and working upon the farm in summer, he continued until he was eighteen years old, when he entered the medical department of Michigan University, at Ann Arbor, where he remained one year, and then entered Rush Medical College, Chicago, from which he graduated in 1882, at the age of twenty-two years, being the youngest man in his class.

Immediately after receiving his diploma, Dr. Snyder located at Kings, Ogle county, and at once engaged in the practice of his profession, but in September of the same year moved to Monroe Center, and has here continued in active practice to the present time. That his choice of a location was a good one is evidenced by his large practice and the estimation in which he is held in the community. In 1884 he was nominated on the Republican ticket for the office of county coroner, was duly elected, and served the full term of four years. In 1890 he was elected township treasurer, a position which he still continues to hold. Reared a Republican, he has since continued to advocate the principles of the Republican party, and is now with his party in favor of the retention of all gained by the late war with Spain.

Dr. Snyder was married September 4, 1889, to Miss Hattie Swett, a daughter of Riley and Mary (Hickox) Swett, who were early settlers of Ogle county. By this union there is one son, Clarendon Swett Snyder, now a lad of seven years.

Fraternally Dr. Snyder is a member of the Masonic order and of the Modern Woodmen of America, in the latter body being examining physician in his local camp. Socially he is a member of the Alumni Association of Rush Medical College and professionally a member of the Fox

River Medical Society. He is a liberal supporter of the various churches and the public schools, and gives aid and encouragement to every enterprise of value to his town and county. In the estimation of his fellow citizens he is held in the highest esteem.

J CHESTER STIRES is a worthy representative of the business interests of Byron, where he is extensively engaged in buying and shipping stock. Of excellent business ability and broad resources, he has attained a prominent place among the substantial citizens of this part of the county, and is a recognized leader in public affairs. He has won success by his well-directed, energetic efforts, and the prosperity that has come to him is certainly well deserved.

Mr. Stires was born February 6, 1852, in Hunterdon county, New Jersey, and belongs to one of the pioneer families of that state, of which his parents, Thomas and Jane (Conover) Stires, were also natives. The father, whose birth occurred in Hunterdon county, in 1808, engaged in farming there until 1854 or 1855, when he removed to Ohio, but in 1856 he became a resident of Byron township, Ogle county, Illinois, where he purchased an improved farm of one hundred and sixty acres. To its cultivation he devoted his energies until called from this life July 1, 1864, and his wife, who survived him some years, passed away in February, 1878. In their family were five sons and five daughters, all of whom reached man and womanhood, with the exception of one son. H. C., the eldest, resides in Byron; Ira owns and occupies the old homestead farm; Mrs. N. J. Hewitt is a resident of Byron; Mrs. Maggie Swackhamer lives in Hunterdon county, New Jersey; Carrie N. died unmarried; Mrs. Hannah Noyes makes her home in Byron; Garret and J. Chester are both residents of that place; and Mrs. Alice Court lives in Creston, Iowa.

Reared on the home farm, J. Chester Stires early became familiar with all the duties which fall to the lot of the agriculturist, aiding in the work of the farm during the summer season and attending the district school during the winter months. He was married in Marion township, Ogle county, December 29, 1875, to Miss Hattie N. Wilbur, who was born in Byron township and was reared and educated in this county. Her father, Charles Wilbur, located here in 1845 and took up a tract of government land in Byron township, which he transformed into a good farm. After his marriage Mr. Stires operated this place, consisting of one hundred and forty acres, until 1890, and also owned and operated another farm of two hundred and thirty acres, being actively and successfully engaged in agricultural pursuits for fifteen years. In 1890 he removed to the village of Byron, where he bought residence property, which he has greatly improved, and now has a very pleasant and commodious home. Here he engages in buying and shipping stock and is one of the most successful dealers in the county. In 1892 he also bought an interest in the Byron bank, and is now one of the four stockholders of that reliable institution.

Mr. and Mrs. Stires are the parents of four children: Mabel, who died at the age of thirteen years; Elva Jane, a well educated young lady who is now successfully engaged in teaching school in Ogle county; Anna L., who is also well educated and is now at home, and Margaret Grace, who completes the family.

Politically Mr. Stires has affiliated with the Democracy since casting his first presidential ballot for Samuel J. Tilden in 1876, and he has taken an active and prominent part in local politics, serving as a delegate to numerous county, congressional and state conventions. In the spring of 1898 he was elected supervisor of Byron township, defeating the Republican candidate who had served for ten years in that office and had always been elected by a large majority. This fact plainly indicates the popularity of our subject, as the township has always been strongly Republican, and his many friends in Byron rejoiced in his triumph, manifesting their enthusiasm by a big rally. He is now serving on the poor farm committee. In 1897 he was elected president of the town board. Mr. Stires is acknowledged to be one of the most enterprising and public spirited citizens of Byron, and for eight years advocated the building of a bridge across the river at that place and was instrumental in at last securing it. He contributed two hundred dollars toward its construction, and was also identified with the building of both elevators at this place.

HORATIO WALES.—Fortunate is he who has back of him an ancestry honorable and distinguished, and happy is he if his lines of life are cast in harmony therewith. Our subject is blessed in this respect, for he springs from a prominent New England family. He was born near Polo, Ogle county, Illinois, November 27, 1852, and is a son of Horatio Wales, Sr, whose birth occurred January 22, 1810, in the town of Wales, Massachusetts, where after clerking for a time he went into business. On coming to Ogle county in 1836, the father located in Buffalo Grove, and having brought with him a stock of goods, he opened a store at that place, which he conducted for a few years. On selling out he bought a tract of government land and engaged in farming until 1876, when he retired from active business cares and spent his last days in Polo, where his death occurred May 5, 1890. At an early day in the history of the county, he took quite an active and prominent part in public affairs and served as sheriff from 1838 until 1840. He attended the Congregational church, and was highly respected by all who knew him.

Royal Wales, the paternal grandfather of our subject, was also a native of Wales, Massachusetts, born in 1773, and died in 1857. For his second wife he married Mrs. Ruby (Porter) Bliss, and Horatio Wales, Sr., was one of the children born of this union. Royal Wales was a son of Oliver and Elizabeth Wales and a grandson of Ebenezer Wales, whose father was Deacon Nathaniel Wales, a son of Timothy Wales. Nathaniel Wales, the father of Timothy, was born in Ide, Yorkshire, England, in 1586, and on his emigration to America in 1662, located at Dorchester, Massachusetts. His father, John Wales, spent his entire life in England.

The mother of our subject bore the maiden name of Mary E. Williams, and was born in Brimfield, Massachusetts, a daughter of Ebenezer and Eliza (Whitwell) Williams. The Williams family was founded in America by Robert Williams, who crossed the Atlantic in 1638, and his descendants down to the grandfather of our subject are as follows: Samuel, probably born in England in 1632, died in 1698; Samuel, born in 1655, died in 1735; Rev. Ebenezer, who graduated from Cambridge in 1709, was born in 1690 and died in 1753; Rev. Chester, born in 1720, died in 1755; Rev. Nehemiah, who graduated from Harvard College in 1769 and was a Congregational preacher at Brimfield, Massachusetts, for over twenty-one years, was born in 1749 and died in 1800; and Ebenezer, grandfather of our subject, was born in 1777, and died in 1856. Mrs. Wales died December 14, 1892.

Horatio Wales, of this review, was educated in the district schools near his boyhood home and in the public schools of Polo, continuing his studies in those institutions until eighteen years of age. On attaining his majority he rented land from his father and continued to engage in agricultural pursuits until 1882. Removing to Polo, he embarked in business at that place in 1885, as a dealer in farm machinery, and from year to year as his business has gradually increased he has enlarged his store room until he now occupies a commodious warehouse and office on the principal business street. He deals in all kinds of agricultural implements, buggies, wagons, wind mills and steam heating apparatus, and has built up a most excellent trade.

In Polo, January 12, 1893, Mr. Wales was united in marriage with Miss Emma Spear. Her father, Captain Joseph L. Spear, was born in Martickville, Pennsylvania, February 1, 1834, and is a son of Rev. John Spear, a minister of the Methodist church, of the New Jersey conference, and his wife, Matilda Wentz, daughter of Joseph and Sarah (Smith) Wentz. On coming to Illinois in 1859, Captain Spear first located in Brookville, and later in Forreston, Ogle county, where he taught school until the outbreak of the Civil war. In August, 1862, he enlisted in Company E, Ninety-second Illinois Volunteer Infantry, was elected first lieutenant of his company and was soon afterward promoted to the rank of captain. He participated in the battles of Lookout Mountain and Chickamauga, was with Sherman on the famous march to the sea, and witnessed Johnston's surrender a few days after Lee's capitulation. On his return from the war he entered in the drug business in Polo, which he successfully carried on until 1896, when he sold out to his son. Just before going to the front Captain Spear was married, in Polo, August 24, 1862, to Miss Mary Carpenter, a native of Delhi, New York, and a daughter of David and Olive (Vegte) Carpenter. Her maternal grandparents were John and Catherine (Shaw) Vegte, and great-grandparents were John and Catharine (Vanderbilt) Vegte. Captain Spear died July 11, 1898. Mr. and Mrs. Wales have an interesting family of three children, namely: Horatio, Frank and Helen.

Politically Mr. Wales is an ardent supporter of the Republican party, takes quite an active interest in political affairs, and has served as chairman of the township Republican committee. Socially he is a member of the Independent Order of Odd Fellows and the Knights of the Globe, while religiously he attends the Presbyterian church, his wife being a member. As a business man he ranks among the foremost in his section of the county and his interests have ever been so managed as to gain him the confidence of the public and the success that should always attend honorable effort.

WILLIAM CAMLING has for many years been one of the most highly esteemed and valued citizens of Ogle county, his home being on section 9, Rockvale township. He is of foreign birth but his duties of citizenship have been performed with a loyalty equal to that of any native son of America, and when the nation was imperiled by rebellion, he went to the defense of the Union and protected the cause of his adopted country on many a southern battle field.

Mr. Camling is a native of Holland, born near Zealand, August 10, 1842, but was only two years and a half old when brought to America by his father, Cyrus Camling, who was probably a farmer in the old world and served for several years in the army of the Netherlands. In the United States he was employed as a day laborer and made his home near Grand Rapids, Michigan, where his death occurred about 1876. He held membership in the Lutheran church in Milwaukee, Wisconsin, and in political sentiment was a Republican. He had by his first wife one child, a son, and by his second had three children: Lane, who married a Miss Van Horn and is engaged in fruit farming in Michigan; Katie, who died at the age of seven years; and William, our subject. For his second wife he wedded Miss Jane Van Heltz, by his third wife had no children.

On first crossing the Atlantic the family located in Buffalo, New York, where they made their home until William Camling was six years of age, and then removed to Milwaukee, Wisconsin, where he was reared and educated in the public schools. At the age of fourteen years he left home and began the battle of life for himself, his first employment being in the hay field, where he worked with a hand rake for three months. He was only seventeen when he joined the boys in blue, enlisting in January, 1862, at Cold Springs, Wisconsin, in Company F, Second Wisconsin Cavalry. The regiment first went to St. Louis, Missouri, where it remained for about three months while being equipped, and then proceeded to Springfield, that state, under command of Colonel C. C. Washburn, while Company F was under the command of Captain Forrest. The summer was spent in fighting bushwhackers on the road from Springfield to Helena, Arkansas. Arriving in the latter place in the fall of that year they there spent the winter, and during 1863 were engaged in many skirmishes and also participated in the siege of Vicksburg and in the battle of Jackson, Mississippi. Returning to Vicksburg they were on garrison duty there during the winter of 1863-4, and in the spring of the latter year went up the Red river, finally landing at Austin, Texas, where they were kept on the lookout for hostile Mexicans until the fall of 1865, when they were mustered out at that place and sent to Madison, Wisconsin. In that city Mr. Camling received his discharge papers and arrived home on Christmas.

During the following winter he worked as a day laborer, and then hired out to a farmer for a couple of years. He continued to make his home in Wisconsin until 1869, when he came to Illinois and located at Rochelle, where, as a teamster, he entered the employ of the Chicago and Iowa Railroad, then in course of construction. For seven years he followed teaming, three years of which time he was in the employ of Joseph Strom in delivering coal, and for the same length of time was with Miles Braiden, who was in the coal, lumber and ice business. In 1876 he purchased eighty acres of his present farm in Rockvale township, to which he has added from time to time as his financial resources have increased, including tracts of forty, forty-eight and eighty acres, until he now has a valuable farm of two hundred and forty-eight and a half acres, which he has placed under excellent cultivation and improved with good and substantial buildings, that stand as monuments to his thrift and industry.

On the 23d of April, 1864, Mr. Camling was united in marriage with Miss Mary Colditz, who was born May 6, 1846, a daughter of William and Mina (Shmutzler) Colditz, in whose family were five children, the others being Minnie, who is now the widow of Frederick Troeger and lives near Elida; F. W., who married Clara Boeswetter, but both are now deceased, his death occurring in 1886; Augusta, wife of William Schroeder, of West Bend, Wisconsin; and Lizzie, wife of Charles Wilke, of West Bend. The father of these children brought his family to America in 1854 and located in Wauwatosa, Wisconsin, where he died about three months after his arrival, at the age of forty-six years. To Mr. and Mrs. Camling have been born seven children, namely: William, at home; Clara, who died at the age of six years; Cyrus, at home; Charles, who died at the age of sixteen; James and Belle, both at home; and Harrison, who is still attending the district schools. All of the children have been provided with fair common-school educations.

In his political affiliations Mr. Camling is a Republican, and he has most acceptably served his fellow-citizens as road commissioner three years and school director twelve years. Socially he is an honored member of Oregon Post, No. 116, G. A. R., and religiously was at one time identified with the Lutheran church, but since coming to Ogle county has not united with any church organization. Brave and fearless, and of a rather venturesome disposition, he was always the first to volunteer for any perilous undertaking during the Civil war, and has ever shown the same spirit when occasion demands in days of peace, and is therefore justly numbered among the valued and useful citizens of the community.

JOHN BISTLINE.—Among the representative and prosperous farmers of Ogle county, the record of whose lives fills an important place in this volume, it gives us pleasure to commemorate the name of this gentleman, who now owns and operates a well improved and valuable farm of two hundred acres on section 14, Forreston township. Like many of our best citizens, he comes from the old Keystone state, his birth occurring in Perry county, Pennsylvania, September 6, 1831. His father, Joseph Bistline, was a native of Schuylkill county, Pennsylvania, and there married Miss Mary Reipseimer. For a number of years he followed farming in Perry county, and there died in 1849.

In the county of his nativity John Bistline passed his boyhood and youth, and the limited education he received in its public schools has been greatly supplemented by reading and study in later years, so that he is almost wholly a self-educated man. Before coming west he spent four years in Center county, Pennsylvania, but in 1857 we find him en route for Illinois. From Chicago he rode horseback to Stephenson county, swimming his horses across the streams as no bridges had then been built in this region. During the two years he remained in that county he worked for thirteen dollars per month. Coming to Ogle county in 1859, he rented land in Forreston township for two years and in the meantime did his own housekeeping. In 1861 he made his first purchase of one hundred and sixty acres of land in the same township and to the work of improvement and cultivation at once turned his attention. He led one of the steers used in breaking the first furrow upon the land, and soon had one hundred acres under cultivation. In the spring of 1862 he built a small house upon the place, the lumber for which he hauled from Freeport. Later he bought more land, and now has a fine farm of two hundred acres under excellent cultivation and well improved with good and substantial buildings, including a commodious and comfortable residence.

Returning to Perry county, Pennsylvania, Mr. Bistline was married there, in 1871, to Miss Mary M. Ewing, who was born in Dauphin county, that state, and when a child of thirteen removed with her family to Perry county. Later she spent six years with an uncle in Baltimore, Maryland, but was mostly educated in Middletown, Dauphin county.

Mr. Bistline uses his right of franchise in support of the men and measures of the Republican party, but has never cared for political preferment, though he was elected and most acceptably served as township trustee for two terms. His estimable wife is a member of the Lutheran church of Forreston. Although Mr. Bistline came to this state as a young man with no capital, he has by untiring labor, perseverance and good management succeeded in accumulating a handsome property, and has also won the confidence and high regard of all with whom he has come in contact by his straightforward way of doing business and by his pleasant, genial manner.

MALCOLM C. ROE, M. D.—Among the prominent practitioners and leading citizens of Ogle county, and a gentleman who has for over a quarter of a century been actively identified with its progress and development, the subject of this sketch deserves special mention. He is a native of Ogle county, born at Light House Point, October 31, 1842. His father, John Roe, was born in Pennsylvania, near Philadelphia, in 1800. He grew to manhood in his native state and there received a fairly good education. At the age of twenty-one years he removed to Kentucky, and at Eddyville, Lyon county, engaged in teaching a private school. While residing in that state he was united in marriage with Miss Elizabeth A. Lyon, a native of that state and daughter of Colonel Matthew Lyon. Colonel Matthew Lyon was born in Wicklow county, Ireland, and in boyhood emigrated to America, and stopping in Halifax, Nova Scotia, worked in a printing office some years. He then removed to Vermont where he published the Scourge of Aristocracy, and in 1776 became a lieutenant in a company of the "Green Mountain Boys." He became a very prominent man in that state, married a daughter of Governor Thomas Chittenden, was fined $1,000, and imprisoned four months in Vergennes, Vermont, under the alien and sedition law. After his death congress returned to his heirs the fine of $1,000 with compound interest. While in jail he was elected to congress, was in congress eight years from Vermont, twelve years from Kentucky, and was territorial delegate from Arkansas at the time of his death, was paymaster during the Revolution, colonel of militia, member of the legislature, judge, and founded the town of Fairhaven, in 1783. He there built a saw and gristmill, established a forge, and engaged in other manufacturing enterprises. (For a more extended account of the Lyon family see Johnson's Universal Encyclopedia.)

To John and Elizabeth A. Roe nine children were born. Matthew Humphrey, born in Kentucky, died in infancy. Uriah C., born in Kentucky, now lives in Franklin Grove, Illinois, where he is engaged in the practice of medicine. Dr. Franklin M. Roe, of Downers Grove, Illinois. Giles Boliver, born in Sangamon county, Illinois, died in Chana, Illinois. Matthew Cartwright, born in Sangamon county, is a farmer living near Grand Junction, Iowa. John H., born in Sangamon county, spent the years from 1853 to 1893 in Kentucky, but is now living in Chana. While residing in Kentucky he was engaged in the practice of law, and was also in the life insurance business, being general agent of the Equitable Life Insurance Company of New York. Buelah Minerva, born at Light House, Ogle county, is now the wife of J. C. Mayberry, and they reside in Chattanooga, Tennessee. Frances Maria is the wife of John Conlon, a farmer and stock-raiser, residing in Milan township, De Kalb county, Illinois, now dead. Malcolm C. is the subject of this sketch.

Leaving Kentucky, Dr. John Roe moved to Sangamon county, Illinois, where he engaged in the practice of medicine for a few years, and then came to Ogle county and located at Light House Point, where he resumed practice. From Light House he went to Chicago, but did not long remain there, going from there to Rockford, Illinois, and then to White Rock township, Ogle county, and later to Malta, DeKalb county, finally going to Nebraska, locating at Beatrice, Gage county, where he died in 1871.

The subject of this sketch was but two years old when his father moved to Chicago. He accompanied his parents to the several places in which they located, in the meantime gaining such knowledge as was possible in the common schools. It was his aim and intention, however, to obtain a higher education, thus fitting himself for a professional life. To that end he entered Mt. Morris Seminary, and later Western Union College and Military Academy at Fulton, Illinois. This was in 1861, and the war for the union commencing, the school was badly broken up, and he therefore remained there but one year. Later he took up the study of medicine, and entering Bennett Medical College, Chicago, he pursued the regular course and was graduated from that institution. In 1871 he took up a post-graduate course in the Physio-Medical College at Cincinnati, and graduated from it in 1872. He commenced the practice of his profession in 1869 in Ogle county, and in 1875 removed to Chana, where he has since continued to reside, building up a practice of which he may well be proud.

Dr. Roe was united in marriage with Miss Sarah P. Sturtevant, a native of Cleveland, Ohio, and daughter of Benjamin D. and Annie (Martin) Sturtevant. In 1857 the family came to Ogle county, and located in White Rock township, where the father carried on farming in connection with contracting and building. He was born in Barton, Vermont, while his wife was born in Cheshire county, New Hampshire. They had a family of six children, two of whom died in infancy. The four yet living are George N., who lives one-half mile west of Chana, Milton E., a farmer of White Rock township, living on the old homestead; Sarah P., wife of our subject; and Emma L., wife of James M. Miller, of Rockford, Illinois.

To Dr. and Mrs. Roe five children have been born: Effie A. is deceased; Milton H. is a farmer living on the north side of Chana; Dr. John B. is engaged in the practice of his profession at Chana, Illinois; Ada M. is the wife of Rev. S. D. Bartle, of Oasis, Iowa; S. Maud is living at home; Malcolm R. is living at home and attending the village school.

In politics Dr. Roe is a Democrat. In 1885 he was elected a member of the board of supervisors and served two years. After an intermission he was again elected in 1896. During the Cleveland administrations he was a member of the pension board. Fraternally he is a Mason, a member of the blue lodge at Oregon and the commandery at Dixon, Illinois. In educational matters he is especially interested, his aim being to have the schools of his place of residence on a par with the best of those in larger places. In fact there is no enterprise of a public nature but finds in him an earnest advocate. He is popular not only as a physician, but as a citizen as well.

JUDSON AGARD WAITE, a prominent representative of the farming and stock raising interests of Ogle county, owns and operates a valuable farm on section 15, Rockvale township, whose neat and thrifty appearance well indicates his careful supervision. Substantial improvements are surrounded by well-tilled fields, and all of the accessories and conveniences of a model farm are there found.

Mr. Waite was born upon that place, January 6, 1862, a son of Adoniram Judson and Amelia (Agard) Waite. The father was a native of Washington county, New York, born July 5, 1821, and was a son of Clarke G. and Abigail (Phillips) Waite, the former born April 3, 1787, the latter May 14, 1791. The great-grandfather of our subject was Peleg Waite. Adoniram J. Waite, the father, was reared in the county of his nativity and received a common-school education. Until twenty-eight or thirty years of age he remained there and was married December 8, 1842, to Miss Caroline Bull, by whom he had three children, namely: Missouri Lorina, who married William A. Steffa and lives in Oregon; Alton Perry, who married Annie Greenawalt and is now deceased; and Alzina, who married John Allen and resides in Oregon. The mother of these children departed this life in July, 1860. The father continued to engage in agricultural pursuits in Washington county, New York, until about 1850, when he removed to Erie county, that state, making his home there until April 8, 1853. He then joined his two brothers, Clarke G. and Elverton J. Waite, who had located in Ogle county, Illinois, in 1837. Here he purchased one hundred and ninety acres of wild land, to the cultivation and improvement of which he at once turned his attention.

On the 29th of June, 1861, Adoniram J. Waite was again married, his second union being with Mrs. Amelia (Agard) Landon, who was born November 9, 1822. Her parents, Joshua and Lucy (Sibley) Agard, were natives of Wilmington, Connecticut, the former born April 16, 1789, the latter June 18, 1792. In the family were five children, as follows: Maria, Mary, Amelia, Austin and Hannah, also a half sister, Malissa Ann, all now deceased with the exception of Mrs. Waite, who has been twice married, his first husband being Horace Landon, Jr., a son of Horace Landon, of Collins, Erie county, New York. By that union she had two children: Newton, who married Annie Lyons, and is engaged in farming in Tennessee; and Sarah Maria, wife of Charles Rathbun, who is engaged in the coal business in Streator, Illinois, and is secretary and assistant manager of the Star Coal Company. Judson A. Waite, of this review, was the only child born of the second marriage. Joshua Agard served in the Revolutionary war, was in the battle of Monmouth, New Jersey. The father died January 22, 1897, honored and respected by all who knew him. He had had several light strokes of paralysis, but on the morning of the day of his death was feeling quite well at breakfast, but twenty minutes after leaving the table he had another stroke and was unconscious until he passed away at two o'clock in the afternoon. He was one of the prominent and influential citizens of his community, was a supporter of the Republican party, and took quite an active part in local politics. He served as supervisor and school trustee, holding both offices for a number of years. In early life he was a member of the Baptist church, but after coming to this state never united with any congregation.

Mr. Waite, whose name introduces this sketch, attended the district schools near his home and supplemented his early education by two years' attendance at the Mt. Morris Academy, leaving here in 1882. Thus well fitted for life's responsible duties he returned to the old homestead and has since devoted his attention to general farming and stock raising with most gratifying results. He is the owner of four hundred and thirty acres of arable land in the home place, besides one hundred and forty-five acres elsewhere, all under the highest cultivation and well improved. Upon the farm are three large barns and other outbuildings besides a neat and comfortable residence. For a number of years he has been interested in stock-raising, making a specialty of shorthorn and Durham cattle and Chester white hogs, and at one time also raised Morgan horses. However, he still has upon his place thirteen good horses. Mr. Waite is an ardent supporter of the Republican party and its principles and for six years has most capably and satisfactorily represented his township on the board of supervisors, during which time he has served on the committees on equalization, bridges, public buildings, printing and education. He has also been town clerk for seven years and in all of the relations of life has been found true and faithful to every trust reposed in him.

PETER R. MEYERS, who resides on section 11, Lincoln township, is a native of Ogle county, and was born on the farm where he now resides, December 23, 1843, and is the son of Jonathan and Elizabeth (Redman) Meyers, the former a native of Dauphin county, Pennsylvania, born January 23, 1812, and the latter of Baden,

Germany, and who came to the new world a young lady, locating first in Pennsylvania, and later coming to Ogle county, where she was united in marriage with Mr. Meyers. In early life Jonathan Meyers learned the trade of stone mason, following that occupation in Hagarstown, Maryland, to which place he removed. From Maryland he came to Ogle county, being one of the pioneers of 1837. On coming to this county he took up a claim in what is now Lincoln township, a portion of which is now comprised in the farm of our subject. He was accompanied to this county by his brother, Jacob Meyers, who was well known to the early settlers, and whose descendants are yet residing in the county. When the land came into market, Jonathan Meyers entered and purchased four hundred and forty acres, and later eighty acres additional. He died on the farm which was his home for more than a half century, his death taking place July 16, 1893, at the age of eighty-one years. His wife passed away in 1877, and their remains lie interred in the cemetery at West Grove.

Peter R. Meyers is the eldest of a family of seven children, of whom six lived to mature years and have families of their own. He grew to manhood on the home farm, and from the time old enough to render any assistance, made himself useful in the cultivation of the farm. His education was limited to the common-schools of the early days of the county.

Mr. Meyers was married in Forreston, Ogle county, January 17, 1867, to Miss Sarah Jane McLane, a native of Ogle county, and daughter of Richard McLane, a native of Maryland, but an early settler of Ogle county. By this union four children were born. Lewis F. is a farmer of Lincoln township. Edwin H. is a farmer of Maryland township, on the old McLane farm. Charles A. makes his home with his brother Lewis, while Ettie May is a young lady residing at home.

After his marriage, Mr. Meyers moved to the McLane homestead, which he occupied and cultivated the farm for twenty-seven years, during which time he made some permanent improvements to the place. In 1894 he succeeded to a part of the old Meyers homestead and removed to the old place. In addition to the two hundred and thirty-seven acres of the Meyers homestead, he owns one hundred and sixty acres of the old McLane homestead. Both tracts are well improved, and the farm presents a very neat and attractive appearance.

Politically Mr. Meyers is a stanch Republican, and has supported that party ticket since casting his first presidential vote for Abraham Lincoln in 1864. He has been somewhat active in local politics, but not as an office seeker. He has, however, served as township trustee, school director, and such minor offices. In the fifty-five years that he has resided in the county—his entire life—he has been brought in contact with many of the best people, and wherever known he is regarded as a man of exemplary habits, a good citizen, one willing to do all he can for his native county and state.

EDWARD E. PRICE, who is now living retired in the village of Byron, is a self-made man, who at an early age started out to make his own way in the world. He now represents a valuable property, all of which he has accumulated by his own perseverance and industry. A native of Wales, he was born in Montgomeryshire, January 1, 1836, and there remained until fourteen years of age. In 1849 he crossed the broad Atlantic to join his brother, David Price, who was then living in Utica, New York. There he worked on a farm during the summer season for a year or two, also engaged in teaming one summer, and spent one winter working in a tanyard, remaining there for about four years. In the meantime his brother had come west to Illinois and settled in Winnebago, where he has since made his home, residing in Rockford at the present time retired from active business.

In 1855 Edward E. Price also removed to Winnebago county, where he worked on a farm by the month for some time. There he married Miss Sarah Goodhue, a most estimable lady, who is said to have been the first child born in Winnebago county. Her father, Squire Goodhue, was numbered among its first settlers and opened up a farm at Kishwaukee. After his marriage Mr. Price took charge of the Goodhue homestead and he and his wife cared for her parents until they were called to their final rest, and then succeeded to the place, which Mr. Price operated for twenty-five or thirty years. In 1890 he removed from Kishwaukee to Byron, Ogle county, where he bought residence property and has since lived retired. In 1898 he purchased lots and erected a good, neat and substantial residence which is now his home.

Mr. Price has a family of seven children, two sons and five daughters, namely: Edward J., a resident of Byron, Thomas C., of David Junction; Mrs. Leora L. Helson, of Byron; Mrs. Lillian Poole, of Rockford, Mrs Alberta Blakesley, of Wisconsin, and Lizzie, of Beloit, Wisconsin, and Lenora E. lives in Beloit.

Politically Mr. Price has been identified with the Republican party since its organization, casting his first vote for John C. Fremont in 1856, and has supported every candidate of the party for the presidency since that time. He is enterprising and progressive, and through his own unaided efforts has attained success in life and won the respect and esteem of a large circle of friends and acquaintances.

JAMES PANKHURST, M. D., of Grand Detour, one of the leading physicians of Ogle county, was born in Westfield, Sussex county, England, January 18, 1845, and is the son of John and Mary (Welfare) Pankhurst, the former a native of Sussex county, England, born in 1811, and the latter of Hastings, England, born in 1805. The paternal grandfather, John Pankhurst, Sr., who was a wheelwright by trade, was also a native of England, where his entire life was spent.

John Pankhurst, the father of our subject, was also a wheelwright by trade, which occupation he followed until coming to America, in 1850. Convinced that in his native land he could never rise higher than a common wheelwright, with no opportunity to provide for the future, he determined on coming to the United States. With his family he took passage on a sailing vessel, and after a voyage of five weeks he landed in New York. Our subject has but a faint recollection of the voyage, but as a reminder he still retains in his possession the box in which the provisions of the family were stored during the voyage.

After spending a few weeks in Alexandria, Pennsylvania, the family came west to Carroll county, Illinois. Leaving there his

JAMES PANKHURST, M. D.

family, John Pankhurst trudged on foot to Grand Detour, where he obtained a responsible position with the Grand Detour Plow Company, and here brought the family. He did not, however, remain but one year, when he went to Jackson county, Iowa, where he also remained one year. Being offered the foremanship in the wood department of the plow company, he returned to Grand Detour, and here spent the remainder of his days. He remained with the company for ten years after its removal to Dixon, but still retained his home in Grand Detour. His death, the result of an accident, occurred July 14, 1896. His good wife passed away September 26, 1894, at the age of eighty-nine years. Both were devoted members of the Church of England, and were firm in the faith. They were the parents of eight children,—Stephen, John, William, Sarah, Edward, Selina, James and Jane. Of these, John died in infancy, and Sarah in early childhood. In politics, John Pankhurst was a stanch Republican. He was a highly respected citizen of the village, esteemed for his many excellent qualities of head and heart.

The subject of this sketch was but six years of age when he came to Ogle county, and in the district schools of Grand Detour township he received his primary education. When the Civil war broke out he was but sixteen, and one year later, on the 2nd of June, 1862, he enlisted in Company H, Sixty-ninth Illinois Volunteer Infantry, under Colonel Tucker, and was mustered into the service at Chicago. He was stationed at Camp Douglas, Chicago, doing guard duty, and was continued there the term of his service, being discharged September 27, 1862.

Returning home after receiving his discharge, our young soldier commenced work in the plow factory, and until June, 1865, worked in the summer and attended school in the winter. In the meantime, as the opportunity was afforded him, he read medicine under the instruction of Dr. C. E. Loomis, of Grand Detour, and in the fall of 1865, entered the medical department of the University of Michigan at Ann Arbor, where he remained until the following spring. He then entered the office of Dr. J. B. Snyder, then practicing in Grand Detour, but now of Polo, Illinois. In 1867 he went to Rush Medical College, Chicago, and finishing the prescribed course, was graduated from that institution in February, 1868. After receiving his diploma, the Doctor returned to Grand Detour and formed a partnership with his former preceptor, Dr. Snyder, which continued one year. He then purchased his partner's interest, since which time he has been alone in practice.

Dr. Pankhurst has been thrice married, and by his first union there was one daughter, Bessie C., who is now in Chicago, and is a student in the Armour Institute. His second union was with Miss Frances Foxley, a native of England, and their marriage was celebrated May 17, 1884. She departed this life November 24, 1894. The Doctor was again married, January 22, 1896, his third union being with Miss May U. Sheffield, who was born January 28, 1861, and daughter of Amos A. and Elizabeth (Scofield) Sheffield, of whom mention is made elsewhere in this work.

Politically Dr. Pankhurst is a Republican, and is at present a member of the Republican central committee of Ogle county. He has always taken a commendable interest in politics, but never in a sense of being an office seeker. Believing it the duty of every citizen to exercise the rights of franchise, he endeavors to keep posted in the political issues of the day that he may intelligently do his duty. It is, however, as a physician that he is best known, and his professional duties require the greater part of his time. He is a member of the Ogle County Medical Society and the Northern Illinois Medical Association, in the meetings of which he takes an active part. He is medical examiner for the New York Life Insurance Company, of New York, the New York Mutual and the Union Central Life Insurance Company, of Cincinnati, and others. Religiously, he and his daughter are members of the Episcopal church. The Doctor is a good physician, a loyal citizen, a kind neighbor, and steadfast friend of those with whom he has so long been associated, and he and his wife are held in high esteem.

MICHAEL N. SWINGLEY is one of Ogle county's honored pioneers and most highly esteemed citizens, having made his home here almost continuously since September, 1845. As an agriculturist he has taken an active and prominent part in its growth and development, and given his support to those enterprises which he believed calculated to advance the general welfare. He now owns and operates a well improved farm of seventy acres on section 15, Leaf River township.

Mr. Swingley was born in Washington county, Maryland, March 10, 1822, a son of Hon. Michael Swingley, also a native of that state and a grandson of Nicholas Swingley, a native of Pennsylvania. His great-grandfather was born in Switzerland and was among the first settlers of Lancaster county, Pennsylvania. At an early day Nicholas Swingley removed to Washington county, Maryland, where his son Michael was reared. The latter, on attaining to man's estate, wedded Miss Mary Newcomer, also a native of Maryland. He owned and operated the old Swingley homestead and reared his family there, but in 1845 emigrated to Ogle county, Illinois, taking up his residence in Mt. Morris township, where he bought a claim and entered land amounting to about eight hundred acres. Here he opened up and improved a large farm, supplied with good buildings. He was one of the honest yeomanry and successful business men of the county. He was a soldier of the war of 1812, and held a number of official positions of honor and trust in Maryland, representing his district one or more terms in the state legislature. He died in Ogle county in 1852, and his wife, who survived him many years, passed away in February, 1870. To them were born eight children, five sons and three daughters, all of whom are still living with the exception of one son. Benjamin, the eldest, is now living retired in Mt. Morris; Samuel is a resident of Kansas City, Missouri; George died in St. Louis; Michael N., of this review, is the next in order of birth; Mrs. Elizabeth Allen resides in Mt. Morris; Mrs. Mary Baker lives in Polo; Mrs. Martha Highbarger makes her home in Montana; and William lives in Oregon, Illinois.

Michael N. Swingley is indebted to the common schools of his native state for his educational privileges, and there he grew to manhood. Coming with the family to Ogle county in 1845, he was put to work at driving an ox team used in breaking prairie and soon became familiar with all the arduous duties which fall to the lot of the pioneer.

In the fall of 1846 he returned to Maryland where he spent the winter, and on again coming to this state resumed work on the home farm. About the 1st of April, 1849, he started overland for California, overtook a train in Nebraska, and reached his destination in August of that year. He engaged in prospecting and mining until the spring of 1850, when he started for home by way of the Nicaraugua route. He was obliged to spend the whole winter on the Isthmus, finally in the spring secured passage on a vessel bound for Cuba, where he was again delayed until a vessel arrived which would take him to New Orleans. However, he at length reached home in 1851 and resumed farming in Mt. Morris township, where he carried on operations until 1860.

In August, 1854, in that township, Mr. Swingley married Miss Susan Welty, who was born in the same neighborhood as our subject. Her father, John Welty, was also a native of Washington county, Maryland, and in 1846 came to Illinois. He improved a farm in Mt. Morris township, on which he reared his family. His wife, who bore the maiden name of Mary Wolff, departed this life in 1875. Mrs. Swingley was reared and educated in Mt. Morris township. Our subject and his wife have two children: Mary is the wife of Leroy Her, of Leaf River township, and has two children: Verna, who is a student in the Leaf River schools; and Ray, who is attending the home school. Cora is the wife of James Wilson, of Winnebago county, Illinois, and they have four children: Lottie, Altha and Nellie, who are attending the home school, and Harry, at home.

In 1855 Mr. Swingley removed to Polo, where he made his home until 1859, and then again made an overland trip to California. This time he located in Sacramento City, where he engaged in the livery business for about two years, returning to Ogle county in February, 1861. For several years thereafter he followed farming in Mt. Morris township, and in 1869 removed to Stephenson county, Illinois, where he operated rented land for about three years. On his return to Ogle county, in 1873, he purchased his present place in Leaf River township, on which a fairly good house was standing and which was slightly improved. To its further development and cultivation he has since devoted his energies with marked success, and now has a well-improved farm pleasantly situated three miles northwest of Leaf River.

Mr. Swingley cast his first presidential vote for James K. Polk in 1844, and has never wavered in his allegiance to the Democracy. In religious faith he is a Lutheran, while his wife holds membership in the Christian church, and they stand high in the community where they have so long made their home. Those who know them best are numbered among their warmest friends, and no citizens in Leaf River township are more honored or highly respected.

JACOB RICE, deceased, was numbered among the pioneers of 1837, and, like all others who came at that early day, he experienced the privations incidental to the settlement of a new country. He was born in Washington county, Maryland, and was the son of Jacob and Mary (Roland) Rice, both of whom were natives of the same county and state, and of whom special mention is made in the sketch of Isaac Rice, on another page of this work.

In his native state our subject commenced his education in the common schools, and on coming to Ogle county he attended a pioneer school taught by his older brother, Joshua, who engaged in teaching soon after their arrival. He was a well educated young man and gave his younger brothers excellent instruction. In 1843 he left school and assisted his father on the farm in Mt. Morris township, continuing with him until he was twenty-seven years old, when he rented one hundred acres of land in Maryland township and commenced life for himself.

On the 11th of December, 1851, he was united in marriage with Miss Elizabeth Zeigler, a native of Jefferson county, Virginia, born September 7, 1833, and daughter of Jacob and Margaret (Stanger) Zeigler, the former born in Washington county, Maryland, January 15, 1795, and the latter in Alsace Loraine, at that time in the kingdom of France, but which is now a part of Germany, September 12, 1796. She came to this country with her parents when but eight years old. They came to America in 1830 and first located in Jefferson county, Virginia, but four years later moved to Clark county, Ohio, where he engaged in farming in connection with his trade as cooper. In 1841 he came to Ogle county and settled in Leaf River township, where he took up three hundred acres of government land, paying the regular price of one dollar and twenty-five cents per acre for the greater part of it. A portion of the land had been staked as a claim by another party on which he had erected a small cabin. For this he had to give a small bonus. He was permitted to enjoy his new possessions but a very short time, his death occurring in 1843. Jacob Zeigler and wife were the parents of eight children, as follows: Mary Ann, born July 22, 1818; Lavina, January 1, 1821; Caroline, October 16, 1823; Margaret A., March 4, 1826; Samuel C., January 23, 1828; John D., March 27, 1830, Elizabeth, September 7, 1833; Jane C., June 11, 1840. Mrs. Zeigler died October 29, 1874. In politics Jacob Zeigler was a Whig, and, religiously, a Methodist. The family were of some note in the old world, a granduncle of Mrs. Rice being an officer under the first Napoleon, serving with him in many of his wars.

To Jacob and Elizabeth Rice three sons were born—William A., August 4, 1854; Frederick N., August 5, 1859; and Eldridge E., December 3, 1863. All are residing at home.

On the death of his father our subject moved to the home place, which comprised one hundred and sixty acres of choice land. There he continued to farm during the remainder of his life. In addition to general farming he was engaged somewhat extensively in stock raising, in which he was quite successful. About 1884 he was stricken with creeping paralysis, and after lingering along for ten years passed peacefully away, February 2, 1894. In politics he was for many years a Republican, but in 1884 he voted for St. John, the Prohibition candidate for president, and continued to vote with the Prohibition party until the end of his life. He never aspired to any official position, but served as school director for years. Religiously he was a Methodist, holding membership with the church in Mt. Morris. He was a firm believer in Christ, and died in the full assurance of faith.

Mrs. Rice still lives upon the old home place, and like her husband is respected by all who know her. She is also a member of the Methodist Episcopal church, and has a lively interest in all that concerns her fellowmen. She well remembers hearing her mother tell of crossing the ocean in a sail vessel, being three months upon the water. She has also a vivid recollection of the journey made by the family to Illinois. They started from their Ohio home with some stock and barnyard fowls, and in coming into the state were stuck fast in a snow drift. Her mother brought the first turkeys that were ever brought into northern Illinois. When they came to the county wild game was very plentiful. Wolves were in great numbers, and often when Mrs. Rice was sent after the cows she could hear the wolves on all sides. Her father dying so soon after their arrival, her mother was compelled to attend to all the farm duties, and often hired her grain hauled to Chicago, where it was disposed of. Those were days of trial and hardships which those of the present generation can have no conception, but they had to be endured. Out of it all has grown the finest country on the face of the globe, and to such men and women as Jacob Rice and his wife the credit is due.

HENRY COFFMAN. Prominent among the energetic, progressive and successful business men of Ogle county are the gentlemen composing the firm of Coffman Brothers, extensive breeders and dealers in pure blooded shorthorn cattle, in which business they have been engaged for the past eight years. They are representatives of one of the old and prominent families of the county, being sons of Abraham Coffman, who was born in Washington county, Maryland, May 5, 1818. John Coffman, the grandfather, was also a native of that state, and in 1840 came to Ogle county, where he pre-empted a large tract of land, and, in company with several families, the Coffman family drove across the country with teams.

Abraham Coffman, our subject's father, located on a tract of eighty acres in Maryland township, to which he added by subsequent purchase until he had a valuable farm of two hundred and eighty acres. This he broke and improved with good buildings, making it one of the most desirable places in the locality. In this county he married Miss Caroline Wagner, also a native of Washington county, Maryland, and a daughter of Henry Wagner, who settled in Ogle county as early as 1838, but died a few years later at the age of forty-five. For several years Mr. Coffman continued to operate his farm in Maryland township, becoming one of its most substantial and well-to-do citizens, but his last days were spent in retirement in the village of Forreston, where he bought residence property. There he passed away July 11, 1895, at the age of seventy-seven years, honored and respected by all who knew him. His estimable wife is still living in Forreston at the age of seventy-three. To this worthy couple were born eight children, all of whom reached years of maturity, but only two are now living: Henry, of this review, and Isaiah T., the junior member of the firm of Coffman Brothers, who was born on the old homestead and like his brother was educated in the local schools. Those deceased are as follows: Elizabeth, who married William A. Harris, a business man of Adeline, Ogle county, and died there leaving one daughter; Mary A.; Amanda; Ada Alice; Joseph N., who died at about the age of nineteen years, and Charles Eugene, who resided in Iowa with his brother, Henry W., and died in Illinois at the age of twenty-seven years.

Henry W. Coffman was born January 3, 1849, on the old homestead on section 5, Maryland township, where he now resides, and is the second in order of birth in his father's family. After reaching man's estate he went to Grundy county, Iowa, where he bought land, but in 1883 became a resident of Ackley, that state, where for seven years he successfully engaged in the agricultural implement business. He built up an excellent trade, but finally sold out to an advantage and returned to Ogle county. In partnership with his brother he took charge of the home farm, and in connection with general farming have engaged in the breeding of shorthorn cattle since 1891, having upon their place a fine herd of fifty thoroughbreds, with Cruickshank, a registered bull, at the head. As upright, reliable business men, the brothers have become widely known, and in all their undertakings have been unusually successful.

On the 27th of October, 1887, in Hardin county, Iowa, Henry W. Coffman was united in marriage with Miss Carrie Walker, a daughter of Jacob Walker. She was born in Clinton county, Pennsylvania, but was mostly reared and educated in Hardin county, Iowa. Her father removed from the latter state to Illinois in March, 1896, and is now engaged in business in Freeport. He is a carpenter by trade and formerly followed contracting and building. To Mr. and Mrs. Coffman have been born four children, namely: Raymond A., Merritt J. and Hazel Ruth, all living, and Wava Gleo, deceased. The home of this family is one of the most hospitable in Ogle county; the stranger within its doors are made to feel at ease; and their many friends and acquaintances are always sure of a hearty welcome. In politics Mr. Coffman is independent.

ELIAS G. BOWERS, an energetic and progressive farmer residing on section 10, Brookville township, has spent almost his entire life in Ogle county, and as one of its public-spirited citizens uses his influence in advancing its welfare, materially aiding all beneficial schemes for promoting its prosperity. Mr. Bowers was born in Northumberland county, Pennsylvania, March 15, 1844, but in June of that year was brought to this county, where amid frontier scenes he grew to manhood.

His father, Henry Bowers, was also a native of Northumberland county, Pennsylvania, born in October, 1808, and was a son of Jacob Bowers, a farmer by occupation, who reared his family in that county, but spent the last years of his life in Stark county, Ohio. Henry Bowers wedded Miss Mary Magdalene Garman, a native of Northumberland county and a daughter of Martin Garman. During his early life Mr. Bowers was employed on public works, principally canal and bridge building, but in May, 1844, started by team, with several other Pennsylvania families, for Ogle county, Illinois, and on his arrival here bought a claim of one hundred and sixty acres and turned his attention to farming. He developed a fine farm from the unbroken prairie, in 1850 erected thereon a large brick residence and later a large barn, and was acknowledged to be one of the most skillful and successful agriculturists of the locality. Having prospered in his new home he was able to spend his last years in retirement from active labor and in 1865 removed from the farm to Forreston, where he passed away February 4, 1882. The mother of our subject had died in August, 1850, and he subsequently married again, his second wife dying in April, 1872.

Elias G. Bowers, the only child born to his parents, was reared on the home farm where he now lives and acquired his education in the district schools of the neighborhood. On the 1st of April, 1864, he enlisted for three months in Company D, One Hundred and Forty-second Illinois Volunteer Infantry, which was assigned to the Army of the Tennessee. He was on guard duty most of the time, along railroads, and was honorably discharged on the expiration of his term of enlistment, but he later joined Company I, Ninety-second Illinois Mounted Infantry, which became a part of Kilpatrick's cavalry. The regiment proceeded to North Carolina, where they remained until the war was over. Mr. Bowers was mostly on detailed duty with a wagon train, and when hostilities ceased and his services were no longer needed he was discharged at Chicago in August, 1865, and returned home.

After the war Mr. Bowers ran a threshing machine and engaged in other labors until the fall of 1867, when he went to Pennsylvania, spending five years in Northumberland and Dauphin counties. He was first employed by a company engaged in manufacturing lumber, but the last two years was interested in the hotel business with his brother-in-law, at Lykens, Dauphin county. Disposing of his property in the east, he returned to Ogle county in 1873 and took charge of the old home farm. He has since remodeled the residence and outbuildings and now has one of the best improved places in the locality.

While in Northumberland county, Pennsylvania, Mr. Bowers was married, December 26, 1869, to Miss Sarah Engle, who was born, reared and educated in that county, and is a daughter of Abram Engle. Five children were born of this union: Alice, wife of Harvey C. Good, of Carroll county, Illinois; Henry W., who is now a member of the First South Dakota Volunteer Infantry, and is one of the brave boys now stationed at Manila; and Agnes, William A. and John J., all at home.

Mr. Bowers cast his first presidential ballot for Samuel J. Tilden, in 1876, and has always supported the Democratic party. For the past twenty years he has taken quite an active and prominent part in local politics, and has most creditably served his fellow citizens as constable, justice of the peace, township assessor, treasurer, and as supervisor for four years, during which time he was a member of several important committees. He was also a member of the school board for several years, and served as clerk of the district eight years. Socially he is a prominent member of Brookville Lodge, I. O. O. F., which he has represented in the Grand Lodge eight years, and in which he has passed through all the chairs and is now past grand. He also belongs to the Grand Army post at Forreston, and is one of the most popular and influential citizens of his community.

EDWARD C. BUTERBAUGH, who resides upon his fine farm of two hundred and forty acres on section 11, Mt. Morris township, is a native of Ogle county, and was born in this county July 8, 1863. He is the son of Henry and Catherine (Hershey) Buterbaugh, the former born July 22, 1819, in Bedford county, Pennsylvania, and the latter of Washington county, Maryland, born June 25, 1821. Henry Buterbaugh was the son of Stephen and Susan Buterbaugh, who were natives of Pennsylvania and Maryland, respectively.

Henry Buterbaugh received but a limited education in the common schools of his native county and was reared to farm life. After his marriage with Catherine Hershey, November 18, 1844, he removed with his bride to Ogle county, Illinois, coming west with a team in 1847. On his arrival he purchased a farm of two hundred and forty acres of land in Mt. Morris township, to which he later added two hundred and forty acres more, giving him an estate of four hundred and eighty acres. He was an active and prosperous farmer, a member of the German Baptist church, and was a good friend and neighbor. In politics he was a Democrat, and for many years served as school director of his district. He died March 22, 1883, and his remains were laid to rest in Silver Creek cemetery. His wife is yet living and makes her home in the village of Mt. Morris. Like her husband, she is a member of the German Baptist church, a true Christian woman, and one deserving the love and esteem in which she is held. They were the parents of eight children. Emma married William Thomas, but is now deceased. Alice married Willoughby Felter and resides on the old homestead. John, Joseph, Mary, Ella and Martin are deceased. Mary married George Thomas and became the mother of three children.

Edward C. Buterbaugh, the subject of this sketch, is the youngest member of the family. He was reared on the home farm and in the district school received his education. At the age of seventeen he commenced life for himself, renting the home farm and engaging in its cultivation. Two years later he became sole proprietor of the place. On the 14th of December, 1882, he was united in marriage with Miss Mary Bopp, who was born in Washington county, Maryland, December 21, 1862, and daughter of John and Matilda (Secore) Bopp, the former born in Dauphin county, Pennsylvania, October 16, 1829, and the latter in Adams county, Pennsylvania, September 14, 1828. They were the parents of six children, as follows: John H., born September 2, 1856; Benjamin F., January 26, 1858; William T., August 13, 1859; Mary E., December 2, 1862; Emma J., December 2, 1866; and Ida M., September 26, 1871. The three sons and the mother are now deceased, the latter dying October 31, 1896.

After residing in Washington county, Maryland, until 1864, John Bobb removed with his family to Montgomery county, Ohio, where they resided eleven years, Mr. Bopp engaging in farming. In 1876 they came to Ogle county, Illinois, to make a permanent home.

To Mr. and Mrs. Buterbaugh four children have been born: Edith, December 18, 1883; Clinton, June 23, 1885; Pearl, October 21, 1886, and Chester, December 11, 1887. The latter died September 5, 1888, after an illness of two weeks. The remaining children are all attending the public school, and it is the design of the parents to give them good education.

After giving his entire time and attention to the cultivation of his farm until 1893, Mr. Buterbaugh rented the same, but still remained upon the place, and has given his attention to stock raising exclusively. He makes a specialty of the red polled cattle and Poland-China hogs. He has also a number of draught and road horses, but in all probability give his attention to roadsters. He thoroughly understands the stock business, and in that line has met with good success. Since coming into full possession of the farm, he has made upon it many valuable improvements, and keeps it at all times under a high state of cultivation. In politics he is a Democrat, and a stanch advocate of the principles of the party, but he is not a politician in the common acceptation of the term. As a farmer he has thoroughly demonstrated his abilities. As a citizen he enjoys the respect of all who know him.

SAMUEL W. POWELL, residing on section 1, Buffalo township, a prosperous farmer and stock raiser, has been a resident of Ogle county since May 2, 1854. He was born in Washington county, Maryland, December 3, 1834, and is a son of Upton Powell, a native of the same county and state, who was born in 1801. The paternal grandfather, Jonathan Powell, was a native of Wales, a seafaring man in early life, but who settled in Washington county, Maryland, at an early day.

Upton Powell grew to manhood in his native county and received a limited education in the common schools of that early day. In his youth he learned the miller's trade, an occupation he followed until he went to farming, while yet residing in Maryland. He there married Miss Anna Smith, a native of Maryland, of German ancestry, and they became the parents of seven children, all of whom grew to mature years. Mary Ann died a single lady. Susan married John N. Winders, and is now a widow, residing in Polo, Illinois. Samuel W. is third in order of birth. John A. is residing in Polo. Jacob H. is also living in Polo. Catherine is the wife of John M. Davis, a substantial farmer of Buffalo township, of whom mention is made elsewhere in this work. William is a farmer of Pine Creek township.

Fully convinced that better opportunities were open before him in the great Prairie state, and having in Ogle county a number of old friends and neighbors, Upton Powell determined here to find for himself and family a new home. In the fall of 1853, he came out and selected a location in Pine Creek township, purchasing a partially improved place of four hundred and fifty-one acres, and in April, 1854, left his old home with his family and arrived here May 2, 1854. With characteristic energy, he commenced to improve the place, in due time erecting a good residence, barn, and various outbuildings. From time to time he added to his possessions until he became the owner of over eight hundred acres of good farming land. He was quite prosperous and became a well-known citizen of the county. He lived upon the old place for some years, and then moved to a farm near Polo, where his death occurred about 1883. His wife passed away some years previously.

In his native county our subject spent his boyhood and youth, assisting his father upon the farm and in the mill, in the meantime attending the common school as the opportunity was given him. He came with the family to Ogle county and continued to assist his father for some years, dividing his time between the saw mill and the farm. He was married January 20, 1860, to Miss Sarah Hays, a native of Washington county, Maryland, and daughter of Henry Hays, also a native of the same county and state, and who likewise came to Ogle county in May, 1854, locating in Pine Creek township. By this union three sons were born. William H. is married and is engaged in farming in Black Hawk county, Iowa. John Upton and George W. yet reside at home, assisting in the farm work, and with their father are making a business of fattening cattle and hogs for the markets. They are also interested in a meat market at Mt. Morris, and also furnish dressed meat for a market in Oregon.

After his marriage Mr. Powell located on the sawmill place, and carried on the mill and engaged in farming for three years. In 1864 he purchased the farm where he now resides, consisting of but one hundred and sixty acres at that time. He later added one hundred and sixty acres more, and still later fifteen acres, making the home farm contain three hundred and thirty-five acres. He has also three hundred and sixteen acres in Pine Creek township, divided into four small farms, and has fifty acres in Grand Detour township. The home farm presents a very neat and attractive appearance with its fine residence and barn, numerous outbuildings, fruit and ornamental trees. Everything about the place denotes the energy and thrift of the owner. In addition to the cultivation of grain, he has given much attention to stock raising, making a specialty of Poland-China hogs.

Politically Mr. Powell is a Democrat, having voted the ticket since casting his first presidential vote for James Buchanan in 1856. He has been honored by his friends and neighbors with various local offices, serving as highway commissioner some eighteen or twenty years and as supervisor one term, in 1894-5. After an interval of two years he was again elected in 1898 and is now serving in that capacity. During his first term he was on several important committees, and is now a member of the equalization and of the finance committee. Interested in the public schools, he has served as school director for some twenty-five or thirty years.

An active and enterprising man, Mr. Powell is highly regarded by all who know him, and his friends are not confined to those of his own party. Broad-minded and liberal, he commands the respect of all. In the forty-five years of his residence in Ogle county he has been an active factor in its progress and has done his full share in its development. Success has crowned his efforts, but no one envies him for that he has, knowing that it has been gained by honest efforts.

CHARLES AYRES, deceased, was a prominent farmer of Woosung township, one well known in Lee and Ogle counties. He was born in Huntingdon county, Pennsylvania, September 13, 1824, and was the son of Ludlum and Susanna (Sharer) Ayres, who emigrated from Pennsylvania to Illinois in 1845, locating in Franklin Grove, Lee county, where they remained until 1860, when they moved to the southern part of the state, where they spent about one year, and then returned to Lee county, where the remainder of their lives were spent. They had a family of eight children, two of whom died in childhood. Those growing to maturity were Charles H., Matthew, John, William, Thomas and Ludlum Smith.

The subject of this sketch spent his boyhood and youth in his native state, and in the schools of that state received his education. This was, however, supplemented by attendance in the schools of Dixon, after the removal of the family to this state. He remained with his parents until twenty-two years old, when he began life for himself, cultivating a farm and operating two threshing machines during the seasons. He was united in marriage June 1, 1855, with Miss Mary J. Grush, who was born March 7, 1834, and daughter of Isaac and Catherine (Burns) Grush, the former a native of Lancaster county, Pennsylvania, and the latter of Huntingdon county, in the same state. Isaac Grush was the son of Isaac Grush, Sr., a native of Germany, and a farmer by occupation, who died in Lancaster county, Pennsylvania. Isaac Grush was by trade a miller, and also followed the trade of cooper. In 1846 he came with his family to Ogle county, and located in Pine Creek township, where he purchased a farm of one hundred and sixty acres, which he operated until within a few years before his death, when he retired from active life, and died at the residence of his son in Paul City, Nebraska.

Isaac and Catherine Grush were the parents of ten children, eight of whom grew to maturity—Philip, John, William, James, Mary J., Elizabeth, Emma and Catherine. Two died in infancy. Mrs. Catherine Grush passed to her reward in 1851, and later Mr. Grush married Mrs. Catherine (Lutz) Eshelman, a widow, and by this marriage there was one daughter, Vernie.

To Charles and Mary J. Ayres eight children were born. Elsie M., born June 17, 1856, died June 2, 1892. Samuel R., born December 28, 1857, is now living in Hardin county, Iowa, he married Miss Delia Miller, of Washington county, Maryland, and they have a son, Charles L. Johnnie E., born December 28, 1859, died January 15, 1861. Alma S., born January 15, 1861, is now the wife of C. E. Parks, and they have one child, Clarence C., born January 1, 1888; they reside on the old homestead. Lillie S., born December 31, 1863, married John Lampen, and they live in Pine Creek township. Henry P., born August 15, 1869, died June 6, 1895. Charles, born August 5, 1866, died March 17, 1867. Lena May, born June 28, 1872, died February 6, 1875.

Mr. Ayres purchased the farm on which his widow now resides, on section 8, Woosung township, from his brother William, who entered the land from the government. In 1855, soon after his marriage, he built a small house, which is now used as an ice house. The second house in which the family lived was erected a few years after, and is now used as a shop. In 1874 he erected the house in which the family now live, and which is a commodious and comfortable structure. As his means would permit, Mr. Ayres added to the improvements of the place, erecting a large barn, and putting up other outbuildings, setting out fruit and ornamental trees, and otherwise adding to the attractive appearance of the farm. He was a practical farmer and endeavored to keep up with the times in the way of improvements.

In politics, Mr. Ayres was a Republican, and a stanch advocate of the principles of the party. He served his neighborhood as school director for a number of years, as he always felt an interest in the public schools. He was also road commissioner a number of years. Religiously he was a member of the United Brethren church, in which he took great interest, being a firm believer in the Christian religion. His wife is also a member of that church. Mr. Ayres passed from this life November 1, 1880, his death being from asthma and consumption. He was a good man, and his death was a sad loss not only to his faithful wife, who was always a comfort and stay to him, but to the community as well. His friends were numerous in both Lee and Ogle counties.

THOMAS DIXON is one of the retired farmers who are living at their ease in the village of Byron, and who know right well how to take care of the property they accumulated in their younger years by untiring industry and economy. For a period of over forty years he was actively and successfully engaged in agricultural pursuits in Ogle county, but has now laid aside business cares to spend his remaining years in ease and retirement.

Mr. Dixon comes from across the sea, being a native of England, born in Cumberland county, February 10, 1834. His father, John Dixon, was a native of the same county and a son of Thomas Dixon, a farmer of that region. There the former grew to manhood and married Miss Ann Thompson, an English lady, who died in her native land about 1841. He was again married, but his second wife also died in England. In 1855 he and his family emigrated to the United States, and on reaching the shores of this country proceeded at once to Ogle county, Illinois, arriving here in the fall of that year. He purchased a farm in Marion township and to its further improvement and cultivation devoted his energies until failing health caused his retirement. Although he was not well for some years, he lived to the ripe old age of seventy-eight, dying July 19, 1873.

In his family were four children, two sons and two daughters, but the latter are both deceased. Sarah died unmarried, and Anna married Joshua Chain, of Byron, and died leaving three children. Our subject is the older son. Paul, born in England, in 1838, came with the family to the new world in 1855, and was married here to Miss Addie Millis, a native of Ogle county, and a daughter of John Millis, who was a pioneer of southern Illinois, and from this state went to California during the '50s. On his return he bought a farm in Marion township, Ogle county, where he successfully engaged in agricultural pursuits for a number of years. Later he rented his farm and bought residence property in Byron, where he spent the last years of his life. After his marriage Paul Dixon engaged in farming for a number of years in Marion township, where he owned and occupied a farm of over one hundred acres, which he placed under a high state of cultivation. After the death of his wife he removed to Dixon, Illinois, where he now resides. He has two daughters, Eva and Sarah, both well educated young ladies. The latter attended the public schools of Byron and also the Rockford Commercial College, and is now successfully engaged in teaching in Ogle county.

Thomas Dixon, of this review, was a young man of twenty years on the emigration of the family to America, and he was of great assistance to his father in developing and carrying on the home farm. After arriving at mature years he took charge of the place and business, remaining with his father until the latter's death, and caring for him during his declining years. Subsequently he purchased the interests of the other heirs and succeeded to the old homestead, on which he made many substantial and useful improvements. After operating it for some years he sold and purchased a farm of one hundred and fifty acres in Scott township, near Stillman Valley. He located thereon, and for a year was engaged in building and improving the place, erecting a good residence, barn, cribs and other outbuildings, and converting it into one of the best improved farms of the township. This work completed he rented it, and in 1897 removed to Byron, where he now lives, enjoying the rest he has so well earned and so truly deserves. The Republican party has found in him an earnest advocate of its principles since he cast his first vote for General U. S. Grant in 1868, and he has never missed a presidential election since that time. Although not a member of any religious denomination he attends and gives liberally toward the support of the Methodist Episcopal church. He and his brother are well known in Byron and Ogle county as men of exemplary habits and sterling worth, and this brief sketch of their lives will be read with interest by their many friends.

WILLIAM STAHLHUT, an enterprising farmer residing on section 9, Mt. Morris township, is a native of the township, born August 7, 1855, but is of German descent, his parents, August and Frederika (Bruns) Stahlhut, being natives of Hanover, Germany, the former born April 28, 1809, and the latter January 4, 1818. They were reared and married in their native land, and in 1849 came to the United States with a party of immigrants, coming direct to Mt Morris township, some of the party having relatives in this county. The father of Mrs. Stahlhut, the maternal grandfather of our subject, was an officer of high rank in the German army, and commanded a portion of the German troops at the battle of Waterloo.

August Stahlhut was a stonemason by trade. On his arrival in Mt. Morris, he found himself a stranger in a strange land, the language of the people being unfamiliar to him. He came, however, with the intention of becoming an American citizen, and to that end assimilated himself to his new surroundings. He at once found employment at his trade, working on the new building of the Rock River Seminary, and on various private dwellings in course of erection. He continued to work at his trade and saving his earnings until he had accumulated sufficient to buy a farm, after which he turned his attention to agricultural pursuits, and only occasionally working at his trade. August and Frederika Stahlhut were the parents of four children, the last born dying in infancy. August, born in November, 1841, in Germany, came with his parents to this country when in his eighth year. Here he grew to manhood, and during the dark days of the rebellion, when the president issued his call for more men, he offered his services to his adopted country and took his place within the ranks in Company K, Ninety-second Illinois Volunteer Infantry. With his regiment he went to the front, and after being wounded in a skirmish near Jonesboro, Tennessee, he was taken prisoner and later confined in the dreaded Andersonville prison, where he recovered from his wound, but was starved to death. Henry, born November 19, 1850, married Laura Feidt, and they have two children. He is a farmer in Mt. Morris township. William, our subject, was next in order of birth.

William Stahlhut, our subject, was reared on the home farm in Mt. Morris township, and until eighteen years old attended the district school, receiving a fair common-school education. He was early learned the meaning of work and was required to do his share of the farm work. Leaving school at the age of eighteen years, in partnership with his brother, he purchased eighty acres of land and they commenced farming for themselves.

On the 23d of December, 1875, Mr. Stahlhut was united in marriage with Miss Lydia C. Thomas, born October 19, 1850, in Mt. Morris township, and daughter of Ezra and Elizabeth (Rice) Thomas, both of whom were natives of Washington county, Maryland, and who were among the early settlers of Ogle county. They were the parents of six children: William R., Jacob O., Martha J., Mary E., Lydia C. and Benjamin F. Mr. Thomas died at his home in Mt. Morris, of blood poisoning, March 20, 1880. His wife survived him, dying March 22, 1888. In politics he was a Republican.

To Mr. and Mrs. Stahlhut seven children have been born, the first dying in infancy. Olive C., born March 14, 1878; Charles A., born November 29, 1881, died December 13, 1882; Benjamin A., born April 26, 1884; William H., May 22, 1886; Edward Earl, December 23, 1888, and Jesse T., born July 23, 1894. Those living are all yet residing with their parents, and all are being given good education.

After his marriage Mr. Stahlhut continued to farm with his brother, and in February, 1887, he purchased forty acres more and has now a fine farm of one hundred and sixty acres, which is under a high state of cultivation. He has confined himself to no special fads, but has engaged in general farming. He has been raising mostly road horses, but has raised some Norman draft. Of cattle he has raised Hereford, but is now mostly engaged with Durhams.

In politics Mr. Stahlhut is a Republican. He cast his first presidential vote for Rutherford B. Hayes in 1776, and has since continued to vote the party ticket. He has held several local offices, including school director, school trustee and supervisor. In the latter office he served two terms and was a member of the board during the railroad bond trouble, which ran for a number of years. His wife is a member of the Lutheran church, as is also his daughter, Olive. Active and enterprising, Mr. Stahlhut keeps abreast with the times, lending aid and encouragement to all worthy enterprises. With his family, he is held in the highest esteem, having many friends in all parts of the county.

FREDERICK H. LEWIS.— Prominent among the more intelligent, active and enterprising citizens of Marion township is the gentleman whose name introduces this biography. His reputation for integrity and industry is second to none in the county, and being a man of rare intellectual attainments, he is authority on many questions with the people of the community. He owns and occupies a fine farm of two hundred acres on section 15, Marion township, and is successfully engaged in its operation.

Mr. Lewis is a native son of Ogle county, his birth occurring on the farm where he now resides December 22, 1849. His father, Homer D. Lewis, was born near Ware, Massachusetts, in January, 1822, and was a son of David Lewis, also a native of Massachusetts, who with his family came to

Illinois in 1837. His sons drove across the country with wagons and the family settled in Marion township, Ogle county, where he cleared and developed a farm, one mile west of the home of our subject. Here Homer D. Lewis grew to manhood and married Miss Adaline Bacon, also a native of the old Bay state and a daughter of Squire Bacon, who came west and died in Illinois. Mr. Lewis entered one hundred and sixty acres where his son is now living and soon transformed the wild land into highly cultivated and productive fields. To his original farm he later added two adjoining tracts of forty acres each, making a fine farm of two hundred and forty acres, which he improved with good buildings. He was one of the most active and successful farmers of the township and at one time owned seven hundred acres of valuable land, all of which property was acquired through his own industry, enterprise and good management. He was honored with a number of responsible official positions. From his farm he removed to Stillman Valley, but subsequently took up his residence in Rockford, where he passed away November 29, 1897, at the age of seventy-five years. His wife survives him and still resides in that city.

Frederick H. Lewis is the only son living in a family of five children. Laura M., his oldest sister, is the wife of H. H. Hurd, of Stillman Valley; Mary is the wife of Nathan James, of the same place; Carrie A. is the wife of William S. Ives, of Byron township, Ogle county; and Lucy is the wife of John L. Keep and resides with her mother in Rockford.

The subject of this review was reared in much the usual manner of farmer boys, and the knowledge he acquired in the district schools has been supplemented by a course in the Rockford High School and also in the Commercial College of that place. During his youth he assisted his father in the operation of the home farm and then purchased eighty acres adjoining, on which he resided for ten years. At the end of that time he bought the old homestead, which he had previously rented, and in its skillful management he is acknowledged to be one of the most progressive and systematic farmers of the community.

On the 27th of December, 1871, in Marion township, Mr. Lewis was united in marriage with Miss Lucy A. Johnson, a daughter of Rev. G. S. Johnson, who served as postmaster of Stillman Valley continuously for about a quarter of a century. He was a native of Massachusetts, an early settler of Illinois, and was a direct descendant of John Alden, who came to America on the Mayflower, and for some time engaged in merchandising in Rockford, but spent the last years of his life in Stillman Valley. Mrs. Lewis was born in Ohio, but was reared in Ogle county, and being well educated she became a successful and popular teacher. Our subject and his wife have a family of six children, all at home, namely: Charles, Harry, Julia, Fred and Frank, twins, and George. The daughter is a graduate of the Stillman Valley High School and is quite proficient in music, and the youngest son is now attending the high school at that place.

Mr. Lewis is a member of the G. O. P., being an ardent Republican since casting his first vote for General U. S. Grant in 1872. He is a director of the Scott & Marion Township Mutual Fire Insurance Company, has been an active member of the school board for twenty years, and has served as its president and also clerk of the district most of the time. He is now serving his second term as township trustee, and he has most capably and faithfully discharged the duties of every position he has been called upon to fill, whether in public or private life. He is one of the official members of the Congregational church of Stillman Valley, to which his family also belong, and in the best social circles of the community they occupy an enviable position.

FREDERICK ZICK, Ph. D., teacher and lawyer, is a prominent citizen of Polo, and one of the ablest lawyers practicing at the bar of Ogle county, having the mental grasp which enables him to discover the best points in a case. A man of sound judgment, he manages his cases with masterly skill and tact, and is regarded as one of the ablest jury advocates in this section of the state. He is a logical reasoner, able debator and forcible in argument, uniting a rare gift of oratory with the most convincing logic that arouses the emotion and convinces the judgment.

A native of Illinois, Mr. Zick was born in Thompson township, Jo Daviess county, October 20, 1858, and is a son of Frederick and Mary (Denchman) Zick, both natives of the province of Waldec, Germany, the former born about 1816 and the latter about 1832. They were married in their native land and came to America in 1852, landing at New York after a long and tedious voyage. After a short time spent in the metropolis they proceeded westward and located in Jo Daviess county, Illinois, where the father engaged in farming until 1877, when he laid aside all business cares. He then spent one year in Galena and his last days in the country near that city, where he passed away in 1879. His wife died in Jo Daviess county in 1866. To them were born two sons: John, who lives on a farm in Jo Daviess county; and Frederick, of this review. The paternal grandfather of our subject, John Zick, spent his entire life in Germany.

Frederick Zick, our subject, is indebted to the district schools of Jo Daviess county for his early educational privileges, and he received his early training at farm work. When he arrived at his majority he decided to change his occupation, and took a preparatory course for teaching at the German-English College, then located at Galena, Illinois. He taught school two terms and graduated from the Northern Illinois College, Fulton, Illinois, in 1884. He read law one year with Judge McCoy, at Fulton, and then read one year in the law office of John J. Cole, Esq., at La Crosse, Wisconsin. He was admitted to the bar in the territory (now state) of North Dakota in 1886, and there entered upon the practice of his profession. He was state's attorney two years for Cavalier county, North Dakota, and in 1891 located at Seattle, Washington, where he remained for two years and a half, during which time he gained an enviable reputation as a criminal lawyer. While at Seattle he tried many criminal cases, and appeared for the defense in two noted murder trials. He tried the case of S. N. Saddler, who was charged with murder in the first degree for stabbing a Greek fisherman on West street in Seattle, and secured his acquittal on the theory of self-defense. He tried the case of Mattia Leoni and Joseph Puccia, two Italians charged with murdering George Richards, on Mercer island, in Lake Washington

FRED ZICK.

GERTRUDE M. ZICK.

They buried the body in the lake and Leoni then went to Canada, where he was arrested and brought back for trial. Mr. Zick defended them on the theory of self-defense, and Leoni was convicted of manslaughter and sentenced to eighteen months in the penitentiary, and Puccia to three months in the county jail as accessory after the fact. In August, 1893, he came to Polo, Illinois, where his wife's parents reside, and here he has since been engaged in practice, meeting with a well-deserved success.

In Polo, on the 29th day of April, 1890, was celebrated the marriage of Mr. Zick and Miss Gertrude M. Sanborn, a native of Ogle county, a graduate of the Northern Illinois College, of Fulton, a successful teacher in our public schools, and a daughter of Ambrose and Elizabeth (Good) Sanborn. In his political affiliations our subject is a Republican. He is city attorney of Polo, has one of the largest law libraries in the county, has a large office and probate practice and is well versed in all and everything necessary to make him a successful practitioner. Socially, he joined the Knights of Pythias while at Seattle and was elected a representative to the Grand Lodge in 1893. He is a member of the Knights of the Globe and also of the Mystic Workers of the World, and is one of the supreme directors of the Mystic Workers. Personally Mr. Zick is a little over medium height, well proportioned, with black hair, grey eyes and strong features that indicate force and determination.

HENRY LANDIS THOMAS.— Among the leading and representative agriculturists of Ogle county, none stands higher in the estimation of his fellow men than the subject of this review, who owns and operates a fine farm of two hundred acres on section 18, Rockvale township. He was born in Maryland, October 24, 1838, a son of Joshua and Salina (Landis) Thomas, natives of Washington county, that state, the former born March 8, 1811, the latter March 7, 1812. The paternal grandparents were Henry and Catherine Thomas, in whose family were the following children: Mrs. Susan Hoffan, deceased; Mrs. Ruan Newcomer, a resident of Washington county, Maryland; Joshua, father of our subject; Elias and Elizabeth. Our subject is the third in order of birth in a family of seven children, the others being: Permelia M., widow of Robert Hitt, of Polo, Illinois; Mary Catherine, wife of H. M. Funk, a hardware merchant of Polo, Illinois; L. F., who married Olga Smith, and conducts a paint, oil and sash store at Polo; Jacob Oskie, deceased; John, who married Martha Seyster and operated the old home farm; Lewis Ferdinand; and John Edwin. The mother of these children departed this life September 22, 1854, at the age of forty-two years, six months and fifteen days, and the father was again married, his second union being with Susan Felker, by whom he had five children: Ettie, deceased; Robert Lee, who married May McGuffin and lives on the old home farm; Frank F. and Olin M., who are also living with their mother on the home place; and one who died in infancy.

Joshua Thomas, our subject's father, was educated in the common schools of Maryland and throughout life followed agricultural pursuits. He first came to Ogle county in the fall of 1839, and purchased two hundred acres of government land for himself and father, who came here in 1840, it being bought at the land office in Dixon at one dollar and a quarter per acre when it came into market. After securing his land, Joshua Thomas returned east, but the following year brought his family to their new home, making the trip overland. All of his land was unbroken with the exception of about three or four acres, which had been placed under cultivation, and the only building upon the place was a log house, but to its further improvement and cultivation he at once turned his attention and soon converted the wild tract into a most desirable farm. In 1850 he made a trip to the gold fields of California by way of the overland route, in company with Mr. Pitzer and Captain Swingley, of Brodie's Grove. He met with fair success on the Pacific slope and returned to Illinois in 1852 by way of the Isthmus of Panama and settled down to farming again. In politics he was a pronounced Democrat, and being one of the most prominent and influential men of the community, he was often called to public office, serving as school director fifteen years, school trustee three years, and director of the Ogle County Agricultural Society from 1853 until 1860. He also served as president of that organization for a time. He departed this life March 18, 1884.

Henry L. Thomas, of this review, was only two years old when brought by his parents to Ogle county, and he was reared about two miles south of his present home, his early education being acquired in a little log school-house a half mile from his boyhood home. He continued to assist his father in the operation of the home farm until his marriage, which was celebrated December 20, 1866, Miss Mary Ellen Felker becoming his wife. He then rented a farm of one hundred and thirty acres in Pine Creek township, on which he lived for three years, and for the same length of time rented his present farm, which then belonged to George W. Phelps. The following two years were spent on a farm of two hundred acres in Mt. Morris township, and at the end of that time he purchased one hundred and sixty acres of his present farm. Before moving to this place, however, he rented the A. F. Weaver farm, of eighty acres, for one year, and then located upon his own farm, to which he has added a tract of forty acres, making a valuable farm of two hundred acres, which he has placed under excellent cultivation and improved with good and substantial buildings. He is interested in stock raising to some extent.

Mrs. Thomas is a daughter of Abraham and Catherine Felker, the former born in Washington county, Maryland, July 6, 1802, the latter in Franklin county, Pennsylvania, April 24, 1811. Her grandfather was a tanner, but her father followed farming in the east, and on coming to Illinois in 1855, settled in the town of Mt. Morris, where he spent three years and then moved to a farm in Ogle county, which he had previously purchased. Mrs. Thomas' education was begun in the schools of Maryland, and after coming to this state attended the public schools and academy at Mt. Morris. Nine children have been born to our subject and his wife, namely: Lillie May, born January 15, 1868, died January 6, 1876; Edgar Felker, born July 29, 1869, is a dentist by profession and is now at home. While serving as a member of the committee on the Fourth of July celebration, he had his finger injured by a skyrocket and had to have it amputated; Florence Edna, born April 11, 1871, is the wife of

Charles Zoller, manager of the Union Tea Company at Omaha, Nebraska; Noble Fillmore, born December 12, 1872, married Susan Young, by whom he has a little son, and they live in Mt. Morris township, where he is engaged in farming; Ada Ellen, born December 19, 1875, died in infancy; Charles Henry, born April 3, 1877; Freddie Henderson, born December 15, 1879, and Catherine, born March 26, 1882, are all at home; Nellie Maude, born February 19, 1885, is attending the district school.

Mr. Thomas has always affiliated with the Democratic party, and is to-day a strong advocate of the free coinage of silver. He has served as school director for nine years, and is at present school trustee. His wife and three daughters are members of the Lutheran church and he gives to its support. He is widely and favorably known throughout the community in which he has so long made his home, and he has a host of warm friends.

HON. CHARLES SCHNEIDER, mayor of Oregon, and cashier of the First National Bank, of that city, is a native of the city, and was born October 19, 1843, and is the son of John M. and Rebecca (Etnyre) Schneider, the former a native of Bavaria, and the latter of Washington county, Maryland. John M. Schneider was born June 8, 1808, and in his native country grew to manhood. He came to the United States in 1834, locating first in Baltimore, Maryland, where he remained for a time, removing from there to St. Louis, and later to Galena, Illinois. In 1839 he settled in Oregon, which at that time contained two log houses. He was a tailor by trade, but at Oregon opened first a grocery store and engaged in the grocery business, later establishing a clothing store and continued in the clothing business up to the time of his death, which occurred September 30, 1893. He was a successful business man and accumulated a good estate. In politics he was a Democrat, and religiously a Catholic. His wife, who was born at Smithsburg, Washington county, Maryland, August 20, 1808, was the eldest child of John and Catherine Etnyre, and came with her parents to Ogle county in 1839. In religious belief she was a Lutheran. She died in the spring of 1895. They were the parents of three children, Charles, Mary and Ellen. Both daughters died in young womanhood.

Charles Schneider was reared in Oregon, and after obtaining his primary education in the public schools, entered the University of Notre Dame, at South Bend, Indiana, where he completed his course. After leaving that institution he returned to Oregon and clerked for a time in a store, and in 1870 entered the banking house of Bayard & Company, as bookkeeper. One year later this bank was converted into the First National Bank of Oregon, Illinois, and in 1873 Mr. Schneider was elected cashier, which position he has since held. He was a little later elected one of the directors of the bank, and is still serving as such. The bank was chartered in 1871 with a capital of fifty thousand dollars. The present officers are George A. Mix, president; J. L. Rice, vice-president; and Charles Schneider, cashier. In addition to those named the directors are William H. Guilford and John Matmiller.

Mr. Schneider was married September 14, 1871, to Miss Fannie Weller, a native of Martinsburg, Virginia, and daughter of Daniel and Mary (Timmons) Weller. At an early day her parents located in Pine

Creek township, Ogle county, where she grew to womanhood. Her father was born in Baltimore, Maryland, December 1, 1805, and died in Ogle county, December 26, 1890. Her mother, who was a daughter of John Timmons, was born in Martinsburg, Virginia, and died November 11, 1886. With the exception of her brother Charles, now living in Pine Creek township, Mrs. Schneider is the only one of her family now living. To Mr. and Mrs. Schneider eight children have been born—Frank B., Charles J., William D., Leo, Mary, Bert A., Ellen and George E., all of whom are living but Mary, who died in infancy.

Mr. and Mrs. Schneider are members of the Catholic church. In politics he is a Republican. In 1885 he was elected alderman and was re-elected three times. In 1893 he was elected mayor of the city, re-elected in 1895, and again in 1897, and is yet serving in that office. No other mayor ever served such a length of time. He is a public-spirited citizen, and believes in pushing things, desiring his city to take a position which it is entitled by its natural advantages. He is keenly alive to the demands of the age, and under his administration the city of his birth will not suffer in comparison with others. He is treasurer of the Rock River Electric railroad, a new enterprise of which he is one of the promoters.

JOSIAH A. HAYS, a well-to-do farmer of Buffalo township, resides on a well improved farm on section 11, lying near the city of Polo. He has been a resident of the county since the spring of 1854, coming here from Washington county, Maryland, where he was born March 17, 1843.

He is a son of Henry Hays, a native of the same county and state, who was born in 1808, and who grew to manhood in his native county and married Miss Sarah Eakle, who was likewise a native of Washington county. The good reports from Ogle county, sent by friends who had settled here, made him determine to follow their example, and accordingly, in the spring of 1854, accompanied by his family, he came to the county and located in Pine Creek township, where he purchased one hundred and sixty-three acres of choice land and engaged in farming, an occupation in which he was engaged in his native state. On that farm he resided a number of years, and then moved to Polo, and there spent the last years of his life, dying there in 1889, his death being the result of an accident, having been run over by a railroad train.

The boyhood of our subject was spent in his native state, and in the common schools he commenced to obtain an education. He was but eleven years old when he accompanied his parents to Ogle county. He is one of a family of eight children, all living but one. On his arrival in Ogle county he assisted his father in the cultivation of the home farm, and usually in the winter months attended the public schools. He remained with his parents until after he attained his majority, and was of great assistance to them in developing the farm. In March, 1865, he enlisted under the last call of the president for men to fill up the depleted regiments. He became a member of Company F, Eighteenth Illinois Volunteer Infantry, joining his regiment at Little Rock, Arkansas. While the war was soon afterwards ended, his regiment was retained in the service, doing guard duty through Arkansas, until in December, 1865, when it was mustered out of service at Pine Bluff, Arkansas, the men receiving their discharge at Springfield, Illinois.

On receiving his discharge Mr. Hays returned to his old home and again engaged in agricultural pursuits. On the 28th of December, 1866, he was united in marriage, at Freeport, Illinois, with Miss Louisa Ann Martha Fox, a native of Albany, New York, and daughter of John Fox, an Englishman, who later came to Illinois and settled in Macoupin county, where Mrs. Hays was reared, and where he died in 1856. His widow later married John Greenfield, and now resides in Grundy Center, Iowa. She is also English born, and is now about eighty-four years old. Mrs. Hays is one of a family of three children, and the sole survivor. One brother, John A. T., was a soldier in the Southern army, while the other, F. B., was a soldier in the Union army, and died while in the service of his country.

The spring after his marriage Mr. Hays moved to Harden county, Iowa, where he purchased eighty acres of land and opened up a farm. He remained on that farm two years, then sold out and rented for two years, then moved to Grundy county, in the state, and purchased one hundred and sixty acres and commenced the development of a new farm. After remaining there ten years and putting the farm under a high state of cultivation, he sold out, and in 1883 returned to Ogle county and purchased the farm where he now resides, on which he has made some permanent and valuable improvements, including the remodeling of the house.

Mr. and Mrs. Hays have two daughters. Martha Ellen is now the wife of James Woolsey, and they have three children—Frank E., Eugene Hays and Murial May.

They reside on a farm in Buffalo township. Fanny Belle is the wife of William Dew, of Buffalo township, and they have four children—Perry W., Elmer, Mary Lavina and Josie Louise.

Politically Mr. Hays has been a Republican since attaining his majority. His first presidential ballot was for Abraham Lincoln in 1863, a time when the votes of every true unionist counted for something. He has never cared for office, but while residing in Iowa he served as justice of the peace, township treasurer and secretary of the school board. He is a member of the Methodist Episcopal church at Polo, of which body his wife is also a member. In whatever concerns the church they take an active interest, having at heart a love for the cause. Although absent from the county for some years he never lost interest in his old home, and is happy to be again numbered among its representative citizens.

CORNELIUS BOWMAN is the possessor of a handsome property which now enables him to spend his declining years in the pleasurable enjoyment of his accumulations. Until recently the record of his life was that of an active, enterprising, methodical and sagacious business man and farmer, who bent his energies to the honorable acquirement of a comfortable competence for himself and family, but he is now living retired in the village of Harper.

Mr. Bowman was born near Berlin, Somerset county, Pennsylvania, August 13, 1831, and is a son of John Bowman, who was born on the same farm in 1792. His paternal grandfather was a native of Germany and was one of the first settlers of Somerset county, where he opened up the farm on which both our subject and his father were born. The latter married Elizabeth Marteeny, who was born near Somerset, Somerset county, of English ancestry. He spent his entire life upon the old homestead engaged in agricultural pursuits, and there died in 1844 at the age of fifty-two years. His wife long survived him, dying in 1890 at the advanced age of eighty-four year. To them were born thirteen children, but only six reached years of maturity and four are now living, namely: Uriah, who owns and operates the old homestead; John J., a farmer of Somerset county; Chauncey, also a farmer of Somerset county, who served through the war of the Rebellion and was wounded at the battle of Gettysburg, and Cornelius, of this review. Cyrus, the oldest of the family, was a farmer by occupation and spent his entire life in Somerset county. Levina married Aaron Geiger and also died in that county.

Upon the old homestead Cornelius Bowman grew to manhood, and in the schools of the neighborhood obtained a limited education, which has been greatly supplemented by reading and study at home. During early life he successfully engaged in teaching for several terms. On the 27th of February, 1852, he was united in marriage with Miss Theresa Hanger, also a native of Somerset county, Pennsylvania, and a daughter of Jacob Hanger, who was born there and belonged to an old family of the county. Of the twelve children born of this union three died in infancy and John died from an accident at the age of nine years. Those living are Harvey, who resides on the home farm in Ogle county, Illinois; Norman, who is married and engaged in business in Webster City, Iowa; Grant, at home; Rebecca, wife of Fred F. Nicodemus, of Forreston, Illinois; Mrs. Rosanna E. Costello, who is now keeping house for her brother Harvey; Agnes M., wife of Henry Fisher, who lives near Forreston; Mary, wife of Jacob Piper, a farmer of Forreston, and Verna, at home.

During the first year of his married life Mr. Bowman operated a rented farm in Somerset county, Pennsylvania, and then in connection with his brother he bought a tract of land which they developed into a good farm and cultivated for thirteen years. In the meantime he served as school director and township assessor. Coming west in 1865 he first located in Lee county, Illinois, where he rented the Colonel Dement farm for one year, but at the end of that time he became a resident of Ogle county, where he has since made his home. He rented a farm in Forreston township for one year and then bought a tract of eighty acres, to the cultivation of which he devoted his time for several years. On selling that place he bought the old David Raisinger farm of two hundred acres in Forreston township, and located thereon. When the railroad was laid out across his land, he divided some of his property into town lots and started the village of Harper. He built a store room and embarked in merchandising at that place, leaving his sons to operate the farm, and continued to actively engage in business there for seventeen years. In the meantime he served as assistant postmaster, and later as postmaster being connected with that office for sixteen or seventeen years. Besides his village property and the farm already mentioned he owns a well improved and valuable farm in Carroll county, Illinois, comprising one hundred and sixty acres, and has four hundred and eighty acres of improved land in Cheyenne county, Nebraska. He was one of the organizers of the Forreston Fire Insurance Company, of which he has been a stockholder, director and secretary for seven years, and he has been actively identified with all enterprises which he believed calculated to advance the interests of the community in which he lives and promote general prosperity.

Originally Mr. Bowman was a Whig in politics, casting his first vote for General Winfield Scott, and since the formation of the Republican party he has been one of its stanch supporters. He has taken quite an active and prominent part in local politics, and has filled a number of township offices, being commissioner of highways six years, school director for a number of years, and supervisor two terms, during which time he served on some important committees. He and his wife are among the original members of the Reformed church of Forreston, contribute liberally to its support and assisted in the erection of the house of worship. For the success he has achieved in life Mr. Bowman deserves great credit, for he started out in life with but little capital, and the prosperity that has come to him is due to his own industry, enterprise, perseverance and good management. He is to-day one of the substantial men of the county, as well as one of its honored and highly esteemed citizens.

JOHN J. LEBO is a wide-awake and energetic farmer of Forreston township who owns and operates a well-improved and valuable farm of one hundred and twenty acres conveniently situated within a mile of the village of Forreston. He is a native of Pennsylvania, born near Harrisburg, in Dauphin county, September 18, 1847, and is a son of Phillip Lebo, a native of the same county. The grandfather, John Lebo, who was born of French parentage, was a pioneer of Dauphin county, where he opened up a farm and reared his family. On reaching man's estate Philip Lebo married Miss Barbara Meyers, also a native of Dauphin county and a daughter of Jacob Meyers, who was a represntative of one of its honored pioneer families. Mr. Lebo owned and operated a fine farm of one hundred and fifty acres near Elizabethville, Pennsylvania, was one of the prominent and influential citizens of his county, and was called upon to serve in a number of local offices of honor and trust. In the county of his nativity he died in April, 1886, at about the age of eighty-four, having survived his wife for some years.

In the family of this worthy couple were twelve children, of whom ten reached years of maturity, namely: Philip, a prominent business man, who is now engaged in the manufacture of lumber in the state of Washington; John J., our subject; Eliza A., twin sister of John J., and the wife of C. S. Hartman, of Dauphin county, Pennsylvania; Mrs. Sarah M. Herner, a widow residing in Harrisburg, Pennsylvania; Aaron S., who is married and engaged in blacksmithing in the state of Washington; William, who married but is now deceased; Mrs. Ann Reams, a widow living in Harrisburg; Rebecca J., wife of John Mayer, of Washington; Mary D., wife of John D. Hartman, of Dauphin county, Pennsylvania; and Emanuel N., a contractor and builder of Harrisburg.

John J. Lebo passed his boyhood and youth in Dauphin county, Pennsylvania and received a good common-school education.

which has been greatly supplemented by reading and observation in later years. He remained under the parental roof until reaching man's estate and in Dauphin county was married, June 2, 1870, to Miss Sarah Lark, who was also born, reared and educated in that county, and is a daughter of Daniel and Susan Lark, natives of Pennsylvania. Two children have been born of their union, namely: Cora E., now the wife of Rev. D. N. Frantz, a minister of the Reformed church now located at Stonington, Illinois, and Harry E., who is attending school in Dixon.

For several years after his marriage Mr. Lebo operated rented land in his native county, but in 1877 he came west, joining old Pennsylvania friends in Ogle county, Illinois. After renting for about four years he bought eighty acres in Forreston township on which he now resides, and erected thereon a good house and substantial out-buildings, but in 1890 his residence was destroyed by fire, together with a large part of the household goods. Later in the season he built his present comfortable home and barn, and now has one of the best improved farms of the locality. To the original purchase he added a forty-acre tract adjoining and now has one hundred and twenty acres, which he has placed under excellent cultivation. In connection with general farming he is also interested in stock raising and has upon his place a good grade of horses, cattle and hogs.

Politically Mr. Lebo is a lifelong Republican, having cast his first presidential vote for U. S. Grant in the fall of 1868, and as a delegate to the county conventions of his party he has done much to advance its interest in this section of the state. For eighteen years he has been a member of the school board and secretary of the district for about the same length of time, but has never sought nor desired office, preferring to give his undivided attention to his business interests. Socially he is a member of the Knights of the Globe and the Mystic Order, and religiously both he and his wife are members of the English Lutheran church. They are widely and favorably known and their friends are many in Ogle county.

WILLIAM C. DIEFFENBAUGH.— Among the successful and enterprising farmers of Ogle county, who have accumulated a competency through their own exertions and economy, and who thoroughly understand their chosen calling, is the subject of this biographical notice, who resides in section 14, Forreston township. He was born in Montour county, Pennsylvania, February 6, 1840, a son of Conrad Dieffenbaugh, a native of Columbia county, Pennsylvania, where he grew to manhood and married Catherine Stamm, also a native of the Keystone state. The father, who was a farmer by occupation, spent his entire life in Pennsylvania, dying there in 1882. In the family were the following children: Benjamin, a farmer of Pennsylvania; William C., our subject; David E., a resident of Sandusky county, Ohio; Franklin, a resident of Wood county, Ohio; Charles, who lives in Kansas, twenty-five miles west of Wichita, Mrs. Mary Ellen Brown, a widow residing in Cheney, Kansas; and Sarah Ann, who died at the age of ten years.

During his boyhood and youth William C. Dieffenbaugh received a good common-school education and was reared on the home farm, remaining with his father until he attained his majority, and assisting him in carrying on the place. He continued to work for his father for one year and then went to Columbia county, Pennsylvania, where for two years he was engaged in raising broom corn during the summer and manufacturing it into brooms during the winter months at Bloomsburg. In the spring of 1864, he came to Ogle county, Illinois, but after working on a farm in Forreston township for one summer, he went to Carroll county, where he remained for four years.

Returning to Ogle county, Mr. Dieffenbaugh married Miss Anna Heitman, a native of Maryland, who died here in 1871, and of the two children born of that union one died in infancy and the other at the age of thirteen months. He was again married in Ogle county, September 25, 1873, his second union being with Miss Margaret Timmer, a native of the county, who was reared amidst scenes incident to pioneer life. As a child she remembers seeing deer approach the house in search of food, and the wolves often made the night hideous by their howls. Her father, Frederick Timmer, was a native of Germany, but was reared in Maryland, where he married Miss Margaret Jane Fry, who was born in that state, but whose father was an Englishman, her mother a German. Mr. and Mrs. Timmer were honored pioneers of Ogle county, and here reared their family of ten children, all of whom reached man and womanhood, and with but one exception all are still living. They are as follows: John F., a farmer of Forreston township; Elias A., a farmer of Maryland township; Margaret, wife of our subject; Mary Ellen, deceased; Sophia, wife of John Rebman, a farmer of Ogle county; Helen E., wife of Chris Zumdahl, of Ogle county; Henry, a resident of Forreston; Frank, who owns and operates the old home farm; Emma, a resident of Forreston, and Charles, a farmer of this county. Mr. and Mrs. Dieffenbaugh have a family of seven children, namely: Anna, who was educated in the schools of the home district of Forreston, and is now the wife of Harry Acker, a farmer of Brookville, Illinois; John and Jesse, who assist their father in the operation of the home farm; Frances Luella, at home; Benjamin C., a student of the Forreston high school; Harvey F., at home; Walter F., who died at the age of fifteen months; and Emma May, who is attending the home school.

For a number of years after his marriage, Mr. Dieffenbaugh rented land and engaged in farming and raising broom corn during the summer, while through the winter he continued to engage in the manufacture of brooms. In 1884 he purchased his present farm of one hundred and sixty acres on section 14, Forreston township, and the following year located thereon, since which time he has devoted his energies to general farming and stock raising with most gratifying results. He has remodeled the house and made other improvements upon the place which add to its value and attractive appearance.

Politically Mr. Dieffenbaugh is identified with the Democratic party, but aside from voting has never taken a very active part in political affairs. He is a warm friend of our public school system, and is now most capably and satisfactorily serving his fourteenth year as president of the district school board. Religiously both he and his wife are earnest and faithful members of the Zion Reformed church at Forreston. His sterling integrity, inflexible honesty, and general high principles, have won him the respect of every community in which he has resided, and he is to-day one of the most esteemed and valued citizens of his portion of the county.

JOHN REYNOLDS, one of the leading and representative farmers and stock raisers of Woosung township, and who resides on his fine farm on section 9, was born June 24, 1844, in county Roscommon, Ireland, and is the son of Thomas and Mary (Graham) Reynolds, both natives of the same county in Ireland.

In 1840 Thomas Reynolds came to the United States, taking passage in a slow sailing vessel, and landing in New York. He remained in that city but a very short time, going from there into Pennsylvania, where he secured work on a railroad. He remained in Pennsylvania about two years, and then went to Dayton, Ohio. He had now accumulated sufficient funds to send for his family, which he accordingly did, and in due time they joined him at Dayton. After remaining in that city until 1865, he concluded to come to Illinois. Locating in Woosung township, Ogle county, he purchased a farm and engaged in agricultural pursuits. Industrious as the day was long, he made a success in life, becoming a thorough and practical farmer. He continued farming until within a few years of his death, when he retired from active life and lived retired, still, however, remaining on his farm. His death occurred December 16, 1891, at the age of ninety years. He was a fine type of the Irish gentleman, and was a hale and hearty old man, retaining his mental faculties until the last. His good wife died February 15, 1881. They were the parents of five children, of whom our subject is the oldest. Winifred, who is the wife of John Donavan, is living in Dayton, Ohio. Martin, who was in the Fourth Ohio Cavalry and served through the entire Civil war, is now making his home with our subject. Patrick, who married Bridget Dalton, is living on the old home place in Woosung township. Mary died in infancy. In politics Thomas Reynolds was a Democrat, and religiously was a Roman Catholic.

The subject of this sketch spent his boyhood and youth in Dayton, Ohio, and in the public schools of that city received his education. At the age of fifteen, he quit school and commenced working in a furniture factory. He remained in that employment but a short time and then ran a stationary engine in a foundry for several years. In 1865, he came to Ogle county, joining his father, who had come about one month previously. On his arrival he took the management of his father's farm, although he had no previous experience in farming. His success has been wonderful in this respect, as it is not often that one takes up the life of a farmer after having spent years in other employment and makes of farming a success.

Mr. Reynolds continued to manage his father's farm until his marriage, November 28, 1882, to Miss Mary Doyle, who was born August 29, 1857, in Livingston county, New York, and daughter of Darby and Mary (Dalton) Doyle, her father being a farmer by occupation. Both parents were natives of Tipperary county, Ireland. They left their native land in 1852, and crossing the Atlantic, made their way to Livingston county, New York, where they were married, and resided about five years. From that county they moved to Lexington, Kentucky, where they remained four years, coming from there to Ogle county and locating on a farm on section 12, Woosung township, where the family has since continued to reside. Mr. and Mrs. Doyle had a family of six children: Mary, wife of our subject; James, living in Lexington, Kentucky; Catherine, deceased; Lizzie, wife of William Callahan, who is living on the farm of Mr. Doyle; two daughters, who died in infancy. Mrs. Doyle died September 23, 1897. Mr. Doyle is yet living on the old homestead. Religiously he is a Roman Catholic, and politically a Democrat.

Four children have come to bless the union of Mr. and Mrs. Reynolds. Mary Winifred, born March 17, 1885, is now attending school at St. Clara Academy, Sinsinawa, Wisconsin; Catherine Frances, born February 15, 1888; James Martin, born July 4, 1889, and Elizabeth Lauretta, born February 21, 1893, are attending the district school.

After his marriage, Mr. Reynolds moved to his present farm, which he had previously purchased and which comprises two hundred acres of excellent land. The farm has been placed under a high state of cultivation, and everything about the place denotes the master mind of its owner. He raises Durham short-horn cattle, Poland-China hogs and Morgan horses. Each year he markets about one hundred head of hogs. Commencing life with but little else than a stout heart and willing hands, he has been quite successful in life, and has no reason to regret making Ogle county his permanent home.

In politics Mr. Reynolds is a Democrat, but in local affairs he votes for the man and not party. For thirteen years he has served as school director, and for five years was road commissioner. He was also a member of the board of supervisors for four years, during which time he was on several important committees, including the committee on education and the building committee. A public spirited man, he has the confidence of his friends and neighbors in a remarkable degree. Religiously he is connected with the Catholic church, of which his wife is also a devoted member.

JOHNSON LAWRENCE, a well-known and prominent farmer residing on section 1, Eagle Point township, is a representative of one of the old and honored pioneer families of Ogle county—one who has borne its part in her development and prosperity for over sixty years. He was born on the old homestead where he still resides, June 17, 1844, and is a son of John Lawrence, whose birth occurred in Kent county, England, in 1801. Leaving home in 1817, he crossed the broad Atlantic and after spending one year in Philadelphia, Pennsylvania, went to Ontario, Canada, locating north of Toronto, where he engaged in farming. There he married Miss Lydia Johnson, a native of that country, where they continued to make their home until 1838, which year witnessed their arrival in Ogle county, being among its first settlers. In Eagle Point township the father bought a claim of one hundred and eighty-three acres, of which only a few acres had been broken and a log cabin erected thereon. To the further improvement and cultivation of the place he at once turned his attention, and when the land came into market he entered it from the government. He was one of the representative and most active farmers in the county and from the raw land soon developed a tine farm. He met with a well-deserved success in his operations and by an upright, honorable life commanded the respect and esteem of all who knew him. He was one of the original members of the Methodist Episcopal church of Buffalo Grove, gave liberally of his means to its support, and always took an active and prominent part in church work. He died on October 31, 1886,and his estimable wife passed away in November, 1888, the remains of both being interred in the Polo cemetery, where a substantial monument marks their last resting place.

Johnson Lawrence, of this review, is the youngest in a family of seven children, two sons and five daughters, namely: Nancy, who married Philetus Peck and settled in Nebraska, where she died in 1867; Susana, who married Albert Slater and resides in Jefferson, Marion county, Oregon; Mary, wife of J. C. Williams, of Denver, Colorado; Jordan who is now living retired in Polo; Catherine, who married Moses Culver and died in Nebraska; Maria, wife of Isaac Appleford, of Dixon, Illinois; and Johnson.

Our subject was reared in much the usual manner of a farmer of his day, and his early education, acquired in the common schools near his boyhood home, was supplemented by a year's course in Mt. Morris College, then known as the Rock River Seminary. On the 4th of September, 1862, he enlisted as a private in Company D, Ninety-second Illinois Volunteer Infantry, which was assigned to the Army of the Cumberland, and with which he participated in the battles of Franklin and Trynne, Tennessee. In August, 1863, he was transferred to the mounted infantry, and later took part in the engagements at Hoover's Gap, Shelbyville and a series of skirmishes.

With his regiment he was the first at Lookout Mountain and Chattanooga, and besides taking an active part in the battles there, he also bore his part in the engagements at Chickamauga and Ringgold, Georgia, and in the Atlanta campaign, where the regiment was almost constantly under fire. During this time he was changed from Wilder's brigade to Kilkpatrick's cavalry division, with which he remained until the close of the war. He was with Sherman on his memorable march to the sea, and later took part in the battles of Bentonville, Waynesborough, Georgia, and Aiken, South Carolina. The regiment was then left in the south and was finally mustered out at Concord, North Carolina, after which he went to Chicago, where he was discharged in July, 1865. On his return home he resumed his farming operations and continued to aid in the work on the old homestead until 1875, when he took complete charge of the same. He is a thorough and systematic farmer and has met with excellent success in his life-work. Besides the home farm, comprising one hundred and eighty-three acres, he also owns a farm of one hundred and sixty acres, three miles south of the former. For over twenty years he has been engaged in feeding and dealing in stock and annually ships from three to five car loads of cattle and one or two car loads of hogs. He has also found this business quite profitable, and is to-day one of the most substantial and reliable citizens of his community.

In Polo, April 8, 1870, Mr. Lawrence married Miss Julia E. Read, a native of Ogle county and a daughter of George D. Read, an early settler of Ogle county from New York, who came here when a young man, in 1836, and served as postmaster of

Buffalo for a number of years. Here he wedded Mary Wamsley, also a native of New York. His death occurred in 1882, and she passed away in 1884. Mr. and Mrs. Lawrence have one daughter, Lillis, now a student in the home school.

Politically Mr. Lawrence has been a lifelong Republican, casting his first presidential ballot for General U. S. Grant, in 1868, and supporting every Republican candidate for that office since then. He has taken quite an active and influential part in local politics, and has served five or six years as assessor of Eagle Point township, and has been a delegate to a number of county and congressional conventions of his party. In 1893 he was elected supervisor, and so acceptably did he fill that office that he has been continually reelected, being the present incumbent. In 1898 he was elected chairman of the county board and is now filling that position with credit to himself and to the entire satisfaction of his constituents. In whatever position he has been called upon to serve he has discharged the duties in a most efficient and creditable manner. He is an honored member of the Grand Army of the Republic, and his wife is a member of the Independent Presbyterian church of Polo. They stand high in the community where they have so long made their home and those who know them best are numbered among their warmest friends.

JOHN S. KOSIER is a well-known contractor and builder of Byron, of whose skill many notable examples are to be seen in Ogle county. Thoroughly reliable in all things, the quality of his work is a convincing test of his own personal worth and the same admirable trait is shown in his conscientious discharge of the duties of different positions of trust and responsibility to which he has been chosen.

Mr. Kosier was born in Perry county, Pennsylvania, June 29, 1830. His ancestors originally made their home in Wurtemburg, Germany, but during the seventeenth century they were driven out by the French and sought a home on this side of the Atlantic, becoming pioneers of Berks county, Pennsylvania. The great-grandfather of our subject, Jonathan Kosier, removed from that county to what is now Perry county and there reared his family, including George Kosier, our subject's grandfather, who was born in Berks county. The father, John Kosier, spent his entire life in Perry county, was a prosperous farmer and a highly respected citizen of his community. He married Maria Rice, a native of Juniata county, Pennsylvania, and a daughter of Henry and Margaret (Thomas) Rice. Her father was one of a family of twenty-one children, twelve sons and nine daughters, whose parents, Zachariah Rice and wife, lived to advanced ages. The Rice family is also of German descent and was founded near Bradywine, Pennsylvania, during the seventeenth century.

In the county of his nativity John S. Kosier spent his boyhood and youth, attending the common schools to a limited extent, but he is mostly self-educated since reaching man's estate. There he also learned the carpenter's and joiner's trade, which he followed in Pittsburg in 1851. Coming to Illinois in 1852, he worked at his trade in Rockford for one year, and in the spring of 1853 came to Byron, where he has since carried on operations as a contractor and builder with marked success.

In January, 1854, Mr. Kosier was united in marriage with Miss Rebecca N. Bull, a daughter of John Bull, one of the pioneers of the county, and they began their domestic life in the village of Byron, where he purchased an unfinished residence the following year. That place continued to be his home until 1890, when it, with its entire contents, was destroyed by fire. Subsequently he erected his present residence, which is heated by a furnace and supplied with all modern conveniences, being one of the best in the village. He is now one of the oldest contractors in the state, having carried on operations in Ogle county for forty-five years and on all sides are seen many evidences of his skill and handiwork. He has not only erected most of the buildings in Byron, but has also built many houses and barns throughout the surrounding country.

Mr. Kosier's first wife died in October, 1858, leaving two children: Frances M., now deceased, was a well-educated lady, who was one of the successful and popular teachers of Ogle county; and Charles B., a carpenter and joiner, is married and resides in Byron. Mr. Kosier was again married, December 27, 1859, his second union being with Miss Elizabeth Titus, of Rockford, who was a native of New York, but when a child went to Michigan and later came to Illinois. Her father, Jarvis Titus, was an early settler of Winnebago county, this state, where Mrs. Kosier was principally reared and educated. By the second marriage there are four children: Lucy Adella, wife of C. C. Kennedy, of Hinckley, Illinois; Rebecca E., wife of Captain H. C. Newcomer, of the engineering corps of the United States army, who is now located at Memphis, Tennessee, and has charge of the levees on the Mississippi and Arkansas rivers; Belle L., a well-educated young lady now engaged in teaching; and Albert, who is a first-class carpenter and is now with his father.

In his political affiliations, Mr. Kosier was first an old-line Whig, but in 1856 joined the Republican party, and has since been one of its stanch supporters. He takes an active part in local politics and campaign work, and as alternate delegate to the national convention of 1880, he assisted in the nomination of James A. Garfield for the presidency. For nearly forty years he has served continuously as a delegate to the county and congressional conventions of his party and has done some very effective work in promoting its interests. He has never sought office, but has served as village trustee, commissioner of highways and member of the school board, in a most capable and satisfactory manner. In 1858 he became identified with the Masonic fraternity and to-day is one of the most prominent members of Byron Lodge, No. 274, F. & A. M., of which he has been master twenty-two years and uninterruptedly for eighteen years, while for the same length of time he has represented the lodge in the Grand Lodge. He also belongs to Winnebago Chapter, No. 24, R. A. M., at Rockford. For forty-five years he has been a resident of Ogle county, has taken an active interest in its growth and development, and is to-day an honored member of the Old Settler Association, serving as its president. He has attended its meetings and taken part in its proceedings for many years, and in 1897 made a speech in reply to the address of welcome. He is one of the best known men in the county, and it is safe to say that none are held in higher regard or have more friends than John S. Kosier.

ADAM BUTTELL, the founder of the Buttell Piano Manufacturing Company, Oregon, Illinois, was born in New York city, April 21, 1855, and is the son of Philip and Margaret (Lieb) Buttell, the former a native of Alsace, France, but who in early life removed to Bavaria, and later to the United States, locating in New York city. He was a cabinet and piano maker by trade, and was an expert in that line. His death occurred in New York city some years ago. In politics he was a Republican, and religiously a Catholic. His wife was also a member of the Catholic church. They were the parents of four children: Adam, the subject of this sketch; George, residing in New York city, where he is engaged in the grocery trade; John, also of New York, engaged in general merchandising; and Margaret, living in New York.

The subject of this sketch was reared in New York city, where his education was obtained. He began when of sufficient age to learn the trade of piano making, working with his father, who, as already stated, was an expert in that line, understanding the manufacture of pianos in all its branches. He there perfected his knowledge of the trade, and later was employed in the best establishments of the east. In April, 1889, he left for the west, locating at Des Moines, Iowa, where he started a factory for himself, under the name of Adam Buttell Piano Company, which was later changed to Adam Buttell & Sons. The excellence of this piano, and the purity of its tone, soon commanded attention, and it was not long before the Buttell piano was placed in the best homes in Des Moines, and was the delight of the lovers of good music. He was able to compete with the oldest piano factories in the country in placing his instruments. In 1895, he removed his factory to Oregon, under the auspices of the National Piano Company, of which company he took the superintendency. This move was made to get a good water power and to be near the great centers of trade. This arrangement lasted until June 1, 1897, when he resigned his position with the National Piano Company, and re-established the Adam Buttell & Sons Piano Company. The latter company has been increasing its trade, and has met with flattering success in the sale of its pianos. As in Des Moines, they are able to compete with the oldest piano makers, and have a bright future before them. As with all new work, it takes time for the people to learn of its merits, but the Buttell piano has met with success far beyond the company's fondest hopes, which demonstrates beyond a doubt the excellence of this instrument, its rich, pure tone, its durability, and also that people appreciate a perfect piano. They have been placed in Chicago, throughout the state of Iowa, Illinois, Michigan, Nebraska, Wisconsin, Missouri, and other states.

The Buttell piano is an upright, embracing all the modern improvements, and is an artistic and beautiful piece of workmanship. From the special and superior construction of its sounding board, the tone enhances with age. The evenness of the scale holds it longer in tune than other pianos. All the material in these pianos is of the highest grade and selected with great care, always with the aim of producing the best and most harmonious effects in tone. Another feature of this piano is that Mr. Buttell is ever present, and supervises in the minutest detail the putting together of every part of his instruments. This feature, with his long experience, is of the highest importance. Mr. Buttell sells direct to the people in this section of the country, and his son John looks after its sale in Des Moines, Iowa.

Mr. Buttell was married in New York city, August 14, 1876, to Miss Anna Marie Geis, daughter of Jacob Geis. She is a native of Germany, born at Budeskeim on the Rhine. Her parents, who are both deceased, came to the United States in 1872, locating in New York, where they both died. By this union there were six children--John Jacob, George Joseph, Frank Adam, Catherine, Richard Arthur, and Harold Stanton. Of these, Catherine died in childhood, while the two oldest are in business with their father. In politics Mr. Buttell is a Republican, and fraternally he is a member of Oregon Lodge, No. 420, A. F. & A. M., and of Des Moines Lodge, No. 18, A. O. U. W., of Des Moines, Iowa.

It is very fortunate for the city of Oregon that the Buttell Piano Company has been located there. In addition to its justly acquired fame of being the most beautiful located town on the far-famed Rock river, it will have the distinction of being the home of one of the best piano manufactories in this country.

CHARLES P. CHEESEMAN, a leading and representative farmer of Eagle Point township, residing on section 34, was born near Toronto, Canada, July 17, 1837. His father, Alfred Cheeseman, was a native of England, born near London, in Kent county, May 8, 1812, and there grew to manhood, learning the shoemaker's trade, which he followed for some years. In early manhood he married Miss Susan Lawrence, also a native of England and a daughter of John Lawrence. In 1836 they emigrated to Canada and took up their residence near Toronto, but three years later came to Ogle county, Illinois. At Buffalo Grove, Mr. Cheeseman took up a claim, erected thereon a log house and began to break, fence and improve his little farm, but in the spring of 1842 he sold the place and removed to Chambers Grove, Carroll county, where he purchased Michael Ayers' claim to two hundred and forty acres. A few acres had been broken and a log house built, in which the family lived while the father opened up his farm. In 1857 he built a comfortable brick residence, a good barn, set out a fine orchard and made a fairly well improved farm of his place. There he spent his remaining years, dying December 26, 1894. His first wife, the mother of our subject, passed away February 2, 1854, and he subsequently married Miss Frances P. Buck, who died seven weeks previous to her husband's death.

Our subject is the oldest of the children born of the first union; Robert D. is a farmer residing near Shannon, Illinois; Elizabeth A. is the wife of Christopher L. Shirk, of Richland City, Richland county, Wisconsin; Mrs. Mary Saterly is a widow residing near Shannon, Illinois; Rachel is the wife of Charles Gross, of Summerville, Tennessee; Nancy Jane is the wife of William J. Griswold, of Milledgeville, Illinois; Rhoda died in infancy; Iantha, deceased, was the wife of Jabez Todd, of Milledgeville; Emma married Dr. Robert McPherso, of Carroll county, and died in California. There were four children by the second marriage, namely: George W., a resident of Daggett, Illinois; Josephine, of Chicago; Samuel B., of South Dakota; and Lafayette, of Chicago.

C. P. CHEESEMAN.

On the home farm in Carroll county Charles P. Cheeseman passed his boyhood and youth, attending the district schools a few months during the winter, and aiding in the farm work during the remainder of the year. He remained with his father until reaching man's estate and on leaving home went to Nodaway county, Missouri, where he worked for one year on a farm four miles south of Maryville. The following year was passed in Doniphan county, Kansas, where he engaged in farming and staging. In the spring of 1860 he went to Denver and from there to the Rocky mountains, and engaged in freighting across the plains for a year.

On the 14th of November, 1861, Mr. Cheeseman manifested his patriotism and love of country by enlisting in Company H, Second Kansas Cavalry, under Captain Gunther and Colonel W. F. Cloud, the regiment being assigned to the Seventh Army Corps. He participated in numerous skirmishes, including those at Lone Jack, Missouri; Cane Hill, Arkansas; Prairie Grove and Coon Creek, Missouri. He had some ribs broken and sustained a rupture by being thrown from his horse and for a short time was confined in the hospital at Fort Scott. Later he was on duty with a scouting detachment made up of soldiers from the hospital and thus spent four months in Kansas and Missouri. After rejoining his regiment at Springfield, Missouri, he participated in the capture of Fort Smith, Arkansas, and on a scouting expedition took Dardanelles. He took part in the Shreveport campaign under Steele, and from there went to Hot Springs, participating in number of battles and skirmishes, including the battle of Prairie Deann, the taking of Fort Camden and the engagement of Poison Springs, where fourteen hundred Union men were engaged in battle with seven thousand rebels, and where the former lost their artillery and the latter lost about twenty-two hundred men in killed and wounded. After the battle of Jenks Ferry, Mr. Cheeseman was transferred to the ambulance corps and while taking wounded to Pine Bluff, Arkansas, was captured, but was soon released. He then proceeded with his charges to Little Rock, where he remained for six months, and later rejoined the command at Fort Smith, remaining there until mustered out on the expiration of his term of service, March 7, 1865, at Little Rock.

Mr. Cheeseman then returned to his home in Elwood, Kansas, but a few weeks later came to the old homestead at Chambers Grove, Carroll county, Illinois, and for two years assisted his father in carrying on the farm. In that county he was married, December 25, 1867, to Miss Hannah M. Hyzer, a native of Delaware county, New York, and a daughter of Peter and Elizabeth (Hoyt) Hyzer, who settled in Carroll county, Illinois, in 1855, and there spent their remaining years. The father died in 1891, the mother a few years previous. The children born to Mr. and Mrs. Cheeseman are as follows: Tina, who married David Buchanan, and died leaving one son, Robert Grant, who is now living with our subject; Harvey J., who carries on the home farm; Lenny, who died in infancy; Susie, wife of Vernon Finkle, of Sanfordville, Illinois; James, Albert and May, all at home.

After his marriage, Mr. Cheeseman located on a farm in Lee county, Illinois, where he operated rented land for three years, and then removed to Story county, Iowa, where he was engaged in agricultural pursuits for two years. On returning to this state he purchased the farm of eighty acres in Eagle Point township, Ogle county, where he still resides, and to its improvement and cultivation he has since devoted his energies with marked success. He is a natural mechanic, very handy with tools, and has conducted a wagon and repair shop since locating here. He cast his first presidential vote for Abraham Lincoln, in 1864, and has since been a stanch supporter of the Republican party and its principles. Socially he is a charter member of George Crider Post, No. 575, G. A. R., of Milledgeville, and is one of the most highly respected and honored citizens of the community in which he lives.

REUBEN S. MARSHALL.—If one desires to gain a vivid realization of the rapid advance in civilization which the last few decades have brought about, he can listen to the stories of the men who are still living among us, and by no means overburdened with years, can tell of their boyhood. The log cabin home, the still ruder school-house with its rough seats made of slabs, its limited range of studies and its brief terms, arranged on the subscription plan, the routine of work at home, unrelieved by any of the modern devices by which machinery is made to do in a short time what formerly occupied the entire year—these and many similar descriptions will bring up in sharp contrast the advantages of to-day. The subject of this sketch, a highly respected citizen of Mt. Morris township, residing on section 11, has many interesting reminiscences of this sort.

Reuben S. Marshall was born in Clinton county, New York, October 4, 1827, and is the son of Caleb and Louisa (Sanburn) Marshall, both of whom were natives of Stowe, Vermont, the former born November 5, 1778, and the latter July 15, 1798. Her father later served in the war of 1812. Soon after their marriage Caleb Marshall and wife removed to Clinton county, New York, where all their children were born. They were numbered among the early settlers of that county, which was their home for many years. They were the parents of six children, as follows: Caleb S., born January 21, 1819; Almira E., August 21, 1820; Lucien, May 14, 1822; Phila, July 21, 1824; Mary K., September 23, 1825; and Reuben S., our subject.

Caleb Marshall served in the same regiment, under Colonel Baker, in which was his father-in-law, Mr. Sanburn. By trade he was a dyer and puller, and in his day the cloth was all dyed and pulled by hand. He also learned the trade of a cooper, which he followed to some extent while yet residing in the east, but never after coming west.

In November, 1834, the Marshall family started for Illinois, but on arriving at Cleveland, Ohio, they heard alarming reports about the Indians and concluded to stop for a time until there should be no further trouble from hostile Indians. They remained in Ohio about two years. In October, 1836, Caleb Marshall left his family in Cleveland and came to Ogle county, Illinois, and made claim to a half section of land in Mt. Morris township, the present home farm of our subject. Lake navigation having suspended when he was ready to return to Cleveland, he walked the entire distance back to that city.

On the 22d of February, 1837, the family left Cleveland for their new home, coming by team arriving at Oregon, on the 19th of March, being about four weeks on the road. After remaining in Oregon about three weeks, they crossed the river, proceeding to their claim, where a small log house, 12 x 14, was erected, into which the family moved. An addition was subsequently built of about twelve feet, and that cabin was the family home for some years. For a time there was nothing but a dirt floor, but finally a floor of puncheons was laid. The roof was made of "shakes," held down by weight poles. It was a rude structure, but it was the abode of hospitality. As soon as the frost was out of the ground some five acres were broken and their first crop planted, consisting of two acres of wheat, one acre of oats, an acre and a half of sod corn, and a half acre of potatoes.

On arriving in Ogle county, Caleb Marshall found himself the possessor of sixteen dollars and a half, and a two-horse team; with that capital he had to provide for his family until he could so improve his farm as to make it productive. This was no easy thing to do in a new country where there was no markets nearer than Chicago, save Galena, which in many respects was not as good. Often has our subject gone to the former place with a load of wheat and without a cent to defray expenses. In those trips he was usually commissioned to buy something for neighbors. In Chicago payment was made in paper currency, but in Galena only gold and silver were used. It was difficult to carry out a neighbor's commission at the latter place when no one in this vicinity had gold or silver to pay. Taxes, however, had to be paid in gold or silver and it was fortunate that such a town as Galena was convenient. When one did not have produce to sell at that point, they would go to the lead mines at that place and work long enough to get sufficient gold or silver for taxes. The first trip our subject made to Chicago with wheat was when he was fifteen years old, and it required seven days in going and coming with a team of horses.

Caleb Marshall was twice married. By his first union there was one daughter that grew to womanhood, married and went still farther west. After a wedded life of about two years, his first wife died, and he subsequently married Louisa Sanburn, as already stated. His death occurred May 17, 1860, his wife having passed away August 12, 1858. In politics he was an old-line Whig until the birth of the Republican party, when he voted for its first presidential candidate, John C. Fremont. Fraternally he was a Mason of high standing in the east. Religiously he was a Congregationalist, as was also his wife. He was a man of strong character, a kind husband and father, and a good neighbor.

Reuben S. Marshall was in his tenth year when he accompanied his parents to Ogle county. His educational advantages were very limited and confined strictly to the common school, attending a few days each winter term until he was seventeen years old. The longest that time he continuously attended was for twenty-one days. He was one of the first pupils to attend a school taught by John A. Wagner, there being but nine enrolled during the term. The school house was the typical one of logs, with puncheon floor and slab seats. On leaving school he settled down to a life of hard work, and in the sixty-two years that he has resided in Ogle county, he has certainly done his full share of the work necessary to its development.

Mr. Marshall was married January 15, 1850, to Miss Matilda Steffa, a native of

Washington county, Maryland, born July 29, 1831, and daughter of William and Elizabeth Steffa, both of whom were natives of the same county and state, and who came to Ogle county in 1844. By this union twelve children were born. William C., born March 6, 1853, married Mary Rowe, and they have two children. He is living in the town of Mount Morris. Mary E., born May 23, 1854, died September 19, of the same year. Emma May, born May 23, 1855, married Dr. H. C. Clements, and they reside in Chicago. They have one child. Ira W., born August 24, 1857, married Delia Smith, and they have two children. They are living in Mount Morris township. Charles E., born January 30, 1859, died September 2, 1859. Albertus S., born July 27, 1861, married Martha Price, and they reside in Oregon, where he is in the hotel business, as proprietor of the Sinissippi House. Francis E., born June 12, 1863, married Anna Smith, and they reside in Mount Morris township. Ida E., born February 3, 1866, is living at Oregon. John C., born September 10, 1867, married Grace Koontz, and with their two children they are living in Mount Morris township. Grace A., born April 24, 1869, married John M. Rinehart, and they have one child. They are living in Iowa Falls, Iowa. Viola, born December 11, 1870, married David Bock, and they have three children. They make their home with our subject. Oliver E., born March 21, 1873, is living in Iowa Falls, Iowa, where he is engaged in the drug business. Mrs. Marshall died February 24, 1873. She was a devoted wife and mother, and her place in the home circle left a void that could not be filled.

Mr. Marshall has in his possession some rare old papers that he prizes very highly, among them the Ulster County Gazette, under date January 4, 1800, containing the notice of the death of George Washington, which occurred on the 14th of December, 1799, some twenty days previously. To realize something of the progress made in means of communication, one has but to think of the death of the most noted man in the country, and yet it required nearly three weeks to carry the news a few hundred miles. Now the death of a man in any part of the civilized world is known everywhere within a few minutes after the occurrence. Another one of the papers in Mr. Marshall's possession is the New England Weekly Journal, of Monday, April 3, 1728. He has also the New York Morning Post, of Friday, November 7, 1783. The last named contains notices of several slave sales. Think of slave sales in New York!

In politics Mr. Marshall is a Republican, with which party he has acted since the "Pathfinder," John C. Fremont, was nominated for the presidency in 1860. He has always manifested an interest in politics and local affairs. He has held the office of school director for thirty years and that of road commissioner for thirty-three years. He served two terms as a member of the board of supervisors, and was one of the building committee for the erection of the present court house in Oregon. While a member of the board he served as chairman of the claim committee for two years, and chairman of the salary committee one year. Fraternally he was for many years connected with the Odd Fellows, but is not at present in fellowship, his age and the distance from the lodge preventing. Religiously he is identified with the Lutherans, holding membership with the church in Mt. Morris.

In the sixty-two years in which Mr. Marshall has lived in Ogle county what wonderful changes have been made! Then a thinly settled country, with neighbors few and far between. Now, a perfect hive of industry, the country thickly settled with a prosperous people. When he came to the county there were but three log cabins in Oregon and but three in the vicinity, and not one between Oregon and Freeport, and only seven in the latter place. He was here when the notorious Driscolls were executed and when they committed their worst crimes. In the early days it was not always easy to even get enough to eat. He remembers that on one occasion his father went to Ottawa for provisions, soon after their arrival here, and while he was gone the family ate up everything but some dried beans. On those beans and some gophers that the boys killed the family lived for several days.

Notwithstanding the hardships endured, it was not always dark and gloomy. There was a bright side to pioneer life. People were as hospitable as the day was long. There was little conventiality. Boys and girls used to go barefooted until they were quite large. The country dance was a source of amusement. The boys would go for their girls on horseback, and taking them on behind away they would go, and "dance till broad daylight." Spelling-schools and husking-bees were another source of amusement often indulged in. All in all they had a good time, and few pioneers would be willing to exchange their experience for those of a later day. Mr. Marshall has no cause to regret becoming a pioneer of Ogle county. He has been blessed " in basket and store," and has to-day more than a section of as fine land as one would care to see, and "the wolf has always been kept from the door."

JAMES H. DONALDSON, an active and enterprising farmer residing on section 1, Buffalo township, about three miles from Polo, is a native of Ogle county, and was born in Brookville township, November 30, 1854. His father, Walter Donaldson, was a native of England, born on the line between England and Scotland, but on the English side, in 1819. William Donaldson, the grandfather, was of Scottish birth, as was also his wife.

In 1821 William Donaldson came with his family to the United States, landed in Vermont and afterward settled in New York. Later he moved to Canada, where he lived some years, and in 1839 came to Ogle county and settled in Eagle Point township, being among the first settlers of that township. Taking up a claim in Buffalo Grove, he opened up a farm, purchasing the land when it came into the market. Walter Donaldson came with his parents to the county and took up a claim in Brookville township and at once began its improvement. He later went to Canada, and near Toronto married Miss Sarah Sylvester, a native of Canada, but of Scotch and Irish parentage. After his marriage he returned with his bride to his farm in Ogle county and here spent the remainder of his life, becoming one of the enterprising and successful farmers, and a highly honored citizen. He served his township as a member of the board of supervisors, and in other official positions. He died on his old farm November 28, 1888, while his wife passed away about six years previously. They were the parents of three children, the others being William, a farmer of Lincoln township, and Ellen, wife of Arthur McMaster, of Fowler, Colorado.

The subject of this sketch grew to manhood on the old home farm and was educated in the schools of the neighborhood. He remained with his father till his death and carried on the old place for several years after. He was married in Whiteside county, Illinois, January 15, 1889, to Miss Agnes McNeil, a native of Whiteside county, where she was reared. In the schools of Sterling, that county, she finished her education, and for some years prior to her marriage engaged in teaching in the public schools. She is a daughter of Robert McNeil, a native of Scotland who came to the United States when a young man, located in Whiteside county, and there engaged in agricultural pursuits. He married Jean Lyle, also a native of Scotland, and daughter of James Lyle, a pioneer of Ogle county. To Mr. and Mrs. Donaldson three children have been born—Robert W., Harold J. and Mildred.

Mr. Donaldson continued to live on the family homestead until 1893, when he removed to Rock Falls, Whiteside county, Illinois, where he rented a place for a few months while looking for a new farm. In the fall of 1893 he decided on his present place and immediately made the purchase. On the 1st of March, 1894, he moved to the farm and has no cause to regret his choice of location. He is now engaged in general farming and stock raising and is meeting with a fair degree of success.

The first presidential vote cast by Mr. Donaldson was in 1876, when he voted for Samuel J. Tilden, since which time he has voted the Democratic ticket, his last presidential vote being for John M. Palmer, in 1896. He was not with the majority of his party on the financial question, and is yet proud to be classed among the so-called "gold Democrats" of his party. Religiously he and his wife are identified with the Presbyterian church at Polo. Fraternally he is a Mason and is a member of the lodge at Polo. He has passed through all the chairs, and was worshipful master of the lodge in 1897 and in 1898, during which time he represented the lodge in the grand lodge of the state. A lifelong resident of the county, his interests are here, and he is always willing to do all he can to make the county occupy an exalted rank among the counties of the state.

CAPTAIN WILLIAM T. DODDS, who is now living retired in Byron, is one of the veterans of the Civil war, and bears an honorable record for brave service in the cause of freedom and union, and in the paths of peace he has also won an enviable reputation through the sterling qualities which go to the making of a good citizen.

The Captain is a native of Ohio, born in Nile township, Scioto county, August 7, 1831, and is of Irish descent, his grandfather, James Dodds, being a native of the Emerald Isle. He was reared and educated on the Isle of Man and on crossing the Atlantic to America became a resident of Pennsylvania. Major John B. Dodds, the Captain's father, was born in the Keystone state in 1797 or 1798, and there passed his boyhood and youth, acquiring a good practical education for that early day. He was a second cousin of General Scott, and a first cousin of Governor Samuel Black, one of the most prominent men of Pennsylvania in his day. When a young man Major Dodds went to Scioto county, Ohio, where he engaged in school teaching for several years with marked success. He married Ann Tucker, a native of that state and a daughter of John Tucker, and they began housekeeping upon a farm in Scioto county. He became one of the most prominent and influential men of the county, was honored with a number of official positions, and served as sheriff for one or more terms. During the Mexican war he was commissioned major and detailed as recruiting officer. In 1855 he determined to try his fortune farther west and moved to Ellisville, Fulton county, Illinois, where he spent his last years in retirement, dying there in 1883. His first wife, the mother of our subject, had died in Ohio, at the age of fifty-one. Later he was again married and had by the second union three children. Harvey, the oldest child of the first marriage, died at the age of eleven years. David T. came to Illinois in 1853, and for a number of years engaged in merchandising at Ellisville, but finally located on a farm in Fulton county. From there he went to Chattanooga, Tennessee, where he engaged in the real estate business and was very successful. He died there about 1892. Martha married Nelson Moore and died soon afterward. Sarah J. married Samuel Edward, a farmer in Fulton county and is now deceased. William T., our subject, is the next of the family. J. W. served as first lieutenant of Company B, Forty-seventh Illinois Volunteer Infantry during the Civil war, and is now treasurer of Fulton county, making his home in Lewiston.

Captain Dodds grew to manhood in Scioto county, Ohio, and received a common-school education, which has been greatly supplemented by reading and study in subsequent years. In 1853 he went with his brother David to Fulton county, Illinois, and spent nearly a year with his uncle, James Schearer. Later he engaged in farming with his brother-in-law, Samuel Edwards, for a year or two, and in 1859 crossed the plains with ox teams to Pikes Peak, being about eight weeks on the way. Prospects not being good, he and one comrade went to Kansas and in Brown county he took a quarter section of land. Returning to Fulton county, Illinois, he built a boat and ran a ferry across Spoon river at Ellisville, in 1860, and did a profitable business.

Feeling his country needed his services Captain Dodds laid aside all personal interests in 1861, and joined the boys in blue as a private of Company C, Seventeenth Illinois Volunteer Infantry, but was soon promoted to the rank of sergeant. With his regiment he went to Missouri, and after his first engagement at Fredericktown, Missouri, was commissioned first lieutenant. Later he participated in the battles of Belmont, Fort Henry, Fort Donelson, Shiloh and Corinth. At the battle of Fort Donelson he received a gunshot wound and at Shiloh was again wounded. He commanded his company at Shiloh and Corinth and was called captain though never commissioned such. When he entered the service he weighed one hundred and sixty-five pounds, but on resigning, in 1863, his weight had been reduced to one hundred ten and a half.

On the 14th of September, 1863, in Ogle county, Captain Dodds was united in marriage with Miss Ellen W. Ercanbrack, a native of Little Falls, New York, and a daughter of William S. Ercanbrack, who located here in 1845. The children born of this union are Albert R.; Charles A., a traveling salesman, who is married and resides in Joliet, Illinois; Jessie B., wife of Fred Nott, a merchant of Byron, Ogle county; Grace

Ellen, wife of W. E. Cort, a successful lawyer of Lewiston, Montana; and William B., who was drowned in the Rock river at the age of seventeen years.

After his marriage Captain Dodds located at Byron, and for one year carried the mail, one day to Oregon and the next to Rockford, but at the end of that time sold his route. In 1865 he removed to Peoria, where he engaged in the grocery business six or seven years, and from there went to Canton, Fulton county, where he was interested in the grain business for two years. On selling out in 1873, he returned to Byron and assisted his father-in-law on the farm for a year. He then went on the road as salesman for a Chicago house, and during the thirteen years he traveled was with three different firms, his route being in this state the entire time. He had a large trade and built up a good business for each house. He was very successful in this line. On leaving the road, he bought an established hardware business at Byron, which he successfully carried on for eleven years, selling out in September, 1892. He was one of the most enterprising and progressive business men of the county, and seemed to prosper in all his undertakings so that he is now quite well-to-do, while he lives retired from active business.

In 1852 the Captain cast his first presidential ballot for General Winfield Scott, and in 1856 supported John C. Fremont, since which time he has been an uncompromising Republican, but he has never cared for official honors, preferring to give his undivided attention to his business interests. He has always been a strong supporter of temperance. He is a Knight Templar Mason, belonging to the blue lodge No. 15 of Peoria, and the chapter and commandery of Peoria, and is a thirty-third degree Mason, and he is also a prominent member of the Grand Army Post of Byron. A man of strong individuality and indubitable probity, one who has attained to a due measure of success in the affairs of life, and whose influence has always been exerted for the good of the community, this honored veteran assuredly demands representation in this volume.

PETER S. MEYERS. While "the race is not always to the swift nor the battle to the strong," the invariable law of destiny accords to tireless energy, industry and ability a successful career. The truth of this assertion is abundantly verified in the life of Mr. Meyers, a well-known and highly respected citizen of Forreston township, residing on section 28.

He was born near Harrisburg, Dauphin county, Pennsylvania, January 7, 1831, and is of French descent, his great-grandfather having come from France and settled in Berks county, Pennsylvania. The grandfather, Jacob Meyers, was a native of that county, and the father, Peter Meyers, was born at the same place September 11, 1805. The family was established in Dauphin county when the latter was a lad of nine years, and as a pioneer of that region Jacob Meyers materially aided in its development and upbuilding. There his son Peter grew to manhood and married Hannah Thoffstall, also a native of Pennsylvania. He continued to carry on the old home farm for a number of years, but in 1852, with his family, he came to Ogle county, Illinois. With his three sons and one son-in-law, he purchased eight hundred acres of land in Forreston township, adjoining the present village of that name, and he, himself, located on the farm where our subject now resides, making his home there until called from this life in 1891, at the age of eighty-six years, eleven months and twenty-two days. His wife preceded him a number of years, dying in 1870. Our subject is the youngest of their four children, the others being as follows: Eliza, who married Joseph Fisher and died in Ogle county; Jacob P., who at one time was a harness-maker in Mt. Carroll, Illinois, and later at at Fort Dodge, Iowa, for some years, but is now living retired at Waterloo, that state; and John, who is engaged in the real estate business at Spokane Falls, Washington.

Peter S. Meyers grew to manhood in Pottsville, Pennsylvania, where he learned the cabinetmaker's trade, and also painting and fancy graining, at which he worked for a number of years. In 1852 he accompanied the family on their removal to Ogle county, and in addition to helping his father on the home farm, he worked at cabinetmaking for neighboring farmers and in West Grove. In October, 1857, at White Oak Grove, Ogle county, he was united in marriage with Miss Sarah Adams, who was born in Northumberland county, Pennsylvania, in 1830, and was reared there, coming to Illinois when a young lady, and they began their domestic life upon his farm in Forreston township. In 1853 and 1854 he had hauled stone and erected the only stone house in the township. This neat and substantial structure is still standing, making a pleasant home for the family. Mr. Meyers now gives his entire time and attention to agricultural pursuits and is the owner of two fine farms of one hundred and sixty acres in Forreston township. He is a charter member of the Forreston Fire Insurance Company and gives a cheerful support to all enterprises which he believes calculated to prove of public benefit.

Mrs. Meyers died in 1871, leaving three children, namely: Millmon Riley, who was an engineer on the Illinois Central railroad for several years; Alfred Alexander, who owns and operates a farm of one hundred and sixty acres near Polo, Ogle county; and Louisa Jane, wife of Henry Tice, a business man of Polo. In Forreston township, February 8, 1872, Mr. Meyers was again married, his second union being with Miss Melinda Hoffa, a daughter of Jacob Hoffa. She was born in Northumberland county, Pennsylvania, but was reared in Ogle county. Of the eight children born of this union seven are now living, namely: Sarah Ann, wife of Edward E. Haller, whose sketch appears elsewhere in this work; William H., a farmer of Forreston township; Hannah H., wife of Frank Diehl, a farmer of the same township; Melinda A., at home; Daniel P., a student in the Forreston school; Jacob C., at home; Edith E., who died at the age of six years; and Lucien G., who is attending the home school.

Mr. Meyers manifested his patriotism and loyalty to country during the Civil war by enlisting at Dixon, in February, 1864, in Company E, Fifteenth Illinois Volunteer Infantry, and entered the service as corporal. With the Army of the Cumberland, the regiment participated in many skirmishes, and later joined General Sherman's command at Morehead City, and with him marched to the sea. They took part in the grand review at Washington, District of Columbia, then went to Louisville, Kentucky, Leavenworth, Kansas, and later to Smoky Hill, and were finally discharged at Leavenworth in August, 1865. Mr. Meyers first united in Oregon Post, but is now a member of the Grand Army Post at Forreston. He cast his first presidential vote for General Winfield Scott, the Whig candidate, but since the organization of the Republican party in 1856, he has fought under its banner. He has been honored with various official positions, serving as highway commissioner over fifteen years, township treasurer twelve years, and school director twenty-two years, being president of the board most of the time. He was made a Mason in Pennsylvania, and is now a member of Mt. Morris Lodge, F. & A. M. At the age of fourteen years he joined the Reformed church, and is now a member of the church of that denomination at Forreston, while his wife holds membership in the English Lutheran church. Upright and honorable in all the relations of life, he has the esteem and confidence of all who know him and this brief sketch of his life will be read with interest by his many friends in Ogle county.

GEORGE WINDLE, a thoroughly progressive farmer and stock raiser, residing on section 15, Mt. Morris township, was born in Shenandoah county, Virginia, November 18, 1841, and is the son of William and Mary (Kretsinger) Windle, the former a native of the same county and state, born in 1807, and the latter in 1806. His father was the son of George Windle, a wagon manufacturer, also a native of Shenandoah county, Virginia. His father, the great-grandfather of our subject, was a native of Germany, who emigrated to this country, located in the Shenandoah valley, and there spent the remainder of his life. George Windle died at the age of eighty-nine years in Shenandoah county. He was the father of nine children—William, Samuel, Joseph, Amos, Richard, Branson, George, Elizabeth and Margaret.

William Windle received his education in the common schools of his native county, and after leaving school took his regular place upon his father's farm and assisted in its cultivation. Later he became the possessor of a farm known as the "Cedar Creek farm," which he continued to cultivate until his removal to Ogle county in 1855. On coming to this county he rented land for about nine years, and in 1864 purchased two hundred acres of Mrs. Hess, in Pine Creek township, and there resided until his death in 1879. To William and Mary Windle ten children were born, all of whom are yet living—John, Cornelius, Lydia, Maggie, George, William, Joseph, L. W., Jackson and Isaiah. The father died in July, 1879, and the mother in 1875. They were both members of the Lutheran church. In politics he was a Jacksonian Democrat.

In his native state the subject of this sketch began his education in the common schools, attending during the winter terms. He accompanied the family to Ogle county, arriving here at the age of fourteen years. Here he also attended the district schools during the winter and in the summer giving his entire time to his father in the cultivation of the farm. After attaining his majority, he entered Rock River Seminary, which he attended three terms, closing his school life in that institution. At the age of eighteen years he commenced to learn the carpenter's trade under Isaiah Speaker, and served an apprenticeship of two years. He then worked at the trade as a journeyman until 1866. In 1863, in company with twelve others, he started from Mt. Morris for Pike's Peak, Colorado, going overland with a team, being thirty days en route Arriving at Denver, he commenced work at his trade and continued there about ten months. He then concluded to return home, and started back with a mule team. Arriving at the Missouri river, he took the stage for State Center, Iowa, and from the latter place he came as far as Polo by railroad, and from there to his home in Mt. Morris township in a buggy. During the winter of 1865-6 he taught school in Mt. Morris township, and in the fall of 1866 he purchased eighty acres of Mrs. Annie Rine, and to that farm he removed and there lived until 1872, when he went into the mercantile business at Mt. Morris, in which he continued two years. He then traded his stock of goods and his eighty-acre farm for his present farm of two hundred and forty acres, on which he has since continued to live.

On the 20th of September, 1865, Mr. Windle was united in marriage with Miss Mary E. Sprecher, born in Ogle county, Illinois, June 6, 1843, and the daughter of Philip and Catherine (Houk) Sprecher, natives of Washington county, Maryland. Her father was a farmer by occupation, and came by teams to Ogle county, Illinois, in 1839, settling on section 25, Mt. Morris township, where he purchased three hundred and sixty acres of land, to which he later added one hundred and sixty acres, giving him a valuable farm of five hundred and twenty acres. Philip and Catherine Sprecher were the parents of eleven children, five of whom died in early childhood, the remainder reaching years of maturity—Daniel, George, John, Adasale, Ann and Mary E. Both parents are now deceased. In politics he was a Democrat. Both were reared in the Lutheran faith, but later united with the Advent church.

To Mr. and Mrs. Windle six children have been born: Charles Elmer died August 24, 1881, his death resulting from an accident, being injured by a traction engine, and only living thirty-six hours after the accident occurred. Mary Catherine married J. H. Harnly, of Auburn, Illinois, and they are now living in Eldora, Iowa, where both are employed as teachers in the Industrial school; Addie married Prof. Ira R. Hendrickson, by whom she had two children, one, Ruth Mary, now living. He is engaged in teaching in Lamar, Missouri; Orpha Irene is teaching in Mt. Morris township; William, teaching in Mt. Morris township; Philip W. is living at home; Thurlow died at the age of sixteen days. Mr. and Mrs. Windle have adopted a little boy, taking, when but five months old, Clifford Neff Windle. They have also made a home for a young miss from Chicago, Clara Fallaskson, thirteen years old. These deeds speak well for the kindly disposition of Mr. and Mrs. Windle.

In politics Mr. Windle is a Democrat, and as a member of the Democratic party he has taken an active interest in its well being, attending the various local conventions and giving of his time to advance the cause. He has served as a delegate to the state convention of his party, and is now serving as a member of the congressional committee. Interested in educational affairs, he served for twelve years as a member of the school board. Religiously he is identified with the Methodist Episcopal church, being one of the trustees. He takes an active interest in the work of the church, and does his full duty in maintaining its services.

In his business relations Mr. Windle has been quite successful, and in addition to the home farm he owns one hundred and seven acres southwest of Mt. Morris, and also three hundred and twenty acres in Buena Vista county, Iowa. His farm is well stocked and is kept in excellent condition and under a high state of cultivation. In 1876 he set out a large number of shade and ornamental trees which add to the attractive appearance of the place. His dwelling house has been remodeled, making it a fine country residence. In stock he is making a specialty of Durham short-horn cattle, Chester white hogs and Norman horses. In addition to his farm work, he is agent for the Aultman & Taylor Company, and the Rumely Company, manufacturers of steam engines and threshers, and is also dealing to some extent in real estate. He is a very busy man, very industrious, and it is no wonder that success has crowned his efforts. While he is not numbered among those who claim to be pioneers, he has yet resided in Ogle county for about forty-four years, and it is but just to say that in that time he has done what he could to advance the business and commercial interests of the county, and is deserving of the high honor and respect in which he is held.

JOHN L. SMITH, one of the honored pioneers and highly esteemed citizens of Ogle county, who now makes his home in Leaf River, was born at Sharpsburg, Washington county, Maryland, April 2, 1832, and is a son of Abram Smith, who spent his entire life there. Our subject, with his mother and maternal grandfather, came to Ogle county, Illinois, in 1839, and here he grew to manhood amid scenes common to frontier life, early becoming familiar with every department of farm work. When quite young he began to earn his own livelihood and the success that he has achieved is due entirely to his own unaided efforts.

On the 3d of October, 1854, Mr. Smith was united in marriage with Miss Susan A. Myers, a native of Washington county, Maryland, and a daughter of Jacob Myers, who came to this county in 1837, entered government land and developed a farm, on which he died in 1876. Here Mrs. Smith was reared as one of a large family of children. Five children were born to our subject and his wife, namely: Mary E., who died at the age of four years; Harriet C., wife of John Palmer, a farmer of Ogle county; Lydia H., wife of Jacob Palmer, also a substantial farmer of Leaf River township; and Elmer G. and Jacob M., who assist their father in carrying on the home farm.

After his marriage Mr. Smith operated the Myers homestead for six years and then made his first purchase of land, consisting of one hundred and twenty-seven and a half acres in Leaf River township, which he soon transformed into a fine farm, placing the land under a high state of cultivation and erecting thereon good and substantial buildings that stand as monuments to his thrift and enterprise. As his financial resources increased, he added to the original purchase until he has three hundred and twenty acres all in one body, and he has also bought one hundred and twenty acres of the Myers homestead. All the property is well improved and quite valuable. Mr. and Mrs. Smith commenced their married life in limited circumstances, but prosperity has crowned their combined efforts and they are now numbered among the substantial and well-to-do citizens of the community. Besides their farm property they own a good home in Leaf River, where they are now living retired, surrounded by all of the comforts and many of the luxuries of life. They and their family hold membership in the Christian church at that place and are held in high regard by all who have witnessed their successful struggle with adversity. In his political views Mr. Smith is a pronounced Republican, but has never cared for official honors, preferring to give his undivided attention to his business interests. He takes considerable interest in educational affairs, and for twelve years most acceptably served as township trustee. For almost sixty years he has watched with interest the growth and development of this region, and has been no unimportant factor in its upbuilding and prosperity.

AMOS F. MOORE, who resides on section 34, Woosung township, is not only a prominent agriculturist, but is an up-to-date business man and stock raiser, with a reputation which is confined not alone to the state of Illinois, but he is well and favorably known in almost every part of the country, especially where the people are interested in fine thoroughbred horses. He was born March 11, 1832, in Ackworth, Sullivan county, New Hampshire, and is the son of John and Mehitable (Foster) Moore, the former born December 31, 1795, in Petersborough, New Hampshire, and the latter October 9, 1798, in Hillsborough, New Hampshire.

John Moore was the son of Samuel and Jennie (Thompson) Moore, also natives of New Hampshire. Samuel Moore was the son of Deacon Samuel Moore, who moved from Londonderry, New Hampshire, to Petersborough, in the same state, in 1751. The ancestor of Deacon Samuel Moore was John Moore, who was murdered February 1, 1692, in the massacre of Glencoe. His wife escaped and that night a boy baby was born, John Moore, who moved to Londonderry, New Hampshire, in 1718, and who is the progenitor of the Moores in America. This John Moore married Janet Cochrane, and to them were born seven children, of whom Deacon Samuel Moore was second in order of birth. Deacon Samuel Moore married Margaret Morrison, and they became the parents of six children, of whom Samuel, the grandfather of our subject, was third in order of birth. Samuel Moore served in the Revolutionary war, and was mustered in at the time of the alarm at Lexington, April 19, 1775. He also served in the war of 1812. He married Jennie Thompson, July 24, 1784, and by this marriage were eleven children, of whom John Moore, the father of our subject, was the sixth. Samuel Moore died February 5, 1844, at the age of eighty-seven years. He was a farmer by occupation, a very stoutly built and robust man, and our subject well remembers him breaking a colt when well past eighty years old.

John Moore grew to manhood in New Hampshire, and was a mechanic and farmer. In the winter he engaged in the manufacture of spinning wheels and reels, and in the summer engaged in farm work. He was united in marriage with Mehitable Foster, on the 13th of April, 1824. She was a daughter of Aaron and Mehitable (Nichols) Foster, who were the parents of ten children, eight sons and two daughters. One of their sons, Rev. Aaron Foster, was a minister and was the father of the Home Missionary Society, having given public utterance to the first words spoken in favor of the enterprise. Another son, Lieutenant Amos Foster, was stationed at Fort Dearborn, Chicago, for a few years. He purchased ———— lots on the section where the ———— the Chicago & Northwestern ———— is now located, and ———————————————— He was ———————————— Bay, ————————————————————— Another son, Dr. John H. Foster, later removed to Chicago, where he ———— after his deceased brother's ————. He also became interested in Chicago real estate, purchasing what is now known as Lincoln Park, for which he paid ———————— per acre. In after years ———————— of it for twenty thousand ———— an acre for park purposes. Our subject built the first fence put up in that vicinity, while he was ———————— D————. The D———— died in ———————————————————— of the sons, ———— Foster ———— the town of Muscatine, Iowa. He was a prominent horticulturist ———— was the father of the Agricultural ———— at Ames, Iowa. To John Moore ———————————— were born, two ————————————. Of ———— who ———————————— in ————, New York; ———————— in Polo, ————; Amos F———————————— E. is living in ——— Moore ————————————————————— New ———————— real education was received in ————————— hard knocks,"

as he expresses it. He began to work for himself at a very early age. When eleven years old he was put out to work for neighboring farmers, and when fifteen years old he came west to Chicago, where his uncle, Dr. John Foster, was then living. He assisted his uncle for a time in collecting his rents, and in various ways. In 1849 he unloaded the first rail from the vessel to be used in the construction of the Galena Union railroad, his uncle being a director in the company. In that same year, when out horseback riding, he was favorably impressed with the land, and his uncle purchased him a farm, which comprises now the city of Evanston, for which he paid fifteen hundred dollars. Having an attack of the ague, Mr. Moore returned east in the fall of 1849, and the next year his uncle wrote him that a lot of fanatics wanted to buy the farm for twenty-five thousand dollars. He sold the land, but now thinks that instead of being fanatics, those desiring to purchase were very far-seeing men.

In the latter part of 1851, Mr. Moore returned to Chicago, where he engaged in the foundry business, having built the largest foundry in the city. In 1853 he came to Ogle county and purchased land, but continued in business in Chicago until 1856, when he took up his permanent residence in the county. On the 6th of October, 1856, he was united in marriage with Miss Marcia A. Cutts, who was born November 13, 1838, in ———— county, Maine, and daughter of ———— Hiram and Eunice (Brown) Cutts, the former a native of Portsmouth, New Hampshire, born in ————, and the latter a native of the same city, born February 2, 1802. Captain Hiram Cutts was the son of Thomas Donald Cutts, who was probably a merchant in Portsmouth. Hiram Cutts followed the sea for many years, in the merchant service, trading all over the world. In his family were nine children,—Joseph B., Alzira, Hiram, Thomas, Emily, Harriet, Elizabeth, Marcia and George. In politics he was an old-line Whig. In September, 1846, with his wife and family, he came to Ogle county, and located on a farm in Buffalo township, where the city of Polo is now located. For the erection of his house, barns and fences, he hauled all the lumber from Chicago. He died on his farm April 5, 1850, at the age of fifty-two years. His wife survived him, and died November 28, 1884.

To Mr. and Mrs. Moore seven children have been born: John died at the age of four months; Albert C. is a graduate of the State University, Champaign, and is now in the employ of the Oregon Short Line railroad. He is the owner of several ranches in that state. A. Foster is a practicing physician and surgeon, of Dixon, Illinois. George H. is now attending the University of Wisconsin, at Madison. Fred L. is at home. Stata M. is also at home, and is her father's stenographer. Frank is attending the high school in Polo.

Mr. Moore erected his dwelling house upon his farm in 1856, but did not commence active farming operations until the spring of 1857. To his original purchase of one hundred and twenty acres, he has added from time to time until his home farm now comprises six hundred acres of fine land, which is kept under the highest state of cultivation. Before moving to his farm, in 1856, he planted a large apple orchard, and has since been adding to it until it is now one of the largest in the northern part of the state. In 1860 he made an artificial pond on his farm, the water from which he used for stock purposes until wind mills came into general since which time it has been used as

In 1865 Moore Morgan horses since been engaged is now the United

breds. the cago, there Horse came one

In the inter- farming community he takes a commendable interest. In 1892 he became a member of the Farmers' Institute, and in 1893 was appointed director in the same, a position which he still holds. In 1897 he was elected the Institute and is He is also a state

stanch with fore the

served as fifteen years, and been board of range 8, for the same three years he was a of commissioners from He was the man that made and carried it to the supreme certain whether the Illinois could take land when and where it pleased. In all that he did the rights of the people were always in view, and it is a pleasure to him to think that he has secured their rights at times when they might have been irrevocably lost. He is a man of the people, and believes the people have rights which corporations are bound to respect. While not a politician in the common acceptation of the term, he has on more than one occasion made his influence felt with politicians. In the winter of 1898-9 1898-9 he assisted in securing an appropriation of one hundred thousand dollars toward the formation of a new agricultural college to be located somewhere in the military tract. His ideas on the subject were such as to command the respect of the members of the assembly, resulting in the appropriation as stated. As president of the Farmers' Institute he has given the subject of agricultural instruction much thought, and he can clearly express what he thinks. As a citizen of Ogle county he at all times has its best interest at heart, and freely gives of his time and means to advance its interests. To such men great credit is due for the proud position which the county occupies among the one hundred and two counties of the state.

JOSHUA THOMAS. Among the pioneer settlers of Ogle county this gentleman is especially worthy of notice in a work of this kind for he was prominently identified with the development and prosperity of this section of the state for many years, and being possessed of a rare amount of energy, proved a valued member of the young and rapidly growing community.

Mr. Thomas was born in Washington county, Maryland, March 8, 1811, a son of Henry and Catherine (Schecter) Thomas. In their family were eleven children, whose names and dates of birth are as follows: Susanna, February 19, 1809; Joshua, March 8, 1811; Elias, January 27, 1813; Ezra, July 21, 1815; Ruanna, March 23, 1817; Abraham, April 17, 1819; Lydia, March 12, 1821; Julian, June 4, 1823; Samuel, August 26, 1825; Elizabeth, February 10, 1827; and Wilhelmina, February 27, 1829.

In the county of his nativity, Joshua Thomas grew to manhood, receiving a common-school education and obtaining an excellent knowledge of every department of farm work. There he was first married, February 7, 1833, to Miss Salina Landis, who was born March 7, 1812, and they became the parents of the following children: Permelia Margaret, born November 30, 1833; Mary Catherine, October 24, 1836; Henry L., October 24, 1838; William Howard, June 19, 1842, died October 28, 1843; Jacob Oscar, born March 3, 1845, died October 21, 1845; Lewis Ferdinand, born September 25, 1846, and John Edwin, born January 23, 1849. The wife and mother was called to her final rest September 22, 1854, at the age of forty-two years, six months and fifteen days.

For his second wife, Mr. Thomas married Susan Felker, who was born in Washington county, Maryland, August 11, 1832, a daughter of Abraham and Susan (Wingert) Felker. Her father was born in Franklin county, Pennsylvania, in 1802, and was a son of John Felker, a native of Germany, who came to America at the age of twelve years and was bound out to pay his passage. He was a tanner by trade, but most of his life was devoted to farming, his home being in Franklin county, Penn-

JOSHUA THOMAS.

sylvania. He became a loyal and devoted citizen of his adopted country and as a soldier took an active part in the Revolutionary war and the war of 1812. In Lancaster county, Pennsylvania, he married Catherine Wilt, and to them were born five children: Barbara, Catherine, Abraham, Henry and Elizabeth. John Felker was a self-made man in every sense of the word and in business affairs was remarkably successful, giving all his children one hundred and sixty acres of land before his death. At one time he traveled from Franklin county, Pennsylvania, to Washington county, Maryland, where he purchased between twelve and fifteen hundred acres of land, carrying the money in silver and gold in the pockets of his saddle, and was unmolested. In addition to his landed property, he also owned many slaves. He died suddenly of cholera morbus and his wife survived him less than a year. During his youth Abraham Felker, father of Mrs. Thomas, removed with his family to Maryland, and in the subscription schools of that state obtained his education, and when not in school aided his father on the farm. At the age of twenty-one he married Susan Wingert, by whom he had two children: Catherine, widow of F. M. Tice, of Mt. Morris, Illinois; and Susan, wife of our subject. The mother of these children died August 16, 1832, when Mrs. Thomas was only five days old. In 1833, the father married Catherine Wingert, a sister of his first wife, and a daughter of Jacob and Elizabeth (Binkley) Wingert, farming people, in whose family were eleven children: John, Henry, Hannah, Susan, Elizabeth, Catherine, Jacob, Joseph, David, Adam and Daniel. Mr. Wingert died near Greencastle, Pennsylvania, about 1860, having visited Mrs. Thomas a short time before his death. Mr. Felker had eleven children by his second marriage, namely: Sarah married Theodore Hewitt, of Washington county, Maryland, and after his death wedded Henry Sharer, a retired merchant, by whom she had one child, Charles H. Her death occurred in 1892. Hiram married Sabina Sprong and lives in Kansas City, Missouri. David married Delilah Taylor and lives in Nebraska. John B., a prominent physician of Amboy, Illinois, married Jennie Miller, of Pennsylvania, and died in 1888. Samuel died at the age of four years. Willoughby married Alice Biuterbaugh and lives in Leaf River township, Ogle county. Mary Ellen is the wife of Henry Thomas, a sketch of whom appears elsewhere in this volume. Noble F. married Alice Fox and is engaged in the practice of medicine in Amboy, Illinois. Jennie is the wife of J. O. Thomas, of Mt. Morris township, Ogle county. Alice Louisa is the wife of Almon King, and lives in Redwood, Minnesota. Hannah Josephine died at the age of fourteen years. The mother of these children died in 1880.

The children born to Mr. and Mrs. Thomas are as follows: Ettie, born August 17, 1863, died at the age of fourteen months, being scalded to death by pulling over a cup of coffee on her face and breast. Robert Lee, born August 3, 1865, married May McGuffin and has two children: Joshua Samuel, born September 27, 1865, and Ralph L., born August 17, 1866. He and his brother, Frank Felker, born May 12, 1867, carry on the home farm for their mother. Olin Madison, born October 27, 1872, was paralyzed at the age of four years by being given the wrong medicine, the druggist having made a mistake in the prescription. At the age of twelve he received another stroke and at sixteen could not speak for a time. The youngest child died in infancy.

In 1840, Mr. Thomas brought his family to Ogle county, Illinois, where the fall previous he had purchased a tract of government land, and here amid pioneer scenes he began life anew, carrying on operations as an agriculturist until his death, which occurred March 18, 1884. In 1850 he went to California and spent two years in the gold fields of that state, meeting with fair success. He was one of the leading and prominent citizens of his community, was an ardent supporter of the Democratic party, and was held in high regard by all who had the pleasure of his acquaintance. He was a director of the Ogle County Agricultural Society for seven years, and served as its president for a time. He was also officially connected with the schools of his district and in all the relations of life was found true and faithful to every trust reposed in him.

On the 1st of May, 1898, a cyclone struck the Thomas farm, tearing down the barn, but did not injure any of the horses. It also took the roof off the house and Mrs. Thomas was unaware of what had occurred until she looked out and saw the storm disappearing. The farm consists of two hundred and fifty acres of valuable land under a high state of cultivation, and is most capably managed by the sons. Mrs. Thomas, who is a most estimable lady, is a member of the Methodist Episcopal church, and is a sincere and earnest Christian, beloved by all who know her.

GEORGE WASHINGTON CARR, one of the foremost and enterprising agriculturists of Rockvale township, is a native of Pennsylvania, being born in Fulton county, February 10, 1849. He is the son of George W. and Margaret (McLean) Carr, natives of Center and Huntington counties, respectively. The former was born in September, 1819, and the latter in 1823. Mr. Carr was a farmer in Center county, where he resided until his twenty-third year, when he removed to Fulton county, where he was united in marriage to the mother of our subject. In 1884 Mr. and Mrs. Carr moved to Ogle county, but being dissatisfied with the country, they went still further west to Wichita county, Kansas, where Mr. Carr purchased three hundred acres. Ten children have blessed this marriage. James married Elizabeth Row, who died in 1876. He afterward married Katie Angel, and they reside in Ogle county; Ellen is the wife of James Stevens. Their home is in Mt. Morris township; George W. is the third child; Erven married Sadie Angel, a sister of Mrs. James Carr; William died at the age of thirty, of brain fever, the result of typhoid pneumonia. He was unmarried; McClure resides in Wichita county, Kansas; Mary died when six years of age, of diphtheria; Silvester, the eighth child, died when eighteen months old; E. D. is foreman of an electric car line in Omaha, Nebraska, and the youngest child, Amanda, is the wife of Furd Avey. Mr. Carr died July 18, 1898, and his wife is residing with Mrs. Avey.

Our subject bent all his energies toward a good education, and helped his father until his twentieth year, when having finished his schooling, he farmed with his father for two years, and then came west and settled in Ogle county. He rented eighty acres in Mt. Morris township for a term of three years, and then rented the farm of the Reverend Robert Hitt, also for three years. After the expiration of this lease, he re-rented the land in Mt. Morris township for a period of four years, which place he left for his present property in Rockvale, giving in part payment eighty acres in Mt. Morris township.

Mr. Carr's first wife was Miss Ella Moats, who was born in Ogle county, and who was the daughter of Daniel and Margaret Moats. By her he had three children: Margaret, born February 17, 1877, died in infancy. Albert, born April 27, 1878, is living with his maternal grandfather. He received his earlier schooling at the district school, and is now attending the normal school at Valparaiso, Indiana, where he is taking a commercial course, and where he expects to remain for the next two years. In the summer he assists his father about the home farm. Maudie, born March 4, 1882, died June 3, 1882, at the age of three months. The mother of this family died January 17, 1884, of consumption, in her twenty-eighth year. She was a highly respected member of the German Baptist church.

February 8, 1887, Mr. Carr married Miss Martha Alexander, who was born in Huntingdon county, Pennsylvania, September 19, 1867. She was the daughter of Randall Alexander, a farmer of Huntingdon county, and his wife, Martha Kuntzman, and was one of twelve children, namely: George W., William, Colter, John, Mary, Rosy, Katie, Rachel, Martha, Sadie, Maggie and Rosa. To Mr. and Mrs. Carr have been born two children, namely: Nora, born April 9, 1886, and Herbert, born April 17, 1887. Both are attending the district school. Our subject carries on, in addition to general farming, the breeding of fancy stock. He has at the present writing about one hundred and fifty Berkshire pigs, sixty head of Durham cattle, and fourteen head of Norman draft horses, from which he frequently sells at handsome prices to the Chicago market.

Mr. Carr is a Republican in politics, and stoutly upholds the party to which he belongs. He has served as school director for several years with great credit to himself and much benefit to the community. He is a prominent and representative citizen of Rockvale, and is held in high esteem by all who know him.

JAMES H. JUDSON, M. D., who resides upon a fine farm in section 14, Buffalo township, has been a resident of Ogle county a half century, coming here in May, 1848, in company with his parents, Roswell and Lois (Perkins) Judson. The family trace their ancestry back to William Judson, a native of England, who emigrated to this country in 1634, settled in Massachusetts, and lived four years near Concord, and then moved to Stratford, Connecticut. Some of the family later returned to Massachusetts, and there Samuel Judson, the grandfather of our subject, was born and reared. His son, Roswell Judson, was born in Massachusetts, October 6, 1795. He grew to manhood in his native country and then moved to Delaware county, New York, where he married Lois Perkins, a native of that state. They lived for some years on a farm in Delaware county, about four miles from Delhi, but with that laudable desire to better himself, he determined to make a home on the broad prairies of Illinois. Accordingly, in 1848, he came to Ogle county and entered a tract of three hundred and twenty acres of land in Buffalo township, where our subject now resides. Erecting a good substantial dwelling, he commenced to otherwise improve the place, setting out an orchard, shade and ornamental trees, and placing the land under cultivation, in due time he had one of the best farms in the county. On that place he continued to reside until called from this life. He died in 1883, his good wife preceding him some nine years, having died in 1874. Their remains were laid to rest in the cemetery at Polo, where a neat and substantial monument has been erected to their memory. They were the parents of three children, of whom our subject is the youngest, the others being Emily M., wife of Benjamin Pierce, of Franklin county, Iowa, and Ann C., wife of John Malone, of Dane county, Wisconsin.

James H. Judson was born near Delhi, Delaware county, New York, August 20, 1839, and was but nine years of age when he accompanied his parents to Ogle county, which has since been his home. His education was begun in the common schools of his native state, and on his arrival here he entered the public schools of Ogle county. Later he entered Rock River Seminary, at Mt. Morris, where his literary education was completed. Commencing the study of medicine, in 1863 he entered Rush Medical College, and finished his medical education in the session of 1864 and 1865. Immediately after taking the degree he enlisted as a private in Company D, One Hundred and Forty-second Illinois Volunteer Infantry, for one hundred days. He was almost immediately transferred to hospital duty and made assistant surgeon, and as such served during his term of enlistment.

Mustered out of service in October, 1864, Dr. Judson returned to his home and commenced the practice of his profession in connection with farming. For a number of years he gave personal attention to every detail of farm work, but finally rented the place and gave more of his attention to his practice. He still, however, looks after his farming interests, and professionally visits Polo every afternoon. His farm has increased in area until he now owns over four hundred acres of as fine land as there is in Buffalo township.

Dr. Judson was married in Ogle county, June 5, 1866, to Miss Margaret R. Myerly, a native of Maryland, born near Baltimore, and daughter of John Myerly, also a native of Maryland, who came to Ogle county in 1844 and engaged in farming. He later moved to Powesheik county, Iowa, where his last days were spent. To Dr. and Mrs. Judson four children have been born. Frank E. now resides in Hancock county, Iowa, where he is engaged in farming in connection with the practice of veterinary surgery. Emma L. is the wife of Charles Hildebrand, a farmer of Buffalo township. George D. is a veterinary surgeon, residing in Polo. He was a soldier in the Spanish-American war, being a member of Company D, Sixth Illinois Volunteer Infantry. He was detailed as brigade veterinary surgeon, and as such served until the close of the war, being with his regiment in Porto Rico. When the war ended and he received his discharge he resumed the practice of his profession at Polo. Grace L., the remaining member of the family, resides at home.

Politically Dr. Judson is a stanch Republican. His first experience was in the exciting campaign of 1860, resulting in the election of Abraham Lincoln, and followed by the Civil war. His ballot has ever since been cast for the presidential nominees of his party. While he is strong in the advocacy of the principles of his party, he has never been an office seeker, although he has served in some local official positions. He has been a member of the board of supervisors, held the office of road commissioner, and for about twenty-five years was on the school board, a part of which time he was president of the district. He and his wife are members of the Methodist Episcopal church at Polo. Fraternally he is a member of the Independent Order of Odd Fellows at Polo, and also a member of the Grand Army of the Republic at Polo, being surgeon of the post. As a citizen he is progressive, ever ready to assist every worthy object. Well known throughout the county, he is held in the highest respect by all.

JACOB H. PRICE, who resides on section 13, Buffalo township, is a well known farmer and stock-raiser, and has the reputation of being one of the best farmers in the township, which is evident from the neat appearance of his place. He is a native of Ogle county, and was born in Pine Creek township, June 26, 1854. His father, John W. Price, was born in Berkeley county, West Virginia, in 1824. The family are of Welch descent, and settled in Pennsylvania, from which state John Price, the grandfather of our subject, removed to Berkeley county, West Virginia. After residing in that county for some years, he removed with his family to Ogle county, Illinois, and took up a claim in Pine Creek township, where he opened up a farm and spent the last years of his life.

John W. Price came with his father to Ogle county. He was then in his sixteenth year, strong and active, and assisted in the work of transforming the place from its native wilderness to a most productive farm. His primary education was received in the schools of his native state, but on coming to this county he entered Rock River Seminary at Mt. Morris, completing his school life in that institution. He then engaged in teaching and was therefore one of the pioneer teachers in the county. He married Nancy Rowland, a native of Jefferson township, West Virginia, and a daughter of Henry Rowland, another one of the early settlers of the county. Purchasing a farm of two hundred acres in Pine Creek township, he commenced its cultivation and there reared his family. On reaching his three score years and ten he was called to his reward, his death occurring June 7, 1894. His wife survived him some two years, passing away November 8, 1895. They were both devout members of the German Baptist church and active workers in the same. Their family comprised eight children. Clara E. is now the wife of O. B. Ringer, of Pine Creek township. Jacob H. is second in order of birth. L. C. is now a resident of Marshall county, Iowa. Hattie E. is the wife of John Heckman, a minister of the Brethren church, residing in Buffalo township. Oliver L. is engaged in the mercantile business in Oregon, Illinois. Gussie is the wife of William Lampin, a farmer of Pine Creek township. Collin C. is also a farmer of Pine Creek township, and a minister of the Brethren church. Henry died when one year old.

On his father's farm in Pine Creek township, Jacob H. Price grew to manhood, and in the district school of the neighborhood received his education. He remained under the parental roof until after he attained his majority, assisting in the work of the home farm. He then rented a farm and began life for himself. A little later he purchased one hundred acres of his present farm, which was then partially improved, and at once commenced its further improvement. Subsequently he purchased sixty acres more, giving him a fine farm of one hundred and sixty acres. He has lately erected a large and substantial residence with all the modern improvements, including furnace heat, bath rooms, hot and cold water throughout the house. It is one of the best country residences in the county. His barn, granaries, and other outbuildings are also of the best, thus showing him to be a very practical man in all things, one who believes that a farmer should enjoy some of the blessings of this life as well as others.

Mr. Price was married in Ogle county, February 24, 1881, to Miss Lillie M. Spickler, a native of Washington county, Maryland, who came to Ogle county in infancy with her parents. Her father, C. B. Spickler, was also born in Washington county, Maryland, in 1830. He was twice married, his first wife dying in Maryland, leaving one daughter, Maggie, now the wife of Daniel Stauffer, a farmer of Pine Creek township. He later married Miss Ellen Newcomer, a native of Maryland, and Mrs. Price is second in their family of four children. The others are Emma, residing with her parents; Henry, a minister in the German Baptist church; and Eddie, a student at Polo. To Mr. and Mrs. Price one daughter has been born--Rhoda Ellen, born October 8, 1898.

Mr. Price was reared in the faith of the German Baptist church, and has adhered to its teachings, believing them to be in conformity with the sacred scriptures. He holds membership with the church in Pine Creek township, and has for some years been a deacon in the same. His wife is also a member of the same church.

In addition to general farming, Mr. Price has made a specialty for some years of raising stock for the markets, annually feeding and shipping from one to six car loads of cattle and about three car loads of hogs. In this branch of his business he has been quite successful.

CHARLES HIRAM BETEBENNER, of Oregon, Illinois, a descendant of one of the old families of Ogle county, was born in Pine Creek township, March 9, 1851, and is the son of Samuel and Rebecca (Strauss) Betebenner, and the grandson of John Betebenner, a native of Maryland of German ancestry. Samuel Betebenner was born December 15, 1805, in Washington county, Maryland, where his youth and early manhood were spent. He was united in marriage September 15, 1831, to Rebecca Strauss, of Hagerstown, Maryland. While reared to farm work, at the age of twenty-two he apprenticed himself to a plasterer, and in two years' time he had become so proficient at the trade that he was recognized as a journeyman. He had learned to play the fife, and play it well, and when General LaFayette visited this country, in 1825, he had the high honor of playing the fife at a reception given to the noble French patriot when he passed through Frederick City, Maryland. In 1861, though too old to be admitted into the army of the Union, yet he was young enough to play the fife and its shrill notes were heard at Polo, Illinois, when the muster roll was open to help raise the Fifteenth Regiment Illinois Volunteer Infantry.

In 1842, having heard so much of the beauty and richness of the Rock river country, Samuel Betebenner concluded to visit it. He spent the summer in Ogle county, and was so much pleased with the country that he concluded to locate here and made some preparations to that end, after which he returned to Maryland. On the 15th of May, 1844, with his wife and three children, he started for his new home, making the journey overland with teams, being seven weeks on the road. On the way they endured many hardships, but were never discouraged. Arriving here Mr. Betebenner took up a claim in Pine Creek township of three hundred and twenty acres, which he immediately began to improve. A part of this tract he owned through life, selling the remainder to his son John. In addition to this tract, he later purchased forty acres in Mt. Morris township. His trade was of great assistance to him in the new country and naturally aided him in supplying his family wants and advancing his farm interests. Deer and other wild game were in abundance when he began to build up a new home and these luxuries were almost daily served at his table. He was among the workmen who plastered the first state house at Springfield. What a record was his life, connecting as it did two generations! His youth was spent with the soldiers of the Revolution and the compatriots of Washington, and his eyes greeted the great LaFayette, and the clear notes of his fife resounded in his ears. He lived to see and help build up a new civilization in the great west and become one of its factors. He set a noble example to the rising generations, and may they emulate his virtues. He departed this life December 12, 1895, in his ninetieth year, and the funeral services took place at the opera-house in Oregon the following Sunday.

Rebecca (Strauss) Betebenner was the daughter of Hiram and Christy A. (Glosbrenner) Strauss, and was born in Hagerstown, Maryland, July 4, 1808. Her father was by profession a physician. Both of her parents lived and died in Maryland. Samuel and Rebecca Betebenner were the parents of eight children. Thomas H. is a farmer and land speculator residing in Carthage, Missouri. Robert V. resides in California, where he is engaged in contracting and building. Samuel G., a mason by trade, resides in Polo, Illinois. Narcissa, now the wife of Benjamin Hanna, is living in Polo. Ella, wife of Abner Newcomer, is living near Polo. John resides on the old homestead. Eliza, who married Thomas Emmert, now lives in Tarkio, Missouri. The subject of this sketch completes the family. Mrs. Rebecca Betebenner survives her husband, and resides at Polo, Illinois, patiently waiting the day when she, too, shall be called up higher.

Charles H. Betebenner was reared on the home farm, and in the home school received his primary education. After spending some time in Rock River Seminary, he entered Beloit College, where he spent two seasons in study. Later he engaged in merchandizing at Dysart, Iowa, for about a year and a half, and then returned to Oregon and clerked for Artz & Ray for four years. He then engaged in the mail service, running from Chicago to Dubuque, Iowa. This took up about four years. Later he was nominated on the Independent ticket for sheriff of Ogle county, and was elected by twenty-six majority, running against John Bailey, the regular Republican nominee. This was one of the hottest campaigns in the history of Ogle county. After his term of four years he engaged in tile manufacturing and contracting, as a member of the firm of Sammis & Co.

Mr. Betebenner was married March 20, 1879, at Polo, Illinois, to Miss Inez Sammis, daughter of C. W. & Emily A. (Helm) Sammis. She was born LaSalle, Illinois, but came with her parents to Ogle county when she was a child. Her parents were natives of New York, coming to Illinois in 1841, locating at what was then known as Buffalo Grove, LaSalle county. They had six children--Fred H., Inez, Grace, J. Uriah, E. Payson and Stata. Grace married Seward Woodruff, and they are living in Oregon. Stata is the wife of A. F. Matthews, of Chicago. Mr. and Mrs. Betebenner are the parents of three children--E. Payson, Ruth W. and Charles Sammis. E. Payson died in 1883.

Mr. and Mrs. Betebenner attend the Presbyterian church. In politics he is a Democrat. Fraternally he is a member of the Masons and the Independent Order of Odd Fellows. In 1898 he was appointed superintendent of the Ogle county almshouse and is now in charge of that institution.

JAMES DONALDSON, an honored pioneer and highly respected citizen of Ogle county, has resided here since May, 1839, and for many years was prominently and actively identified with its agricultural interests. He bore his part in the early development and prosperity of this region, but is now living retired upon his farm on section 12, Eagle Point township, only three miles northwest of Polo.

A native of New York, Mr. Donaldson was born on the shores of Lake Champlain, Washington county, January 4, 1821, and is a son of William Donaldson, who was born in Northumberland county, England, May 5, 1795, of Scotch ancestry, and there grew to manhood. There he was also married to Miss Isabella McDonald, who was born at Berwick on the Tweed, England, of Scotch ancestry. Being reared on a farm, the father early became familiar with all the duties which fall to the lot of the agriculturist, and engaged in farm work in his native land until 1820, when he emigrated to America and first located in Washington county, New York, where he continued to engage in agricultural pursuits for four years, during which time two of his children were born. His next home was at Little York, Ontario, Canada, and there he engaged in his chosen occupation for fifteen years. Coming to Ogle county, Illinois, in 1839, he bought a claim of three hundred and twenty acres in what is now Eagle Point township, forty acres of which had been placed under cultivation and a log house erected thereon. In that primitive residence the family lived while the farm was being developed and improved. Later a good frame house was built, also a good barn and outbuildings, and an orchard set out. The father was one of the most enterprising and successful early farmers, and having prospered in his life work, he was at length able to lay aside all business cares and spend his last years in ease and retirement. He sold the farm to his youngest son, and upon a part of the place erected a residence where he lived until called from this life in March, 1870, at the age of seventy-five years. His wife survived him for some time, passing away in November, 1884, and both were buried in Fairmont cemetery, where a substantial monument marks their last resting place.

In the family of this worthy couple were nine children, four sons and five daughters, all of whom reached years of maturity. Walter, the eldest, was born in England and spent his last days in Brookville township, Ogle county; James, our subject, is the next in order of birth; John is now living retired in Morengo, Illinois; Margaret is the wife of John S. Miller, an old settler and substantial farmer of Eagle Point township, Ogle county; Isabella is the wife of Patterson Pringle, of Morengo; William was a resident of Ogle county, but is now deceased; Elizabeth is the wife of Eber Smith, of Buffalo township, this county; Jane is the wife of Alexander Hawver, of Dedham, Carroll county, Iowa; and Flora W. is the wife of John Brace, of Dedham, Iowa.

James Donaldson, of this review, was about eighteen years of age when he accompanied the family on their removal to Ogle county, and he was of great assistance to his father in opening up and developing the farm from wild land. When his services were not needed at home he would work for others at farm labor. He and his brother Walter were experts in the use of the ax and in the groves of this region were employed in getting out the timbers for many of the houses and barns of the early settlers. Until twenty-five years of age he continued to aid in the operation of the home farm and then located upon a one-hundred-acre tract in Eagle Point township which his father gave him. To its improvement and cultivation he devoted his attention with most gratifying results and made his home thereon for a quarter of a century, during which time he bought more land adjoining, making a valuable tract of four hundred and eighteen acres. Later he built on the farm where he now resides and now has one of the best improved farms of the township. There is a large and substantial residence and good outbuildings. Mr. Donaldson met with most excellent success in his farming operations but for the past ten years has lived retired, enjoying a well earned rest.

On the 31st of May, 1848, was celebrated the marriage of Mr. Donaldson and Miss Locada J. Seavey, who was born in Sandwich, New Hampshire, January 8, 1831. Her father, Joshua Seavey, was a native of Rye Beach, the same state, and there grew to manhood and married Miss Betsy Webster, a cousin of the great statesman, Daniel Webster. In 1840 Mr. Seavey came to Illinois and settled near Dixon, in Lee county, where Mrs. Donaldson was reared. To our subject and his wife were born nine children, namely: Elizabeth Isabel, who died at the age of sixteen years, Mary Josephine, who died at the age of fourteen; Walter Atwood, who died at the age of fifteen; John James, who died at the age of six; Alice, who married M. P. Strall and lived in Iowa, where she died in September, 1891, leaving ten children; Emma Frances, who married Zelus L. Shafer and also lived in Iowa, where she died in October, 1891, leaving an infant daughter, Emma Frances, who now lives with our subject and is attending the home school; William, who is married, and he and his brother carry on the home farm; Gertie, wife of Nelson B. Sweet, a farmer of Eagle Point township; and Sherman B., who owns and operates a farm in Buffalo township, this county. There are now fourteen grandchildren and two great-grandchildren. On the 31st of

May, 1898, Mr. and Mrs. Donaldson celebrated their golden wedding, at which time all of their living children and grandchildren in this vicinity were present, and a most enjoyable time was passed.

Politically, Mr. Donaldson is a Jeffersonian Democrat, having cast his first presidential ballot for James K. Polk in 1844, and for each succeeding candidate of his party but two. In 1896 he supported Palmer and Buckner on the gold Democratic ticket. He has never desired office, preferring to give his attention to his own interests. For sixty years he has been a resident of Ogle county and has watched with interest almost its entire growth and development. He has seen the wolves and deer disappear, town and villages spring up, the railroads and telegraphs introduced, and the wild land transformed into fine farms and good homes. He has borne his part in the work, and has ever been recognized as one of the valued and useful citizens of his community, one honored and respected by all who know him.

JAMES WESLEY CARR, a skillful and thorough farmer residing on section 19, Rockvale township, is a native of Pennsylvania, born in Fulton county, September 4, 1843, and is a representative of an old family of that state. His grandfather, George Carr, was probably a native of Center county, that state, as it was there he made his home from early life, his time and attention being devoted to agricultural pursuits. He married Louise Sanders and to them were born three children: Samuel, a laborer, resided in Blair county, Pennsylvania, until his death in 1896; George W., our subject's father, and William, a carpenter, who was residing in Fulton county, Illinois, at the time of his death.

George W. Carr was born in Center county, Pennsylvania, and remained there until he attained the age of twenty-two, attending the common schools during the winter months and aiding his father in the work of the farm through the summer season. On leaving home he came to Fulton county, Pennsylvania, where he continued to engage in the occupation to which he had been reared. He wedded Miss Margaret McLean, who was born in Huntingdon county, Pennsylvania, in 1823, a daughter of Eli McLean, and to them were born eleven children, of whom our subject is the eldest. Ella, the next in order of birth, is now the wife of James H. Stevens, a farmer of Mt. Morris township, Ogle county; George W. is represented on another page of this work; John Ervin married Sarah Angel and lives in Rockvale township, Ogle county; William died at the age of thirty-eight years; McClure married Annie Beard and lives in Wichita county, Kansas; Elliot Duffield married, and is foreman for an electric line at Omaha, Nebraska; Mary Jane died at the age of five years; Sylvester died at the age of two years; and Amanda and Ferdinand Avery, of Rockvale township, Ogle county.

During his boyhood and youth James W. Carr pursued his studies in the district schools near the old home farm in Fulton county, and aided in the labors of the fields. After leaving school at the age of nineteen, he devoted his entire time to the work of the farm until attaining his majority. During the following two years he was employed by Reuben Faust in Franklin county, Pennsylvania. He then came west and settled in Mt. Morris township, Ogle county, Illinois, where he worked by the month for a year, but in 1870 located upon a farm of one hundred and fifty acres, which he rented for three years. The following three years were spent on Mr. Phelps' farm of two hundred and seventy-nine acres, and for the same length of time he lived on the David Gloss farm of one hundred and sixty acres. In 1876 he bought one hundred and eight acres, lying partly in Mt. Morris and partly in Rockvale townships. As his financial resources have increased he has kept adding to his property, purchasing eighty acres in 1878, and since then two tracts of forty acres, one of which was timber land, and in 1894 purchased one hundred and thirty acres in Mt. Morris township, making three hundred and ninety-eight acres in all. This property he has placed under a high state of cultivation and improved until it is now one of the best farms in the community.

On the 15th of November, 1868, Mr. Carr was united in marriage with Miss Lizzie Rowe, a daughter of Henry Rowe, of Franklin county, Pennsylvania. She was born in Maryland, in 1840, and died October 10, 1877. Four children were born of that union: Alice, born July 10, 1869, died September 4, 1889, from dropsy brought on by catching cold while attending college. Charlie, born October 6, 1871, was married, in June, 1894, to Belle Goodrich, a daughter of George and Fulelia Goodrich, and they now have one child, Charlie Guy, born in March, 1898. Charlotte, born November 4, 1873, died with measles in April, 1877. Harvey, born September 4, 1876, was educated in the district schools and Mount Morris College, and now assists his father on the farm.

Mr. Carr was again married, March 4, 1879, his second union being with Miss Katie S. Angel, who was born in Maryland, October 19, 1855, and is the second child in the family of Uriah and Mahala (Koontz) Angel, who brought their family to Illinois in 1878. By the second marriage six children have been born, namely: Orville B., born December 23, 1879, died February 20, 1880; Elmer B., born July 20, 1881, died January 29, 1882; Mina Pearl, born September 12, 1883, is at present attending the home school, Wilbur J., born September 12, 1885, died of diphtheria September 19, 1894; Alva Harrison, born February 13, 1887, died August 25, 1889; and Vernie May, born May 2, 1890, is attending the district school. The wife and mother is a consistent member of the Lutheran church.

The Republican party always finds in Mr. Carr a stanch supporter of its principles, but he has never cared for the honors or emoluments of public office, preferring to devote his entire time and attention to his business interests. He has, however, served as school director for three years. On coming to Ogle county he had but one hundred and ninety dollars, and the success that he has achieved in life has been due to his own industry and well-directed efforts.

SQUIRE ROLFE. Prominent among the successful and energetic farmers of Marion township may be found the subject of this biographical notice, whose home is pleasantly located on section 15, and who is considered one of the most industrious and worthy citizens of Ogle county. Besides his home farm of one hundred and sixty acres, he owns another valuable place of one hundred and thirty acres in the same township, known as the old Blye homestead

This he purchased in 1895, has made some substantial improvements upon it, and now has two valuable and desirable farms.

Mr. Rolfe was born in Tompkins county, New York, September 21, 1829, and is a son of Chester Rolfe, a native of New Jersey, and a grandson of Samuel Rolfe, also a native of New Jersey and a pioneer settler of Tompkins county, New York, where the father grew to manhood. There he married Matilda Kirkendall, a native of New York, and in Tompkins county they made their home throughout the remainder of their lives. He died in Rockford, Illinois, at the home of his son, Henry, while on a visit to his son, but his remains were taken back to New York and interred by the side of his wife, who had passed away several years previously. Their family consisted of five sons and four daughters, all of whom grew to man and womanhood, but only our subject and three sisters are now living. Henry came west and located in Ogle county, but later removed to Rockford, where he spent his last years. Levi, the oldest son, was a pioneer of Waukesha county, Wisconsin, where he opened up a farm and continued to live until his death. Edgar and Frank both died on the old homestead in New York in early manhood.

Squire Rolfe obtained a good common-school education and remained under the parental roof until eighteen years of age, when he went to Enfield Center, New York, to learn the carriagemaker's trade, serving a three-years' apprenticeship. For a year or two he worked as a journeyman, but in the fall of 1853 he and his brother Henry came to Illinois and settled in Ogle county, where he continued to follow his trade for four years. The brothers purchased eighty acres of land in Marion township, in 1855, which they at once commenced to improve and cultivate, it being operated by Henry for two or three years, when he went to California. During the war Squire Rolfe engaged in carriage making and also had charge of the farm, and when his brother returned they carried it on together for a few years. They finally sold and bought a farm of three hundred and twenty acres in Scott township, to the further development and cultivation of which they devoted their time and attention for five years. They erected thereon a good house and barn and made many other useful and valuable improvements. Selling out at the end of that time Squire Rolfe purchased his present home farm in 1873, and has converted it into one of the best and most attractive places in Marion township. In connection with general farming he is also interested in breeding and dealing in a good grade of horses, cattle and hogs.

On the 11th of March, 1874, in Marion township, Mr. Rolfe was united in marriage with Miss Mary A. Comstock, daughter of Hiram and Jane (Lamphier) Comstock. She is a native of Herkimer county, New York, born November 22, 1847, and came west with her step-father, Nathan Bly, in 1854, and located in that township, where she was principally reared and educated. Mr. Rolfe cast his first presidential ballot for General Winfield Scott, four years later supported John C. Fremont, and for many years was identified with the Republican party, but in 1896 supported the Democratic nominee. For forty-four years he has been identified with the interests of this county, and in all enterprises tending to benefit the people of the community, morally, socially or financially, he has been an earnest and cheerful worker, and now while traveling down the sunset hill of life he has reason to be comforted that his years and labors have not been in vain.

DAVID NEWCOMER, M. D., for more than a quarter of a century has been a resident of Mount Morris, where he has been actively engaged in the practice of his profession. He is a native of Franklin county, Pennsylvania, born near Greencastle, July 26, 1830, and is the son of Daniel and Barbara (Stoner) Newcomer, both of whom were natives of Maryland, the former born in November, 1800, near Hagerstown, Washington county, and the latter in June, 1801, near Lightersburg, in the same county. Daniel Newcomer was the son of Peter Newcomer, also a native of Maryland and a farmer and miller by occupation. On both the paternal and maternal sides the family trace their ancestry to Switzerland.

At the age of twenty-four Daniel Newcomer married Barbara Stoner, and they became the parents of seven children, as follows: Elizabeth, born in 1822, married John Brandt and they had seven children. They removed to this county at an early day, but both are now deceased. John, born in 1826, married Catherine Middour, and they had five children, two of whom are living. He died October 2, 1872, but his widow is yet living and makes her home in Chicago. Cyrus B., born in 1828, married Elizabeth Haws, and to them were born seven children. He died in 1896, but his widow is yet living in Mount Morris township. David, next in order of birth, is the subject of this sketch. Daniel W., born in 1832, married Margaret Walter, and to them were born five children. They now reside in Polo, where he is living a retired life. Martin S., born in 1838, married Anna C. Funk, and six children were born of this union. His wife dying, he later married Miss Bergstrum. They now reside in Decatur, Illinois. He is a minister of the Church of God. Barbara, born in 1835, married Abram Miller, and they became the parents of eleven children. Mr. Miller is deceased, and his widow now resides near Freeport, Illinois.

Shortly after his marriage, Daniel Newcomer moved to Franklin county, Pennsylvania, where he engaged in agricultural pursuits, reared his family, and there continued to reside until 1865, when he came to Ogle county and located in Buffalo township, where the remainder of his life was passed. He died in 1875, his wife preceding him some years, dying in 1873. In early life he was an old two line Whig, with which party he continued to act until it ceased to exist. Having a dislike for slavery, he naturally became a Republican on the organization of that party. He lived to see slavery abolished and the union of states restored. With the Republican party he continued to affiliate until his death. Religiously, he was identified with the River Brethren, as was also his wife. He was a man of deep religious convictions and endeavored to walk in the footsteps of the Master.

The subject of this sketch remained at home until he attained his majority. His primary education was obtained in the common schools of the neighborhood, which was supplemented by attending Shady Grove Academy, in Perry county, Pennsylvania, where he remained one year. He then engaged in farming, continuing in that line for three years. At the age of twenty-four he entered the office of Dr. James Brotherton, of Waynesboro, Pennsylvania, and read medicine under his instruction for a time, and later entered Jefferson Medical College, Philadelphia, taking the regular course, and graduating therefrom in 1859. On receiving his diploma, he went to Upton, in his native state, opened an office and commenced the practice of his profession. He was building up a good practice at that place when the war for the union commenced. Offering his services to his country, he was commissioned assistant surgeon of the Twenty-sixth Regiment Pennsylvania Volunteer Infantry, and immediately went to the front. His service began in May, 1862, being mustered in at Camp Curtin, near Harrisburg. From Camp Curtin he was sent to St. Joseph hospital, a military hospital in Philadelphia, where he remained two months, and then joined the Army of the Potomac under McClellan, taking part in the campaign in the Chickahominy valley, being in the seven days' fight in the Wilderness. While in this campaign he was taken quite sick and resigned his commission. Returning home he resumed his practice as soon as his health would admit. He remained at home about a year and a half and again went into the service as acting assistant surgeon, being stationed at Beverly hospital, in New Jersey, where he remained until about the close of the war, when he again returned to Upton. From that place he later removed to Martinsburg, West Virginia, where he remained four and a half years, in the meantime building up a fair practice. In March, 1871, he came to Mt. Morris, and for twenty-eight years has attended to the ills of the people of that city and vicinity, meeting with very gratifying success.

On the 18th of November, 1851, Dr. Newcomer was united in marriage with Miss Mary Shelley Funk, a native of Franklin county, Pennsylvania, born April 30, 1831, and the daughter of Jacob and Catherine (Shelley) Funk, both of whom were also natives of Pennsylvania, the former born in 1803, and the latter in 1806. By occupation Jacob Funk was a farmer. He never came west, but died in his native state February 6, 1850. His wife survived him many years, dying March 27, 1891. They were the parents of twelve children—Henry, Elizabeth, Rebecca, David, Mary, Christian, Cyrus, Susan, Joseph, Annie C., Martin S. and Jacob. Catherine Funk was the daughter of Christian and Madeline (Hershey) Shelley, both natives of Pennsylvania, and both born in 1769.

To Dr. and Mrs. Newcomer six children were born, two of whom died in infancy. The living are: (1) Catherine, born May 30, 1855, married N. W. Sollenberger, and they have three children—Harry C., Hugh Hale and Earl. Mr. Sollenberger is engaged in farming in North Dakota. (2) Barbara Alice, born June 18, 1856, married Rev. J. W. Thomas, a minister of the general synod of the Lutheran church, recently located at Lanark, but now residing at Mt. Morris. (3) David W., born November 20, 1858, married Nellie McFadden, and they have six children—Henry, Edward, David, Frank, Minnie and Earl. They reside in Kansas City, Missouri, where he is engaged in the undertaking and livery business. (4) H. C., born April 30, 1861, married Rebecca Kosier, and they have two children—Sidney and Francis. They reside in Memphis, Tennessee, where he has charge of an engineering corps. He is a graduate of West Point, in the class of 1886, graduating at the head of his class. He holds the commission of captain in the regular army, but is now attached to the engineering corps.

Politically Dr. Newcomer is a Republican, but his professional duties have always been such as to prevent him from taking a very active part in political affairs. While preferring to give his time to his profession he served as president of the village board in a commendable manner. For years he has been connected with the Ogle County Medical Society, and for several years was its president. Fraternally he is a member of the Masonic Order, Knights of Pythias, and John Smith Post, G. A. R., of Mt. Morris. He is a member of the Lutheran church, and for two years served as deacon. He is very popular in the county of his adoption, not only as a physician, but as a citizen, and his friends are numerous indeed.

JAMES MYERS is one of the representative pioneers and honored citizens of Ogle county, where he first located in the spring of 1837. For many years he was actively identified with the agricultural interests of this section of the state, but is now living retired in the village of Leaf River, enjoying the rest which should always follow a long and busy career.

Mr. Myers is a native of Maryland, born in Washington county, July 22, 1829, and is a son of Jacob Muers, whose birth occurred in the same state in 1800. On reaching manhood the latter married Miss Elizabeth Her, also a native of Maryland. The father, who was a farmer by occupation, emigrated to Illinois in 1837, driving to Wheeling, West Virginia, and thence proceeding down the Ohio and up the Mississippi and Illinois rivers to Peru, this state. From that place he drove across the country to Ogle county and in Leaf River township laid claim to four hundred and twenty-four acres, which he later entered from the government. At that time the country was all wild and unimproved, no roads constructed or bridges built. Mr. Myers was compelled to go to Peru to mill, and would haul part of his grain and pork to Chicago, where he bought most of his supplies, while at times he did his marketing at Mt. Carroll and Grand Detour. In crossing sloughs his wagon would often stick fast in the mud and he was obliged to take the load off and carry it to firmer ground. On hills or elevations he put up stakes as land marks to guide him across the open prairies. He had two plows with wooden moll board, and his harrows had wooden teeth, and with these rude implements he managed, however, to break and cultivate his place. He located first in Maryland township, where he built a log house with a mud and stick chimney, but after living there two or three years he elected a more substantial residence of hewed logs upon his claim in Leaf River township. He also built a separate kitchen and good outbuildings, which in later years were replaced by modern frame structures. Upon his farm he passed away in the spring of 1876 at the age of seventy-six years, and his wife died in 1892, at the age of eighty-two.

Fifteen children were born to this worthy couple, and with the exception of one all reached man and womanhood, and five sons and five daughters are now living. William, who married and settled in Winnebago county, Illinois, is now deceased; James is the second eldest son; Henry is a farmer of Linn county, Iowa; Jacob is a farmer of Stephenson county, Illinois, and John and David are both farmers in Ogle county. The sisters are Amanda, wife of Silas Snyder, both now deceased; Mary, deceased wife of John Piper; Susan, wife of John L. Smith; Adaline, wife of Joseph Kendall, a farmer of Ogle county; Sarah, wife of Joseph Folder, of Ogle county; Catherine, wife of Jacob Shriver, of Ogle county; and Martha, wife of George Grove, of Ogle county.

James Myers was a lad of eight years when he came with the family to Ogle county, and here he grew to manhood, assisting in opening up and developing the home farm. After attaining his majority he operated the place for four years, and then bought eighty acres of land in Ridott township, Stephenson county, which he converted into a fine farm, it being one of the best improved places in the township. He erected thereon a commodious frame residence, a good barn, granary and other outbuildings, and placed the land under a high state of cultivation. For twenty-four years he was actively and successfully engaged in farming upon that place, but now rents the farm and lives retired in Leaf River, where he bought a lot and built a comfortable residence.

At Freeport, Illinois, September 30, 1857, Mr. Myers was united in marriage with Miss Caroline Matilda Allen, who was born in Luzerne county, Pennsylvania, April 12, 1838. Her parents, Peter and Sarah Allen, also natives of that county, came to Illinois in 1854, and bought an improved farm in Ogle county, where they spent their last years.

On national issues, Mr. Myers is a supporter of the Democratic party, but at local elections he votes independently, supporting the man whom he believes best qualified to fill the office. He and his wife are earnest and faithful members of the Christian church, assisted in its organization, and he has served as deacon and trustee since it was started, while Mrs. Myers gave the lot, adjoining their own home, on which the church was built. Their many sterling traits of character have endeared them to all, and it is safe to say that no couple in the community have more or warmer friends than Mr. and Mrs. Myers.

AMOS A. SHEFFIELD, deceased, was a well-known farmer of Grand Detour township, and the proprietor of the Sheffield House, in the village of Grand Detour. He was born September 5, 1828, in North Stonington, Connecticut, and was the son of Amos and Nancy (Baldwin) Sheffield, both of whom were also natives of the Nutmeg state. In his native state he remained until he was seventeen years old, when he accompanied his parents to Otsego county, New York, where they made a permanent home. His father was a wheelwright by trade, and followed that occupation almost exclusively in Connecticut, but on his removal to New York he engaged in farming, only occasionally working at his trade. His last days were spent in Otsego county, his death occurring many years ago.

In his native state our subject received a limited education, but his native shrewdness served him instead of the thorough school training that he would have been pleased to have had. He remained at home and assisted his father until after attaining his majority. His marriage was celebrated October 9, 1852, when Miss Elizabeth Scofield became his wife. She was born in

AMOS A. SHEFFIELD.

MRS. A. A. SHEFFIELD.

Otsego county, New York, March 5, 1833, and is the daughter of Hezekiah and Vashti (Cole) Scofield, both of whom were natives of New York. Before leaving New York, one son, William Eugene, was born. In infancy he accompanied his parents to Illinois, and here grew to manhood, and March 6, 1879, married Miss Elizabeth M. J. Foxley, born January 15, 1855, and a daughter of John and Jane (Reynolds) Foxley, her father being a farmer in Grand Detour township. By this union two sons were born—Arthur E., born April 9, 1887, and Nelson F., born January 30, 1890. In politics William E. Sheffield is a Republican, and has served as supervisor of his township one term, six terms as township clerk, three years as school director, twelve years as notary public, and is at present justice of the peace. He is a member of Grand Detour Camp, No. 3683, M. W. A., Ulysses Grant Garrison, No. 11, K. G. For some years he has been engaged in the general mercantile business in Grand Detour, and has a very satisfactory trade. All four of the brothers belong to the same camp of M. W. A. 3683.

Upon coming to Illinois about 1855, Mr. Sheffield first located in Lee county, near Dixon, where he purchased a farm of one hundred acres, which was their home for two years. Selling that farm, he moved into Dixon, where he remained two years. In November, 1861, he moved to Grand Detour, and for two or three years cultivated a rented farm, and then bought a farm in the township, about two miles north of the village, of six hundred and seventeen acres. However, he made his home in the village where the family still reside. In 1864, he purchased the present home of the family in the village, and soon after remodeled the house, adding to its dimensions, making it the commodious house as it now exists. When the repairs on the house were all completed, it was opened as a hotel, which he named after himself, the Sheffield House. His attention ever after was divided between his hotel and farm, and on the latter he raised a good grade of stock in which he took considerable pride.

After coming to Illinois, four more children were born: May C., now the wife of Dr. James Parkhurst, of Grand Detour; Charles A., of whom mention is made further along in this sketch; Mark S. and Amos H., who are carrying on the home farm.

Charles A. Sheffield was born October 15, 1862, in the village of Grand Detour, and was educated in its public schools. His life has mainly been spent on the home farm, but he has on occasions engaged in other lines of business. In 1888 he took charge of the butter making in the creamery of Buell Brothers, Rock Falls, Illinois. In 1882 he took a position with an engineering corps at Sioux City, Iowa, engaged in surveying a road through Iowa, and was with the corps for some time. In politics he is independent in local elections, but on general issues he affiliates with the Democracy. In 1894 he was elected constable of his township and served four years. In 1896 he was elected highway commissioner, which position he yet fills. On the 20th of June, 1895, at Milwaukee, Wisconsin, he was united in marriage with Miss Lottie Burhyte, daughter of John and Matilda (McIntyre) Burhyte, of Fond du Lac, Wisconsin.

Amos A. Sheffield departed this life January 22, 1898. Three brothers and one sister yet survive him, as follows: George H., a merchant of Holley, New York; Rev. Charles A., a minister of the Baptist church, of Topeka, Kansas; Dr. D. A., an old practitioner, of Dixon, Illinois; and Mrs. Julia Lyon, of Gilbertsville, New York.

Mr. Sheffield was reared in the Baptist faith, in which in early life he was a member. Fraternally he was a member of Grand Detour lodge, A. F. & A. M. In politics he was a Democrat of the old school, a stanch advocate of the principles of the party. He filled a number of local positions of honor and trust, including commissioner of highways, constable, school director, and was also postmaster of Grand Detour for two terms under Cleveland, and was reappointed by McKinley. After his death Mrs. Sheffield received the appointment, and is now discharging the duties of the office. He was a man of sterling character and worth, thoroughly honest, of good business ability, and his death was mourned not alone by his faithful wife and family, but by a large circle of friends and acquaintances.

STEPHEN B. SHUART, president of the Byron Bank, of Byron, Illinois, has a wide reputation as a most capable financier and occupies a position of no little prominence in business circles in Ogle county. His life demonstrates what can be accomplished through energy, careful management, keen foresight and the utilization of powers with which nature has endowed one, and the opportunities with which the times surround him.

A native of Ohio, Mr. Shuart was born in Ashtabula county, May 15, 1837, and is a son of Stephen Shuart, who was born in New Jersey, of German ancestry, the family having been founded in that state at an early day. The father was reared, however, in New York and there married Miss Mary Beckwith, a native of Allegany county, New York. About 1836 he removed to Ashtabula county, Ohio, but spent his last years in Gerard, Pennsylvania, where his death occurred.

When a lad of thirteen years Stephen B. Shuart left home to begin the battle of life for himself as a farm hand. His early school privileges were limited and he is mainly self-educated, having devoted considerable time to reading and study in later years. Coming west in 1857, he spent the first winter in work upon a farm near Rockford, Illinois, but the following spring witnessed his arrival in Ogle county, where he has since made his home. Here he also worked on a farm during the summer season and the first winter attended a country school, but during the winter of 1860 pursued his studies in the high school at Mt. Morris.

His patriotism and loyalty to country were manifest May 24, 1861, by his enlistment in Company H, Fifteenth Illinois Volunteer Infantry, as a private. The regiment was assigned to the Western Army, and was first under General Fremont in Missouri. Later they participated in the battles of Shiloh, Corinth, Hatchie's Run, the second battle of Corinth; was in a number of engagements around Vicksburg, and helped to take that stronghold. Then followed the battles of Big Black and Jackson, after which they returned to Vicksburg, and from there went to Natchez, Mississippi. Mr. Shuart veteranized and returned home on a sixty days' furlough, rejoining his regiment at Nashville, Tennessee. He was then with Sherman on the memorable march to the sea. While his company was acting as rear guard at Ackworth, Georgia, about two hundred and fifty of the regiment, including our subject, were taken prisoners by Hood and sent to Andersonville, where they were incarcerated until the spring of 1865. They were then taken to Vicksburg, where they were deserted by their guard after hearing of the assassination of President Lincoln. Mr. Shuart soon returned north, and at Springfield was honorably discharged in May, 1865, and reached home on the 4th of July.

The following year he engaged in farming in Marion township, Ogle county, where he first purchased forty acres of wild land, which he soon converted into highly cultivated fields. He bought more land from time to time until he had one hundred and seventy-five acres, on which he erected a good residence and made many other improvements which added to its value and attractive appearance. Renting his farm in 1887, he removed to Byron, where he was first engaged in buying, selling and shipping stock, and also conducted a butcher shop for a few years and then sold. In 1892, in partnership with other gentlemen, he purchased the Byron Bank, was elected president and is still filling that position. They do a general banking business and their patronage extends throughout the county. Besides his own comfortable home in East Byron, Mr. Stewart has other residence property, and is to-day one of the substantial and prosperous citizens of the community.

In Ogle county, Mr. Shuart was married in 1866, to Miss Julia A. Whittaker, a native of the county and a daughter of John Whittaker, one of its first settlers. She died in 1887, leaving one daughter, Emily, now the wife of Albert Kosier, of Byron. Mr. Shuart was again married, in Allegany county, New York, in 1888. His second union being with Miss Cynthia Londesberry, who was born, reared and educated in that state.

In political sentiment, Mr. Shuart is a pronounced Republican, casting his first presidential vote for Abraham Lincoln in 1860, and he has rendered his party effective service as a delegate to state and county conventions. Socially he is a member of Byron Lodge, F. & A. M., with which he has been officially connected for several years, and both he and his wife are members of the Eastern Star, in which she is serving as treasurer and Mr. Shuart as worthy patron. He is a courteous, affable gentleman, and, above all, wherever he is found, whether in public or private life, his integrity is above question and his honor above reproach. Byron owes much to him and numbers him among her valued citizens.

HON. FRANCIS BACON, one of the leading attorneys of Oregon, Illinois, is well known, not only throughout the county of Ogle, but throughout the state. He is a native of the city, and was born August 21, 1858, his parents being Captain Bowman W. and Almira M. (Robertson) Bacon. His father was a native of Huntington Mills, Luzerne county, Pennsylvania, born October 5, 1823, and came with his parents to Illinois in 1839, locating in Sterling, Whiteside county. His education, begun in the public schools of his native state, and continued in the schools of Sterling, was completed in Rock River Seminary, quite a noted institution in the early days, and which he entered in 1846. After completing his literary studies he went to Oregon, and entered the office of Henry A. Mix and commenced the study of law.

A strong union man, B. W. Bacon offered his services to his country in the hour of its peril, and on the 15th of August, 1862, entered the army, receiving a commission as captain of Company C, Seventy-fourth Illinois Volunteer Infantry. His regiment was assigned to the Army of the Cumberland under General Buell. With his regiment and company, Captain Bacon took part in the battle of Perryville, Kentucky, and was in various skirmishes in pursuit of Bragg. He was also in the battles of Stone River, Liberty Gap, and was in the Tullahoma expedition. Following this he was in the fight at Chickamauga, Mission Ridge, Buzzard Roost, Calhoun, Adairsville, Dallas, Lost Mountain, and the battle of Kensaw Mountain, in which he was severely wounded in the right and left arms, causing the amputation of the right arm July 12, and of the left a week later. Too weak to stand these operations he died July 21, at Nashville, Tennessee, with his devoted wife at his side. He was a brave and gallant officer, cool and self-possessed in the hottest of battle, and always at his post of duty. He was patient and cheerful throughout his severe sufferings to the end. For gallant and meritorious service a commission as colonel was sent him from the war department, but his death occurred before it was received.

Captain Bacon was married February 1, 1852, to Mrs. Almira M. Fuller, née Robertson, widow of William W. Fuller, in his day one of the most prominent attorneys of Oregon, and an uncle of Margaret Fuller. She was born in Ripley, Chautauqua county, New York, November 27, 1824, and came to Illinois in 1840 in company with her parents. In 1841 she entered Rock River Seminary, from which she was later graduated. She then became preceptress in that institution, a position she held until her marriage with Mr. Fuller, which took place March 3, 1847. Mr. Fuller died August 17, 1849. After the death of her husband, Mrs. Fuller lived in widowhood about two and a half years and then married Captain Bacon, with whom she spent twelve happy years. Partly to divert her mind and to be the better fitted to superintend the education of her only son, Francis, she entered the Illinois Normal University in 1866, from which she was graduated in 1870. She died in May, 1896, at Oregon, where she was held in high esteem for her mental attainments as well as for her estimable qualities as a Christian woman.

Francis Bacon, the subject of this sketch, grew to manhood in his native city, and after attending the public schools entered the Highland Military Academy, at Worcester, Massachusetts, from which he was graduated in June, 1877. He then took a regular law course in the Columbian Law School, Washington, District of Columbia, and was admitted to the district bar in April, 1879, being the youngest person admitted at that time, not yet having reached his twenty-first year. From the law school he graduated the following June. In January, 1880, he entered upon the practice of his profession at Oregon, and soon acquired a prominent position and recognition as an able attorney. In 1881 he was elected city attorney of Oregon, and re-elected in 1883, but later resigned. In 1887 he was elected mayor of Oregon, and re-elected in 1889. During his last term as mayor, the city was run and maintained, and various improvements made, without levying any city tax.

This was probably the only case of the kind in a city the size of Oregon.

Mr. Bacon was married at Dixon, Illinois, June 23, 1881, to Kizzie H. Kennedy, a daughter of William Kennedy, and niece of Mr. Oliver Ernest. Two children have been born to them—Francis Everett and Marion Eugene.

In addition to carrying on a very lucrative law practice, Mr. Bacon conducts a large stock farm of nearly four hundred acres near the city limits, giving it his personal superintendence. He makes a specialty of breeding Aberdeen-Angus cattle, in which he has been quite successful. He is also a large feeder, and ships annually several car loads of cattle. For some years he has taken considerable interest in military affairs, and is now captain of Company C, Sons of Veterans Regiment Illinois State Militia. The services of his company were offered to the general government during the war with Spain, but were not accepted, but the company was afterwards on duty at Virden, Illinois, during the coal strike of 1898.

Mr. Bacon has an established reputation as a trial lawyer, and is engaged in nearly all of the jury cases. Perhaps his greatest successes have been in criminal cases, and but two or three criminals defended by him have been committed to Joliet. While serving as mayor all indebtedness against the city was cancelled and many material improvements were made, among which was the extension of the city water works, and beneficial changes at the pumping station and in the fire department. The streets were carefully attended to, stone crossings being laid upon all the principal thoroughfares, and the streets of the city were lit by electricity. Mr. Bacon has always affiliated with the Republican party and his services have been in demand in the various campaigns in the discussion of the principles of the party. Mr. Bacon is a man of fine physique, with a corresponding heart, and either as a private citizen, in a professional capacity, or in his official duties, is one of the most approachable and genial of gentlemen, and well deserves the high honor bestowed upon him by his fellow citizens.

JOHN H. DAVIS, a retired farmer, residing on section 14, Buffalo township, one mile east of the city of Polo, has been a resident of Ogle county since 1864. He was born in Washington county, Maryland, May 18, 1846. His father, William Davis, was a native of the same county and state, born about 1824. He there married Margaret Rohrer, likewise of Washington county, Maryland, and they became the parents of five children, as follows: John H., the subject of this sketch; William, a farmer of Pine Creek township; Martha, wife of Hugh L. Henry, of Johnson county, Kansas; James, living in Buffalo township; and Mary L., wife of Columbus Sheeley, of Pine Creek township. The father died in 1856, a young man of thirty-two years, leaving a widow and five children. With true motherly devotion she determined to do the best she could by the fatherless ones. In 1864 she came with the family to Ogle county and made a permanent location in Pine Creek township, and there she still resides, making her home with her daughter.

The subject of this sketch was but ten years old when his father died, and but eighteen when he accompanied his mother to Ogle county. The oldest born, much depended upon him in the care and improvement of the farm, and his opportunities for obtaining an education were very limited. It may be said that he is almost wholly self-educated, the knowledge acquired being principally obtained in the school of experience. Soon after his coming to the county he bought an interest in a threshing machine, and for several seasons engaged in threshing grain for farmers throughout the county.

Mr. Davis was married in Pine Creek township in February, 1870, to Miss Maria C. Powell, also a native of Washington county, Maryland, but who came to Ogle county in childhood. In the public schools of this county she received the greater part of her education. She is a sister of Samuel C. Powell, a sketch of whom appears on another page of this work. By this union six children were born, two of whom are now living—Gertie B., a young lady, at home; and C. O., a student of Eureka College, of the class of 1899. The deceased are Carrie, who died at the age of five years; Anna, who died when eighteen years old; Ray, at eight months; and Minnie Lee, when about five months old.

After his marriage Mr. Davis rented a farm in Pine Creek township a few years, and then bought a farm of one hundred and sixty acres in the same township, on which he resided for twenty-seven years. In 1885 he purchased the farm where he now resides and which he rented until the spring of 1897. He then came to the place and has since made it his home, although he rents out the land and is practically living retired. Since coming to this farm he has built a good house and barn, and otherwise improved the place. He still owns the Pine Creek farm, and in addition has seventy-eight acres in another locality, and sixty-two acres in still another locality. Success has crowned his efforts, having commenced life almost empty-handed, but he has been industrious and persevering, and the result is seen in the property which he has accumulated and his well-tilled fields.

Politically Mr. Davis is a Republican, and he has been identified with that party since casting his first presidential vote for General Grant in 1868. From that time to the present he has supported every presidential nominee of the party. While residing in Pine Creek township, he served as road commissioner for several years, was a member of the board of supervisors two terms, and for years was a member of the school board. Both he and his family are members of the Pennsylvania Corners Christian church in Pine Creek township, and are earnest Christian people.

For thirty-five years Mr. Davis has been a resident of Ogle county, coming here in his early manhood. He has been an active factor in the development of the county, especially of Pine Creek township. Modest in his bearing, he has calmly gone on his way doing that which seemed to him best, and enjoying the respect and esteem of those with whom he was brought in contact. While still in his prime he has accumulated a competency and believes in enjoying life while he can.

LEWIS MORING is one of the progressive and enterprising farmers of Forreston township, where he owns a fine farm of one hundred and sixty-three acres on section 1, which has been transformed into one of the best and most desirable homesteads of the locality. The land has been brought to an excellent state of cultivation, and is embellished by a good and substantial set of farm buildings. A flourishing orchard serves to add to the comfortable appearance of the premises, and supplies the household with the luxuries of the season.

Mr. Moring was born in Forreston township, November 27, 1857, and is a son of Frederick Moring, who was born in Germany in 1811, and there married Dorothea Foshea, also of German birth. In 1848 they emigrated to America and joined some friends from their native land who had previously located in Ogle county. In Maryland township the father bought a tract of eighty acres, built a little house thereon, and continued the improvement and cultivation of the land for several years. He finally sold the place and came to Forreston township, where he purchased about six hundred acres in three different tracts. He located on section 18, when he opened up a farm of two hundred and forty acres, which he improved with good buildings. Upon that place he died January 19, 1889, and his wife passed away December 23, 1890, the remains of both being interred in the Prairie Dell cemetery. Lewis is the youngest in their family of eight children, three sons and five daughters, all of whom are still living and are heads of families. The others are Mrs. Dorothea Bower, of Ogle county; Mrs. Mary Timmer; Mrs. Louisa Dorman; Mrs. Lizzie Hodger; Frederick; Mrs. Ella Garles; and Henry.

Lewis Moring was reared in much the usual manner of farmer boys, attending school in winter, and assisting in the work of the farm during the summer months, and he remained with his father until he reached man's estate. He then rented a part of the farm, which he operated for a number of years. He was married in Forreston township, March 8, 1883, to Miss Caroline Zundahl, a native of Maryland township, Ogle county, and a daughter of Christopher Zundahl, one of the early settlers of the county. Nine children bless this union, namely: Lizzie, Alvin, Anna, Ida, Clara, Mabel, Esther, Ruth and Laura.

In the spring of 1883, Mr. Moring located upon his present farm, to the further development and improvement of which he has since devoted his energies with most gratifying results, converting it into one of the most desirable farms of the township. He has been a life-long Republican, casting his first vote for James A. Garfield, and he is now serving his third term as school director. He and his wife are active and prominent members of the Prairie Dell Presbyterian church, with which he is officially connected, serving as deacon, and both are workers in the Sunday school. Socially he is a member of Florence Lodge, M. W. A. He is well known in his part of the county as a man of exemplary habits, of upright character and sterling worth, and he and his estimable wife have the respect of the entire community.

PROF. JOHN G. ROYER, president of Mt. Morris College, has an excellent reputation as an educator, and is well known throughout the United States. He was born in Hartleton, Union county, Pennsylvania, April 22, 1838, and is the son of Jacob and Susan (Myers) Royer, both of whom were natives of Pennsylvania, the former born in October, 1797, and the latter in 1801. The paternal grandfather, John Royer, was born in Lancaster, Pennsylvania. He married Anna Grove, a native of the same state. He was a minister of the German Baptist church, preaching the gospel as the opportunity was afforded him, and also attending to the duties of his farm. Jacob Royer also engaged in agricultural pursuits, following that vocation during his entire life. He was an earnest and devoted member of the German Baptist church, of which body his wife was also a member. They were the parents of seven children. Isaac, born October 25, 1821, married Anna Shellenberger, and they became the parents of four children. Both are now deceased. Abraham, born October 11, 1824, married Sarah Kleckner, and three children blessed their union. He was a soldier in the One Hundred and Forty-eighth Pennsylvania Volunteer Infantry, and lost his life in the battle of Petersburg, in May, 1864. His widow is yet living in Wisconsin. Jacob, born October 17, 1827, married Elizabeth Strickler, and to them were born seven children. Both are living in Union county, Pennsylvania, where he is engaged in farming. Elizabeth, born October 17, 1829, married William Royer, and they also reside in Union county, Pennsylvania, where he is farming. Mary, born February 19, 1832, died April 18, 1858. John G., our subject, was next in order of birth. Samuel, born June 3, 1840, married Mary Mumert, and they have one child. They reside in Miami county, Ohio, where he is engaged in farming. The mother of these children died in August, 1868. In early life Jacob Royer was a Whig, but voted for Buchanan in 1856, on account of the fact that he was a former schoolmate of Buchanan. After that he voted the Republican ticket until his death, which occurred in April, 1876.

The subject of this sketch was reared on a farm, and received his primary education in the common schools. He later attended the academy at Mifflinsburg, Pennsylvania, but completed his literary course at Union Seminary, New Berlin, Pennsylvania. Before completing his education, however, he taught several terms of school, commencing at the age of sixteen years. He was but twenty years old when he left the seminary. He then determined to make teaching his life work, and in connection with the preaching of the gospel, has since engaged in that profession. Commencing in the graded schools of his native state, he taught for about five years, and then, at the age of twenty-five, went to Darke county, Ohio, and engaged in teaching in the graded schools until 1871, the last six years of which time he was principal of the schools at Webster and Versailles. In 1871 he went to Burnettsville, White county, Indiana, and for four years was principal of the high school at that place. He then accepted the superintendency of the high school at Monticello, Indiana, and was there eight years. From Monticello he came to Mt. Morris and was assigned the chair of English literature in Mt. Morris College. One year later he was elected president of the college, since which time it has been under his control. Since taking active charge the college has met with a fair degree of success and gained in popularity with the people.

On the 8th of December, 1860, Prof. Royer was united in marriage with Miss Lizzie Reiff, born November 30, 1838, a native of Union county, Pennsylvania, and a daughter of Christian H. and Susan (Titlow) Reiff, both of whom were natives of Pennsylvania. Both are now deceased, the latter dying in 1870, and the former in

1896 He was a manufacturer of agricultural machines, including threshers and hullers, being the inventor of a clover separator. They were the parents of ten children, of whom Mrs. Royer was sixth in order of birth. Religiously they were members of the German Baptist church. Politically he was first a Whig and then a Republican.

To Prof. and Mrs. Royer eight children were born. (1) Galen, born September 8, 1862, married Anna Miller, of Mt. Morris, and to them have been born five children— Bessie, Daniel, Catherine, Ruth and Anna. They reside in Mt. Morris, and he is secretary of the General Mission Board of the Brethren church. He is also connected with the Brethren Publishing Company. (2) Susan, born July 10, 1865, married Prof. E. S. Young, of Canton, Ohio, and they have five children—Katie, Vinna, Marguerite, Ida May and Paul. Prof Young is now president of Manchester College, North Manchester, Indiana. (3) Mary, born June 16, 1867, is at home. (4) Ida, born October 27, 1868, married J. M. Myers, and they have one child, Galena. They reside at Cando, North Dakota, where he is engaged in the mercantile business. (5) Nettie, born March 31, 1870, married J. A. Brubaker, and they have four children— Madge, Ralph, Bernice and Nellie. He is secretary and general manager of the Chain Stay Fence Company, of Sterling, Illinois. (6) Lillie, born November 18, 1872, is a teacher in the high school at Cando, North Dakota, and she owns one-half section of land near that place. (7) Josephine, born October 9, 1875, is also residing at Cando, North Dakota, where she is the owner of a quarter section of land. (8) Myrtle, born July 18, 1880, is a student in Mt. Morris College. All but Mary are graduates of Mt. Morris College. Galen is also a graduate of Juniata College, of Huntingdon, Pennsylvania.

Politically Prof. Royer is a Republican, but gives little time to political affairs, his college work commanding his entire time, except that given to ministerial labors. He is a logical and convincing speaker, a thorough student of the word of God, and a firm believer in the inspiration of the Bible. For forty years he has given his time to teaching the youth of the land, and his instruction has always been of a nature to make better citizens, to fit them not only for their proper station in this life, but prepare them for the life to come. The world is always the better for such men.

JAMES CAMPBELL, a retired farmer who now makes his home in Byron, Illinois, is of sturdy Scotch ancestry, and has inherited the traits of industry, thrift and economy peculiar to that people, that always bring to them success in their various occupations. He was born in the city of Forfar, near Dundee, Scotland, November 4, 1829, a son of John and Jane (Fairweather) Campbell, also natives of that country. The father, who was a tobacconist by trade, emigrated to the New World in 1831 and first settled in Philadelphia, but later removed to Miami county, Ohio. He sent for his family who joined him in Philadelphia. In Miami county, he first lived on a farm but later removed to the city of Piqua. In his family were five children, four sons and one daughter, all of whom reached years of maturity. In order of birth they were as follows: Robert and William, now deceased; James, our subject; David Angus, who was a soldier of the

Civil war and is now a resident of Pickaway, Ohio; and Ann, deceased.

The subject of this review was reared on a farm in his native land and had good common school advantages in early life. Coming to America in 1853, he joined his parents in Ohio, and remained with them a few years, assisting in the operation of the home farm. He was married in Miami county, August 22, 1860, to Miss Margaret A. Linn, a native of that county, and a daughter of William Linn, who removed from Pennsylvania to Ohio in an early day, settling in Pickaway about 1822. Mrs. Campbell was provided with excellent school privileges, supplementing the education acquired in the common schools by a course in the Troy high school and the Oxford Female College, and for six years she successfully engaged in teaching. By her marriage to our subject she has become the mother of seven children, namely: John, a resident of Storm Lake, Iowa; Jane A., wife of C. E. Johnson, who lives near Bridgewater, South Dakota; Margaret M., wife of Charles Bowie, of Tacoma, Washington; Mary G., a trained nurse of Chicago; Belle, wife of William Kelly, of Chicago; William L., a druggist and business man of Byron; and Elizabeth Ada, who is now a student in a business college in Rockford, Illinois.

After his marriage Mr. Campbell engaged in farming in Ohio for five years, but in 1865 came to Ogle county, Illinois, and purchased an improved farm of eighty acres in Byron township about five miles from the village of Byron. As his financial resources increased he added to the original purchase until he had two hundred and eighty acres of valuable land, on which he made many excellent improvements, including the erection of a pleasant residence and good barns and outbuildings. He successfully engaged in the operation of his farm until 1897, when he rented the place and removed to Byron, where he has since lived retired from active labor in a comfortable home of his own.

Politically Mr. Campbell has been identified with the Republican party since casting his first presidential vote for Abraham Lincoln in 1860, and he has been honored with a number of responsible positions in his township, being treasurer for the long period of twenty-six years, supervisor for four consecutive years, during which time he was a member of several important committees. He has also served as highway commissioner and a member of the board of education, besides being a delegate to a number of county conventions of his party. He and his wife are now connected with the Congregational church of Byron, and previously were for thirty-two years active and prominent members of the Middle Creek Presbyterian church. They are esteemed residents of Byron and taken an active interest in the welfare of the community, aiding all beneficial schemes tending to improve its moral, educational or social status.

JOHN BECK, a retired farmer living on section 33, Woosung township, is a well-known German farmer who has made a success in life. He was born in Hessen, Darmstadt, Germany, in 1822, and is the son of John and Elizabeth Beck, both natives of the same country. They were the parents of one son, our subject, and one daughter, Katherine, who is now deceased. The wife and mother dying, he was again married, and by the second union there were five children, of whom two are yet living—Leonard, on the old home farm in Tazewell county, Illinois, and Elizabeth, now the wife of Jacob Meyers, a retired farmer of Pekin, Illinois.

John Beck, Sr., was a shoemaker by trade, which occupation he followed in his native land. In 1832 he came to the United States and first located in Franklin county, Pennsylvania, where he remained until 1845, working at his trade. Saving some money, he came to Illinois and settled in Tazewell county, where he secured one hundred and sixty acres of land and spent the remainder of his life as a farmer. He died in 1881 at the age of eighty-five years.

The subject of this sketch was but ten years of age when he accompanied his father to the United States. In his native land he commenced to acquire an education in the parochial schools, but on coming to this country the opportunity was not given him to attend the public schools here but a comparatively short time. As soon as he was old and large enough he engaged in farm work in Pennsylvania, at which he continued until he was eighteen years old, when he took up the tanner's trade, at which he worked until he came to Illinois in 1856. Four years previous to his coming he had purchased eighty acres of land through the agency of his father in Tazewell county. On his arrival he settled on his farm and at once commenced its improvement. He there remained until 1867, when he sold the place and came to Ogle county and purchased his present farm in Woosung township, comprising two hundred acres.

Mr. Beck was married in Pennsylvania to Margaret Hanstein, and to them have been born five children: John F., who married Margaret Coon, of Frederick county, Maryland; William, who is in the west; Alfred, a prosperous farmer of Buffalo township, now residing in Polo; Clara, who remains at home with her father, and Amos, a farmer of Nemaha county, Kansas.

Mr. Beck has followed general farming, the raising of grain and stock, and is one of the highly esteemed citizens of the county. All that he has has been acquired by his own industry and good management. Commencing life a poor boy, working for small wages, he has persevered, toiling early and late, and success has come to him, and he is now enabled to lay aside business cares and take life easy during the remainder of his days. His good wife died in 1873.

ANDREW F. LONG, who resides on section 15, Lincoln township, owns and operates a fine farm of one hundred and sixty acres, two miles from Haldane. He has been a resident of the county since 1845, a period of fifty-four years, coming here a lad of eleven years. He was born near Hagerstown, Washington county, Maryland, June 20, 1834, and is the son of Rev. Jacob Long, a native of Washington county, Maryland, born in 1784, and who was the son of Isaac Long, a native of Pennsylvania, of German ancestry. Isaac Long removed from Franklin county, Pennsylvania, to Washington county, Maryland, at a very early day. Jacob Long grew to manhood in his native county and there married Catherine Friedley, a native of Franklin county, Pennsylvania, and daughter of Andrew Friedley, born in Pennsylvania of Swiss descent.

Jacob Long was a minister in the German Baptist church, but as a means of livelihood engaged in farming during his entire life. In 1845, in company with about a dozen families, he left his native state and came to Ogle county, Illinois, being about five weeks en route. He settled on the farm where our subject now lives, entering a tract of six hundred and forty acres, and at once commencing its improvement. He was very prosperous, being as industrious as the day was long. As a minister of the Brethren he established what is known as the west branch of the Brethren church, and during his life was very active in its work. He was a good man and accomplished much good in the community in which he lived. His death occurred February 17, 1868. His wife survived him some years, dying May 3, 1879, when nearly ninety years old. They were the parents of twelve children, ten of whom grew to mature years, and four yet surviving. Hannah is the wife of Daniel Singer, of Maryland Station, Ogle county. Samuel is a retired farmer of Gove county, Kansas. Rebecca is the widow of Jonathan Smith, of Pawnee county, Nebraska. Andrew F. is the subject of this review.

Andrew F. Long came with his parents to Ogle county, and on the home farm grew to manhood, in the meantime attending the common schools and assisting in the work of the farm. He remained with his parents until the father's death, when he succeeded to the home place. He was married in Lincoln township, February 26, 1857, to Miss Ann Maria Wallace, a native of Washington county, Maryland, and daughter of James Wallace, a native of the same county and state, who moved west with his family in 1845, settling in Lincoln township, where he opened up a farm and reared his family. By this union nine children have been born. Isadora died at the age of nine years and six months. Laura Alice grew to womanhood, married Hiram Goode, and after his decease she wedded Henry Davidson. She died in July, 1896, leaving four children, of whom one was by the first marriage, and three by the last one. The youngest born, Vinna P. Davidson, is now an inmate of our subject's home. Grace A. is the wife of B. F. Miller, of Wright county, Iowa. Cora Edna is the wife of D. H. Newcomer, a farmer of Mt. Morris township. Mary Esther is the wife of J. C. Muller, a carpenter by trade, but who owns a nice farm in Mt. Morris township. O. C. A. is a farmer in Lincoln township. Rosella L. P. is living at home. Arthur J., a well educated young man, is a successful teacher in his native county.

Mr. and Mrs. Long commenced their domestic life on the farm where they yet reside, and which has been their home for forty-two years, and his home for fifty-four years. They are well known, especially in the western part of the county, and by all who know them are held in the highest esteem. The only official position held by him has been in connection with the public schools, serving as a member of the school board and clerk of the same. His first political views were those held by the Whig party, the party with which his father was identified. He attained his majority at the time of the birth of the Republican party, to which he has since gave adhesion. Both he and his wife are earnest and devoted members of the west branch of the German Baptist church, and in the simple and Apostolic teachings have the utmost faith. As a citizen he has always endeavored to be true and loyal, doing his duty faithfully and well. In the development of the county he has done his part.

HENRY J. SCHRADER is one of Ogle county's honored sons and most active and progressive business men. Throughout his career of continued and far-reaching usefulness his duties have been performed with the greatest care, and business interests have been so managed as to win him the confidence of the public and the prosperity which should always attend honorable effort.

Mr. Schrader was born in Leaf River township, January 11, 1844, a son of William Schrader, who was born in Ohio in 1812, and came to Ogle county about 1842. He took up land in Leaf River township and developed a fine farm of one hundred and twenty acres, upon which he successfully engaged in agricultural pursuits until life's labors were ended, passing away in 1875. Here he married Mrs. Mary Myers, née Her, a native of Maryland, who came to this state with her father, David Her, a pioneer of Ogle county of 1837. She first married Peter Myers, by whom she had two children, and by the second union there were three children, of whom Henry J., our subject, is the eldest; Samuel is a farmer of Ogle county; and Sarah is the wife of William Beebe, also of this county. The children by the first marriage were Peter L. Myers, of Ogle county, and Hettie, wife of Wilson Hubble, both now deceased. The mother died some years before her second husband.

On the home farm Henry J. Schrader passed his boyhood and youth in much the usual manner of farmer boys, assisting in the labors of the fields during the summer season and attending the district schools during the winter months. He remained with his father and operated a part of the farm until twenty-four years of age. On the 13th of February, 1868, in Ogle county, was celebrated his marriage with Miss Tena Light, a daughter of John Light, whose sketch appears elsewhere in this work. Three children bless this union: Joseph, who died February 15, 1875, at the age of eighteen months; Mary, who was well educated in the schools of Leaf River and Mt. Morris, November 2, 1898, married Charles T. Schelling, of Leaf River; and Lewis M., a graduate of the Leaf River schools, also attended the United Brethren College at Huntington, Indiana, for one year, and is now learning telegraphy at Stillman Valley.

After his marriage Mr. Schrader located on a farm of one hundred and sixty acres near Egan, to the further improvement and cultivation of which he devoted his energies with marked success. He built a good residence, barn, granary, cribs and other outbuildings, and later bought another farm of one hundred and sixty acres in the same locality, making his home there for three or four years. He then bought seventy-seven acres on the northern line of the county in Leaf River township, and to-day owns three valuable farms aggregating four hundred acres, which he has placed under excellent cultivation. In March, 1889, he rented his farms and moved to the village of Leaf River, where he bought a lot and built a pleasant residence that is now his home. His time is now devoted to the management of his estate, and he is still one of the most active, energetic and enterprising men of the community.

Mr. Schrader cast his first presidential ballot for General U. S. Grant in 1868, and continued to affiliate with the Republican party for some years, but now gives his support to the men and measures of the Prohibition party, and is an earnest advocate of the cause of temperance. At the present time he is acceptably serving as a member of the town board, but has never been an aspirant for political honors. The family are members of the United Brethren church and hold an enviable position in the social circle of the community in which they make their home.

JAMES I. MASON, residing on section 22, Buffalo township, is one of the substantial farmers of Ogle county. He is a native of the county, and was born in Buffalo township, November 12, 1843. He traces his ancestry back to Sampson Mason, who was an officer in Cromwell's army, and who emigrated to America in 1650, locating in Massachusetts. James Mason, the grandfather of our subject, was a native of Rhode Island, and his son, Edward Mason, was a native of the same state, born November 12, 1810. The family emigrated to New York, settling in Cayuga county, when Edward was a lad of ten years. In that county James Mason engaged in agricultural pursuits and there spent the remainder of his life.

Edward Mason grew to manhood in Cayuga county, and received a limited education in its common schools. When he arrived at man's estate he determined to come west with a view of bettering his condition in life. In Milwaukee, Wisconsin, he was united in marriage with Miss Debra Van Wormer, a native of Onondaga county, New York, and daughter of Isaac Van Wormer, and immediately after he came with his bride to Ogle county and located in Buffalo Grove, where he had previously made a claim. This was in 1837, and he, therefore, became one of the pioneers of the county.

On making the county his permanent home, Edward Mason immediately commenced to improve his claim, and as soon as the land came into market he purchased the same from the government. He became a very prosperous farmer and opened up three different farms, among which was the one now occupied by our subject. On this farm he later located and spent the last years of his life. He died September 3, 1886, while his wife preceded him, passing away in October, 1881. Their remains were laid to rest in the Fairmont cemetery, where a neat monument has been erected to their memory.

James I. Mason is the only child living of Edward and Debra Mason. He grew to manhood on the home farm, and in the common schools received his primary education. He later entered Mt. Carroll Seminary, which he attended for a time, and then went to Aurora, completing his school life in Jennings Seminary, at that place. Choosing farming as his life calling, he remained with his father until the latter's death, when he succeeded to the old homestead, and has since been successfully engaged in general farming. In addition he has for about twenty years engaged in feeding and dealing in pure blood shorthorn cattle, and also a good grade of horses. In all that he has done he has met with a fair degree of success. His fine farm of three hundred and ten acres, lying two and a half miles southeast of Polo, is always kept under a high state of cultivation and always attractive to the eye. By birth and training a farmer, everything about the place gives evidence of the fact.

On national issues Mr. Mason always votes the Republican ticket, but on local issues, he votes for the man he considers the best qualified for the office. For himself he never cared for, nor would he accept any office. Born in Ogle county before it had taken any advanced steps in general progress, his growth has been cotemporaneous, and he has been an eye witness of nearly everything that has changed for the better, and he takes a just pride in the achievements of the past while having a lively hope for the future.

SOLOMON DAVIS, deceased, was one of the large number of persons to come to Ogle county from Washington county, Maryland, and who became the most substantial citizens, making of the county of their adoption one of the best in the great state of Illinois. He was born in Boonesborough, Washington county, Maryland, December 28, 1825, and in his native county grew to manhood and received a common-school education. In his youth he learned the trade of tailor, and followed that occupation for some years. He was the son of Edward and Mary (Smith) Davis, both of whom were natives of Pennsylvania.

On the 10th of August, 1848, our subject was united in marriage with Miss Rebecca Fletcher, daughter of Louis and Dela (Shafer) Fletcher, who were natives of Maryland, of which state she was also a native. In the fall of 1855 he came with his family to Ogle county, where he worked at his trade until 1861, when he opened a restaurant and grocery store in Mt. Morris, in which line he was fairly successful. He continued in that trade until his death, October 3, 1897. In politics he was a Democrat, and while a strong union man he did not enter the service in the Civil war, but had one brother, John Davis, killed at the battle of Gettysburg. His father and mother came to Ogle county in the same year that he made settlement, in 1855. The father served as postmaster of Mt. Morris for a time, as did our subject.

To Solomon and Rebecca Davis twelve children were born. Laura J., born July 22, 1849, married Thomas Avey, and they made their home in Mt. Morris. She died leaving two sons. Louis D. married Miss Ella White, and was living at Marshalltown, Iowa, when he met his death by accident. He left a wife and six children. Otho F. married Kittie McMullen, of Lincoln, Illinois, where they now reside, and where he follows his trade of carpentering. Anna F., born February 22, 1855, married December 28, 1873, James H. Depue, and they live in Chicago, where he is employed as car inspector. Mary D., born April 12, 1857, married Albert Lookabaugh, a blacksmith of Mt. Morris, where they now reside. Charles V., born August 27, 1858, died of paralysis at the age of twenty-nine years. He was a printer by trade. Eva C., born October 30, 1860, married Fred Petrie, and they live in Clinton, Iowa, where he is employed on the police force. Ida E., born October 31, 1862, died in childhood. Hattie M., born May 9, 1864, married James Miller, and they now reside in Clinton, Iowa, where he has a position with a wholesale drug house. Benjamin S., born May 24, 1866, married Annie Sharp, and they live in Washington, District of Columbia, where he has a position in the war department, a position that he has held since 1888. Seymour S., born May 29, 1868, married Elizabeth O'Leary, and they reside in Chicago, where he is engaged in the milk business. Florence R., is living at home.

Mrs. Davis has been a member of the Methodist Episcopal church since she was ten years old, and has always taken an active interest in the work of the church, endeavoring to do her full duty in the Master's service. She was born in Boonsborough, Washington county, Maryland, April 9, 1830. Of her seven brothers, two were killed in the war for the union, Robert being killed at the battle of Bull's Run, and Charles at the battle of Liberty Gap. Her parents also came to Mt. Morris in 1855, her father following the calling of an auctioneer. He served in the war of 1812, and the sword that he carried in that war is yet in the possession of Mrs. Davis. When the Masons of Mt. Morris have a gathering or a funeral to attend they borrow that sword, Mr. Fletcher having been a prominent Mason. He was also a member of the Odd Fellows and the Sons of Temperance. In the latter organization he was quite prominent, being a stanch temperance advocate. He was a member of the M. E. church for many years in Maryland and served as Sunday school superintendent for about thirty years, also served as magistrate in Maryland for a number of years. Politically he was a Whig. He died in Mt. Morris in 1857.

WILLIAM L. PALMER. The world instinctively pays deference to the man whose success has been worthily achieved, and who has fought his way unaided from an humble to an exalted position in the business and social world. Self-reliance, conscientiousness, energy, honesty—these are the traits of character which insure the highest emoluments and greatest success, and to these may be attributed the success that has crowned the efforts of Mr. Palmer. For many years he has been prominently identified with the business interests of Ogle county, carrying on operations as an agriculturist on section 17, Leaf River township, and as a merchant, grain dealer, etc., at Myrtle.

Like many of the most enterprising and progressive citizens of the county, Mr. Palmer is a native of Maryland, born in Washington county, October 22, 1832, and is a son of John and Elizabeth (Wetty) Palmer, who were born, reared and married in the same county. In 1847 the family started for Illinois by team, and finally arrived in Ogle county on the 2d of June, of that year. The father bought a farm in Mt. Morris township, opened up a claim, and continued its further improvement and cultivation until called from this life in the fall of 1865. His estimable wife died two years later. In their family were ten children, five sons and five daughters, of whom only four are now living.

Being a lad of thirteen years when he came to the county with his parents, William L. Palmer was of great assistance to his father in the development and improvement of the farm. After reaching man's estate he continued its operation for some years, but in 1864 removed to Leaf River township, where he bought four hundred acres, the only improvements on the same being an old house and frame barn. He has added to the original purchase until he now has five hundred acres of valuable land in

W. L. PALMER.

the home place, has erected thereon a commodious brick residence, a large and substantial barn with a basement, and other buildings, making it one of the best improved farms of the locality. Mr. Palmer has not confined his attention alone to agricultural pursuits, but has branched out into other lines of business. As the Great Western railroad runs through his land near his home, he secured the establishment of a station upon his place, and to it was given the name of Myrtle. He has been a most prominent and active factor in the growth and development of the village, built an elevator there, established a store and also a creamery. The first and last of these are carried on by a stock company, of which he is president and the largest shareholder. He erected the store building, donated a lot for the church, and in every possible way has advanced the interests of the village. Besides the property already mentioned he owns eighty acres of good timber land in Byron township.

On September 20, 1860, in Rockford, Illinois, Mr. Palmer married Delana Kate Hammond, who was also born and reared in Washington county, Maryland, and they have become the parents of eight children, of whom six are now living, namely: Alfred, who runs the elevator at Myrtle and is engaged in the grain and stock business at that place; Anna E., wife of David Rowe, a farmer of Leaf River township; Louisa, wife of W. H. Wagoner, of the same township; Ella, wife of Daniel Emory, of Byron township; Kate, wife of Alva Stine, of Leaf River township; Quimby, who is married and engaged in farming on the home place; Elson and Bertha May, both at home.

Mr. Palmer has been a life-long supporter of the Republican party, casting his first presidential ballot for John C. Fremont in 1856, and for every nominee of the party since that time. Being a warm friend of our public school system he has efficiently served as a member of the school board for a number of years, but has never cared for the honors or emoluments of political office, preferring to give his undivided attention to his extensive business interests. As a public spirited and enterprising citizen, however, he gives his support to all objects tending to advance the welfare of the community along any line, and is recognized as one of the most useful and valued residents of the county.

CLARK K. MATTESON, a representative and prominent farmer of Ogle county, owns and operates a fine farm of one hundred and forty-four acres on sections 21 and 22, Rockvale township. He was born in Green Island, Schenectady county, New York, September 29, 1836, and is descended from good old colonial stock. His parents, Spink and Tabitha (Waite) Matteson, were both natives of Rensselaer county, New York, the former born June 27, 1802, the latter April 18, 1797. The paternal grandparents, Moses and Amy (Matteson) Matteson, were both born in the town of Westerly, Rhode Island, but were not related prior to their marriage. The grandfather was a sleigh-maker by trade, but after his removal to Rensselaer county, New York, was engaged in farming. In his family were twelve children, of whom nine reached years of maturity, namely: Spink, Laura, Gorah, William, Abel, Almeron, Horatio and Daniel. Amy Matteson was a daughter of David and Sarah Matteson, who removed from Rhode Island to Rensselaer county, New York, in 1789, and settled in the town of Berlin. Their children were Lydia, Gideon, Ishmiel, Deborah, Titus, Job, Phebe, Sarah, Daniel and Amy.

Spink Matteson grew to manhood in Berlin and Petersburg, Rensselaer county, but never went to school only three days in his life, the teacher having struck him with a whip over the eye, producing a scar which he carried to his grave. At the age of twenty-two, he learned the blacksmith's trade, which he followed for three years, then followed market gardening for fifteen years, and subsequently engaged in general farming on rented land. He married Tabitha Waite, who was born April 18, 1797, a daughter of Peleg G. and Mary (Greene) Waite, the former born October 23, 1761, the latter March 24, 1766. Mrs. Waite was a niece of General Greene, of Revolutionary fame. She and her husband also removed from Rhode Island to Rensselaer county, New York, at an early day, going by way of the marked trees along the regular Indian trail. In their family were ten children, whose names and dates of birth were as follows: Greene, September 26, 1784; Clark G., April 3, 1787; Marcey, April 4, 1789; Thomas, May 1, 1791; Benjamin, April 27, 1793; Alice, July 6, 1795; Tabitha, April 18, 1797; Mary, April 30, 1799; Lois, December 8, 1801; and Laura, November 4, 1804. All reached years of maturity, and in their younger days were dressed in clothes spun and woven by the mother. The subject of this sketch is the older of the two children born to Spink and Tabitha (Waite) Matteson. The other, Harlow L. Matteson, was born in Petersburg, Rensselaer county, August 2, 1840, and is now living in Clark county, Illinois. He wedded Mary Etta Odell, who was born in the same place and died in 1879, leaving two children, Giles B. and Oren. Subsequently he married Henrietta Fager, of Forreston, Ogle county, Illinois, by whom he has three children: Laura Winnifred, Harrison Fager and Glenn Harlow. He owns a good farm of one hundred and sixty acres in Clark county.

Our subject spent the first twenty-two years of his life in the county of his nativity, attending school in winter until seventeen and assisting in the farm work during the summer. When fourteen his parents moved to the town of Petersburg, where he was sent to school. Under the old rate bill at that time those who paid the school tax on all taxable property were allowed to send their children to school during the winter, while those who refused were not. In the summer there was generally enough public money to carry on the schools without the special tax. After leaving school he worked at odd jobs of various kinds, but principally farming. At the age of twenty-two he went to Granville township, Washington county, New York, where he worked by the month for two years. There he was married and subsequently engaged in farming on rented land for eight years. Coming to Illinois in March, 1868, he purchased his present farm in Rockvale township, Ogle county, of E. J. Waite, of South Oregon, and here has since made his home while engaged in agricultural pursuits.

On the 20th of November, 1859, Mr. Matteson was united in marriage with Miss Sarah M. Northrup, who was born in Granville township, Washington county, New York, October 13, 1842, a daughter of John H. and Elvira (Eldred) Northrup, also natives of that place, the former born in 1813, the latter in 1828. The father, who was a farmer by occupation, was a son of Clark and Mary (Holmes) Northrup, natives of Londonderry, New Hampshire, and New York, respectively. Their children were Reynolds, Carr, Sarah, Mary, Penelope, Elizabeth, Annie, Emeline, John H. and Ephraim. Mrs. Matteson is the second in order of birth in a family of ten children, the others being Josephine, James C., Penelope H., Mary Elizabeth, Chloe E., Addie and Emma, twins, John Carr and William R. The father of these children died in June, 1894, at the age of eighty-one years, and the mother passed away in May, 1889, at the age of sixty-one.

Five children have been born to Mr. and Mrs. Matteson. John C., born in Granville, Washington county, New York, April 9, 1862, was married February 20, 1886, to Katherine Elizabeth Taylor, who was born in Racine county, Wisconsin, September 16, 1864, a daughter of T. D. and Mary (Kirkham) Taylor, natives of Massachusetts and England, respectively. To John C. Matteson and wife have been born five children: Charles Edward, born November 27, 1886, died at the age of three months; Clark Valentine, born February 14, 1888, and Mary Permelia, born June 3, 1890, are attending the district schools; John Dwight, born February 27, 1893, and Henry Albert, born May 31, 1896, are both at home. Charles Ferdinand, the second child of our subject, was born September 17, 1864, and died of measles March 21, 1877. The third died in infancy. Emma E., born October 25, 1869, died July 8, 1870. The fifth died in infancy.

In his political views Mr. Matteson is a pronounced Republican, and he has been honored with a number of important official positions in his township, being clerk for fourteen years, school treasurer nine years, school director a short time, road commissioner one term, pathmaster a number of years, and justice of the peace for the past seven years. His official duties are always most faithfully and conscientiously performed. Socially he belongs to Oregon Lodge, No. 420, F. & A. M., Rock River Chapter, No. 151, R. A. M., and Economy Camp, No. 131, M. W. A., in which he has passed through the various chairs. He has also been vice-president of the Old Settlers Association, and a member of the Republican county central committee. His estimable wife holds membership in the Methodist Episcopal church of Oregon.

Mr. Matteson can relate many interesting incidents of early pioneer days and of life in the east. He was in the midst of the Anti-Rent Indian troubles of Rensselaer county, New York. This land was owned by the heirs of Rensselaer, and they refused to sell any of the land to the settlers, preferring to rent at high rates. The settlers finally took the law into their own hands, and, dressed as Indians, they would harass and bother the collectors and agents, sometimes tarring and feathering them until they had secured their demands to be permitted to purchase the land upon which they lived. He also lived there when Millerism was at its height, when the people of that denomination tore down their churches, expecting Christ to come October 22, 1843. Mr. Matteson also has a very clear recollection of the old training days of the state militia. One company had a brass cannon, captured when General Burgoyne surrendered. His great-grandfather, Warren Matteson, was a gunner in the Revolution. Our subject has one of the first geographies published in the United States, containing only a map of New England. He still has in his possession Noah Webster's Third Reader, published in 1802; The Principles of the Government of the United States, by Pardon Davis, in 1823; an old campmeeting songster, 1836; a rhetoric reader, 1835; a Bible which belonged to his grandfather Waite, printed in Edinburg, Scotland, in 1791; and Bunyan's Holy War, printed by John Melcher, in 1794. Besides these cherished possessions he has a pewter platter, which his paternal grandmother owned, also a cup and saucer, soup tureen, neckerchiefs, and thread that she spun. He also has the Masonic apron and sash which belonged to his father over sixty years ago, and many other interesting relics relative to the early pioneer and Revolutionary days.

HARVEY M. SHOEMAKER.—The fine farm belonging to this gentleman on section 15, Eagle Point township, invariably attracts the eye of the passing traveler as being under the supervision of a thorough and skillful agriculturist, and a man of good business qualifications. He is one of the most extensive stock dealers and shippers in Ogle county, and always carries forward to successful completion whatever he undertakes. He was born November 27, 1839, on the farm where he still resides and has borne his part in the development and upbuilding of this region.

Pierson Shoemaker, the father of our subject, was born in Butler county, Ohio, January 16, 1800, and was a son of Michael and Elizabeth (Long) Shoemaker, the former of German, the latter of English descent. The great-grandfather of our subject on the paternal side was an early settler of New Jersey, where Michael Shoemaker was born, but at an early day the latter removed to Ohio and later to Indiana, becoming pioneers of both states. During his youth Pierson Shoemaker learned the carpenter's trade, which he followed in early life. In 1828 he removed to Union county, Indiana, and later to Sullivan county, that state, where he was married, November 20, 1833, to Miss Elizabeth Parker, who was born on the Blue Ridge mountains in Grayson county, Virginia, February 18, 1809. Her father, Lemuel Parker, was one of the first settlers of Sullivan county, Indiana, where he removed from Tennessee on horseback. Soon after his marriage, in 1833, Mr. Shoemaker came to Illinois, and after spending the winter in the vicinity of Peoria, in the spring of 1834, he took up his residence in Ogle county. At that time the country between his home and Galena and Dixon was almost an unbroken wilderness, and the Indians, who were still quite numerous here, stole his team of horses, leaving him only a yoke of oxen to break and improve his land. He was the first settler in his part of the country, and his nearest neighbor was a Mr. Kellogg, of Buffalo Grove, who located there in 1833. Mr. Shoemaker secured a claim of about three hundred and twenty acres in Eagle Point township, built a log house, and at once turned his attention to the improvement and cultivation of his land. He entered a half-section and when the land came into market he purchased it from the government. Later he built a commodious residence, hauling the pine lumber, doors and windows from Chicago, and all of his marketing in early days was done either in that city or Galena, it requiring fourteen days to make the round trip to Chicago. Although he came to the county empty-handed, he succeeded in accumulating a handsome property by his own labor, enterprise and good management. He was a successful farmer, a substantial and reliable citizen, and besides his farm owned good business property in Polo. From his farm, he removed to that place and erected the Orient House, which he successfully conducted for twenty-five years. He was one of the original members of the brick United Brethren church, which was located on his land, having deeded it to the church for their house of worship and cemetery. He was a consistent Christian and an active church worker. He died in Polo, July 3, 1890, at the age of eighty-two years, his wife October 19, 1892, at the age of eighty-three, and both were laid to rest in the brick Church cemetery, Eagle Point township, where a monument has been erected to their memory.

In their family were the following children who reached years of maturity: Elmer, deceased, was married and lived in Eagle Point; Mary wedded Dr. M. C. McPherson, who engaged in the practice of medicine in Eagle Point, but both are now deceased; Joseph died at the age of twenty-one years; Harvey M. is the next of the family; J. M. is a resident of California; Laura is the wife of Joel B. Buswell, of Elk Horn township; Sarah is a resident of Polo; Lemuel died in Florida, January 30, 1890; and Elizabeth is the wife of E. C. Williams, of Polo.

Amid pioneer scenes, Harvey M. Shoemaker passed his boyhood and youth on the old home farm and is mostly self-educated as his early school privileges were limited. He and his brothers helped to operate the farm, and after his father's removal to Polo, he took charge of the same,

which he later purchased. To its further improvement and cultivation he has since devoted his attention in connection with stock feeding and dealing. He feeds from one hundred to one hundred and eighty head of steers for the market and about two hundred head of hogs annually, and ships his own stock. So successful has he been in his life work, that he is now the owner of seven hundred acres in one body and improved with two sets of farm buildings.

In Stephenson county, Illinois, April 6, 1865, Mr. Shoemaker was united in marriage with Miss Marian P. Rowand, who was born, reared and educated in Ogle county. Her father, Andrew Rowand, was a native of Scotland, born near Paisley, and when a young man came to America in 1832, locating first in Canada, where he participated in the Rebellion. There he married Miss Elizabeth Losson, a Scotch lady, who came to the new world on the same vessel as her future husband. In the fall of 1838 they went to New York, and the following spring came to Ogle county, Illinois, Mr. Rowand buying land and developing a farm in Eagle Point township. There he passed away in the winter of 1887, and Mrs. Shoemaker's mother died in 1854. To our subject and his wife have been born three children: Andrew P., residing on the home farm with his father, married Nellie Smith, who died leaving one son, Harvey B. Elizabeth W. and Marian P. are also at home.

Since casting his first presidential vote for Abraham Lincoln, Mr. Shoemaker has been a stanch supporter of the Republican party, but has never cared for the honors or emoluments of public office, though he most efficiently served as highway commissioner for about fifteen years. His wife and daughters are members of the United Brethren church, and the family is one of prominence socially in their community. Mr. Shoemaker is widely and favorably known as an upright, reliable business man whose word is considered as good as his bond.

JOHN E. KINDELL, a most progressive and successful agriculturist, is the owner of a beautiful farm on section 11, Byron township, Ogle county. His methods of farm management show deep scientific knowledge combined with sound practical judgment that the results show that "high class" farming as an occupation can be made profitable as well as pleasant.

Mr. Kindell was born on the 15th of April, 1835, in Miami county, Ohio, and is a son of Joseph Kindell, who was born on Sherman creek, in Pennsylvania, and there grew to manhood. The grandfather, Joseph Hunter, was also a native of Pennsylvania and was one of the first settlers of Miami county, Ohio. The father, with two brothers, John and William Kindell, cleared farms in that county, and all became quite well-to-do. Joseph Kindell's place comprised three hundred and sixty acres of rich and arable land, and to its development and cultivation he devoted his energies until called to his final rest in 1851. In Miami county, he married Miss Martha Hunter, who was also a native of the Keystone state and removed to Ohio with her father. Eleven children blessed this union, seven sons and four daughters, of whom six sons and three daughters reached years of maturity. James, the eldest, was a soldier of the Civil war and after that struggle removed to Iowa, later to Kansas and finally settled in Arkansas. Rev. William was a minister of the United Brethren church, labored earnestly for its interests and died in Mercer county, Ohio. David was also a soldier of the Civil war and now resides in Iowa. John E., of this review, is the next of the family. Martha is the wife of William Manchester, a veteran of the Civil war residing in Iowa. Joseph is living in Lima, Ohio. Baxter is a farmer in Iowa. Alexander is a farmer in Ohio. Samuel also makes his home in Iowa. Mary E. died at the age of ten years. Priscilla died in Mercer county, Ohio.

On the home farm in Ohio, John E. Kindell passed his boyhood and youth and was given fair common-school advantages, attending school during the winter months and aiding in the farm work during the summer season. He was married in Pickaway, Miami county, Ohio, August 27, 1857, to Miss Jenet Stuart, who was born near Edinburg, Scotland, a daughter of James and Ellen (Simpson) Stewart, natives of the same country. Mrs. Kindell's paternal grandfather was quite wealthy and belonged to the nobility. The father was given good school privileges, being educated in Edinburg for the ministry, but after his marriage he located on a farm in his native land and devoted his attention to agricultural pursuits for a few years. In 1842 he emigrated to America and settled at Paris, Illinois, where he took up six hundred and forty acres and built thereon a large frame house and had it well furnished, but after residing there for about three years, he rented the place and located near Cincinnati, Ohio. Being in poor health he contemplated returning to Scotland, but died near Cincinnati. Mrs. Kindell, who was principally reared and educated in Ohio, was one of a family of six children, all born in

Scotland. Ellen Sprong, the eldest, is still a resident of Ohio. Elizabeth married a Mr. Zider, a noted educator, who died in St. Louis, Missouri. Mary is the wife of Thomas Plummer, of Braymer, Caldwell county, Missouri. John enlisted in an Ohio regiment during the Civil war and served for six months. In the fall of 1861 he came to Illinois with our subject and his wife and after being here for about a year he re-enlisted in Company C, Seventy-fourth Illinois Infantry. He was wounded at Spring Hill and Franklin, Tennessee, and died from the effects of the same.

Mr. and Mrs. Kindell have become the parents of eight children, namely: Walter, a railroad man, is married and resides in Farmland, Indiana; William L. married and located in Elgin, Illinois, where he worked in the watch factory, but died at home at the age of twenty-three years; Augustus E., who is now in the Klondike, is married and owns a place near Tacoma, Washington; John Stewart is married and engaged in farming in Byron township, Ogle county; Ida Jenette is the wife of Robert Hench, railroad agent at Kent, Stephenson county, Illinois; Rosa Florence is at home; Lillie is the wife of Frank Lowe, telegraph operator at Byron, on the Great Western railroad; and Mary Ellen, at home.

For two years after his marriage Mr. Kindell operated the old home farm in Ohio, but in the fall of 1861 we find him a resident of Ogle county, Illinois, where he rented land the first year. In the spring of 1862 he bought eighty acres, of which thirty-seven acres had been placed under cultivation, fenced and a little frame house erected thereon. To the further development and improvement of his place he at once turned his attention, and later added forty acres adjoining, making a good farm of one hundred and twenty acres, on which he has erected a large and well appointed house, also good barns and outbuildings, has set out forest and ornamental trees, and the neat and thrifty appearance of the place testifies to his careful supervision and his skill in his chosen calling.

The Republican party has always found in Mr. Kindell a stanch supporter of its principles, but he is not a politician in the sense of office seeking, his time and attention being wholly occupied by his business interest. He has, however, most efficiently and satisfactorily served as member of the school board for several years. He and his family hold membership in the Middle Creek Presbyterian church, and in the best social circles of the community they occupy an enviable position, while their many friends are always sure of a hearty welcome at their hospitable home.

JOHN H. PHILLIPS, an active and enterprising farmer residing on section 16, Lincoln township, is a native-born citizen of Ogle county, the date of his birth being April 13, 1852. His father, Jacob Phillips, was a native of Washington county, Maryland, born in 1822, while his grandfather, William Phillips, was a native of Pennsylvania, but who later settled in Maryland. They both came to Ogle county in 1844 and together entered three hundred and twenty acres of land on section 15, Lincoln township, and at once commenced the improvement of the tract, and in due time had as fine a farm as one would wish to see. The grandfather died some years after locating here. Jacob Phillips was married, November 25, 1847, to Miss Mary

E. Brantner, a native of Maryland, and who grew to womanhood in her native state. By this union there were six children that grew to mature years. Lucinda is now the wife of Jacob Waltermire, and they reside in Marshall county, Iowa. John H., of this review, is next in order of birth. George W. resides in Gage county, Nebraska, where hs is engaged in farming. Effie Irene is the wife of Elias Henshaw, of Hancock county, Iowa. Lewis A. resides in Brown county, Kansas. Samuel C. is living in Nebraska. On the old home place the father passed the last days of his life, his death occurring July 27, 1887. The mother yet resides on the old farm, enjoying the love of her children and many friends.

The subject of this sketch grew to manhood in his native township and was educated in the home schools. He remained with his father and assisted in the cultivation of the farm until the father's death. He later bought the interest of the other heirs and succeeded to the home farm, where he has since continued to live. He was married in Freeport, Illinois, February 21, 1883, to Miss Elizabeth C. McCoy, a native of Ogle county, Illinois, born, reared and educated in Mt. Morris, and a daughter of Walter Bond McCoy, a native of Washington county, Maryland, born in 1816, and who grew to manhood in his native county, and there married Mary Ann Huyett, a native of the same county and state. They moved to Ogle county in 1840, and settled in Mt. Morris township, where he engaged in farming, and where they reared their family. Later they moved to Eagle Point, where the father died March 30, 1879. His wife passed away in 1878. They had a family of eight children, seven of whom grew to mature years. Sarah J. is the wife of Abraham South, and they reside in Quitman, Nodaway county, Missouri. David is now residing with our subject. Mrs. Nancy Taylor is now living in Hardin county, Iowa. Archibald Franklin resides in Wright county, Iowa. The next living one is Mrs. Phillips, wife of our subject. Mary Ann married Walter Hedrick, but is now deceased. Edward died in California, and Charles in infancy.

Immediately after marriage, Mr. and Mrs. Phillips took up their residence on the farm where they yet reside, and on which he has made some substantial improvements, including the remodeling of the residence, and the erection of a large barn and various outbuildings. Two children have come to bless their union— Clarence O. and Sylvia N., both of whom are in attendance at the home school.

Politically Mr. Phillips is a stanch Republican, having given adhesion to that party since casting his first presidential vote for Rutherford B. Hayes, in 1876. He was elected and served six years as constable of Lincoln township. He has also served as director of his school district, and as a delegate to various conventions of his party. Fraternally he is a member of the camp of Modern Woodmen of America, at Haldane. Life-long residents of the county, Mr. and Mrs. Phillips take a lively interest in all that concerns its well being. Their friends are many and they are worthy of the esteem in which they are held.

ELMER E. BAER.—Like many other residents within the bounds of Ogle county who started out in life with naught but an abundance of determination and indefatigable industry, and who have succeeded through their own diligence, energy and economy, we classify the gentleman whose name stands at the head of this shetch. He was born in Berlin township, Somerset county, Pennsylvania, February 26, 1876, and the following April his parents removed to Carroll county, where our subject was reared. He attended the public school at Millidgeville, and at the age of thirteen proceeded to learn the printer's trade. When he was fourteen years old he ended his school days and devoted his entire time to his trade in the Free Press of Millidgeville. This required a period of four years, and at the expiration of that time he came to Rochelle where he worked from the fall of 1892 until the following spring. He then removed to Waterloo, Iowa, and shortly afterward returned to Illinois, and resided at Marseilles until August, 1893. The following year he spent in Millidgeville, Pennsylvania, and in August, 1894, he entered the office of the Register at Rochelle. At the breaking out of the Spanish-American war, the editor, G. W. Dicus, lieutenant of the militia, was called to Porto Rico, and Mr. Baer leased the business for the following year. Although it has been under his supervision but a few months, it already shows the result of his good judgment and management.

Mr. Baer is the youngest of three children, the eldest of whom died in infancy. The second child, Susie M., is the wife of A. L. Poffenberger, and resides at Kastota, Minnesota. The parents of this family are Jacob H. and Mary (Blough) Baer, both of Somerset county, Pennsylvania, who came west in 1876 and purchased a farm in Carroll county. Mr. Baer was actively engaged in the management of this property till 1885, when he retired from active business life. Six months previous to his death, which occurred in 1887, he was manager of a hotel in Millidgeville, in which town his wife still resides.

On the 3rd of October, 1898, our subject was united in marriage to Emma E. Beck, a daughter of John Beck. In politics our subject is a stalwart Republican, always giving his support to the principles of his party. He has never cared for position in public office, preferring to give his undivided attention to his business interests. He is a keen-sighted and honorable man of business, and possesses the confidence and respect of the community.

CYRUS NICODEMUS, an enterprising groceryman, has been an important factor in the business affairs of Polo for a number of years and his popularity is well deserved, as in him are embraced the characteristics of an unbending integrity, unabated energy and industry that never flags. He is a leading merchant of the city, and as a public-spirited citizen is thoroughly interested in whatever tends to promote the moral, intellectual and material welfare of the community.

A native of Pennsylvania, Mr. Nicodemus was born in Woodbury township, Bedford county, October 2, 1846, a son of Conrad Nicodemus and grandson of Jacob Nicodemus. The latter was a native of Maryland, and was a farmer and lumberman by occupation, owning and operating a sawmill. He died about 1856, at the age of sixty years, from the efforts of an injured leg, which was crushed by a timber falling upon it. His wife bore the maiden name of Susan Allebaugh.

Conrad Nicodemus was born in Bedford county, Pennsylvania, and came west in the fall of 1867 after his children had emigrated to the Mississippi valley. He followed farming in his native state and continued to engage in the same occupation during the nine years of his residence in Ogle county, Illinois. From here he moved to Iowa, where he lived until 1896, and it was there that his wife died December 12, 1881. In her maidenhood she was Sarah Hefley, a native of Blair county, Pennsylvania, born in 1819, and a daughter of Samuel Hefley, who was born in Maryland and died at the age of forty-nine years. In the spring of 1896, Mr. Nicodemus went to live with a daughter in Appleton, Minnesota, where he departed this life November 25, 1898, at the age of seventy-eight years. Politically he was a Democrat, and religiously a faithful and consistent member of the Methodist Episcopal church. In his family were eight children, of whom six are living, our subject being the third in order of birth, and with the exception of himself all reside either in Iowa or Minnesota.

The boyhood and youth of our subject were spent upon his father's farm in Woodbury township, Bedford county, Pennsylvania, until seventeen years of age, and during the winter months he pursued his studies in the district schools of the neighborhood. In February, 1865, he enlisted in the Ninety-ninth Pennsylvania Volunteer Infantry, and was mustered into the United States service at Chambersburg, Pennsylvania. The regiment was first sent to City Point, Virginia, and later took part in the battle of Hatchie's Run and the siege of Petersburg, and then went in pursuit of Lee's fleeing army, returning by way of Berksville to Richmond. For three days during this time they were without food. It required a twelve days' march from Richmond to Washington, District of Columbia, and at Bailey's Cross Roads they were reviewed by General Hancock. On reaching the capital they participated in the grand review, and then marched back to Arlington Heights, being finally mustered out at Philadelphia June 28, 1865.

Mr. Nicodemus returned to the old home in Woodbury township, and continued to work for his father for a year. On coming to Ogle county, Illinois, in September, 1866, he stopped first at the Pine Creek settlement, where he was employed by an uncle for eighteen months. On the 7th of November, 1867, he was married in Pine Creek township to Miss Sarah Stauffer, a daughter of John E. and Rebecca (Haight) Stauffer. Her father is a native of Pennsylvania, and is now a retired farmer living in Polo. She was born in Sandusky county, Ohio, but when a child was taken by her parents to Elkhart, Indiana, and in 1865 became a resident of Illinois.

After his marriage Mr. Nicodemus began working at the carpenter's trade. He also rented a farm, which he operated for six years, and then came to Polo, where he clerked in a grocery store for ten years. At the end of that time he embarked in the same business for himself, in partnership with Samuel Brenner, who later sold his interest to W. W. Kline, the firm remaining Nicodemus & Kline for seven years. They then sold out to Garman & Handshaw, and for the following seven months Mr. Nicodemus did nothing while looking around for a favorable opening. In company with Mr. Newcomer, he bought the store of Mr. Woolsey, which they conducted under the firm style of Nicodemus & Newcomer for four years, or until January, 1898, when our subject sold his interest to his partner. The following November he and Lester A. Brand purchased a stock of groceries and opened a store on Exchange street, where he is now greeting his old friends. He has met with a well-deserved success in his business undertakings, and besides his mercantile interests he now owns a fine quarter-section of land in Iowa. He and his wife attend the Methodist Episcopal church of Polo, and have the respect and esteem of all who know them. Socially he affiliates with the Independent Order of Odd Fellows, the Knights of the Globe and the Grand Army of the Republic, and politically is identified with the Democratic party.

HON. JAMES P. WILSON, ex-member of the general assembly of the state of Illinois, resides on section 10, Woosung township. He was born June 7, 1854, in Blair county, Pennsylvania, and is the son of Franklin and Susan (Dridenbaugh) Wilson, both of whom were also natives of the Keystone state. By occupation the father was a farmer, and in 1856, when our subject was but two years old, he came with his family to Illinois and located in Lee county. He later purchased land in Palmyra township, that county, which he improved, and where the remainder of his life was spent, dying there November 4, 1870. His wife is yet living, and now makes her home in Sterling, Illinois. In their family were five children, four of whom lived to maturity, and three yet living. Theodore met his death December 9, 1898, by falling from the tower of his windmill in Palmyra township, Lee county. Stewart is now living on the old homestead in Lee county. Mary F., widow of C. C. Fisk, is residing in Sterling, Illinois, with her aged mother. Rebecca died in childhood. James P., our subject, was the youngest of the family.

On the old homestead, in Lee county, Illinois, the subject of this sketch grew to manhood, and received his primary education in the public schools of his township. He subsequently attended the high school in Dixon, Illinois; and completed his school life in Knox College, Galesburg, Illinois, which he attended in 1872 3-4. Leaving school, he taught school in Woosung township for a time, and then, in partnership with his brother, Theodore, farmed in Lee county one year.

Mr. Wilson was married, February 8, 1877, to Miss Mary E. Rogers, of Palmyra, Lee county, Illinois, daughter of W. L. and Hannah (Fellows) Rogers, pioneers of Lee county. Her father, a native of Canada, settled in Lee county in 1839, while the Fellows family, who were of Puritan stock, from New Hampshire, settled in the same county in 1834. By this union were born two children—Franklin B., who was a graduate, with honors, of the Dixon High school, and who was also a student of Stienman Commercial College, of Dixon, and Jay P.

In the fall of 1876, Mr. Wilson purchased one hundred and sixty acres of land in Woosung township, comprising a portion of his present farm, and soon after his marriage moved to the place, making it his home to the present time. To his original purchase he has added eighty acres, giving him an excellent farm of two hundred and forty acres. Since coming into his possession, he has made many valuable improvements, keeping up with the times in every particular. While he has been successful, he has yet met with severe loss. On the 3d of October, 1896, his fine large barn, with its contents of hay, grain and machinery, was totally consumed by fire, entailing a loss of five thousand dollars. He has followed general farming and stock raising, and usually feeds from seventy-five to one hundred head of cattle per year. He endeavors to consume on the place all the grain and hay that he raises.

In politics Mr. Wilson is an ardent Democrat, a stanch advocate of the principles of the Democratic party. Since attaining his majority he has taken quite an active part in political affairs and has served almost continuously in some local office. In 1881 he was elected supervisor of the newly organized township of Woosung, and his election was contested by citizens of the old township of Buffalo, of which Woosung had formed a part. The contest was warmly pressed, but resulted in the recognition of the newly organized township, and confirmed the validity of the election of Mr. Wilson. In 1884 he was elected chairman of the board of supervisors, a position which he filled to the satisfaction of all concerned. In 1886 he was elected a member of the thirty-fifth general assembly of Illinois, re-elected in 1890 and again in 1892. During his term he took an active part in the contest between Palmer and Oglesby for the United States senate, and which resulted in the election of General Palmer. He introduced a valuable bill, which, however, failed of adoption, making railroad and warehouse commissioners elective, instead of appointive. The measure was carried in the house, but defeated in the senate. In 1891 he was chairman of the appropriation committee and of the revenue committee in 1893. He also served on various special committees, and was an influential member of the house. In educational matters he has always taken a commendable interest and for years served on the school board. While living in a Republican legislative district, he has always held the respect of his political opponents and usually polls a good Republican vote. In his home neighborhood his popularity has always been great.

JAMES M. CLAYTON is one of the many residents of Ogle county who started out in life with naught but an abundance of determination and indefatigable industry, and a strong and healthy constitution, and who have succeeded through their own diligence, energy and economy. He is now able in his declining years to lay aside all business cares and live retired at his pleasant home in Stillman Valley, where he is surrounded by all the comforts and many of the luxuries of life.

Mr. Clayton was born in Brimfield, Massachusetts, November 18, 1814, and when a young man, through the influence and solicitation of an older brother, made application to and had his name changed by a legislative enactment from Crouch to Clayton. His paternal grandfather was of German descent and a soldier in the American Revolution, while the father, Ephraim Crouch, who was born and reared in Vermont, took up arms against Great Britain in the war of 1812. When a young man the latter went to Massachusetts, where throughout the remainder of his life he engaged in farming and the butcher business. There he married a Miss Stebbens.

As his parents were in very limited circumstances, Mr. Clayton's educational privileges were limited, being able to attend school only a few months during the winter. His training at farm work was not so meager, however, and during his youth he worked on the farm of Colonel Brown and gave his wages to his father until he reached manhood. On the 2nd of April, 1837, in company with Colonel Brown, Hon. A. F. Brown and Samuel Patrick, he started for the Rock river valley, Illinois, going down the Hudson river from Hartford to New York city, by vessel to Philadelphia, by canal to Pittsburg, down the Ohio and up the Mississippi rivers to St. Louis, where changed boats and then proceeded up the Illinois river to Peoria, by team to the Rock river and by stage to Dixon. Mr. Clayton arrived in Ogle county May 2, and until the following August worked by the day at Byron. He next worked by the year for Joseph Sanford, and from that gentleman purchased a partially improved claim of one hundred and sixty acres, on which a log house had been constructed. His brother-in-law, Solomon Small, who arrived here in 1838, located upon the place, while our subject continued to work for others for a few years.

In the fall of 1841, in Byron, Mr. Clayton married Miss Harriet Norton, who was born and reared in New York, and was one of a family of ten children, five sons and five daughters. Her father, Rev. Isaac Norton, a Free Will Baptist minister, settled in this county in June, 1837. The young couple made their home in Byron until the spring of 1842, and when Mr. Clayton sold his first place and took a claim of one hundred and twenty acres adjoining the village of Stillman Valley, which he subsequently entered and still owns. After erecting a log house thereon, he moved in and began to break and improve his land. In 1868 he built a neat, substantial and commodious residence, and later erected two barns and other outbuildings, set out an orchard and a number of forest and ornamental trees, and transformed the wild tract into a beautiful and attractive farm. His financial resources having increased he purchased an adjoining farm of one hundred and fourteen acres, making in all two hundred and thirty-four acres of valuable and well improved land, which he successfully operated for forty years, but now leaves the active management of the farm to younger hands, while he spends his declining years in that ease and retirement which should always follow a long and useful career. He has lived in Stillman Valley since 1882 and there owns two good residences.

Mr. Clayton has been called upon to mourn the loss of his estimable wife, who passed away December 12, 1887. Of the seven children born to them, three are now deceased, two having died in childhood. Adelaide, the eldest, is the wife of Wallace Revell, a prominent business men of Stillman Valley, whose sketch appears elsewhere in this volume. Nellie is the widow of Rev. James Robertson, a minister of the United Brethren church, and she resides in Forreston, Illinois. George is a farmer residing in Stillman Valley. Edgar is also a farmer of Ogle county. Hattie is the wife of Eli Hoysington, a farmer and dairyman of Ogle county. Carrie is the wife of William Sovereign, formerly a business man of Stillman Valley, where he now resides. Lena died when a young lady; Delia Ann at the age of two years; and William H. at the age of three months.

Politically Mr. Clayton is a stanch Republican, having supported that party ever since its organization. He cast his first presidential vote for Martin Van Buren in 1836, and in 1840 supported Tippecanoe and Tyler, too. He has never sought or cared for official preferment, but when a young man once served as constable in Byron. He has ever used his influence to secure good schools and teachers, and for some years was a most efficient member of the school board. For sixty-one years he has watched with interest the wonderful changes that have taken place in this county, has borne an important part in its upbuilding and development, and his name should be among the foremost on its roll of honored pioneers. He is one of the charter members of the Stillman Valley Congregational church and his life has ever been such as to commend him to the office and respect of all with whom he has come in contact either in business or social life.

SAMUEL KNODLE, one of Forreston's esteemed representative citizens, was born in Washington county, Maryland, November 21, 1827, where he grew up and attended school in the district school in the neighborhood. In the spring of 1841 he came west with his parents to Illinois and settled in Mount Morris. The journey was a long and tedious one, coming as they did by wagon through Cumberland, Wheeling, Virginia, Zanesville, Ohio, Crawfordsville, Indiana, Attica, Indiana, and through Illinois by way of Ottawa, until they reached their destination, Mount Morris. Upon their arrival they found but a few settlers, among which were the Hitts, McCoys and Meyers. Samuel Knodle's father, Jonathan Knodle, was a native of Maryland and was born in 1795. His mother, Barbara (King) Knodle, was born in 1795 in Pennsylvania. His father was a successful mechanic, and in the early days, at Mount Morris, manufactured cradles and Hussey reapers, the first built in this country. He also had shipped to him, from the east, a printing press and brought his nephew, Emanuel Knodle, west to run it. He for a long time printed the Rock River Register, which was first published in 1841, and was the first publication in Ogle county. Jonathan Knodle for a period conducted a store in Mount Morris, but retired from active business life, and lived at ease until his death in 1854. Mrs. Knodle, the mother of our subject, died in 1882 at an advanced age and her remains lie in Mount Morris cemetery beside those of her husband. The subject of this review had five brothers and two sisters. Peter, now deceased, a resident of Mount Morris; Jacob, a wagonmaker and painter, residing at Mount Morris; Jonathan, a carpenter, deceased; Samuel, the subject of this sketch; Joseph, a carpenter residing at Oregon; Elizabeth, the widow of John Winders, William, a carpenter, living at Oregon; Mary Catherine died in infancy.

Such educational advantages as the primitive settlement offered Samuel Knodle secured and after his school days earned his living at farm work and teaming until 1850, when with a few companions he set out for the gold mines of California. The party consisted of Messrs Lott, Fink, Boner, Davis, Fonck and Samuel Knodle, all living in the neighborhood of Mount Morris. They set out on their long journey March 19, 1850, and by tedious travel over land arrived at their destination the following October. On their way they stopped sixteen days at Salt Lake City to rest up, and camped at Nevada City, when they set to work to dig for gold. Mr. Knodle spent eighteen years in mining and prospecting in

California, Arizona, British Columbia and Washington. His perilous life as a miner and mine-owner was terminated by an accident sustained in defending his camp from the hostile raids of the Apache Indians. In the struggle, four of a party of six were killed outright, the remaining two, of which Mr. Knodle was one, were severely injured, he losing the entire use of his right arm from a weapon in the hands of an Indian. After the accident he returned to Mount Morris, arriving there in 1868. He remained at Mount Morris one year, and in 1869 started a business in Forreston, which he has conducted ever since.

Mr. Knodle is a stanch Republican, and cast his first presidential ballot in 1852, for Winfield Scott. It is said that a child is unerring in its affections, and the truth of the saying is evinced in his popularity with the little folks, who greet him as "Uncle Sam." Mr. Knodle has witnessed the growth of Ogle county, having been a resident since before the era of railroads, when as a farm hand he was obliged to haul grain to Chicago, and Peru, and groceries from Savannah. He is a man of sterling qualities, of wide experience in human affairs, a persistent reader and deep thinker, and because of these qualifications, an entertaining companion.

DANIEL SIMS, Sr., one of the honored pioneers and highly esteemed citizens of Ogle county, has for the long period of sixty years successfully engaged in agricultural pursuits on section 12, Byron township, where he has a fine farm of one hundred and sixty acres, which he has developed from wild land. On coming to the county in 1838, the greater part of this region was still in its primitive condition, few settlements having been made and the land was raw and unimproved. He has borne an active and prominent part in transforming the unbroken wilderness into fine farms and assisted in opening up the country to civilization. His first crops he hauled to the Chicago market with an ox-team and as there were no good roads his team and wagon often got stuck in the mud.

Mr. Sims was born in Luzerne county, Pennsylvania, August 31, 1817, and is a son of John Sims, a native of the same county, who was a soldier of the war of 1812 and was stationed on Long Island. For his services in that struggle he received a land warrant. In Luzerne county he married Miss Catherine Hoover, a native of New Jersey, and in 1838 they emigrated to Ogle county, Illinois, where the father bought a claim of about eighty acres and opened up a farm in Byron township, making a number of improvements on the same and continuing its cultivation for some years. Here his wife died, but his death occurred in Iowa, where he made his home during his last days. Daniel is the oldest of their children, six sons and five daughters, all of whom grew to manhood and womanhood, but only three sons and two daughters are now living.

Daniel Sims was reared in Bradford county, Pennsylvania, and had but limited school privileges, so that he is mostly self-educated. During his youth he began working as a farm hand, and throughout life has devoted his energies to agricultural pursuits. On coming to Ogle county in 1838 he entered eighty acres of government land on section 12, Byron township, and later purchased an adjoining tract of eighty acres, which he has converted into a highly cultivated and well improved farm. His first home, which was a little log cabin, has long since been replaced by a comfortable frame residence and good and substantial outbuildings have also been erected.

Mr. Sims was married in Ogle county, in 1845, to Miss Christina Bunton, a native of Dundee, Scotland, where she continued to make her home until eighteen years of age. Eleven children were born of this union, but only the following are now living: Mrs. Mary Ferguson, a widow living in Iowa, Henry, a resident of Nebraska; David and Albert, also of Nebraska, Jessie, wife of James Turner, of Byron township, Ogle county, and Daniel living in Iowa; Ella grew to womanhood and married, but is now deceased; while the others died in childhood.

Originally Mr. Sims was an old-line Whig in politics, casting his first vote for William Henry Harrison in 1840, but since the organization of the Republican party he has been one of its stalwart supporters. Religiously he and his wife are consistent members of the Middle Creek Presbyterian church, and by all who know them they are held in high regard.

GEORGE MURRAY.—Canada has furnished to the United States many bright, enterprising young men who have left the Dominion to enter the business circles of this country with its more progressive methods, livelier competition, and advancement more quickly secured. Among this number is Mr. Murray, one of the most enterprising and progressive farmers and stock breeders of Ogle county, his home being on section 17, Buffalo township.

Mr. Murray was born near Toronto, Ontario, Canada, November 15, 1850, and is a son of Thomas Murray, a native of Scotland, born in the city of Edinburg, September 26, 1818. When a young man the father came to the new world, locating in Ontario, Canada, in 1836, and there he followed the blacksmith's trade throughout the remainder of his life, dying January 17, 1866. He was married in Canada, in March, 1848, to Miss Louisa Graham, also a native of Scotland, her birth occurring in Dumfrieshire, June 28, 1826. She crossed the Atlantic with a brother and also took up her residence in Ontario. She survived her husband for thirty years, spending her last days with her son in Illinois, where she passed away January 27, 1896. She was the mother of eight children, five sons and three daughters, of whom four sons and two daughters are still living, namely: Mary, who acts as housekeeper for our subject; George, of this review; Thomas, a farmer of Holcomb, Ogle county; John, who is married and engaged in farming in Lee county, Illinois; Robert; and Mrs. Margaret Copenhaver, who also resides with our subject and has two sons, George and Robert.

George Murray was reared in Ontario, Canada, and received a good common-school education, which well fitted him for life's responsible duties. As a young man he came to Illinois, in 1872, and took up his residence in Taylor township, Ogle county, where for one year he worked by the month as a farm hand. He then rented a farm, which he operated for the same length of time. Since then he has given the greater part of his time and attention to the breeding of fine stock, in partnership with his brother importing and dealing in pure-blooded Percheron, Clydesdale and French coach horses. The firm of Murray Brothers became well-known

JOHN H. NYE.

among breeders and dealers in different states and they sold their horses quite extensively throughout the west, doing a large and profitable business. The partnership was dissolved in 1886, but our subject continued to engage in the business until 1893. His first purchase of land consisted of seventy-five acres in what is now Woosung township, but after residing there for three years, he sold the place and in 1881 located upon his present farm, consisting at that time of one hundred and eighty-two acres. Upon the place he has made extensive improvements, which add greatly to its value and attractive appearance, making it one of the most desirable farms of the locality. He has enlarged its boundaries so that they now contain two hundred acres of valuable land under a high state of cultivation and improved with a large neat residence, corn cribs, granaries, barns, etc. He has also given considerable attention to the raising of Galloway cattle, and still feeds annually from one to four car loads of cattle and a car load of hogs for the market. He started out in life for himself with nothing but his own indomitable energy and through his own efforts has acquired a comfortable competence, being to-day one of the substantial men of the county.

Mr. Murray cast his first presidential vote for Grover Cleveland and continued to affiliate with the Democracy until 1896, when he supported William McKinley, the Republican candidate. For a number of years he has served as a member of the school board and has been president of the district. He is also connected with the library association and has served as one of its trustees and directors. He and his sisters hold membership in the Independent Presbyterian church of Polo, and he is also a member of the Knights of the Globe. He is held in high regard by all who know him, and he has a host of warm friends throughout the county.

JOHN H. NYE, deceased, was for many years a well known and highly esteemed citizen of Ogle county. He was a native of England, born near Dover, and was the son of James and Harriet Nye, both of whom were natives of the same country, the father there spending his entire life. He was a pipemaker by trade. After the death of her husband, his widow came to the United States, afterwards marrying a Mr. Marsh, her husband being a farmer in Lincoln township, Ogle county, where her death occurred in 1876, when about seventy-eight years old.

John H. Nye received his education in the common schools of his native land. At the age of nineteen he came to the United States, landing in New York, where he spent the succeeding three years learning the carpenter's trade, apprenticing himself to a Mr. Beebe. He then came to Ogle county and located in Mt. Morris. This was in 1853. His first work here was for Mr. Marston, who had the contract for the carpentry work on the seminary, then in course of construction. After leaving Mr. Marston he engaged in business for himself, locating just southeast of the village. He continued contracting and building until 1860, when he commenced farming in Mt. Morris township, on a farm the property of his wife, comprising two hundred and twenty acres. He later purchased a farm of one hundred and sixty acres in Lincoln township, which he rented, while still continuing to remain upon the farm in Mt. Morris township. In

1867 he left the farm with his family and removing to Mt. Morris he lived a retired life until 1882.

On the 2d of October, 1860, Mr. Nye was united in marriage with Miss Catherine Coffman, born in Washington county, Maryland, July 24, 1820, and daughter of James and Anna (Palmar) Coffman, natives of Pennsylvania. By occupation he was a farmer. In 1840 he came to Ogle county and located in Pine Creek township. With his family he came through by team, in a large wagon, usually called a "prairie schooner." They passed through Virginia, Ohio and Indiana, and were six weeks en route, although they stopped some two weeks near Dayton, Ohio. The greater portion of the land was yet owned by the government, and believing there was a great future for the country, Mr. Coffman purchased six quarter-sections in Ogle county, and nearly as much in Sangamon county, paying the government price of one dollar and twenty-five cents per acre. This land he at once commenced to improve, and in 1842 built a small brick house for occupancy, brick being more easily obtained than lumber, as there was a brick-yard within six miles, while lumber had to be hauled from Chicago. The previous year, however, he erected a gristmill on Pine creek. On settling here their nearest neighbor was three miles away and their market was Chicago. On the present site of Mt. Morris there was but one solitary building, afterwards known as the old seminary building. This building remained until a few years ago.

James and Anna Coffman were the parents of eight children. Edward married Catherine Price, and they became the parents of ten children. They lived in Pine Creek township, where he died in 1889. By occupation he was a farmer. Catherine, widow of our subject, was next in order of birth. Barbara married Daniel Sprecher and to them were born eleven children. They are both deceased. Aaron died in California in 1894. He was prospector. Sarah married David Fearer, who is now deceased. She is the mother of six children and now resides in Kansas. Susan married John Widney, and to them were born three children. They are living in Ohio, where he is farming. David married Susan DePue, by whom he had two children. He died many years ago. James Coffman, the father, was not permitted to live to see the great changes that have since taken place in Ogle county, his death occurring in April, 1847, while yet in the prime of life. His wife survived him several years. Both were highly esteemed, and their death was a sad loss to the new country in which they had cast their lot.

To our subject and wife two children were born. Frank Coffman, born November 21, 1861, was a young man of more than ordinary ability, a graduate of Mt. Morris College. He died in Dakota, June 3, 1886, greatly lamented by a large circle of friends. Ulysses, born April 12, 1864, married Ella Green, of Chicago, who died in California in 1896. He received his literary education in Mt. Morris College, and is a graduate of the Chicago Musical College. He is a teacher of music of marked ability. At present he is employed in the postoffice at Mt. Morris. Our subject first married Miss Maria Beebe, by whom he had four children—Sarah, Harriet, Emma and Anna.

In November, 1882, Mr. Nye moved with his family to Beadle county, South

Dakota, and entered a homestead of one hundred and sixty acres, and a tree claim of one hundred and sixty acres. In 1893 they left Dakota and returning to Illinois, located in Maywood, a suburb of Chicago, where they remained until January, 1896, when they went to Los Angeles, California. In that beautiful city, on the 28th of February, 1898, Mr. Nye passed to his reward. He was a devout member of the Methodist Episcopal church, and died in the hope of the resurrection. Fraternally he was a Mason, and politically a Republican.

A few weeks after the death of her husband, Mrs. Nye left Los Angeles, and after visiting relatives in Douglas county, Kansas, in April, following, returned to her old home in Mt. Morris, where she is surrounded by many of her old friends, and where she can make the most of this life. Like her husband, she is a consistent member of the Methodist Episcopal church, a true Christian woman.

ORLO W. NORTON.— When after years of long and earnest labor in some honorable field of business, a man puts aside all cares to spend his remaining years in the enjoyment of the fruits of his former toil, it is certainly a well deserved reward of his industry.

"How blest is he who crowns in shades like these
A youth of labor with an age of ease,"
wrote the poet, and the world everywhere recognizes the justice of a season of rest following an active period of business. Mr. Norton spent his last years living retired at his pleasant home in Stillman Valley and his history is one that shows the accomplishment of well directed labor.

He was born in Genesee county, New York, June 18, 1825, and was of a family of English extraction which was founded in Massachusetts as early as 1640. His grandfather, Henry Norton, was born in Guilford, Connecticut, in 1753, and was one of the heroes of the Revolutionary war who participated in the battle of Lexington, where the colonial troops won their first victory. Gould G. Norton, the father of our subject, was born in Vermont, in 1800, and was the youngest in a family of six children, five sons and one daughter. In 1805 the family removed to Essex county, New York, and in 1816 settled in Genesee county, that state, where Gould G. Norton grew to manhood and married Mary Hyde, a native of the Empire state, whither her father, Jesse Hyde, had removed from Vermont at an early day. Her grandfather was Captain Thomas Hyde, of Norwich, Connecticut, who held a captain's commission in the Revolutionary war.

The father of our subject successfully engaged in merchandising and also in farming in Genesee county, New York, until 1830, when he removed to Orleans county, that same state, but seven years later returned to the former county, locating in the part which afterward became Wyoming county. In 1846 he came west and settled in Hartland, Waukesha county, Wisconsin, where he resided for two years while traveling for a mercantile house. At the end of that time he brought his family to Ogle county, Illinois, and entered on hundred and sixty acres of land in Scott township, where he developed a good farm. On their arrival here of most the land was still in its primitive condition, deer and other wild game was plentiful, and the few settlers were widely scattered, their nearest neighbor on the east being nine miles distant. The father erected a stone house which is still standing and to the improvement and cultivation of his land at once turned his attention. Here he spent the remainder of his life, dying June 22, 1886, at the ripe old age of eighty-six years. His worthy wife passed away in April, 1877. He was one of the most prominent and influential citizens of his community, was a friend of education and a stanch supporter of our public schools. He was a self-educated as well as a self-made man, but by hard study and close application he fitted himself for a teacher and successfully followed that profession for a number of terms. He was supervisor of his township ten years, and township trustee for a number of years.

Orlo W. Norton was the oldest in a family of five children, three sons and two daughters, all of whom reached years of maturity. Emma C. married Hon. O. B. Young, of Stillman Valley. Mary E. B., a resident of Oakland, California, is a lady of superior education and excellent business ability. She taught for twenty-five years in the Rockford, Illinois, Seminary, and the State Normal of California, and is now secretary of the Social Settlement in West Oakland. Henry B. was educated at the Illinois State Normal and was also a teacher by profession, being employed in the State Normal at Emporia, Kansas, for five years. As his health failed he spent two years among the Indians and then went to California, where he followed his chosen profession for a time. He was an ordained minister of the Congregational church, and often lectured on scientific subjects. His death occurred June 22, 1885. Gould Hyde Norton, now a resident of Eustis, Florida, was also engaged at the Illinois State Normal, and in 1861 enlisted as lieutenant in the Thirty-third Illinois Volunteer Infantry, which was largely composed of teachers and pupils belonging to that school and was commanded by the president, Colonel Hovey. Mr. Norton was wounded by a ball in the breast at the battle of Vicksburg, and being unfit for further duty he was discharged with the rank of captain. Later he moved to Vicksburg and served as captain of police in that city. He was the first man to build a house at Arkansas City, Kansas, where he traded with the Indians on Buffalo range for three years. Later he was colonel of the First Kansas Cavalry and participated in the Indian wars on the frontier. In 1876 he removed to Florida and has since engaged in the nursery and orange-growing business. He is a prominent member of the Grand Army of the Republic and at one time was in command of the department of Florida. He had a family of five children, four sons and one daughter, of whom three sons were in the Cuban war and one was killed when fighting with Colonel Roosevelt's rough riders.

Reared in New York, Orlo W. Norton obtained a good practical education in the common schools of his locality and the high school of Varysburg, and in early life successfully engaged in teaching in that state. In 1845 he accompanied his father on his removal to Waukesha county, Wisconsin, and three years later became a resident of Ogle county, Illinois. He opened up a farm in Scott township on the opposite side of the road from his father's place, and there successfully engaged in agricultural pursuits for forty-five years, being recognized as one of the most industrious and enterprising farmers of the locality.

On the 25th of January, 1853, Mr. Norton was united in marriage with Miss Margaret Lanckton, who was born, reared and educated in Genesee county, New York, and engaged in teaching in that state and in Illinois prior to her marriage. Her father was Aaron Lanckton, of Wheatville, New York. She died in 1862, leaving three children, namely: Ada C., now the wife of Malcolmb D. Norton, of Eustis, Florida; Mary L., wife of Charles H. Tallmage, of Columbus, Ohio; and Charles H., who died unmarried in Dakota, in 1886, at the age of twenty-four years. Mr. Norton was again married at Laporte, Indiana, September 21, 1863, his second union being with Mrs. Elmira L. Carruth, widow of Amos Carruth, and daughter of Frederick Palmer, who moved to Michigan at an early day. She is also a native of Genesee county, New York, and was there reared. By the second marriage there are three children: Harriet M. is the wife of Elmer Johnston of Des Moines, Iowa; Arthur A. completed the regular course and graduated from Harvard University with the degree of A. B. in 1898, and after taking the post-graduate course at that famous institution of learning, had the title B. S. conferred upon him, and Edna R. is the wife of Harvey Watson, of Normal, Illinois.

In 1893 Mr. Norton rented his farm and removed to Stillman Valley, where he purchased a cottage. Politically he first affiliated with the Free Soil party, but was a Republican from the organization of that party. His first vote was for Martin Van Buren, and in 1856 for John C. Fremont. He took an active and prominent part in public affairs, especially along the lines of education, and for years was a member of the school board. He also served as township clerk eight years, justice of the peace the same length of time and supervisor two years, his labors in behalf of his fellow citizens giving the utmost satisfaction. He with his wife held membership in the Congregational church and stood high in social circles of the community. Those who knew him best numbered him among their warmest friends, and no citizen in Stillman Valley was more honored nor highly respected. Mr. Norton died October 31, 1898.

JACOB KAPPMAN.—It is said that biography yields to no other subject in point of interest and profit, and it is especially interesting to note the progress that has been made along various lines of business by those of foreign birth who have sought homes in America—the readiness with which they adapt themselves to the different methods and customs of America, recognize the advantages offered and utilize the opportunities which the new world affords. Such a man is Mr. Kappman, who is now one of the wealthiest and most prosperous farmers of Ogle county, his home being on section 20, Leaf River township.

He was born in Hohenzollern, Prussia, February 29, 1828, and was there reared to manhood, but is self-educated in German as well as in the English language. Before leaving the fatherland he was married, in 1856, to Miss Mary Schetter, who was also of German birth. In his native land he continued to carry on farming until 1858, when he crossed the Atlantic and came direct to Illinois, joining his brother, John Kappman, who had located here a few years before, but later removed to South Dakota. Our subject arrived in Ogle county in October, 1858, and at first rented land, which he operated for one year. He then purchased a tract of forty acres, on which he now resides. The land had been broken, but no building erected, and his first home here was a small house which he erected. To the further improvement and cultivation of the land he devoted his entire time and attention, but for a few years it was a hard struggle to support himself and family. As his financial resources have increased, however, he has bought more land from time to time, until he now owns seven hundred and forty-seven acres. His home farm, comprising two hundred and forty acres, is improved with a commodious and comfortable residence, supplied with luxuries. Good barns and outbuildings have also been erected, and the place is now one of the most desirable in the locality.

Mr. and Mrs. Kappman have a family of seven children, four sons and three daughters, namely: Adolph, who is married and engaged in farming in Leaf River township; Christian, at home; Joseph, who is married and also carries on operations as an agriculturist in Leaf River township, and William, who assists his brother Christian in the operation of the home farm; Mary, wife of William Betz, of Winnebago county, Illinois; Susan and Anna, both at home.

In his political views Mr. Kappman is a strong Republican, and cast his first presidential vote for Abraham Lincoln in 1860. He served as school director in his district for several years, but has never cared for official honors. In religious faith he and his wife are devout Catholics, and helped to build the church of that denomination at Seward. He is now the possessor of a handsome property which now enables him to spend his declining years in the pleasurable enjoyment of his accumulations. He came to this country in limited circumstances, and with no capital started out in a strange land to overcome the difficulties and obstacles in the path to prosperity. His youth dreams have been more than realized, and in their happy fulfillment he sees the fitting reward of his earnest toil.

JAMES H. MAGNE, of Haldane, has spent more than a half century of his life in Ogle county. He was born in Rochester, New York, March 30, 1835, and is a son of Charles Magne, a native of Connecticut. The family are of French extraction, the first of the name settling in Connecticut in a very early day, and there Charles Magne, Sr., the grandfather of our subject, was born. He later removed to New York and settled near the city of Rochester. During the second war with Great Britain he served his country faithfully, and was wounded at the battle of Queenstown Heights. His death occurred in 1835.

Charles Magne, the father of our subject, grew to manhood in New York, but returned to Connecticut and there married Mary A. L. Noble, a native of that state. He was a ship carpenter by trade, and soon after his marriage moved to New York city, where he was employed at his trade. In 1847 he came west with his family and located at Buffalo Grove, Ogle county, where he remained two years engaged in carpentry work and in farming. He then moved to what is now Lincoln township, bought one hundred and sixty acres of land near the present village of Haldane and opened up a farm. He later added eighty acres to his tract, giving him a fine farm of two hundred and forty acres, which he improved. He there spent the last years of his life, dying in February, 1857, at the age of forty-eight years. His wife survived him and reared the family, passing to her reward in 1895, at the age of eighty-two years. They had a family of three sons and three daughters, who grew to mature years, our subject being the eldest. The others were Charles A., living retired in Haldane; Lucretia E. Mantle, of Brookville township; Horace, living retired in Polo; Abalena, who died a single lady; and Adaline, now deceased, who married Gavin R. Cross, of Ogle county.

James H. Magne came to Ogle county with his parents when a lad of thirteen years and here grew to manhood, assisting his father in opening up and operating the home farm. Before leaving his native state he secured a fair education in the common schools, but the greater part of his knowledge has been obtained since attaining his majority by reading and observation. After his father's death he remained with his mother and carried on the farm, and cared for her in her declining years. He later sold his interest in the farm to the other heirs and then purchased a farm of eighty acres between Maryland and Haldane, to which he removed and further improved the place. He remained on that farm until his removal to the village of Haldane, in 1894. While on the farm he was engaged to some extent in buying and selling stock for a few years. Purchasing residence property in Haldane, he rebuilt and remodeled the house and now has a very neat and comfortable home.

Mr. Magne returned east, and, in Clinton county, Pennsylvania, January 27, 1881, married Miss Emma J. Wilson, a native of that county and state, where she was reared and educated. She is the daughter of Joseph B. Wilson, a stonemason by trade and a native of Pennsylvania. He is now deceased, but his widow is now living with Mrs. Magne. By this union there was one child, Linus E., a student of the home school.

Politically Mr. Magne is a Prohibitionist, but was originally a Democrat, casting his first presidential vote for James Buchanan, in 1856. From the fact that he considers the liquor traffic the worst foe to society, he has given his adhesion to the Prohibition party, the only party that is fighting the gigantic evil. By casting his vote with that party he believes that he is at least registering his will, and that the party is exercising an educational influence. Mrs. Magne is a member of the Evangelical church of Haldane. When he came to Ogle county there was little to give promise of the great future before this section of the country. There was not a railroad in the state, and very few towns of any importance. Farm houses were few and far between, and the whole country was almost in its virgin state. He has lived to see a change that the most optimistic person could not have conceived, and while his part may have been a humble one he has done what he could in the change that has been accomplished.

ISAAC SPENCER, who resides on section 10, Eagle Point township, is a well-known farmer and stock raiser, one who is numbered among the pioneers of northern Illinois, having been a resident of this section since 1839. He was born near Collinsville, Connecticut, January 31, 1832, and is the son of Naaman and Diantha (Benham) Spencer, both of whom were natives of the Nutmeg state. The paternal grandfather, John Spencer, was also a native of the same state, but the family is of English origin.

Naaman Spencer grew to manhood in his native state, and his marriage with Diantha Benham was celebrated July 16, 1811. In early life he learned the cooper's trade, and also the trade of a miller, following one or the other occupations while yet residing in the east. In 1833 he moved with his family to Bradford county, Pennsylvania, cleared and opened up a little farm, and there remained until 1839, when he came to Illinois, and settled on the north side of Elkhorn grove, in Carroll county, where he rented a small place, and there resided for some five or six years. He then purchased a claim of forty acres, where his son now resides, on which was a log house, and about thirty acres of the land having been broken. He there began to farm, and at the same time worked at the cooper's trade, erecting a small shop, where he made flour barrels, and carried on quite a business. The product of his shop he would haul principally to some river point and sell the same. When the land came into market he made his entries and secured his title. On that farm he spent the last years of his life, dying January 3, 1873, when nearly eighty-five years old. His wife passed away September 11, 1861. They had a family of four sons and four daughters that grew to mature years. William married and settled in Stephenson county, but is now deceased. Fanny married Elias Woodin, but is now deceased. Alanson settled at Elkhorn Grove, but is now deceased. Allen is a resident of Eagle Point township. Mrs. Lucinda Jenkins is a widow, residing in Iowa. Naaman is a resident of Milledgeville, Illinois. Diantha married Lewis Porter, but both are now deceased. Mrs. Clarinda Case, a widow, residing in Eagle Point township. Isaac, the subject of this review, is the last in order of birth.

Isaac Spencer was but nine years of age when he accompanied his parents to Illinois, and but fourteen when his father settled on the farm where he now resides. His education was obtained in the pioneer schools of Carroll and Ogle counties, but his attendance in the school room was not of long duration. He remained at home and assisted his father in the shop and on the farm until after he had attained his majority. He was married on the 26th of September, 1861, to Romelia Maxwell who was born in the town of Delhi, Delaware county, New York, February 25, 1832, and daughter of Heman and Paulina (Ballard) Maxwell, the former a native of Delhi, Delaware county, New York, and the latter of Bridgeport, Connecticut. In 1840, Henry Maxwell moved with his family to Chautauqua county, New York, where they lived a few years, and then moved to Pennsylvania. In 1850 they came to Illinois, and located in Eagle Point. He was a wagon-maker by trade, and followed that occupation at Eagle Point for some years. He lost his wife in 1875, and later moved to Red Oak, Montgomery county, Iowa, where his death occurred in 1883.

After his marriage, Mr. Spencer took charge of the home farm, and has since made many valuable improvements to it in the way of a new dwelling, barn, storehouse, etc., and has now a well improved and valuable place. In addition to general farming, he has given attention to raising good graded stock, and is accounted one of the successful farmers of the township.

Politically Mr. Spencer is a stanch Republican, having been an advocate of the principles of the party since its organization. He has never wanted nor would accept any office, willing at all times that others should have the honors and emoluments attached to office holding. When he came to northern Illinois, it was indeed a wilderness, and in the sixty years he has resided here he has witnessed changes hard to realize, changes as wonderful as were ever wrought by Aladdin's lamp. In the transformation he has borne his part.

ALEXANDER ANDERSON, residing on section 7, Woosung township, is the owner of one hundred and ninety-seven and a half acres of as fine land as there is in the township. He is a native of Ogle county, born on the home farm in Woosung township, June 11, 1872, and is the son of Alexander and Agnes (Spence) Anderson, both of whom were natives of Scotland, and who came to the United States in 1850, coming direct to Ogle county and locating in Eagle Point township, where he engaged in farming for about three years. He then moved into Woosung township, purchased eighty acres of unimproved land, and at once commenced the establishment of a permanent home, and there resided until death. He was a very successful farmer, and from time to time added to his estate until he had six hundred and forty acres of fine land, the greater part of which was under cultivation. As a breeder of stock, he was likewise successful, and always had on his place many head of cattle and hogs. He was not a member of any church, but was reared in the Presbyterian faith. A man of retiring disposition, he did not force either himself or his views on others, and therefore never asked or sought public office. In politics he was a thorough Republican. His death occurred August 27, 1887, and his remains were laid to rest in the East Jordan cemetery. His wife is yet living, and is yet residing upon the old home farm. They were the parents of two children: Alexander, our subject; and Ellen E., who is still at home with her mother.

James Anderson, the paternal grandfather, also a native of Scotland, came to the United States the same year as did the father of our subject, and made his home with him until his death in 1866. In his family were five sons and one daughter.

The subject of this sketch grew to manhood on the old home farm, and in the public schools of the neighborhood received his education. This was supplemented, however, by a course in the business college at Dixon, Illinois. He was thus well prepared for the active duties of life. He was but fifteen years old when his father died, leaving the care of the large estate to him, since which time he has cultivated and superintended the farm, meeting with fine success. Like his father before him, he has shown himself a thorough and reliable farmer, practical in all things. He ships from one hundred to two hundred hogs per year, besides one or two car loads of cattle. He has shown himself a man of superior character and business ability, strong in his inherited Scotch characteristics of integrity and thrift.

In politics Mr. Anderson is a Republican, and since the spring of 1898 he has filled the office of township clerk. In religion he is connected with the United Brethren church, and is an active worker in both the church and Sunday-school. He is president of the Young People's Society Christian Endeavor, Rock River conference of United Brethren in Christ, and is trustee of the United Brethren Camp Grounds of Polo. Fraternally he is a member of the Knights of the Globe, and has passed all the chairs in the local lodge. He is also a member of Polo Lodge, I. O. O. F., of which he is past grand; and of Polo Encampment, No. 117. While yet a young man, he is well-known in various parts of the county and has many friends. His home is one of the best in the township, and his farm one of the best improved.

MATTHEW P. BULL, an enterprising agriculturist of Ogle county, is the owner of a fine farm on sections 6 and 11, Byron township, and his management of the estate is marked by the scientific knowledge and skill which characterize the modern farm. The Bull family is of English descent and was among the pioneer settlers of Chester county, Pennsylvania. At an early day our subject's great-grandfather, Richard Bull, removed to Perry county, the same state, and opened up a farm on which the grandfather, William Bull, and father, John Bull, were both born, the latter in 1794. There he grew to manhood and when the war of 1812 broke out he joined the army, being stationed most of the time at Buffalo as private clerk to his colonel. He was married in Perry county to Miss Jane Linn, also a native of the county, and a daughter of William Linn. Upon the old homestead they resided many years, but finally sold and came west, arriving in Ogle county, Illinois, May 1, 1851. Here Mr. Bull purchased three hundred acres of land and developed the farm on which his son now resides. He erected good and substantial buildings upon his place, and successfully engaged in its operation until called from this life in September, 1863, at the age of sixty-nine years. His wife died in Pennsylvania about 1846, before the emigration of the family to Illinois. The family of this worthy couple consisted of twelve children, ten of whom, two sons and eight daughters, reached years of maturity, but only our subject and two sisters are now living,—Mrs. Jane Milligan, of Mason City, Iowa, and Elizabeth G., a resident of Rochelle, Illinois. Our subject's only brother was Robert Henry, who married and owned and operated a nice farm in Ogle county, on which he died in 1875.

Matthew P. Bull was also born on the old homestead in Perry county, Pennsylvania, April 9, 1833, and was provided with a good common school-education, which was supplemented by a year's attendance at the Bloomfield Academy. He was eighteen years of age when he accompanied the family on their removal to Illinois, and was of great assistance to his father in opening up the new farm and preparing it for planting. On the death of the latter he succeeded to a part of the estate and he and his brother subsequently bought an adjoining farm. For some years they engaged in their cultivation together, but finally the property was divided and our subject still lives on the old home farm. He has enlarged and remodeled the residence, built a large barn and good outbuildings and made many other valuable improvements upon the place, and is acknowledged to be one of the best and most successful farmers of the community. In connection with general farming he has also been engaged in raising a good grade of stock and is now interested in the milk business.

In Byron township, December 17, 1873, was celebrated the marriage of Mr. Bull and Miss Mary E. Linn, the only daughter of John R. Linn, another of Ogle county's early settlers, formerly from Pennsylvania. Mrs. Bull was born and reared in the Keystone state, and by her marriage to our subject has become the mother of six children: John L., who died in 1888, at the age of fourteen years; Margaret Isabelle, a music teacher, at home; Roberta, who is engaged in school teaching and also resides at home; Mary R. and Nancy M., twins, who are attending the Rockford high school; and Grace Grant, a student in the home school.

Since the organization of the Republican party in 1856, Mr. Bull has been one of its stanch supporters, but he has never sought nor desired political preferment. As a friend of education and our public school system, he has ever used his influence to secure good schools and teachers and for some years was a most active member of the school board. He and his wife hold membership in the Middle Creek Presbyterian church and their lives have been such as to commend them to the confidence and esteem of all who know them.

GEORGE POOLE is a retired farmer residing in Polo. He was born near Toronto, Canada, January 31, 1835, and is the son of William and Nancy (Johnson) Poole, the former a native of county Wexford, Ireland, born in May, 1803, and the latter near Toronto, Canada, May 12, 1814. William Poole was the son of George Poole, a hatter by trade, and likewise a native of Ireland, who came to America in middle life and established himself in business at his trade in Cincinnati, Ohio. He remained there a few years, then came to Ogle county, Illinois, making his home with his son, William, until his death in 1859, at the age of eighty-six years. His wife died in the old country. They were the parents of five children, all of whom grew to maturity.

William Poole grew to manhood in his native country, and after coming to America learned the the carpenter's trade. At the age of twenty-one years he started for America, taking passage in the sailing vessel Maria, and was twice shipwrecked. He finally landed in America, going direct to Toronto, Canada, where he worked a year or two for an uncle who advanced the money for his passage across the ocean. After being released from this obligation, he commenced work at his trade, at which he continued until the spring of 1839, when he came to Ogle county, Illinois, and located in what is now Brookville township. He came here with his brothers-in-law, John Lawrence and John Sanborn, and jointly they secured about eight hundred acres of land, for which they paid the government price of of one dollar and twenty-five cents per acre, besides paying the squatter's claim, as nearly all the land in this vicinity had been settled on by squatters, who located on it for the purpose of holding until they could sell out to some actual settler. On the division of the tract about three hundred acres went to Mr. Poole. Not a rod had been turned and he must make every improvement necessary. He first erected a stone house on his portion and then started to break and cultivate. He there continued farming until his death, which occurred September 18, 1886, at the age of eighty-three years. In 1831 he married Miss Nancy Johnson, both of whom were natives of Pennsylvania. Abraham Johnson was by occupation a farmer, and when but a lad he entered the British service in the Revolutionary war as a wagon boy. His wife's father, Mr. Hommon, was killed by an Indian, about one-half mile from Fort Frederick. To William and Nancy Poole were born six children, George, Abraham, Joseph, John, Catherine and one who died in infancy. In politics William Poole was an Abolitionist, and with the Free Soil party acted until the organization of the Republican party, the principles of which were so nearly identical with those he had been advocating, that he gave adherence to the new party, believing that with it the country would the sooner become in reality a free country. He was not an office-seeker, but served one term as justice of the peace and was road commissioner for a time. Religiously, he was an Episcopalian. His wife is still living at the age of eighty-five years and is making her home with our subject.

George Poole was but four years of age when he accompanied his parents to Ogle county, and here he has since continued to reside, a period of sixty years. He was educated in the school at Old Town, and was one of the first pupils to attend the school at that place. The first teacher was John Frisbie. He continued to attend school, principally in the winter months, until he was twenty years old, in the meantime assisting in the farm work. He then gave his whole time to his father, and continued to work for him until he was twenty-six years old.

On the 11th of October, 1860, Mr. Poole was united in marriage with Miss Sabina Strock, born July 22, 1836, in Bedford county, Pennsylvania, and daughter of Jacob and Catherine (Longnecker) Strock, the former a native of Franklin county, Pennsylvania, born in 1806, and the latter of Bedford county, in the same state, born in 1810. They came to Ogle county in 1854 and settled in Buffalo township, where Mr. Strock engaged in farming, at which he continued for some years. Later he removed to Polo, where he lived a retired life, and where his death occurred in November, 1882. His wife died in 1895, at the age of eighty-five years. They were the parents of nine children—Sabina, Henry, John, David, Nancy, Susanna, Abram, Elizabeth and Jacob. All are yet living. To our subject and wife four children have been born, one of whom died in infancy. The living are Frank, Nellie and John.

On his marriage, Mr. Poole received from his father a small farm and at once commenced its cultivation. After living there for seven years, he sold the same and purchased a farm of three hundred acres on sections 13 and 14, Eagle Point township, where he resided until his removal to Polo, in 1892. In his farming operations he was quite successful, and was regarded as one of the leading farmers in the township. He carried on general farming and stock raising, including the raising of short horn Durham cattle, Poland China hogs, and Norman draft horses. His farm was always kept under a high state of cultivation, and everything about the place showed that it was under the care of a practical man.

After years of hard toil, Mr. Poole concluded that he would retire and live a less active and laborious life. In 1895-6, he built his present fine residence on Barber avenue, Polo, which is the abode of hospitality. In politics he is an ardent Republican, and has served his fellow citizens in various local offices. For eleven years he was supervisor of Eagle Point township, and was a member of the board when the railroad trouble of the county was at its height. He was a valuable member of the board, and his services were appreciated by the people of his township, as is attested by his continual re-election. An energetic, enterprising man, he was always willing to work for the best interest of his township and county. He was greatly esteemed throughout the county.

MORTIMER S. BREWSTER.—The natural advantages of this section attracted at an early day a superior class of settlers—thrifty, industrious, progressive and law-abiding—whose influence gave permanent direction to the development of the locality. Among the worthy pioneers of Ogle county the Brewster family holds a prominent place. The results of the labor and self-denial of these early settlers are manifest in the comfortable homes and fertile, well-arranged farms which we to-day see.

It was August, 1837, that Mr. Brewster arrived in this county, and he has since taken an active and prominent part in its development. His life has been devoted to agricultural pursuits and he is still successfully carrying on the old homestead on section 1, Byron township. He was born in Broome county, New York, August 8, 1820, and is a son of James Brewster, a native of Connecticut. The grandfather, David Brewster, was born in one of the New England states and when quite young entered the Continental army during the Revolutionary war. At an early day he removed with his family to the Empire state, where James Brewster grew to manhood. In Albany county, New York, the latter married Miss Chloe Palmer, who was also a native of Connecticut, but removed with her parents to the former state when young. For some years he followed farming there and then removed to Bradford county, Pennsylvania, where he was similarly employed for a few years. In 1837 he came to Illinois by way of the Erie canal and Great Lakes, and proceeding thence by team finally arrived in Ogle county, where his friend and old neighbor, Mr. York, had located a year or so previously. Mr. Brewster rented land the first summer and then took a claim of about four hundred acres on section 1, Byron township, entering three hundred and twenty acres when the land came into market. Subsequently he sold some of his land but improved a farm of two hundred acres and made it his home until called to his final rest. He built a log house in which the family lived while he opened up and developed the farm, but it has since been replaced by a more commodious frame residence. He died at the ripe old age of eighty-four, having survived his wife some years. In their family were ten children three sons and seven daughters, all of whom reached years of maturity, but only our subject and his sister Caroline are now living.

Mortimer D. Brewster was a lad of seventeen years when he accompanied the family on their removal to this state and in the task of converting the wild land into a rich and productive farm he bore an active part. His school privileges were limited and he is mostly self-educated. He remained under the parental roof and on his father's death took charge of the farm, which has been his home for sixty-one years. It is one of the best improved and most highly cultivated places of the locality.

In Roscoe, Illinois, in 1856, Mr. Brewster was married, the lady of his choice being Miss Caroline Alden, a native of Bradford county, Pennsylvania, who in 1837 came with her father, Adonijah Alden, to Ogle county, settling in Marion township, near Byron. They have become the parents of six children, all living: Henry M., cashier of the Farmers & Merchants bank of Byron; Willis J., who is helping to carry on the home farm; Augusta and Edwin P., twins, the former the wife of Daniel Sims, of Cherokee county, Iowa, and the latter at home; Walter H., who is married and engaged in teaching at Saint Ann, Illinois; and Lucians D., at home.

In politics Mr. Brewster was originally a Whig, casting his first presidential ballot for the candidate of that party in 1844, and since its dissolution he has been an ardent Republican. He and his wife are faithful members of the Middle Creek Presbyterian church and are held in high regard by all who know them for their sterling worth and many excellencies of character.

ANDREW NEWCOMER, deceased, came to Ogle county in 1846, and for a period of nearly forty years occupied a prominent position in the community, and with an acquaintance as extensive as any man in the county. He was born November 25, 1810, in Washington county, Maryland, and was a descendant of Wolfgang Newcomer, who came from Germany to America more than a century ago. His boyhood was spent in his father's mill, when not in attendance in the common schools. In his youth he learned the carpenter's trade, which occupation he followed for about fifteen years after attaining his majority, working in various places in the states of Maryland and Virginia. Many of the public and private buildings in those states show the mark of his handiwork. In the fall of 1832 he located in the town of Boonsborough, Maryland, and immediately afterward united with the Methodist Episcopal church. His conversion was thorough and genuine, and he soon commenced taking an active interest in the work of the church and in the affairs of the community, becoming prominent in all lines of benevolent work, which prominence was maintained while residing in the place. During the winters of 1832-3-4, he taught school, and during the summers worked at his trade.

Mr. Newcomer was first married May 1, 1834, to Eliza Hamilton, a sister of Rev. William Hamilton, D. D., of the Baltimore conference of the Methodist Episcopal church, and an aunt of Ex-Governor W. T. Hamilton, of Maryland. She died April 2, 1875, at Mt. Morris, Illinois. On the 21st of March, 1876, Mr. Newcomer married Sarah E. Smith, in Winnebago county, Illinois.

Mrs. Newcomer was born February 6, 1827, in Luzerne county, Pennsylvania, and is the daughter of Samuel and Rebecca (Reynolds) Rose, the former a native of Philadelphia, Pennsylvania, and the latter of New Jersey. By trade her father was a hatter, but after his marriage he removed to the country and engaged in farming, an occupation that he followed until his death, March 18, 1841. In October following, his widow moved with her family to Winnebago county, Illinois, settling in Rockford. Samuel and Rebecca Rose were the parents of seven children—David, Benjamin, Ann, Maria, Sarah E., Samuel and Jacob, all of whom are deceased, with the exception of Maria and Mrs. Newcomer. In her native state the latter received a good common-school education. She was first married September 29, 1846, to Lucius J. Smith, a native of Ohio, then residing in Rockford, and a son of John and Maria (Ferris) Smith, also natives of Ohio. Immediately after their marriage they moved to a farm in Winnebago county, where Mr. Smith engaged in farming for two years. They then removed to Stephenson county, where he bought a farm of one hundred and twenty acres, and there they lived until his death, October 4, 1867. They became the parents of six children, two of whom are deceased. Frances A., born May 28, 1847, married Jefferson Stephens, of Winnebago county, Illinois. They later moved to Fillmore county, Nebraska, where he died in August, 1880. She is now living in Mt. Morris. Arthur L. married Eliza Ackers, August 18, 1878, and they now reside in San Francisco, California, where he is employed as a traveling salesman. Edward died in infancy. Volney E. died at the age of sixteen years. Emily L. lives at Mt. Morris. Frank C. married Emma Yearing, of Trenton, Missouri, May 24, 1887, and they live in Colorado Springs, Colorado, where he is the division superintendent of the Rock Island railroad. After her husband's decease Mrs. Smith remained on the farm for seven years, and then removed to Winnebago, Winnebago county, Illinois, where she was living at the time of her marriage with Mr. Newcomer. Lucius J. Smith was a good, Christian man, a member of the Methodist Episcopal church, one ever ready to lend a helping hand to those in distress, and his house was the abode of hospitality. He was a well-read man, and kept himself posted on the events of the times. He was honored and beloved by all who knew him.

While yet residing in Boonesborough, Maryland, for a short time during the years 1843-4, Mr. Newcomer was connected with the publication of "The Odd Fellows." The western fever was upon him, however, and hearing good reports from his old friends and neighbors who had settled in Ogle county, Illinois, he determined to emigrate. Accordingly, in 1846, he came to Mt. Morris, and soon afterwards opened a furniture store and undertaker's establishment, a business in which he continued about twenty years. Selling his furniture store in 1867, he embarked in the grocery trade in which he continued until his death, May 20, 1885.

The death of no man in Mount Morris ever affected the community more deeply than that of Andrew Newcomer, for he was public official and private citizen. In politics he was a Republican, a firm believer in the principles of the party. He served his township as a member of the board of supervisors, and from 1852 until his death he was almost continuously a justice of the peace. Few men ever served in the latter office with more signal ability, and few, if any, of his decisions were ever overruled by the higher court on appeal. He also served as school director and school trustee at different times, and in other official capacities. His business qualifications were more than ordinary, and his honesty was not questioned. There are few men whose names appear oftener on the records of the probate court than does that of Andrew Newcomer as executor, administrator or guardian. When he thus served it was certain that every duty would be conscientiously performed. His social qualifications were of a high order. Genial in manner, kind in disposition, old and young delighted to be in his society. He was an excellent reader, having few equals outside of the professional ones, and it is said that during the civil war he would get his daily paper, and going to his store he would be followed by a crowd, who would gather around him and listen while he read the latest war news. He never lost interest in his church, and at all times served his local church in some official capacity, either as class leader, steward, trustee, or Sunday school superintendent. No call of the church was by him unheeded. He was a firm believer in the cause of his Master, and was ever ready to render the best service in his power. He died in the full assurance of of a blessed resurrection.

JAMES D. ANDERSON, a representative and prominent farmer and stock raiser of Ogle county, makes his home on section 3, Eagle Point township, and owns and operates over four hundred acres of valuable and well improved land. He has been a resident of the county since 1845 and is, therefore, numbered among its honored pioneers.

Mr. Anderson was born in the town of Andes, Delaware county, New York, October 12, 1842. His father, John Anderson, was a native of Scotland, born in 1807, and was a son of Joseph and Jane (Clark) Anderson, also natives of that country, where they spent their entire lives. The grandfather was a millwright by trade and reared a family of eleven children. Reared in his native place, John Anderson received a common school education and in early life worked in his father's mill. In 1832 he emigrated to the new world, landing in Nova Scotia, whence he proceeded to Delaware county, New York, where he worked as a millwright and also engaged in farming. He was a natural mechanic and built a mill in that county. There he was married, September 18, 1834, to Miss Margaret Sim, who was also born and reared in Scotland. Her father, Alexander Sim, a native of the same country, was an early settler of Delaware county, New York. In 1845 Mr. Anderson came to Ogle county, Illinois, and made a permanent location upon the farm where our subject now resides. He entered a tract of eighty acres from the government and built a small house, where he resided for some years. He also erected a shop in Eagle Point and engaged in wagon making and repair work. Later he removed the shop to his farm and continued to carry on business there while opening up and improving his farm. As he prospered in his new home, he purchased more land from time to time until he owned about three hundred acres. He built a large, neat residence thereon and made many other improvements, which added greatly to its value and attractive appearance. He was in limited circumstances when he came to the county and by his own labor, enterprise and perseverance he succeeded in acquiring a comfortable home and competence. He continued to make his home upon his farm throughout the remainder of his life, but died in Rockford while on a visit, March 21, 1886. Two years previously he and his wife celebrated their golden wedding, at which time a large number of their friends and neighbors were gathered together at their home to wish them joy. Mrs. Anderson departed this life June 1, 1892, and was laid to rest by the side of her husband in

JAMES ANDERSON.

Fairmont cemetery, where a monument has been erected to their memory. They had a host of warm friends in this community and were held in high regard by all who knew them. Politically, Mr. Anderson was a stanch Republican, and was called upon to fill a number of official positions of honor and trust, including that of justice of the peace, which he filled for a number of years to the entire satisfaction of the public.

James D. Anderson, of this review, is the fourth in order of birth in a family of seven children, the others being as follows: Joseph A., who is married and resides in Wasco county, Oregon; George, who is with his brother in that state; Jane A., wife of G. J. Monroe, of Dysart, Iowa; John, who is married and is engaged in contracting and building in Chicago; Nettie A., widow of W. W. Pierce and a resident of Polo; and Margaret C., wife of George Gibbs, of Ogle county.

James D. Anderson was only three years old when brought by his parents to Ogle county, where he grew to manhood on the home farm and was educated in the common schools. During early life he assisted his father in the farm work and in 1868 took charge of the place and business. After the death of the latter he purchased the interests of the other heirs in the old homestead which he still owns and operates. He has added to it more land until he now has about four hundred acres, which he has placed under a high state of cultivation and improved in an excellent manner. He has built one of the largest and most conveniently arranged barns in the county. He also has a very large cattle barn, good outbuildings, windpumps, etc., so that it might well be numbered among the model farms of the county. For the past twenty years, Mr. Anderson has made a business of feeding stock and annually fits for market from two to six car loads of stock, usually having from sixty to one hundred head of cattle upon his place and from one hundred to one hundred and fifty head of hogs. He is one of the most successful farmers and stockmen of the county and usually ships his own stock.

In Brookville township, Ogle county, Mr. Anderson was married, April 2, 1885, to Miss Addie L. Gibbs, who was born, reared and educated in this county, a daughter of Leonard Gibbs, one of its early settlers. They now have two children: Grace B. and McKinley J.

In politics, Mr. Anderson has been a life-long Republican, and his fellow citizens recognizing his worth and ability have often called him to office. He is now serving his eighteenth year as commissioner of highways, has been treasurer the same length of time, and has served as collector of his township and as a delegate to the county and congressional conventions of his party. For twenty-five years he has been connected with the Eagle Point Mutual Fire Insurance Company and is now serving as its president. He is past grand of Polo Lodge, I. O. O. F., and socially is quite popular. In all the relations of life he has been found true to every trust reposed in him, and he enjoys the confidence and esteem of all who know him.

JOHN GRAHAM is one of the leading and influential citizens of Lead River township, his home being on section 11, and he has taken an active part in promoting the substantial improvement and material development of the county. Although an adopted son of America, his loyalty is above question, for during the dark days of the rebellion he offered his services to the government and for three long years followed the old flag to victory on southern battle fields.

A native of Ireland, Mr. Graham was born near the city of Belfast, in County Antrim, in 1832, and was there reared to manhood. Deciding to come to America in 1856 he took ship at Belfast for Liverpool, England, where he boarded a sailing vessel, which was five weeks in crossing the broad Atlantic. They encountered some severe storms, the mast was blown away, and the vessel was almost a complete wreck when it arrived in New York. In April of that year, Mr. Graham found employment in a brickyard at Newburg, Orange county, New York, but the following fall proceeded to Ohio, where he remained only a short time, however. He spent the winter at Freeport, Illinois, and the following year found work in the harvest fields. He then worked for a Mr. Carpenter in Ogle county until after the outbreak of the Civil war.

Prompted by a spirit of patriotism, Mr. Graham enlisted in 1862, in Company B, Seventy-fourth Illinois Volunteer Infantry, which was assigned to the Army of the Cumberland. He participated in many important engagements and skirmishes, including the battles of Perryville, Kentucky, and Murfreesboro, Tennessee, where they fought for nine days, fighting the old year out and the new year in. He was also in the battles of Lookout Mountain and Missionary Ridge, from there marched to near Knoxville. At Murfreesboro the regiment lost heavily and Mr. Graham was wounded in the left cheek, his eye being badly injured. He did not give up, however, and later took part in the battles of Resaca, Jonesboro and Kenesaw Mountain. At the last named battle he was again wounded, the bone in his right leg below the knee being terribly shattered. This permanently disabled him, and he was sent to the hospital at Louisville, Kentucky, whence he was later transferred to the hospital at Quincy, Illinois. When discharged in June, 1865, he was still obliged to use crutches and he has never fully recovered from his injuries.

Returning to the home of Mr. Carpenter our subject remained there for two or three years, and when sufficiently recovered he resumed farm work. On the 8th of March, 1873, he was united in marriage with Miss Catherine Shriber, a native of Schuylkill county, Pennsylvania, and a daughter of Christian Shriber, who removed from that state to Ogle county and became one of the successful farmers of this region. He died in March, 1890, and his wife, who survives him, is living in Lightsville, a hale old lady of eighty-four years. To Mr. and Mrs. Graham have been born four children: Rosa J., Lilly Dora, Ervin Seymour and Ernest M.

For a few years after his marriage, Mr. Graham operated rented land and then removed to the farm on which he now resides. Although he began life in this country in limited circumstances, he has steadily worked his way upward until he is now the possessor of a comfortable competence. His success has been achieved through his own well directed efforts and the assistance of his estimable wife, who has proved a true helpmeet to him. He now has a fine farm of over two hundred acres of rich and arable land. In his political affiliations he is an ardent Democrat, but he has never cared for the honors or emoluments of public office, preferring to give his undivided attention to his business interests. He is a man of intrinsic worth, esteemed in all the relations of life, and has a host of warm friends in Ogle county.

NELSON B. KIDDER, the efficient supervisor of Woosung township, is one of the leading farmers of Ogle county, owning a fine farm of two hundred and sixty acres in Woosung township, and some three hundred and twenty acres in Jordan township, Whiteside county, Illinois. His home farm is on section 7, Woosung township, which is a highly improved place, with everything in the best order. He is a native of New Hampshire, born in the town of Bristol, Grafton county, January 15, 1834, and is the son of Benjamin and Mary (Doton) Kidder, both of whom were natives of the Granite state. Benjamin Kidder was by occupation a farmer in his native state, and after his removal to Illinois. With his family, in 1856, he left his native state and came to Whiteside county, Illinois, where he purchased land and engaged in farming for eighteen years, and then moved to Woosung township, Ogle county, where the remainder of his life was passed. He died on the farm now owned by our subject, August 6, 1883. He was a man of retiring disposition, and one who gave his undivided attention to his business, family and religious interests. He made a success in life, and was enabled to assist his children. Religiously he was a member of the Methodist Episcopal church, and in politics was a Democrat. He had a family of six children, as follows: Adoniram, of O'Brien county, Iowa; Levi, who died in 1865; Sarah, the deceased wife of J. W. Taylor, of Whiteside county, Illinois; Nelson B., the subject of this sketch; Electa, the deceased wife of H. Taylor, of Powesheik county, Iowa; and Marcellus, of Whiteside county, Illinois.

The paternal grandfather, Benjamin Kidder, was a native of New Hampshire, while his father, the great-grandfather of our subject, was born in England, and emigrated to this country in 1770. He later served in the Revolutionary war, and assisted the colonies in securing their independence.

In his native state Nelson B. Kidder grew to manhood, and there received a common-school education. The knowledge obtained in the school room was but little in comparison to that since obtained by contact with his fellow men, and in reading the general and current literature of the day. He had attained his majority when he came with the family to Illinois, and on his arrival purchased eighty acres of land in Whiteside county, to which he later added one hundred and twenty acres, giving him a fine farm of two hundred acres, eighty acres of which has since been sold, leaving him a balance of one hundred and twenty acres.

On the 30th of December, 1862, Mr. Kidder was united in marriage with Miss Amanda Mingle, a native of Bradford county, Pennsylvania, and daughter of James and Catherine Mingle, both of whom were natives of the same state. She was but ten years of age when she accompanied her parents to Carroll county, Illinois, where they made their permanent home. By this union there were three children: Aldena died at the age of four years and eight months. Irvin is engaged in farming in Woosung township. Fred J. is now a student in the State Normal School, at Dixon, Illinois.

In March, 1874, Mr. Kidder moved to Ogle county, since which time he has been one of its most enterprising citizens, and has taken quite an active part in public life, having served nine consecutive years as school director and six years as commissioner of highways, and in the spring of 1897 was elected to his present position as supervisor of his township, an office which he is well qualified to fill, because of his good business ability and earnest desire for the public good. He has given his attention to general farming, never running off on any fads, and in his life work has met with a reasonable degree of success. For the past twenty years he has been quite an extensive feeder of cattle, and annually prepares a good many head for the general market. A residence of forty-three years in Whiteside and Ogle counties has brought him in contact with many of their best citizens, and wherever he is known he is held in high esteem.

REV. ANDREW STAHLEY, a resident of Ogle county since the spring of 1865, and one of its highly esteemed citizens, was born October 3, 1821, in York county, Pennsylvania, where he was reared and educated in the common schools of the locality. He is of German descent, his grandfather, Andrew Stahley, for whom he was named, being a native of Germany. On coming to America he located in Chanceford township, York county, Pennsylvania. He had a family of four children: Peter, the father of our subject; Joseph, a blacksmith by trade, who came to Illinois and located near Quincy; Stephen, also a blacksmith by trade, who came west; and Sarah, who remained and died in York county,

Pennsylvania. The grandfather died when comparatively a young man. Peter Stahley was born in York county in 1784, and by occupation was a farmer, a calling which he followed during his entire life. During the war of 1812 he was called out, but did not enter the service for the reason the order was countermanded before his company could muster. He married Catherine Tome, also a native of York county, Pennsylvania, daughter of Henry Tome, a farmer of that county. She was one of a family of six children, the others being Fannie, who married Fred Gable, a merchant of Dover, Pennsylvania; Elizabeth, wife of Daniel Guhn, a farmer of York county; Jacob, George and Henry, who lived and died in York county.

Andrew Stahley is the son of Peter and Catherine (Tome) Stahley. After his school days and until he attained his majority, he remained with his parents, assisting his father in the farm work. When he was twenty-one he commenced life on his own account, doing farm work by the day, continuing in that work until he was twenty-eight years old. Being of a religious turn of mind and desirious of serving the Master, he entered the ministry of the Evangelical Association, having prepared himself by constant reading and study for several years. From 1849 until 1869 he traveled about preaching the word, first as a member of the Central Pennsylvania conference, doing missionary work. He then came to Illinois, and as a member of the Illinois conference continued the work for four years. His first station was at Warren, Pennsylvania, where he remained one year. He was then at Pittsburg two years, thence back to Warren, Pennsylvania, and then to the Ohio circuit, in Stark county, that state, where he remained one year. He was then again at Pittsburg one year, when he was elected presiding elder for the Pittsburg district. Later he was sent to Canton, Ohio, where he remained two years, then to Erie, Pennsylvania, two years. From Erie he came direct to Forreston, Illinois, and was assigned to the West Grove circuit, preaching at Forreston and Freeport, and other points in this locality.

Mr. Stahley was first married in 1842 to Miss Charlotte Vogt, a native of York county, Pennsylvania, and daughter of Peter and Paulina (Will) Vogt. She died in York county after a wedded life of five years, leaving one daughter, Delilah Ann, now the wife of Isaac Vogelgesang, a retired merchant and business man of Forreston. In 1852 Mr. Stahley married Miss Sarah Long, daughter of Bishop Joseph Long and Katherine (Hoy) Long. She was a native of Columbiana county, Ohio, her father being bishop of the Evangelical Association. She died in Forrestson, leaving one daughter, Josephine, now the wife of Samuel McLain, of Forreston, a wholesale manufacturer of specialties in medicine. Mr. Stahley married his present wife June 22, 1875. She was Miss Ceres Oakes, a native of Reading, Pennsylvania, and daughter of George and Susan (Cleversy) Oakes. Her father was born October 13, 1782, in Hessen Cassel, Germany, and left that country when eighteen years old, crossing the ocean on an English vessel, and while en route to Nova Scotia received his first lesson in the English language from the captain of the vessel. He came to the United States and settled in Lancester, Pennsylvania. He was married in Nova Scotia to Miss Susan Cleversy, a native of Nova Scotia, born in 1800. They were married November 26, 1826, and became the parents of six children: Serene, born in Lancaster, Pennsylvania, March 13, 1828, became the wife of Francis Knauss, and they reside in Rock City, Illinois. Zero, born in New Ephrata, Pennsylvania, married Robert Mitchell, and they also reside in Rock City, Illinois. Alpha, born at Berne, Pennsylvania, June 5, 1832, was a soldier in the Civil war. He now resides at Quincy, Illinois. Ceres is the wife of our subject. Atlas, born in Johnstown, Pennsylvania, April 9, 1835, was also a soldier in the Civil war. He is now residing in the west. Omega, born in Johnstown, Pennsylvania, April 3, 1838, is a retired business man, living in Oregon. Professionally, George Oakes was a teacher, and taught in both the English and German languages. He was also a fine musician and gave some time to teaching music. He came with his family to Illinois in 1846, but died the following year, his remains being interred in the Dakota cemetery, in Stephenson county. His wife survived him many years, dying in 1890, in her eighty-eighth year. Her remains were interred beside those of her husband.

On retiring from the ministry in 1869, Mr. Stahley became interested in a planing mill, but for many years he has given his time to looking after his business interests in connection with his farming land, owning three hundred and seventy acres in Ogle county and eighty acres in Carroll county. He has never taken much interest in political affairs as generally managed, and for many years did not cast a vote. His first presidential vote was cast for Abraham Lincoln. He now votes as his conscience dictates without regard to party politics. While actively engaged in the ministry, he was instrumental in the erection of several churches, and his labors in that way were appreciated by the good people of Warren, Ohio, and those on the Harmony circuit and in Columbiana county, Ohio. He has not lost interest in good works, but is ever ready to assist in promoting "peace on earth, good will toward men."

EMANUEL M. HARNER.—Almost the entire life of this gentleman has been passed in Ogle county, Illinois, and his name is inseparably connected with the agricultural and industrial interests of this region. His thoroughly American spirit and great energy have enabled him to mount from a lowly position to one of affluence. One of his leading characteristics in business affairs is his fine sense of order and complete system and the habit of giving careful attention to details, without which success in any undertaking is never an assured fact. He owns and operates a well-improved farm on section 2, Leaf River township, and is also successfully engaged in the manufacture of brick.

Mr. Harner was born in Schuylkill county, Pennsylvania, February 28, 1840, and is a son of Christian Harner, whose birth occurred February 26, 1811, in Germany. About 1830 the father emigrated to America in company with a cousin, also a young man, and located in Northumberland county, Pennsylvania, where he worked as a farm hand. There he was united in marriage with Miss Elizabeth Delp, who was born in that state of German parentage. They continued to reside in Pennsylvania until 1840, and then, in company with eight families, drove across the country to Illinois, arriving in Ogle county in May of that year. Mr. Harner took up one hundred and twenty acres on section 11, Leaf River township, on which he erected a log cabin, and he also pre-empted one hundred and sixty acres on section 2. After residing upon the former tract for about two years, he built where our subject now resides on section 2. This was a good log house, in which he made his home until called from this life in 1846, at the early age of thirty-five years. His wife subsequently married again, but continued a resident of Ogle county, dying here March 18, 1869.

Our subject is the second in order of birth in the family of five children, the others being as follows: Edward B. joined the boys in blue during the Civil war, enlisting in 1861, in Company H, Thirty-fourth Illinois Volunteer Infantry. He was killed April 15, 1865, in Chatham county, North Carolina, at which time he was serving as first lieutenant and was on detached duty, having charge of a foraging expedition for his command. Amelia is the wife of John Willoughby, of Legrand, Iowa. Mary Ann is the wife of David Huff, of Leaf River township, Ogle county. Christian F. is married and lives in Kansas.

The first recollections of our subject are of pioneer scenes, for he was an infant when brought by his parents to Ogle county. Wolves were numerous in this region at that time and would often come to the house in the day time and stick their noses under the door. Deer and other wild game were also plentiful, the country was all wild and unimproved, and the few settlers were widely scattered. In common with other pioneers, the Harner family endured many hardships and privations, but as time passed the comforts of civilization were added to their home, the wild land was transformed into good homes and farms, thriving villages sprung up, and the railroad and telegraph were introduced. Mr. Harner has watched with interest the wonderful changes that have taken place, and has been an important factor in the growth and development of the county. As there were few schools here during his boyhood, his educational privileges were limited and he is mostly self-educated.

On the 7th of September, 1861, he enlisted with his brothers, as a private in Company H, Thirty-fourth Illinois Volunteer Infantry, which was assigned to the Army of the Cumberland and they fought together until the brother was killed, participating in thirty-seven engagements. Among the more important was the battle of Shiloh, the siege of Corinth, the battles of Missionary Ridge, Perryville, Kentucky, Stone River, Tennessee, Liberty Gap, Chickamauga, the engagements of the Atlanta campaign, the memorable march with Sherman to the sea, and the battle of Bentonville, North Carolina. He also took part in the grand review at Washington, District of Columbia. At Chattanooga he had re-enlisted December 22, 1863, and at Louisville, Kentucky, was mustered out July 12, 1865, after almost four years of faithful service.

Returning to his home Mr. Harner worked at the carpenter's trade, which he had previously learned. He was married December 23, 1866, to Miss Elizabeth Grove, a native of Leaf River township, and a daughter of Samuel H. Grove, and then rented a farm in that township, which he operated for several years. He lost his wife September 23, 1868, and the only child born to them, Ola Melissa, died at the age of ten months. On the 7th of October, 1869, he wedded Miss Bennettie J. Jackson, who was born in Sharpsburg, Washington county, Maryland. Her father, Josiah Jackson, was a native of England, and on coming to America settled in Maryland, where he was married, in 1840, to Catherine Twig, a native of Sharpsburg. He died in Washington county at the age of thirty-three years, and Mrs. Jackson subsequently removed to Ogle county, Illinois, where Mrs. Harner was reared and educated, being only five years old on her arrival here. Our subject and his wife have four children: Anna S., wife of Ira Ulfers, who has been operator and agent at Maryland Station, Illinois, for about twelve years; Mary C. A., wife of David Kretsinger, a merchant and business man of Egan; Josiah F. O. and Hattie Z., both at home.

Mr. Harner purchased the interest of the other heirs in the old homestead where he has since resided, and has successfully engaged in farming and stock raising. In 1895 he embarked in the manufacture of brick, set up an engine and machinery for that purpose, and the first season turned out one hundred and sixty thousand, the second, one hundred and twenty thousand, and in 1898 ninety-one thousand. He uses a superior clay and makes a most excellent quality of brick, for which he finds a ready sale in the local markets. He was for many years identified with the Republican party, but being a strong advocate of temperance he now supports the men and measures of the Prohibition party. He has served as highway commissioner for three years and as a member of the school board and as its president for some years. Both he and his wife hold membership in the United Brethren church at Egan, of which he is one of the trustees, and by all who know them they are held in high regard.

FRANCIS A. SMITH has for over sixty-one years been prominently identified with the agricultural interests of Ogle county, and is still engaged in farming on section 4, Byron township. As one of its honored pioneers he has been an important factor in the development and prosperity of the county. He is now numbered among the elderly residents of the community and is held in that reverence and respect tacitly accorded those whose lives have been distinguished by integrity and usefulness.

Mr. Smith was born in Palmer, Massachusetts, January 22, 1817, and is of the sixth generation born on the old homestead, which is still in the possession of the family. His ancestors were from Scotland and were among the first to settle in the Massachusetts colony. His father, Robert Smith, spent his entire life on the old home farm, his energies being devoted to agricultural pursuits. He married Hannah Hoar, also a native of the old Bay state and a daughter of Squire Hoar. He died in 1819 when comparatively young, and his wife passed away in 1855. After her husband's death she carefully reared her family, consisting of six sons and two daughters.

Our subject, who is the youngest of the family, grew to manhood on the old homestead, and received a good practical education, attending first the common schools and later the Wilbreham and Amherst Academies. For two terms he taught school in his native state. In 1837, when a young man of twenty years, he came to Illinois, and on foot proceeded from Chicago to Ogle county, where friends from Massachusetts had previously located. He spent the first winter with the Patrick family, and in June, 1838, purchased a claim of four hundred and eighty acres, of which he broke four hundred acres the first year. In 1838 he returned to his old home in Massachusetts, and in the spring of 1839 came back to his present home in Illinois, traveling the entire distance on horseback and alone, making over one thousand miles in twenty-one days. Between Michigan City, Indiana, and Chicago, Illinois, he traveled sixty miles without passing a house.

The following two years he planted crops, but as there was no market for his products, he then abandoned farming and went to work by the month. In the spring of 1841 he started for New Orleans in company with Messrs. White and Reed, taking the first stock marketed in the Crescent City. They made the trip by flat boats and did not arrive at their destination until August, the stock being fed and fattened on the boats. On his return to Illinois, Mr. Smith engaged in teaming for Henry Potwin, who owned and operated several stores, and our subject remained in his employ for about three years, hauling goods from the stores to Chicago and also to the Galena mines.

On the 14th of March, 1844, Mr. Smith was united in marriage with Miss Sarah Brown, who was born, reared and educated in Brimfield, Massachusetts, and is a daughter of Dauphin Brown, one of the honored pioneers of Ogle county, and a sister of A. F. Brown, whose sketch appears elsewhere in this volume. Nine children were born to our subject and his wife, of whom six are still living, namely: Hattie, wife of H. D. Merrill, who lives on a ranch near Los Angeles, California; Albert and Alice, twins, the former a resident of Fairbury, Nebraska, and the latter the wife of Thomas Ferguson, of Rockford, Illinois; Dr. A. H., who successfully engaged in the practice of medicine for about twenty years and died in

Clinton, Iowa, in the spring of 1890; Nellie, wife of Thomas Roberts, of Elida, Winnebago county, Illinois; William H., who died in Nebraska; Harry R., who is married, has one child and assists his father in the operation of the home farm; Julia B., who died in 1883; and Lena Belle, wife of Henry J. Young, of Scott township, Ogle county.

In 1845 Mr. Smith returned to his farm in Ogle county and resumed farming. His first home here has long since been replaced by a commodious and comfortable residence, large barns and other outbuildings have been erected, and many other improvements have been made which add to the value and attractive appearance of the place. In connection with general farming, Mr. Smith has given considerable attention to stock raising, keeping a high grade of cattle and hogs. He has met with excellent success in his undertakings, and is to-day one of the most prosperous and substantial farmers of Byron township, as well as one of its most highly esteemed and honored citizens. Although eighty-one years of age he is still able to follow the plow and to perform the other duties of the farm, and believes he is able to walk twenty-five miles in a day. In 1840 he cast his first ballot for William Henry Harrison, and continued to support the Whig party until the organization of the Republican party, when he joined its ranks and has since been one of its stanch supporters. He has filled the office of commissioner of highways, but has never cared for political honors, but as a public-spirited and enterprising citizen he gives his support to all objects which he believes calculated to prove of public benefit, or will in any way advance the welfare of the people around him. His estimable wife is a member of the Congregational church.

HENRY SCHELLING.—There are numerous fine farms in Ogle county which will compare favorably with any others in the state as regards production and also as to the improvements which have been made upon them. Many of these places are owned by men who have started out in the world with little more than an unlimited amount of energy and perseverance, and who have succeeded in an eminent degree in securing a comfortable home and competence. As a representative of this class of agriculturists, great pleasure is taken in presenting the name of the subject of this notice, who is living on section 26, Leaf River township.

Mr. Schelling was born in Washington county, Maryland, December 16, 1837, a son of Joseph and Catherine (Schaffer) Schelling, who were born, reared and married in Germany. On coming to the new world they settled in Washington county, Maryland, where as a stonemason and plasterer the father carried on operations throughout his active business life. He died there in 1859, and his wife passed away some nine years previously. In their family were ten children, four sons and six daughters, all of whom reached years of maturity, but one daughter is now deceased.

Henry Schelling grew to manhood in his native county, and in early life was provided with fair common-school advantages. In the east he worked for his father as a plasterer and mason, but in 1859 came to Ogle county, Illinois, arriving on the 28th of February, and joining an elder brother, Andrew Schelling, who had located here about 1854. During the first two years spent here he worked as a farm hand. On the 12th of January, 1861, he was united in marriage with Miss Susan Henan, also a native of Maryland, and a daughter of William Henan, a pioneer of Ogle county, where she was mostly reared. They began their domestic life upon rented land, which Mr. Schelling operated for six years, and then made his first purchase, consisting of a tract of three hundred and twenty acres of timber land. He at once began to clear and fence the land, and it was not long before he had transformed the wild tract into a well cultivated farm. Later he bought more land, and is now the owner of two good farms adjoining his other and aggregating four hundred and twenty-three acres, pleasantly situated in Leaf River township, only a half mile from the village of that name. He has recently purchased one additional tract of seventy acres. While opening up his farm he made his home for a number of years in a frame house, which had previously been erected thereon, but it has since been replaced by a large, neat and substantial residence, while two large barns, a granary, windpump, water works, cribs, sheds, etc., have also been built, making it one of the best improved farms of the township.

Mr. and Mrs. Schelling are the parents of eleven children, namely: Frank and Albert, who are both married and are engaged in farming in Leaf River township; Charles, who is married and assists in the operation of the home farm, Dallas, who is married and carries on farming near Waterloo, Iowa, Arthur, who is married and engaged in farming in Leaf River township; Bert and John, both at home; Mary, wife of Homer Stanley; Irena, wife of Samuel Clevidense, a farmer near Polo, Ogle county; Lilly, who is engaged in teaching school and resides at home, and Jennie, also at home.

Mr. Schelling cast his first vote for Abraham Lincoln and continued to support the Republican party for some time, but believing the temperance question the most important issue before the people, he now gives his allegiance to the Prohibition party. He has never sought or desired public office, though he has acceptably served as highway commissioner and as a member of the school board in his district. Both he and his wife are faithful members of the United Brethren church of Leaf River and enjoy the esteem and friendship of a large circle of friends and acquaintances. For almost forty years he has been a resident of the county, and during that time he has witnessed much of its growth and development and has given his support to every enterprise for its advancement, being one of its most public spirited and progressive citizens.

AUGUST F. KORF, section 1, Lincoln township, is one of the most prosperous farmers in Ogle county. In his home farm he has three hundred and thirty acres, a well improved and valuable farm, while he is also the owner of three hundred and twenty acres in another part of the township, which is well improved. He is a native of Germany, born in Lippe Detmold, May 2, 1843, but has been a resident of Ogle county since July 10, 1848. His father, Louis Korf, was also a native of Germany, born in 1797. He there grew to manhood and married Mary Cosha, also a native of that country. In his native land Louis Korf engaged in herding, an occupation in which there was but a bare living. He desired something better, and to that end, in company with a number of immigrants, he left for the United States. They set sail from

Bremen for New York in a slow sailing vessel, and in due time landed in New York, from which place they came direct to Ogle county, where they joined some German friends. They landed in the county on the 19th of July. The survivors of that company celebrated the event July 19, 1898, their semi-centennial.

The second year after his arrival Louis Korf purchased eighty acres of land in Maryland township on which he erected a log cabin, with two rooms, one and a half stories in height, into which he removed with his family and commenced life in earnest in this new world. Like almost all others of his race, he was industrious and thrifty, and from time to time added to his possessions until he became one of the well-to-do farmers of the township. On that farm he died in July, 1871, at the age of seventy-five years. His wife passed away September 28, 1869. They had a family of six children who grew to mature years, as follows: Minnie, wife of William Mondhanker, of Baileyville, Illinois; Dorotha, who married John Pothost, both of whom are deceased; Elizabeth, wife of Frederick Todman, of Forreston township; Frederick, a farmer of Forreston township; Henry, of Jasper county, Iowa; and August F., of this review.

The subject of this sketch was but five years old when he came to Ogle county, and here his entire life has since been passed. His educational advantages were very limited, confined principally to the common schools. The knowledge since acquired has been obtained by experience with the world. The youngest son, he remained with his parents during their declining years, helping to relieve them of much of the cares incidental to old age. He was married in Maryland township, Ogle county, March 9, 1870, to Miss Doratha M. Zumdahl, also a native of Germany, born in Sabberhauser, Germany, April 7, 1848, and who came to Ogle county, in 1850, where she grew to womanhood and received her education. Four sons have come to bless their union. August C., born February 23, 1871, yet resides at home and is assisting in carrying on the home farm. Jesse A., born January 14, 1874, is now a student in the Northern Illinois Normal school, at Dixon, Illinois. George F., born May 10, 1877, is a student of Heidleburg University, Tiffin, Ohio. William H., born October 31, 1880, is a student of the Forreston high school.

After his marriage, Mr. Korf took his bride to his father's home, where they resided until 1881, when he bought his present farm to which they removed and where they have since continued to reside. The farm has been greatly improved in the past few years by the remodeling of the dwelling house and the erection of needed outbuildings. The place now shows the work of a master mind, and the thrift of its owner. Mr. Korf has in addition to his home farm one of three hundred and twenty acres in sections 11 and 12, Lincoln township. Much of his property has been acquired since his marriage, and is the result of his own wise management, assisted by his estimable wife.

Politically Mr. Korf holds to the views and principles of the Democratic party. His first presidential vote was cast for George B. McClellan, in 1864. In local elections he does not confine himself to his party ticket, but votes for the men he considers the best qualified. The only official position held by him is that of member of the school board, a position that he held for about twelve years.

During the Civil war the sympathies of Mr. Korf was on the side of the union, and in March, 1865, he offered his services to his adopted country and joined Company F, Fifteenth Illinois Volunteer Infantry, joining his regiment at Morehead City, North Carolina, remaining with it until after the close of the war. After the close of hostilities his regiment was ordered first to Louisville, Kentucky, and later to Leavenworth, Kansas, where it was mustered out. His discharge was received at Springfield, Illinois.

Mr. Korf and family are members of the Reformed Church of America, their local church being at West Grove. In that organization Mr. Korf has been one of the elders for some years. In the work of the church he manifests the liveliest interest. The family are held in the highest esteem wherever known. For fifty-one years Mr. Korf has been a resident of Ogle county, and although he was quite small when he came here, he has yet a vivid recollection of the hardships endured during the first few years after the arrival of the family. He has, however, lived to see a vast change, and the county of his adoption take front rank among its sister counties of the fair state of Illinois.

MILO A. JONES has demonstrated the true meaning of the word success as the full accomplishment of an honorable purpose. Energy, close application, perseverance and good management—these are the elements which have entered into his business career and crowned his efforts with prosperity. To-day he is the leading hardware merchant of Byron, Illinois.

Mr. Jones is a native of New York, born in Jewett, Greene county, April 29, 1841, and his father, Benjamin Jones, Jr., were also natives of the Empire state, where the family was founded by Welsh emigrants at an early day in the history of this country. The father grew to manhood in Greene county, and there married Miss Catherine Peck, who was also born in New York, and died in Greene county, in 1892. There he still resides, a hale and hearty old man of ninety-three years, honored and respected by all who know him. By occupation he was a farmer and met with success in his chosen calling. Milo A. is the oldest in his family of seven children, five sons and two daughters, the others being Edward, a resident of Greene county, New York; Charles, who is engaged in mercantile business at Albequerque, New Mexico; Frank, who went to Colorado after reaching manhood and there died; Sumner, a business man of Greene county; and Mary, wife of Herbert Kipp, a merchant of Greene county.

Amid rural scenes on the home farm, Milo A. Jones passed his boyhood and youth. On the 29th of August, 1862, he joined the boys in blue as a member of Company F, One Hundred and Twentieth New York Volunteer Infantry, which was assigned to the army of the Potomac, and with his regiment participated in a number of important engagements, including the battles of Fredericksburg, Chancellorsville and Gettysburg. At the last named he received a gunshot wound in the left thigh which permanently disabled him. For several months he was confined to the hospital at Baltimore, and when partially recovered was ordered to Washington, District of Columbia, where he was on duty in the provost marshal's office for about a year. He was then put in the detective service, and was in the provost marshal's office another year, remaining there until hostilities ceased, when he was mustered out in July, 1865.

Returning to his home in New York, Mr. Jones remained there a short time, but in February, 1866, we find him en route for Illinois. He located in Winnebago county, where he rented land and engaged in farming for a few days. There he was married, in March, 1869, to Miss Sarah E. Brown, a native of that county, and a daughter of Samuel Brown, one of its honored pioneers, having made his home there since 1836. He is now deceased, but the mother is still living, a hale old lady of about ninety years, and makes her home with Mrs. Jones in Byron. She has three children. Captain John E. Brown, the only son, valiantly fought for the old flag and the cause it represented during the Rebellion, and commanded his company in that war. He received an excellent education, being a graduate of Lombard University, and for some years successfully engaged in teaching, but is now a railroad man with the Missouri Pacific and resides in Kansas. The other daughter, Alice, is the wife of S. P. Wilson and resides in South Haven, Michigan. Mr. and Mrs. Jones have two children: Ellen, now the wife of Henry Weld, a farmer of Marion township, Ogle county; and Alice, at home.

For a few years after his marriage, Mr. Jones operated the old Brown homestead, and later engaged in the grain and stock business at New Milford for several years. After coming to Byron in the fall of 1883, he continued that business and was instrumental in forming the stock company which erected the first elevator at this place. In 1888 he purchased an interest in a hardware store, and in partnership with William Dodds carried it on for several years, but in 1897 he purchased the latter's interest and is now alone in business. He carries a full and complete line of shelf and heavy hardware, stoves, tinware, buggies, wagons and agricultural implements and enjoys a large and lucrative trade, receiving a liberal patronage from the people of Byron and surrounding country.

Politically Mr. Jones has been a lifelong Republican, casting his first vote for Abraham Lincoln in 1864, but he has never taken a very active part in politics aside from voting. While a resident of Winnebago county he served as deputy sheriff for two years, but has never sought office, preferring to give his time and attention to his extensive business interests. Fraternally he is an honored member of the Masonic lodge of Byron, and the Ancient Order of the United Workmen and the Grand Army post at Rockford. As a business man and citizen he merits and receives the respect and confidence of the entire community, and since coming to Byron he has made a host of warm friends.

HON. TIMOLEON O. JOHNSTON, editor and proprietor of the Oregon Reporter, is a native of Wisconsin, born in Franklin, Iowa county, June 30, 1849, and is the son of Wesley and Sarah L. (Phelps) Johnston. The family are of Irish ancestry, the paternal grandfather being a captain during the war of the Revolution, coming to this country at an early day. He was a prosperous merchant of New York city, where his death occurred. Wesley Johnston was born in New York city, April 1, 1817, and inherited from his father a shrewd business capacity, which favored him in the world of trade. He received a good education, and, at the age of twenty, with a good portion of money he left the great metropolis and started out in the world to seek his fortune. Aside from substantial financial backing he had a good stock of courage, determination and energy. St. Louis was his first stopping place, and the pleasure he experienced on this trip, which was mainly by water, suggested to him a position on one of the magnificent packets then on the river, and he succeeded in getting a clerkship on one of the boats plying between St. Louis and New Orleans. This position was of value to him in after life, as it brought him in contact with the various phases of human life and nature, and it also added to his capital. His next position was as clerk in a hotel in that once famous resort, Sulphur Springs, near St. Louis. He there became acquainted with prominent men of wealth, and later a company was formed for the purchase of several thousand acres of timber land near St. Louis, and Mr. Johnston was put in charge of the cutting. This was a gigantic task and brought young Johnston in contact with another phase of mankind, as he had in his employ hundreds of laborers of all classes.

In 1841 Mr. Johnston came to Ogle county, Illinois, where his brother James, an extensive farmer, was then living, and whose lands lay just east of the village of Oregon. He there established an office and employed himself in loaning money for a few years. Later he formed a partnership with J. C. T. Phelps, his brother-in-law, and engaged in merchandising. They were well fixed financially, and also had unlimited credit, and established a number of trading posts in Illinois and Wisconsin. This partnership lasted for sixteen years.

They had stores in Peru and LaSalle, in LaSalle county, and while living at Peru, Mr. Johnston was elected county treasurer of LaSalle county during one of the most exciting periods of the county's existence. From Peru they went to Polo, Illinois, and established themselves in the banking business. Soon the great state of Texas attracted the attention of these gentlemen, and ever ready to embrace opportunities for business, they started in 1857 for that southwestern empire, locating at Austin, where they opened a general store, and also had business at other points. They were quite successful, but the air soon became full of secession, and these business men were looked upon with suspicion. The Southern confederacy was formed, and before the battle of Bull's Run their goods were confiscated, and they returned to Illinois, satisfied to get out with their lives.

In 1865 Mr. Johnston retired from active trade and established a real estate and loan office at Oregon, which he continued up to the time of his death, which occurred September 5, 1893, at the residence of his daughter, Mrs. Wagoner, where he had made his home since the death of his wife. The funeral services were conducted by Rev. Barton Cartwright. He had accumulated a valuable estate, which, with his honored name, he left to his heirs. He was a man of fine social qualities, a good conversationalist, which, added to his vast experience and stirring events in his life, made him a very interesting companion. He was quite domestic in his taste, fond of his family and friends, and they were of him, and loved him. He had erected for himself and family, at Oregon, a large and handsome residence, in which, surrounded by his family, he spent his declining years. He died, mourned and regretted by all.

In 1848 Mr. Johnston married Sarah Louise Phelps, daughter of Judge John and Sarah (Carlin) Phelps, cousin of Governor Carlin, this state, her father being the founder of Oregon. He was a native of Bedford county, Virginia, and came to Illinois early in the thirties. In 1835 he located in Ogle county, where he had staked a claim in 1833, his attention having been called to this beautiful location by Colonel William Hamilton, son of Alexander Hamilton. A two-story log house was built in 1834, in the erection of which his brother-in-law, James C. T. Phelps, so long and prominently connected with Ogle county, assisted. This house was situated just below where the old Catholic stone church now stands. This house was used by the first circuit court held in the county. John Phelps was the first probate judge to hold court in the county, which was also held in this house. He was a man of the people, and was elected and served as a member of the legislature. John Phelps was born in Bedford county, Virginia, August 9, 1790, and died April 2, 1874. His wife died in 1879. They had three children—James C. T., who died at his home in Kansas City, Missouri, December 24, 1895; Sarah L., and Napoleon B., the latter dying in New Orleans, December 10, 1857. The family were related to Governor Carlin, of this state. Mrs. Johnston was born in Lebanon, Tennessee, March 27, 1817, and her mother, Sarah Regan Carlin, was born in Nashville, Tennessee, April 29, 1797. She came to Ogle county with her father in May, 1835, where she first met Wesley Johnston, to whom she was married June 8, 1848, by S. Wooley, a justice of the peace, at her father's house, over the old store, No. 118 North Third street, corner Washington and Third streets. She departed this life October 4, 1889. She was a devout Christian woman, a devoted wife and mother, and was much beloved by all who knew her. She was a member of the Episcopal church, of which body Mr. Johnston was also a member. In politics he was originally a Democrat, but later became a Republican. They were the parents of four children: Timoleon O., our subject; Sarah Alice, who married S. G. Jones, but is now deceased; Eva E. and James W., the latter being in business in Chicago.

The subject of this sketch was educated at Sinsinawa Mound and at Rock River Seminary, Mt. Morris. After learning the printer's trade in the office of the Oregon National Guard, he went to Vinton, Benton county, Iowa, and was there connected with the Vinton Semi-Weekly Eagle for about three years. He then returned to Oregon and purchased an interest in the Ogle County Reporter, February 16, 1872. At the end of six months he purchased the entire interest in the plant and became sole proprietor. From that time to the present he has continued in charge of the paper, a longer period of time than the publisher of any local paper in the state.

Mr. Johnston was united in marriage December 30, 1869, at Vinton, Iowa, to Miss Mary E. Shockley, daughter of Philip and Mary Shockley. Her parents are yet living in Vinton, Iowa, and celebrated their golden wedding in June, 1898. To Mr. and Mrs. Johnston three children have been born. May Aileen is now the wife of William L. Katzenberger, of Baltimore, Maryland; John P. is in the office with his father. He married Hattie E. Sutphen, of Rochelle, and daughter of Peter M. and Maggie (Kelly) Sutphen. They have one child, Timoleon O. The remaining member of the family is Lillian Eidola, who was married to William F. Rudolphy, of Chicago, April 27, 1898.

Mr. Johnston has taken an active and leading part in the politics of Ogle county. He was elected alderman in 1877-8, and then in 1879-80. In 1883 he was elected mayor and served one term. He was elected secretary of the Republican Editorial Association, of Illinois, in 18—, and was elected president of the Press Association at the Bloomington convention, in 1888, and has been secretary of the Republican Editorial Association of Illinois. He was secretary of the Old Settlers' Association of Ogle county, and has been vice-president of the same since the death of his father and served as president of the same in 1896. He has been delegate to various conventions from time to time, and is now on the State Editorial Republican committee. In May, 1897, he was appointed, by Governor Tanner, as trustee of the Southern Illinois State Normal University at Carbondale, Illinois.

Fraternally Mr. Johnston is a member of the Masonic order, holding membership with Oregon Lodge, No. 420, R. A. M., Rock River Chapter, No. 151, and Dixon Commandery, and the Modern Woodmen of America. He is also a member of Oregon Lodge, No. 94, I. O. O. F., and of the Independent Order of Improved Red Men.

The Ogle County Reporter, which has so long been conducted by Mr. Johnston, is a Republican journal, and one of the leading papers of the county. It is a seven column quarto, and is issued every Wednesday, being ably edited by its proprietor, who makes of it a bright newsy sheet. A good job office is connected with the paper, where first-class work is done.

Mr. Johnston is the only representative now in Ogle county of two prominent and leading families who were early settlers in the county, and who left their mark on its civilization. He is a worthy representative of these families and holds up their honored name. He has an ample fortune mostly derived from the estate of his father, and is liberal in aiding all public enterprises that center in the development of the county and in charitable work. He has a host of friends, not only in Ogle county, but throughout the state.

REV. N. J. STROH, deceased, was a man deserving of the highest honors, one who gave the best years of his life for the betterment of his fellowmen. He was born in Liken's Valley, Pennsylvania, May 5, 1798, and after receiving a fairly good education in the grammar schools of his native county he entered college under the direction of Rev. Lockman, a minister of the Lutheran church, who educated for the ministry a number of young men, with the design of having them enter the missionary field. After completing his course Mr. Stroh was ordained to the ministry by the Lutheran Synod of Pennsylvania. This was about 1823. After preaching for a number of churches in the east, with a view of restoring his health which had been impaired, he came west, traveling throughout Illinois and other states.

Returning east, in 1826, Mr. Stroh was united in marriage, near Newville, Pennsylvania, with Miss Elizabeth Givler, born December 2, 1807, and by this union ten children were born: Maria, November 23,

REV. N. J. STROH.

1828, Luther M., April 17, 1830; Muehlenberg, July 28, 1832; Martha E., September 6, 1835; Rhenius, April 27, 1837; Christavius A., September 16, 1840; Alfred E., March 6, 1842; Augusta C. and Cecelia A., twins, February 16, 1844; and Josephine, June 6, 1848.

After remaining and preaching in the east for a number of years, Rev. Stroh, in 1845, came to Ogle county, Illinois, and located at Oregon, where he resided one year, in the meantime organizing the Lutheran church at that place. He then moved to Mt. Morris and purchased two large farms, on one of which he made his home, and there resided for many years engaged in agricultural pursuits, and preaching the gospel in regions roundabout. He organized the Lutheran church in Mt. Morris, and for a number of years ministered to its spiritual wants. After a long and useful life, he was called to his reward January 1, 1897, being in his ninety-ninth year. His wife died November 10, 1894. She was a good woman, a worthy helpmeet to her husband and a devout member of the Lutheran church. In politics Mr. Stroh was a Democrat, but he did not mingle much in political affairs. He was much beloved by the people, not alone of his own religious communion, but by all others, and his death was sincerely mourned. "Truly a prophet in Israel has fallen."

Maria E. Stroh, the first of the children born to Rev. and Mrs. Stroh, grew to womanhood and July 4, 1846, was united in marriage with Philip R. Bennett, a merchant doing business in Oregon, who was born in Massachusetts, October 10, 1824. He departed this life March 1, 1855. They became the parents of four children: Frederick W., born September 11, 1848; Walter S., August 4, 1850; Arthur V., September 30, 1852; and Philip, January 31, 1855. Mrs. Bennett, January 4, 1860, was again married, her second union being with William Schultz, a native of New York state, born May 23, 1823. By this union four children were born: William, September 21, 1860; John R., July 26, 1862; Mary L., April 12, 1864; and Katie L., February 13, 1866.

For some years Mr. Schultz was engaged in the real estate business in Mt. Morris. Later he moved to Oregon and continued in the same line of business with gratifying success. He died in Oregon February 28, 1879. As a business man he was enterprising, ever ready to assist in any enterprise that would be of benefit to his adopted city and county. In politics he was a Republican, and religiously a Lutheran, being a member of the church at Oregon.

After the death of her husband, Mrs. Schultz moved with her son Walter to Grand Island, Nebraska, where she resided for some years. In October, 1896, she returned to Mt. Morris to care for her aged father, who died a few months later. She still makes her home in the village where she is so well known and where she is surrounded by many old friends.

MICHAEL GARMAN, now living in retirement in Forreston, is one of Ogle county's pioneer citizens, and a gentleman whose life has contributed largely to its development along industrial and educational lines. He dates his residence in the county since May 28, 1842. He was born in Lebanon county, Pennsylvania, January 10, 1821, and there lived until six years of age, removing with his parents to Northumberland county, in the same state, where he was educated and grew to manhood. After his school days, he became an apprentice to the shoemaking trade, but because of its close confinement he soon gave it up and selected a healthier life at farm work on his father's farm. In 1842, he came west with his parents, and settled in what was then Mt. Morris township, his father purchasing two hundred acres, and beginning its cultivation.

On the 16th of April, 1844, Mr. Garman was united in marriage with Miss Elizabeth Fagar, a daughter of Coonrod and Hosanna (Fisher) Fagar. She was a native of Northumberland county, Pennsylvania, born March 17, 1823, and came west with her parents the same year in which the Garman family settled here. By this union were eleven children as follows: Sarah Ann and John Henry, who died in infancy; Joel Ezra, a farmer residing near Adelaine; Louise Josephine, Lucinda Rebecca, Emma Frances, and Helen Ada, who died in infancy; Lucy Alice, wife of Harvey Alters, a farmer of Lincoln township, Ogle county; Ida Honora, wife of Alfred Meyers, a farmer of Woosung township, Ogle county; Newton Alvan, a merchant of Sioux City, Iowa; and Gerard Michael, who enjoys a fine dental practice in Chicago. Mrs. Garman, the mother of these children, lived to see the living ones married and settled comfortably, and then passed away September 2, 1898.

Michael Garman lived in Lincoln township, until 1880, and by his frugality and industry, acquired a competency in choice and well-improved farm property. While yet residing in Mt. Morris township, he held the office of assessor two years, and from 1844 to 1848, was town treasurer. He was township trustee for twelve years and school director of district No. 1 twenty-four years. In Lincoln township he was supervisor one year and assessor two years, school trustee ten years, president of the school board in Forreston nine years, and president of the town board one year. He holds the remarkable record of service in educational affairs, continuously since 1844. His first presidential ballot was cast for James K. Polk, in 1844, and he is yet a stanch Democrat.

Mr. Garman's ancestors came from Germany to America some years prior to the Revolutionary war. His grandfather, Michael Garman, was a native of York county, Pennsylvania, and was born in 1747. He had a creditable military record, and served seven years in the Revolutionary struggle, and was taken prisoner by the enemy in the battle of Brandywine. He had the rank of sergeant, and, being a blacksmith by trade, had the entire management of the blacksmith department during the war. The hardships endured brought on an illness which terminated in his untimely death, January 8, 1800. He married Susanna Sheets, who was born in Lancaster county, Pennsylvania, August 16, 1768. They were united in marriage in Dalton county, Pennsylvania, in 1785, and became the parents of six children: Catherine, wife of John Wertz, a farmer of Northumberland county, Pennsylvania; Martin, who followed the trade of shoemaker in Northumberland county, Pennsylvania; Benjamin, who died in infancy; Jacob, who in early life learned the trade of tailoring, but who later became a farmer, and who removed with his family to Illinois in 1844; Michael, the father of our subject, and George, a farmer of Northumberland county, Pennsylvania.

Our subject's father was born September 29, 1798, in Northumberland county, Pennsylvania, where he attended school, and afterwards learned the blacksmith's trade, at which he worked until twenty-six, when he was elected constable, in which office he served until 1833. On the 21st of June, 1826, he married Rebecca Mace, daughter of John Mace, a farmer of Lebanon county, Pennsylvania. To this marriage there was born one child, Michael, the subject of this sketch. The father died August 11, 1870, his remains being buried in West Grove cemetery, Lincoln township. His wife survived him, dying February 24, 1874, and her remains were interred beside those of her husband's.

Mr. Garman's maternal great-grandfather, Jacob Mace, was born in Lebanon county, Pennsylvania, and followed farming. In 1750, he married a Miss Baker, and one of the children of this marriage was John Mace, the father of our subject's mother. John Mace was born in Lebanon county, Pennsylvania, and married Miss Margaret Jacoby, daughter of Jacob Jacoby, and by this union were four children: Mary, Rebecca, Jacob and John.

Mrs. Michael Garman, the wife of our subject, was one of a family of twelve children, eight surviving as follows: Daniel, residing in Forreston, Samuel, living in Lincoln township; Sarah Fagar Maze, living in Forreston township; Isaac, of Brookville township; Peter, of Forreston township; David, of Willow Springs, Kansas; Henry, of Osage county, Kansas; and Hosanna, wife of Daniel Hoelshue, living at Herndon, Northumberland county, Pennsylvania.

Mr. Garman and family are devout members of the Evangelical association. He is among Forreston's and Ogle county's most highly esteemed citizens, and the confidence and regard in which he is held is evidenced daily in his advice and counsel being sought, and his assistance being rendered in the settlement of estates. His life has been an open book, and he has freely given of his time to aid in the general improvement of his county, and has especially been helpful in social, educational and religious affairs.

JOHN S. HASTINGS, one of Ogle county's most thrifty and energetic farmers, whose home is on section 8, Marion township, was born in Clark county, Ohio, September 19, 1846, and is a son of Edmond Hastings, who was born in one of the New England states, and when a young man went to Ohio. In Clark county he wedded Miss Mary Ann Sheaff, a native of New York, and a daughter of John Sheaff, a pioneer of that county, who removed from Pennsylvania to New York, and from there to Ohio. Coming west in 1850, Mr. Hastings located on a tract of wild land in Ogle county and at once commenced the improvement and cultivation of his place. He was joined by his wife and family the following year, and continued the operation of his farm until his death, which occurred in 1856. His widow subsequently married John M. Hinckle, now deceased, and now makes her home with a daughter in Oregon, Illinois, a hale and hearty old lady of seventy-four years. By the first union there were four children: Mary, who married, and died leaving a family; Emma C., wife of a Mr. Frace, of Holcomb, Illinois; John S., of this review; and Peter E., a business man of Oregon.

Brought to Ogle county during childhood,

John S. Hastings was reared by his mother upon the home farm in Marion township, and obtained his education in the common and higher schools of the county. Although only sixteen years of age, he enlisted in February, 1864, in Company F, Thirty-fourth Illinois Volunteer Infantry, and joined the regiment at Oregon. He participated in many important engagements, including the battles of Rocky Faced Ridge, Buzzard Roost, Resaca, Rome, Georgia, Peach Tree Creek, the siege of Atlanta, the battle of Goldsboro, and the march with Sherman to the sea. Later he took part in the battle and capture of Savannah, Bentonville, South Carolina, and Averyboro, and at the close of the war participated in the grand review at Washington, District of Columbia. He was always found at his post of duty, valiantly fighting for the old flag and the cause it represented, and when hostilities ceased was honorably discharged in July, 1865. He was never confined to the hospital and lost no time from his regiment.

After his return home Mr. Hastings attended school in Rockford for three months and then began work on the home farm, which he continued to operate after his marriage until 1880, when he purchased the place where he now resides. It comprises one hundred and twenty acres of highly cultivated and well improved land, on which he has erected a large barn and other out-buildings, making it one of the most desirable farms of the locality. He thoroughly understands his chosen calling and has met with a well-deserved success.

At Oregon, Ogle county, in December, 1876, was celebrated the marriage of Mr. Hastings and Miss Rachel J. Page, who was born, reared and educated here, her father, Robert Page, having come to the county at an early day from Ohio. Four children bless this union: Charles E., at home; Mabel L., who was well educated in the schools of Byron and is now a successful teacher; Herbert J. and Eva B., both at home.

In his political affiliations Mr. Hastings has always been an ardent Republican, casting his first presidential ballot for Gen. U. S. Grant in 1868. For several years he was an efficient member of the school board and was president of the district. Fraternally he is a Master Mason, belonging to the blue lodge at Byron, and is also an honored member of the Grand Army post. He is a public-spirited, enterprising citizen of known reliability, and has the confidence and esteem of all with whom he comes in contact either in business or social life.

HENRY A. PARKS one of the enterprising farmers of Ogle county, resides on section 22, Woosung township. He was born January 15, 1847, in Palmyra, Lee county, Illinois, and is the son of Hiram P. Parks and Martha (Moon) Parks, early settlers of Lee county. Hiram P. Parks was born at Malone, New York, in 1806, and resided there until twenty-two years of age, when he came to Illinois and located in what is now Palmyra township, Lee county, which was his home until his death in 1885. His first tract comprised one hundred and twenty acres, to which he later added fifty acres. In politics he was a Republican in later life, and religiously was a Baptist. In his family were eight children, seven of whom are yet living. Mary first married Rodney Mason, of Lee county, and afterwards John Lawrence, of the same county. Rebecca, one of the first white children born in Lee county, married Thomas Ayers, who is now deceased, and a brother of William Ayers. She now resides in Dixon, Illinois. Wainwright married Lydia Sayres, who died leaving two children who reside in Dixon. Bruce is a farmer residing near Dorchester, Nebraska. Henry A. is next in order of birth. Frederick is in the flour and feed business in Seward, Nebraska. Abner, when last heard from, resided in St. Louis, Missouri. Eunice married William Ayers, and they now reside in Hardin county, Iowa.

The subject of this sketch grew to manhood on the home farm in Lee county, and was educated in the public schools. When seventeen years of age he entered the store of Willis G. House, of Dixon, Illinois, where he remained five years as a clerk. About 1869, in company with his brother, Wainwright, and his cousin, Clinton Coe, he bought three hundred and twenty acres of land in Woosung township, Ogle county. They were all single men, and kept "bach" while improving their place. After working the farm for several years and putting it under good improvement, they divided the land, one hundred and sixty acres falling to our subject, which is comprised in his present farm.

On the 24th of July, 1872, Mr. Parks was united in marriage with Miss Marcia L. Hathaway, who was born in Grand Detour, Illinois, and daughter of Stephen and Sophronia (Wetherby) Hathaway, the latter being the first white woman to locate in that village. By this union were two daughters who died in infancy. They have now one daughter, Selma Ione, who is a joy and a comfort to them.

Stephen E. Hathaway, the father of Mrs. Parks, was born in Barnard, Windsor county, Vermont, October 15, 1815, and there grew to manhood. In 1836 he came west and located in Grand Detour, where he engaged in work at his trade of wagonmaker, a business which he has followed throughout life. For the last ten years, however, he has lived retired, making his home with our subject. Sophronia Wetherby was a daughter of Charles and Sarah (Hurd) Wetherby, and was born in Worcester, Massachusetts, August 31, 1816. She was a maiden of sixteen or seventeen when she came with the first colony to Grand Detour. Among those in that colony were Leonard Andrus, Willard and Harry House and Mrs. Willard House. They crossed the river by ferry, and in going over Mrs. House playfully declared her intention of being the first white woman to set foot in Grand Detour, but Harry House, in jest, detained her, while Miss Wetherby, taking advantage of the opportunity, stepped ashore, and therefore was the first. To Stephen Hathaway and wife two children were born—Marcia L., now Mrs. Parks; and Wells F., now a resident of Dixon. Mrs. Hathaway died October 12, 1867.

Commencing life without means, Mr. Parks has been fairly successful, and what he has he owes to no one save his faithful wife, who has been to him a true helpmeet. They have toiled together and the result is shown by their home surroundings, their place being in excellent repair, and everything about it showing that it is controlled by a master mind. In politics he is a Republican, and religiously a Baptist, holding membership with the church in Dixon. In the work of the church he has taken great interest, and contributes liberally of his means to its support. He has taken interest also in educational matters, and has served as school director for some years, and has filled other offices in the township with credit to himself and to his constituents.

ERASTUS W. SCHRYVER, who owns and operates a valuable farm of one hundred and sixty acres on section 34, Eagle Point township, first came to Ogle county in the spring of 1839, and throuhgout the greater part of his life has been prominently identified with its agricultural interests. He was born in Andes, Delaware county, New York, September 16, 1829, a son of Matthew and Ann (Webster) Schryver, also natives of that county. The maternal grandfather, Elijah Webster, was a near relative of the great statesman, Daniel Webster. The father of our subject, who was born in 1797, spent his early life in his native state, working at farm labor, on the canal or at anything he could find to do. Coming west in 1839, he took up a claim of one hundred and sixty acres of land in what is now Eagle township, Ogle county, upon which he built a cabin, which was the home of the family for a number of years, while he fenced, broke and cultivated his farm. He set out an orchard, later built a good frame house and barn, and transformed the wild land into highly cultivated fields. He departed this life in 1872, his wife December 13, 1880, and both were buried in the United Brethren church cemetery, where a monument now marks their last resting place. Both were active members of the Methodist Episcopal church, were consistent Christian people, and had the respect and esteem of all who knew them.

Erastus W. Schryver is the third in order of birth in a family of six children, five sons and one daughter, who reached years of maturity. John Henry, the eldest, married and settled in Ogle county, where he died in 1867; Jesse is a farmer of Eagle Point township; Samuel B. also located here after his marriage, but later removed to Hardin county, Iowa, where his death occurred in 1897; George is a farmer of Minnesota; and Eliza Jane Ann is the wife of Henry Landers, of Hardin county, Iowa.

The subject of this review was a lad of ten years when he came with his parents to Ogle county, and in the development and improvement of the old home farm he bore an important part, remaining with his father until he attained his majority. His school privileges were limited, so that he is mostly self-educated. In 1850 he went to California by way of Omaha, where a wagon train was made up to cross the plains. The party started with four yoke of oxen, but on reaching their destination had but one yoke remaining, having been six months and fifteen days upon the road. Mr. Schryver arrived at the mines September 16, of that year, and for nearly three years was engaged in hunting the yellow metal with a fair degree of success. In the spring of 1853 he started eastward, leaving San Francisco February 1, and by way of the Isthmus of Panama and Aspinwall proceeding to New York city, where they arrived on the 28th of that month. From New York he went to Chicago and from there home.

In Eagle Point township Mr. Schryver bought eighty acres of land, only five acres of which had been broke and a few fruit trees set out. To the further improvement and cultivation of his farm he at once turned his attention, and in 1856 he erected thereon a good residence. Selling the place in 1864, he went to Idaho by means of teams and engaged in mining for a year and a half, returning to Ogle county by the same means in the fall of 1866. He then purchased his present place of one hundred and sixty acres, and he now owns another farm of eighty-seven and a half acres two miles farther east. Upon his home place he has built a commodious and pleasant residence, a good barn, granary and cribs, and has set out an orchard and ornamental trees, and now has one of the neatest and best improved places of Eagle Point township. In connection with general farming he is interested in breeding and raising stock of good grades, and is accounted one of the successful farmers and stock-raisers of the county.

On the 16th of April, 1857, in Ogle county, Mr. Schryver was united in marriage with Miss Lucinda Landes, a native of Niles, Michigan, and a daughter of Solomon and Elizabeth (Detamore) Landes, natives of Rockingham county, Virginia, where they were reared and married. The father, who was born in 1806, took his family to Michigan at an early day, and after spending six years there, came to Ogle county, Illinois, in October, 1835, being among the first settlers here. He took up a claim, and from the wild land developed a good farm, upon which he died in 1893, honored and respected by all who knew him. He was twice married, Mrs. Schryver's mother having died in 1866, and both were laid to rest in the United Brethren church cemetery. Mr. and Mrs. Schryver have passed almost their entire lives together, as they were reared in the same neighborhood, attended the same school, and in company with her family she went to California with him in 1850, and returned together by way of the Isthmus. After their marriage she accompanied him on going to Idaho, and their married life has been a most happy one, as they have shared with each other its joys and sorrows, its adversity and prosperity. They have two sons: Albert, residing on the home place, is married and has three children: George, Lucinda and Erastus; and Fletcher, a farmer of Eagle Point township, is married and has one daughter, Anna.

Politically Mr. Schryver has been a lifelong Democrat, casting his first presidential ballot for Franklin Pierce in 1852, while in California. At local elections, however, he endeavors to support the best men for the office, regardless of party affiliations, but he has never sought nor desired political preferment for himself. His life is exemplary in many respects and he has the esteem and confidence of the entire community in which he has so long made his home and where he is so widely known.

SOLOMON BELL BOWERMAN, M. D., a prominent and successful physician and surgeon of Leaf River, Ogle county, was born near Harrisburg, Dauphin county, Pennsylvania, March 3, 1830, a son of John A. Bowerman and grandson of William Bowerman, both natives of the Keystone state. The kingdom of Holland, which has given to the world one of its hardiest races of people, sheltered the paternal ancestors of our subject, but the family was founded in Lancaster county, Pennsylvania, at an early day. On reaching manhood John A. Bowerman, our subject's father, married Miss Ann Maria Woland, a native of Dauphin county and a daughter of John Woland, who was born in Lancaster county, Pennsylvania. They continued to make their home in that state throughout life, the mother dying in 1854 and the father in 1894, at the ripe old age of eighty-five years. By occupation he was a farmer. They reared a family of seven children, four sons and three daughters, all of whom are still living.

In the county of his nativity Dr. Bowerman spent his boyhood and youth, received good common-school advantages and also attended the Perrysburg Seminary for a time. Subsequently he engaged in teaching school there for several years. He first came to Ogle county, Illinois, in 1858, and taught school for a time in Leaf River township, but in the spring of 1859 returned to his native state. He had previously devoted his vacations and leisure time to the study of medicine for some years, and on his return to Pennsylvania took his first course of lectures at the old Philadelphia Medical College. After completing the course he returned home and engaged in practice in his old neighborhood until the outbreak of the Civil war.

The Doctor was then serving as lieutenant-colonel of the uniformed militia of Pennsylvania, and in November, 1862, enlisted for one year in Company A, One Hundred and Seventy-second Pennsylvania Volunteer Infantry. On the organization of the company he was elected first lieutenant, and in January, 1863, was promoted to the captaincy, in which capacity he served until mustered out at the close of his term in September, 1863. He was first on detached duty and had charge of the artillery at Yorktown, Virginia, but later the regiment was transferred to the Eleventh Corps, Army of the Potomac. During the winter of 1863-4 Dr. Bowerman attended two courses of medical lectures at Philadelphia, and was later engaged in practice for a short time, but in 1864 re-enlisted in his country's service, and was commissioned captain of Company A, Two Hundred and Tenth Pennsylvania Volunteer Infantry. With his command he participated in the battles of Hatcher's Run, Dapey's Mills, Gravelly Run, the engagements in front of Petersburg, and the battle of Five Forks. They continued the pursuit of the rebel army until Lee surrendered to Grant at Appomattox Court House. Our subject was breveted major and commanded the regiment in front of Petersburg and at Five Forks, and later took part in the grand review at Washington, District of Columbia, in which city he was mustered out in August, 1865.

Returning to Philadelphia, Dr. Bowerman again attended lectures for three terms, and was graduated from the Eclectic Medical College of Philadelphia, in the class of 1866. After two years practice at his old home in Dauphin county he came to Illinois, arriving in Ogle county, August 20, 1868. Locating in Lightsville, he resumed practice and as time passed his patronage rapidly increased until he had all that he could attend to, and he still enjoys a large and remunerative practice.

Dr. Bowerman was married in Ogle county, in 1873, to Miss Margaret Motter, a native of Pennsylvania, and a daughter of Leonard Motter, who located here in 1859. They have become the parents of four children, as follows: Hughlins E., acquired his literary education in the home school and the Wells school of Oregon, and after studying medicine with his father for some time, he attended lectures at Bennett Medical College, Chicago, where he was graduated in the class of 1897. He is now successfully engaged in practice with his father. Adda is the wife of Elmer Myers, of Leaf River township. Anna and Minnie are both at home with their parents. Mrs. Bowerman is a member of the Evangelical church, and the family is one of prominence in the best social circles of the community.

Politically the Doctor is identified with the Republican party, and he has taken an active and prominent part in public affairs. He served for two years as assessor of his township, four years as justice of the peace and as supervisor two terms. While a member of the county board he was chairman of the committee on education, for nine years was a member of the local school board, and has been an important factor in raising the standard of the schools in Ogle county. Fraternally he is an honored member of the State Eclectic Medical Society, and he stands deservedly high among his professional brethren. Wherever he goes he wins friends and has the happy faculty of being able to retain them. His popularity has made him a great favorite in all circles.

NOAH PRESTON, a representative and leading farmer of Marion township, residing on section 33, is a fair specimen of the sturdy agriculturist who have so largely assisted in the development of Ogle county. Here he has met with success in his undertakings and is now the owner of two valuable farms near the village of Byron.

Mr. Preston was born in Oneida county, New York, November 29, 1838, and is a grandson of Noah Preston, Sr., an early settler of that county, who was born in 1763, in Connecticut, and was reared in that state. He was a soldier of the war of 1812, and died April 9, 1835, while his wife, Honor Preston, who was born May 28, 1766, died November 22, 1847. The birth of the father, John S. Preston, occurred in Oneida county, in 1804, and there he was married, May 14, 1834, to Miss Amanda Tuttle, a daughter of Lyman Tuttle. She died in Oneida county, and he was again married, December 27, 1837, his second union being with Mrs. Elmira Robbins, also a native of Oneida county, and a daughter of Amasa Barnes. Mr. Preston was a well-educated man and for nine years successfully followed the teacher's profession in the Empire state. Later he located on a farm and devoted his attention to agriculture. In 1854 he came to Ogle county, Illinois, arriving here May 10, and joining his brother, who had located here in 1852. He purchased land and improved the farm on which our subject is now living, making his home there until called from this life September 2, 1879, at the ripe old age of seventy-five years. His wife survived him for some time, dying May 13, 1888, at the age of seventy-seven, and both were laid to rest in Stillman cemetery. Noah is the eldest of the four children born of the second marriage of both parents, the others being John D., a resident of Shelbina, Shelby county, Missouri; Amanda, widow of Silas Noble, of Marion township, Ogle county; and Sarah A., widow of Dr. Delos Hurlbut and a resident of Iowa.

Noah Preston was a lad of fourteen years when he came with his parents to Ogle county, and on the home farm grew to manhood. After arriving at mature years he took charge of the farm and cared for his parents during their declining years. On their deaths he came into possession of the place and now gives his entire attention to its cultivation and improvement. On the 4th of June, 1865, in Marion township, was celebrated his marriage with Miss

Ruth A. Baker, a daughter of Warren Baker, of Oneida county, New York. She came to Ogle county with her brother, Amasa Baker, who graduated at Mt. Morris College and engaged in teaching here for some years. Later he went to Kansas, there married and spent the remainder of his life. Mrs. Preston is also a native of Oneida county, New York, and was educated at the Holland Patent Academy, New York, where she was a classmate of President Cleveland's two sisters and one brother. She has often heard the President's father preach. After leaving school she successfully engaged in teaching in her native state and also after coming to Ogle county, in 1861. Mr. and Mrs. Preston have a family of six children, as follows: Olive, now the wife of Elsworth McNeal, a farmer, mechanic and carpenter, of Marion township; Lucy, wife of Henry Alfred, a farmer of the same township; Nellie, Edna, Rossiter and Myrtle, all at home. The children have all been well educated and are an honor to their worthy parents.

Since casting his first presidental vote for Abraham Lincoln in 1860, Mr. Preston has been a stalwart supporter of the men and measures of the Republican party, but he has never cared for official honors. He has ever used his influence to secure good schools and for some years was an active and capable member of the school board. In the Methodist Episcopal church he and his wife hold membership, and in the esteem and confidence of their fellow citizens they hold an enviable position.

DANIEL WORTHINGTON YOUNG, one of the prominent and highly respected residents of Rockvale township, is the subject of this sketch. He was born July 4, 1844, on his father's farm in Oregon township. He received his education first at the district school and later at Mount Morris, where he attended the Rock River Seminary. He is the son of William and Nancy (Long) Young, who left their home in Maryland for the "far west" in 1843. They were farmers by occupation, and when coming to Illinois made the journey by team, the only method of traveling across the country in pioneer days, and which required about three months' time. They went direct to Ogle county, where Mr. Young's death occurred in 1889. He rests in Salem meeting house cemetery, Pine Creek township. Mrs. Young was born in 1819, and was the daughter of Daniel and Elizabeth Long, and married Mr. Young at the age of sixteen. She was one of twelve children, nine girls and three boys, all of whom grew to maturity. Her death occurred in 1870, at the age of fifty-one.

Mr. and Mrs. Young were blessed with ten children. Elizabeth, the eldest, is living at Mount Morris, and is the widow of Samuel Price. George married Mary Wagner, and they occupy the homestead in Oregon township. William and Joshua died when very young. Daniel Worthington, of this writing, was the fifth child. Henry married Miss Grover, of Manson, Iowa, and is a physician of considerable note at that place. Mary, the seventh child, died when two years of age. B. Frank is a pharmacist in Manson, Iowa, where he married Miss Nettie Grover, a sister of Mrs. Henry Young. Amanda married Henry C. Munn, and is living in Pine Creek township. The youngest child, Charles C., died at the age of four years.

Mr. Young, the subject of this sketch,

attended school and helped his father until he was twenty-one years of age, when he left school and farmed with his father until his marriage, four years later; at the expiration of this time he rented land in Oregon township, where he and his family resided for two years, moving later to Mount Morris township, where they lived for eleven years, and in 1883 moved to Rockvale, where Mr. Young purchased one hundred and sixty acres on section 19. This property, under his management, has become a well-regulated and valuable tract, yielding its owner a handsome income.

When twenty-five years of age Mr. Young was united in marriage to Ann Elizabeth Wagner. To them five children have been born. The eldest child, Edith, is at home with her parents. She received her education at the district school and at Mount Morris Seminary. Susie also received her education at the above named school. She is the wife of N. F. Thomas, a farmer of Mount Morris township, and is the mother of one child, H. Worthington. Charles Worthington is, at the present writing, at home. He has just finished a course of pharmacy at the Normal School, Valparaiso, Indiana, preparatory to entering business. Nannie, the fourth in order of birth, married R. C. Gaffin, a farmer in Leaf River township. They have one child, a daughter, Dorathy M. The youngest child, Alice, is living at home, attending the district school.

Mrs. Young is the daughter of Joseph and Susan (Scheeter) Wagner, and is the seventh in order of birth. Her parents came to Oregon township in the pioneer days, and purchased three hundred and twenty acres, at a dollar and twenty-five cents per acre. They made the journey overland by team, stopping at Springfield, Ohio, for the winter, and reaching Ogle county, in 1837. Mr. Wagner was a clear-sighted and successful man of business. He supervised the work on his farm in Oregon, and was a stock-dealer and shipper; he was also a banker, having been connected with the Exchange Bank, of Oregon. Mr. Wagner died March 10, 1889, and his wife, three months earlier.

Mrs. Young is a member of the German Baptist church. Her great-grandparents were people of considerable prominence, as were their children after them. Captain B. R. Wagner, who was for several terms sheriff of Ogle county, died in 1897 from the effects of a bullet received in the battle of Shiloh. Three uncles served in the war. Captains D. C. and Nehemiah were captured and held as prisoners of war at Macon, Georgia.

Our subject is a Republican in politics, but has never cared for a position in public office, nor for social organizations. He is strictly a home man, more interested in his family and the education of his children than in anything else, his children being more than ordinarily bright and well educated.

GEORGE HETTIGER, the leading merchant tailor of Oregon, Illinois, is a native of Louisville, Kentucky. His father, Joseph Hettiger, was born in Munich, Bavaria, and came to the United States at the age of five years with his father, Jacob Hettiger, who died in Evansville, Indiana, although he first settled in Louisville, Kentucky, where Joseph grew to manhood and spent the remainder of his life, his death occurring April 4, 1879. He was by occupation a contractor and builder. In politics he was a Union Democrat, and during the rebellion was a member of the home guards. Religiously he was a Roman Catholic, of which body his wife is also a member. He married Susanna Lehnen, a native of Trier, Germany, born near Frankfort on the Main. She came to the United States with her parents, who settled in Dubois county, Indiana. She is still living in Louisville, Kentucky. Joseph and Susanna Hettiger were the parents of ten children, as follows: George, our subject; Mary, wife of Edward Kurtz, of Chicago; Ferdinand, living in St. Louis, Mo.; Johanna, in a convent in Mexico; Martin, living in St. Louis; Susie, who died in childhood; Susie (2), who died in infancy; Frank, living in New Orleans, and Edward, who lives in Louisville, Kentucky.

The early life of our subject was spent in his native city, where he attended the parochial schools, and at the age of sixteen years commenced to learn the tailor's trade. After completing his trade, he first went to St. Louis, where he worked as a journeyman, and later worked in Cincinnati, Chicago and other places, finally locating in Bloomington, Illinois, in 1878, where he lived nine years, and in 1887 came to Oregon, Illinois, where he has since continued to reside. On coming to Oregon he first engaged as cutter for Mr. Snyder, and remained in his employ for five years. He then commenced in business for himself on Washington street, between Fourth and Fifth, where he yet remains.

Mr. Hettiger was married July 15, 1875, at Columbus, Ohio, to Kate Whiteaker, of Fort Wayne, Indiana, daughter of D. L. and Sarah (Zimmerman) Whiteaker. Her father was a prominent lawyer of Fort Wayne, Indiana, but is now deceased. Her mother is yet living, making her home in Grand Rapids, Minnesota. They had a large family, but all are now deceased, but the wife of our subject; Robert E., living in Minnesota; and Rosa, wife of Samuel Stell, of Dixon, Illinois. An uncle of Mrs. Hettiger, John Whiteaker, was at one time governor of Oregon, and is still living at Eugene City, in that state.

Mr. and Mrs. Hettiger are the parents of three children: George Eugene, Jessie May and Robert E. The last named died in infancy. Miss Jessie received a fine musical education, and in this direction is possessed of much talent. She is proficient on the violin and piano, and these instruments she has played frequently in public in the different cities of the state. Her brother, who is also a good pianist, often accompanies his sister. October 18, 1898, Jessie M. Hettiger was united in marriage with Herman Leborich, The National clothing merchant of Oregon.

Religiously Mrs. Hettiger is a member of the Christian church. In politics Mr. Hettiger is a Republican, and has taken an active part in public matters. He is a progressive and representative citizen of Oregon, and was elected alderman of the third ward in 1896 and re-elected in 1898. He is a member of Oregon Lodge, No. 420, F. & A. M., Economy Camp, M. W. A., and of the Knights of Pythias. His son is also a member of Oregon Lodge, F. & A. M.

Mr. Hettiger is a thorough merchant tailor, and understands every branch of the business. He is regarded as one of the best cutters and fitters in the county, his suits being neat and artistic, and always giving satisfaction.

WILLIAM H. MILLER, furniture dealer and undertaker, Mt. Morris, Illinois, is a worthy representative of the mercantile interests of the place. He is a native of Washington county, Maryland, born July 23, 1850, and is a son of Upton and Maria Louisa (Davis) Miller, both of whom were natives of the same county and state, the former born March 2, 1828, and the latter October 1, 1831. They were married April 22, 1849, at Bakersville, Maryland, where her father, Solomon Davis, was engaged in the tailoring business. Her father never came west, but spent his entire life in his native state. Upton and Maria L. Miller became the parents of six children. William H., the subject of this sketch. Cyrus, born February 23, 1852, died young. Eliza Jane, born July 8, 1855, married B. F. Thomas, and six children were born to them. She died February 5, 1897. He is engaged in business in Oregon, Illinois. John D., born October 26, 1858, married Carrie Stone, and they had six children, three of whom are now deceased. He is engaged in the harness business at Mt. Morris. Mary Elizabeth died in infancy. Thomas M., born September 1, 1863, is making his home with our subject.

In 1857 Upton Miller came with his family to Ogle county, locating in Mt. Morris, where he worked at his trade of carpentering and cabinet making until the close of the Civil war, when he commenced the undertaking business, buying out Andrew Newcomer. In 1872 he added the furniture department, and in time did the leading business in the place, carrying a large and complete stock. In 1892 he retired from active business, since which time he has done a little in the cabinet-making line, but has practically been living a retired life. His wife died September 25, 1886, her death being quite sudden, caused by hemorrhage of the lungs. She was a kind and loving wife and mother, a member of the Lutheran church, in which faith she died. He was again married, in 1888, chosing as a companion Mrs. Catherine (Koontz) Newcomer. In politics he is a Republican, and religiously is identified with the Brethren.

The subject of this sketch came to Ogle county with his parents in 1857, and in the schools of Mt. Morris obtained his primary education. This was supplemented by an attendance at Rock River Seminary, now Mt. Morris College, which ended his school life. After leaving school, he learned the undertaking business, and in 1887 went to Sterling, Illinois, where Professor Sullivan had organized a class in embalming. In 1896 he attended Champion College of Embalming, from which he received a diploma. He has since passed a successful examination by the state authorities, and is ranked as one of the best embalmers in the state. For twenty years he worked for his father, at the expiration of which time he purchased the business, and is now sole proprietor of the best furniture establishment in Mt. Morris, and one of the best in the entire county. He carries a fine line of the best grades of furniture, and always endeavors to keep up with the times.

Mr. Miller was united in marriage December 25, 1878, with Miss Mary Ellen Wallace, born in Mt. Morris township, Ogle county, July 27, 1860, and a daughter of Lawrence and Elmira L. (Leek) Wallace, the former a native of Maryland, born August 26, 1824, and the latter of Pennsylvania born August 2, 1841. Her father came to Ogle county a young man, and is numbered among its early settlers. He is the son of Otho and ———— (Duggan) Wallace. His father was a farmer and came west at an early day. Louisa (Leek) Wallace is the daughter of Jacob and Emily (Allen) Leek, the former born January 25, 1797, and the latter July 7, 1811. The former died in Pennsylvania, and later his widow came to Ogle county, locating in Lincoln township, where she lived until within three or four years of her death, when she moved to the home of her daughter, Mrs. Wallace, in Mt. Morris township. Lawrence Wallace and wife are the parents of seven children, of whom the wife of our subject is the eldest. Susan, born July 10, 1863, married Henry Bearman, a farmer of Mt. Morris township, and they have three children. Emily, born December 16, 1865, married Gray Watts, also a farmer of Mt. Morris township, and they have three children. Lewis, born December 10, 1867, is engaged in well drilling. William H. born October 2, 1873, died at the age of eighteen months. John, born February 5, 1877, is farming in Mt. Morris township. Ida, born March 6, 1880, married Elmer Baker, and they reside in Mt. Morris. Lawrence Wallace is a carpenter by trade, and has followed that occupation the greater part of his life. He is now living on a small farm in Mt. Morris township, practically retired.

To our subject and wife three children have been born: Maude Louisa, born July 25, 1882; Edith May, February 27, 1884; and Florence Eva, July 29, 1886. They are giving their children good educational advantages, thus preparing them for useful lives. The entire family are members of the Lutheran church, Mr. Miller being secretary and treasurer of the church in Mt. Morris. All are active workers in the church.

Fraternally, he is a member of Elysian Lodge, No. 56, I. O. O. F., of Mt. Morris, and has passed all the chairs. He is at present permanent secretary of the lodge, which position he has held since passing through the chairs, a period of nearly twenty-five years. Politically he is a thorough Republican, and he has been quite active in local politics. He has been town clerk for the past twenty years, village treasurer since 1890, and school treasurer since 1892, and is now serving in each of these offices. These facts testify as to the standing of Mr. Miller in the community which has been his home from early childhood, a period of forty-two years. Suffice it to say that no man in the community is more highly honored.

ALFRED HARRISON, a highly esteemed and worthy citizen of Byron, Illinois, who is now living retired from active business cares, was born in Yorkshire, England, July 12, 1832, and is a son of George and Mary (Brown) Harrison, who spent their entire lives in that country, where the father worked as a common laborer or at farming. In the family were three children, of whom one died in childhood, and Mrs. Emma Wise is now a resident of the city of York, England.

Our subject had but little opportunity of attending school in early life, and is therefore almost wholly self-educated. He was reared on a farm, where he began work when a mere boy. Saving his earnings, he and his aunt, Elizabeth Steele, came to America in 1855, taking passage on a sailing vessel, the Albion, at Liverpool. They were six weeks upon the Atlantic and encountered one fearful storm, which did much damage to the rigging. The ship carried five hundred passengers and a crew of fifty men, and finally arrived at New York in safety. Mr. Harrison and his aunt proceeded at once to Rockford, Illinois, where they joined some English friends, and for two seasons he worked by the month in Winnebago county. In 1864 he bought forty acres of land in Byron township, Ogle county, which was covered with timber, and upon his place erected a small shanty, in which he lived for some years, while he cleared, fenced, broke and improved his land. To the original purchase he later added twenty acres adjoining, making a good farm of sixty acres, on which he erected a large and substantial residence, good barns, sheds, etc., converting it into one of the best improved and most desirable farms of the locality. For thirty-six years he successfully engaged in its cultivation, but in 1895 sold the place and removed to Byron, where he bought a lot and erected a neat residence that is still his home.

Mr. Harrison was not only without means on his arrival in this country, but had borrowed money to pay his passage, and the success that he has achieved here is certainly well deserved. By his own labor, enterprise and economy he has accumulated a comfortable competence, and is now able to spend his declining years in ease and quiet. In political sentiment he is a Democrat, but formerly was a Republican, casting his first ballot for Abraham Lincoln, and later supporting Grant for the presidency. He has never aspired to office, preferring to give his undivided attention to his business interest. He and Mr. and Mrs. Wright were among the first settlers of this section of the county, and our subject worked for them for several years. In 1876 he and their son visited the Centennial exposition at Philadelphia, where they spent three weeks in sightseeing. They also visited New York city, had a most pleasant and profitable time, and returned home feeling much better.

HENRY SCHRADER has been one of Ogle county's worthy and honored citizens since August, 1840, and was for many years actively identified with its agricultural interest, but is now living retired upon his pleasant farm three miles east of Leaf River. Like many of our best citizens he is a native of Maryland, born in Washington county, September 8, 1817. The father, Henry Schrader, Sr., was born in the same state, of German parentage, and in Washington county engaged in farming during early life. Selling his place there in 1827, the father removed to Mansfield, Richland county, Ohio, where he resided for a few years, and from there went to Wayne county, Indiana, where he developed a farm in the midst of the forest and spent his remaining years, dying in 1888, while his wife died three or four years previously. In his native state Henry Schrader, Sr., was united in marriage with Catherine Longman, who was born near Hagerstown, of German parentage, and until 1827 they made their home on the Schrader farm in that state. Our subject is one of a family of nine children, seven sons and two daughters, but only two are now living, the other being Mrs. Sophia Layman, of Dublin, Wayne county, Indiana.

During his boyhood and youth Henry Schrader, Jr., assisted his father in opening up and carrying on the home farm, and at the age of twenty years began working for others as a farm hand. In 1840 he came to Illinois with his father and brother and located in Ogle county, where he worked for a cousin, Isaac Avery, for one year, and the following year also engaged in farming for others. The father and brother returned to Indiana later.

On the 10th of October, 1842, Mr. Schrader led to the marriage altar Miss Mahala Iler, also a native of Washington county, Maryland, and a daughter of David and Mary (Hannon) Iler, who were born in the same county, and came to Illinois in 1837 with a colony of Maryland people. Mr. Iler settled at North Grove, in Leaf River township, Ogle county, where he developed a farm and spent his last years, dying at the advanced age of eighty-four. His wife survived him and departed this life at the age of eighty-five years. To Mr. and Mrs. Schrader were born five children, namely: Thomas, who married and died in Ogle county, leaving one child; Frank, a resident of Lightsville; Albert, a farmer of this county; George, who is carrying on the home farm; and Harriet, who married Martin Light, but is now deceased.

After his marriage Mr. Schrader rented land for several years and then bought a small place at North Grove, where he operated in connection with rented land for some time. Selling that farm in 1866, he purchased eighty acres which were under cultivation and fenced. He erected thereon a small house into which the family moved, and has since made many valuable and useful improvements, which make it one of the most attractive places of the locality. Besides his property he also owns a small farm near Lightsville, on which his son Albert is now living.

Politically Mr. Schrader is an old Jeffersonian Democrat, but cast his first vote for William Henry Harrison in 1840, and has since supported every presidential candidate of the Democracy. He has served his fellow citizens as school director and pathmaster, and in all the relations of life has been found true to every trust reposed in him. He and his estimable wife are faithful members of the Christian church at Leaf River, and as honored pioneer and highly respected citizens deserve prominent mention in their county's history.

CHARLES FRUIT, an enterprising farmer, residing on section 2, Taylor township, came to the United States in 1869, and has since been a resident of Ogle county and a thorough American citizen, one having at heart the interests of his adopted country. He was born near Gottenborg, Sweden, November 15, 1849, and is the son of Gus and Johanna (Anderson) Fruit, both natives of the same country, and who came to this country in the spring of 1875 and settled in Taylor township, where the husband and father worked at his trade of carpentering. They were the parents of six children, three of whom are now deceased. John died at the age of twelve years. Charles is the subject of this sketch. Edward died at the age of seven years. Matilda married C. A. Jacobson, and they reside in Falkeping, Sweden, where he is employed in the machine shops of a railroad company. Carrie died when two years old. Alda married John Larson, and they live in Taylor township where he is engaged in farming.

Charles Fruit grew to manhood in his native country and there obtained a fair education in the public schools. Desiring to

CHARLES FRUIT.

better his condition in life, and knowing of the possibilities in the new world, he determined, if the opportunity was ever afforded him that he would emigrate to that land where even the very poorest might realize his heart's desire. When but twenty years old, he secured his parents' consent to try his fortunes in this land. Leaving his native land on one of the ocean liners he crossed the ocean and after a voyage of eighteen days, during which time they encountered some pretty severe weather, they landed at New York, and from there proceeded direct to Rockford, Illinois, where he remained one year engaged in various employments, and then came to Ogle county and located in Taylor township, where he purchased a small farm some five years later, having in the meantime assisted in the construction of the Chicago & Iowa railroad.

Mr. Fruit was married August 20, 1884, to Miss Annie Bronson, of Chicago, Illinois, and by this union two children were born, Ellen and Vanner, both of whom are now attending the district school. This wife died October 30, 1889, and Mr. Fruit, December 31, 1891, married Miss Selma Anderson, daughter of Carl and Johanna Anderson, natives of Sweden. The three children born of this union are George, Henry and Irma, the first named now being a student in the district school.

Since locating on his present farm Mr. Fruit has given his attention to general farming. He has improved the place by tiling the land and the erection of wind mills, the building of necessary outbuildings, and the planting of orchard and shade trees. He has served his township as town clerk two years, town collector two years, and is now a school director. In politics he is a Republican. Religiously he is a Methodist, holding membership in the Methodist Episcopal church at Light House. He comes of a patriotic family, his paternal grandfather, J. Fruit, serving in the war which his country had with Denmark.

CHARLES BUSH. Among the progressive, energetic and successful farmers and stock dealers of Ogle county, who thoroughly understand the vocation which they follow, and are consequently enabled to carry on their calling with profit to themselves, is the subject of this sketch. He is actively engaged in agricultural pursuits on section 3, Eagle Point township, where he owns a valuable and well improved farm.

Like many of our best citizens, Mr. Bush is a native of the Empire state, born in Roxbury, Delaware county, March 25, 1834. His father, Nicholas Bush, was born in the same county, May 31, 1803, and was a son of John Bush, a native of Fairfax, Virginia, and a hero of the Revolutionary war, having aided the colonies in their struggle for independence. The great-grandfather of our subject was of English extraction and an early settler of the Old Dominion. At the close of the Revolution John Bush was discharged and mustered out in New York city, and then took up his residence as a pioneer in Delaware county, New York, where, in the midst of the wilderness, he cleared and developed a farm. There he died at the ripe old age of eighty years.

On reaching man's estate, Nicholas Bush was married in his native county to Miss Lydia Wolcott, a native of Greene county, New York, and a daughter of Gideon Wolcott, an early settler of that county. He was a native of England and a son of Francis Wolcott, who spent his entire life in that country. For some years after his marriage Mr. Bush continued to engage in farming and lumbering in New York, but in 1856 he started for Illinois, and on reaching Ogle county he purchased eighty acres of land in Eagle Point township, on which our subject now resides. A small house and barn had already been built and thirty-five acres fenced and broken. To its further improvement and cultivation he at once turned his attention, later erected larger and more subjectial buildings and added to the original purchase ninety acres. In connection with general farming he also engaged in stock raising. During his residence in New York he affiliated with the Odd Fellows society, but never joined the order here. He died September 13, 1890, at the advanced age of eighty-seven years, and his wife departed this life July 2, 1878, at the age of seventy-eight years, both being laid at rest in Eagle Point cemetery, where a neat monument has been erected to their memory. In their family were only two children, the daughter being Nancy, who married and died in Ogle county in 1858.

Charles Bush, the only son, grew to manhood in Delaware county, New York, and completed a good education at Pottsville Academy. In that county he was married April 4, 1855, to Miss Hepsebah Booth, who was reared and educated there. Her parents, Levi and Phœbe (Harley) Booth, were natives of Connecticut and early settlers of Delaware county, being one of the first families to locate there. Mr. and Mrs. Bush have one daughter, Clara, now the wife of Joseph Sprecker, of Polo, by whom she has two children, Hepsebah and Charles Harry. She was born in Pittsford, Hillsdale county, Michigan, but was reared and educated in Ogle county, being a graduate of the Polo high school. She engaged in teaching for a time and her parents also followed that profession, both in their native county and after coming to Ogle county, Illinois, Mrs. Bush being a prominent teacher here for several years.

In March, 1856, Mr. Bush accompanied his father on his removal to this county and assisted in carrying on the home farm for some time, after which he took complete charge of the same. In 1859, however, he went to Michigan and lived for some time in Hillsdale, Adrian and Allegan, being a conductor on the Michigan Southern & Northern Indiana railroad for ten years. He then returned to the farm in Ogle county, and has since successfully managed the same. He has also engaged in feeding and shipping stock, and in his undertakings has met with well deserved success. He has made many improvements upon his place, including the erection of a commodious and comfortable residence, a large granary and other outbuildings, so that he now has one of the most desirable farms in this part of the county.

Although his father was a Jeffersonian Democrat, Mr. Bush has been identified with the Republican party since casting his first vote for John C. Fremont in 1856, and has since supported every presidential candidate of that party. As one of the leading and influential citizens of his community, he takes an active interest in local politics, has been a delegate to many county, congressional and state conventions, has served as township clerk fourteen years and been a member of the school board some years. He has proven a most competent and trustworthy official, and commands the confidence and respect of all with whom he comes in contact either in private or public life. He is quite prominent in Masonic circles, being a Knight Templar, a member of the blue lodge and chapter in Polo and the commandery at Dixon. His estimable wife holds membership in the Methodist Episcopal church at Eagle Point, and like her husband has a host of friends in this community.

BENJAMIN DOUGHTY, who, after the labors of a long and busy life, is spending his later years in ease and retirement in the village of Byron, has made his home in Ogle county since January 16, 1858, and bore an active part in its early development and upbuilding. A native of England, he was born in Yorkshire, April 12, 1830, and is a son of Thomas and Mary Doughty, who spent their entire lives there. The father engaged in farming or worked at anything which he could find to do, and died at the advanced age of eighty-nine years. Benjamin was the oldest of his five sons, all of whom reached manhood, but two are now deceased, while the other two, William and Thomas, still reside in England.

Benjamin Doughty was reared on the farm and during his youth received a very limited education, but by reading and observation in subsequent years he has become a well-informed man. He was married in Yorkshire, November 23, 1857, the lady of his choice being Miss Elizabeth Wright, a native of that county, who was reared in the same village as her husband. A few days after their marriage they started for the new world, taking passage at Liverpool, November 28, on a sailing vessel, which finally reached New York, January 8, 1858, after a long and tedious voyage of six weeks, during which they experienced much rough weather and several severe storms, which carried away some of the sails. On landing they came at once to Illinois, and after stopping a short time in Franklin Grove came to Byron, where they joined Mr. Doughty's uncle, John Doughty, who had located here about 1842 or 1843.

Our subject went to work on a farm in Winnebago county for Alfred Bridgeland, also a native of England, and remained with him about seven months. Returning to Ogle county in 1859, he secured a position with Mr. Spalding, with whom he and his wife lived for one year. In 1859 he made his first purchase of forty acres of land, which he began to improve in 1861, at the same time operated rented land. He fenced his place, erected thereon good and substantial buildings, and continued the work of development and cultivation for many years. As time advanced and he prospered in his undertakings he added more land to the original purchase, first forty acres and then twenty acres, making in all a fine and valuable farm of one hundred acres, pleasantly located three miles and a half from Byron. He successfully carried on farming here until 1860, when he sold out and purchased property in Byron, where he has since lived retired from active labor, in the enjoyment of the fruits of his former toil. The success that he has achieved in life is due entirely to his own unaided efforts, as he was in rather limited circumstances on coming to America, but by hard work, close application and guided by a sound judgment he has made for himself a comfortable home and competence.

Mr. Doughty has been called upon to mourn the loss of his wife, who passed away October 20, 1889, and was laid to rest in

Middle Creek cemetery, Winnebago county. In 1890 he was joined by his cousin, Miss Emily Doughty, who has since been his housekeeper. This estimable lady is also a native of Yorkshire, England, and a daughter of Charles Doughty. She came alone to America, and in 1892 returned to Yorkshire on a visit to family and friends. During the five weeks she remained in the old world she visited the cities of York and Leeds, and also the beautiful seaport town and pleasure resort of Scarborough. She has heard Spurgeon preach, has been in London, and has also seen Buckingham palace and Windsor castle.

On becoming an American citizen, Mr. Doughty cast his first presidential vote for Abraham Lincoln in 1864, and has since supported the Republican party. He has efficiently served as a member of the village board of Byron, and his duties, both public and private, have always been most faithfully and conscientiously discharged. Both he and his cousin were reared in the Episcopal faith, and are held in high respect by all who know them.

NICHOLAS N. SHAVER, deceased, was a native of Delaware county, New York, born September 11, 1809, and was the son of Jacob P. and Catherine Shaver, both of whom were natives of the same county and state, the former born May 20, 1775, and the latter April 14, 1784. They were the parents of seven children. Catherine Shaver died in her native state, after which her husband came west, where his death occurred many years ago.

In his native state Nicholas N. Shaver grew to manhood, and in the common school received a limited education. He was reared to the life of a farmer, an occupation that he followed during his entire active life. He was twice married, his first union being with Miss Hannah Nicholson, who was probably a native of Delaware county, New York. Their marriage was celebrated May 13, 1840, and to them were born five children, three sons and two daughters: Arthur J., born February 21, 1841; Robert S., March 12, 1843; Mariette, April 24, 1845; Sophia, October 17, 1847; and Edward, October 15, 1850. The mother of these children died in 1852.

On the 19th of June, 1854, Mr. Shaver was united in marriage with Miss Kate Voorhees, who was born in Sullivan county, New York, November 14, 1814, and the daughter of John C. and Nancy (Brown) Voorhees, natives of New York, but of German descent. They were the parents of nine children, who lived to be men and women. By occupation he was a farmer, one who attended strictly to his own affairs, and enjoyed the respect and confidence of his friends and neighbors. He never came west, but passed the last days of his life amid the familiar scenes of his native state. His wife also passed to her reward in her native state.

Soon after his second marriage Mr. Shaver came with his wife and family to Ogle county and located in Buffalo township, where he purchased a farm and engaged in agricultural pursuits. He was a good farmer, very industrious, and success crowned his efforts. In his old age he laid aside the cares of the farm and moved into the city of Polo, to enjoy the fruits of a life well spent. For years his face was a familiar one on the streets of the city, and those meeting him had a kindly greeting and a pleasant word.

Politically Mr. Shaver was a Democrat, and a firm believer in the principles of the party as expounded by Jefferson and Jackson. He was never, however, an office seeker, content always that others should have whatever honors office holding contained. He was a member of the Presbyterian church, in the doctrines and teachings of which he had unbounded faith. His good wife, who survives him, is also a member of that church. His death occurred February 19, 1886, and his remains were laid to rest in the cemetery at the brick church in Eagle Point township, there to wait the resurrection day. "Blessed are the dead who die in the Lord, for they shall rest from their labors and their works shall follow them."

JOHN B. WOODCOCK, a well-known and prominent agriculturist, residing on section 33, Marion township, has for over fifty-four years been connected with the history of Ogle county and few, if any, have done more for its upbuilding. He has been a champion of every movement designed to promote the general welfare, a supporter of every enterprise for the public good, and has materially aided in the advancement of all social, industrial, educational and moral interests.

Mr. Woodcock is a native of Canada, born near Prescott, Ontario, on the St. Lawrence river, October 1, 1823, and belongs to quite an honored and distinguished family, which was founded in New England soon after the arrival of the Mayflower. His ancestors were originally from England and for several generations resided in the United States. His great-grandfather on the paternal side took up arms against the mother country in the Revolutionary war, and for three years fought for the freedom of the colonies. One of his sons was also in the same struggle. The grandfather, Jonathan Woodcock, was a native of Connecticut, but about 1790 removed to Canada, making his way through the dense forests with an ox team for about four hundred miles, it being a most tedious and remarkable trip. In the midst of the wilderness he hewed out a farm and there made his home until called from this life, at the age of fifty-five years. His wife lived to the advanced age of ninety-one years and died in Marion township, Ogle county, Illinois.

Freeman Woodcock, the father of our subject, was born in the province of Ontario, Canada, March 12, 1802, and was there reared amid pioneer scenes. He married Miss Elizabeth Bass, also a native of Canada, who was born in Ontario, October 14, 1800, and was a daughter of John Bass, whose early home was in Vermont. In Canada, Freeman Woodcock carried on business along various lines, being engaged in farming and merchandising, and also the manufacture of furniture, boots and shoes. In the spring of 1844 we find him and his family *en route* for Illinois, joining our subject in Ogle county. In Nashua township they purchased about five hundred acres of partially improved land, but after operating it five years sold the place and in 1850 bought two hundred acres on sections 27, 31 and 32, Marion township, on which our subject now resides. Here a flouring mill, propelled by water power, had previously been built on Stillman creek, and this the father conducted until it was destroyed by ice in the spring of 1857. It was rebuilt, however, the same season, but soon proved unprofitable and the building was moved away and used for other purposes. With the mill Mr. Woodcock purchased about three thousand acres of land, and in connection with milling engaged in agricultural pursuits. He was one of the most prominent men of his township and was often chosen to positions of honor and trust. He died on the homestead in Marion township, October 11, 1860, and his wife passed away November 15, 1870. They were earnest and consistent Christian people, holding a membership in the Methodist Episcopal church.

Their family consisted of three sons and two daughters. Lucy, the eldest, married T. G. Anderson, a minister of the Methodist Episcopal church, and she died in Lafayette township, Ogle county, leaving three daughters and one son. John B., our subject, is the next in order of birth. Albert was a man of superior attainments, who graduated at Union College, New York. He then studied law, was admitted to the bar and engaged in practice until elected treasurer of Ogle county for a term of two years. Later he was elected county clerk and for sixteen years held the latter office. In 1862 he enlisted in the Ninety-second Illinois Volunteer Infantry, was elected captain of his company and was subsequently promoted to major, being mustered out as such at the close of the war. He then resumed the duties of county clerk, was afterwards elected county judge for a term of two years, and was appointed internal revenue collector of the district, holding that position until the consolidation of the districts in 1883. President Arthur appointed him consul to Sicily, and he held that responsible post for four years, during which time he resided at Catania, at the base of Mt. Etna. On his return home he served as land commissioner for two years for the U. P. R. R. Co. He made two trips to California and finally settled in Los Angeles, where he died in 1894. He was three times married and by the first wife had two children. His last wife still survives him. Alanson, the next of the family, is engaged in farming near Fort Scott, Bourbon county, Kansas. Sarah, the widow of Rev. A. G. Smith, resides in Byron township, Ogle county.

During his youth John B. Woodcock attended the academy at Gouverneur, St. Lawrence county, New York, and after coming to Illinois, at the age of eighteen years, he attended the Mt. Morris Academy. He arrived here in September, 1844, and for several years assisted his father in the work of the farm and mill. As deputy in his brother's office, he discharged the duties of county clerk when the latter was at the front during the Civil war, and continued to fill that position for five years, during which time he resided in Oregon. Later he used to assist in the office for five or six months out of the year. On his father's death he succeeded to the old homestead, and has since given the greater part of his time and attention to its management, with results which cannot fail to be satisfactory. He added to his farm until he had three hundred acres of valuable land, which he placed under a high state of cultivation, but has since given some of this property to his children.

On the 15th of May, 1848, in Lafayette township, Mr. Woodcock was united in marriage with Miss Lucy Martin, who was born in Ontario, Canada, September 15, 1829, a daughter of Richard and Belinda Martin, who settled in the southern part of the county in 1838. Of the six children born to this union, four are now living, namely: Ella E., Walter S., Antoinette and John D., all at home. They have received fair educations, attending the local schools and those at Byron and Oregon.

Mr. Woodcock cast his first vote for Zachary Taylor in 1848, in 1856 supported John C. Fremont, and has since been an uncompromising Republican. He has filled a number of local offices, but has never been a politician in the sense of office seeking. For many years he and his wife have been faithful members of the Methodist Episcopal church, to which his parents also belonged, and socially he is connected with Oregon lodge, A. & A. M. Those who know them best are numbered among their warmest friends, and no citizens of the community are more honored or highly respected.

JACOB F. SWANK, one of the leading citizens of Forreston and of Ogle county, and who is engaged in the ice business in connection with farming, was born in Somerset county, Pennsylvania, February 13, 1853, and is the son of Michael and Adeline (Baker) Swank, both of whom were natives of Pennsylvania, the Swanks being of German descent. In the spring of 1865 Michael Swank came with his family to Illinois and located near Dixon, Lee county, where he remained three years, giving his attention to the cultivation of an eighty-acre farm which he rented, and also to his trade of a carpenter. In the spring of 1868 he removed to Forreston township, Ogle county, where he purchased eighty acres of land and at once set about its improvement. The farm was located near the village of Harper, and on it he continued to reside until 1889, when he removed to Pennsylvania and lived a retired life. He, however, continued to work at his trade for many years, assisting in the erection of many of the buildings in Forreston.

Our subject was twelve years old when he accompanied his parents to Illinois. His education, begun in the public schools of his native state, was completed in the schools of Lee and Ogle counties. While confined to the common schools he is yet a well-informed man. On removing to Ogle county he was fifteen years old and was required to do his full share of the farm work, his father giving much of his time to work at his trade. In 1873 he commenced life for himself, renting his father's farm of eighty acres, together with sixty acres from other parties.

On the 12th of March, 1874, Mr. Swank was united in marriage with Miss Henrietta Foy, daughter of Ludwig Foy, an early settler of Brookville township, but who later moved to Forreston township. She was a native of Pennsylvania, but reared in Ogle county. Mrs. Swank took a special interest in organizing a camp of Royal Neighbors in Forreston and was elected oracle of the camp. By this union six children have been born. Cora M. is the wife of Charles W. Timmer, a farmer of Lincoln township; Adeline A., Louis, William M., Arthur F. and Clifford, all of whom are yet at home. Of the brothers and sisters of Mr. Swank, Melinda is the widow of Charles Brant, and lives near Shannon, Carroll county; Edward lives in Sedgwick, Kansas; Samuel lives in Pennsylvania. His mother died in Ogle county, but his father is yet living in Pennsylvania.

Of the brothers and sisters of Mrs. Swank, Edward is deceased; Louis lives in Lena, Illinois, where he is engaged in business; Henry reside in Freeport, where he is engaged in the grocery trade; Catherine is the wife of Simon Geating, a farmer of Lincoln township; Louisa, widow of George Lawber, living in Freeport; Maggie, wife of E. H. Binkley, a real estate dealer of Cherokee, Iowa.

Mr. Swank is the owner of one hundred and eleven acres of excellent farm land which he cultivates, together with forty acres additional which he rents. In politics he is a Republican, and in political and local affairs he has always taken an active part. No enterprise for the public good but meets with his hearty co-operation. He was elected a director and secretary of the Harper Creamery Association in 1890 and served three years, or until it was sold to the Elgin syndicate. He was one of the directors of the Forreston Mutual Fire Insurance Company; was elected president of the Ogle County Farmers Institute in February, 1897, and re-elected in February, 1898. He was appointed a delegate to the Farmers National Congress by Governor Tanner, which met in St. Paul, Minnesota, in September, 1897, and was re-appointed to the Farmers National Congress which met at Ft. Worth, Texas, and served with signal ability. He has contributed more or less to the public press, and was the correspondent of the Forreston Herald for six years. Fraternally, he is a member of the Modern Woodmen of America, and was elected venerable consul of the camp, and, religiously, he and his family attend the United Evangelical church, of which he is a trustee. He was also a member of the building committee and was secretary of the committee, and is the present secretary of the board of trustees.

In educational affairs Mr. Swank has always taken great interest, serving on the school board and giving freely of his time to advance the best interests of the schools. For eight years he served as secretary of the board of directors, and is now one of the trustees. In 1886 he was elected commissioner of highways and served three years. For ten years he has been a member of the county board of supervisors, and has been one of its most active and influential members. He was a member of the board when the court house was built, and cast the deciding vote for its erection. He was a member of the bridge committee that built the bridge at Oregon, and also appointed on the committee of the bridge across Rock river at Grand Detour. In the building of bridges in Maryland, Brookville and Grand Detour and other points he gave of his time as one of a committee charged with their erection. In whatever position he has been called on to fill he has given his best efforts and always in the interests of the people. He is a man in whom the people can trust, knowing that they will not be betrayed.

J H. MILLER, who is now living in Mt. Morris, is a native of Mt. Morris township, Ogle county, and was born December 24, 1865. His father, Abraham Miller, was born June 21, 1831, in Franklin county, Pennsylvania, and was of German extraction. He grew to manhood in his native county and received a very limited common-school education, the knowledge afterwards acquired being received in the school of experience. He was early taught to work, however, and assisted his father in the work of the farm, finally taking the management thereof. He was married November 24, 1853, to Miss Barbara Newcomer, daughter of Daniel Newcomer, a native of Washington county, Maryland, but who removed to Franklin county, Pennsylvania, and there spent the remainder of his life. By this union there were born eleven children, as follows: Elizabeth, born September 24, 1854; Mary A., May 3, 1856; Barbara, December 1, 1858; Emanuel, May 26, 1861; David M., June 10, 1863; J. H., our subject; Edna M., June 5, 1867; Martha, June 11, 1870; Abraham, March 29, 1874; Emma S., June 15, 1876; Silas E., March 21, 1878. Of these Elizabeth, Barbara and Edna are deceased.

Believing that he could better his condition in life, Abraham Miller left his native state with his family and came to Ogle county, Illinois, in 1865, and on his arrival purchased ninety-five acres of excellent farming land and commenced its cultivation. He later purchased one hundred and five acres adjoining, giving him a valuable farm of two hundred acres. He subsequently deeded seven acres of the same to the railroad company, on the completion of the road to Mt. Morris. On that farm he spent the remainder of his life, dying July 2, 1898. His widow is now residing with her daughter Emma, near Freeport, Illinois. She is of Swiss extraction. Politically Abraham Miller was a Republican, and religiously was identified with the River Brethren. His wife is also connected with that church.

The subject of this sketch grew to manhood in his native county, receiving his primary education in the common schools of Mount Morris township. He then entered Mount Morris College, which he attended for a time, but did not take the regular course. After leaving school he assisted his father on the farm for a time, or until he attained his majority, when he went to Nebraska and remained there about five months. He then returned home and again assisted his father in the cultivation of the home farm remaining two years.

Again seized with the western fever, he went to Kansas, where he remained for a few months, going from there to Omaha, Nebraska, where he entered a business college and remained about two months, being compelled to leave on account of ill health. From Omaha he went to Vinton, Iowa, and there remained about five years, with the exception of a short period when he returned to Ogle county for his bride. While in Vinton he was employed in a grain elevator, and also in farming.

Mr. Miller was united in marriage with Miss Myrtle Rine, December 24, 1890. She was born April 21, 1866, in Ogle county, and is the daughter of Benjamin and Melissa (Fish) Rine, and is the oldest in a family of four children born to her parents. To Mr. and Mrs. Miller, two children have been born: Mable D., born May 8, 1893, and Harold Guy, January 29, 1898.

In September, 1894, Mr. Miller returned to Ogle county, taking charge of his father's farm, the father being in poor health. He remained on the farm until the fall of 1898, when he moved to the village and purchased the livery stable of H. L. Smith, which he disposed of in 1899.

Politically Mr. Miller is a stanch Republican, and has held various local offices, including that of town clerk. He is a member of the Modern Woodmen of America, and is the present venerable counsel of the camp at Mount Morris.

JOHN H. HELM. Sound judgment combined with fine ability in mechanical lines has enabled the subject of this biography, a prominent contractor and builder of Byron, Illinois, to attain a substantial success in life. He was born in Chemung county, New York, July 31, 1834, and is a son of Phineas Helm, a native of Orange county, that state. The father enlisted in the army during the war of 1812, was ordered out, but did not engage in active service. He was married in Chemung county to Miss Betsy Smith, also a native of the Empire state. He was a cabinetmaker by trade and carried on business for a number of years in Southport, New York, where he remained with his family and spent his last days. His wife survived him only a few months, dying at the same place. In their family were four sons and one daughter, namely: Floyd, who married but is now deceased; Samuel, still a resident of Southport; Phineas, deceased; Mrs. Mary Ann Winkler, deceased; and John H., of this sketch.

During his boyhood and youth John H. Helm pursued his studies in the schools of Southport, New York, and there learned the carpenter's and joiner's trade. In 1861 he came to Illinois and located in Rockford, where he worked at his trade for one year, and then came to Byron, where he continued to follow his chosen occupation. In response to the President's call for more men during the dark days of the Rebellion, he enlisted December 29, 1863, in Company B, Ninety-second Illinois Mounted Infantry, which was assigned to the Army of the Cumberland. With his regiment he was engaged in scouting, skirmishing and picket duty until July, 1864, when he was taken ill and sent to the hospital, first at Chattanooga and later at Nashville, Jeffersonville and the marine hospital at Chicago, being confined at these places for several months. He was finally discharged at Chicago, July 21, 1865, and returned to Byron to recuperate. The following year he was able to resume work at his trade, and has since engaged in contracting and building most of the time. A great many of the public buildings and private residences bear testimony to his handiwork and architectural skill.

Just previous to coming to Illinois Mr. Helm was married in Ohio, April 1, 1861, to Miss Sarah Babcock, who was born and reared in Steuben county, New York, a daughter of Elias Randall Babcock, of that state. She departed this life November 15, 1889, and of the four children born to them three are now deceased. Grace died at the age of six years, Albert at the age of one year, and William H., a pharmacist of Byron and Stillman Valley, died at home December 31, 1894, at the age of twenty-three years. Mrs. Anna Schafer, the only one now living, is her father's housekeeper. She has one son, William Helm Schafer, aged three years.

Mr. Helm's father was a Clay Whig, and our subject cast his first presidential ballot for Millard Fillmore in 1856, but has since supported the men and measures of the Republican party. In June, 1889, he received the appointment of postmaster of Byron under President Harrison and most capably and satisfactorily discharged the duties of that office for four years, his daughter acting as deputy. He was made a Mason in Byron Lodge, F. & A. M., several years ago, and for four terms has served as master of the lodge, which he also represented in the grand lodge of the state for the same length of time. He is also a prominent member of the Grand Army post at Byron, of which he is past commander, and by his fellow citizens he is held in high regard, receiving the respect and confidence of all with whom he has business or social relations.

GEORGE R. RHODES, who is engaged in farming on section 6, Grand Detour township, and who for some years was one of the leading contractors and builders of Springfield, Illinois, was born July 27, 1833, in Frederick county, Maryland, and is the son of Peter and Elizabeth (Foaster) Rhodes, both of whom were also natives of Frederick county, Maryland, the former born in 1794. The paternal grandfather, Jacob Rhodes, was a blacksmith by trade, and followed that occupation during his entire life. He never came to this state, but died in Maryland many years ago.

In his youth Peter Rhodes learned the carpenter trade, an occupation he followed during his active life. In 1863, he came to Illinois, and located in Rochester, Sangamon county, where his death occurred in 1878. His wife died some years ago. They were the parents of ten children—Amanda, William H., John T., George R., Martha E., Ann O., Alice E., Katherine, James W. and Fannie. All are yet living save Ann O. In politics Peter Rhodes was a Jackson Democrat, a firm believer in the principles of the party as proclaimed by Jefferson and Jackson. He was a member of the Episcopal church.

The subject of this sketch was reared to manhood in his native state, and in the common schools received his education. At the age of eighteen he left school and worked with his father at the carpenter trade until 1856, when he came to Illinois and located at Springfield, where he continued to work at his trade. The firm of Rhodes Brothers, contractors and builders, was formed, and for many years did a prosperous business, erecting many of the best public and private buildings in the city, among them the splendid building of the Young Men's Christian Association. He continued in contracting and building until 1889, when he moved to his present place of residence, and engaged in agricultural pursuits. The farm consists of one hundred and sixty acres, and is under excellent improvement.

Mr. Rhodes has been twice married, his first union being with Miss Mary C. Lakin, and their marriage was celebrated February 23, 1862. She died in 1869. His second marriage was with Mrs. Ella Miller, *née* Bovey, their union being formed September 2, 1874. Mrs. Rhodes was born May 8, 1852, in Ogle county, Illinois. She is the daughter of Samuel and Barbara (Funck) Bovey, both of whom are natives of Washington county, Maryland, and who came to Ogle county in the spring of 1846, and located in Grand Detour township, where his death occurred in 1891. Miss Ella Bovey married Samuel S. Miller in 1860, and his death took place December 25, 1869. At the time of his death he was managing the farm of his father-in-law.

To Mr. and Mrs. Rhodes six children have been born. Clinton B., born June 26, 1875, is now in the government mail service, running between Pontiac and Chicago. Charles L., born January 20, 1879, is attending Steinman Business College, Dixon, Illinois. Robert S., born July 24, 1882, died April 9, 1885. George T., born June 15, 1885, is attending the district school of Grand Detour township. Harry

D., born January 14, 1889, is also in school. Ethel May, was born February 7, 1897.

In politics Mr. Rhodes is a Democrat, and for nine years served as a member of the board of supervisors of Sangamon county from Springfield. He made an efficient member, being a practical man, one who looked after the best interests of the public, and who did not serve just to please politicians. He also served for nine years as fire marshal of Springfield, a difficult and responsible position which he filled to the satisfaction of the people. Mrs. Rhodes is a member of the Christian church, with which she has been connected for a number of years, and in the teachings of which she has the utmost faith. She is now living in the home of her childhood where she has many friends. Although comparatively a newcomer, Mr. Rhodes is well known and universally esteemed.

LOUIS J. OTTO, a thorough and skillful farmer and business man of more than ordinary ability, is a representative of the agricultural and stock raising interests of Ogle county, his home being on section 3, Forreston township, where he has a good farm of one hundred and sixty acres. A native of the county, Mr. Otto was born in Maryland township, May 27, 1854, and is a son of Christian Otto, who was born about 1803, in Lippe, Germany, where he was reared and married to Miss Mary Pepperling, a German lady. He followed farming in his native land. About 1848 he crossed the Atlantic and proceeded at once to Chicago, where he secured a team, and then drove across the country to Ogle county, where some friends from Germany were living in Maryland township. There he purchased a tract of eighty acres, and later bought a similar amount, making a good farm of one hundred and sixty acres, which he commenced to improve and cultivate. He died there in 1862, and his wife passed away in February, 1861. In the family of this worthy couple were four sons and two daughters, all of whom married and became heads of families. They are Dora, wife of David Haselbrook, of Riley county, Kansas; Henry, a farmer of Stephenson county, who owns and operates a farm adjoining that of our subject; Louis J., of this review; Lizzie, wife of Henry Stuckenburg, who lives on the line between Ogle and Stephenson counties; August, who operates the old homestead; and Fred, who owns and operates a valuable farm of six hundred and forty acres in Riley county, Kansas.

Reared in Ogle county, Louis J. Otto remained with his mother and assisted in carrying on the old homestead. After the father's death two hundred and eighty acres were added to the place, making a valuable property of four hundred and forty acres. This they cleared from all indebtedness and transformed into a well cultivated and highly improved farm. Our subject acquired his education in the schools of Maryland township. There he was married, December 29, 1879, the lady of his choice being Miss Anna Fosha, who was born and reared in Stephenson county. Her father, John Fosha, was a native of Germany, was brought to America when a child and reared in Maryland whence he came to Illinois when a young man. He married Minnie Shineman and located on the Stephenson county line, where he now resides. Our subject and his wife have eight children, namely: Nettie, William, Henry, Emma, Minnie, Mary, Roy and Walter, all at home.

For four years after his marriage Mr. Otto lived on a part of the old homestead, of which he owned eighty acres, and on selling that place in the spring of 1884 he removed to his present farm, which he has greatly improved by making an addition to the house, building a large barn, and placing the land under excellent cultivation. He is acknowledged to be one of the successful and progressive farmers of Forreston township, and in connection with general farming is interested in dairying and stock-raising, keeping a high grade of stock, both cattle and hogs. On national issues he supports the Democratic party, but at local election votes for the man whom he believes best qualified to fill the office regardless of party affiliations. He has most acceptably served as school director for thirteen years, and as clerk of the district for eight years. Socially he is a member of Florence Camp, M. W. A. He was reared in the Catholic church, but he and his wife now attend the German Reformed church, and in the social life of the community occupy an enviable position, having the respect and esteem of all who know them.

BURTON D. KRIDLER, of the well known firm of Strickler & Kridler, Polo, Illinois, was born in Luzerne county, Pennsylvania, November 18, 1843, and is the son of John and Lydia (Ransom) Kridler, both of whom were also natives of Luzerne county, the former born August 15, 1809, and the latter December 15, 1815. She is a daughter of Colonel George Palmer Ransom, a native of Connecticut, born in 1761, but who removed with his father, Samuel Ransom, to Wyoming Valley, Pennsylvania, then a portion of Connecticut, but now Luzerne county, Pennsylvania. On the 26th of August, 1776, Samuel Ransom was commissioned captain of a company to be organized, and later with his company was ordered to join Washington's forces. With him, Captain Ransom took his son George, a lad of less than sixteen years, who acted as orderly sergeant. Their first battle was at Millstone, January 20, 1777. They also participated in the battles of Brandywine, Germantown, Bound Brook and Mud Fort. Captain Ransom was killed in the Wyoming massacre, July 3, 1778. As it happened his son George was not present at the time, but arrived on the scene a few days later, and helped bury his father and other victims of the carnage. He was later taken prisoner and taken to Montreal, where he was held until the following June, when he made his escape on a raft in the St. Lawrence river. After many hardships he succeeded in reaching a settlement in Vermont, and later rejoined the army, remaining until the close of the war, when he was honorably discharged.

John Kridler was reared in his native county, and received a very limited education, attending school for a short time when he was but seven years of age, and but one half day when he was eleven years of age. When nineteen, he commenced to learn the wagon-maker's trade, serving an apprenticeship of two years, for which he was to receive twenty-two dollars and fifty cents per year. Completing his trade, and having rested for a time and visiting his old home, he hired out to a carriage-maker at ten dollars per month, working for him four months. He then went into business for himself, and for a time had a hard struggle to make both ends meet. He was persevering and industrious, however, and from his earnings paid off a mortgage on his father's place. On the 8th of September, 1835, he was united in marriage with Miss Lydia Ransom, at which time his entire cash capital consisted of eight dollars. Soon after his marriage he moved to Susquehanna, Pennsylvania, where he opened up a small farm. After spending eighteen years of his married life trying to make headway in his native state, he concluded to try the prairies of Illinois. Accordingly, in 1853, he moved to Carroll county and purchased a farm of three hundred and twenty acres, about twelve miles west of Polo. From the beginning he was successful, and in addition to his home farm, in due time he became the owner of two other farms in Carroll county, which yielded him a generous return for his investment. After residing on his farm for thirty-one years, he moved to Polo, and there made his home during the remainder of his life. He died June 30, 1897. His wife is yet living in Polo. They were the parents of nine children. George H. was a member of the Fifteenth Illinois Volunteer Infantry, and was wounded at the battle of Shiloh. He died while on his way home. Sabina is the wife of Alexander Windle, and they are living in Iowa Park, Texas; B. D. is the subject of this sketch; W. H. is living in Omaha, Nebraska; S. R. is a physician of Red Oak, Iowa; Emma L. married Orris Mosher, and they reside in Walnut, Iowa; Marian H. is the wife of Dr. D. F. Hallett, and they reside in Red Oak, Iowa. Two died in childhood.

The subject of this sketch was ten years old when he accompanied his parents to Carroll county, Illinois. In the public schools of that county he received his primary education, which was supplemented by an attendance at Mt. Carroll Seminary. At seventeen, he quit school and commenced clerking in the general store of Pierce & Barber, Polo, at the munificent salary of seventy-five dollars per year. He remained with that firm for three years, but with an increase of salary, and then entered the Commercial College, at Poughkeepsie, New York, one of the best institutions of the kind in the country. After remaining there one year he removed to Polo and went into the livery business where Griffin's stables now stand. He remained in that business for about two years and then traded his livery stable for a grocery store. After being in the grocery business for about two years, he met with serious reverses which forced him to the wall, leaving him several hundred dollars in debt. He is happy to say, however, that in due time he paid out one hundred cents on the dollar. After meeting with his loss, he went on the road for a time as traveling salesman for a wholesale notion house, and was also engaged in the patent right business. In 1882 he again went into the mercantile business, purchasing an interest in the furniture store of William Strickler, to which they added dry goods, and later other departments.

On the 20th of December, 1867, Mr. Kridler was united in marriage with Miss Eliza Baker, daughter of Daniel and Mary C. (North) Baker, both of whom were natives of Michigan, as was their daughter. He is yet living, and makes his home with our subject. His wife died in March, 1888. By this union there was one son born, F. B., who is engaged in the grocery and notion trade, in which line he has been for the last eight years. He is a graduate of the Polo high school, and is a good business man.

In politics, Mr. Kridler is a Republican, but is not a partisan. He prefers to give his time and attention to his business interests rather than to politics. He has been in business with Mr. Strickler for about seventeen years, their store now being more than double its original size, covering a space of thirteen thousand five hundred square feet. They handle almost everything that is sold in the large department stores, and their trade is constantly increasing. They are up-to-date business men, and have the confidence of the people.

MRS. MARY J. JOINER, whose farm is in Eagle Point township, about three and a half miles west of Polo, is a worthy representative of one of the prominent and influential pioneer families of Ogle county, dating her residence here from November, 1837. She was born in Delaware county, New York, October 29, 1831, and is a daughter of Robert Smith, a native of Scotland, who was born in 1796, and grew to manhood there. He was a weaver by trade, but after his emigration to the United States, in 1827, he located in Delaware county, New York, and turned his attention to agricultural pursuits. There he was united in marriage with Miss Deborah Broadwell, a native of the Empire state and a daughter of Ezra Broadwell, who fought for American independence as a soldier of the Revolutionary war and was a pioneer settler of Delaware county. In 1837 Mr. Smith brought his family to the west and settled in Eagle Point township, Ogle county, when the whole region round about was almost an unbroken wilderness; wolves and deer were often seen and the Indians had not all left for their new home beyond the Mississippi. A wonderful transformation has since taken place in the county and in these changes the Smith family bore an active and prominent part. The father entered one hundred and sixty acres of land in Eagle Point township, of which ten acres had been broken, as he purchased the claim from another gentleman, and he bought the land from the government when it came into market. He first built a log house, in which the family lived for a number of years while he was opening up and developing his farm, but it was later replaced by a good frame residence, and good barns and other out-buildings were also erected. He spent his last years in retirement in Polo, and there passed away November 28, 1881, at the ripe old age of eighty-five years. He was one of the valued and honored citizens of his community, having the respect and confidence of all who knew him. He was twice married, Mrs. Joiner's mother, who died in 1843, being the first wife. To them were born three children, the son being Henry Smith, who, in August, 1862, enlisted in the Ninety-second Illinois Infantry for service in the Civil war and died in the hospital at Nashville, Tennessee, February 13, 1863.

Mrs. Joiner was reared in Ogle county, and on the 1st of February, 1855, gave her hand in marriage to William Joiner, a native of Vermont, who was born October 23, 1830, and came west with his parents, Alvin and Anna Joiner, in June, 1837. He grew to manhood on his father's farm in Pine Creek township, Ogle county, and was educated in the common schools. He and his bride began their domestic life upon the old homestead in that township, which he owned and occupied for a number of years. It comprised about one hundred and forty acres, to which he added by subsequent purchase until he had a very valuable farm under a high state of cultivation and well improved. He was a successful farmer and a very prominent and influential citizen of the community in which he lived. On leaving his farm in Pine Creek township he removed to the old Smith homestead in Eagle Point township, where his death occurred May 18, 1864. He filled several official positions of honor and trust, including those of tax collector and assessor, and was a leading and active member of the Baptist church of Pine Creek. His remains were interred in the Oak Ridge cemetery, and a marble slab marks his resting place. He left two children. Henry, the older, is a farmer of Eagle Point township; he is married and has six children—Beulah, Pearl, Irma, Vera, Edna and Etta Marie. Paulina is the wife of William Made, of the same township, and they have four children—Henry W., Mary A., Nellie E. and Robert S., all attending the home school. The mother of these children died March 22, 1877. By a second marriage Mrs. Joiner had one daughter, Bertha, who married Wilson Bellows, of Buffalo township, and is the mother of one child, Robert. Mrs. Joiner is a most estimable lady, loved and respected by all who know her for her many excellencies of character, and this brief sketch of her life will be read with interest by her many friends throughout the county.

McFARLEN J. WEST, who is now living a retired life on his farm within the corporate limits of the village of Leaf River, is one of the most prosperous and successful business men of Ogle county, with whose interests he has been identified since November, 1856. He was born in Monroe county, New York, January 24, 1835, and is a son of Nathaniel R. West, a native of Massachusetts, born in 1787. The family is of English origin and was founded in the old Bay state at an early day in colonial history, and the paternal grandfather of our subject was a soldier of the Revolutionary war. Nathaniel R. West was reared in his native state, and when a young man removed to Monroe county, New York, where he subsequently married Miss Esther Barker, a native of Rensselaer county, that state, and a daughter of Richard Barker, of Monroe county, of Scotch ancestry. Mr. West spent the remainder of his life as a farmer there, dying in 1837 when our subject was only two years old. The mother carefully reared her children to habits of thrift and industry and finally came west with her sons to Illinois, locating at Leaf River, where she died in 1873, at the age of sixty-eight years.

McFarlen J. West is the youngest of the four children, two sons and two daughters, who reached years of maturity. Amasa B. came to Illinois in 1844 and entered a tract of land in Ogle county, a part of which now lies within the limits of the village of Leaf River. He located thereon in 1856, making it his home for a number of years, but finally sold and removed to Wisconsin and spent his last days near Sparta, dying there in 1884. Alma B. married John G. Randall and settled in New York, but later removed to Wisconsin, where her death also occurred. Jane A. married Henry Downer and is now deceased.

The subject of this review grew to man-

M. J. WEST.

hood in Monroe county, New York, and was educated in the common schools and in Lima Seminary. It was in 1854 that he came west and purchased two hundred acres of land adjoining his brother's place in Ogle county. At the end of two months, however, he returned to his eastern home and did not locate permanently here until 1856, when he began the work of cultivation and improvement. His brother had already made some improvements upon his place, including the erection of a residence, and there they all lived together for several years, while our subject developed his own place. Here he was married May 7, 1863, to Miss Margaret E. Waggoner, a native of Pennsylvania and a daughter of Henry R. Waggoner, who removed here from the Keystone state in 1848. She was educated at Mt. Morris, and prior to her marriage was a successful teacher. Her brother, Prof. Joseph Waggoner, was the first principal of the Mt. Morris school. Mr. and Mrs. West began their domestic life upon his farm and soon afterward commenced to build their present residence, which is a large, neat and substantial dwelling, surrounded by good barns and outbuildings. To his original purchase he added until he had three hundred acres, through which the railroad passes, and he has since laid off and platted a portion of the present town. He has sold several acres of his farm and still owns two hundred and twenty-five acres. He has ever taken a deep and commendable interest in the growth and development of the village, has materially aided in its advancement and prosperity, and was one of the organizers of the Leaf River Bank, of which he is an original stockholder and director. He has given a hearty support to all enterprises that tend to the improvement of the place and to those interests which are calculated to advance the moral, intellectual or social welfare of the community.

The children born to Mr. and Mrs. West are as follows: Henry S. is married and is the present cashier of the Leaf River Bank; Elsie E. is a cultured and refined young lady, who graduated at Cornell University, in Iowa, and was a teacher in that institution for two years, but resigned to accept her present position as general secretary of the Young Woman's Christian Association with headquarters at Detroit, Michigan. She makes her home with her parents. Wilbur M. is a business man of Duluth, Minnesota. George A. died in September, 1897, at the age of twenty-three years. They also have an adopted son, Fred D. West, son of Mr. West's sister. He is a well-educated young man and is now serving as postal clerk or mail agent.

Mr. West cast his first presidential ballot for Millard Fillmore, later was identified with the Republican party for some years, but being a strong temperance man and believing that to be the great question before the people, he joined the Prohibition party, with which he now affiliates. Although he has never sought office, he was elected a member of the village board and served as trustee for some years. He and his wife were among the original members of the Methodist Episcopal church of Leaf River, and he is now the oldest member of the class at that place. Earnest and sincere Christian people, they are active and zealous workers in the church, and for many years Mr. West has served as one of its officers. Wherever known they are held in high regard and their friends throughout Ogle county are numerous.

JOHN LIGHT, who is now living retired in Leaf River, has been identified with this section of the state for more than sixty-one years, and has contributed to its material progress and prosperity to an extent equalled by but few of his contemporaries. He early had the sagacity and prescience to discern the eminence which the future had in store for this great and growing country, and acting in accordance with the dictates of his faith and judgment he reaped, in the fullness of time, the generous benefits which are the just recompense of indomitable industry, spotless integrity and marvelous enterprise.

Mr. Light was born July 17, 1812, in Dauphin county, Pennsylvania, in that portion which now forms a part of Lebanon county. His ancestors were originally from Germany, but for many generations the family made their home in Pennsylvania, it being founded in Lancaster county by John Peter Light in 1739, and for several years its representatives were among the most substantial men of that region. Martin Light, father of our subject, was born there, and married Miss Barbara Overalls, also a native of Lancaster county and a daughter of Christian Overalls. She had a paternal uncle who was a soldier of the Revolutionary war. Martin Light followed farming in his native county, but when it was divided his farm lay in Lebanon county. There he continued to live until called from this life.

John Light had limited advantages in early life, and is almost wholly self-educated. Leaving home in 1836, he went to Ohio, where he spent one winter, and in 1837 came to Ogle county, Illinois, locating in Leaf River township, where he assisted the family with whom he came west in building a house and in breaking prairie. He returned to Pennsylvania in the fall of that year, but in the spring of 1838 he again came to Ogle county and bought a claim, comprising three-quarters of a section, for which he paid three hundred dollars. This he later entered from the government and built thereon a log house. As it was covered with timber, he opened up a prairie farm first and then began to clear and cultivate his timber land.

In 1845, Mr. Light was united in marriage with Miss Catherine Sengar, who was born in Pennsylvania, in 1824. Her father, Michael Sengar died when she was a child and her mother subsequently married again. With the family she come to Illinois in 1843. Mr. and Mrs. Light began housekeeping in true pioneer style in a little log cabin with wooden benches for chairs, a homemade bedstead and other rude furniture then so common in the homes on the frontier. Two or three years later this home was replaced by a good frame residence, and subsequently a regular Pennsylvania barn with a basement was also built. In connection with farming Mr. Light engaged in merchandising for some years, starting in business at Lightville with a small stock of groceries, but as he prospered in the undertaking he increased his stock from time to time until he had a good general store, which he conducted for ten years. When he began business he hauled his goods from Chicago, the trip occupying from seven to twelve days. After operating his first farm for twenty-one years, he rented it and moved to Stephenson county, where he bought three hundred and twenty acres, and later a similar amount, it being divided into four farms of a quarter section each. In that county he made his home for twenty years, but since 1885 has lived retired in the village of Leaf River. Besides the property already mentioned he owned more land in Ogle county, and at one time was the largest land owner and tax-payer in Stephenson county, and owns a substantial home in Leaf River. On coming to the state he had no means, and like the immortal Lincoln, he made rails for several years, splitting some thirty thousand of them. His success is attributed to his own industry, economy and sound judgment, as well as to his integrity and fair dealing.

To Mr. and Mrs. Light were born seven children, four sons and three daughters, to each of whom he gave a farm of one hundred and sixty acres. In order of birth they are as follows. Tena, wife of Henry Schrader, of Leaf River; Martin, who is married and engaged in farming in Ogle county; John, Jr., a farmer of Stephenson county, who died, leaving a wife and two children; Catherine, wife of Dr. John Penningburg, a physician of Herman; Henry, who is married and is engaged in the practice of veterinary surgery in Rockford; Mary, wife of Riley Motter, a farmer of Stephenson county; Joseph, a farmer of Stephenson county, who was accidentally killed in October, 1898, and left a wife and eight children. The parents are consistent members of the United Brethren church and have the respect and esteem of all who know them on account of their sterling worth and exemplary lives.

C. W. JOHNSON, residing in Grand Detour, is a native of West Virginia, born in Jefferson county, May 27, 1845, and is the son of Aaron H. and Marietta (Boone) Johnson, the former a native of Virginia, born January 10, 1821, and the latter of Boonsborough, Maryland, born July 17, 1822. Aaron Johnson was the grandson of Thomas Johnson, a Revolutionary soldier who fought throughout the entire war. Marietta Boone was a daughter of Daniel Boone, who was one of the family owning the site of the present city of Boonsborough, Maryland, and who was a grandnephew of the renowned Daniel Boone, of Kentucky. In early life Aaron Johnson followed his trade of shoemaker, continuing in that occupation as long as he remained in his native state. In October, 1846, he came with his family to Ogle county, coming through the entire distance by wagon. On his arrival he took up a tract of two hundred and fifty acres in Pine Creek township, where he continued to remain and farm until his death June 22, 1867. His wife is yet living and makes her home with her children. They were the parents of eight children, six of whom grew to maturity: Charles W., the subject of this sketch; J. C., living in Fulton county, New York; H. N., living in Dixon, Illinois; Mary V., who died at the age of thirty-one years; Susan K., wife of Frank H. Wilber, living near Polo; and A. M., living east of Polo on the home farm. In politics Aaron Johnson was originally an old line Whig, but became a Republican on the organization of that party. He was an earnest member of the Christian church, of which body his wife is also a member.

The subject of this sketch came to Ogle county when but one year old, and in the public schools of Pine Creek township he received his primary education. This was supplemented by an attendance at Rock River Seminary, at Mt. Morris. After attending one term, his patriotism got the better of him and he enlisted April 24, 1864, in Company I, One Hundred and Fortieth regiment, Illinois Volunteer Infantry. He went first to Camp Butler, near Springfield, Illinois, and from there he went with his regiment to Memphis, Tennessee, where they were assigned to guard the Memphis & Charleston railroad. In the discharge of this duty they had a number of skirmishes with guerrillas, but were in no regular battle. At the close of his term of service he was mustered out October 29, 1864, and has yet in his possession the card of thanks issued and signed by Abraham Lincoln.

On his return home, Mr. Johnson again entered the seminary at Mt. Morris and remained one term. After leaving school, he worked for his father two years, then taught school in winter and farmed in summer for the next seven years. On the 29th of December, 1868, he was united in marriage with Miss Saville M. Bovey, who was born March 5, 1850, in Grand Detour township, and daughter of Samuel and Barbara (Funk) Bovey, both of whom were natives of Washington county, Maryland, the former born November 5, 1814, and the latter December 8, 1816. Samuel Bovey was a farmer, and in 1840 came to Ogle county and located in Grand Detour township, where he resided until his death in January, 1891. His wife died August 20, 1888. They were the parents of ten children, five of whom grew to maturity. Lydia married J. H. Brubaker, and they live in Anthony, Kansas. Saville M. is the wife of our subject. Ella B. is the wife of George R. Rhoades, and they are living on the old home farm in Grand Detour township. Katie is the wife of H. N. Johnson, and they reside in Dixon, Illinois. Barbara is the wife of D. M. Fahrney, and they also live in Dixon. To Mr. and Mrs. Johnson six children were born. Clarence died in infancy. Bertha O., born November 8, 1870, married Jerome F. Cox, and they live on our subject's farm in Grand Detour township. Nellie J., born January 21, 1873, married Amos L. Palmer, and they reside in the village of Grand Detour. Francis M., born January 22, 1875, is living with his father. E. May, born December 21, 1876, is living with her parents. Bessie L., born March 19, 1886, is also living at home.

In the spring of 1869 Mr. Johnson commenced farming for himself, renting the farm of his father-in-law in Grand Detour township, and in 1874 purchased one hundred and sixty acres from the heirs of Peter Newcomer. To his original purchase, as his means increased, he made additions, until he has now four hundred and seventy-nine acres of well improved and valuable land. In addition to the raising of grain, he has made a specialty of raising Poland China hogs, having usually on his place from one hundred to one hundred and fifty head. He has also had on his farm a number of Morgan and Norman horses, and Durham shorthorn cattle. Conservative in his work, he has been quite successful in what he has undertaken, and is numbered among the prosperous farmers of the county.

In politics Mr. Johnson is a Republican. He has been collector one year; highway commissioner eight years; school trustee eight years; school director two terms; justice of the peace sixteen years; and is now serving his seventh year as supervisor of his township. While on the board he has been chairman of the judiciary, educational, fees and salaries, and poor farm committees, and a member of the claim committee. He has represented his party twice in state conventions at Springfield, and in his party work he has always endeavored to keep the rights of the people in view. He is a member of the Christian church, as is also his wife and family, and in the work of the church takes a deep interest. Fraternally he is a member of the Grand Army of the Republic, holding membership with Post No. 116, at Oregon.

DANIEL CASE is a man whose genial temperment, sound judgment and well-proved integrity have brought to him the esteem and friendship of a host of acquaintances far and near. On coming to the county in March, 1874, he located on section 8, Marion township, and for some time his attention was entirely occupied by agricultural pursuits, but since 1888 he has made his home in Stillman Valley, and in connection with his farming interests he has since dealt in all kinds of farm machinery.

Mr. Case is a native of New Jersey, born in Hunterdon county, June 22, 1842, and is a son of Hon. John H. Case, whose birth occurred in the same county in 1807. His grandfather, Daniel Case, commanded a company and served with distinction in the war of 1812. From wild land he developed the farm in Hunterdon county on which our subject and his father were both born. On attaining to man's estate the latter married Miss Elizabeth Bennett, a native of Warren county, New Jersey, and a daughter of Isaac Bennett, who was an early settler of Warren county, but spent his last days in Hunterdon county. Throughout life John H. Case followed farming on the old homestead and was one of the most prominent and influential men of his county. He was called upon to fill many local positions of honor and trust and for two or more terms represented his district in the state legislature with credit to himself and to the entire satisfaction of his constituents. He died in 1869, at the age of sixty-two years, and his wife who survived him for some time, passed away in 1893, at the age of eighty-three. They were the parents of eight children, four sons and four daughters, namely: Sarah, wife of Jonas Robins, of Hunterdon county, New Jersey; Phœbe, deceased wife, of Joseph Hart; Isaac B., who owns and operates the old homestead; Catherine died at the age of twenty-eight years; Daniel, of this sketch; Dr. Nathan, who was engaged in the practice of medicine in Rigglesville, New Jersey, for several years, but is now deceased; Howard, a commission merchant of New York city; Elizabeth, wife of Anderson Conover, of Foreston, Ohio.

In the county of his nativity, Daniel Case grew to manhood and had the advantages of a good education, completing his studies at the Raraton high school. On leaving the school room he assisted his father in the labors of the home farm for some years, and thus obtained a good practical knowledge of the occupation which he has made his life work. In Hunterdon county, September 23, 1873, he led to the marriage altar Miss Mary M. Smith, a native of the county, and a daughter of Robert Smith, one of the substantial farmers of that locality. Three children have been born of this union: Robert G., Elizabeth and Emma, all of whom have been well educated and are now at home.

In the spring following his marriage, Mr. Case came to Ogle county, Illinois, and in Marion township purchased one hundred and sixty acres, to which he subsequently added an adjoining one hundred and twenty acres, making a fine farm of two hundred and eighty acres, which he placed under a high state of cultivation and improved until it is one of the most desirable places of the community. In connection with general farming he also engaged in breeding and raising a good grade of stock—horses, cattle and hogs. In 1888 he rented the farm and removed to Stillman Valley, where, as previously stated, he is now doing a successful business as a dealer in farm machinery, mowers, binders, etc.

Mr. Case has been called upon to mourn the loss of his estimable wife, who passed away May 1, 1898, and was laid to rest in Stillman Valley cemetery. She was a faithful member of the Congregational church, to which he and his family also belong. Socially he affiliates with the Modern Woodmen of America and the Knights of Pythias, and has held office in both orders. Politically his support has always been given the Democracy since casting his first vote for General George B. McClellan in 1864. In Marion township he served on the school board for a number of years, and since coming to Stillman Valley has occupied a similar position. He has identified himself with every enterprise for the public good and is justly numbered among the valued and useful citizens of the community.

W. H. CUNNINGHAM, one of the leading merchants of Polo, and vice-president of the Exchange Bank of the same city, was born in Washington county, Maryland, May 20, 1841, and is the son of Joseph and Elizabeth (Sprickler) Cunningham, both of whom were natives of Washington county, Maryland, the former born in 1808, and the latter in 1822. Joseph Cunningham was the son of David Cunningham, also a native of Maryland, and who followed the occupation of a cooper during his entire life. In his family were six sons and two daughters. In the common schools of his native state Joseph Cunningham obtained his education, and at the age of twenty-two years went into the mercantile business, opening up a general store at Cunningham's Cross Roads, now Cearfoss, Maryland. He continued in that business for nearly forty years, retiring from the same about fifteen years before his death, which occurred December 15, 1875. He was united in marriage with Miss Elizabeth Sprickler, by whom he had eleven children, four only now living—W. H., Andrew, Miley and Mary. With the exception of two, all died young. Those two were John, who died at the age of sixty years, and George, when fifty-six years old. The mother is yet living in Washington county, Maryland. In politics Joseph Cunningham was an old-line Whig until the organization of the Republican party, when he gave adhesion to that organization, the principles of which he advocated during the remainder of his life. For some years he served as justice of the peace, and also school director a number of years.

The common schools of his native county afforded the only opportunity for our subject to obtain an education, but he made the best use of his opportunities until he was sixteen years old, when he quit the school room that he might begin in earnest the battle of life. One year later, in 1858, he came to Ogle county, and for two years worked on a farm owned by Henry Newcomer. At the expiration of that time he went to Polo and commenced clerking in the grocery store of H. N. Murray, the same store and in the same line of business in which he himself is now engaged. For five and a half years he continued in Mr. Murray's employ, and then, in partnership with John Bingaman, purchased the stock of the Murray estate and continued the business. This partnership lasted for nineteen and a half years, when Mr. Bingaman withdrew, since which time he has continued alone.

On the 15th of June, 1868, Mr. Cunningham was united in marriage with Miss Delilah Sanford, who was born in Buffalo township, and daughter of Harrison and Bridget (Deyo) Sanford, the former born in Middletown, Delaware county, New York, February 16, 1812, and who died July 1, 1866, and the latter born in the same county and state, March 14, 1814, and who died October 19, 1869. They were married in 1835. Harrison Sanford came west in 1835 in company of a party of New York people, and took up some land in Buffalo township, and followed farming for a number of years. He then went to Oldtown and established a hotel there, which he ran until 1854, when he came to Polo and built a hotel where the Exchange National Bank now stands, and called it the Sanford House. He occupied that house for some years. In 1870 the building was torn down, and the present building erected by the stockholders of the Exchange National Bank, of which Mr. Cunningham is vice-president.

To Mr. and Mrs. Cunningham four children have been born: Cora is living at home with her parents. F. S. is assisting his father in the store. Fannie married Frank Brown, and they have two children. They reside in Sycamore, where he is engaged in the grocery and drug business. Carrie died May 7, 1891, at the age of seventeen years.

In addition to his mercantile business, Mr. Cunningham has been connected with the Exchange National Bank since it was organized, April 15, 1871, being one of its charter members. Since 1885 he has filled the office of vice-president of the same. He is a good business man, conservative in all things, and has the entire confidence of the business community. In politics he is a Republican, but not a partisan. Fraternally he is a Mason, holding membership with blue lodge at Polo, and the commandery at Dixon.

GEORGE SMITH, who is operating a farm of three hundred and twenty acres on section 32, Woosung township, is a good representative of the young, enterprising farmers of Ogle county. He was born in Rockbury, Washington county, Maryland, April 21, 1861, and is the son of John V. and Sarah (Smith) Smith, both of whom were natives of Washington county, Maryland. They were the parents of four children: George, our subject; Fannie E., wife of Fred Seelemur, a farmer of Jones county, Iowa; Jennie G., wife of Frank H. Wilson, of Buffalo township; Ida E., wife of James Hawkins, of Coleta, Whiteside county, Illinois; and Anna D., wife of Elmer R. Osterhoudt, residing on the home place, and assisting in carrying on the farm. The great-grandfather, John Smith, was a native of Maryland.

The paternal grandfather, Solomon Smith, was a native of Frederick county, Maryland, a farmer by occupation, who spent his entire life in his native state. He married Elizabeth Hutzel, a native of Washington county, Maryland, and their children were John V., the father of our subject; Susan L.; Jacob L., a farmer of Buffalo township; and Adam W., a real esstate dealer of Lincoln, Nebraska. The great-grandfather on the mother's side was John Hutzel, also a native of Maryland.

Sarah E. Smith, the mother of our subject, is the daughter of John and Mary Smith, both natives of Maryland. John Smith came to Illinois at the same time as did the father of our subject. He located on the farm which was later purchased by his son-in-law, and which is now the home of our subject

John V. Smith was reared in his native state, and he there married. In his native state he worked for wages, and he there remained until 1865, when he came to Ogle county, Illinois, and the first year after his arrival, rented and cultivated a farm in Woosung township. He was then one year on a rented farm in Pine Creek township, after which he removed to the farm now owned by his heirs. He made a humble start in Ogle county, having not to exceed one hundred dollars on his arrival here, but he was industrious and attentive to business, and left at his death a fine estate. In politics he was a Republican, but was never an office seeker or a politician in the common acceptation of the term. He believed it to be the duty of every voter to cast his ballot intelligently and as his best judgment dictated. In religion he was a Lutheran. He died at his home in Woosung township, March 5, 1888, at the age of forty-nine years and ten months. He was a good man and had no fears of death. His widow is yet living, and is making her home with her husband's brother, Jacob L. Smith, of Buffalo township.

The subject of this sketch was but four years old when he came with his parents to Ogle county. He grew to manhood on the home farm, and was educated in the common schools and in the high school at Polo. On attaining his majority, he rented the home farm for one year, and the next worked the place in company with his father. He was married December 21, 1887, to Miss Harriet E. Wilson, who was born in Buffalo township, and a daughter of Jesse and Ann E. (Hyatt) Wilson, the former a native of Baltimore, Maryland, and the latter of Washington county, same state. Mr. Wilson came to Ogle county soon after his marriage and located in Buffalo township, where he still resides. Mrs. Smith was one of their five children, the others being Sarah E., wife of Daniel Isham, of Buffalo township; Newton, who died in childhood; Charles W., a merchant of Polo; and Franklin H., who lives with his parents.

Since attaining his majority, George Smith has been working the home farm. The estate is yet intact, and since the death of the father the children have made some valuable improvements on it, having erected a large barn and other outbuildings. In politics he is an ardent Republican. Mr. and Mrs. Smith have one son, John W. The family are highly esteemed in the community in which they reside and their friends are many.

SPENCER LAWSHE, who is retired from active business, is now a leading and highly respected citizen of Byron. Since coming to this state in 1856 he has been principally engaged in agricultural pursuits, and has by shrewd judgment, excellent management, and fair business transactions, acquired sufficient property to enable him to give up active labor and enjoy the results of his former toil.

SPENCER LAWSHE.

Mr. Lawshe is a native of New Jersey, his birth occurring in Hunterdon county, December 24, 1826. His grandfather, Jacob Lawshe, who was of German descent, lived to the remarkable age of ninety-nine years. The father, Henry Lawshe, who was also a native of New Jersey, grew to manhood in Hunterdon county, and there married Sarah Carter, who was born in the same county and was a daughter of Henry Carter. Mr. Lawshe was a weaver by trade but also engaged in farming, and met with good success in his undertaking, accumulating a competence. He died in his native state in 1870, and his wife passed away a few years previously. Six children, five sons and one daughter, constituted their family, namely: William, who married and settled in New Jersey, but later removed to Austin, Illinois, where his death occurred; George married and spent his entire life in New Jersey, Spencer is the next of the family; Hannah is the wife of John Dilts, a farmer of New Jersey; Lewis H. married and spent his entire life in New Jersey; and Jacob R. is a business man of Newark, that state.

Until eighteen years of age Spencer Lawshe remained with his father, assisting in the labors of the home farm and attending the local schools to a limited extent, his education being mostly self-acquired since reaching manhood. He served a three years' apprenticeship to the tanner's and currier's trade, and then followed that occupation for five years in his native state. There he married Rachel Tomlinson, who died after a short married life of a year and a half. After her death he came west to Rockford, Illinois, in 1856, and for one year operated a rented farm in Winnebago county. He then located near Freeport and followed the same occupation there for three years. In 1860 he became a resident of Carroll county, where, after renting for one year, he purchased a farm of two hundred and forty-five acres. While there he was again married, March 20, 1864, his second union being with Miss Ruby A. Rogers, who was also born, reared and educated in Hunterdon county, New Jersey. Her father, Major Rogers, was a native of Connecticut, from whence he removed to New Jersey when a young man, and was married there to Elizabeth Bodine, a native of that state, and in 1856 they came to Carroll county, Illinois, locating on a farm. In the east Mr. Rogers worked at his trade of shoemaking and also taught vocal music.

After carrying on his farm in Carroll county for about five years, Mr. Lawshe sold and moved to Rockford, where he purchased residence property and engaged in the express business for sixteen years. In 1884 he became a resident of Ogle county, and first bought one hundred and seventy-two acres of good farming land in Rockvale township, two miles from Byron, which was well improved, and to which he later added an adjoining tract of one hundred and twenty acres, making a valuable place of two hundred and ninety-two acres. His time and attention were devoted to its further improvement and cultivation until the spring of 1897, when he rented the farm and removed to Byron, where he has since lived retired.

Of the eight children born to Mr. and Mrs. Lawshe, six are now living. Major R. died in childhood. Emma is the wife of Sherman Taylor, a farmer of Marion township; Alice died at the age of twelve years; George H. is a farmer of Shelby county, Iowa. Carrie is the wife of Amos Blanchard, a farmer of Ogle county; Charles S. is a business man of Chicago; J. Franklin is in California, and Fred H. is at home.

Politically Mr. Lawshe was first identified with the Whig party, casting his first vote for Zachary Taylor, but joined the Republican party on its organization and has since fought under its banner. He has never cared for the honors or emoluments of public office, but has always faithfully discharged his duties of citizenship and has supported those interests which he believed calculated to prove of public benefit.

HENRY R. MEYERS, a prosperous and enterprising farmer residing on section 13, Lincoln township, owns and operates two hundred acres of land. He is a native of the township, born January 16, 1848. His father, Jonathan Meyers, was born in Dauphin county, Pennsylvania, in 1812. His grandfather, Jacob Meyers, was a native of Germany. In his native state Jonathan Meyers grew to manhood, and in his youth learned the mason's trade. In early manhood he went to Hagerstown, Maryland, and there worked at his trade a few years, then came west and settled in Ogle county. This was in 1837. Here he took up a claim of several hundred acres of land in Lincoln township, and later entered several tracts and opened up three or four farms. He became in due time a very prosperous and well-to-do farmer. He was married in this county to Elizabeth Rodman, a native of Germany, who came to the new world a young lady, with an aunt, and after residing in Pennsylvania a few years came west and located in White Eagle, Maryland township, Ogle county, where she was residing at the time she gave her hand in marriage to Jonathan Meyers. They became the parents of four sons and three daughters and all but one grew to mature years. Peter R. owns and operates the old homestead. Lydia is the wife of Lewis Boby, of Forreston. Sarah is the wife of Benjamin McCutcheon, of Forreston. Henry R. is next in order of birth. Jonathan R. resides in Forreston. Elizabeth is the wife of Joseph E. Garman, of Maryland township. Aaron R. died at the age of three years.

On one of his farms in Lincoln township Jonathan Meyers located with his bride, and there they reared their children. To his agricultural interests Mr. Meyers gave his undivided time and attention, caring nothing for the honors or emoluments of public office. He was a thoroughly practical farmer, and withal industrious, and it is no wonder that success crowned his efforts. His wife was called to her reward January 16, 1890, and he followed her July 15, 1893. They were members of the Lutheran church, good Christian people, and worthy of the respect in which they were held.

Henry R. Meyers spent his boyhood and youth on the home farm and was educated in the West Grove school. He was early given his regular duties to perform in operating the home farm and grew up to be a thoroughly practical farmer. He remained at home with his parents until he was twenty-nine years old, being a great help to his parents. He was married in Lincoln township, January 13, 1878, to Miss Rebecca Elizabeth Mase, also a native of Lincoln township, Ogle county, and daughter of John M. Mase, a native of Pennsylvania, who there grew to manhood and came to Ogle county a young man, here marrying Miss Ellen Meyers, a native of Maryland, who came to Ogle county when but two years old with her father, Jacob Meyers, who was also a native of Maryland. By this union four children were born, of whom but one is now living, Oliver Grant, a young man at home. Roy died at the age of fourteen months, Luella at seven months, and Sylvia at eight months.

Soon after his marriage, Mr. Meyers erected a dwelling house on his present farm, and in the fall of the same year moved to the place where he has since resided. After moving to the place he turned his attention to its further improvement, erecting a good substantial barn, granary, and various outbuildings, set out an orchard, planted shade and ornamental trees, remodeled the house, until he to-day has one of the best-improved farms in the township.

Politically Mr. Meyers is an earnest and enthusiastic Republican, advocating the principles of the party even before he attained his majority. His first presidential vote was cast for U. S. Grant in 1872, and he has since supported the Republican candidate at every presidential election. He was elected and served as commissioner of highways for nine consecutive years, but has never wanted public office. Fraternally he is a member of the Odd Fellows lodge at Forreston. As a citizen he is held in high esteem, and a progressive man he lends aid to all worthy enterprises.

WILLIAM ELLIS, who is now living retired in the village of Byron, is one of the oldest and most highly esteemed citizens of Ogle county. Years of quiet usefulness and a life in which the old-fashioned virtues of sincerity, industry and integrity are exemplified have a simple beauty that no words can portray. Youth has its charms, but an honorable and honored old age, to which the lengthening years have added dignity and sweetness, has a brighter radiance, as if some ray from the life beyond already rested upon it.

Mr. Ellis was born in Attleboro, Massachusetts, June 22, 1808, and is a representative of a family of Welsh origin, who was founded in Dedham, that state, by an old gentleman and his seven sons at an early day. The grandfather, Richard Ellis, was a native of Massachusetts, as was also the father, Hon. George Ellis, who, on reaching manhood, married Miss Polly Fisher, who was born near Dedham. They located on a farm in Attleboro, where they reared their family and spent the remainder of their lives. The father was one of the most prominent and influential men of the community, and for one or more terms ably represented his district in the state legislature. In the family were nine children, four sons and five daughters, who reached years of maturity, but Daniel and Darwin are now deceased; William is the subject of this review; George Otis is a resident of Middleboro, Connecticut; Adelia, Maria and Emeline all married, but are now deceased; Mrs. Catherine Plymton is a widow living in Pawtucket, Rhode Island; Harriet is the wife of Otis Putney, of Pawtucket, Rhode Island; and Elizabeth died when young.

William Ellis grew to manhood on the old home farm in Massachusetts, and had fair school advantages. He learned the jeweler's trade at Attleboro, serving a three years' apprenticeship, and continued to follow the business there for a few years. At Middleboro, Connecticut, in 1845, he married Miss Justina Abbott, a native of that state and a daughter of David Abbott, who belonged to an old and historic family. She had six uncles who were ministers in the Methodist Episcopal church and one who followed the legal profession. To Mr. and Mrs. Ellis were born seven children, four of whom are now living, one son and three daughters, namely: Adelaide J. married David J. Simpson, of Byron, Illinois, who is now engaged in gold mining in Utah, and their daughter, Helen Barnum, is now the wife of Charles Beggs, who is connected with the Standard Oil Company at Pittsburg, Pennsylvania. Eleanor F. married Robert Spottswood, who is engaged in the grain and lumber business in Winnebago, Illinois. Fred W. is interested in railroading at Fall City, Washington. Harriet is the wife of Labra Spoor, a merchant of Byron. Those deceased are Frances A., Frank H. and George B.

After his marriage Mr. Ellis and his brother George Otis engaged in the manufacture of buckles and buttons at Middleboro, Connecticut, for a number of years, but in 1852 he came to Illinois and first located at Rockford, where he worked in the factory of Clark & Utter for about eight years. He then purchased a farm six miles from that city and successfully engaged in agricultural pursuits until 1889, when he sold the place and the following year moved to Byron, where he purchased property and has since lived retired, enjoying a well-earned rest. His faithful wife passed away in April, 1891, at the age of sixty-three years.

In politics Mr. Ellis was originally a Jackson Democrat, casting his first vote for Old Hickory, but on the organization of the Republican party in 1856 he joined its ranks and has since been one of its stalwart supporters. On the 20th of September, 1849, he was made a Mason in Harmony lodge at Waterbury, Connecticut, and still holds membership there, being its oldest living member. In the summer of 1898 he and his daughter, Mrs. Simpson, made a trip east and spent three months in visiting in Massachusetts, Connecticut, Rhode Island, Pennsylvania, New York and Ohio. Although over ninety years of age he is still hale and hearty and has the appearance of a man not to exceed seventy, as he is erect and active, while his hearing is good and his eyesight only slightly impaired. Nature deals kindly with the man who abuses not her laws.

SAMUEL KNODLE, dealer in watches, clocks, jewelry, silverware and diamonds, Mt. Morris, Illinois, has now the distinction of having been engaged in the mercantile business a longer period of time than any other man in the village. He was born in Fairplay, Washington county, Maryland, a hamlet eight miles south of Hagerstown, the county seat, August 4, 1820. He attended the public school at Fairplay from the time he was nine years old until he was sixteen, from which time he applied himself studiously to the acquisition of an academic education, in the meantime assisting his father in his store of general merchandise. Following this he had a clerkship in the store of Major E. Baker, and later a clerkship in the general commission house of Meixsell & Struebaker, of Baltimore. Leaving the latter position in the fall of 1839, he returned to the place of his nativity and again took a position in his father's store, which he filled until the fall of 1842.

On the 13th of January, 1843, Mr. Knodle was united in marriage with Miss Ellen

Dick, who was born at Winchester, Virginia, June 12, 1823. In May, following, they removed to Boonsborong, Maryland, where he engaged as teacher in the public shcool, and continued to fill that position until January, 1846, in the meantime having been in partnership with his brother, Josiah, in printing and publishing a weekly newspaper called The Odd Fellow. The paper was not a fraternal paper, as its name would indicate, but purely a local paper. Having a taste for newspaper work, in January, 1846, he removed to Williamsport, Maryland, and purchased of Judge Daniel Weisel, The Republican Banner, a Whig newspaper founded by him January 1, 1830. Six volumes of this paper are yet in possession of Mr. Knodle, and they embrace the history of several of the most exciting political campaigns recorded in the annals of the country, notably that of the Andrew Jackson and Henry Clay contest for the presidency in 1832.

After purchasing the material of the office of The Republican Banner, Mr. Knodle then commenced the issue of The Times, which he continued to edit and publish until the fall of 1848, when he sold the office and removed back to Fairplay, and engaged as a teacher of the public school there, in which he continued until March, 1856. In April of the same year he came to Mt. Morris, expecting to secure the public school at this place, but circumstances favoring his embarking in the jewelry trade he relinquished his time-honored profession, and on the 20th of May, 1856, he opened a jewelry shop in rooms in the Eldorado House, then conducted by the late Jonathan Mumma. From that day to the present time he has pursued that avocation.

During his residence in Mt. Morris, in connection with his regular business, he has been identified with all the various newspaper enterprises up to 1879. In 1858-9, he conducted the Northwestern Republican for an association of citizens who purchased the office of Atwood & Metcalf, who had established the paper in the fall of 1857. In 1860-61, he managed the Independent Watchman, whom a like association of business men had bought of Col. M. S. Barnes, who had purchased the office of the former association. This ended his newspaper business in Mt. Morris until July, 1876, when he again embarked in the business, in the establishment of The Independent, owned by a corporation company, Mr. Knodle owning nearly one-half of the stock, consisting of a well-equipped job printing plant, which was added to the newspaper outfit, the job office having been conducted by him since 1872. In May, 1877, the Independent Company sold the the office to Henry Sharer, and his son, John, then immediately commenced the publication of the Ogle County Democrat, with Mr. Knoole, as manager of the typographical department and proof reader.

Mr. Knodle had a family of nine children. Emanuel Luther was born at Boonsborough, Marland, April 17, 1844, and died July 23, of the same year. Washington Irving, born June 13, 1845, died December 29, 1845. Charles William, born at Williamsport, Maryland, April 13, 1847, died January 16, 1848. Mary Ann, born at Fairplay, Maryland, July 3, 1849, died December 16, 1849. Edwin Wilme, born at Fairplay, December 6, 1850, is now living near Monroe, Wisconsin. Jane Elizabeth, born at Mt. Morris, Illinois, June 8, 1857, married John A. Walker, February 14, 1880, and they are now residing in Mt. Morris. Lillie

Belle, born in Mt. Morris, January 5, 1860, married George Ellot Coffman, January 16, 1879, and they now reside in Thayer, Kansas. Thomas Oscar, born in Mt. Morris, August 29, 1863, died August 25, 1865. Ernest Elmer, born in Mt. Morris, October 5, 1868, married Miss Mary Carpenter, April 10, 1893, and they now reside in Rockford, Illinois.

Mr. Knodle's father, Samuel Knodle, Sr., was born in Adams county, Pennsylvania, April 23, 1784, and was married at Hagerstown, Maryland, January 3, 1806, to Miss Jane Cutshaw, who was also born in Adams county, Pennsylvania. What time they removed to Maryland is not known, but some time prior to 1810, at about which time his father built the first house at the place which was afterwards known as Fairplay, where his parents continued to reside until the day of their death, his father dying May 29, 1851, and his mother January 23, 1865.

Since coming to Mt. Morris, Mr. Knodle has been quite active in local affairs. He was clerk of the township of Mt. Morris from 1858 to 1861, and in 1860, 1861, and 1868, served as village clerk. In 1871 he served as village trustee and president of the board. In 1883 he was elected village clerk, and has been annually re-elected, making twenty years service in that office. In 1876 he was collector of the township of Mt. Morris. Few men have the good will of their fellow men in a higher degree.

CHARLES W. GARNHART, a wideawake and progressive farmer residing on section 25, Marion township, four miles and a half south of Stillman Valley, is a man whose sound common sense and vigorous, able management of his affairs have been important factors in his success, and with his undoubted integrity of character have given him an honorable position among his fellowmen. His birth occurred in Northumberland county, Pennsylvania, August 27, 1834, and he is a representative of one of the old honored families of that state. There his great-grandfather, Peter Garnhart, and grandfather, Balsar Garnhart, were also born, and the latter was a pioneer of Northumberland county, his early home having been in the southern part of the state. John Garnhart, father of our subject, was born on the same farm in Northumberland county where his son's birth occurred, and there he grew to manhood and followed farming for some years. He married Louisa Moress, also a native of Pennsylvania, and a daughter of Squire Moress. In 1840 they started across the country to Illinois with two teams and arrived in Ogle county during the fall. That winter the father purchased the farm on which our subject now resides, but the only improvement found thereon at that time was a rude log cabin, while about thirty acres had been broken by the plow. Acre after acre was soon placed under cultivation, and in due time a pleasant brick residence was erected, and also a good barn with a basement, making it one of the best improved farms of the county. For many years Mr. Garnhart was one of the most active and successful farmers of the community, but spent his last years in retirement in Rockford, passing away at his home there July 26, 1870. His first wife died on the home farm and he subsequently married again.

By the first union there were seven children, six sons and one daughter, of whom Charles W., our subject, is the eldest;

Harry married and located on the old homestead where his death occurred; George W. is a farmer near Polo, Illinois; David P. served as a soldier during the war of the Rebellion and now resides on a farm in Stephenson county, Illinois; Mary C. is the wife of Wallace Walters, of Calhoun county, Iowa; Aaron, who was also a soldier in the Civil war, later became a business man of Davenport, Iowa, and there died; and John W. is a farmer of Pine Rock township, Ogle county.

Charles W. Garnhart was a lad of fifteen years when the family came to Ogle county, and being the eldest son he was early inured to the arduous task of developing wild land into productive and well cultivated fields. He also assisted in making improvements upon the place. He received good common school advantages and at the age of nineteen years began life for himself by working by the month for Peter Smith for two years. He then learned the carpenter's and joiner's trade, which he followed for about the same length of time. He rented land in White Rock township and successfully engaged in farming on his own account. In the spring of 1862 he bought his first land, which was an improved land of one hundred and twenty-eight acres in Pine Rock township, and after operating it for about six years he bought eighty-eight acres adjoining, making a fine farm of two hundred and seventeen acres, upon which he made many substantial improvements. He lived there until 1877, when he purchased the old homestead and rented the former place. He started out in life for himself empty-handed, and for his work received but small wages. This did not discourage him, however, and he is to-day the owner of two valuable farms, which have been obtained through his own labor, economy and well-directed efforts.

In September, 1861, in Ogle county, Mr. Garnhart led to the marriage altar Miss Caroline Lilley, who was also born in Northumberland county, Pennsylvania, and when a child of thirteen years was brought to Illinois with her parents, David and Catherine Lilley, who settled in Marion township, Ogle county, in the spring of 1847. Of the five children born to Mr. and Mrs. Garnhart two died in infancy. Those living are Lawrence D., a carpenter and joiner, now residing in Minnesota; William H., who assists in carrying on the home farm; and Clarence W., a carpenter and joiner residing at home.

Mr. Garnhart has been an ardent Republican in political sentiment since casting his first vote for John C. Fremont in 1856, and he has taken quite an active and prominent part in local politics. At the age of twenty-two he was elected a member of the school board, and served as such for twenty-five or thirty years, most of the time being president of the board, also serving as clerk part of the time. He has also filled the office of commissioner of highways for sixteen years, and being the present incumbent he has two more years to serve. His official duties have always been most promptly and faithfully discharged, and he is now most capably and satisfactorily filling the office of township trustee. In all the relations of life he has been found true to every trust reposed in him, and well merits the high esteem in which he is held by all who know him.

MAJOR EDWARD FELLOWS DUTCHER.—Among the remaining early settlers of Ogle county is that distinguished lawyer, soldier and pioneer whose name heads this sketch. He was born April 2, 1828, in Canaan township, Litchfield county, Connecticut, on the Housatonic river. His education was obtained at the Lenox Academy, at Lenox, Massachusetts, and in a school at Salsibury, Connecticut. Later he took up the profession of law, and in 1836 entered the law office of Woods & Morse, at Lockport, New York, and began his reading. He read in this and other offices until 1842, when he was admitted to the bar in Orleans county, New York, and soon afterwards formed a partnership with Judge Royal Chamberlain for practice in that county, locating at Lynden. In 1846 he became imbued with a desire to go west, and in that year he is found located at Oregon, Ogle county, Illinois, with his office open for business.

Major Dutcher is the son of Captain Ruluff Dutcher, who was born at Dutcher's Bridge, Litchfield county, Connecticut, a farmer by occupation, a soldier of the war of 1812, serving as captain of a company. His father, the grandfather of our subject, was Captain Ruluff Dutcher, who was born in 1738 and who served through the war of the Revolution, entering the service first as corporal in Captain James Hudson's company of Major Skinner's regiment of light-horse militia. His name appears on the rolls of the war department as having "marched June 20th. Time when discharged, August 3d. Days in service, 38." Later the war records show him with the rank of captain of a company of Major Sheldon's regiment of light horse in 1776. This roll contains special remarks relative to his service. This Revolutionary captain was a son of a Hollander whose name was also Ruluff, and who was born on the ocean while his parents were *en route* to America. He died January 17, 1736.

The mother of our subject was Lucinda Howe, daughter of Elisha Howe, of English ancestry. She was a cousin of Admiral Howe, of the English navy. She died at Amboy, Illinois, August 27, 1874, in her eighty-seventh year, and her remains were interred at Oregon. The paternal grandmother, Jane Dutcher, *née* Ashley, was the daughter of John Ashley, who was a general in the Revolutionary war. The second daughter of John Ashley, Mary, married John Fellows, who was also a general in the war for independence. John Fellows' son, Edward, was a colonel in the same war, and is the one from whom the subject of this sketch is named. Revolutionary records also show that William Bull, the first husband of Jane Ashley, was a surgeon in the Revolutionary war and died from smallpox, and that later Jane married Major Dutcher's grandfather.

Ruluff and Lucinda Dutcher were the parents of nine children, as follows: Frederick R., born December 21, 1804; Caroline M., born July 1, 1806; William A., born January 7, 1809, and died in 1850; Emeline J., born June 1, 1812; Elisha Wells, born in 1815; Edward F., our subject; Catherine L., born November 15, 1820; Samuel A., born January 7, 1823; and Elizabeth S., born May 10, 1825. Emeline, who married Herman B. Bushnell, was matron of the Soldiers' Home, Quincy, Illinois, for three years. Her only son, Lieutenant Pierre Bushnell, was killed during the Civil war. Caroline M., who married Frederick A. Sterling, died at her son's home in St. Louis, January 3, 1898, at the age of ninety-two years. Her only daughter married

Joseph H. Choate, the distinguished lawyer of New York city. Samuel A. is living at Farley, Iowa.

Major Dutcher was reading law at Lockport, at the time of the burning of the steamer Caroline, at Schlosser. To him was given the important charge of going to Buffalo for a capias for the arrest of the British officer under whose orders the vessel was burned. During the Canadian trouble of 1837-8, Major Dutcher was arrested at Hamilton, Ontario, and held a prisoner for four days as a rebel, together with seventeen other Americans, whose sympathies for the Canadians brought the action of the higher powers against them.

It was not long after Mr. Dutcher opened his office at Oregon before the people of this section of the country became satisfied that he was a lawyer of no mean ability. In fact he soon took front rank among the members of the profession, and before the war for the Union commenced he was recognized as the leading criminal lawyer of the northwestern part of the state. He was of Revolutionary stock of patriotic ancestors, and when the war broke out and a blow was aimed at the union his ancestors had helped create, it was his second nature to take a hand and help parry that blow. Accordingly his name is found on the muster roll in August, 1862. He was soon after commissioned second lieutenant, with authority from Governor Yates to recruit a company, which he soon had ready, and it was assigned to the Seventy-fourth Illinois Volunteer Infantry. On the organization of the regiment he was elected major, and with his regiment he reached the front October 1st, and was assigned to the Army of the Cumberland. In all he recruited some four hundred men for the army. With his regiment he took part in the battle of Champlain Hill, and the skirmishes in pursuit of General Bragg. He was also in action at the battles of Perryville, Lancaster, Knobb Gap, Overall Creek, Stone River and in all the skirmishes and marches in which his regiment was engaged, until he received his discharge in March, 1863, on account of disability. For seventy days after the battle of Stone River, Major Dutcher was in command of his regiment, and was in the expedition to Franklin, Tennessee, under General Jeff C. Davis, the object being to intercept Forrest and Wheeler. On leaving the army he returned to Oregon, and on regaining his health resumed the practice of his profession.

Major Dutcher was united in marriage, in 1849, to Elizabeth C. Van Valkenburg, a native of Kinderhook, New York. This union was blessed with six children. Edward S. was a resident of St. Louis, Missouri. He is now deceased. William H. lives at Oregon, and has served as United States deputy marshal for the northern district of Illinois. Ruluff E. married Maggie Terwilliger, and they reside in Council Grove, Kansas. George A. married Laura McCary, and they reside in Oregon. Katie S. and Mary A. died in childhood. Mrs. Elizabeth C. Dutcher departed this life May 13, 1876. In 1879 Major Dutcher married Sarah (Marsh) Scripter, of Batavia, New York, who died in June, 1893.

Major Dutcher has always been an earnest Democrat, though generally in advance of his party, politically. He has lived in a county and district some fifty years which has been largely Republican, yet he has been true to his early training, but discussing freely what he conceived to be the errors of his party. In 1849, in a series of able articles, he denounced in unmeasured terms the "black laws" of 1845. These papers brought upon him much censure from the members of the Democratic and Whig parties who supported those laws. In the days of Knownothingism he took an advanced position in the advocacy of the doctrine which he claimed every foreigner coming to the United States to reside should adopt— he should be required to file his intention to become a citizen, and that a court having jurisdiction should be the scene of this action within ninety days after his arrival. In that way only should aliens be allowed to enter government land, and then only upon the further condition that said alien should become a naturalized citizen within six years thereafter, and in case of failure to secure such citizenship, such lands should revert back to the general government. Later legislation has shown the soundness of these views and his far-seeing mind.

The major has always taken an active part in political matters, but living in a district where his party was in the minority, political preferment even if desired was out of the question. He severely denounced the verdict of the electoral commission, and has always held that Tilden was duly elected. He was a delegate to the Democratic convention that nominated Horatio Seymour for president, and has twice been chosen presidential elector for Illinois.

Major Dutcher has been in active life for nearly a half century in this and adjoining circuits, and has acquired a reputation in criminal law practice excelled by none. Up to within a few years he was connected with almost every important criminal trial in this circuit, and in every case of homicide with which he was connected he has saved his client from the death penalty save one, and this one exception was when he was appointed by the court to defend a prisoner in the absence of his attorney, and had no time to prepare for trial. With his thorough knowledge of criminal jurisprudence, his analytical mind quick to grasp all the salient points of a cause, his intuitive estimate of the character of evidence, his clear, logical arguments and forceful reasoning, win for him the respect and attention of the court and the confidence of the jury. Courtly and fair in the conduct of cases was another attribute he possessed. This, together with his willingness to give his best efforts to the poor client, as well as the one who could produce a handsome retainer, made him the ideal lawyer. His phenomenal memory was another aid in his profession, and in the longest trials he rarely took notes.

During the war the Major generally had two horses with him, and many a weary or wounded soldier, unable to keep up, had his sore feet relieved, or his limbs rested, or saved from capture by the rebels, by riding the major's horses, while he would jog along afoot. He has always held to the immortal principle embodied in the Declaration of Independence, that "all men are created equal." He is to-day an active member of the Grand Army of the Republic, and has aided hundreds of soldiers in securing their pensions without charge.

In addition to his practice the Major has been an extensive breeder of fine horses, an animal of which he is very proud. He has raised some very fast horses and has materially aided in improving the stock of this noble animal in Ogle and adjoining counties. After a residence of over a half century in Oregon, and although he has passed his four-score years, he is yet hale and hearty, with form erect, and his mental powers unimpaired. He was reared in the Episcopal faith, and his religious views incline in that direction. Genial in manners, he has always had many warm friends.

SILAS WRIGHT LEWIS, a leading resident of Rockvale township, and a thorough and experienced farmer, was born in Saratoga county, New York, November 18, 1843, and is the son of the late Stephen Lewis and his wife, Judith Maria (Boyce) Lewis, natives of Herkimer county, New York, the former born November 25, 1818, and the latter October 23, 1822. Mr. and Mrs. Lewis were married June 30, 1839, and are the parents of two children, Caroline, who married George Clancy, and died in 1863, and Silas Wright.

When the subject of this sketch was a child of five years, his father, believing that the west afforded greater opportunities for advancement and progress, moved his family to Buffalo, and thence to Chicago by way of the great lakes, which place he left for Oregon, Illinois, moving later to Rockvale township, where he rented successively, for periods of two years each, the farms of Hiram Read, William Irvine, John James, Hiram Getchell and the Hill farm. Later he purchased two hundred acres on section 9, where he lived until his death, which occurred October 25, 1879, and where his wife still resides at the comfortable age of seventy-seven.

Mr. Lewis' grandparents, John and Elizabeth (Millis) Lewis, were natives of Saratoga county. They were farmers by occupation, and emigrated to Ogle county in 1879, where they resided until their death. His great-grandparents on both sides, took part in the great struggle that gave us our freedom, and which was the first step toward the position which we now occupy, one of the foremost nations of the earth.

Our subject first attended school at the home of Mrs. Ditwilder, and later, in an old log house which was converted into a school-room. When not attending school Mr. Lewis assisted his father about the farm, and at odd times picked up carpentering and blacksmithing, at which he became very proficient. He is still actively engaged in the cultivation of his farm, a valuable tract of two hundred acres.

December 15, 1871, our subject was united in holy matrimony, to Mary Palmer, who was born on the 9th of October, 1851, and is a daughter of Harry and Lydia (Beeler) Palmer. Mr. and Mrs. Lewis are the parents of four children: Elma, the eldest, died of scarlet fever when but two years of age; Zelda May, born in 1875, is the wife of Lawson Stine. They have a bright little son of three years, and are living on the Frank Knode farm; Stephen, a typical specimen of young America, was born October 25, 1878, and remains at home to assist his father in the management and superintendence of the home farm; Lydia, the youngest child, was born in 1881, and is the wife of George E. Smith. They reside at the home of our subject and are the parents of a fine daughter born January 7, 1899, Mary P. Smith.

Politically, Mr. Lewis is a Republican, and takes a keen interest in all affairs of state. He is at present holding the office of school director, in which capacity he has served for three terms. He has also served as pathmaster. It seems hard to realize, in looking over Mr. Lewis' farm, that these lands now in such excellent state of cultivation, were so recently the home of the deer, and other wild game, but America is nothing if not progressive and to her people belong the credit of this progression. It is to the agriculturists, however, that we owe our standing as the greatest grain-producing country in the world.

JOHN SHELLY, a prominent and influential farmer residing on section 11, Forreston township, Ogle county, was born in Blair county, Pennsylvania, August 15, 1850, and is a son of Abram and Elizabeth (Snively) Shelly, who were also natives of Pennsylvania and were married in Blair county, where the father carried on operations as a farmer until 1870. Coming to Illinois in that year, he spent one year in Ogle county, and then located in Carroll county, where he bought an improved place and again turned his attention to farming. There he spent his last years, dying September 25, 1875, at the age of seventy-two years, ten months and twenty-three days. His wife, who survived him for a number of years, passed away in 1896, at the age of eighty-five years, three months and fifteen days. Besides our subject, the other children of the family were as follows: Jacob, a traveling salesman residing in Shannon, Carroll county; Mrs. Susan Breneman, of Lenark, Illinois; Mrs. Henry Shirk, of Shannon; Mrs. Lizzie Hoffee, who makes her home near Grundy Center, Iowa; Mrs. Barbara Shirk, of Carroll county; Mrs. Sarah Stonrock, of Cedar county, Iowa; Mrs. Louisa Bowers, of Kansas; and Mrs. Albert Puterbaugh, of Plattsburg, Missouri.

John Shelly received a good common-school education in his native state and was a young man when he came with the family to Illinois. Here he assisted his father in the operation of the home farm until the latter's death. In Forreston township, Ogle county, December 4, 1877, he led to the marriage altar Miss Barbara Shirk, also a native of Blair county, Pennsylvania. Her father, Rev. Joseph Shirk, a minister of the Dunkard church, was born in Lancaster county, that state, in 1827, and in Pennsylvania grew to manhood. He married Miss Rebecca Miller, a native of Bedford county, Pennsylvania, born in 1834, where he engaged in farming for a number of years. On coming west in 1865 he first located on a farm in Forreston township, Ogle county, near Harper, but one year later removed to another farm on section 11, the same township, where he engaged in agricultural pursuits for some years. Since 1895, however, he has lived retired in Shannon, enjoying a well-earned rest. Mrs. Shelly is the oldest in her family of four children, two sons and two daughters, the others being Robert, a farmer of Carroll county; Jennie, at home with her parents; and Porter, who now operates the old home farm. Our subject and his wife have three children, Ida M., who is now attending the Shannon high school; Harry N. and Oscar. They lost their oldest child, Alvin, who died at the age of two and a half years.

For three years after his marriage Mr. Shelly engaged in agricultural pursuits on the Blair farm in Carroll county, and then bought the place on which he now resides on section 11, Forreston township, Ogle county. It was then but slightly improved, and the house was in a rather dilapidated condition, but during the eighteen years of his residence here he has made many changes, has set out forest and ornamental trees, has built a commodious and pleasant residence, erected good outbuildings and now has one of the neatest and best improved places of the township, comprising eighty acres. In connection with general farming he is engaged in the dairy business, and for this purpose keeps on hand from ten to fourteen cows. Formerly he was interested in breeding and raising stock, and kept a good grade of cattle and hogs. He commenced life for himself in limited circumstances, and by his own labor and enterprise and the assistance of his estimable wife, he has become one of the prosperous and well-to-do farmers of the community in which he lives. He has always been a supporter of the Republican party, but has never aspired to office, though he has capably served as school director for ten years, and as clerk of the district. Religiously, both he and his wife are worthy members of the German Baptist church, and are held in high esteem by all who know them.

JOHN FRANKLIN SPALDING, of Byron, Illinois, is undoubtedly one of the best business men of Ogle county. Industry, enterprise and energy have been the crowning points of his success, and his connection with various business enterprises and industries have been of decided advantage to this section of the state, promoting its material welfare in no uncertain manner.

Mr. Spalding is a native of Illinois, his birth occurring in Winnebago county, January 30, 1843. The Spalding family is of English extraction, and was founded in the United States in 1619 by two brothers, one of whom settled in Connecticut, the other in Maryland. From the former, who bore the name of Edward, our subject is descended. His great-grandfather, John Spalding, was a native of Connecticut, and served with distinction as a colonel in the Revolutionary war. The grandfather, Harry Spalding, died at the early age of thirty-six years.

S. S. Spalding, the father of our subject, was born in Bradford county, Pennsylvania, in 1816, and in 1835, when a young man of nineteen years, he came to Illinois. An older brother, John Franklin Spalding, had located here several years previous and died in Chicago in 1832, while two other brothers, Asa and James, also came here in 1835, and Harry arrived several years later. S. S. Spalding and his two brothers spent the winter of 1835-6 in Peru, Illinois, and in the summer of 1836 came to Ogle county and located in Byron township. Our subject's father took a claim two miles west of the village of Byron and opened up a farm of five hundred acres, becoming one of the prominent and substantial farmers of the county. He was married here to Miss Lydia Ann Weldon, a native of Strasburg, Pennsylvania, and a daughter of John Weldon. She came to this state with Asa Spalding and died in November, 1860, while her husband passed away in January, 1869. To this worthy couple were born six children, of whom two daughters died in childhood. Those living are John Franklin, of this review; D. W., a resident of Chamberlain, South Dakota; Mrs. Alice Danforth, of California, and Mrs. Susan Stout, of St. Paul, Minnesota.

Upon the home farm in Byron township, Mr. Spalding of this sketch grew to manhood, and the early education he acquired in the district schools of the neighborhood was supplemented by a year's attendance at an academy in Monroe, Connecticut. On his return to Ogle county, he spent one year on the farm with his father, but in July, 1862, he joined the boys in blue as private in Company B, Ninety-second Illinois Volunteer Infantry, which was assigned to the Army of the Cumberland. Later he was promoted to the rank of sergeant and participated in the battles of Chickamauga, Lookout Mountain, Missionary Ridge, the Atlanta campaign, the March to the Sea, and the engagements at Goldsboro and Raleigh. At Jonesboro he was disabled by a gunshot through the right shoulder and also through the left arm, and at Raleigh had a horse killed under him, while at Chickamauga his gun was shot to pieces. For three long years he followed the old flag to victory on southern battle fields, being mustered out at Concord, North Carolina, in June, 1865.

On his return home, Mr. Spalding commenced working by the month on a farm, and the following year operated rented land. On the 20th of December, 1866, was celebrated his marriage with Miss Emily L. Reed, who was born and reared in Byron, her father, Lucius Reed, being a native of Vermont and a pioneer of Ogle county. They now have four children: Carl S., who is married and engaged in business in Byron; Lucius Reed, an electrician, who now has charge of the electric light plant at Kirkland, Illinois; Roy V. who has prepared himself for the legal profession, graduating from the law department of the State University in June, 1898; and Ralph D., who is attending the home schools, and in five years has been neither absent nor tardy.

In 1868 Mr. Spalding purchased a farm of one hundred and twenty acres, which had been placed under the plow and fenced. He erected thereon good buildings and engaged in its cultivation until 1875, when he sold the place and bought residence property in Byron, where he has since made his home. In 1873 he began to take contracts for building bridges and has followed that business continuously since with marked success, never having had an accident happen through any fault of his own to a bridge he constructed. He build them of wood, iron and stone, but mostly of iron and stone, and has constructed more bridges in Ogle county than any three men together. He spent three weeks in the lobbies of the legislature trying to get the act passed authorizing the building of the Byron bridge, and later had the contract for part of the work on that structure. In 1876 he erected four store buildings on Main street, Byron, which were lost by fire two years later, and in 1878 he built the Commercial Hotel, which he conducted for five years in connection with his other business. He also built a livery stable and carried it on for ten years. He has a ranch in South Dakota and is extensively interested in stock growing. He is one of the most active, progressive and successful business men of the community and the prosperity that has crowned his efforts is certainly well deserved.

Since casting his first vote for General U. S. Grant in 1868, Mr. Spalding has been an ardent Republican, and has ever taken an active and prominent part in political affairs. He has most capably and satisfactorily filled the offices of school director, commissioner of highways, village trustee, etc., and in 1888 was elected supervisor. So acceptably did he serve in that position that he has been constantly re-elected up to the present time, and was chairman of the board for two years. He has also been chairman of almost every committee and as superintendent had charge of all the business connected with the building of the court house. He has taken an active interest in all public improvements and is recognized as one of the most progressive and public-spirited citizens of the county. He has served as a delegate to the county and state conventions of his party, and during the fortieth general assembly was one of the three sergeants at arms and also through a called session. Socially he is a prominent member of the Grand Army post at Byron, in which he has served as commander, and he was also one of the trustees and a member of the building committee during the erection of the Methodist Episcopal church at that place, of which his wife is a member.

Mr. Spalding holds a commission given by Governor Fifer, in 1892, as a member of the National Nicaragua Canal convention, which held its first meeting at Saint Louis in June, 1892, and met the following year in November, in New Orleans. There were twenty-two commissioners appointed for the state of Illinois.

BENJAMIN WOLF, a farmer residing on section 36, Woosung township, was born November 13, 1839, in Huntingdon county, Pennsylvania, and is the son of Jacob and Elizabeth (Layman) Wolf, both of whom were natives of Pennsylvania, the former being born about 1804. He was a shoemaker by trade, an occupation which he followed throughout life. He remained in Pennsylvania until 1850 when he came to Ogle county and located in Pine Creek township, but still continued to work at his trade. His death occurred in 1875. In his family were nine sons, two of whom died in childhood. The living are Samuel, a farmer of Powesheik county, Iowa; Henry, a shoemaker of Polo, Illinois; George, a farmer of Powesheik county, Iowa; Jacob, a carpenter, residing in Polo; Benjamin, our subject; Joseph, a fruit grower of Los Angeles county, California; and John, a harness maker, residing in Iowa.

In his native county our subject commenced his education in the public schools. He was eleven years old when the family came to Ogle county, and in the public schools of this county he finished his education. As soon as physically able he engaged in farm work for wages, and continued in such employment until in July, 1861, when he enlisted in the Thirty-fourth Illinois Volunteer Infantry, under Colonel Van Tassel. His regiment was assigned to the second division of the fourth army corps, under Sherman and saw considerable hard service. With his regiment, Mr. Wolf participated in the battles of Shiloh, Mission Ridge, Liberty Gap, Rome, Georgia. Prior to the engagement of Stone River, while his regiment was on the extreme right of the army, it was compelled to retreat, and about fifty men of the regiment, including Mr. Wolf, were captured by Confederate cavalry, but after being held about one hour, were re-captured by Union cavalry. He thus probably escaped a long confinement at Andersonville, the notorious rebel prison.

In the siege before Atlanta, while holding his haversack and drawing his rations, Mr. Wolf was struck by a rebel bullet, and two of his ribs were broken. He was sent to the hospital, where the next four months were spent. He was one week in the field hospital, and the remainder of the time in the hospitals at Chattanooga and Nashville. During the latter part of his disability he was removed to the hospital at Mound City, Illinois, where he was taken with the smallpox. After his recovery he was transferred to the veteran reserve corps, where he spent the remainder of his term of service at Rock Island, guarding prisoners. He was discharged and mustered out of service July 2, 1865, after giving four years of his time to the government.

After receiving his discharge, Mr. Wolf returned to his home in Ogle county, and renting a piece of land in Pine Creek township, he engaged in farming on his own account. He was married March 8, 1866, to Miss Susan Sterner, who was born in Freeport, Illinois, and daughter of John and Fietta (Sheets) Sterner. She was an orphan girl, her mother having died when she was only one year old. By this union there were three daughters born: Marietta, now the wife of Frank Ackert, of Dixon, but who is in the postal service between Chicago and Council Bluffs, Iowa; Grace E., wife of Charles Hempleman, a farmer of Pine Creek township; and Gertrude S., still at home.

After his marriage, Mr. Wolf rented the farm now owned by William Clark, in Pine Creek township, on which he remained three years. He then purchased his present farm of eighty acres, which has since been his home, and where he has been engaged in general farming and stock raising. When purchased the place was unimproved, and with characteristic energy he went to work to put it in order. All the buildings on the place were erected by him, and after a lapse of some years, it presented an entirely different appearance. It is now one of the best improved in the township. For the past five years he has rented the cultivated portion of his farm, but retaining the pasture land, and has given his entire time to stock raising. He yet remains on the farm.

Mr. Wolf has taken an active interest in educational matters, and has served six years as director in his school district. He is a stanch Republican and cast his first presidential vote for Abraham Lincoln. Fraternally he is a member of Post No. 84, G. A. R., of Polo. Mrs. Wolf is a member of the Pine Creek German Baptist church.

ARON CASS, deceased, was for years one of the most enterprising citizens of Rochelle, a man to whom the entire community delighted in doing honor. He was born in Tompkins county, New York, July 2, 1833, and was the son of Moses and Elizabeth (Mott) Cass, natives of Connecticut, but early settlers of Tompkins county, New York. For a number of years Moses Cass was engaged in the mercantile business in Watkins, New York, in which line he met with signal success. He never came west, but died in 1856 in Watkins, New York.

In early childhood, Aron Cass accompanied his parents to Watkins and there spent his boyhood and youth, completing his studies at Starkey Seminary, North Hector, New York. As a result of his training in that seminary he learned to prize the advantages of education above almost everything else. On leaving that institution he engaged in the manufacture of lumber in connection with his father and brothers, but his lungs being weak, he was advised by a physician to seek a change of

ARON CASS.

climate, and accordingly, in 1855, he followed an older brother to Ogle county, Illinois, locating at Rochelle, where he established himself in the mercantile business, a pursuit for which he had inherited a taste. He continued in that line until the outbreak of the Civil war, at which time he closed out his interests.

On the 11th of May, 1869, Mr. Cass was united in marriage with Miss Susan M. Smith, who was born in Marion township, Ogle county, June 23, 1847, and daughter of Peter and Sarah (Foster) Smith. (See sketch of Peter Smith.)

Six children came to bless the union of Aron and Susan M. Cass: Edward, of whom further mention is made in this sketch; Margaret Austin, wife of W. P. Landon, formerly pastor of the Presbyterian church and now a lawyer of Rochelle; Annie Amelia, who is taking a four-years course in Smith College, Northampton, Massachusetts; Ruth Frances, living at home and attending school; Charlotte May, who died at the age of one year, and Willie B., who died at the age of ten years.

From 1876 until 1881, Mr. Cass served as a director of the Rochelle National Bank, sharing in its management with his father-in-law, Peter Smith. He then re-established himself in business in the dry goods trade, and conducted a successful business for several years. From time to time he was a silent partner in several firms in Rochelle, assisting them with his means and wise counsels. On retiring from active business, he invested his means principally in farming lands. He was a good business man and was uniformly successful in all his undertakings. From 1891 to 1893, he served as mayor of Rochelle, and made a good executive officer. He did not seek the office, and in fact was averse to holding office, and in his case it was an exemplification of the office seeking the man and not the man the office.

Mr. Cass prided himself on his vigorous health and excellent constitution, but in the fall of 1893 he contracted muscular rheumatism, which caused him some alarm. In the latter part of February, 1894, he consulted Dr. N. S. Davis, one of the best physicians and diagnosticians in the country, who pronounced him apparently a sound man, slightly run down with stomach trouble, which ought to yield to treatment. From that time, however, he remained indoors, and for four days previous to his death, which occurred March 1, 1894, was confined to his bed. The morning of the day on which he died found him so much better that he was able to walk unassisted to an adjoining room. Late in the afternoon, however, his condition suddenly changed and it was but a few hours before he was at rest, his spirit having gone to join his Maker.

Politically Mr. Cass was a Democrat, with prohibition tendencies, although most liberal in his views. He was an independent thinker, while his clear perceptions and sound judgment were generally recognized and appreciated in all his business connections. He possessed a popular reading knowledge of law and took great interest in points of legal controversy. In striking contrast to a mind tempered with a keen sense of humor, was a capacity for thought which attempted to weigh all things considerately. His home life was a model one, and his pre-eminent characteristic in the family circle was love. He loved his family with all the intense devotion of his nature, and they in turn loved him. He could not do too much for them, and they reciprocated all his service. He was a member of the Presbyterian church.

While his family was to him so much and so dear, his goodness of heart extended to his fellowmen, and with unassuming modesty he performed many acts of mercy, which only his Maker and the recording angel have knowledge. His favorite motto was "With charity for all," and that charity he endeavored to extend to all. His death, therefore, was not alone mourned by his family and relatives, but by many who were recipients of his favors, and, in fact, by all who knew him. Recognizing the impossibility that all should be famous, he felt assured that in the eyes of an all-wise Judge he who performed even the humble duties of every-day life would not lose his reward. That he performed well all such duties a host of friends who are left behind will attest.

Edward Cass, the eldest son of Aron and Susan M. Cass, was born in Rochelle, Illinois, August 6, 1870, and died on the twenty-eighth anniversary of his birth, August 6, 1898. He grew to manhood in his native city, and after graduating from the high school he took a four years' course, including the preparatory year, in the university at Lake Forest, Illinois, and then spent one year in Amherst College, Massachusetts, from which he was graduated in 1893. A three years' course in the Harvard Law School followed, and after graduating from that institution he was admitted to practice in the courts of Illinois. On the first of January, 1897, he began the practice of his profession in Chicago, first with Green, Honore & Robbins, and later with Samuel Lynde. He was a very bright young man, and had just completed arrangements for entering a still more important field of labor, when death cut short his rapid advancement. Quiet, modest and unassuming, he was possessed of unusual power of intellect, and his death deprived the state of Illinois of one of its brightest young men, and one who doubtless would have advanced to the front in his profession, to which he gave his best talent and thought. In his professional work he was very thorough. He had resolved to reach the top round, and spared no amount of time, expense or labor in obtaining the best possible mental equipment. In the midst of his preparation, while at the law school, his father died. This threw upon him a multitude of business details and responsibilities. Most young men would have stopped their studies, but he assumed the extra load and pressed steadily on, being a student and business man at the same time. Likewise he was husband and father to his mother and sisters. No outside inducement, however attractive, nor laborious details within his professional work, swerved him from his purpose. This patient perseverance, combined with his natural endowments and good sense, would have brought him to the very front in the legal profession. Few, even of his intimate acquaintances, knew what complete devotion to a lofty purpose possessed this quiet, modest, polite young man. His family life was beautiful, and his thoughtfulness for each member of the family was most strikingly manifested on his death bed. He desired to take his father's place in the family and this he did to a remarkable degree. The beautiful companionship between the son and father as they walked and talked together will be remembered by many. His father's wishes were always a law to him, and the words and desires of the father were often spoken of by him to his friends.

When about nineteen years old, Edward united with the Presbyterian church, and from that time to the day of his death he was a steadfast, earnest Christian man, a firm believer in the Word of God. He not only read but studied his bible. He also read and studied church history and religious literature, spending his last Sunday at home in reading aloud a life of Christ. A friend has said of him, "Many were his virtues—few his faults." Certainly a noble tribute, and one well deserved.

LEVI M. BELLOWS, one of the substantial farmers of Eagle Point township, and who resides on section 23, has been a resident of Ogle county for a little more than half a century. He was born in Delaware county, New York, December 25, 1842, and is the son of Hoton and Sarah (Banker) Bellows, both of whom were natives of the same county and state. Hoton Bellows was born in 1809, and was the son of Jotham Bellows, who removed from one of the New England states to Delaware county, New York, at a very early day. The family is of English ancestry, and were pioneers in New England. Sarah Banker was a daughter of Squire Banker, a member of the Society of Friends. She died in Ogle county about 1850.

Hoton Bellows, who was a farmer by occupation, came to Ogle county in 1848, joining here his father's family, who had come out a few years previously. He came to Chicago by way of the great lakes, and by teams from that city to Ogle county, locating on section 23, in what is now Eagle Point township. He purchased a tract of land and opened up a farm. For forty years he was a leading citizen of the township, a good farmer, a kind neighbor, and one ever ready to oblige a friend. His death occurred in 1888, while that of his wife occurred December 24, 1844, in the forty-first year of her age. To Hoton Bellows and wife four sons and three daughters were born. Mary is now a widow and resides in Eagle Point township. Relief resides in Marion county, Kansas. Mrs. Sarah E. Hodge is now living in Lawrence, Kansas. Benjamin R. settled in Eagle Point township, where his death occurred. Levi M. is the subject of this sketch. Orison settled in Carroll county, and later died there. Talman C. resides in Buena Vista county, Iowa. For his second wife Hoton Bellows married Miss Cornelia Decker. To them five children were born, four of whom are still living: Charles, Emery, Adelbert and Jotham.

Levi M. Bellows was six years old when he came with his parents to Ogle county. He here grew to manhood, and in the public schools received but a limited education. He remained with his father until he reached mature years, when he rented land and engaged in farming on his own account. He was married in Carroll county, Illinois, February 20, 1867, to Miss Anis M. Wolcott, a native of Green county, New York, and daughter of Francis C. and Mary Ann (Robinson) Wolcott, who removed from New York to Ogle county and later to Carroll county, Illinois. By this union nine children were born, of whom five are yet living. Francis C. died in early childhood. Rose married Harry Stokes, and died in August, 1897, leaving two children, Merna Belle and Levi S., who now live with their grandparents. Walter E., a young man, is now assisting in operating the home farm. Harry R. died February 24, 1899. Hattie, a twin sister of Harry, died in infancy. Wilson H. is yet at home. Mary A. also lives at home. Edith Belle died in childhood. Fanny is a student in the home school.

Immediately after marriage, Mr. and Mrs. Bellows commenced their domestic life on his father's farm. In the winter following he purchased eighty acres, which he farmed in connection with his father's place. He has since added to his original purchase, and is now the owner of about three hundred acres. He has endeavored to keep up with the times in the way of improvement, putting out fruit and ornamental trees, tiling the place, and building a neat and substantial residence, two good barns and other outbuildings. In addition to the raising of grain, he has engaged to some extent in feeding and fattening cattle for the markets, usually shipping one or two car loads per year and about fifty to one hundred head of hogs. He has been fairly successful in life, and has no reason to complain.

The first presidential ballot cast by Mr. Bellows was in 1864, when he voted for Abraham Lincoln, since which time he has given his earnest support to the men and measures of the Republican party. He has taken quite an interest in local politics, and frequently represents the Republicans of his township in the various conventions of the party. He has served for some years as justice of the peace, and being a friend of education and the public schools, has served as a member of the school board. He is a member of the United Brethren church in Eagle Point township, the old brick church, of which he is one of the trustees. He is an active worker in the Sunday school, and served several years as superintendent. Mrs. Bellows is also a member of the same church, and is interested in its work. Both are well-known, especially in the western part of Ogle and the eastern part of Carroll counties. All who know them hold them in the highest respect.

REV. HOLMES DYSINGER, D.D., pastor of the Lutheran church, at Polo, is a well known and popular divine in the Lutheran church, with a national reputation as a minister and a teacher. He was born in Mifflintown, Juniata county, Pennsylvania, March 26, 1853, and is second in a family of seven children born to Joseph and Mary Amelia (Patterson) Dysinger, both of whom are natives of the same county and state, and where they yet reside. Joseph Dysinger, by trade, is a carpenter and builder, an occupation which he followed for some years, later following farming, a vocation in which he has been engaged for about thirty-five years. In politics he is a Democrat, and has served his fellow citizens in various official positions, including assessor, collector and school director. Religiously he is a Lutheran, as also his wife. She is a daughter of William and Catherine (Echo) Patterson, the former a native of England, a blacksmith by trade, who died at the age of sixty-eight years, and the latter a native of Lancaster county, Pennsylvania. The paternal grandfather, John Dysinger, when a young man moved from Dauphin county, Pennsylvania, to Juniata county, in the same state, and there followed the occupation of a farmer. He died at the residence of his son, Joseph, with whom he made his home for a time before his death. He married Sarah Kauffmann, whose father was an Omish preacher in Pennsylvania, and who died at an advanced age. At one time John Dysinger was quite wealthy, but lost his fortune. He had three uncles in in the Revolutionary war.

In the public schools of his native county our subject received his primary education, and at the age of seventeen commenced teaching. For three years he taught in the country schools and was then employed in the schools of Mifflintown, where he taught two years. He then entered Pennsylvania College, at Gettysburg, and after pursuing the regular course, graduated from that institution in 1878. After he received his diploma he taught Latin and Greek in the preparatory department of his Alma Mater for four years, in the meantime finishing the course and graduating from the Lutheran Theological Seminary, located at Gettysburg. In 1882 he was invited to accept a chair in the college at Mt. Pleasant, North Carolina, and was a teacher in Latin and Greek. Later he was with the college at Newberry, South Carolina, where he continued five years. He was then called to the presidency of Carthage College, Carthage, Illinois, and filled that position for seven years, during which time he greatly strengthened the institution. His resignation was accepted with reluctance, as he had the entire confidence not alone of his own church, under whose auspices the college was conducted, but by the entire community as well. Leaving the college, he accepted the call of the Lutheran church at Polo, to become its pastor. While teaching had been his regular profession, for years he had been a regular ordained minister of the church, preaching at such times as his other duties would admit. He is a fluent and eloquent speaker, and is one of the most popular pastors that has ever served in Polo. The church to which he ministers, was organized in 1870, and the house of worship erected in 1872. The parsonage was built in 1898.

Mr. Dysinger was married at Blairsville, Pennsylvania, September 22, 1886, to Miss Ada Frances Ray, a native of that city, and daughter of Samuel and Margaret (Johnson) Ray, the former a native of county Armaugh, Ireland. By this union four children have been born—Mary Ray, Cornelia, Margaret Eloise and Helen Frances.

In politics, Mr. Dysinger is thoroughly independent, believeing in giving his support to the best men regardless of their political belief, especially in local affairs. Fraternally he is a Mason, holding membership with the blue lodge at Polo. In every enterprise for the best good of his adopted city and county, he cheerfully lends his aid and influence, and in charitable and moral reform, he is always in the lead.

MAJOR CHARLES NEWCOMER, for many years engaged in the banking business at Mt. Morris, is personally as well known as any man in Ogle county. He was born in Washington county, Maryland, August 22, 1825, and is of Swiss origin, his paternal ancestor, Wolfgang Newcomer, emigrating from Switzerland in 1749, and locating in Philadelphia, Pennsylvania. He married an American-born woman, removed with her to Lancaster county, Pennsylvania, and they became the parents of three sons, Henry, Christian and Peter, who located in Washington county, Maryland. Henry was the grandfather of the Major, who belongs to the fourth generation. His father,

Samuel Newcomer, was a native of that county and state, while his mother, Sarah Fridly, was a native of the state of New York. They emigrated to Illinois in the summer of 1845, the father securing the title to three hundred acres of land adjoining the village of Mt. Morris. Here the father died four years later, the mother surviving him until January, 1882. They were members of the Evangelical Lutheran church and took an active part in organizing the church and society of that denomination in Mt. Morris.

Major Newcomer came to Ogle county with his parents. He was then but twenty years of age. The Mexican war, which followed a little later, brought with it the acquisition of California with its newly discovered gold fields. Great excitement followed the discovery of gold and a vast emigration set in towards the gold fields. In company with his relatives, Samuel W. Chaney, George and Michael Swingley, on the 1st of April, 1849, our subject started to California with an ox team. St. Joseph, Missouri, being the principal outfitting point for the overland emigrants, they went to that point, secured their outfit for what was then known and called "the plains," crossed the Missouri river early in May, and started out into an unsettled country, uninhabited except by Indians and three government forts garrisoned by United States soldiers—Forts Kearney, Laramie and Hall. The Mormons, however, had a settlement south of the emigrant trail at Salt Lake. The Indians were not as a rule hostile, unless imposed upon.

The party to which the major belonged traveled and camped alone the greater part of the way, frequently coming in site of Indian camps and villages, and were never molested or disturbed by them. They saw vast herds of buffalo on the plains, in some instances numbering thousands in a herd. Antelope were plenty, but they did not see any deer until they got into the Sierra Nevada mountains, where they saw plenty of the black tailed deer, mountain sheep, and occasionally a grizzly bear. Traveling with oxen was slow and tedious. Meeting a camp of Mormon traders at the crossing of Green river, in Wyoming, they exchanged their outfit and surplus supplies for saddle horses and pack mules, and traveling faster, they arrived at the mining region on Bear river, August 1, 1849. Their provisions being nearly exhausted, as well as their cash, they found it necessary to commence work without delay. One dollar per pound was the minimum price of supplies. Luxuries, such as potatoes, onions, etc., were dearer. Picks and shovels were worth one ounce of gold ($16.00) each.

Mining on Bear river was not sufficiently remunerative to satisfy the party, so they prospected on the Uba, the north fork of the American river, but with indifferent success. Finally they succeeded in finding satisfactory "diggin's" near where the city of Nevada is now located, and built the first cabin in the embryo city. Being moderately successful, and well pleased with the outlook and surroundings, Major Newcomer was making plans for a probably permanent abode on the Pacific coast, when the intelligence of the death of his father reached him, entirely changing the course of his after life. Returning to his home in the summer of 1850, and purchasing the interest of the heirs of his father's estate, he became the proprietor of the homestead and occupied the same until the spring of 1876, when he disposed of it.

On the first of August, 1877, in company with Dr. Isaac Rice, now deceased, he established the Bank of Mount Morris, becoming sole proprietor in 1880, and continuing the same until January 1, 1899, when he sold out to Joseph L. and John H. Rice, the former being the son of his former partner.

Major Newcomer was united in marriage with Miss Rosalie D. Blanchard, July 13, 1853. She was a native of Jefferson county, New York, and preceptress of Rock River Seminary at the time of her marriage. She died at the homestead, November 11, 1872, leaving three sons—Frank F., at present a resident of Texas; Charles E. and Lyle C., residents of New Mexico. On the 2d of June, 1889, Major Newcomer married Miss Maria Hitt, daughter of Rev. Thomas Hitt, who was one of the pioneers of Ogle county. She was born on the Hitt homestead, adjoining the village of Mt. Morris, was a student in Rock River Seminary, and afterwards continued the study and completed a course of music, both vocal and instrumental, at a conservatory in Washington City. For several years she was music teacher in Rock River Seminary, as scores of old students from its classic halls can testify.

In public life the Major has been an active and prominent factor. In 1853 he was appointed and served under Elias Baker, as deputy sheriff of the county, and in 1855 was elected sheriff without opposition. In November, 1861, he was elected to represent Ogle county in the constitutional convention, and upon the adjournment of the convention was appointed by President Lincoln paymaster in the United States army, with the rank of major, and was assigned to duty in the military division of the Department of the Cumberland, with headquarters at Louisville, Kentucky. Colonel William Allen, chief paymaster of that department, placed him in charge of the field payments of the Army of the Cumberland, including the entire forces of Generals Sherman and Thomas. His subordinates numbered forty paymasters and clerks. He retained that position until the close of the war, when he was mustered out of the service and returned home to assume the duties of civil life. Since returning home for more than twenty-one years he was actively engaged in the management of his bank. On the 1st of October, 1885, he was selected by the court to adjust the embarrassed condition of the suspended Bank of Forreston, which he succeeded in doing to the satisfaction of the assignor and creditors. In whatever position he has been called upon to fill, every duty has been conscientiously performed. He has always had the confidence of the community in which he has lived, and all have a good word to say of him.

FRED J. DEUTH, one of Forreston's enterprising merchants, owns and manages a well-stocked hardware establishment. He was born in Ost Friesland, Germany, October 6, 1852, and in his native land was reared and educated. After his school days were over he assisted his father in the cultivation of the farm, until 1870, when the family came to America and located in Forreston township, Ogle county, where the father rented a farm. He continued farming in Forreston township during the remainder of his life, dying in May, 1897. His remains were interred in White Oak cemetery, Forreston. His wife, who was a Miss Tina K. Scharman, was a daughter of Kreine and Margaret (De Vreis) Schurman. Mr. and Mrs. Deuth were the parents of the following named children: George J., living on a farm in Stephenson county; K. J., living in Minnesota; Fred J., our subject; Jacob J., a farmer of Forreston township; and August, a farmer of Lincoln township.

Fred J. Deuth, in 1877, married Miss Anna H. Abels, a daughter of Herman Abels, a farmer of Lincoln township. Her parents, Herman and Margaret Abels, came to America in 1855, and settled near German Valley. To Mr. and Mrs. Deuth nine children have been born, -Tina F., Herman, Johnnie F., Annie Carrie, Frederick George, Martha M., Bertha M., Esther Lillian and Emma Augusta. Of these Anna is deceased.

On a farm in Forreston township Mr. Deuth remained until the fall of 1883, when he came to the city of Forreston and engaged in the hardware business, in company with a Mr. Marr, purchasing the establishment of Middlekauff Bros., and the firm became Marr & Deuth. This partnership lasted three years, terminating on account of the death of Mr. Marr. The firm then became Deuth, Hemphill & Co., which lasted for nine years. It was then Deuth & Abels for one year, then Deuth & Rebman, three years, and since December 13, 1897, Mr. Deuth has been sole proprietor. He carries a full line of stoves, builders' hardware, agricultural implements, etc. The store is the oldest in Forreston and was established in 1866.

In politics Mr. Deuth is a Republican, and cast his first presidential vote for R. B. Hayes, in 1876. He has been quite active in political and local affairs, and for fourteen years served as road commissioner, and also as a member of the board of education for nine years. The family are members of the Presbyterian church. He is a very popular, affable, friendly, bright business man, and is recognized as a leader of the community. A self-made man in the true sense of the term, he has worked his way steadily upwards until he is now the possessor of a comfortable competence. No man in Forreston has more friends or is held in higher respect than the subject of this sketch.

JOHN AND JAMES NICHOLS are numbered among the most enterprising, energetic and industrious agriculturists of Eagle Point township, where they own and successfully operate a fine farm of two hundred and eighty acres on section 14. They were born upon that place, December 31, 1861.

Their father, John Nichols, was born in the town of Andes, Delaware county, New York, in 1818, and was a son of William Nichols, a native of Martha's Vineyard, Massachusetts, and a representative of an old English family, his ancestors being among the Pilgrim Fathers who settled in that state early in the seventeenth century. William Nichols was a sailor and followed the sea for a number of years. He was married at Martha's Vineyard and later removed to Delaware county, New York, where he was one of the pioneers. There John Nichols, Sr., was reared and educated, receiving fair school advantages. In 1836, when a young man of eighteen years, he came with his father's family to Illinois and located in what is now Eagle Point township, Ogle county. Here they took up a claim, built a residence and turned their attention to the development and cultivation

JAMES NICHOLS.

of a farm in the midst of the wilderness, the grandfather spending the last years of his life here. John Nichols, Sr., remained with his parents until after he attained his majority. He entered a tract of eighty acres where the family now resides and soon converted the wild land into a good and well cultivated farm, improved with substantial buildings. Being a successful farmer, he bought more land, becoming the owner of a fine place of one hundred and twenty acres. He was an efficient member of the county board of supervisors for a number of years, and held other positions of honor and trust, the duties of which he most capably and satisfactorily performed. He died upon his farm May 28, 1880, honored and respected by all who knew him. In Ogle county he had married Miss Christiana Byers, who was born and reared in Delaware county, New York, a daughter of James and Jane (Scott) Byers, both natives of Scotland. Mrs. Nichols survived her husband for a number of years, passing away April 27, 1897, and both were laid to rest in the United Brethren cemetery at the brick church in Eagle Point township. They were formerly members of that church, were among the original members and helped to build the church, but later in life united with the Presbyterian church at Polo, Mrs. Nichols having been reared in that faith. To this worthy couple were born six children, namely: Elizabeth, wife of George Adee, who is now living retired in Sycamore, Illinois; Russell B., a farmer of Eagle Point township; Nettie, wife of Barnabus Wright, of Polo; Olive, who was formerly a teacher but is now keeping house for her brothers; and John and James, of this review.

As soon as old enough to be of any assistance, John and James Nichols began to aid their father in the operation of the home farm, and since the father's death have purchased the interests of the other heirs in the place, which they are now so successfully carrying on. By subsequent purchase they have added to it and now have a fine farm of two hundred and eighty acres under a high state of cultivation and well improved. They are thorough and systematic farmers and as stock feeders have also met with excellent success, fattening for market about three car loads of cattle and one hundred and twenty hogs annually. They ship their own stock and find the business quite profitable.

Since casting their first presidential ballot for James G. Blaine, in 1884, the Nichols brothers have been ardent supporters of the Republican party and have never missed a presidential or state election. James takes quite an active interest in local politics, has been a delegate to numerous county and congressional conventions of his party, was assessor of his township for five consecutive years, and for several years has also been president of the township board of trustees of the public schools. He is a member of Buffalo Grove Garrison, No. 3, K. of G., of Polo, and both he and John are members of the Eagle Point Mutual Fire Insurance Company. They are well-known and highly respected, and have been prominently identified with the upbuilding and prosperity of the community where they have spent their entire lives, as upright and honorable business men who command the confidence of all with whom they come in contact.

CAPTAIN JOSEPH M. MYERS is unquestionably one of the strongest and most influential business men whose lives have become an essential part of the history of Forreston and Ogle county. Born on the 2nd of December, 1837, in Mount Morris township, and reared in Ogle county, his interest in its growth and advancement have always been uppermost in his thoughts, and every effort tending toward its improvement, strained to the utmost. He is one of the eight children of Benjamin and Mary (Rothruck) Myers, the former a native of Pennsylvania, and the latter of Washington county, Maryland, he and his twin brother, now deceased, coming first in order of birth. Mary is the wife of John H. Mullen, a resident of Columbus Junction, Iowa. John is a resident of Mount Morris township. Ruth Ann, the third child, is deceased. Samuel is a resident of Leaf River. Sarah J. is the widow of Norton S. Goodrich and lives in Winnebago, Illinois. The youngest child, David, died in infancy.

Captain Myers' parents were among the first settlers of Ogle county, having come to Illinois in 1837. His father was a stonecutter and worked at his trade after reaching Ogle county. When Captain Myers was a child of four years, his parents moved near Adelbar, Maryland township, where they lived until his mother's death, in 1851. After this sad event the Captain was obliged to earn his own living, which he did at farm work, attending school during the winter seasons. In August, 1861, he enlisted in Company H, Thirty-fourth Illinois Infantry. He took an active part in several notable engagements, among which were Shiloh, Corinth, Stone River, Liberty Gap and Missionary Ridge. He also took part in various battles of the Atlanta campaign, in Sherman's march to the sea and the campaign in the Carolinas. At Kenesaw Mountain he received a slight wound. Captain Myers received an honorable discharge, in Chicago, having been mustered out of service at Louisville, Kentucky, July 18, 1865.

After the close of the war, Captain Myers went to Forreston and engaged in the livery business until May, 1874. He then clerked in a general store until April, 1876, and from that time until 1877 he was proprietor of the Commercial hotel. Selling out the hotel business, he accepted a position with the Illinois Central Railroad Company as baggageman at Forreston, which position he held until his appointment as postmaster, discharging his duties in the latter capacity very creditably until the expiration of his term, April 1, 1893. Captain Myers then established an insurance agency, to which he now gives his time and attention, and which has become representative in the volume of business written for. On the 1st of November, 1898, he was again appointed postmaster of Forreston, an indication of his popularity and the esteem in which he is held by the community.

In the year 1871, Captain Myers was united in marriage to Barbara A. Geeting, a native of Germantown, Ohio. She is a daughter of George and Nancy (Wagner) Geeting, who settled in Ogle county in 1854. To this union two children were born: George, a telegraph operator at Harper, and Florence, residing at home. Our subject is a Knight of the Globe and a member of the Grand Army of the Republic. He has been constable for four years, tax collector for two years, assessor three years, member of the board of education three years, town council three years and is now holding the office of village treasurer and notary public; was president of the old settlers association for the year 1895. He has frequently been a delegate to county, congressional and senatorial conventions, and has been township and county committeeman in public affairs. Captain Myers is a stanch Republican, voting at every presidental election since casting his first ballot for Abraham Lincoln, at Mt. Morris. He is a man of sterling integrity, always courteous and affable, has the confidence of the community, and the regard of the citizens of Forreston.

EDMOND D. HUGGANS is one of the active and enterprising farmers of Ogle county. He resides on a well improved farm of three hundred and twenty acres on section 20, about two miles southwest of Polo, and has been a resident of the county since the fall of 1854. His father, David G. Huggans, was a native of Green county, New York, and was the son of William Huggans, of Irish parents, who married a Scotch lady. William Huggans was an early settler of Green county, New York, and near the Catskill mountains, in the heavy wilderness, cleared a farm and provided himself and family a home. The last years of his life were passed in that place.

David G. Huggans spent his boyhood and youth in his native county, receiving in its primitive schools a limited education. He there married Miss Polly Griffin, a daughter of Daniel Griffin, who was likewise an early settler of Green county. She was born in Delaware county, in the same state. After marriage David G. Huggans located in Delaware county, where he engaged in farming for some years, and also in the manufacture of lumber. In 1854 he came to Illinois, first locating in Lee county, and later moving to Whiteside county. In 1861 he came to Ogle county and purchased land in what is now Woosung township. He subsequently moved to Labette county, Kansas, where he lived four years, and then returned to Ogle county, where his death occurred in 1894. His wife died while they were residing in Lee county, soon after removing west. They had a family of eight children, of whom six sons yet survive. Daniel Uriah grew to manhood, married and settled in Ogle county, but died in 1894. Kimber resides in Labette county, Kansas. James G. is a farmer of Jones county, Iowa. John P. is residing in the same county. Richard W. is a farmer of Buffalo township. Edmond D. is the subject of this sketch. William S. is also a farmer of Buffalo township.

Edmond D. Huggans came to Ogle county when thirteen years old. After the death of their mother the brothers bought a farm of two hundred and forty acres in partnership, adjoining the farm of their father. They lived and worked in partnership for several years, later purchasing more land. With his brother William he bought out the other brothers, and the two continued together for some years, owning two farms comprising five hundred and sixty acres. They also engaged in buying and shipping stock together for about fifteen years, meeting with fair success. They then dissolved partnership, Edmond D. taking the farm where he now resides. Since the dissolution of co-partnership he has confined his operations to general farming and stock raising, and is considered one of the best farmers in the section where he resides.

Mr. Huggans was married in Ogle county, December 29, 1892, to Miss Jennie Maxwell, a native of Whiteside county, Illinois, and daughter of William Maxwell, a native of Scotland, but an early settler of that county, where he yet resides and is living a retired life. By this union one son has been born, Allen Maxwell.

Mr. Huggans was reared a Democrat and cast his first vote for General Hancock in 1880. Always a strong advocate of temperance, and firmly believing that from the old parties no permanent laws can ever be obtained, or any earnest efforts put forth for the suppression of intemperance, he has for the past eight years voted with the Prohibition party. Fraternally, he is a Mason, a member of the blue lodge and chapter at Polo and the commandery at Dixon. As a citizen he is loyal to the best interests of his adopted county and state, and has given the best years of his life to the permanent improvement of the county. He has been an industrious man and the results are shown in the fine farm that he owns and the personal property that he possesses. All who know him hold him in high esteem.

GEORGE W. JONES is the owner of three valuable and well-improved farms, and in his home place, which is pleasantly located two and a quarter miles south of Stillman Valley, he has four hundred acres of rich and arable land. He is numbered among the self-made men of the county, his accumulations being the result of his own industry, perseverance and good management, and the exercise of a naturally good judgment, both in regard to agricultural pursuits and business matters. He came to Ogle county in June, 1850, and since that time this has been the field of his operations, and the center of his interests and hopes.

Mr. Jones was born in Harlem township, Delaware county, Ohio, October 13, 1824, and is a son of Samuel Jones, whose birth occurred in Luzerne county, Pennsylvania, 1801. The grandfather, Samuel Jones, Sr., was a native of Wales and a pioneer of Luzerne county, where he cleared and improved a farm, following farming there until 1819, when he removed to Delaware county, Ohio, and in Harlem township again developed a farm from wild land. Samuel Jones, Jr., was a young man of eighteen years when the family removed to the Buckeye state, and was of great assistance to his father in opening up the farm. Here he married Miss Maria Cockrell, a native of Virginia and a daughter of Edward and Elizabeth (Dawson) Cockrell, pioneers of Delaware county. For several years after his marriage Mr. Jones carried on operations as a farmer in Ohio, but in 1849 came to Ogle county and took up three hundred and twenty acres of land with Mexican war land warrants. In Pine Rock township he built a residence and developed a farm of one hundred and sixty acres, giving to his children the other one hundred and sixty-acre tract. He died upon that farm July 3, 1889, at the advanced age of eighty-eight years, honored and respected by all who knew him. His first wife departed this life in 1845, and his second wife only survived him three months and eight days.

George W. Jones, our subject, is the oldest child of the first union, which was blessed by eleven children, four sons and seven daughters, all of whom reached years of maturity with the exception of one daughter. By the last marriage there were two sons and three daughters. Oliver Perry, next younger than our subject, was a soldier of the Mexican war and died in Pueblo; John Butler is living retired in Minnesota; Lorinda married William Howe and died in Delaware county, Ohio; Elizabeth is the present wife of Mr. Howe, who still resides in that county; Maria Jane married George Lilley and is now deceased; Katie Ann died in Delaware county during childhood; Elmira is the wife of Lawrence Wren, of Chana, Ogle county, Illinois; Emma is the wife of Nehemiah Woodruff, of Shamburg, Page county, Iowa; Lucy Ann married William Gifford, who died in the service of his country during the Rebellion, and she later married Samuel G. Morrison, but is now deceased, and Samuel B. is a resident of Delmar Junction, Iowa. The children of the second marriage were William H., who died after reaching manhood; Alice, wife of O. W. Campbell, of Ashton, Lee county, Iowa; Mary, who died in childhood; Irene M., widow of John Giles and a resident of Texas, and Philip P., a resident of East Chain Lakes, Martin county, Minnesota.

In the county of his nativity, George W. Jones was reared and educated, and was there married November 23, 1848, the lady of his choice being Miss Jane Woodruff, whose brother married Mr. Jones' sister. She was born in Pennsylvania, but when a child of three years was taken to Ohio, where she was reared. Four children have been born to our subject and his wife. Ann Mary is now the wife of George Smith, a substantial farmer of Marion township, Ogle county; Elizabeth is the wife of D. A. Harlaman, of the same township; Emma T. is the wife of Walter Stagle, a farmer of Marion township; Oliver Perry married and died at the age of forty-four years, leaving a large family.

In 1850 Mr. Jones came to Ogle county, making the journey in a home-made covered wagon with a blue box, and arriving at his destination in June, after twenty-two days spent upon the road, and they brought with them their few household effects and wearing apparel, all home-made. They camped out at night. Mr. Jones left Ohio with thirty-six dollars and arrived here with thirty-one, which, with his team and equipments, constituted his entire worldly possessions. He bought a cow and a stove, and began life here in earnest, working by the day for others for the first year. He then operated rented land for several years, his first purchase consisting of a tract of eighty acres of raw land in Pine Rock township, which he broke and cultivated, and to which he later added another eighty adjoining, making it his home until 1882, when he sold the place for ten thousand eight hundred and eighty dollars. He then bought eighty acres in the same school district, but sold it two years later and purchased one hundred and sixty acres in Greene county, Iowa, which he disposed of six years later at a good profit. He also bought one hundred and sixty acres in three pieces in Pine Rock township, this county, which he sold at the end of that year, and at the same time owned considerable land around Chana. He is still the owner of three fine farms, aggregating five hundred and fifty-eight acres. This includes the home farm previously mentioned, fifty-two acres north of Stillman Valley, sixty-six acres in Pine Rock township, and forty acres at Black Walnut Grove, and is valued at over forty thousand dollars.

Mr. Jones supported Zachary Taylor, Winfield Scott and John C. Fremont for the presidency, and each succeeding candidate of the Republican party, and he has ever taken an active and commendable interest in public affairs. He has held a number of official positions of honor and trust, the duties of which he most capably and satisfactorily discharged. These include the offices of justice of the peace, township collector and trustee, and was also a member of the school board. He and his estimable wife are earnest and consistent members of the Methodist Episcopal church, and are held in high regard by all who have the pleasure of their acquaintance. Mr. George W. Jones has just passed his seventy-fourth year; his sight is good, and his business qualifications are remarkably good for his age. He has just deeded each of his four children land in Ogle county, valued at two thousand five hundred dollars.

LEWIS PETRIE, a well-known farmer of Lincoln township, resides on a well improved farm of one hundred and fifty acres on section 15, and which is one mile north of Haldane. He is a native of the county, born in Maryland township, May 7, 1849. His father, Jonas Petrie, was a native of Washington county, Maryland, born April 1, 1809, while his grandfather, Philip Petrie, probably of the same county, was of German parentage. The latter was a commissioned officer in the Revolutionary army, and the sword that he carried in the service is now in possession of our subject. His death occurred in 1854, in Maryland township, Ogle county.

Jonas Petrie was reared in his native county and there married Miss Emily Weaver, also born in Washington county, Maryland, and they became the parents of eight children, all of whom grew to mature years, and but one now deceased. Frances married Daniel Stoffer, and they now reside in Adeline, Ogle county; David resides in Black Hawk county, Iowa; Jonas is living in Union county, Iowa; Jacob came west, but married and remained on the old home farm in Maryland township, Ogle county, Illinois. He is the deceased one. Upton resides in Iowa Falls, Iowa; Freeland resides in Clinton, Iowa; Mary C. is the wife of Samuel Bovey, of Black Hawk county, Iowa; Lewis, of this review, completes the family.

In early manhood Jonas Petrie was engaged in freighting over the mountains of his native state. The favorable reports from old friends and neighbors who had come to Ogle county induced him to come also. He arrived in this county with his family in May, 1840, and first located in Mt. Morris township. He only remained there a year or two, however, and then entered two hundred and forty acres of land in Maryland township, to which he removed. His farm was within two miles of the present village of Adeline. He there reared his family, and later moved to Forreston, where he lived a retired life, dying there July 23, 1880. His wife survived him but a few months, passing away in November of the same year. They were laid to rest in the cemetery at Adeline. They were highly esteemed people. By his friends and neighbors he was elected to various local offices of honor and trust. He was a member and active worker in the United Brethren church, as was also his wife.

On the old home farm in Maryland township, Lewis Petrie grew to manhood, and in the district schools received his education. He remained at home, assisting his father in the management of the farm until the latter's removal to Forreston. He was married in Stephenson county, Illinois, August 24, 1869, to Miss Margaret Ellen Heitman, who was born near Hagerstown, Washington county, Maryland, and daughter of Joseph Napoleon Heitman, a native of Germany, who removed to the United States when a young man, locating in Maryland, where he followed his trade of stone mason. He was married in Martinsburg, Virginia, to Miss Anna Fry, a native of what is now West Virginia. After his marriage he came to Stephenson county, Illinois, arriving in that county in 1852. To Mr. and Mrs. Petrie five children have been born. Anna May died at the age of six years. Charles A. will graduate in the Northwestern Dental College in the class of 1899; he has taught seven terms of school in his home district. Carrie A. is the wife of Oliver Long, a farmer of Lincoln township. Daisy A. and Howard A. are yet at home, and are students in the home school.

After his marriage, Mr. Petrie located on the old home farm, which he operated a number of years, and in the meantime purchased the farm where he now resides and to which he removed with his family in 1882. Since his removal to his present farm he has made many improvements on the place, including the erection of a large and neat residence, large barn and various outbuildings, and the planting of orchard and shade trees. He now has one of the best farms in the township.

Politically, Mr. Petrie is a Democrat, the principles of which party he has advocated during his whole life. His first presidential vote was cast for General Hancock. For about twenty years he has served as school director, and for a large part of the time as president of the board. No other office has he cared for, and he only would serve as school director from the fact that he took great interest in the public schools. A lifelong resident of the county, he has always had its best interests at heart, and has done what he could to subserve those interests.

WILLIAM STOCKING, senior member of the firm of William Stocking & Company, bankers of Rochelle, is well-known throughout Ogle and adjoining counties as a man of strict honor and integrity, possessing fine business qualifications, one having the best interests of his adopted city and county at heart, and who has doubtless done as much as any other one man to advance those interests. He was born in Ashfield, Franklin county, Massachusetts, January 3, 1827, and is the son of Herod and Lydia (Ames) Stocking, both of whom were natives of the same county and state, the former born in April, 1795. By occupation the father was a farmer and followed that vocation during his entire life. In 1832 he moved with his family to Cuyahoga county, Ohio, and seven years later to Ogle county, Illinois, settling in Monroe township, where he took up a claim of one hundred and twenty acres of government land and at once began the development of a fine farm. On that farm he spent the greater portion of his life, dying in 1888, at the age of ninety-three years. A few years prior to his death he retired from active life, passing away at the residence of his son. Always an active man, he retained the full possession of his faculties till the last, and outlived his second wife. During the second war with Great Britain he served his country as one of its brave defenders. Politically he was a stanch Democrat. Herod Stocking was the son of Abraham and Abagail (Smith) Stocking, both of whom were probably born in Massachusetts, the former living to the age of ninety years, and the latter until eighty-five years old. Of the ten children born to Herod and Lydia Stocking, two only are now living, Lewis, of Lynnville township, and our subject.

William Stocking was five years old when he accompanied his parents to Cuyahoga county, Ohio, and but twelve years old when he arrived with them in Ogle county, and here his entire life has since been spent, a period of three score years. He well remembers the trip from Ohio to Illinois, coming through as they did with teams. The country was new and it was quite interesting to the boy. His education, which was begun in the common schools of Ohio, was completed in the primitive schools of Ogle county, attending as he did generally during the winter months. But in those primitive schools he laid the foundation of a practical business life which has been successful, and which has brought him honors and the esteem of his fellow men.

Continuing with his father, and assisting in the cultivation of the home farm, until he was twenty-one years old, he then took up one hundred and sixty acres of land from the government and the first year broke twenty acres, thus beginning life for himself. His first crop of wheat he hauled to Milford with an ox team and sold for forty-five cents per bushel. Success seemed to crown his efforts from the start, and he is now the owner of one thousand acres in one body, lying in White Rock and Lynnville townships. For some years he was extensively engaged in buying and selling stock, and in that line of business was likewise successful.

In 1872 he became interested in the Rochelle National Bank, and was connected with that institution until 1881, when he sold his stock and severed his connection with the bank. He then bought a controlling interest in the First National Bank of Rochelle, which was later changed into a private bank and business continued under the firm name of William Stocking & Co. The bank is recognized as one of the sound financial institutions of the county, and has a large line of deposits.

In Monroe township, Ogle county, June 27, 1847, Mr. Stocking was united in marriage with Miss Lydia Crill, a native of Oneida county, New York, and daughter of Henry Crill, one of the pioneer settlers of Monroe township. Four children were born of this union. Horace married Alma Weeks, and is now living on the home farm. They have four children. Dexter died at the age of three years. Aurora married George Terry, a manufacturer of Chicago, in which city they reside. George E. is connected with the bank in Rochelle. He married Helene S. Stanton, by whom he has three children.

In politics Mr. Stocking is a Republican and for years has been active in the councils of the party. He has been likewise active in county and municipal affairs, and while residing in White Rock township served as supervisor three terms, and also five terms in the same office in Flagg township, since removing to Rochelle. On the board he was one of the most active and influential members. As a member of the city council of Rochelle, he was chairman of the committee on water works and was chiefly instrumental in securing so fine a plant, and took part in putting in the same. Since 1881 he has served as mayor of the city, a term of office which has probably no parallel in the state in the same office. He has been of great assistance in getting the city of Rochelle free from bonded indebtedness. That his services have been appreciated, a reference to the length of time which he has served is all that need be said.

SOLISTINE GUIO, is a well known citizen of Ogle county, residing about four miles north of Polo, on section 32, Lincoln township, where he owns and operates a well-improved farm of one hundred and sixty acres, and also owns eighty acres additional in the same township. He was born in Summit county, Ohio, near Akron, October 14, 1835. His father, Peter Guio, was a native of Canada, of French extraction, but who emigrated to Ohio when a young man, locating on a farm in Summit county. He there married Miss Josephine Moushang, a French lady, who was reared in Summit county, Ohio. They became the parents of four sons and five daughters, all of whom grew to mature years. Of the family, two sons and two daughters are now living. The living are Solistine, of this sketch; Peter, who resides near Salt Lake City, Utah, where he owns a ranch, and also keeps a public house and stage station; Levina, widow of J. B. Lamb, of Chicago; and Mrs. George Culver, of Kalamazoo, Michigan. The mother of these children died in Ohio in 1845, and about four years later the father removed with the family to Branch county, Michigan, and settled near Gilead, where he engaged in farming and reared the family. He died there about 1854.

The subject of this sketch spent his boyhood and youth in Ohio and Michigan, being about fourteen years old when he accompanied his father to the latter state. He had good common school advantages in his native state, and also attended the common schools of Michigan for a short time. When about seventeen years old he commenced life for himself, working on a farm. He continued at that work in Michigan until the spring of 1860, when he went to Kansas with the idea of making that his home. However, he did not long remain there, but in the fall of the same year came to Ogle county and commenced working by the month. After being thus employed about one year, he rented a farm and began farming for himself. He later bought a threshing machine, and during the seasons for thirty-five years was engaged in operating the same, in all probability being the oldest operator of a threshing machine in Ogle county.

Mr. Guio was married in Ogle county February 27, 1868, to Miss Mary Pyter, born in Lancaster county, Pennsylvania, and daughter of George Pyter, also a native of the same county and state, who there married Mary Sweigard, likewise a native of Pennsylvania. He moved with his family to Ogle county, Illinois, in 1857, and here Mrs. Guio grew to womanhood and was mostly educated. To Mr. and Mrs. Guio nine children have been born. Rosella, living with her parents. Louisa is the wife of Eugene Reed, a farmer of Buffalo township. Sarah is the wife of James Mayburn, of Ogle county, and they have one child, Nellie, a bright little girl of three summers. George, who is assisting in carrying on the home farm. Henry, Oliver, Amos, Lillie and Fanny, complete the family.

After their marriage, Mr. and Mrs. Guio

commenced their domestic life on a farm near where they now reside. His first purchase of land was a tract of eighty acres, and later purchasing one hundred and sixty acres adjoining, he has now a fine farm of two hundred and forty acres, all of which is under cultivation. Coming to this county a poor man, by his own industry, assisted by his estimable wife, he has accumulated a fine property and is now one of the substantial citizens of the county.

Politically Mr. Guio gives his support to the Republican party on national issues, but in local elections he votes independently, casting his ballot for the men he considers best qualified to fill the offices for which they aspire. For nineteen years he has served as a member of the school board, a part of which time he was president of the board. He has also served as road commissioner. His wife and daughter, Rosella, are members of the Methodist Episcopal church. The entire family are highly esteemed wherever known.

ABRAHAM FELKER WEAVER, a well-known farmer and highly esteemed citizen of Rockville township, Ogle county, was born in Washington county, Maryland, December 2, 1838. His father, Samuel Weaver, was born in Huntingdon county, Pennsylvania, June 27, 1799, and was married November 14, 1824, to Elizabeth Felker, whose birth occurred in Washington county, Maryland, June 14, 1805. He died August 14, 1839, and she passed away June 4, 1875. In their family were seven children, namely: John, born June 24, 1825, died July 14, 1825; Catherine Wilt, born June 23, 1826, married Daniel Binkley, of Washington county, Maryland; George, born November 15, 1829, died October 1, 1884; Elizabeth, born July 20, 1832, died February 27, 1837; Mary A., born November 24, 1834, died June 18, 1838; Louisa, born September 5, 1836, died October 25, 1894; and Abraham F. completes the family.

Our subject was only eight months old at the time of his father's death, and was reared by his mother in his native county, where he acquired his primary education. In July, 1857, at the age of nineteen years, he came alone to Ogle county, where his brother had located two years before, and the first summer he worked for various persons in the county. For one year he was in the employ of Charles Samis, and for six months was with Daniel Zellars. He then purchased a half interest in a threshing maching, and in the fall of 1860, when the threshing season was over, he hired out to Benjamin Swingley for three months. The following year he was again engaged in threshing, and at the end of the season entered the Mt. Morris Seminary, where he pursued his studies for three months. He and his cousin, David Felker, then bought a new machine, and in the spring of 1863 Mr. Weaver rented a small farm which he operated until harvest time, when he resumed threshing while making his home with his uncle Abraham Felker. With his thresher he traveled extensively through the southern part of the state. At the end of this season he returned to Maryland, where he spent four or five months. In 1862 he made his first purchase of land, consisting of eighty acres, in Forreston township, which he sold about 1867. He then purchased a farm in 1870, with like improvements, and in 1876 moved on the same.

On the 28th of April, 1864, Mr. Weaver enlisted in Company I, One Hundred and Fortieth Illinois Volunteer Infantry, under Captain James W. Cartwright and Colonel Lorenzo H. Whitney, and was mustered in at Dixon. After the regiment was equipped at Springfield, they proceeded to Cairo and on to Memphis, Tennessee, and to Lafayette. Mr. Weaver's company, together with Companies I and F, were detailed to guard a bridge five miles from Lafayette, which the rebels burned at every opportunity. Our subject was wounded September 5, 1864, in a skirmish with Forrest's men and is now a pensioner of the government. They returned to Memphis, Tennessee, where they remained for two or three weeks. While there the time for which they enlisted expired, but they were held for nearly three months; a part of which time he was on the sick list. They were mustered out of service at Camp Fry, at or near Chicago, Illinois.

Mr. Weaver married Miss Jennie W. Briggs, who was born March 30, 1851, a daughter of Joseph and Louisa E. (Case) Briggs. Her father was born June 16, 1806, and died July 11, 1856, and her mother was born August 31, 1810, and died May 10, 1891. To Mr. and Mrs. Weaver were born four children: Grace E., born January 7, 1877; Mabel L., September 5, 1879; Charles H., July 3, 1882; and Lillian E., May 17, 1887. All are living with the exception of the youngest, who died February 13, 1888. Our subject has also been called upon to mourn the loss of his estimable wife, who passed away October 30, 1892.

Politically Mr. Weaver is a silver Democrat, and he has most capably and satisfactorily served as school director for fifteen years and as road commissioner for three years.

ADDISON COFFMAN, one of the representative and prominent agriculturists of Ogle county, operates a fine farm of two hundred and eighty-four acres on section 12, Maryland township, and also has another well improved and valuable farm of two hundred and sixty acres in the same township, which he rents. He is one of Ogle county's honored sons, his birth occurring on the farm where he now resides, August 24, 1843.

His father, Samuel W. Coffman, was a native of Washington county, Maryland, born in 1811, and was a son of John Coffman, who was born on the Atlantic ocean, while his parents were removing from their old home in Germany to the United States. They were among the pioneers of Washington county, Maryland. There Samuel W. Coffman grew to manhood and married Catherine Doney, a native of the same county and a daughter of Timothy Downey, also an early settler of the county. Mr. Coffman engaged in farming there until 1840, when he came to Ogle county, Illinois, in company with two other families. He entered a tract of two hundred and eighty-four acres in Maryland township, on which his son now resides, erected thereon a log house and began to improve and cultivate his land. He also entered other tracts, but later sold these. In subsequent years his first home here was replaced by a more commodious and modern residence, and the wild land on which he located was converted into a fine farm. His last years were spent in retirement in the village of Baileyville, Illinois, where he died in 1887. His first wife had died in 1876 and he later married again.

By the first union there were ten children, six sons and four daughters, of whom two sons and four daughters reached man and womanhood, namely: John D., who is living retired in Chicago; Mrs. Naomi Dunn, of Freeport, Illinois; Catherine, deceased wife of Valentine Wallace; Susan, wife of S. W. Griffith, of Marshalltown, Iowa; and Matilda, a resident of Freeport.

The subject of this review was reared on the home farm and had very limited school advantages. He remained with his father until reaching manhood and then took charge of the homestead, which he later purchased of the other heirs. His whole life has been devoted to agricultural pursuits and he has met with marked success, his landed possessions now aggregating five hundred and forty-four acres of fertile and valuable land, which he has placed under a high state of cultivation and well improved. Upon the home farm he has erected a large barn with a basement.

In Maryland township, June 29, 1879, was celebrated the marriage of Mr. Coffman and Miss Sarah Wagner, a native of Ogle county and a daughter of Jonathan Wagner, who settled here as early as 1840. By this union three children were born: Samuel and Jonathan Emory, who assists their father in the operation of the farm, and Eusebia, who died at the age of four years. The wife and mother departed this life in 1885, and Mr. Coffman was again married in Maryland township, December 5, 1887, his second union being with Mrs. Emma Stover, a native of the township and sister of his first wife. In November, 1871, she gave her hand in marriage to John Stover, and they went to New York city on their wedding trip. Returning they stopped in Chicago and left that city on the night of the great fire. Mr. Stover located in Sangamon county, Illinois, where he engaged in farming until his death, which occurred in July, 1875. He left two daughters, Marian and May, who are both well educated and the former is now a stenographer in Freeport. There is one son by the second marriage: Frank F.

Since casting his first presidential vote for Abraham Lincoln, in 1864, Mr. Coffman has been a stalwart supporter of the Republican party, but he has never cared for office, though he has served for three years as commissioner of highways. He is one of the leading and popular citizens of his community and wherever known he is held in high regard.

WILLIAM M. CLARK, a practical and successful farmer, residing on section 30, Pine Creek township, is a native of Huntingdon county, Pennsylvania, born November 14, 1832, and is the son of Isaac and Nancy (Campbell) Clark, both natives of County Antrim, Ireland. Isaac Clark came to the United States in 1832 and located in Huntingdon county, Pennsylvania, where he remained until 1850 and then removed to Jefferson county, in the same state, where he spent the remainder of his life. He was a good and faithful citizen of his adopted country and state and filled a number of local offices, serving as collector, constable and school director. He died when about seventy-one years of age. His wife survived him and died in 1895, when eighty-two years of age. They were the parents of eleven children, ten of whom grew to maturity. William M. is the subject of this sketch. Thomas remained in Pennsylvania until 1887, and then came to Ogle county, where he remained two years, going from here to the state of Washington, which is his present home. Elizabeth is the wife of George A. Currier, of Pennsylvania. Mary is the wife of Samuel Montgomery. They left Jefferson county, Pennsylvania, came to Ogle county, where they remained ten years, then went to Wright county, Iowa, where they now reside. Sarah married David Currier, of Clarion county, Pennsylvania. Nancy married Peter Butler, now of Jefferson county, Pennsylvania. Samuel, when less than eighteen years of age, enlisted in the One Hundred and Third Pennsylvania Volunteer Infantry, was captured at Plymouth, North Carolina, spent some time in Andersonville prison, from which he was taken to Charleston, South Carolina, and from there to Florence, South Carolina, where his death occurred about two weeks before peace was declared. James remained in Jefferson county, Pennsylvania, until about 1874, when he went to California, and from there to Oregon. Later he went to British Columbia, where he accumulated a fortune, after which he returned to his old home in Jefferson county until 1880, when he went to the state of Washington, and is now living on Puget Sound. Issac died at the age of twenty-seven years. John died when six years old. Elizabeth married George A. Currier and resides in Pennsylvania.

The subject of this sketch spent his boyhood and youth in Jefferson county, Pennsylvania. When thirteen years old he was apprenticed to learn the shoemaker's trade, but after serving six months, left his master and returned home. He was then hired out by his father for five dollars per month to work on a farm. When sixteen he was apprenticed to a blacksmith to learn his trade. When his employer broke up some months after, he abandoned the idea of learning the trade, and for some three years was employed in and about the iron works. From that time until 1854 he was engaged in lumbering, at which he cleared about five hundred dollars, two hundred of which he gave to his father. With the remainder he went to California and located in Plumas county, and for two years was engaged in mining for others. He then went to Sierra county, where he engaged in mining on his own account. He was there at the time the vigilance committee was organized to rid the the county of rascally officials. He remained in California until November, 1860, engaged in mining with fair success. He returned home by way of the Isthmus of Panama. In February, 1861, he came to Ogle county on business, and liking the country, he purchased one hundred and sixty acres of land in Pine Creek township, which he rented out until after his marriage.

On the 12th of July, 1866, Mr. Clark was united in marriage with Miss Amanda Yates, daughter of Charles and Catherine (Ninick) Yates, the former a native of England, and the latter of German parentage. Mrs. Clark was born in Frederick county, Maryland, and when seven years old came with her mother to Ogle county, her father having died when she was but three years of age. She was born March 12, 1839, and was one of a family of nine children. Of these John resided in Ogle county until his death, about 1893. Lucinda married Emery Foxwell, a well-known banker of Baltimore, but is now deceased. George died in Ogle county June 7, 1878. Elizabeth married Benjamin Cummings, for years a resident of Ogle county, but who died in Kansas. She now resides in Vinton, Iowa. Mary L. died in childhood. Isaac died at the age of seventeen. Rebecca married

Joseph Mumma, of Ogle county. Edward, when sixteen years old, went to the state of Washington, where he now resides, engaged in farming.

After their marriage, Mr. and Mrs. Clark lived for a year and a half upon the first farm that he purchased. In 1868, they removed to their present place of residence, which then consisted of one hundred acres. He has since added to his possessions until he has now a section of good land, which he has leased for a number of years. Much of his time has been given to stock raising, it being his aim to use up all the grain and hay raised on his farms. He usually feeds from two to five car loads of cattle and hogs per year. He has always been a stanch Democrat, and never hesitates to advocate the principles of his party. Fraternally he is a Master Mason, and a member of the Independent Order of Odd Fellows, having joined the latter order in 1856. He is a member of both subordinate lodge and the encampment. As a farmer, he has proved a success, keeping up with the times in the various improvements made, and entering heartily into his work. In regard to the future he is an agnostic in belief.

CHARLES FISHER.—Wherever there is pioneer work to be done men of energy and ability are required, and success or failure depends upon the degree of those qualities that is possessed. In wresting the land of Ogle county from its native wilderness; in fitting it for the habitation of men; in developing the natural resources of the community, few if any have done more than Mr. Fisher and it is mete and proper that for the arduous and important labor he performed he should receive due reward.

Here he has made his home since the 8th of June, 1839, and for many years he was actively identified with the agricultural interests of Byron township, but is now living retired in the village of Byron in the pleasurable enjoyment of his accumulations.

Mr. Fisher was born in the town of Westboro, Worcester county, Massachusetts, July 21, 1818. The early home of his ancestors was in England, but the family was one of the first established in the old Bay state. His grandfather, Samuel Fisher, and his father, Nahum Fisher, were both born on the old homestead in Worcester county, the latter March 15, 1788. On attaining man's estate he became prominently identified with public affairs, and for several terms most ably and satisfactorily represented his district in the state legislature. He also served as justice of the peace for many years, and his decisions were rendered without fear or favor. During the war of 1812 he was one of the gallant defenders of his country, and afterward received a pension in recognition of his services. He received a good education, was engaged in surveying for a time, and was an excellent business man of known reliability. He married Miss Betsy Harrington, also a native of Westboro, Worcester county, born May 15, 1787, and after her death, which occurred October 2, 1851, he was again married. His death occurred in his native place March 27, 1865.

By the first marriage there were ten children, six sons and four daughters, all of whom grew to man and womanhood, but only three sons are now living: Charles, of this review; Samuel D., a resident of Westboro, Massachusetts; and Joseph, who lived retired at Montpelier, Vermont, for many years, where he was a neighbor and ac quintance of Admiral Dewey. He died December 22, 1898.

Reared in Westboro, Charles Fisher obtained an excellent education, being a student in the Leicester and Westminster Seminaries and also the Baptist Academy at Worcester. At the age of eighteen he commenced teaching and for two winters successfully followed that profession in his native state. In May, 1830, he started for Illinois in company with a brother and a sister, Mrs. Parsons and her children, driving two teams. The trip was a long and tedious one and they did not arrive at their destination until June 8. Though not a professor of religion at that time, Mr. Fisher observed every Sabbath during the journey. In Ogle county he joined his brother-in-law, Luke Parsons, who had located here three years previously. Our subject purchased a claim of two hundred and forty acres in Byron township, of which fifteen acres had been cleared, but later sold that place and purchased Mr. Parsons' farm after the death of his brother-in-law. He then devoted his energies to its further improvement and cultivation, and as prosperity crowned his efforts he was subsequently able to purchase an adjoining tract of sixty acres, making in all a fine and valuable farm of two hundred and ten acres near the present village of Byron, in Byron township. Being the owner of the horses with which he had driven from his eastern home, he was able to be of use to the community in which he located by engaging in teaming between this county and Chicago, hauling lumber, and other supplies for the settlers. In this way he not only aided those around him but also added not a little to his income.

On the 10th of November, 1850, in Byron township, occurred the marriage of Mr. Fisher and Miss Harriet N. Salisbury, who was born in Townsend, Windham county, Vermont, August 2, 1827, a daughter of Barnard and Arethusa (Duncan) Salisbury, also natives of the Green Mountain state. The father was born in Brattleboro, March 30, 1786, and was descended from a family of German origin, which at an early day was founded in England, and from there its representatives came to America, settling in New England. Mr. Salisbury was a pioneer of Townsend, Vermont, where he ever afterward made his home, successfully engaged in agricultural pursuits. On returning from a visit to our subject and his wife he was taken ill with cholera at Pulaski, New York, and died July 4, 1854. His wife passed away December 27, 1832. In the family of this worthy couple were ten children, of whom nine reached years of maturity, but only Mrs. Fisher, Mrs. Arethusa Merwin, of New Haven, Connecticut, and Henry Salisbury, of Schenectady, New York, are now living. Coming west in 1849 to visit a sister, she accepted a position as teacher in Ogle county, and while thus engaged she became acquainted with her future husband. Theirs was the first marriage celebrated in the Byron church. The children born of this union are Harriet E., wife of J. B. Tinker, a business man of Mason City, Iowa; Mary J., wife of George Rood, of Byron, Ogle county; Alice A., wife of Charles B. Kosier, a carpenter of Byron, Illinois; Charles M., a business man of Mason City, Iowa; Arthur C., a lawyer by profession, who is now serving as lieutenant-colonel of the Third Illinois Volunteer Infantry at Porto Rico; Elsa L., at home; and Nahum H., a business man of Janesville, Wisconsin.

Mr. and Mrs. Fisher began their domestic life on his farm in the new residence which had just been completed, but has since been enlarged and remodeled. Good barns and other outbuildings were also erected, and under the skillful management of our subject the farm was made to yield bountiful harvests in return for the care and labor bestowed upon it. For thirty-seven years he successfully engaged in its operation, but in 1887 rented it and removed to the village of Byron, where he erected a neat residence and has since lived retired.

In political sentiment Mr. Fisher was originally a Whig, and cast his first vote for William Henry Harrison in 1840, but in 1856 he joined the newly organized Republican party, and of later years has been a supporter of the men and measures of the Prohibition party, as he is a strong temperance man. He served as commissioner of highways for about fourteen years, and for several years was a most active and prominent member of the school board, doing much to advance the grade of schools in this section. He provided his own children with good educational advantages, all being graduates of the graded schools of Byron, while some of the sons attended Wheaton and Mt. Morris Colleges, and the younger members were students in the Rockford Business College. All became successful and popular teachers with the exception of the oldest, who never followed the profession. For over half a century the parents have been worthy members of the Congregational Church at Byron, and their lives have ever been in harmony with its teachings. Mr. Fisher has served as deacon since 1881, and as a public-spirited and progressive citizen he gives his support to all enterprises which he believes calculated to advance the moral, educational or material welfare of his town and county.

DAVID H. LAMONT, dealer in hardware, stoves and tinware, Holcomb, is one of the leading merchants of the place, an enterprising citizen, and one who enjoys the respect and confidence of the entire community in which he lives. He is a native of Jo Daviess county, Illinois, born September 27, 1863, and is the son of Hans and Alice (Lamont) Lamont. Although of the same name, the parents were not related. They were both natives of Ireland, and became the parents of nine children, three of whom are now deceased. The living are Mary, Sarah, John, Stewart, Alice and David. The deceased are William, Thomas and Albert. In 1848, a year that Irishmen have cause to well remember, he came to the United States and for ten years was in the employ of the Baltimore & Ohio railroad, in the meantime accumulating a little money with which to begin life in earnest. In 1858 he came west and located in Jo Daviess county, Illinois, where he continues to reside. He was a good man and made friends wherever he lived.

In his native county our subject grew to manhood and was educated in the public schools. At the age of seventeen he commenced to learn the tinner's trade with his brother John, and has since continued to follow the trade with a reasonable degree of success and satisfaction. In 1890 he started a tin and hardware store in Stillman Valley, which he continued to run for three years, but believing there was a better opening in Holcomb, he removed to the latter place, where he now carries a fine line of hard-

DAVID H. LAMONT.

ware, stoves and tinware, and has built up an excellent trade.

On the 19th of February, 1896, Mr. Lamont was united in marriage with Miss Dora A. Gates, a native of Ogle county, and a daughter of Jacob Gates, who is now deceased, but who was an early settler of that county, and a man greatly esteemed wherever known.

In politics Mr. Lamont is an unqualified member of the Republican party, a party with which he has been identified since attaining his majority. Soon after his removal to Holcomb he was appointed postmaster of the place, an office which he has since continued to hold to the satisfaction of the patrons of the office. He is at present a member of the school board at Holcomb, giving of his time freely to advance the interests of its public schools. Fraternally he is a member of the Knights of the Globe. Religiously he is a Baptist, and in the work of the church he takes an active interest, and is at present superintendent of the Sunday school. He makes a good superintendent, and the school has flourished under his charge. As a business man he attends strictly to business, and is ever ready to encourage any enterprise that he believes will best conduce the interests of his adopted city and county. He enjoys the respect and confidence of the entire community in which he lives.

BENJAMIN D. SEIBERT, deceased, though not numbered among the pioneers of Ogle county, was yet an early settler, and a man who attained prominence in the industrial affairs of the county, and was numbered among its most enterprising and prosperous citizens. Like many of the best citizens of the county he was a native of Washington county, Maryland, born in Hagerstown, April 9, 1816. He was the son of John Seibert, also a native of the same county and state, and who was by occupation a farmer. The father never came west, but spent his entire life in his native state.

In his native county our subject grew to manhood and there received a common school education. The knowledge obtained in the school room was supplemented by that gained in the school of experience, by contact with his fellowmen. He was always observing, and with an eye to the main chance, he was quite successful in whatever he undertook. In 1858 he came to Ogle county and located in Mt. Morris township, about four miles north of the village, where he purchased three hundred acres of good land and engaged in agricultural pursuits. From time to time he added to his possessions until at the time of his death he was the owner of over one thousand acres of excellent farming land.

Mr. Seibert was united in marriage with Miss Hannah Thompson, a native of Canada, and daughter of Henry and Sarah B. (Straw) Thompson, the former born in Connecticut in 1791, and the latter in New Hampshire in 1800. Her father died in Canada in 1847, while her mother survived him many years, dying at the residence of Mrs. Seiber, December 29, 1878. They were both members of the Methodist Episcopal church. To Mr. and Mrs. Seibert three sons were born, all of whom are yet living. John V., born March 17, 1870, married Florence Wolfe, and they have one child, also named Florence. They reside in Mt. Morris. Benjamin D., born March 20, 1872, resides in Mt. Morris.

Alfred T., born September 1, 1874, is attending the law department of the Illinois University, in Chicago.

While Mr. Seibert was the owner of several fine farms in Ogle county, he gave his time principally to the real estate and loan business. He had considerable Chicago property and much farming land throughout northern Illinois. A brother, Dr. John Seibert, was a well-known physician in Chicago before the great fire in that city. He also practiced medicine in Milwaukee for about ten years. He was a ripe scholar, a graduate of the University of Pennsylvania. During his life he amassed considerable property in his adopted city of Chicago. He died in that city October 9, 1896.

After a long and useful life, Mr. Seibert passed to his reward, April 9, 1889. His wife died April 7, 1895. Both were devout Christian people, he a member of the German Baptist church, and she of the Methodist Episcopal. For many years she was president of the Women's Christian Temperance Union of Mt. Morris, and in both temperance and church work was quite active. In politics he was a Democrat. Both enjoyed the love and esteem of a large circle of friends, and their death was sincerely mourned.

GEORGE BRAND is now retired from the labors of a long and active life and is spending his declining days in the midst of ease and plenty at his comfortable home in Polo. For many years he was engaged in agricultural pursuits, and his position financially is the result of his own unaided industry, coupled with the sound common sense and excellent business capacity with which nature endowed him.

Mr. Brand was born near Utica, New York, October 12, 1828, and is a representative of a good old Scotch family, his parents being James and Jenette (Ferris) Brand, natives of Dumfrieshire, Scotland. The father was born in the village of Ecclessechan, January 16, 1799, and was a cousin of Thomas Carlyle, a native of the same village. The grandfather, William Brand, was a man of strong religious convictions and was one of the organizers and buildings of the first church in Ecclessechan. He spent his entire life in Scotland, and when a young man followed the weaver's trade. He was a son of Robert Brand, of whom little is known at the present time.

At the age of fourteen years, James Brand, our subject's father, was apprenticed to the carpenter's trade, at which he worked until he attained his majority, and then went to Newfoundland, sojourning there for eighteen months. On his return to Scotland, he was married in 1822 to Jenette Farries, who was born in Ecclessechan, March 10, 1799, a daughter of George and Lucy Farries, who in later years crossed the Atlantic to Prince Edwards Island, where they spent their last days. They came to Utica, New York, in 1880. Mr. and Mrs. Brand became the parents of ten children, namely: William and Lucy, both born in Ecclessechan; George, born in Utica, New York; James, born in Toronto, Canada; Jenette, John (deceased) and Robert, all born in Canada; and Henry, Mary and Anna, born after the family came to Ogle county, Illinois. After their marriage the parents continued to reside in their native village until 1828, when they sailed from Greenock, Scotland, bound for America, but were becalmed two weeks on the coast of Ireland, finally landing in New York city after six weeks spent upon the water. The family first located at Utica, New York, where they made their home until 1830, and then removed to Toronto, Canada, spending one year at that place. The father then purchased a farm twenty miles north of the city, and in the midst of the almost unbroken forest they lived for some years. It was during this time that the McKenzie rebellion occurred, with which he was a sympathizer. While living there he worked at his trade, as a shipbuilder, on the lakes. Selling his land in Canada in 1840, he came to Ogle county, Illinois, and located on a farm northwest of Polo, in Brookville township, where he was actively engaged in farming until 1852. He died in April, 1873, and his wife March 13, 1871, honored and respected by all who knew them for their sterling worth and many excellencies of character.

George Brand had little opportunity of attending school up to the time the family left Canada, but he made the best of his advantages after coming to Illinois, and is a well-informed man. He remained with his father until twenty-three years of age, and then purchased eighty acres of land, for which he went partly in debt. During the busy season he operated a corn sheller and threshing machine and continued in that vocation for thirty-four consecutive years. It is needless to say that he soon lifted the debt on his first purchase, and from time to time he bought more land until he owned two fine farms, one of one hundred and twenty acres and the other of one hundred acres. These he sold in 1875 and 1876, and purchased two farms a short distance north of Polo, aggregating two hundred and twenty-nine acres. He successfully engaged in general farming and stock raising until 1888, when he retired from active life and removed to Polo, where he is now enjoying a well-earned rest.

At Freeport, Illinois, March 21, 1854, Mr. Brand was united in marriage with Miss Leonora Sanburn. Her paternal grandfather, Jonathan Sanburn, was probably a native of New Hampshire, and descended from John or William Sanburn, who, with their grandfather, Rev. Stephen Bachelder, came to this country in 1630, from Holland, whither they had fled from England because of religious persecution. They were sons of John Sanburn, of England. John P. Sanburn, Mrs. Brand's father, was born in New Hampshire, in 1797, and in early life removed to Montreal and later to Toronto, Canada, whence he subsequently moved to Ogle county, Illinois, in 1839, and bought a farm of two hundred and fifty acres near Buffalo Grove. Here he died in 1872. In York township, York county, Canada, he married Miss Susan Johnson, who was born there in 1801, and died in 1866. Her father, Abraham Johnson, was born near Philadelphia, Pennsylvania, about 1772, and died about 1867-8. Throughout life he followed the occupation of a farmer. During the war of 1812 he moved to Canada, as he was a British sympathizer, his parents having been Tories during the Revolutionary war. He first located in Nova Scotia, but later made his home near Toronto. He married a Miss Fisher and to them were born thirteen children, of whom six are now living, and of these Mrs. Brand is the third in order of birth.

The children born to Mr. and Mrs. Brand are as follows: Lester A., who is engaged in the grocery business with Cyrus Nicodemus, in Polo, married Mary Wolf, of

Brookville, Ogle county, and they have two children, Alpha and Iva; Mary died at the age of nine months; George Mortimer, a baggage clerk at the Union depot, St. Paul, Minnesota, married Annie Kates, and they have two children, Milton and Leonora; John James, who is employed in a shoe factory in Rockford, Illinois, first married Ella Hanna, by whom he has one son, George, and for his second wife married Emma Hawes; Hiram Douglas, a successful dentist of Tacoma, Washington, married Ellen Lemon and they have two children, Ellen and Iva; Robert Miles, a promising young attorney of Chicago, married Luella Gibson; Kate A. is the wife of Sherman Donaldson, a farmer living near Polo, and they have one son, George; and Ambrose Alexander, who married Ellen Runnell, is a dentist of Chadwick, Carroll county, Illinois.

In his political views, Mr. Brand is an independent Democrat, and for fifteen years he most acceptably served as school director in his district. He is a prominent member of the Masonic fraternity, belonging to the blue lodge and chapter in Polo and the commandery in Dixon. He is a pleasant, genial gentleman, of high social qualities and has an extensive circle of friends and acquaintances in Ogle county, who esteem him highly for his genuine worth.

AUSTIN WRIGHT SPOOR, deceased, was for many years a well known citizen of Ogle county, having many friends, and enjoying the respect and esteem of all with whom he was brought in contact. He was born in Clarence Hollow, Erie county, New York, August 16, 1837, and was the son of Orsemus and Sophia (Cole) Spoor, both of whom were natives of New York, the former born September 12, 1802. He was the son of William and Christine Spoor, the former born January 20, 1769, and the latter July 30, 1774.

Orsemus Spoor was reared in his native state, and there married Sophia Cole. In 1840, he came west with his wife and family, locating first in Buffalo Grove, Illinois, but in the spring of 1841 removing to Byron, Ogle county, where in partnership with William Wilkinson, he erected the first grist mill built in the northern part of the county. He died, however, in the fall following, leaving a widow with a family of six children to care for. In addition to his Ogle county interests he had some property in Chicago, but not knowing its location his widow and children lost track of it and never acquired rights in it. After surviving her husband eleven years, his widow was called to her reward, dying in 1852.

The subject of this sketch was but three years old when he accompanied his parents to Ogle county, and but four years old when his father died. He remained with his mother until twelve years old when he went to East Troy, Wisconsin, to make his home with an uncle, Sylvanus Spoor. After remaining about three years in the family of his uncle, he felt an earnest desire to return home, fearing that something was wrong. On his way back he stopped over night at the house of an acquaintance, where he learned from acquaintances returning from his mother's funeral that she was dead.

Deciding on remaining in Byron, Mr. Spoor made his home with his brother, who was engaged in the hotel business, and for a time assisted him in the work, and later was his brother's partner for about two years. He then engaged in carrying the mail between Byron and Rockford for one year. The following year he drove the stage between Rockford and Dixon, and was then engaged in farm work for two years. Following this he carried mail between Byron and Stillman Valley, and between Kishwaukee and Rockford for four years.

The war for the union being in progress, Mr. Spoor determined to assist in maintaining the union, and accordingly in July, 1862, he enlisted in Company B, Ninety-second Illinois Volunteer Infantry, and was mustered into the service September 4, following. For the first twelve months he was on detached duty, driving an ambulance wagon, after which he was assigned to duty at the headquarters of General Kilpatrick as veterinary surgeon. The war closing, he was mustered out of service June 22, 1865, at Concord, North Carolina.

Returning to his home, in 1866, Mr. Spoor secured a position as traveling salesman for a Chicago house, and for several years was upon the road. On the 23d of September, 1869, at Polo, Illinois, he was united in marriage to Miss Anna Brand, a native of Polo, and daughter of James and Janet (Farries) Brand, both of whom were natives of Scotland. James Brand was born in the village of Ecclessechan, Dumfriesshire, Scotland, January 16, 1799, and was a second cousin to the renowned Thomas Carlyle, who was born in the same village. At the age of fourteen he was apprenticed to learn the carpenter's trade. After serving his time he came to America, where he remained about eighteen months, working as a journeyman, then returned to Scotland, and in 1822 was united in marriage with Janet Farries. After his marriage he remained in Scotland until 1827, when he again came to the United States, sailing from Greenock and landing in New York, after a voyage of six weeks. For two weeks he was becalmed in mid-ocean. With his family, he first made his home in New Hartford, near Utica, New York, where he was engaged in building power looms in cotton factories. In 1830 he removed to Toronto, Canada, where he lived one year and then bought a farm twenty miles north of that place, and was there during the Canadian rebellion, in which he took no active part, though his sympathies were with those in rebellion. Selling his farm, in 1840, he came to Ogle county and settled on a farm northwest of Polo, in Brookville township. After some twelve years of active farm life in Illinois, Mr. Brand lived in ease and retirement until called to the upper and better world, his death occurring April 5, 1873. In politics he was a Democrat and for years served as school treasurer and director. He was a member of the Old School Presbyterian church, and was very strict in his family. James Brand was a son of William Brand, one of the founders of the first church in the village of Ecclessechan, a weaver by trade, and who died in his native town. He was the son of Robert Brand. Janet Farries was a daughter of George and Lucy Farries, her father being a farmer by occupation, and who emigrated to Prince Edward island, where his death occurred.

To James Brand and wife ten children were born. William and Lucy, the latter being the wife of W. A. Hatfield, were born in Scotland. George was born in New York. James, Jr., Janet (widow of Benjamin Walkie,) John and Robert born in Canada. Mary, now Mrs. John Elward, and Anna, now Mrs. Spoor, were born in Illinois.

To our subject and wife two sons were born, Harry and Albert, both of whom assist the mother in conducting the hotel. The latter was married October 12, 1898, to Miss Mary Agnes Perrine, daughter of John Perrine, of Oregon. The sons, it may truly be said, were born to hotel life, having given their time to little else since their age would permit active work in any line. They are accommodating young men, and their mother thoroughly understands the wants of the traveling public, and each try to make life pleasant to those who make the Spoor House their temporary abode. A more homelike house cannot be found, while the table is well supplied with all the delicacies of the season.

After his marriage Mr. Spoor opened a grocery and confectionery store in Polo, which he conducted for two years, when he sold out, and the following year was with the Elward Harvester Company. He was next engaged in the produce business with Charles F. Barber, continuing in that line until 1879, when he moved to Oregon, leased the American House for five years and conducted the same with signal ability. He then leased the Sinissippi House four years, but in the spring of 1888 purchased the American House, made many substantial improvements in the same, refurnished it and renamed it the Spoor House. He conducted the house in first-class style until his death May 28, 1894. In politics Mr. Spoor was a Democrat, and for a time served as an alderman from his ward, but would not accept any other office, preferring to give his time and attention to his business interests. In 1878 he united with the Episcopal church and continued a faithful member during the remainder of his life. Fraternally he was a member of the Masonic order, blue lodge and chapter, Knights of the Globe and Grand Army of the Republic. A worthy citizen, a kind and loving husband and father, his death was sincerely mourned by all who knew him in this life. Like her husband, Mrs. Spoor is also a member of the Episcopal church. She is greatly esteemed by all and her friends are many, not only among those among whom she has spent her entire life, but by all who have accepted her hospitality.

DANIEL H. STAUFFER, one of the progressive farmers of Ogle county, owns and operates a fine farm on section 19, Pine Creek township. He was born in Stark county, Ohio, February 4, 1853, and is the son of John E. and Rebecca (Haight) Stauffer, the former being a native of Pennsylvania, but who is now a resident of Polo, Illinois. In 1854, John E. Stauffer left Ohio with his family and moved to Elkhart county, Indiana, where they made their home for thirteen years. Soon after the close of the Civil war, they came to Ogle county, locating on the place which is now the home of our subject. On that farm the father toiled until 1880, when he rented the place and moved to Polo where he has since lived a retired life. To John E. and Rebecca Stauffer twelve children were born, ten of whom are now living. John W. is now residing in Glendale, Arizona, where he is engaged in the fruit business. Sarah E. is the wife of Cyrus Nicodemus, a merchant of Polo. George W. is a farmer of Pine Creek township. Christina is the wife of Solomon Solenberger, a retired farmer of Polo. Mary E. is the wife of Abraham Miller, of Buffalo township. Ananias is a farmer of Buffalo township. William is a farmer of Pine Creek township. Rebecca is the wife of Frank McDowell, of Polo. Anna is making her home with her parents in Polo.

The subject of this sketch was thirteen years old when he came to Ogle county. His education, commenced in the public schools of Elkhart county, Indiana, was completed in the public schools of Ogle county. He assisted his father on the farm until he attained his majority, when he rented a portion of the home place and worked it on shares. The following year he purchased eighty acres in Pine Creek township, but had to assume the greater part of the purchase price. This eighty was about three miles from his present home, and on the Dixon road. It is now owned by John Ambrose. Removing to his new purchase, he there lived for fourteen years, having in the meantime added eighteen acres to the tract. In 1890 he sold the place and bought the old homestead where he has since made his home. In 1892 he erected his present commodious and comfortable residence, and, since becoming the owner, he has erected all the other buildings now on the place. He has followed general farming, and is regarded as one of the best farmers in the county.

On the 15th of October, 1876, Mr. Stauffer was united in marriage with Miss Maggie C. Spickler, daughter of C. B. and Sarah (Plumb) Spickler, her father being a retired merchant in Polo. By this union there have been seven children, two of whom are deceased—Florence, Charlie B., Ollie C., Ellen R., Henry M., Bertha P. and Emma R. The parents met with a sad bereavement in the loss of their two eldest sons. On New Years day, 1896, the boys were skating on Rock river, and both fell into an air hole and were drowned.

Politically Mr. Stauffer is a Republican, having been an advocate of the principles of the party since casting his first vote. Religiously he is a member of the German Baptist church, and for ten years served as deacon in the same. He has always taken an active interest in the work of the church, being a firm believer in the Christian religion and in the teachings of his church. His wife is also a member and active worker in that body. Both are highly esteemed by all who know them. Mr. Stauffer has been quite successful in life, and his success has been attained by his own efforts, assisted by his faithful helpmeet. He is the owner of one of the finest homes and best farms in this rich and productive county.

LEONARD ANDRUS, deceased, the founder of the village of Grand Detour, and one of the first settlers of Ogle county, was a man of energy, and one who clearly saw the possibilities of the beautiful Rock river country. He was born in Cornwall, Vermont, in 1805, and was a son of Cone Andrus, a native of Connecticut. He traced his ancestry back for many generations on both his father's and mother's side, both families being early residents of the New England states. His father's family went from Connecticut to Vermont, and later to Malone, New York, in which place he grew to manhood. After due preparation he entered Middleberry College, where he spent two years. He did not complete the full course, but on the death of his father he left college and returned home. Cone Andrus was a farmer by occupation, and while of retiring disposition, was a man of good business ability. One of his brothers was the father of the celebrated Bishop Andrews. In his family were four children who grew to maturity: Leonard, the subject of this sketch; William, who died in Malone, New York; Lucius, who spent his life in Brooklyn, New York; Albert, who lived and died in Malone, New York; and George, who lived in Malone until late in life, and then moved to New Jersey, where his death occurred. Cone Andrus died in Malone, New York.

After attaining his majority Leonard Andrus went to Rochester, New York, where he engaged in the mercantile business until 1833, meeting with fair success. Not satisfied, however, and believing the west a better place for a young man, in the fall of 1833, he came west as far as Constantine, Michigan, where he remained until the spring of 1834, when he made his way to the Ohio river, and started down that stream to St. Louis, with the idea of making that city his future home. Before locating, however, he concluded to go on a prospecting tour through northern Illinois, having heard something of the beauty of that country, and believing that the time would soon come when it would be settled by a thrifty and enterprising people.

Arriving at Dixon he took a canoe and went up the river until he came to the great bend, the beauty of which and the possibility of founding here a great manufacturing point, for which there seemed sufficient water power, he made his claim. At that time there were but few settlements in all this region, and they were far between. The settlement at Kellogg's grove and at Dixon were those nearest to this point. Returning east he settled up his business, and in the spring of 1835 returned, stopping, however, at Constantine, Michigan, where he had relatives living. From that point Willis and Willard A. House, twin brothers, accompanied him. Mrs. Sarah I. House, the wife of Willard A. House, came a little later, arriving here July 4, 1835. She was the first white woman in Grand Detour. She later gave birth to a daughter, Gertrude, who was the first white child born in Grand Detour.

Soon after his arrival Mr. Andrus became associated with Flint & Walker, proprietors of the old stage line, which connection was continued but a short time. In 1836, in company with Russell Green, Amos Bosworth, William G. Dana, Marcus and Dennis Warren, he formed the Hydraulic Company, for the improvement of the water power and the erection of mills, and in 1837 the company commenced to build the dam, race and sawmill and make other improvements. Among the number to come to Grand Detour was John Deere, who afterwards became the noted plow manufacturer, and who made a world-wide reputation and a colossal fortune. Mr. Deere was a blacksmith, and opened a shop, and in addition to the job work that came to him, he engaged in the manufacture of shovels and pitchforks. With Mr. Andrus, two years later, he formed a partnership, and under the firm name of Andrus & Deere they commenced the manufacture of plows. The fame of the Grand Detour plows was soon established throughout the west, and the firm did a good business. Mr. Deere later withdrew and moved to Moline, where he continued the business and established his fame.

The Hydraulic Company built the first grist mill in northern Illinois. It was to have commenced running on the 4th of July,

1830, and was to form part of the celebration of that day, but it failed to start, and it was one year later before it was in successful operation. Its success was immediate, and it had more patronage than it could well accommodate, with its three run of stone.

When Mr. Deere removed to Moline, Mr. Andrus continued the business alone until it became too large for him to manage without help, when he took in Amos Bosworth, his brother-in-law, as a partner, which partnership continued until Mr. Bosworth's death, in 1862. After running the business alone again for a time Mr. Andrus formed a partnership with Theron Cummins, which partnership lasted until the death of Mr. Andrus.

On the 3d of June, 1838, Mr. Andrus was united in marriage with Miss Sarah Ann Bosworth, a native of Royalton, Vermont, and daughter of Amos and Susan (Wheelock) Bosworth, both of whom were also natives of Royalton, Vermont, and who were among the early settlers of Grand Detour. By this union three children were born—Caroline C., who died at the age of eight years; William C., and Leonard, of the Dixon National Bank, Dixon, Illinois.

In early life Mr. Andrus was a Henry Clay Whig, a great admirer of that grand old statesman. On the dissolution of the Whig party, he became a stanch Republican, and was an earnest advocate of Republican principles until his death. He was always in public life, and filled almost every local official position. He also served as a member of the legislature, making a good, working member of that body. His acquaintance with the public men of his day was quite extensive, and his influence was always felt. He was a man of the people, and had at heart the interests of the people. The founder of the village of Grand Detour, he was connected with almost every enterprise that was introduced into the village. He was a pioneer among pioneers, and experienced all the hardships common to those who engage in the development of a new country, but he lived to see his adopted county and state take front rank, and most of the great inventions that have made our whole country famous. In the development of the country and the various industrial enterprises, he certainly bore well his part, and his name will not soon be forgotten. His death, which occurred February 18, 1867, was entirely unexpected, having contracted pneumonia and living thereafter but a few days. His death was a sad loss to the business and local interests of his adopted county, of which he was such a worthy citizen.

GEORGE E. HIESTAND, the leading liveryman of Oregon, Illinois, was born in Leaf River township, Ogle county, October 28, 1854, and is the son of Benjamin and Lydia (Rice) Hiestand. The father was a native of Ohio, and by occupation was a farmer. He came to Illinois in the thirties, and located in Leaf River township, where he took up a section of land from the government, which he improved and cultivated up to the time of his death, which occurred February 6, 1855. Leaf River at that time was one of the best towns in the county. In politics Benjamin Hiestand was a Whig, taking great interest in the political discussions of the day. A strong temperance man he advocated the cause of temperance publicly and privately. For some years he served as school trustee, and held other offices of honor and trust. He was a leading and influential man in his township, and was held in high respect wherever known. His wife, Lydia, was a daughter of Jacob Rice. She was also a member of the Methodist Episcopal church, a devoted wife and mother. She died June 13, 1884, at the old homestead, which was so long her home. They were the parents of seven children. Susan, now the widow of David Kendall, resides in Leaf River. Urilla is the wife of Thomas L. Potter, and they reside in Mt. Morris. Mary, who married Charles Gaffin, died March 21, 1898. Jacob and John H. both died young. Thomas resides in Mt. Morris township. George B. completes the family.

George B. Hiestand was reared on the old farm, and in the schools of his native township received a common school education. This was supplemented by a term at Mt. Morris Seminary. He was but four months old when his father died. As soon as old enough, in connection with his brothers, he carried on the old farm. Later, in partnership with his brother Thomas he purchased the interests of the other heirs, and together they carried on the farm until 1888, when George purchased his brother's interest and then leased it for three years. In 1893 he sold the place to William Hagerman, and then removed to the village of Leaf River, and in 1895 came to Oregon and opened up a livery stable on Fourth street, which he has since conducted. He has a finely equipped stable with stock, and is withal a very accommodating man.

Mr. Hiestand was married September 4, 1878, to Miss Adell Bly, daughter of Rathburn and Emily (Richardson) Bly. She is a native of Ogle county. Her father was in the Civil war and lost his life in battle. By this marriage are two children, Clarence L. and Lydia E., both of whom are yet at home. Mr. and Mrs. Hiestand are members of the Methodist Episcopal church. In politics he is a Republican. While residing in Leaf River he served as a member of the board of alderman. Fraternally he is a member of the Knights of the Globe and of the Modern Woodmen of America.

WALLACE REVELL is one of the honored veterans of the Civil war whose devotion to his country was tested not only by service on the field of battle but in the still more deadly dangers of a southern prison. This gallant soldier is now most capably and satisfactorily serving as postmaster of Stillman Valley, and is also successfully engaged in the grocery business at that place.

Mr. Revell was born near Niagara, Ontario, Canada, July 19, 1842. His father, William Revell was born in England, in 1817, and in 1834 crossed the broad Atlantic with his father, William, Sr., and family, settling near Hamilton, Ontario, where he grew to manhood. He was married in Canada to Miss Mary A. Bartlett, a native of that country. He was a tailor by trade and continued to follow that occupation in the Dominion until 1848, and when he removed to Conneaut, Ashtabula county, Ohio, but did not remain there long coming to Ogle county, Illinois, in April, 1850. Here he purchased one hundred and twenty acres of raw land in Scott township, erected thereon a house, and then turned his attention to the arduous task of developing a good farm from wild land. During those early days the family experienced many of the hardships and privations incident to pioneer life. The father was one of the most industrious and enterprising men of the county and was fairly successful in his undertakings. He continued to work at his trade until 1858, after which he devoted his entire time to agricultural pursuits. He died in 1885, and his wife, who still survives him, now makes her home with her daughter, Mrs. Graham. Wallace is the oldest of their six children, four sons and two daughters, all of whom reached years of maturity, but two sons are now deceased.

Wallace Revell was a lad of eight years when brought by his parents to Ogle county, and upon the home farm he grew to manhood, acquiring a good knowledge of work and a fair common-school education. Prompted by a spirit of patriotism he enlisted August 11, 1862, in Company K, Ninety-second Illinois Volunteer Infantry, as a private, and with his regiment was assigned to the army of the Cumberland. He participated in the battles of Franklin, Tennessee, and Chickamauga, and spent the fall and winter of 1863 as courier at General Thomas' headquarters. In March, 1864, he joined his regiment in northern Alabama, near Chattanooga, they having been mounted in July, 1863, and afterward served as mounted infantry. In April, 1864, they went into camp at Ringgold, Georgia, and while doing picket duty on Taylor's Ridge, on the morning of April 23, 1864, Mr. Revell, with twenty of his regiment, was taken prisoner, after being twice wounded in the skirmish by gunshots through the left fore arm and right hip. He was first taken to Atlanta, where he was held for about four weeks, and the following four months were spent as a prisoner in Andersonville, where with others he experienced all the horrors and privations of southern prison life. About one thousand of the men were then taken to Charleston, South Carolina, where they were confined in a prison camp for four weeks. From October, 1864, until February 24, 1865, Mr. Revell remained a prisoner, and was then exchanged at Richmond, Virginia. He suffered most while at Charleston, as the prisoners were confined on a low piece of ground. The prisoners were furnished with spades and by digging holes about four feet deep got the brack sh water contained therein and were forced to drink. It made nearly all ill and many died. On being released our subject was still sick and was sent to the hospital at Wilmington, Delaware. He had not fully recovered when discharged.

For two years after the war, Mr. Revell remained at home, and then rented land, purchased a team, and began life for himself. He was married December 11, 1868, the lady of his choice being Miss Adelaide L. Clayton, a daughter of James M. Clayton, whose sketch appears elsewhere in this work. To them were born four children, namely: Charles W., who is with his father in the store and is also serving as deputy postmaster; Nellie M., wife of J. D. Scoon, of West Superior, Wisconsin; Matie, who died at the age of five years; and Chester A., who is attending the home school.

After his marriage, Mr. Revell located in Monroe township where he subsequently bought a small farm, which he operated for eight years and then sold in 1876. During the following fifteen years he lived upon rented land and continued to engage in agricultural pursuits, but in 1890 removed to Stillman Valley and established himself in the grocery business, which he has since successfully conducted. He carries a large and well selected stock and bears an excellent reputation for fair and honorable dealing. In the fall of 1897 he was appointed postmaster, and is now acceptably filling that office. He has been a pronounced Republican in politics since casting his first vote for General U. S. Grant in 1868, and in religious faith he and his wife are Baptists. Socially he is a prominent member of the Odd Fellows society, has filled all the chairs in his lodge, is past grand, and and has represented the local order in the grand lodge. He also belongs to the Knights of Pythias, and is past commander of W. C. Baker Post, No. 551, G. A. R., of Stillman Valley.

HENRY GRAEHLING, who resides on section 22, Eagle Point township, is a worthy representative of that hardy race that have done so much to build up this new country, and who, however lowly their condition in life on their arrival here, by industry and economy manage to accumulate a competency, leaving to their children sufficient means to give them a good start in life. He was born in Alsace, Loraine, Germany, June 28, 1828, and in his native land grew to manhood, and in his youth learned the blacksmith trade, although reared on a farm. Like many other youths in the old country, he dreamed of better opportunities afforded in America than in the crowded cities of the old world. He determined to here try his fortunes, and the resolve was put into execution. Bidding farewell to the friends of his youth he set sail for the promised land, and landing at New York, he proceeded to Pittsburg, Pennsylvania, where he arrived July 11, 1850, joining there some German friends. Securing work in a vise factory, he there worked three years, saving in that time some four hundred dollars, which he lost through a broker or banker. He was so discouraged that he did not have the heart to longer remain in that city. From there he went to Westmoreland county, Pennsylvania, and for two years was engaged in farming.

Mr. Graehling was married in Pittsburg, Pennsylvania, August 8, 1853, to Miss Walburga Beck, who was born in Wurtemburg, Germany, February 25, 1835, and who came with her brother and sister to the United States in 1851, the family locating in Pittsburg. By this union ten children were born, two of whom are deceased. Mary is now the wife of Fred Diehl, of Carroll county, Illinois. Alexander is engaged in farming in Whiteside county, Illinois, where he owns a good farm. James is a farmer of Carroll county, Illinois, where he is the owner of a good farm. George W. also is the owner of a good farm in Carroll county, where he is engaged in farming. Henry is a farmer of Ogle county. Elizabeth is the wife of Andrew Peters, of Carroll county. Gustaf Adolph and Fred Wilhelm yet reside at home. John and Albert were the deceased. They have in all fourteen grandchildren.

After their marriage, Mr. and Mrs. Graehling took up their residence in Allegheny City, Pennsylvania, Mr. Graehling working at his trade. In September, 1856, he came west to Chicago, and there continued seven months, working at his trade, his time being principally given to horseshoeing. His wife joined him in the spring of 1857, and in April of that year they went to Sugar Grove, Lee county, where he again worked at his trade a few months and then moved to Eagle Point, Ogle county, continuing there at his trade. He there made his first purchase of real estate, becoming the owner of a small plat of ground, and a little house and shop. He remained there until September, 1860, when he moved to the place where he now resides. He first purchased five acres of ground, a piece of brush and stumps, moved here his shop, and commenced to clear the land. Later he purchased five acres more, and still later two and a half acres. He improved his little tract, but in 1865 sold his personal property and moved to Polo and gave his time exclusively to his trade for one year. In the spring of 1866, he returned to his place in Eagle Point and worked at his trade in connection with farming. From time to time as his means would permit, he purchased some land until he had a good sized farm. In 1879 he bought an adjoining farm of one hundred and sixty acres, and still later forty acres more. His next purchase was a farm of one hundred and fifty-four acres in Carroll county. At one time he owned five hundred acres of excellent land, but has sold off to his sons a portion, but still owns three hundred acres. His farm is well improved, and he has erected on it a large and neat house, big barn and other outbuildings.

Politically Mr. Graehling is a stanch Republican, his first presidential vote being cast for Abraham Lincoln in 1860. The party ticket he has continued to support from that time to the present. Religiously, he is a member of the Lutheran church at Polo, his wife being a member of the same body. For forty-two years they have been residents of Ogle county, and both are well known and highly respected. Beginning life in limited circumstances, they have endured together many toils and privations. For some years fortune did not seem to favor them, but they toiled on and have now the satisfaction of knowing that they have laid by enough to sustain and keep them in old age, and that their children are also well provided for. They know further that what they have gained has been by honest industry.

SAMUEL DOMER, deceased, was for more than fifty years an honored citizen of Ogle county, one respected by all who knew him. He was born September 3, 1818, near Sharpsburg, Washington county, Maryland, and there grew to manhood, receiving his education in the common schools. In 1839 he left his native state and went to Ohio, where he remained one year, when for some reason he returned to his old home and there remained until 1845, when he came to Ogle county, which remained his home until called to the upper and better world. He was a brickmaker by trade, and on locating in Mt. Morris township, in 1845, he made the brick and built his own home. He soon gave up his trade for the more profitable and healthy occupation of farming.

Mr. Domer was twice married, his first union being with Miss Elizabeth Steffa. After a wedded life of but two years, Mrs. Domer passed away. They had one child, which died in infancy. On the 10th of March, 1852, Mr. Domer wedded Miss Rachel Varner, a native of Fayette county, Ohio, born January 9, 1829, and daughter of William Herman and Cynthia Ann (Knox) Varner, who were also natives of the same county, the former born January 19, 1808, and the latter April 4, 1810. When Mrs. Domer was but a year and a half old her parents moved to Fort Wayne, Indiana. In 1837, when she was but eight years old, they moved to Lee county, Illinois, and in 1850 came to Ogle county, where she has since resided. On the 22d of June, 1892, her mother died at the age of eighty-two years. Her father died about 1837, in Indiana. They were the parents of three daughters, Mrs. Domer being the eldest; Sarah, now Mrs. William Turner, of Lee county, Illinois; Mary L., wife of John Etnyre, of Paine's Point, Illinois.

To Samuel and Rachel Domer were born eight children: Martha Frances, born February 15, 1854, married Charles Reber. She died February 16, 1876. Lydia Ann, born November 27, 1855, died September 9, 1862. Andrew J., born July 29, 1857, married Ida Lewis, and to them four children have been born: Maude, Earl, Minnie and Laura. They reside in Kansas, where he is engaged in farming. William H., born April 20, 1859, married Kate Alter, and four children have blessed their union—Jesse, Ethel, Percy and Bessie. They are living in Mt. Morris. Samuel O., born May 21, 1863, married Emma Shuber, and they have two children, Floyd and Edna. They are living in Polo, Illinois. Franklin V., born September 30, 1868, married Effie Brooks, and they have one child, Mary Eva. They are living in Oregon township. Frederick W., born April 20, 1870, married Anna Fridley, and they have one child, Ray V. They are living on the old homestead in Mt. Morris township. Sarah A., born July 10, 1873, married William W. Koontz, and they reside on the home place in Mt. Morris township.

Mr. Domer commenced farming on a farm of one hundred and sixty acres, on which he lived for twenty-two years. He then purchased another farm, to which he added from time to time until he had a farm of four hundred acres, all of which he had under improvement. This he disposed of and purchased two hundred and ten acres in Mt. Morris township, upon which he lived about twenty years. In 1895 he rented the farm and moved to Mt. Morris, to spend his remaining years in retirement. He was, however, not long for this world, as the summons came for him to depart July 4, 1898. He died of dropsy and heart disease, and his remains were interred in the cemetery at Silver Creek, Ogle county. In politics he was originally an old-line Whig, but on the dissolution of that party he became a Democrat, with which party he acted during the remainder of his life. Interested in the public schools, for many years he served as school director. He never cared to push himself forward in any manner, but was quiet and unassuming in manner, content to fulfill his daily duties of farm and home life, leaving to others the more exacting responsibilities of public life. He left a large circle of relatives and friends to mourn his loss. His widow, who is highly esteemed for her many excellent qualities of head and heart, is yet living in Mt. Morris, where her friends are many.

MARTIN A. FREI, a leading and successful merchant of Forreston, came to the county in 1866 and has here spent one-third of a century. He was born in the village of Nuettermoor, Cantor Leer, Germany, October 10, 1852, and is the son of Aldirk and Anna (Brandt) Frei, both natives of Germany. In his native village he received his education and, there remained until he was thirteen years old, when the family emigrated to the United States and settled in Forreston township, Ogle county, where the father engaged in farming. From 1866 until 1879 our subject remained on the farm and assisted in the farm work, becoming a thorough and scientific farmer. He has yet living one brother and five sisters. Hilka is the wife of John Geisman, living near Shannon. Renskea is the wife of T. Buisker, a farmer of Lincoln township. Gerhardina is the wife of B. Temple, a farmer residing near Shannon. John resides two miles west of Baileyville, in Stephenson county. Lena is the wife of Henry VanDeest, a farmer of Forreston township. Margaret is the wife of L. Pammer, residing at Ashton, Iowa. An older brother, Frederick, preceded the family to the United States. During the Civil war he offered his services to his adopted country, and dying while yet in the service was buried at Monterey, Tennessee. The father of this family died August 18, 1870, and the mother, August 26, 1877.

On the 27th of November, 1877, Mr. Frei was united in marriage with Miss Annie DeGrote, daughter of F. and Tina DeGrote. She was born in Woquard, Emden, Germany, and came to America in 1866 in company with her parents, who settled in Ridott. By this union four children have been born—Ollie J., Tina, Fred and Henry F. Of these, Ollie and Fred are assisting their father in the store. The family are well known and highly esteemed.

In 1879 Mr. Frei left the farm and went to Freeport, where he engaged in the mercantile business, remaining there until 1885, when he came to Forreston and started a general dry goods and grocery business, in which he has since continued with gratifying success. He cast his first presidential vote for Rutherford B. Hayes, and has since been a stanch and uncompromising Republican. He has been town trustee for more than six years, and has been on the school board for three terms, and is the present secretary of that body. He is the secretary of the Retail Merchants Association, and has held different offices of the community. A member of the German Reformed church, he has been superintendent of its Sunday-school for the past six years, and has been a worker of the Sunday-school since 1885. He is a self-made and successful business man, affable and courteous in address, and interests himself in all improvements, and is a factor in the development of his adopted city and county along all lines. He is popular and influential, and his friends are many throughout Stephenson and Ogle counties.

ALFRED R. BINKLEY, now living a retired life in Mt. Morris, is a veteran of the Civil war. He was born in Washinton county, Maryland, January 13, 1847, and is the son of Daniel and Catherine (Weaver) Binkley, the former born in Franklin county, Pennsylvania, in 1818, and the latter in Washington county, Maryland, in 1826. By occupation the father was a farmer, and was a strong, robust man up to the time of his death, in 1860. He was taken sick with some stomach trouble on Friday and died the following Tuesday. The mother is yet living in Morganville, Washington county, Maryland. They were the parents of six children, our subject being their first born. Calvin married Sevilla Butterbaugh, and they reside in Maryland township, Ogle county, where he is engaged in farming, owning one hundred and eighty acres of land. William died in early childhood. Ida married Abram Hawes, and they reside in Morganville, Maryland, where he follows his trade of carpentering. Charles died of typhoid fever at the age of twenty-seven years. Daniel married Eva Downey, and they live in Morganville, Maryland, where he follows farming.

The subject of this sketch remained in his native state until he was sixteen years old, when he came to Ogle county, and here attended school until 1864, when he enlisted in the One Hundred and Fortieth regiment, Illinois Volunteer Infantry, Company I, with which he served until the close of the war. He was on picket duty the greater part of the time and was in several skirmishes. On receiving his discharge at Camp Fry, Chicago, he returned to Ogle county, where he remained a few months. He then went east, and for five years was clerk in a general store at Green Castle, Franklin county, Pennsylvania, after which he again came to Mt. Morris, Ogle county, and clerked for a time. Later he purchased a restaurant, which he gradually turned into a general store, in which line of business he continued until in July, 1895, when he was compelled to retire on account of ill health.

Mr. Binkley was married February 12, 1878, to Miss Laura B. Sprecher, of Mt. Morris, and daughter of Philip and Letha (Castle) Sprecher. They now reside in a comfortable home in Mt. Morris. Mrs. Binkley is a consistent member of the Brethren church, in the work of which she is deeply interested. She is one of a family of eight children, three of whom are now living. Fraternally Mr. Binkley is a member of the Grand Army of the Republic, in which he keeps alive the memory of the days, when yet a youth he went out in defense of his country's honor, and for the restoration of the Union. He has lived to see not only the Union restored, but its boundaries extended, good feeling existing among those who wore the blue and the grey, and a more fraternal feeling than ever existed before.

PETER SMITH, banker, capitalist and retired farmer, was a natural financier who aided much in the development of Ogle county. He was the son of Edward and Anna (Tebow) Smith, and was born in Franklin, Bergen county, New Jersey, December 21, 1808. His American ancestry runs back to one of the members of a little Swedish colony, who settled in Bergen county, New Jersey, in 1624. When twelve years old he moved with his parents to New York city, where he attended school and acquired a good common-school education. His first business venture was in buying and selling fruit, and when but sixteen years old he engaged in the poultry business, and afterwards carried on the manufacture of mustard and cayenne pepper, in which business he continued until he was twenty-one years old. For the succeeding ten years he was in the wood business, and also in buying and selling horses, purchasing his stock in the state of Ohio and selling in New York. He met with success in each line of business, but he believed that he could do still better in the West. Coming to Ogle county, he settled in White Rock township and a few years later he entered six hundred acres of land in Marion and Pine Rock townships (although there were then no townships), and erected a log cabin, 16 x 24 feet, and one and a half stories in height. For miles around neighbors turned out and assisted him in its erection, the time requiring but one day. With his wife and two children he there laid the foundation for his large fortune. While developing his own farm he kept a breaking team of five yoke of cattle to assist other early settlers in the neighborhood. By energy and good judgment it was not long before he owned over one thousand acres of land. His ability lay in wisely directing the work of others. He was collector and constable in Marion township and school director about fifteen years. He continued farming and stock raising until December, 1875, when he moved to Rochelle. For several years he was president of the First National Bank of Rochelle. In 1883 he sold out his interest in this bank, making his investments in well improved farms and loans. Mr. Smith was a life-long Democrat, but had no taste for holding office. He died November 24, 1886, at the age of seventy-eight years, leaving a fortune of a quarter of a million dollars.

May 12, 1831, Mr. Smith married Sarah Foster in New York city. She was born in County Armagh, North of Ireland, July 12, 1809, and was of Scotch-Irish descent. Eleven children were born to them, five of whom died in infancy; a daughter, Emma, died at the age of twenty-four. The following survive: Abbie A., who married Minor Parker, deceased, resides at Steward; Margaret, who married Austin Noe, deceased, resides at Rochelle; Caroline, the wife of Patrick O'Mara, resides in White Rock township; Susan M. married Aron Cass, deceased, mention of whom is made in another article; George F. married Mary Jones, and now lives on the old homestead in Marion township.

Mrs. Smith by her sound sense, industry and economy was a great aid to her husband. She was always a Presbyterian. She died July 9, 1897, at the age of eighty-eight.

FRANKLIN F. PEEK, who resides on section 34, Woosung township, is a well-known citizen of Ogle county, which has been his home since 1838. He was born in Bethel, Windsor county, Vermont, March 2, 1832, and is the son of John and Lucretia (Lamb) Peek, both of whom were natives of Vermont. His father was a farmer by occupation, and politically was a strong Whig and an active worker in the party. He came with his family to Ogle county in 1838, coming by water from Buffalo to Detroit, and from there to Ogle county by teams, being five weeks on the road, arriving in July. He stopped about three months at Grand Detour, where his brother-in-law, John Deere, afterward the famous plow man, was then located. John Deere first married Dennis Lamb, a sister of the mother of our subject, and came west and established himself at Grand Detour where he was working at his trade of blacksmith. He had not then begun the manufacture of plows, which later brought him both reputation and colossal fortune. While residing at Moline his first wife died and he later married her sister, Lucina Lamb.

In the fall of 1838 John Peek bought the claim to two hundred acres, which he afterward entered, now the home of our subject. That place he put under improvement and made it his permanent home He became quite successful financially, and was well known throughout the county. He was quite active in political affairs, but never an office-seeker. At the time of his settlement on his claim there was little else but wolves and rattlesnakes in the vicinity. There was but one house between his place and Dixon, and no settlement north until Oldtown, or Buffalo was reached. At that time and for years after Chicago was the chief market, and to that place they hauled their grain and other produce. With a four-ox team they could haul sixty or sixty-five bushels of wheat, and with a two-horse team about thirty-five or forty bushels, and ten days were required to make the trip with oxen. Our subject speaks of one trip of ten days on which he accompanied his father, of not having but one warm meal during the whole time. They usually carried their provisions with them for they could not afford to pay out what little was obtained for their produce for meals. The money was too badly needed for other purposes. He tells of holding a lantern while the grain was being unloaded at Chicago, and the scoop shovel used for the purpose was left in the wagon and brought home with them, being the first of the kind in the neighborhood. But think of unloading grain in the city of Chicago by the light of a lantern!

John and Lucretia Peck were the parents of nine children, all save one born in Vermont, and all lived to maturity, eight of the number yet living. Samuel C. has been a resident of Calaveras county, California, since 1859; William P., who resides in Amadore county, California, has been a prominent citizen there since 1852. He has filled a number of important offices in his adopted county, serving as supervisor several years, and as a member of the state legislature two terms; George N. is a retired farmer residing in Polo; Jeannette married Fenwick Anderson, of Bureau county, Illinois, who has been a prominent business man and politician, and extensive land owner. She died January 9, 1899; Franklin F., our subject, was next in order of birth; Mellona, who is single, makes her home with her brothers and sisters; John D. died when about thirty-five years old; Henry P. is a resident of Oregon, Illinois; Horace W. is a farmer of South Dakota.

The subject of this sketch was but six years of age when he came with his parents in Ogle county. The first school he attended here was at Sugar Grove, four miles from his home. While attending that school he boarded with a family in the neighborhood and did chores for his board. One year's time would probably cover the entire period of his school life, his attendance being in the winter months for a very short time. When he attained his majority he began life for himself, working at various occupations. Much of the prairie in the vicinity of his home he assisted in breaking and otherwise improving. In 1861 he went to Calaveras county, California, where he remained until October, 1864, when he returned home on account of his father's death and took charge of the home farm. He has since carried it on, his mother making her home with him until her death in February, 1873. Soon after her death he purchased the interest of the other heirs, becoming sole owner.

Mr. Peck was married April 2, 1874, at the home of his uncle, John Deere, in Moline, to Mrs. Mattie Wood, widow of Beeler Wood, of Moline, and daughter of Asa and Luchera (Warren) Eaton, her mother being of the family of General Warren, of Revolutionary fame. The eldest brother of her mother, Daniel Warren, was a colonel in the war of 1812. Mrs. Peck's first marriage was celebrated in Moline, where she lived until her husband's death one year later. She was born in Windsor county, Vermont, where she grew to womanhood. She received a good education at South Woodstock, Vermont, at the Green Mountain Liberal Institute, and when but eighteen engaged in teaching in her native state. Two years later she came west to Champaign county, Illinois, where she had a cousin living, who was the only acquaintance in that locality. She taught the first term of school at Philo, in that county, and then took a position in the public schools of Urbana, where she remained two years. From there she went to Decatur, where she also remained two years, and then went to Moline, where she was teaching at the time of her marriage to Mr. Wood. She was induced to go to Moline from the fact that Mrs. Deere was an old Vermont friend. She is one of a family of eleven children, five of whom are yet living. Besides herself, the living are George W., of Geneseo, Illinois; Mary, wife of Joseph Savage, of Polo, Illinois; Frederick W., who remains on the old homestead in Vermont; and Dr. David D., a practicing physician, of 3147 Indiana avenue, Chicago.

Since taking possession of the old homestead, Mr. Peck has followed general farming and stock raising, feeding usually the grain he grows on the place. He has been a Republican since the organization of the party, but has never been an office-seeker. Since 1891, except two years, he has been serving as supervisor of his township, filling the position to the general satisfaction of those interested. He has ever been active in educational matters, serving many years on the school board. It is, however, as one of the representative farmers of the township that he is best known. On the old homestead he has made many improvements, adding to the beauty and value of the place. The old Galena and Dixon stage road used to cross the farm, and a magnificent row of hard maple trees now on the place was set out by our subject's father along the road. He has made a success in life and has gained the esteem and respect of his many acquaintances, not only for his integrity and upright character, but for his ability and good judgment as well. Mrs. Peck is a cultivated and highly refined lady, of scholarly attainments. Their home and genial hospitality is shared and appreciated by their many friends and guests. In the summer of 1875 they visited their old home in Vermont, and although he had left it when but six years old, Mr. Peck was yet able to recognize some of the old landmarks.

WILLIAM H. STEFFA, the subject of this sketch, was born December 21, 1857, in Rockvale township, Ogle county. He is the son of David and Martha (Hill) Steffa, who were born in Maryland, the former March 19, 1823, and the latter in 1831. By occupation Mr. Steffa was a farmer, and came to Ogle county in 1841 with his parents. Mr. and Mrs. Steffa had ten children, namely: Jacob E., living in Kansas; Barbara A., also living in Kansas; Ella, living in Nebraska; William H., of whom we are writing; Andrew David, a resident of Iowa; J. F. and O. B., of Rockvale; J. M., of Kansas; Effie, of Rockvale, and Lottie, who died when twenty years of age. Mr. Steffa is living with his son, the subject of this sketch. His wife died October 26, 1891.

Our subject attended school and helped his father until eighteen years of age, when he started out for himself, going first to the farm of Joseph Wagoner, where he remained for one year and then worked by the month for eighteen years, after which time he rented the farm of Joshua Thomas for a period of two years. At the expiration of that time Mr. Steffa moved to Hamilton county, Nebraska, where he made his home for one year, moving later to Scott county, Kansas, where he resided for eighteen months, and where he purchased a valuable tract of one hundred and sixty acres, still in his possession. He afterward returned to Ogle county, where he still resides, and where he is still occupied in the management of the highly cultured farm on section 17.

On the 14th of September, 1890, Mr. Steffa married Mrs. Mary Haney, who was born October 29, 1846, and is the daughter of E. T. and Margaret (Howard) Mallory. Mr. Mallory is a native of Yorkshire, England, and was born February 18, 1818. His first wife was from Scotland, where she was born February 13, 1812. When nine years of age, Mrs. Mallory moved with her parents to London, Canada, where she met her first husband, John McGuffin, a Canadian, by whom she had six children. She afterward married Edward T. Mallory, and they are the parents of five children. Mary, the wife of the subject of this sketch; Ellen, who was born July 23, 1849, is the widow of Olwyn Trask, and resides in Austin; Frances A., born April 5, 1851, is the wife of Frank Robinson, a carpenter, also living in Austin; Edward T. was born August 14, 1853. He was president of the Minnesota Stoneware Company, at Red Wing, Minnesota, where his widow still resides.

The youngest child, Thomas Howard, was born February 13, 1854. He married Ann Steffa, and they reside in Chicago, where Mr. Mallory is a traveling salesman for a large brickware concern. Edward Mallory lent his support to the Republican party. He was actively interested in all public affairs, and was school-director and constable at the time of his demise, which occurred November 28, 1856. Mr. Mallory returned to England to visit the home of his childhood, and later with reference to some legacies which were left to him. Mrs. Mallory's death occurred February 13, 1862. Her father was one of the patriots who fought in the Canadian rebellion.

Mrs. Steffa, the wife of our subject, was twice married. Her first husband was Patrick Haney, whom she married March 19, 1863. Eleven children graced this marriage, as follows: George E., born April 6, 1864, married Mary Ebersole, and together with their seven children, they reside in Manson, Iowa. William S., born June 17, 1865, married Minnie Lewis. They have two children, and live near Bailyville, Kansas. Olive E. was born March 3, 1867. She married C. A. Rosecrans, and they have one child. Their home is in Chicago, where Mr. Rosecrans is engaged in the wholesale hardware business. Henry B. was born September 29, 1868, and married Mabel Morton. They have one child and live in Mount Morris township. Lucy Ann was born April 16, 1870, and died two days after her birth. John H. was born April 24, 1871, and makes his home in Chicago, where he is in the employ of his brother-in-law. Mary Edith, born July 1, 1873, married Henry Lohafer. They have one child and lives near Mount Morris. Maggie Irene was born February 9, 1876, and is living at home. Homer C. was born March 26, 1878, and is attending college at Mount Morris. Bessie Pearl, born January 26, 1880, died of appendicitis December 3, 1897. Walter P. was born January 13, 1883, and is living at home, attending the district school. Mr. Haney was a Democrat and gave his support to that party until his death, which occurred July 19, 1882.

Mrs. Steffa is the possessor of three hundred acres in the estate on which they reside. In politics our subject is a Republican, and ardently supports the party to which he belongs. He is a clear-sighted man of business, and has a very high standing in the community in which he resides.

REV. JAMES H. MORE, M. D.—Only those lives are worthy of record that have been potential factors in the public progress in promoting the general welfare or advancing the educational or moral interests of the community. Dr. More has rounded the psalmist's span of three score years and ten, has always been found true to his church, to his country and to his friends, and the world is certainly far better for his having lived.

The earliest ancestor of the family of which our subject has any knowledge is John More, who was of the Grant clan of the Highlands of northern Scotland, and who was married at Forrest to Isabel Duncan, December 22, 1735. Their son John, who was born February 24, 1745, was married in 1770, to Betty Taylor, of Elgin, Scotland, and they lived happily together for the long period of fifty-three years.

Their two children were both born in Scotland, but in the autumn of 1772 the family emigrated to America. They spent the winter in New York city, and in the spring of 1773 ascended the Hudson river to Catskill, crossed the mountains and proceeded through the wilderness to what is now Delaware county, New York. Coming to a favorable spot where the large trees of the forest indicated a fruitful soil, they stopped, and in that wild region made for themselves a home. Two children were born in Scotland, and six children in America. From these worthy pioneers are descended many who have won distinction in the pulpit, on the rostrum, at the bar, and in commercial, financial, medical and educational circles as well as in the humbler walks of life.

James More, grandfather of the Doctor, was the sixth in order of birth in the family of eight children born to John and Betty More. He was born in Roxbury, Delaware county, New York, January 10, 1782, and died May 19, 1866. He married Roxana, daughter of John and Patience (Post) Benjamin. Of the six children born of this union, John Benjamin More, the second in order of birth, was born November 21, 1804, and died in Polo, Illinois, February 24, 1886. In 1829, he married Miss Louisa Jane Kelley, who was born in Middletown, Delaware county, New York, November 6, 1809, a daughter of Phineas and Rosalind Kelley. She makes her home with our subject and is still in the possession of her mental and physical faculties. Her father, a blacksmith by trade, was born in Dutchess county, New York, December 6, 1777, and died at age of sixty-seven years. He was a son of David Kelley, a soldier of the Revolutionary war, who married a Miss Ellis. Mrs. More's maternal grandfather was Jonathan Kelley, whose mother was Priscilla King, and he married Grace Godfrey, a daughter of John Godfrey.

Dr. More, the subject of this sketch, was born in Halcottsville, Delaware county, New York, August 31, 1826, a son of John S. and Louisa J. (Kelley) More, and his boyhood was passed in the town of Roxbury, that county, his education being obtained in the common schools and the academies at Prattsville and Fergusonville, where he prepared for college. He successfully engaged in teaching school for several terms in Roxbury, and later entered the medical department of the University of Buffalo, New York, where he was graduated June 27, 1853. Coming west, he located at Buffalo Grove, Ogle county, Illinois, in May, 1854, and the following August began the practice of his chosen profession with Dr. W. W. Burns. In 1856 he embarked in the drug and book business in Polo, but four years later entered the ministry of the Methodist church as a member of the Rock River Conference, being first stationed at Harvard and later at Richmond, McHenry county. At the latter place he joined the Union army as chaplain of the Ninety-fifth Illinois Volunteer Infantry, which participated in many important engagements in Missouri, Tennessee, Mississippi, Alabama, Arkansas and Louisiana. The regiment was at first in the Seventeenth Army Corps, but later formed a part of the Sixteenth Army Corps, under General A. J. Smith, and was mustered out in August, 1865.

After the war, Dr. More continued his labors in Rock River Conference, was stationed at Mt. Morris two years and Kankakee one year, and in 1868 was appointed presiding elder of the Dixon district, where he remained for four years. During the following three years he had charge of the church at Sterling, was at Sycamore two years, presiding elder of the Freeport district four years, and for a year and a half was pastor of the Western Avenue church, Chicago. While there his health failed and he was forced to resign, in 1883. Going to Biddle county, South Dakota, he opened up a farm and engaged in agricultural pursuits. He found no church facilities for the people of that locality, the young folks were desecrating the Sabbath, and he organized churches and held services around at different settler's cabins. When it became known that he was also a physician, he was forced into the practice of medicine again. He took a great interest in the political affairs of the territory, was a delegate to the constitutional convention, and chairman of the committee on public schools and school lands, embodied in the organic law of the state the best provisions for the safety of school funds of any state in the Union. From this wise legislation the state now has two million dollars drawing seven per cent interest; in each township two sections have been set apart for school purposes, and such safe guards thrown around the school funds as will prevent loss by dishonest officials. The credit of this is almost wholly due to the efforts of Dr. More, and it almost seems that he was sent by Providence to the territory for that purpose.

On leaving Dakota, December 23, 1886, Dr. More returned to Margaretville, Delaware county, New York, where he engaged in various commercial enterprises until 1890, when he returned to Ogle county. He has since served as pastor of the Methodist church at Forreston for three years, but is now living retired in Polo, where he has renewed old friendships. He has ever taken a prominent part in local politics, especially in all that is conducive to the welfare of the city, and being elected alderman in 1891, he immediately made his influence felt, as he had done in other towns where his lot had been cast. He was the chief factor in securing the local prohibition at Sycamore while residing there, and the city council of Polo soon realized that improvements must be made in the streets and sidewalks. The Doctor was instrumental in establishing the street grade and park system which has made Polo one of the neatest little cities of its size in the state. He was appointed engineer and superintendent of public works, and for a nominal salary has given many days of valuable time to surveying and grading the streets, etc., since 1895.

On the 21st of January, 1857, in Polo, Dr. More was united in marriage with Miss Harriet E. Frisbee, also a native of Roxbury, Delaware county, New York, and a daughter of Rev. George and Maria (Smith) Frisbee. Her father, who was also a Methodist Episcopal minister, was born in Rensselaerville, New York, March 23, 1796, and died at Mt. Morris, Illinois, November 4, 1855. He came west in 1846 by way of canal and lakes, having a son who had located at Buffalo Grove four years previously. After spending one year in Mt. Morris, Rev. Frisbee took up his residence in Buffalo township, Ogle county. His first wife had died in 1853, and he subsequently married again and returned to Mt. Morris, where his last days were passed. The genealogical record of the Frisbee family is as follows: Edward Frisbee, of Bradford, Massachusetts, had twins, Ebenezer and Silence, who were born at that place September 5, 1673. Ebenezer was married at Bradford, April 21, 1703, to Hannah Page, and their first born was Ebenezer, who was born there April 14, 1704, and was married at the same place, December 24, 1731, to Silence Brackett. Triplets were born to them, April 28, 1736, and one of these, Benjamin, married Margaret Holley, by whom he had nine children. Benjamin Frisbee, the grandfather of Mrs. More, was the fifth in order of birth in this family. He was born in Sharon, Connecticut, August 17, 1768, and died in Roxbury, New York, February 18, 1841. He was married about 1790, to Ruth Dolph, who was born in Wethersfield, Connecticut, April 18, 1771, and died in Roxbury, New York, May 8, 1835. Rev. George Frisbee, Mrs. More's father, was the second child in their family. The first to come to the new world was Bathazar and Alice De Wolf, who settled in the Connecticut Valley. They became the parents of several children, among whom was Edward, who was born in 1642. To Edward De Wolf and his wife Rebecca was born Charles, 1673 (died 1731), who married Prudence White. Of their nine children, Joseph, the youngest, was born in 1717 and was killed during the French and Indian war, before Louisburgh, in 1757. In 1737 he had married Tabitha Johnson, and the youngest of their three children was Abda, who also entered the Colonial army in the French and Indian war, as did several of his cousins. It was at this time that the name was changed by these young men, who considered it too Frenchy, although it had been borne by English-speaking people for several generations. They adopted the name of D'olph or Dolph. After his return from the war, Abda Dolph went to New Haven, Connecticut, where he was married March 16, 1766, to Mary Coleman, who was born March 4, 1745, a daughter of Nathaniel and Ruth Coleman. Their daughter, Ruth Dolph, was born April 18, 1771, and was married February 8, 1791, to Benjamin Frisbee. One of the eight children born of this union was Rev. George Frisbee, Mrs. More's father.

To Dr. More and wife were born five children, namely: Mary L., who married George C. Marsh, secretary of the Gates Iron Works and a resident of Ravenswood, Chicago; George Frisbee, an expert electrician, now located at Denver, Colorado; Annie, who is clerk in the Sunday school missionary society of the Congregational church in Chicago; Faith, who is engaged in kindergarten work in the same city; and Pauline, who is studying in a kindergarten college in Chicago, and is also assisting in the Riverside public schools in kindergarten work.

In political sentiment Dr. More is a stanch Prohibitionist and has always made his influence for good felt in every community in which he has made his home. He is a Knight Templar Mason and belongs to the blue lodge and chapter at Polo and the commandery at Dixon. His circle of friends is only limited by his circle of acquaintances, and it is safe to say that no man in Ogle county is held in higher respect or esteem than Dr. More.

REV. JOHN J. McCANN is the efficient pastor of the St. Mary's Catholic church, Oregon, Illinois. He was born in Providence, Rhode Island, October 25, 1862, and is the son of George T. and Catherine (Wynne) McCann. His father was a native of Manchester, England, and came to the United States with his parents, the family locating in Providence, Rhode Island, where the parents later died. Felix McCann, the paternal grandfather, married Mary Coleman, whose father, Thomas Coleman, was a colonel in the English army, and who was thrown from his horse and killed. Felix and Mary McCann were the parents of four children—John, James, Susannah and George T., the latter being the father of our subject. By trade George T. McCann was a weaver, and a good one. He first came west on a prospecting tour, and for a time resided in Chicago, from which place he went to Aurora. In Aurora he first found employment in the woolen mills of Mr. Stolp, a factory that did a large and profitable business during the Civil war and for some years after. He had to abandon that business, however, on account of his health. This was, however, shortly before the war. He took his family east again, and resided in Providence, Rhode Island. During the latter part of the Civil war he enlisted, and was mustered into the service as a member of the First Rhode Island Light Artillery, and served until the close of the struggle. His brother James was all through the Rebellion, serving in a company of heavy artillery from Rhode Island. He came west again in July, 1866, and located in Aurora, Illinois, where he yet resides, being foreman in one of the departments of the Aurora Silver Plate Factory. Mrs. Catherine McCann was a native of Ireland, her parents dying in that country when she was a small child. She was the youngest of the family. To George T. and Catherine McCann nine children were born, five of whom are yet living—John J., our subject; Agnes, living with our subject; An-

REV. JOHN J. McCANN.

drew and George C., now residing in Chicago.

Father McCann was but four years old when the family moved the second time to Aurora, Illinois. After attending the public school and being one year in the high school in that city, he entered St. Viateur's College, Bourbonnais, Illinois, in September, 1877, where he remained five years in the study of the classics and philosophy. Leaving college, he studied theology and kindred sciences in St. Mary's Seminary, Baltimore, Maryland, finishing the regular course of clerical studies January 6, 1888, at which time he received ordination at the hands of Cardinal Gibbons. His first ministry was as assistant pastor of St. James church, Chicago, where he remained four years, and was then at St. Phillips church, Chicago, for six months. Leaving Chicago, for a year and a half he was at St. Mary's church, Joliet, and for one year at St. Michael's church, Galena. He was then appointed pastor of the mission of Oregon, Polo and Forreston, by Archbishop Feehan. This was in November, 1894. Since then he has annexed to his charge the Catholic missions at Byron and Ashton. He organized the first Catholic congregation and built the first Catholic church at Byron, in 1895. The mission at Oregon was organized in 1850, by Rev. John Quigley, C. M., of LaSalle, who with other priests celebrated mass in private houses, and in the court house until 1862, when they erected a small stone church in which services were held until the present fine church building was erected in 1891 by the Rev. D. B. Toomey. It is a large brick structure, with a seating capacity of five hundred, and will cost when completed twenty thousand dollars. The Oregon mission has about seventy families, that at Polo about sixty-five families, about forty families in Ashton, and about sixty families in Byron. They have services in each of these places once every two weeks. All the congregations are in a flourishing condition, and that at Polo have in contemplation the erection of a church building. Father McCann is a zealous pastor and a hard worker in the interests of his people and Christianity. He is a man of marked ability and popular with all classes, with many friends and well-wishers throughout Ogle and adjoining counties.

JOHN R NETTZ is numbered among the thriving farmers of Grand Detour township, where he owns and operates a farm of one hundred and twenty acres of fine land. He is a native of Ogle county, and was born in Pine Creek township, October 26, 1853. His parents, Henry and Margaret (Smee) Nettz, are natives of Washington county, Maryland, his father being born in 1816. By trade he was a carpenter, an occupation he followed until coming to Ogle county in 1851. On his arrival here, he located in Pine Creek township, where he purchased land and engaged in farming in connection with his trade. When his sons became old enough he relinquished into their hands the management of the farm, and is now living a retired life. In politics he is a staunch Republican, and religiously is a member of the Christian church, being one of the original members of the church in Pine Creek township. In his family were six children, five of whom are yet living. Thomas F. died in his twenty-first year. Otho J. is a farmer of Cass county, Iowa. Edward A. is living on the old home farm in Pine Creek township. John R. is next in order of birth. Daniel B. and Samuel B. are twins. They reside in Monroe, Wisconsin.

The subject of this sketch grew to manhood on the home farm in Pine Creek township, and was educated in the common school. He was reared to farm life, and until he attained his majority gave his time faithfully to his father. On arriving at man's estate, he worked on farms for wages for several years. On the 5th of August, 1880, he was united in marriage with Miss Marthe Wragg, daughter of Peter and Nancy (Thompson) Wragg, of whom further mention is made in the sketch of John B. Wragg, on another page of this work. By this union two children have been born, a son and daughter, George M., and Cora M. both of whom are at home.

After his marriage Mr. Nettz cultivated a rented farm in Woosung township for two years, after which he rented what is known as the Hershey farm in Pine Creek township, where he remained ten years. In 1893 he purchased his present farm, which is located on sections 5 and 14, Grand Detour township. During the same year he erected a fine barn and remodeled the dwelling house, since which time he has made other permanent and valuable improvements.

For the past six years Mr. Nettz has served as school director of his district, and in September, 1897, was elected road commissioner, which office he is at present filling. In politics he is a Republican, his first presidential vote having been cast for Rutherford B. Hayes, in 1876. He is a worthy member of the Pine Creek Christian church, of which body his wife is also a member. His success in life is largely due to his own industry, integrity and business ability. Both he and his wife are held in high esteem, and they have many friends in Ogle county, especially in Pine Creek, Woosung and Grand Detour townships, where their entire lives have been spent.

WILLIAM WATTS, deceased, who resided on section 23, Pine Creek township, belonged to that sturdy class of pioneers who left comfortable homes in the south and east and braved the hardships of frontier life and succeeded in transforming a wild country into one of the most productive countries in the known world. He was a native of Washington county, Maryland, born January 29, 1818, and is the son of Thomas and Sarah (Knudson) Watts, the former an Englishman by birth, and the latter born in Washington county, Maryland. In his youth Thomas Watts learned the carpenter's trade, but later engaged in farming, an occupation in which he continued throughout the remainder of his life. He never came west, and he and his wife both lived in Maryland. They were the parents of the following named children — John, Nancy, Rachel, Sarah, Joseph, Elizabeth, Thomas, William, Frisby and Abraham.

In his native county William Watts received his primary education in the district schools, attending the same as the opportunity was afforded him until he was seventeen years old, when he commenced to learn the carpenter's trade. After serving an apprenticeship of three years he worked as a journeyman in his native state until 1840, when, in company with George Swingley, Walter B. McCoy and John B. Chana, he left Hagerstown on horseback and started west, traveling through Pennsylvania, Ohio and Indiana, taking about a month in making the trip to Ogle county. They went first through the southern part of Illinois, passing through Springfield, the state capital, which was then but a small village, arriving in due time at Mount Morris.

On his arrival here, Mr. Watts commenced to work at his trade, assisting in the erection of the first dwelling house in the place. After completing the frame of the dwelling house, he went to work on the old seminary building, which was then in course of construction, and continued on that work until it was completed in the spring of 1842. He then purchased the claim of Major Hitt to a half section of land for which he paid five dollars per acre. The major who is the uncle of the present congressman is yet living in Ottawa, Illinois, at the age of ninety years. Although purchasing the land, Mr. Watts did not at once commence farming, but continued to work at his trade until 1850. At that time the land was still in its primitive condition, although about fifty acres had been broken.

On the 29th of October, 1849, Mr. Watts was united in marriage with Miss Anna Ankeny, a native of Washington county, Maryland, born January 22, 1832, and the daughter of Samuel and Elizabeth Ankeny, also natives of the same county and state, who came to Ogle county in 1837, locating in Mount Morris township. By this union there were born eleven children, one of whom died in early childhood. Thomas married Martha Avey and they have two children. They reside in Buffalo township where he is engaged in farming. Albert married Miss Vickey Weller. He is a farmer of Mount Morris township. William married Ella McNett, and they have one child. He is a farmer of Mount Morris township.

Ella married Albert Fahrney, and they have three children. He is a farmer of Buffalo township. James is living with his father and running the home place. John died at the age of twenty-one. Mary and Martha, twins, are living at home. Frisby married Ella Felker. He is a farmer of Pine Creek township. Oliver married Ada Mumma, and he is engaged in the grocery business at Mount Morris.

Immediately after his marriage, Mr. Watts, with his young bride, started for their old home in Maryland, making their bridal tour with a horse and buggy. After spending the winter visiting relatives and friends, they returned to Ogle county in the spring of 1850 and settled upon the farm that Mr. Watts had purchased several years previous, and at once began the battle of life. For forty-nine years they traveled life's journey together, and she was to him a helpmeet indeed, seconding him in all his efforts for success in this world. She was withal a loving mother and her memory is held in grateful remembrance. The summons came to her suddenly in February, 1898, her death being attributed to heart failure. Mr. Watts survived his wife about one year, when he, too, was called to rest.

When Mr. Watts came to Ogle county there were but a few log houses in the town of Oregon, and the whole country was almost in its natural state. Wild game was yet in abundance, and continued plentiful for several years. He was blessed in many ways, and by his own industry and wise management the original three hundred and twenty acres were added to until he became the owner of about fifteen hundred acres of as fine and productive land as there is in Ogle county. In addition to the cultivation of his farm, in times past he gave considerable attention to raising thoroughbred horses.

Although more than four score years have passed since Mr. Watts was born into this world, he was hale and hearty, with strength of mind and body well preserved until the last. The years that have come and gone since he was born have been eventful ones. His birth was cotemporaneous with that of the great state of Illinois, which at that time had but few more inhabitants than has Ogle county at the present time. A long and bloody civil war was fought, four millions of slaves were made free, and in the lapse of time the bonds that held the union together have been strengthened, and there is no longer the sectional feeling that divided the country, but we are truly one people. In what is now the northern part of Illinois, there was not a white man living at the time of his birth. Railroads, steamboats, telegraphs, telephones and the many useful labor-saving agricultural inventions were unknown. It has certainly been a grand age in which to live, and in the progress and development of the country Mr. Watts bore his part. Reared a Democrat, he always voted that party ticket, but never aspired to officeholding, believing he could do more good by attending strictly to his personal affairs.

S. E. BROWN, who has been actively engaged in business in Forreston for many years, is one of the honored sons of that place, and his life is a verification of the fact that the inevitable law of destiny accords to a tireless energy, industry and ability a successful career. Prominent in business circles of Forreston stands Mr. Brown, who conducts a restaurant, bakery and confectionary at that place. He was born August 11, 1844, in Schuylkill county, Pennsylvania, and at the early age of two years was left motherless. Upon reaching his fourteenth year he was apprenticed to the shoemaking trade, at which he worked until 1864, when, on the 13th of September, he enlisted in Company H, Two Hundred and Tenth Regiment, Pennsylvania State Volunteers. Shortly after entering the service he was taken ill and sent to the regimental hospital, but owing to the lingering condition of his disease he was transferred to the McDougal general hospital, from whence he was discharged, and also mustered out of service, receiving his discharge papers May 31, 1865. In 1865 he returned to Dauphin county, and worked in the coal mines from the spring of that year until fall, when he again took up his trade of shoemaking, which he pursued throughout the winter of 1865-66.

On the sixth of April, 1866, Mr. Brown came to Illinois to join his brother who had preceded him, and settled at Lanark, Carroll county. Upon joining him, he worked as a farm laborer until 1867, when he was employed by Jonas Beck, for whom he worked the following eight months. On the 24th of November, 1867, he was united in marriage to Miss Nancy Beyers, a daughter of J. G. Beyers, a pioneer settler of Ogle county, and at that time a prosperous farmer of Brookville township. Two children have blessed this marriage, namely: Agnes, living at home; and John William, express agent at Forreston for the American Express Company. In the fall of 1868 Mr. Brown rented a farm of eighty acres in Brookville township, which he subsequently increased to one hundred and twenty acres, and which he worked until 1894. On the eighth of January he removed to Forreston and went into business in the location which he now owns and occupies. Mr. Brown is one of a family of six children. George, the eldest, is deceased. J. P. is a prosperous farmer in Otter Creek, Carroll county, Illinois. David is a farmer in Dauphin county, Pennsylvania. Sarah is the wife of E. O. Ready, of Kewanee Illinois. Susanna is deceased. The sixth child is the subject of this sketch.

Mr. Brown votes the Republican ticket, and cast his first ballot for Ulysses S. Grant. He is a self-made man, and his valuable farm lands in Iowa, and the business property in Forreston are the results of his energy and good managment, ably assisted by his wife, who seconds his efforts by her constant zeal and activity. He is among the most progressive and public-spirited citizens of Forreston, and gives his support and co-operation to measures tending toward its growth and development.

HOWARD A. MORRIS.—America owes much of her progress and advancement to a position foremost among nations of the world to her newspapers, and no line has the incidental broadening out of the sphere of usefulness more than this line of journalism. Ogle county has enlisted in its newspaper fields some of its strongest intellects—men of broad mental grasp, cosmopolitan ideas and notable business sagacity. Prominent among these is Howard A Morris, of Rochelle, the successful editor and proprietor of the Herald. He comes of a good old Connecticut family who have lived for generations in the town of Danbury, and whose ancestry dates back to the landing of the Mayflower. His great-grand-father was Bethel Morris. His grandparents were Samuel Morris, who died in Danbury in 1864, and Phoebe (Starr) Morris, who died in 1871 at the residence of her son in Chicago. His maternal grandparents were Oliver and Polly (Benedict) Vail. The former went to Connecticut when a boy, and by his frugality and industry he acquired a small farm, and at the time of his death, which occurred while on a visit to his brother in Syracuse, New York, he was the the owner of large and valuable tracts of land near Adrian, Michigan.

The father of our subject was Granville White Morris, who was born in Danbury, Connecticut, on the 17th of November, 1822. He attended the district school from the age of four years until reaching his twelfth year, and from that time until his sixteenth year he was employed in his father's woolen mills during the summer, attending an academy in the winter seasons. The four years following he worked in the mills of Dick & Sanford at Sandy Hook, and in 1842 purchased from his father the woolen mills aforementioned. These he ran until 1848, when he accepted the office of sheriff and served until 1862, under Philo T. Barnum, a brother of the famous showman of that name, and at the same time kept the county house and jail.

In 1862 he opened the Turner House in Danbury, which he ran for a year, and in 1863 came west to Rockford, returning the following year for his family, which he took to LaCrosse, Wisconsin, and in 1865 to Rockford, where they remained for ten years. At the expiration of that time they moved to Chicago where Mr. Morris was employed as general agent by an insurance company, traveling over a territory comprising Illinois, Iowa, Nebraska, Minnesota, Wisconsin, Michigan, Indiana and Missouri. In 1876 Mr. Morris visited Washington, District of Columbia, and the following spring went south intending to locate in Georgia, but was taken ill and returned home, locating in Creston, Illinois, and a few months later removed to Malta, Illinois, where he established the Malta Mail and the Creston Times. In 1881 he sold the former and combined the latter with the Rochelle Herald, of which he was editor until his death, which occurred in March, 1893.

Our subject, Howard A. Morris, was born on the 8th of December, 1851, in Danbury, Connecticut, and came west with his parents in 1864. He received his schooling in the common schools of Rockford, attending later the Rockford Business College, where he remained eighteen months. In 1876 he was employed as a traveling salesman by an insurance firm in Wheeling, West Virginia, and the two years following, for a Detroit firm. The fourth year he was in the employ of the Chicago Baking Company, and spent most of his time between Chicago and Omaha, Nebraska. In 1880 he joined his parents in Malta, remaining until the following year when, in connection with his father, established the Rochelle Herald, of which his father was editor until his death in 1883. Since that time he has been editor and sole proprietor. On the 9th of September, 1880, Mr. Morris was united in marriage to Miss Julia Pease, a daughter of Dan Pease, who was born in Middlefield, Massachusetts, and his wife Rachel (Burzell) Pease, a native of Buffalo, New York, and a daughter of Owen and Mary Burzell. Four children have graced this marriage, namely: Mary Josephine, Jennie M., Howard A., Jr., and Helen M.,

Howard A. having died at the age of five year. Mr. Morris is a member of the Masonic Lodge and Chapter of Rochelle, and Sycamore Commandary, K. T. Politically he is a Republican, always giving his support and ballot to that party. He is an honorable and straightforward man of business, and by this and his courteous and affable manner, commands the respect and esteem of his fellow citizens.

SAMUEL P. MUMMA, the well-known stock dealer of Mt. Morris, is a native of Ogle county, born in Pine Creek township, October 1, 1844, and is the son of Daniel S. and Naomi (Malone) Mumma, both of whom were natives of Washington county, Maryland, the former born June 17, 1818, and the latter September 29, 1820.

Daniel S. Mumma was reared in his native state and received his education in the common schools. At the age of eighteen he came west, making the journey on horseback, in company with his brother. They were so favorably impressed with the country that they returned east, disposed of their property, and in 1837 came to Ogle county for permanent settlement, thus becoming pioneers of the county. On his arrival he made claim to one hundred and thirty acres of land in Pine Creek township, on which he resided for about eight years, when he disposed of the same and purchased a tract of one hundred and sixty acres, on which he lived for some sixteen years. He then rented the place to his son and purchased eighty acres in Pine Creek township, on which he lived about fourteen years, when he moved to Mt. Morris and lived retired until his death. Daniel S. Mumma was the son of John and Mary

(Shafer) Mumma, both of whom were also natives of Washington county, Maryland, and who there spent their entire lives, living to a good old age. They were the parents of six children.

After residing here about three years, Mr. Mumma returned to Maryland and wedded Naomi Malone, daughter of James and Susanna (Albert) Malone, also natives of Washington county, Maryland, and who were the parents of nine children—Elias, Maria, James, Mary, Naomi, Susan, Jane, Ruan, Lizzie. In his native state, James Malone passed to his reward, and later his widow came to Ogle county, where her last days were spent.

To Daniel S. and Naomi Mumma ten children were born. James L., born April 15, 1841, married Sophia Etnyre, and they reside in the village of Mt. Morris; six children have been born to them, of whom three are now living. Mary A., born August 7, 1842, married William Griswold, by whom she had five children, two of whom are deceased; both Mr. and Mrs. Griswold are deceased, the latter dying January 19, 1890, and the former October 23, of the same year. Samuel P. is the subject of this sketch. Margaret, born August 26, 1846, married A. N. Ankney, and they have one child; he is living retired in Mt. Morris. Amanda died in infancy. Benjamin F., born August 11, 1849, married Laura Shafer, and they have one child; he died July 5, 1888, the result of an accident; she later married Frank Stonebraker, and they now reside in Hagerstown, Maryland. Henry C., born September 9, 1851, married Amanda Young, and they have two children; they reside on the home place in Pine Creek township, where he is engaged in farming. Estella F., born February 26, 1853, married Joseph Middlekoff, and they have three children; he is a farmer, and they reside in Pine Creek township. Ella, born February 28, 1855, is living with her mother in Mt. Morris. Elizabeth S., born August 15, 1860, married Harvey Griswold, and they have two children; he is a farmer in Rockvale township.

Daniel S. Mumma died at his home in Mt. Morris, September 10, 1888. His death was calm and peaceful, drooping away like a summer flower in autumn. His widow yet survives, and is living a peaceful and contented life, and waiting for the summons to "come up higher."

After passing through the grammar school of Pine Creek township, Samuel P. Mumma entered Rock River Seminary, finishing his school life in that institution. After leaving the Seminary, he returned to his father's farm and there remained seven years, assisting in farm labor. He then went to Mt. Morris and opened the first meat market in the place, and continued in that line of business for nine years, in the meantime engaged to some extent in dealing in stock. Closing out his meat market, he went into the grain and stock business, in which he continued for four years. Desirous of giving his attention exclusively to the stock business, he disposed of his grain interests, since which time his whole time and attention has been given to the purchase and sale of stock.

On the 22d of February, 1870, Mr. Mumma was united in marriage with Miss Louisa Swingley, a native of Washington county, Maryland, born February 11, 1844, and a daughter of Benjamin and Catherine (Hershey) Swingley, both of whom were also natives of the same county and state. They were the parents of eight children—

Ellen, John, Oliver, Louise, Ann, Laura, Alice and Grace. The latter is now deceased. Benjamin Swingley came to Ogle county in 1845 and located in Mt. Morris township, where he engaged in farming, at which he continued until 1891, when he moved to the village of Mt. Morris, where he is now living at the age of eighty-two years. His wife died June 21, 1893, at the age of seventy-six years.

To Mr. and Mrs. Mumma five children have been born: Willis, born December 22, 1870, married Annie Rice, and they are living in Mt. Morris. Ada, born October 9, 1873, married Oliver Watts, who is engaged in the mercantile business in Mt. Morris. Edgar, born September 24, 1876, is assisting his father in the business, doing much of the buying. Grace, born April 8, 1880, is living at home. Olie, born November 23, 1884, died September 17, 1886.

In politics Mr. Mumma is a Democrat, a party with which he has been identified since casting his first presidential vote for Horatio Seymour, in 1868. He has served his township and village as school director for a number of years, constable for a few years, member of the village board, and clerk of the same. Fraternally he is a member of the Knights of the Globe, and religiously is a Lutheran, as is also his wife, holding membership in the church at Mt. Morris.

It is as a business man and stock dealer that Mr. Mumma is best known, handling about eighty car loads per year, and doing a business amounting to fully one hundred thousand dollars per year. He is a good judge of stock and is always willing to live and let live. The farmers of the community know that they can trust him, and for that reason he handles such a large amount of stock per year. His reputation as a fair dealer is beyond question. As a citizen, he is fully abreast of the times, and is always willing to practice what he preaches, doing his share in the development of his village and county.

GARDNER S. PRESTON.—Prominent among the early settlers of Ogle county, who have witnessed the marvelous development of this section of the state during the past half century, and who have, by honest toil and industry, succeeded in acquiring a competence, are now able to spend the sunset of life in quiet and retirement, is the gentleman whose name heads this sketch, and who is a resident of the pleasant village of Stillman Valley.

Mr. Preston was born in Oneida county, New York, June 11, 1828, and is descended from a family of English origin, which was founded in New England at an early day in the history of this country. His paternal grandfather, Noah Preston, was one of the heroes of the Revolutionary war and was wounded while fighting for liberty. He was an early settler of Connecticut, and in 1806 became one of the pioneers of Oneida county, New York, where he reared his family.

Lyman Preston, father of our subject, was born in Connecticut, in 1800, and grew to manhood in Oneida county, New York, where he was united in marriage with Miss Hannah Gillett, a native of Herkimer county, that state. Her father, Rev. Truman Gillett, was a minister of the Free Will Baptist church and a missionary to Canada among the Moravians. Lyman Preston engaged in agricultural pursuits in Oneida county until 1850, when he brought his family to Ogle county, Illinois, and here spent the remainder of his life, dying about 1853. His estimable wife long survived him, passing away in the spring of 1898, at the advanced age of ninety years. In their family were the following children: Mrs. Fanny Lawson, now a resident of Milwaukee, Wisconsin; Gardner S., of this review; Lyman, a business man of Providence, Rhode Island; Mrs. Helen Lewis, of Stillman Valley; and Juliette, who married Colonel York and at an early day removed to Kansas, where her death occurred.

Gardner S. Preston is wholly self-educated, as his school advantages in early life were limited. He was reared upon the home farm in Oneida county, New York, remaining with his father until he attained his majority, and in the fall of 1849 he came to Ogle county, Illinois, where his father had traded for property some time previous. He located on a tract of one hundred and sixty acres of wild land in Marion township, fenced it and commenced the work of cultivation and improvement. He built a stone or gravel house in which he lived for over twenty years while opening up his farm, but it was finally replaced by a more commodious and modern frame residence. He also built good barns and outbuildings, set out fruit and ornamental trees, and continued to improve his place until he had one of the finest farms in the township. He added to the original purchase until he now has three hundred and twenty acres of valuable land, which has been acquired through his own industry and good management as he came to this region almost empty-handed.

Mr. Preston has been twice married, and by the first wife had four children who are still living, namely: Curtis, who is married and engaged in farming in Monroe township, Ogle county; Carrie, wife of George Bird, of Marion township; Frank, who went to the Pacific coast, and since 1893 has been engaged in the vegetable business in California; and J. W., who is now a farmer of Cass county, Iowa. On the 28th of June, 1872, Mr. Preston was married in Ogle county to Miss Lillie Traxlar, a native of the county, and a daughter of Peter Traxlar, who came to this section from Canada during the forties. There are two children by this marriage: Lyman, like his brothers, is married and lives on the old home farm, and Maude is her father's housekeeper. This is her last year at the Rockford Female College, where she has been giving special attention to music. Mrs. Preston, who was a most estimable lady, passed away in February, 1895, and was laid to rest in the Stillman Valley cemetery. She was a sincere and consistent Christian, an active member of the Congregational church, and much esteemed and beloved for her many Christian virtues.

Mr. Preston has also been a faithful member of the Congregational church of Stillman Valley for nearly forty years. He is a stanch Republican in politics, but has never cared for the honors or emoluments of public office, though he has most creditably served as highway commissioner for twenty years, was treasurer of the board, and for several years was an efficient member of the board of education. His support is never withheld from any object which he believes will prove of public benefit, and he is justly numbered among the valued and useful citizens of the community. After the death of his wife in 1895, he removed to Stillman Valley, where he is surrounded by a large circle of friends and acquaintances who appreciate his sterling worth.

GEORGE W. HAMMER, residing on section 36, Lincoln township, is numbered among the active and enterprising farmers of Ogle county. His home farm comprises one hundred and ninety acres, and is a well improved place, while his farm of seventy-four acres in Buffalo township is also well improved. He is a native of Ogle county, born on the farm where he now resides, September 7, 1845, and is the son of John and Eliza (Witmer) Hammer, both of whom were natives of Washington county, Maryland, the former born in 1806, and the latter in 1813. They were married in their native county, and in 1838 moved to Illinois, locating in Springfield, and there resided until 1842. John Hammer was a harness maker by trade, and was working at his trade while residing in Springfield. Leaving that city, he came to Ogle county and settled in Mount Morris where he continued to work at his trade for about three years. During that time he entered eighty acres of land, which was a portion of the farm now occupied by our subject. In February, 1845, he removed to the tract that he had purchased, erected a small frame house, and there resided while otherwise improving the place. He later purchased more land and had a fine farm of two hundred and forty acres. On his farm he commenced the manufacture of brick, which he continued three seasons, during which time he made the brick that went into his own brick residence that he had built. On that farm he continued to reside until his death in January, 1879, at the age of seventy-three years. His wife survives him and now resides in Mount Morris at the age of eighty-five years. They were the parents of six children, all of whom are living and have families of their own. Benjamin resides in Polo. John W. is living in Dixon, Illinois. D. Harry is a prominent citizen of Chicago. Eliza is the wife of Rev. Malachi Newcomer, a substantial farmer of Ogle county. George W. is the subject of this review. Ida is the wife of Edward Baker, a farmer of Pine Creek township.

The subject of this sketch was reared on the farm where he now resides, which he helped to improve. His education was obtained in the district school, but the opportunities that were given him were well improved, and he is to-day a well-informed man. He continued to remain at home until his father's death, when he bought the interest of the other heirs and succeeded to the home place. Since coming into possession he has made a number of valuable improvements upon the place, including the erection of a large basement barn, together with cribs, sheds and various out-buildings. Everything about the place shows the effect of a master mind, one that fully understands what he desires and puts into execution his plans. He is regarded as one of the best farmers and stockraisers in the county.

Mr. Hammer was married in Pine Creek township, February 3, 1870, to Miss Mary C. Miller, a native of Ogle county, and a daughter of David F. Miller, a pioneer of Ogle county, from Washington county, Maryland, and one of the first settlers of Pine Creek township. By this union eight children have been born, of whom D. O., the eldest, is assisting in carrying on the home farm. Clarence is now a student in

Mt. Morris College. Edith is the wife of Albert Coffman, a farmer of Buffalo township. Daisy is the wife of Prof. Ora Foster, a professional teacher, residing near Anderson, Indiana. Eva is yet residing at home. Minnie is a teacher in the public schools of Ogle county. George M. and Ray are attending the home school. Ruth died at the age of two months.

Mr. Hammer cast his first presidential ballot for U. S. Grant in 1868, and from that time to the present has been a consistent Republican. He has never held or desired public office, having no taste for such, and willing that those aspiring for official honors may have all they wish. His business interests have commanded his time and attention. He is well known as a man of strict integrity and honor, one deserving of the confidence of the community which has always been his home.

WILLIAM ALFRED HAMMOND, a well-known and successful farmer and veterinary surgeon residing on section 30, Leaf River township, a mile and a half northeast of the village of Leaf River, is one of the active, enterprising and substantial citizens of Ogle county, with whose interests he has been identified since 1855. He was born in Washington county, Maryland, March 11, 1836, a son of William Hammond, whose birth occurred in the same county, in 1807. The family were pioneers of that region and the grandfather, Peter Hammond, was of German ancestry. On reaching manhood the father married Miss Louisa Santman, also a native of Washington county, where they continued to make their home for some years, his time and attention being devoted to farming. In 1855 he removed with his family to Ogle county, Illinois, and the following year located on the farm where our subject now lives. A small house had previously been built and thirty-five acres placed under cultivation, and to the further improvement and operation of the place he gave his attention for seven years. In 1861, however, he returned to Washington county, Maryland, where he lived retired until called from this life about 1866. His wife survived him a number of years and died at the ripe old age of eighty-two.

In the family of this worthy couple were eleven children, of whom eight are still living, namely: Mrs. Mary Ann Eakle, of Bakerville, Maryland; Rev. Josiah L., a Lutheran minister, now located in Iowa, William A., of this review; Mrs. W. L. Palmer, whose sketch appears elsewhere in this work; Isaiah, a farmer of Washington county, Maryland; C. E., a baker of Sterling, Illinois; Mrs. Susan Miller, of Washington county, Maryland, and Franklin P., a dentist of Texarkana, Texas.

The education of our subject has been acquired through reading, study and observation since reaching years of maturity, as he had no school privileges during his youth. He was nineteen years of age when he accompanied the family on their removal to Ogle county, and was of great assistance to his father in opening up and carrying on the home farm. In 1861 he purchased the place and has made the farm what it is to-day—one of the best in Leaf River township. It comprises two hundred acres of valuable land, which is well improved. Mr. Hammond has rebuilt and remodeled the house, and the other buildings are in harmony therewith. For twenty-eight years he has successfully engaged in the practice of veterinary surgery, and has built up a good practice. In 1873 he removed to Rockford, where for three years he gave his entire time to the practice of his profession, but at the end of that time he returned to his farm and has since engaged in farming in connection with his practice.

At Freeport, Illinois, March 14, 1861, Mr. Hammond was united in marriage with Miss Sarah Williard, a native of Dauphin county, Pennsylvania, who came with her father, Jacob Williard, to Ogle county in 1854, when a child of eleven years, and settled in Leaf River township. Five children were born of this union, as follows: Alcinda, wife of Dr. Ira O. Paul, who is engaged in the practice of medicine in Winnebago, Illinois; William J., who is married and engaged in farming in Mount Morris township, Ogle county; Sarah V., wife of James B. Shierk, a farmer living near Egan, this county; Franklin, a painter, residing at home; and Gertrude, wife of F. J. Marks, a telegraph operator holding a position at Rosalia, Washington.

Politically Mr. Hammond is a stanch Democrat, but has never cared for political preferment. His honorable, upright life commends him to the confidence and esteem of all with whom he comes in contact, and he has a large circle of friends and acquaintances who fully appreciate his sterling worth.

H ON. ISAAC RICE, deceased, for three score years was a resident of Ogle county, and it is but just to say that few men living here were better known or more highly respected among those with whom they associated. He was a native of Washington county, Maryland, the birthplace of some of the best men and women that have made their home in Ogle county. He was born October 28, 1826, and was the son of Jacob and Mary (Roland) Rice, both of whom were natives of Washington county, Maryland. The Rice family were originally from Germany, the great grandparents of our subject being natives of that country.

Jacob Rice was by occupation a farmer, following that calling during his entire life. In 1837, in company with his brother-in-law, John Wagner, he came to Ogle county. Leaving their old home in Maryland, on horseback they passed through the states of Ohio and Indiana, but did not find any place to suit their fancy until they arrived in Ogle county, July 4, 1837. While making their tour of observation they left their families in Ohio. As soon as they determined on a location they sent for their families, and in the meantime a double log house was erected, into which Mr. Rice moved with his family on their arrival. It is said that during the following winter about twenty persons found shelter and a home in that log cabin.

To Jacob and Mary Rice eleven children were born. Barbara married Samuel Maysilles, of Washington county, Maryland. They never came west. She is now deceased. David married Catherine Avey. They came west, and he died in Ogle county some years ago. Joshua is deceased. John came to Ogle county and located in Leaf River township. He married Eliza Kendall, but is now deceased. Susan, widow of Elias Thomas, is now living in Mt. Morris township. Lydia married Benjamin Hiestand, of Leaf River township, but is now deceased. Elizabeth married Ezra Thomas, of Mt. Morris township, and is now deceased. Jacob and Mary were twins. The former is deceased. The latter is the widow of Daniel Etnyre, of Oregon, Illinois. Isaac was next in order of birth. William died at the age of twenty-one years.

On the 1st of December, 1840, Mary Roland Rice departed this life, leaving the husband and eleven children to mourn her loss. Later Jacob Rice married Miss Catherine Funk, a native of Maryland. "Aunt Kittie," as she is familiarly called by all who know her, is yet living at the age of one hundred and two years, and is yet in excellent health and spirits, her lovely character making of her a friend to everyone. Born during the first administration of John Adams, Washington was yet alive, and she has therefore lived while yet there was one ex-president, and under the administration of twenty-three presidents, surviving all save three. She is a member of the Mennonite church, clinging to the faith of her fathers, and trusting in the redeeming grace of her Savior.

On coming to Ogle county, Jacob Rice purchased some twelve hundred acres of land, all of which, with the assistance of his sons, he soon had under improvement. He was a man of marked character, an indefatigable worker, a kind husband, an indulgent father, a good neighbor, and left the world better for his having lived. He was a member of the River Brethren, as was also his first wife, the mother of his children. He died on his farm in Mt. Morris township, April 25, 1870.

Isaac Rice was eleven years old when he accompanied his parents to Ogle county. While yet residing in his native state, he attended the common schools a few terms, and the year following the arrival of the family in Ogle county his father erected a log school house on his place, and in the first school taught therein he was a pupil. On the opening of Rock River Seminary he became a pupil in that institution. At the age of eighteen years he taught his first term of school in the school house erected by his father. For that school he received eighteen dollars per month. Desiring to enter the medical profession, he went into the office of Dr. Francis A. McNeil, of Mt. Morris, reading under his instructions until ready to enter a medical college. In the winter of 1852-3 he entered Rush Medical College from which he was graduated with the class of 1855.

On receiving his diploma, Dr. Rice returned to Mt. Morris, and with his late preceptor began practice. He continued in the profession but a few months, however, when he rented some land and commenced farming. In 1860, he made his first purchase of land, and until 1876 he engaged exclusively in farming and stock raising. He then moved to the village of Mt. Morris and one year later, with Major Charles Newcomer, he established the Bank of Mt. Morris. He never, however, abandoned his interest in agriculture, but continued to give more or less attention to his farms until his death. He became an extensive land owner and his farms were always kept in good condition.

On the 14th of January, 1857, Dr. Rice was united in marriage with Miss Sarah Hiestand, daughter of Henry and Elizabeth (Newcomer) Hiestand. She is a native of Washington county, Maryland, born January 27, 1836, and is third in a family of six children, and was but one year old when her parents came to this county. Three children were born of this union. Roland, born February 10, 1858, died at the age of seven months. Anna, born March 22, 1860, died when she was eighteen years old. Joseph L., born December 23, 1866, is mentioned elsewhere in this work.

In politics Dr. Rice was a thorough and consistent Republican, voting the party ticket and advocating its principles from the very birth of the party. He was a great admirer of our first martyred president, Abraham Lincoln, and supported his candidacy with enthusiasm. His admiration for Lincoln increased after listening to the debate between Lincoln and Douglas at Freeport, Illinois. He took quite an active part in local politics and for two terms represented his county in the lower house of the general assembly of the state, and for four years was a member of the state senate. In both branches he took an active and leading part and was regarded as one of the strong members. He was always a strong temperance man, and while a member of senate endeavored to have passed some temperance legislation. He introduced the first resolution for the submission of the question to a vote of the people in regard to the manufacturing of distilled spirits, and also introduced what was known as the "Hind's bill," which empowered women to have a voice in licensing the sale of intoxicating liquors. While both measures were defeated, they showed conclusively where the Doctor stood on the temperance question.

Religiously the Doctor was a Methodist, being for many years a member of the Methodist church at Mt. Morris. In all the work of the church he took an active and abiding interest. The Sunday school work of the church called forth his best energies, and for some years he was the efficient superintendent of the school of his home church. His talent as a Sunday school worker was recognized by his election as president of the County Sunday School Association.

Dr. Rice was a thorough business man, and his abilities in that direction is unquestioned. Commencing life with very little assistance from his father, he began adding to his possessions until he was numbered among the most prosperous men in the county. His gains were all legitimately made, and not by oppressing any one. He was always lenient with creditors when they were disposed to do right, and there are many men in Ogle county who have reason to be grateful to him for timely assistance rendered and good advice given. He was one of the original stockholders in the First National Bank of Oregon, and for many years owned the controlling interest, and for twenty years was president of the same. He retained connection with the Bank of Mount Morris but about four years, when he sold out to his partner and gave his attention to the bank in Oregon and his extensive private interests. In 1893 he established the Citizens Bank of Mount Morris, to which he gave only supervisory care, his son, Joseph L., attending principally to the business. Always careful and methodical, it is no wonder that success crowned his efforts. Whether on the farm, in the bank, in the church, or in whatever engaged, the same attention was given to the minutest details of the business in hand. During later years he lived practically retired, traveling much of the time, making numerous trips abroad. In 1889, he went as far east as Constantinople and in 1890, and again in 1892, visited England and the continent. He later lectured considerably in northern

Illinois on his travels and various other subjects.

Dr. Rice was a thoroughly conscientious man, one who endeavored to do right by his fellow man, living up to the standard of the golden rule. His death, which occurred May 3, 1897, was not only a sad loss to his family, but to the community in which he had so long resided. He had been ill but a few days and his death was unexpected. The funeral sermon was preached by Rev. A. S. Mason and his remains laid to rest to wait the resurrection day.

JOSEPH L. RICE, president of the Citizens Bank of Mt. Morris, Illinois, is a good representative of the younger business element of Ogle county. He is a native of the county, born in the township of Maryland, December 23, 1866, and is the son of Isaac and Sarah (Hiestand) Rice, pioneers of Ogle county, of whom mention is made elsewhere in this volume. His early life was spent upon the farm, and in the district schools of his native township he began his education. When ten years of age he removed with his parents to the village of Mt. Morris, and for a time attended the public school of that place. Later he entered Rock River Seminary, and after pursuing a partial course, entered the Nortwestern University, Evanston, Illinois, with the intention of taking the complete classical course. At the age of twenty-one, however, he was compelled to abandon his studies on account of weak eyes. For the succeeding four years he was endeavoring to establish his impaired sight. Believing that further rest and travel would be beneficial, he went abroad in 1891, spending several months, during which time he visited the various cities and places of interest in England, Ireland, Scotland, Wales, Holland, Belgium, Germany and France. While in England he visited the noted Oxford University, which to him was one of the most interesting sights witnessed. He returned home by way of Liverpool and New York, stopping for a few days in the latter city. With this trip he was well pleased, the only regret now being that it was not more extended.

On the 19th of January, 1803, the Citizens Bank was established by Mr. Rice's father with our subject virtually in charge, his father giving but little attention to the details of the business. On the death of the father he took sole charge, latter becoming associated with his cousin, J. H. Rice, who has assumed the position of cashier, with our subject as president. The bank is in good condition and in January, 1899, purchased the business and good will of the Bank of Mt. Morris. With the absorption of the business of the latter bank, it gives the Citizens Bank an increased line of deposits and a clientage equal to any bank in the county. With large capital, good business methods, and the confidence of the people, the bank starts on a new career. Like his father, he is trusted by the people, all having a good word to say of "Joe" Rice, as he is familiarly called. In addition to his interest in the Citizens Bank, he is the largest stockholder in the First National Bank of Oregon, and is vice-president of the same.

On the 23d of December, 1895, Mr. Rice was united in marriage with Miss Emily Newcomer, a native of Ogle county, born May 31, 1874, and daughter of Albert and Margaret (Hitt) Newcomer, both of whom are natives of Illinois.

In politics Mr. Rice is a thorough Republican and a stanch advocate of its principles. His business interests, however, have been such as to preclude a very active participation in the work of the party.

HIRAM WOODIN is one of the most enterprising and successful agriculturists of Ogle county as well as one of its most capable financiers, and is a prominent citizen of Eagle Point township. His career proves that the only true success in life is that which is accomplished by personal efforts and consecutive industry. It proves that the road to success is open to all young men who have the courage to tread its pathway, and the life record of such a man should serve as an inspiration to the young of this and future generations and teach by incontrovertible facts that success is ambition's answer.

Mr. Woodin was born July 3, 1837, on the same farm in Hartford county, Connecticut, where his father, Elias Woodin, was also born. The latter married Miss Fanny Spencer, a native of the same county and a daughter of Naaman Spencer. They continued to make their home on the old Woodin homestead in Connecticut for a number of years, the father of our subject being engaged in its operation until 1843, when he brought his family to Ogle county, Illinois, but after spending the winter in Eagle Point, he removed, in 1844, to Carroll county, where he purchased a farm with a few acres broken and a log house erected thereon. The country was still very new, deer and wolves were numerous, and he assisted in killing a bear and capturing a cub upon his own place. He transformed his wild land into a well improved farm, the primitive frontier buildings giving place to a good residence and substantial outbuildings. He died there in the spring of 1864, but his wife long survived him, passing away in April, 1897. Both were buried in Union cemetery, Carroll county, where a monument marks their last resting place. Hiram is the fourth in order of birth in their family of twelve children six sons and six daughters, all of whom reached years of maturity, and five sons and five daughters are still living and are heads of families.

Hiram Woodin was a lad of nine years when he accompanied the family on their removal to Illinois. He attended the common schools to a limited extent, but is mostly self-educated. In the 50s he used to haul grain to Freeport, and selling the grain was paid in the paper money of those days. After holding a few weeks until he desired to spend it he would find it depreciated, often being worth no more than fifty cents on a dollar. Such was the circulating medium of those days. He remained with his father until his marriage, which was celebrated in Carroll county, March 28, 1864. Miss Sarah Ann Jenkins, becoming his wife. Her parents, Henry and Lucinda (Spencer) Jenkins, were natives of New York and Connecticut, respectively and were pioneers of Carroll county, Illinois, where Mrs. Woodin was reared and educated. Our subject and his wife have two children: Walter, who married Ardella Hurless and occupies the old home farm; and Fanny, wife of Frederick E. Becker, a farmer and stock feeder, of Eagle Point township. There is also one grandchild, Archie Woodin.

For one year after his marriage, Mr. Woodin continued to reside in Carroll coun-

HIRAM WOODIN.

MRS. HIRAM WOODIN.

ty, but in 1865 he became a resident of Eagle Point township, Ogle county, where he first purchased ninety acres. As time has passed and his financial resources have increased, he has added to his landed possessions from time to time until he now has three adjoining farms, aggregating nine hundred acres of valuable and productive land. He is to-day the largest land holder in the township and the success he has achieved is due entirely to his own industry, perseverance and sound judgment. Before his marriage he became interested in stock raising and had built up a large and profitable business in that line. He now feeds and ships on an average of eight or ten car loads of cattle annually and three or four car loads of hogs. His first shipment of stock was in 1865 and he arrived with the same in Chicago on the day President Lincoln was shot. As there were no stock yards at that time, he had to pile up ties to the car door and drive the hogs down such a platform to the street. This was accomplished with great difficulty and he then found hard work in disposing of his stock, as business was practically suspended on the announcement of the assassination. Mr. Woodin's son has been a partner in the stock business for the past twelve years and now has charge of most of the shipping.

At each presidential election since 1860 Mr. Woodin has supported the men and measures of the Republican party, but has never sought nor desired political honors. Ever a friend to our public schools, he most efficiently served as school director of his district for some years and has given his aid to every enterprise which he believed would prove of public benefit. In business affairs he is energetic, prompt and notably reliable, and through his own well directed efforts has worked his way upward to a position of affluence, so that he is now one of the most substantial citizens of his community.

HON. OGDEN B. YOUNGS, who was a leading and prominent citizen of Stillman Valley, resided in Ogle county for over sixty years, arriving here in October, 1838. The difference between the past and the present can scarcely be realized, even by those who were active participants in the development of the county. The present generation can have no conception of what was required by the early settlers in transforming the wilderness into a well settled and highly cultivated county.

Mr. Youngs, who for over half a century bore a most active and prominent part in the work of development, was born in Coyahoga county, Ohio, June 13, 1822, and was a son of Thomas A. Youngs, whose birth occurred in New Jersey, in 1790. The grandfather, Benjamin Youngs, was also a native of New Jersey, and was a representative of a family of English origin which was early established in that state. In 1807 or 1808, he removed to Canada, where his children were reared. During the war of 1812, the father, Thomas A. Youngs, decided he did not care to fight against his native land, and as to the British authorities in Canada were enlisting men for their army, he with other young men made their way to Detroit, where they were taken prisoners, being suspected as spies by the American army, but were soon released. They made their way round the lakes to Buffalo, New York, arriving in time for the battle of Lundy's Lane. When General Scott was wounded and brought to Buffalo,

Mr. Youngs assisted in carrying him to the hospital. Being a carpenter and joiner by trade, the father of our subject worked at those occupations in Buffalo for some time and later settled near Cleveland, Ohio, where he was similarly employed. In partnership with a Mr. Scoville, he erected the first sawmill in that region and engaged in the manufacture of lumber. Later he located on a farm three miles from Cleveland but still carried on operations as a contractor and builder for many years. In 1838, however, he brought his family to Illinois, driving across the country with two teams, drawing a wagon and carriage. They crossed the Chicago river on a ferry, as no bridges had then been built, and the city at that time contained a population of three thousand. Their destination was Ogle county where other Ohio families had settled, and on their arrival here the father bought claims to several hundred acres in Scott and Marion townships, entering the land some years later. Their first home was a log cabin to which he built an addition, also of logs, but it was afterward replaced by a good substantial frame residence, while barns and other outbuildings were also erected and a good farm developed from the wild land. In 1818, near Cleveland, Ohio, Thomas A. Youngs married Miss Lydia O'Brien, a native of Vermont, who, when a young girl, removed with her father, Benjamin O'Brien, to Ohio. The latter was a native of Ireland but when a child came to America, and served as sergeant in the war for independence. He often spoke with justifiable pride of seeing General Washington. Thomas A. Youngs served as captain in the Ohio State Militia, and after coming to Ogle county was justice of the peace for several years, and filled other positions of honor and trust in a most creditable and acceptable manner. He departed this life in May, 1871, at the ripe old age of eighty-one years.

Ogden B. Young was the second in order of birth in a family of eight children, four sons and four daughters, who reached years of maturity. George, the eldest, married and settled on a farm adjoining the old homestead, where he reared his family and died December, 1897. Mary and Ruth are still living on the old homestead. Sarah Jane is the widow of Rev. Cleveland and resides in California, as does also her sister, Lydia M. Thomas A. is a retired farmer of Rockford, Illinois. Captain John F. enlisted in 1861 in the Fifth Kansas Cavalry and served through the war. Later he settled on a cattle ranch in California but is now living in Arizona.

Mr. Youngs, whose name introduces this sketch, was sixteen years old when the family came to Ogle county. He had received good school privileges in Ohio, and also attended school here after the country became more thickly settled and the school more proficient. Being thus supplied with a fair education he engaged in teaching, and while visiting his father's family in Canada during the winter of 1844-45 taught school. After his return to Ogle county he had charge of the home school for one winter. He took a claim of one hundred and sixty acres in Scott and Marion townships, entered the land and developed a good farm. He erected a frame house upon his place in 1853, hauling the siding and finishing lumber for the same from Chicago. Here he made his home for some years while engaged in the arduous task of converting the wild land into rich and highly cultivated fields, but it was subsequently replaced by a more commodious and modern residence. Good barns and other outbuildings were also erected, making it one of the well improved farms of the locality. In the spring of 1893, he laid aside business cares and has since made his home in Stillman Valley, enjoying a well earned rest.

In Ogle county, July 19, 1853, Mr. Youngs was united in marriage with Miss Emma C. Norton, a native of New York, who was educated in that state and successfully engaged in teaching there and later in Illinois, having charge of the school in Mr. Youngs' district for a time. She is a daughter of Gould G. Norton and a sister of O. W. Norton, whose sketch appears elsewhere in this work. The children born to Mr. and Mrs. Youngs are as follows: Thomas G., who is now in Alaska, leaving his wife and two children in Spring Valley, Illinois; Henry J., who owns and operates a farm in Scott township, Ogle county; Mary, wife of Arthur Norton, who lives on a cattle ranch in Idaho, Bertha B., wife of Harry R. Smith, a farmer of Ogle county, Alice M., who died at the age of nineteen years, and two who died in infancy.

Originally Mr. Youngs was a Jackson Democrat in politics, casting his first vote for Franklin Pierce in 1852, since which time he has never missed a presidential election. He supported John C. Fremont in 1856, and was ever afterward an ardent Republican. He most capably filled the office of justice of the peace for a few terms, and in 1868 was elected to the state legislature, where he served with distinction on several important committees, including those on counties and agriculture. At intervals he served as supervisor of his township for several years, and has also been assessor, trustee and a member of the school board. His public and private life were alike above reproach, and he had the respect and esteem of all who knew him, while as an honored pioneer he certainly deserves prominent mention in this volume. After a residence here of more than three score years he was called to his reward. His estimable wife is one of the original members of the Stillman Valley Congregational church, and like her husband she has many friends throughout this section of the state.

HON. JAMES A. COUNTRYMAN, one of the representatives of the tenth senatorial district in the house of representatives of the state of Illinois, is one of the best known and highly honored of the citizens of Ogle county, of which he has been a resident for forty-four years. He was born in Herkimer county, New York, May 24, 1840, and was partly educated in the district schools of his native state. He came with his parents to Ogle county in 1885, the family locating in the township of Lynnville. After coming to the county he became a student in Rock River Seminary, at Mt. Morris, and attended that institution of learning for several terms.

Daniel Countryman, the father of our subject, was born in Starkville, Herkimer county, New York, March 31, 1815, and obtained his education in the primitive schools of the early day. He was married in his native county to Miss Sally Phillips, also a native of New York, and who was born in 1818. Six children were born to them, four of whom are yet living — James A., Calvin, Carrie E. and Jennie V. Of these, the first named is the subject of this sketch. Calvin is now in business in the city of Rockford. Carrie E. married

Benjamin F. Allen, and they had a son and daughter, Ada and Daniel. Jennie V. was united in marriage with Wesley M. Longenecker, of Rochelle, and one daughter was born to them, Grace E.

Daniel Countryman was a stock farmer by occupation, and in his life was quite successful. His whole life was spent in the discharge of duty. He was a member of the Lutheran church, but for many years he advocated with voice and pen church union of all evangelical denominations, and from his advocacy of this a very strong and flourishing union mission church, located at Lindenwood, is doing much good in that community. His generous spirit led him into constant deeds of charity, and it was fortunate for others that his ability and frugality gave him ample means to assist others. He lived in the enjoyment of the love and almost adoration of his family, the esteem of his friends, and with the respect of all that he ever met. He died as he had lived, with a benediction on his lips for all, and he left a large circle of sorrowing friends to mourn his loss. He died March 14, 1883, and his widow August 10, 1893. She was also well beloved by all who knew her, a true Christian woman, a loving mother, and steadfast friend and neighbor. The family, which is of German origin settled early in Herkimer county, New York, and there the grandfather of our subject, John I. Countryman, was born.

James A. Countryman was fifteen years old when he came to Ogle county. He remained at home assisting his father in farm work until after he had attained his majority. Farming has been his life work, and that he has made a success of it is attested by his well tilled fields and the excellent stock upon his premises. He was married, February 26, 1873, to Miss Carrie Klinkhart, an adopted daughter of Moses Countryman and wife. This union has been blessed with three sons and one daughter: Floyd M., born July 12, 1874; F. Belle, August 12, 1877; Ralph A., February 11, 1882; and Jay A., April 28, 1886.

Mr. Countryman owns the greater part of the original family homestead, on sections 20 and 21, consisting of eight hundred and eighty acres, which is under a fine state of cultivation. He is a general stock farmer, his specialties being thoroughbred shorthorn cattle, of which he annually fattens and prepares for the market a very large number of head, for which he secures the highest market price. He is also a breeder of the world-wide and justly celebrated Poland China hogs. His reputation in this line is very extensive, having made four shipments of the same to Germany. He has been for many years a breeder and exhibitor of pure bred stock, and has taken many first and sweepstake prizes at the American Fat Stock Show and leading fairs of the country. It is but natural that he should take great interest in this branch of his business.

Since first exercising the right of franchise Mr. Countryman has taken an active interest in political affairs, and has exercised a good influence in the party councils of his party, which, it is needless to say, is that of the Republican party. He has been repeatedly elected and filled responsible positions in his township, and the duties of every office held he has discharged in a faithful manner. He was first elected supervisor of the township of Lynnville in 1875 and re-elected in 1876, and again in 1883-4-5-6, then again in 1890, since which time he has served continuously in the office to the entire satisfaction of his constituents, a period of fifteen years. For two years he was chairman of the board. In the fall of 1898 he was elected one of the representatives of the tenth senatorial district to the Forty-first general assembly of the state of Illinois, and took his seat in that distinguished body January 4, 1899. He is now chairman of the committee on state institutions, and is a member of the following named committees: Agriculture, appropriations, county and township organizations, farm drainage, horticulture, roads and bridges, and state and municipal indebtedness. In the legislation of the house he has taken an active part, and has made an influential member, one whose presence is felt. The life of such a man is well worthy of record, and is certainly an incentive to the young to do well his part, that in time they, too, may receive due honor.

AUGUST KANEY.—Among the enterprising citizens of Forreston township, there is none more energetic or thoroughgoing than the gentleman whose name heads this sketch. His home is on section 18, where he owns a valuable and well improved farm of one hundred and eighty acres, four miles from the village of Forreston, and is successfully engaged in both general farming and stock raising.

Mr. Kaney was born in Maryland township, July 12, 1856, and is a son of Henry Kaney, who was born in Lude, Prussia, March 9, 1817. The father of Henry died when his son was of tender age. In the common schools of his country he obtained his education, attending the same until he was fourteen years old. He then learned the blacksmith trade, and had but completed his term of service when he was forced to serve in the Prussian army for three years. Receiving an honorable discharge from the army, he again took up his trade, at which he continued to work in his native country for some years, when he decided on coming to the United States. In May, 1845, after a six weeks' voyage, he landed at Baltimore, Maryland, from which place, some time during the year, he made his way to Shepardstown, Virginia, where he again worked at his trade, often carrying the iron that he used from Harper's Ferry on his back.

While yet residing in Shepardstown, he was united in marriage, August 29, 1845, with Miss Elizabeth Fosh, who was born in Saben Hausen, Germany, May 17, 1817. The following year they started west in a one-horse wagon, driving to Dayton, Ohio. Thence they proceeded down the Ohio river on a flat boat to Cairo, and by steamer up the Mississippi and Illinois rivers to Peru, and from there drove across the country to Ogle county, joining some German friends in Maryland township. Leaving his family there Mr. Kaney worked in a plow shop at Grand Detour, and a year or two later bought a tract of eighty acres in Maryland township, on which he built a shop of his own and engaged in blacksmithing in connection with the development and cultivation of his farm, but finally gave his entire time to agriculture. In 1861 he bought the farm on which our subject now resides—a place of one hundred and sixty acres, then but slightly improved. He converted the tract into a nice farm, and subsequently bought one hundred and sixty acres across the road, and still later a tract of similar size in the same township. He came to this state empty-handed, and it has been through his own industry, enterprise, perseverance and economy that he is now one of the most substantial, as well as one of the honored and highly respected citizens of Forreston township. He and his wife celebrated their golden wedding August 29, 1895, at which time their children, grandchildren, and great-grandchildren gathered at their home to rejoice with them. Since then he has been called upon to mourn the loss of his estimable wife, who passed away October 10, 1897. To them were born four sons and two daughters, all of whom married and became heads of families: Henry is now deceased; John is a merchant and business man of Forreston; Lewis is a farmer of Forreston township; August is the subject of this sketch; Elizabeth is the wife of August Kilker, a farmer of Maryland township; and Anna M. is the wife of William M. Richter, a merchant of Forreston.

August Kaney was educated in the district schools near his boyhood home, and as soon as he was large enough to be of any assistance he commenced to aid in the farm work, first driving a team used in breaking prairie. His early life was passed under the parental roof, and after arriving at man's estate continued to assist in the operation of the home farm. In Mt. Morris township, he was married March 6, 1879, to Miss Elizabeth Zumdahl, who was born and reared on a farm in Lincoln township, Ogle county, a daughter of Christian Zumdahl. They began their domestic life on the old homestead, and since taking charge of the same Mr. Kaney has built a large neat barn, good granary and outbuildings, and now has one of the best improved places of the locality. He is engaged in breeding and raising a good grade of Durham and short horn cattle and Poland China hogs, and in this branch of his business has also met with success.

Mr. and Mrs. Kaney have four children: August J., Irvin E., Elizabeth D. and Arthur E. all attending the home school, and have lost three: Edward, who died at the age of four years; and Ezra and Sylvia, who both died at the age of two. The parents are active and prominent members of the Evangelical church at North Grove, both have been teachers in the Sabbath school, while Mr. Kaney has served as its superintendent three years and is one of the officers of the church. Formerly he was identified with the Democratic party and voted for Grover Cleveland, but is now a Republican. He is a stockholder and director of the Forreston Mutual Fire Insurance Company and gives his support to all enterprises which he believes calculated to advance the moral, intellectual or material welfare of his township and county.

AMERICUS L. MENDENHALL, M. D., who is engaged in the practice of his profession at Kings, Ogle county, Illinois, was born in Winchester, Ohio, May 21, 1846, and is a son of Dr. Elijah and Mary Angeline (Graves) Mendenhall, the former who was a son of John Mendenhall, being a native of Preble county, Ohio, born January 20, 1816. He was reared and educated in Ohio, and was a graduate of the Ohio Medical College, of Cincinnati. He began practice at Somerville, Ohio, and there remained five years, moving from that place to Winchester, in the same state, and later to Cincinnati, where he remained in active practice until 1872, when he moved to Indianapolis, Indiana, which was his home until his death, November 5, 1897. His wife died two days later, and the two were buried in one coffin, their remains being interred in Oakwood cemetery, Indianapolis. He was recognized as one of the ablest physicians in that city, and one of the best diagnosticians in the profession. A Republican in politics, he gave but little time to political matters, his professional duties requiring his entire time. In his family were four sons: Alonzo, born August 6, 1843, is a practicing physician of Cicero, Indiana. Rev. James W., born November 8, 1844, was a clergyman in the Methodist Episcopal church, and for the four years preceding his death, which occurred June 18, 1892, was editor of the Methodist Review, a position to which he was appointed by the general conference. He had just begun his second term of four years when removed by death. Americus L., our subject, was next in order of birth. Dr. Winfield S., born February 10, 1848, died January 25, 1899. He was for many years a practicing physician of Springfield, Illinois. He was a graduate of Miami Medical College, Cincinnati, Ohio.

The subject of this sketch spent his boyhood and youth in Cincinnati, Ohio. From 1860 to 1864 he was a student in the Wesleyan University, Delaware, Ohio. On the 12th of February, of the latter year, he left school and enlisted in Company F, One Hundred and Eighty-third regiment, Ohio Volunteer Infantry, under command of Colonel Hoge, his company being commanded by Captain Thornton. The regiment was attached to the third brigade, second division, twenty-fifth army corps, of the Army of the Cumberland. With his regiment he took part in the engagements at Franklin and Nashville, Tennessee, and Wilmington, North Carolina, and also in several minor engagements. He enlisted for one year, but served until the close of the war, being mustered out of the service at Camp Denison, Ohio, May 29, 1865.

On returning home our subject entered the Richmond Commercial College, at Richmond, Indiana, from which he was graduated in 1866. He then took a position as bookeeper with the wholesale house of John Shilito, of Cincinnati, one of the largest establishments of its kind in the west. He remained with that house one year, but was not able to endure the confinement, and so resigned his position and entered the Miami Medical College, of Cincinnati, from which he graduated March 2, 1869, in the same class with his brother Winfield. Receiving his diploma, he commenced the practice of his profession at Granville, Indiana, in the fall of 1869, and there remained three years. In 1872 he came to Illinois, locating at Kappa, Woodford county, where he built up an excellent practice, and there remained until 1890, when, on account of failing health of his wife, he removed to Smithfield, Nebraska. He remained in that place until the fall of 1893 when he removed to Kings, which has since been his home, and where he has also built up a good general practice.

Dr. Mendenhall was married at Muncie, Indiana, November 30, 1870, to Miss Louisa Smith, a native of that city, and daughter of William M. and Phoebe Smith, both of whom were natives of Ohio. She died October 12, 1891, leaving four sons: Wilbar, of DesMoines, Iowa; Roscoe, a student of the law school of DesMoines, Iowa; Adelbert, a medical student of the DesMoines Medical College, and Walter, a student of the high school of DesMoines.

The Doctor was again married, June 27, 1895, to Miss Alice Green, of San Diego, California, and daughter of Miner P. Green. She was born in Reedsburg, Wisconsin, but her father was a native of New York.

Dr. Mendenhall is a member of the Illinois State Medical Society, and is also a member and one of the founders of the North Central Illinois Medical Association, of which he was for some years president. During his residence at Kappa, he was a member of the Woodford County Medical Association. A student of his profession, he has been an occasional contributor to various medical journals. Fraternally he is a Mason, and has attained the Chapter degree. He is also a member of the Modern Woodmen of America, of which he has served as physician. In politics he is a Republican, but he does not give much of his time to political affairs, the practice of his profession being more to his taste. In the comparatively short time that he has been a resident of Ogle county he has made many friends, and has the confidence not only of the community where he resides, but of the medical profession of the county.

HENRY SHARER, now living a retired life in Mt Morris, is one among the living pioneers of Ogle county, who has witnessed its growth and development from a wilderness to one of the best counties in the great state of Illinois. He has not only been a witness of the same, but was actively engaged in the great work of transformation, giving many of the best years of his life to the work. His first visit to the state was when he was a youth of seventeen years. At that time he traversed a goodly portion of the state, but did not locate.

Like many others of the best citizens of Ogle county, Mr. Sharer is a native of Washington county, Maryland, born March 29, 1817. He is the son of John and Anna (Newcomer) Sharer, the former a native of Lancaster county, Pennsylvania, and the latter of Washington county, Maryland. They were the parents of three children. Jacob, born in 1807, married and had two children. He came to Ogle county at an early day and died at the age of fifty-six years. Eliza, born in 1809, married Nathaniel Swingley, and to them were born eight children. They were also among the pioneers of Ogle county. Both are now deceased, Eliza dying when about sixty-eight years old. The third child was the subject of this sketch. The mother died in her native county when fifty-six years old. In 1855, after the death of his wife, the father came to Ogle county where his last days were spent, dying at the residence of our subject at the age of seventy-seven years. While residing in Maryland he engaged in milling and farming, but after coming to Ogle county he lived a retired life. John Sharer was the son of Jacob Sharer, a native of Germany, who emigrated to America when in his prime, locating in Lancaster county. Eliza (Newcomer) Sharer's ancestors were from Switzerland, the first of the name emigrating here at an early day.

In his native state Henry Sharer grew to manhood. After receiving his primary education in the common schools of his day, at the age of fifteen he entered St. Mary's College, which was located just north of Frederick City, Maryland, where he remained three years. The college at that time was under the management of Bishop Purcell, the noted Catholic divine, one of the best posted and most popular men in the Catho-

HENRY SHARER.

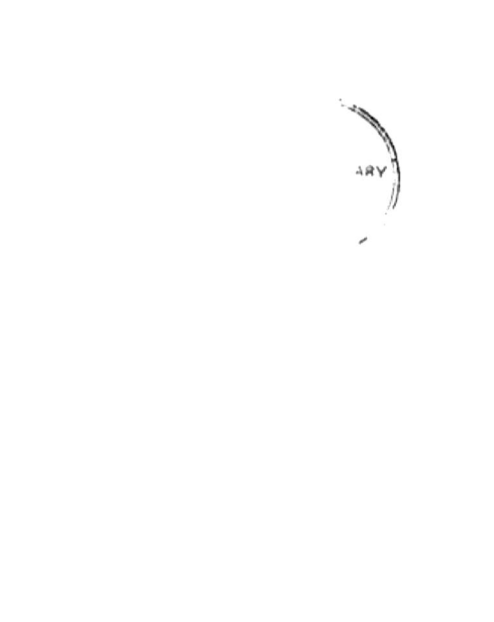

lic church. Leaving St. Mary's College, he went to Jefferson College, located near Canonsburg, Pennsylvania, an institution under control of the Presbyterian church and presided over by President Brown.

After remaining in Jefferson College one year Mr. Sharer returned home at the age of nineteen years, and was variously employed until his removal to Ogle county in 1839. On the 8th of September, that year, he left his old home to seek his fortune in the new and growing west. In company with Jacob Rice and his sister, Mrs. Eliza Swingley, who had been in the west but had returned, they started for Illinois in a double-seated carryall. They passed through the states of Virginia, Ohio and Indiana, arriving in Ogle county in October, being about four weeks on the road. At the time of their arrival the country was very sparsely settled and very little of the virgin soil had been upturned by the plow. The previous year our subject's father came to the county on a visit and had entered a half section of land which was occupied by our subject, and which he purchased in his own name, when the land came into market at the regular price of one dollar and twenty-five cents per acre.

On taking possession of the land entered by his father, Mr. Sharer at once commenced its improvement. About twenty acres had been broken, a portion of which was enclosed by a sod fence. Erecting a log cabin about fifteen feet square, he lived in that while making improvements on the place. That cabin was replaced a few years later by a house of hewed logs.

In 1842, in company with Elias Snively, Mr. Sharer purchased an isolated grove in the eastern part of the county, in what is now Creston township, to which he removed. A log cabin had been erected on the place which for some years was used as a tavern. At the time he moved to his new location, his nearest neighbor was seven and a half miles away, but his cabin being on the main thoroughfare, and no house on the route nearer than twelve miles, it became almost a necessity that it should be thrown open for the accommodation of the traveling public and seekers of a new home. The house was on the stage line between Galena and Chicago. In its construction not a nail had been used; the roof, which was made of clapboards, being held in place by means of long poles weighted at each end. While living in this grove, which was called Brodies' grove, in honor of a former owner, he had several peculiar experiences. Brodie was a brother-in-law of the notorious Driscoll, and was probably not one whit better, having the reputation of being a notorious horse thief, and having to flee the country to escape a like fate that befell the Driscolls. It was at Mr. Sharer's tavern that the Driscolls, father and son, ate their last dinner, being captured, taken to Oregon, and shot the next morning at Washington Grove.

For some years the nearest market was Chicago, and to that village, as it then was, Mr. Sharer hauled his grain, and for his first frame house hauled the lumber from that place. At the time he settled in Ogle county there were but ten or twelve houses in Oregon, and Grand Detour and Oregon were the only two villages in the county. The change that has since been made is truly wonderful.

On the 6th of November, 1845, Mr. Sharer was united in marriage with Miss Cornelia Motter, a native of Washington county, Maryland, born September 21, 1823.

She was the daughter of Jacob Motter, also a native of the same county and state. By this union five children were born: Morton N., born August 16, 1846, died October 10, 1846. John Jacob, born November 28, 1847, is married and has three children. He is living in Mexico. Anna E., born September 10, 1849, married John Swingley, and to them three children were born. They are living in Mt. Morris township, where he is engaged in farming. Luella M., born August 11, 1851, married Wentworth Wheeler, and they reside in Kansas City, Missouri, where he is engaged in the mercantile business. They have one child, Anna M. Cornelia M., born September 19, 1853, died in infancy. Three days after the birth of the last named Mrs. Sharer gave up her life, her death being mourned by a large circle of friends and relatives.

On the 26th of January, 1858, Mr. Sharer married Mrs. Sarah A. (Felker) Hewitt, widow of Theodore Hewitt. She was born in Washington county, Maryland, August 11, 1832, and is the daughter of Abraham and Catherine (Wingert) Felker, both being of German descent. They came to Ogle county in 1855. By this last union one child was born, Charles H., a graduate of Northwestern University, who married Miss Susannah McCosh, a native of Pennsylvania. They have four children, Charles Wentworth, David Max, Sarah Elizabeth and Ruth. He is engaged in the grocery business in Mt. Morris.

In politics Mr. Sharer is a Democrat, the principles of which party he has advocated his entire life. While living in a Republican community, he has yet been honored by his fellow-citizens with a number of local offices. He was a member of the town board eight years, was school director for five or six years and was postmaster of Mt. Morris for four years under Cleveland. Fraternally, he is a Mason, holding membership with Mt. Morris Lodge, No. 96, A. F. & A. M. His wife, who was a member of the Methodist Episcopal church, died June 6, 1892. Well known and highly esteemed, everybody has a good word for Henry Sharer, the pioneer.

ELDER ISAAC TRUMP, a well known minister of the German Baptist church, known as the Brethren in Christ, now in charge of the Chicago district of that body, has been a resident of Ogle county a period of thirty-six years. He was born near Canton, Stark county, Ohio, May 1, 1830. His father, George J. Trump, was a native of Ohio, born in 1807, and was the son of John Trump, a native of Pennsylvania, but of English parentage. In a very early day John Trump moved to Ohio, and located in Stark county, being among its very earliest settlers. He located in the dense forest, erected his cabin and commenced clearing off the timber in order to cultivate the soil. At that time Indians were still very numerous in the vicinity.

On the old homestead of his father, George J. Trump grew to manhood, receiving a limited education in the pioneer schools. In Stark county, Ohio, he married Miss Rachel Weaver, a native of Ohio, and daughter of Valentine Weaver, who moved from Hagerstown, Maryland, to Ohio in an early day. By this union there were three sons and three daughters: Isaac, the subject of this sketch, William, a farmer of Stark county, Ohio; Mrs. Sarah Gibbs, a widow, residing in Ohio; Lyda, wife of Daniel Smith, of Stark county, Ohio; and Levina, wife of John Barnett, of the same county and state.

George J. Trump was a farmer and manufacturer of lumber, having on his farm a saw mill, from which he supplied much of the lumber that was used in the city of Canton in the early days. From that same mill he furnished considerable lumber to the Pennsylvania Central railroad when it was being constructed. He was an active, enterprising and successful business man, and was well known throughout northern Ohio. His entire life was spent in his native county, where his death occurred February 5, 1881. His wife survived him some years, passing away in January, 1896.

The subject of this sketch spent his boyhood and youth in his native county and in the home of his parents, with whom he remained until after he attained his majority. His educational advantages were quite meager, but he received a good business training in his father's lumber office and in the mill. Referring to his early life and experience, Elder Trump thus writes:

"In 1838, father purchased the Rohrer farm, two miles east of Canton, and on the place was a sawmill on the stream called Hunishding, with power to run the mill during the year. At that place I spent many happy days, the cares of life being but few. I worked on the farm during the summer, and during the winter was obliged to ride the horses over the grain in the old log barn or stable. This or the flail, was the only way we had to thresh our grain. When this was done and there was nothing else to do I had the blessed privilege of going through the dense forest to a little log shanty, called a school house, with a few windows, slabs for benches, wooden pins in the logs with boards laid on them for promoted scholars to scribble on, and teachers that would rank in the third or fourth degree. The first morning of their appearance was a scare to the children, as they came with a handful of gads. This was called the gad system. Then the result, if the mind did not work, as they called it, they would mark the back. Thus it would continue for two or three months.

"In 1845, I was obliged to leave the farm and help in the mill, and there spent many a long day, and often until two o'clock at night, when father would take charge until six o'clock in the morning, when it was my turn again. It was as natural for me when in a dangerous place to call on the Lord to help as to eat when I was hungry. This was about the experience of all on this line. At said time a brother, named George, four years old, was drowned near the mill, on a beautiful Sunday evening. Oh, how sad! We did not miss him until the evening meal, when every seat at the table was occupied but the "high-backed chair." Today, when I see an empty chair, I think of that solemn event. In 1844, my parents sent me to the German Reformed church to catechise, as they called it. After going once a week for five or six weeks, I was sprinkled, or baptized as they called it. By thus doing I was received into the church, but am sorry to say had no salvation until I repented and was truly and hopefully converted to God. I was then baptized by immersion. This is salvation, and when thus saved we know it."

Elder Trump was married in Stark county, Ohio, March 27, 1854, to Miss Elizabeth Bowers, a native of Blair county, Pennsylvania, by which union there were four children: Jeremiah W., a farmer of Buffalo township, Henry, a minister of the

German Baptist, or Brethren, church, residing in Buffalo township; Isaac B., who resides near Jackson, Tennessee, and Irvine, who carries on the old home farm in Pine Creek township.

After his marriage, Mr. Trump purchased a forty-acre tract of land in the timber, on which was a log cabin and a steam sawmill. He at once commenced clearing the land, and the same season erected a good residence, at the same time operating the sawmill. For the next eight years he did the work of two men at the mill, while still carrying on his farm. He then sold the land, but retained the mill, purchasing another farm in the vicinity, which he cultivated some two or three years, in connection with his milling business. He then sold the mill, but retained the farm six years longer, engaging exclusively in agricultural pursuits.

In 1863 Mr. Trump sold his farm in Ohio and came to Illinois, arriving in Dixon April 7 of that year. He did not remain there, however, but purchased a farm in Pine Creek township, Ogle county, known as the Brubaker farm, where he actively engaged in farming for twenty years. He then moved to Polo, where he purchased ten acres of land and built the residence where he now resides. While yet residing on the farm, his wife died March 13, 1876, and was laid to rest in the cemetery at Polo. She was a noble woman, well beloved by all who knew her, a member of the German Baptist, known as Brethren in Christ, church, and died in the assurance of faith. The Elder, in speaking of this wife, said: "In the fall of 1855 she was truly and hopefully converted to God, which was an event in the history of my life that I shall never forget. It was the loudest call that ever came to me. I do not think anything less could have moved me to think how poor and needy I was, with all my churchisms. Her Christian life was a constant sermon to me. What a blessing it would be if every home had Christian parents. It would truly be heaven on earth begun."

Some three years after the death of his first wife, in Albany, Whiteside county, Illinois, December 22, 1879, Mr. Trump was united in marriage with Mrs. Mary Winger, a widow, and daughter of Abraham Zook, an early settler of Whiteside county, where, a child of eleven years, Mrs. Trump was taken, and where she grew to womanhood, receiving her education in the public schools. She there married John G. Winger, a native of Pennsylvania and a carpenter by trade. After their marriage they located at Shannon, Illinois, where his death occurred October 16, 1870. By her marriage with Mr. Trump she is the mother of one son, Clayton E., who is yet residing at home.

Elder Trump was converted when about thirty years old, uniting with the German Baptist church, having faith in the apostolic teachings of that body. He soon after became an active worker in the church, and was ordained a deacon, serving in that office seven or eight years. He was then elected to the ministry, second degree, and served in that capacity about ten years, being then promoted to the eldership, or bishopric, which is the third degree. While still actively engaged on his farm, he traveled much in the interest of the church, devoting about one-half his time to ministerial labors. Since removing to Polo he has devoted the whole of his time to the work of the church, proclaiming the unsearchable riches of Christ, and teaching the simplicity of His gospel. He is one of the best known among the Brethren, having visited churches in Illinois, Indiana, Iowa, Nebraska, Kansas, Missouri, Pennsylvania, Michigan and Canada. His friends are many wherever known, and his highest aim is to do his Master's will faithfully and well.

GEORGE H. SHARLAND.— Honored and respected by all, there is no man in Ogle county who occupies a more enviable position in business circles than Mr. Sharland, the well-known dealer in granite and marble monuments at Rochelle, not alone on account of the brilliant success he has achieved, but also on account of the honorable, straightforward business policy he has ever followed. He possesses untiring energy, is quick of perception, forms his plans readily and is determined in their execution; and his close application to business and excellent management have brought to him the high degree of prosperity which is to-day his.

Mr. Sharland was born June 14, 1854, in Torquay, Devonshire, England, a son of George and Sarah (Shapley) Sharland. He is the oldest of their three children, the others being Ellen, wife of Emil Hemmer, of Chicago; and Charles, who is engaged in the nickle-plating business in Denver, Colorado. The father died in 1866 and the mother subsequently married R. E. Edgcombe, who died in Denver, where she now makes her home. Our subject's paternal grandfather, John Sharland, was also engaged in the marble and granite business in Torquay, England, for fity-four years, and was then succeeded by our subject's father, who continued operations there until his death in 1866. The business was carried on by the family for the following two years, and after the mother's second marriage, her husband had charge of the same for one year. In 1870 the family emigrated to America and located in Brantford, Ontario, Canada.

During his boyhood George H. Sharland commenced learning marble cutting with his father and in 1871 went to Chicago, where he completed his apprenticeship. As business was dull along his line during the panic of 1873, he left the city and went to Sycamore, Illinois, where he worked at his trade with N. Latten for two years, at the end of which time he came to Rochelle. On the 10th of March, 1875, in company with his stepfather, he established his present business. The partnership only existed a little over a year and since then Mr. Sharland had been alone in business. From a humble beginning the business has increased until it is now the largest of the kind in northern Illinois outside of Chicago, and he has probably erected more fine and costly monuments than any one in the business outside of the large cities of the state. He understands thoroughly every detail of the business, is a practical mechanic himself, and much of his success is due to his careful methods of filling orders. His trade is not merely local, but he has received orders from distant points as far west as Nebraska and Los Angeles, California, and his present business amounts to about thirteen thousand dollars annually. The monuments manufactured by him compare favorably in superior workmanship and artistic skill with those produced by any establishment of the kind in the west. All the work in his shop is done under his personal supervision, and his productions prove him to be not only a skilled mechanic but an artist and sculptor of undoubted talent. Having business relations with the largest and leading quarries of United States and Europe, he has facilities for securing the best materials at a minimum price and these advantages he shares with his patrons.

On the 24th of November, 1877, Mr. Sharland was united in marriage with Mrs. Mary (Burton) Stringfellow, widow of Clark Stringfellow. She was born in Pittsburg, Pennsylvania, and by her former marriage had three children, one of whom, Dollie, died in childhood. She others made their home with our subject until their marriage. They are Nettie, now the wife of Horace E. Carr, who is engaged in the job printing business in Cleveland, Ohio; and James P., superintendent of the Union Central Telephone Company, of Fremont, Ohio. Two children were born to our subject and his wife, but both died in infancy. Politically Mr. Sharland has always been a supporter of the Democratic party, but aside from voting takes no active part in political affairs, preferring to give his entire time and attention to his business interests.

CHARLES B. NOBLE, now living a retired life on his pleasant farm, on section 8, Buffalo township, and which is within one and one half miles of the corporate limits of Polo, and known as the Winters farm, is an almost life-long resident of the county. He was born in Winnebago county, Illinois, December 5, 1838, and is the son of Daniel Noble, a native of Williamstown, Massachusetts, born in 1815. The family are of English origin, and was among the pioneers of that state. Daniel Noble was a graduate of Williamstown College. In 1835 he came to Illinois and located in Jo Daviess county, and was therefore numbered among its pioneers. He was married in Ogle county, November 2, 1837, to Miss Sarah B. Waterbury, a native of New York, and daughter of John and Phoebe Waterbury, also natives of the Empire state, but who were pioneers of Ogle county, locating at Eagle Springs in 1836. Soon after their marriage, Daniel Noble and his wife moved to Winnebago county, where his death occurred in March, 1839. After his death, Mrs. Noble returned to the home of her father, where she remained until her marriage, February 30, 1845, with George D. Dement. By this second marriage she became the mother of four sons and three daughters. John E. and Daniel W. are deceased. Wallace E. resides in the state of Washington. Mrs. Phoebe Buno and Mrs. Louisa Dallam reside in Denver, Colorado. Helen E. makes her home with our subject, with whom she has spent the greater part of her life. Frank L. resides in Alaska. Mr. Dement died in 1863, and Mrs. Dement then made her home with her eldest son, Mr. Noble, until she, too, was called to rest, July 15, 1893.

Charles B. Noble was the only child of his parents. After the death of his father he was taken and reared by his grandfather Waterbury, with whom he remained until he was sixteen years old. His education was received in the school at Eagle Springs, and well does he remember one morning when about ten years old, in going to school across the prairie, and when within one-half mile from his home, in a hazel thicket, a prairie wolf confronted him and wanted the first claim to the nice, crisp doughnuts in his dinner bag. The small boy had no notion of going dinnerless and stood his ground until Mr. Wolf sneaked off into the brush again. Keeping a sharp look behind, the boy lost no time in reaching the school house. In those days prairie wolves frequently invaded the farms of the settlers.

When sixteen years of age, Mr. Noble, in earnest, commenced life for himself, purchasing at that time three yoke of oxen on time, and giving his personal note in payment. He commenced breaking prairie in Whiteside county, under contract, making his home with his mother. The first season he broke one hundred acres of land and made three hundred dollars. From the proceeds he paid for his team and plows, and then followed breaking for two more seasons. In that time he turned over about three hundred acres of the virgin soil, at times using as many as seven yoke of oxen to the plow. Often his plow would stick so tight in the red roots and "devil's shoe strings" that he had to take two yoke of oxen and hitch them to the back of the plow to haul it out. With the prairie grass knee-deep and wet with dew until about eleven o'clock each day, did not make the work a pleasant one.

Renting a farm in what is now Eagle Point township, he commenced farming, and in 1860 had a crop of about sixty acres. In the spring of 1861 he put in a crop and harvested the small grain. The war for the union was now in progress and men were in demand. In response to the call of the president, on the 5th of September, 1861, he enlisted in Company B, Seventh Illinois Volunteer Cavalry, at the same time furnishing to the government two horses, one of which he used himself and the other by a comrade. With his regiment he joined the Army of the Tennessee, and was soon afterwards detailed as one of the body guard for General Rosencrans. Just before the battle of Iuka, while on detailed duty, he was injured somewhat, and fever setting in he was taken to the field hospital, and a short time afterwards was moved north to the hospital at St. Louis, Missouri. As soon as strong enough, he was detailed as warden, and also for a time was acting steward.

In 1863 he was transferred to the Veteran Reserve Corps and sent to Columbus, Ohio, and from there to Camp Douglas, Chicago, to guard prisoners. He remained at the latter place until February, 1864, when he was ordered to Washington City, and there put with the troops in defense of the city, participating in the battle on the outskirts of the city, near Forts Stevens and DeRussey. Our army succeeded in driving the enemy back, thus saving the capital. While with that corps, he served a part of the time as drummer. After three years of faithful service, he was mustered out September 5, 1864.

Returning home after receiving his discharge, he purchased one hundred and twenty acres of the old Waterbury homestead and again engaged in farming. He purchased the place on time, and after a number of years paid off the obligation, but it was after a long and hard struggle. He later added many improvements to the place and there continued to reside until 1876, when he sold and purchased his present farm, a place of two hundred and eighty acres. A part of the purchase price of this farm he secured time on, but has been so fortunate as to pay off the entire claim, and in addition has made some substantial improvements.

Mr. Noble was married in Ogle county, November 8, 1865, to Miss Phebe Roberts, who was born in Whiteside county, Illinois, February 15, 1842, but was reared in Ogle county. She is a daughter of Orrin and Julia A. (Osterhoudt) Roberts. By this union there are ten children—Jesse D., Addie J., Ella S., Harriet W., Esther H., Lena M., Ruth A., Olive K., Stella B., and John Calvin. The latter died when but four years old. The first named is living in a neat, substantial dwelling built by his father near the family residence, and is now carrying on the home farm.

Politically Mr. Noble is a Republican. His grandfather Waterbury was an Abolitionist, and kept a station on the underground railroad, and his views on the "peculiar institution" he instilled into the mind of his grandson, and the lessons thus early learned were never forgotten. While averse to office holding, he yet served some years on the school board. With one exception, Mr. Noble and family are members of the Polo Presbyterian church, and endeavor to walk in the footsteps of the Master.

Mr. Noble is a natural mechanic, and for a time was employed as a traveling salesman, and in repairing and setting up threshing machines, being with the J. I. Case Company. For about eighteen years he ran both horse and steam rigs, and made a success of it. He also operates one of the largest sorghum plants in northern Illinois, and by extensive experimenting and closely observing the results, he is now manufacturing a very fine quality of syrup. In the past few years he has manufactured over thirty-five thousand gallons of superior syrup. Notwithstanding that he has engaged in these outside lines, Mr. Noble has never neglected his farming. He believes in the thorough cultivation of the soil, and that the farmer should give general attention to stock raising, using as far as possible on the farm all grain that he raises. On account of failing health, however, for the past twelve years he has practically lived a retired life.

JOHN A. McCREA, who is now living a retired life, was for years one of the most enterprising of the business men of Ogle county, of which he has been a resident since 1865. He is a native of Orange county, New York, born under the shadows of the Catskill mountains, September 5, 1827, and is the son of William and Abigail McCrea, the father being a native of Ireland but of Scotch parentage. Soon after his marriage William McCrea with his young wife came to the United States and located in Orange county, New York, where he engaged in farming. He later moved to Monroe county, in the same state, where he remained a number of years, or until he joined his children in Ogle county. The last years of his life were spent in Creston, where his death occurred April 4, 1888.

William and Abigail McCrea were the parents of ten children, all of whom grew to mature years, and of which number three sons and four daughters are yet living. Abraham settled in Malta, Illinois, where he engaged in business, but is now deceased. Samuel H. located at Morrison, Whiteside county, Illinois, where he engaged in the grain and lumber business. He later removed to Chicago and became one of the leading citizens of that city. He served four years as treasurer of Cook county, and was president of the board of trade for some years. He also held other positions of honor and trust in that city, where his death occurred in 1895. John A., the sub-

JOHN A. McCREA.

ject of this review, is next in order of birth. Leander located in Carroll county, Iowa, where he resided some years, then moved to Carroll county, Missouri, where he is now living. Alfred B. resides in Creston, and a sketch of him appears on another page of this work. Mrs. Catherine Covey is a widow residing in Sterling, Illinois. Mrs. Jane Parsons is a widow residing in Carroll, Iowa, with a son. Mrs. Maria Kittle is a widow, residing in New Lisbon, Wisconsin. Caroline is making her home with our subject.

John A. McCrea grew to manhood in Monroe county, New York, and received a good education in the schools of Rochester, New York. Attracted by the discovery of gold in California, in 1849, he set out for the new Eldorado. He went by way of the Isthmus of Panama, taking the steamer Empire City at New York, for Chagres, and after crossing the isthmus took the steamer Oregon for San Francisco, arriving in that city in November, 1849. During the first winter he engaged in running a boat across the bay, but in the spring of 1850 went to the mines in search of the yellow metal. He continued mining for two and a half years with very good success, and then returned home by the Nicaragua route through Central America. In due time he arrived at his old home in Rochester, New York, where he remained until 1854, when he came west to Branch county, Michigan, and located near Coldwater, where he engaged in farming for ten years. Selling his farm, he went to Morrison, Whiteside county, Illinois, to learn the grain and lumber business. In 1865 he moved to Creston, Ogle county, and formed a partnership with his brother Alfred B., and here engaged in the grain, lumber and coal business. They commenced in a small way, but later built an elevator and for many years continued together, doing a thriving business, amounting from two hundred thousand to five hundred thousand dollars per year. The partnership continued until 1892, when our subject withdrew, and has since practically been living a retired life. He has invested some in real estate and has two good farms near the village of Creston aggregating four hundred and fifty acres. While yet in partnership the brothers formed a stock company and started a tile factory. They built up a large trade, selling their products for miles around.

Mr. McCrea was married in Linnville, Illinois, in 1870, to Miss Clara E. Bird, a native of Ohio, and daughter of William Bird, now deceased. She is a well educated lady, and previous to her marriage engaged in teaching. By this union two daughters were born, Ella B. and Florence E., both living at home.

In 1892 Mr. McCrea went to California to look after some mining interests in which he and his brother were interested. He returned again in 1893 and spent the greater part of that year in the mines. He has now in his possession some fine specimens of gold, which he took himself from the mines. He has made several trips to the Pacific slope, and has spent two winters in California since retiring from business. In 1896 he visited Havana, Cuba, where he spent a short time, and during the same trip visited Galveston and New Orleans, crossed the Rio Grande at El Paso into Mexico, and on to southern California. He takes considerable pleasure in traveling, and manages to pick up a great deal of information.

Mrs. McCrea is a worthy member of the

Methodist church, and while Mr. McCrea is not a member, he attends the church with his wife and contributes of his means to its support. Fraternally he is a Mason, holding membership with the blue lodge at Creston, the chapter and commandery at Sycamore, and Medinah Temple, Scottish rite, of Chicago. He is well known in Ogle and adjoining counties, having been a resident of this county for thirty-four years, a little more than a third of a century. His friends are many, and they may be found from the Atlantic to the Pacific ocean. With the sturdy self-reliance of the Scotch race he has made a success in life.

IRA METTLER, now living a retired life in the village of Creston, has been a resident of the state of Illinois since 1840. He was born in Northumberland county, Pennsylvania, October 27, 1817, and is the son of Relph Mettler, a native of New Jersey, born October 11, 1792, and a grandson of Henry Mettler, also a native of New Jersey, and who was one of a family of fifteen children. On the father's side the family are of German descent, but on the mother's side of English descent.

Relph Mettler, who was a blacksmith by trade, grew to manhood in New Jersey, but when a young man moved to Northumberland county, Pennsylvania, where he married Mary Ann Housewert, a native of Pennsylvania, and daughter of Solomon Housewert, of German descent. They became the parents of nine children who grew to mature years, seven of whom are yet living. Mrs. Elizabeth Barnum, a widow, resides in Creston. Ira, of this review, is next in order of birth. Sarah is deceased. Mrs. Rhoda Dudley resides in Cayuga county, New York. Mrs. Fidelia Miller is a widow residing in St. Louis, Missouri. Mrs. Harriet M. Powell is a widow residing in College Springs, Iowa. Mary Ann grew to womanhood, but is now deceased. William J. resides in Creston, Illinois, and James Iliff lives in Great Falls, Montana.

Relph Mettler carried on his trade a few years in Northumberland county, Pennsylvania, and in 1822 moved to Seneca county, New York, and started a blacksmith shop, in which he worked a few years, and then purchased one hundred acres of wild land in Tompkins county, New York, and there moved his family. He began at once to clear the place of its heavy timber, preparatory to its cultivation, and in due time had a good farm. But the west was now holding out its attractions, and he decided on coming to Illinois. In 1840 he traded his farm in New York for land near Rockford, Illinois, and then came west and settled on the place which he began to improve. In the fall of 1841 he returned easton business, and came back by way of the great lakes. While on the lakes he was exposed to bad weather, which caused his sickness and death, November 17, 1841. His wife survived him many years, dying May 27, 1876.

The subject of this sketch accompanied his parents to Illinois and assisted in opening up the home farm. After his father's death he remained with his mother some three or four years, and later purchased a thresher and engaged in threshing grain for a number of years during the season. He also engaged in hauling freight to and from Chicago, and in breaking prairie for a few years. His first purchase of land consisted of two hundred and sixty-five acres in Winnebago county, which he improved, and in 1855 purchased the old home farm, which he operated for three years. He then traded that farm for land and town property at Creston and moved to the place, where he engaged in the real estate business in connection with farming. He assisted greatly in building up the town, and also improved several farms, being one of the most successful farmers and real estate men in the county.

In 1850 Mr. Mettler went to his native state for his grandfather Housewert. While gone, in New York, he met Miss Delia Young. It is the old story. He returned east, and on the 5th of June, 1853, they were united in marriage. By this union there were three children, only one of whom is now living, Edna M., wife of Professor A. D. Stowell, now of Hannibal, Missouri. Stella grew to womanhood, and died August 27, 1876, at the age of twenty-two years. Lewis Burke died November 25, 1860, at the age of four years. The mother of these children departed this life February 16, 1864. She was a devoted member of the Congregationalist church, while her daughter, Mrs. Stowell, is a member of the Methodist Episcopal church.

On the 26th of April, 1870, in DeKalb county, Mr. Mettler was united in marriage with Miss Mary Riddle, born east of Knoxville, Tennessee, and daughter of John and Susan (Anderson) Riddle. Her father first moved with his family from Tennessee to Indiana, and in 1836 moved to DeKalb county, Illinois, where he entered a tract of several hundred acres of land and engaged in agricultural pursuits. He was a man of great business ability, and was often called on by his neighbors to transact for them some business. He served as justice of the peace, assessor and supervisor, as well as in other official positions, and practiced law in the justices' courts. He died at the age of sixty-nine years. His wife survived him a few years.

In early life, Mr. Mettler was an abolitionist and cast his first presidential vote for James G. Birney. On the organization of the Republican party, he became a Republican, and continued to vote that party ticket for many years. A strong temperance man, and in favor of the entire prohibition of the liquor traffic, he has for some years been voting the Prohibition ticket. While not desiring official position, he has been honored by his fellow citizens with several offices of honor and trust. He has been assessor of his township, road commissioner, member of the town board, justice of the peace and police magistrate, having been elected by a good majority. He has also served as delegate to the county and state conventions of his party. Mr. Mettler and his wife are strong believers in the Christian religion, taking the Bible as their guide and rule of practice.

A resident of northern Illinois almost three score years Mr. Mettler is well known, especially in Winnebago, DeKalb and Ogle counties, and he and his most estimable wife are held in high esteem.

THOMAS P. FRANTZ, who is engaged in the meat market business at Holcomb, Illinois, is a veteran of the Civil war. He is a native of Allegany county, Maryland, born September 7, 1841, and is a son of George and Rebecca (Friend) Frantz, both of whom were also natives of the same state, and of their six children, four are yet living. William B., Thomas P., Joseph, and

George D.; John W. and Julia A. are deceased. The paternal grandfather, Joseph Frantz, was a native of Pennsylvania, and was a man of considerable prominence, serving in various local offices, including justice of the peace and county commissioner, in the latter office continuing four years. In 1835 he was elected a member of the legislature and served with signal ability. He was a Jacksonian Democrat, a great admirer of "Old Hickory," and advocated the principles of the party until his death, which occurred about 1850. George Frantz, the father, was also a man of more than ordinary ability, and also served as justice of the peace for some years. By occupation he was a farmer and stock dealer, and was a well-known man in Allegany county, Maryland.

Thomas P. Frantz, our subject, was reared and educated in his native county and state and was educated in Cumberland, Maryland. Before he attained his majority the war for the union was in progress, and his sympathies being on the side of the union, he enlisted September 2, 1861, in Company I, Second Maryland Volunteer Infantry, at Cumberland, Maryland, to serve three years or during the war. For a little more than three years he was in active service, and was many times under fire of the enemy. At one time at Suspension Bridge, with three others, he volunteered to lay plank across the bridge. The bullets rained like hail from the enemy's guns, but they accomplished the work which they set out to do without receiving a scratch. The experience, however, was not very pleasant and he would not care to repeat it unless absolutely necessary. On the 31st of October, 1864, at Cumberland, Maryland, with his regiment he was mustered out of service.

Returning to his home, after receiving his discharge, Mr. Frantz again commenced work at his trade of stone mason, and there remained for two years, at which time he determined on emigrating to Illinois. In 1867 he located near Mt. Morris, and followed his trade in connection with farming, and there remained some years. In 1875 he came to Holcomb and engaged in his present business and has here since continued to reside, building up a most satisfactory trade.

On the 2d of January, 1870, Mr. Frantz was united in marriage with Miss Emma C. Hastings, a native of Springfield, Ohio, and a daughter of Edmond Hastings, who for many years had been a resident of Ogle county. By this union there was born one son, John A., who, grown to manhood, is now in partnership with his father, and is a young man of good business ability.

In politics Mr. Frantz is an uncompromising Republican, and while never aspiring to official position, has yet served as township collector and other minor positions. In whatever he has been asked to do he has tried to do well. He is a good citizen and is held in high esteem.

GEORGE M. REED, who is engaged in the mercantile business at Daysville, is a well known citizen of the county, having been identified with its interests for some sixty years. He was born February 7, 1836, in Gilsom, New Hampshire, and is a son of Lyman and Mehitable (Clark) Reed, the former a native of Vermont, born December 25, 1807, and the latter of New Hampshire, born April 24, 1814. Lyman Reed was a carpenter by trade, and followed that occupation during almost his entire life. In 1839 he located at Daysville, where he spent the remainder of his life, becoming a prominent and influential citizen of the place and of Ogle county. In early life he was politically a Democrat, but on account of the attitude of his party on the slavery question, he became a Republican on the organization of the party, and continued to advocate its principles until called from this life. For many years he served as postmaster of Daysville, was constable for a time, and also filled the office of school director. His death occurred January 8, 1866. His wife survived him many years, dying April 28, 1886. They were the parents of six children. George M. is the subject of this sketch. Mary died in infancy. Virgil E. is a farmer of Nassau township, of whom mention is made elsewhere in this work. Lucy A., Bemis, Edwin E. and John L., all reside in Oregon, Illinois.

The subject of this sketch was but three years old when he came with his parents to Ogle county, and since that time he has been a resident of Daysville. In that village he grew to manhood, and in its schools received a common-school education. In his youth he learned the carpenter trade with his father, and followed that occupation for some years. He continued to reside at home and assisted his father until he was twenty-two years old, when he commenced life for himself. On the 1st of November, 1858, he was united in marriage with Miss Elizabeth A. Thompson, a native of England, born November 1, 1834. She died September 20, 1873, leaving three children. Frank E. is a prominent attorney in Oregon, and is present county judge of Ogle county, having been elected to that position in the fall of 1898. He married Cora Pankhurst, daughter of the bookkeeper of the First National Bank at Oregon. Alice E., now deceased, married Clarence Gardner, a well known attorney of Rochelle, Illinois. One child was born of their union, Freddie. Georgia died at the age of two years.

The second marriage of Mr. Reed was celebrated November 26, 1874, when he wedded Miss Elmira A. McCloud, who was born in Ohio, December 11, 1847, the daughter of Stephen and Ruth (Simpson) McCloud, both of whom were natives of Pennsylvania, but who emigrated to Ohio, and from that state to Daysville, Illinois, in 1849.

In 1868 Mr. Reed opened a general store in Daysville, in which line of business he has continued to the present time with a fair degree of success. His acquaintance throughout the county is very extensive, and wherever known he is held in the highest esteem. In 1859 he was elected constable in his township and served eight years. He has also served as township collector a number of years, as school director for twenty years, and as town clerk for twenty-seven years, and is yet filling the latter office. For twenty-three years he has served as postmaster, and is yet occupying that position. For a time he was a member of the Odd Fellows, but does not now affiliate with the order. Religiously, he is a Methodist, holding membership with the church at Daysville. In politics he is a thorough Republican, and has voted the party ticket since attaining his majority. As a business man he is enterprising and reliable at all times. He carries a general stock of such goods as are in demand in his section. An almost lifelong resident of the county, he has not only witnessed its growth and development, but has contributed his part in making the county occupy its present exalted rank among the counties of the state.

MAJOR J. G. GAMMON, a veteran of the Civil war, and for nineteen years connected with the Illinois National Guards, is now living a retired life in the village of Creston. He is a native of England, born in the city of Bristol, July 6, 1840. His father, Robert Gammon, was also a native of England, and was professionally a sailor, following the sea for many years. His wife died when the Major was but a small lad, and he went to live with an uncle, Henry Gammon, who had no children, and was living in Devonshire, England. In 1854, he accompanied his uncle and aunt to the United States, the family first locating near Buffalo, New York, where they remained two years. In 1856, they came to Illinois and made a permanent location and home in De Kalb county, where the uncle purchased raw land and opened up a farm.

The subject of this sketch remained with his uncle and assisted in the improvement of the farm until January 4, 1862. His adopted country was then in the midst of a Civil war and was calling for men. He had lived long enough in the country to become attached to its institutions, and to all intents and purposes he was a thorough American. On the date mentioned he enlisted in Company L, Fifteenth Illinois Cavalry, and at once went with his regiment to the front. On his arrival at the scene of activities, he was put on detached duty, forming one of the body guard of General Halleck, and later he was in like service under General Grant. At Corinth, he rejoined his regiment, and with it participated in the battle at that place. He was also in the engagements at Bear Creek, Tuscumbia, and later was in Arkansas, hunting and skirmishing with bushwhackers and guerrillas. At the close of his term of service, in January, 1865, he was honorably discharged at Helena, Arkansas.

On receiving his discharge, Mr. Gammon returned home, but he was not content to remain as his adopted country was still engaged in the struggle, and accordingly, on the 6th of March, 1865, he re-enlisted for one year, and joined Company G, Fourth Regiment, General Hancock's Veteran Volunteer Corps, and went to Washington, where he was engaged in doing guard duty until the final close of the war. He later was sent to Camp Chase, where he was engaged in garrison duty. At the expiration of his second term of service he was discharged at Todd's barracks, Columbus, Ohio.

Mr. Gammon again returned to De Kalb county, and located in Malta, but soon after made a trip to England, and visited his native city. He was married May 31, 1866, to Miss Jane Bennett, who was born in Devonshire, England, and a daughter of Henry Bennett, also of Devonshire. Soon after his marriage he returned with his bride to his home in De Kalb county and took charge of the farm of his uncle, and soon after purchased the place, and took care of his uncle and aunt in their declining years. He continued to operate the farm, which consisted of one hundred and sixty acres of fine land, until 1875, when he removed to the village of Creston, which has since been his home.

In 1876 Mr. Gammon joined the Illinois National Guards, and was commissioned first lieutenant of his company, and was soon promoted to the captaincy. While serving with that rank he took the company to Braidwood to preserve peace and protect property at that place. In 1880 he was commissioned major of the first battalion, third regiment. While in the service he was called out a number of times. During the great strike at Chicago in 1894, he spent twenty-one days with his battalion in that city. He made a good and efficient officer, and the men all had confidence in him.

Mr. and Mrs. Gammon have three children. Frank A. is married and is carrying on the home farm in De Kalb county. Henry Bennett is a graduate of the medical department of Michigan University, at Ann Arbor. During the Spanish-American war he was hospital steward of the Thirty-fourth Michigan Infantry, and was with his regiment at Santiago. After his return from the service he was taken sick, and on his recovery was placed in the hospital service at Ann Arbor. Jessie E. is now the wife of B. L. Kittle, of Chicago, and they have two children, Paul and Mildred. In the family of Frank A. Gammon are three children, Neal, Maud A. and Clifford Dewey.

The first presidential vote cast by Major Gammon was for Abraham Lincoln in 1864. He has been a stanch Republican from that time to the present, and has voted for every presidential nominee of the party. Fraternally he is a Mason, holding membership with the blue lodge at Creston, the chapter at Rochelle and the commandery at Sycamore. He is also a member of the Grand Army of the Republic, Post No. 12, at Sycamore. Mrs. Gammon is a devoted member of the Congregationalist church, in the work of which she takes a lively interest. Both are highly esteemed in Creston and wherever known, the Major having many friends, not only in De Kalb and Ogle counties, but throughout the state, wherever his duties have called him.

DELOS W. BAXTER.—Not by gift or purchase or by influence can one rise at the bar, but solely by merit must he gain his reputation, his ability winning him greatness, and enabling him to pass on the highway of life many who had accomplished part of the journey ere he started out. Among the members of the legal fraternity in Ogle county, who have won for themselves prominent places in the ranks of their professional brethren, is the gentleman whose name introduces this sketch, and who is successfully engaged in practicing in his native city. He was born on the 29th of July, 1857, in Rochelle, where he was a pupil of the common and high schools until his eighteenth year, when he entered the law department of the Iowa State University, graduating in 1881, having previously read in the office of M. D. Hathaway. He commenced practicing for himself on the 1st of July, 1882, and with the exception of a short time with Mr. Hathaway and later with Mr. Gardner, he has conducted his practice alone.

At Huron, South Dakota, our subject was united in marriage to Georgia Ambrose, formerly of White Rock township, Ogle county, a daughter of George and Ann (Hess) Ambrose. Politically, Mr. Baxter is a Republican, who staunchly upholds the principles of his party. He has been state senator since 1896. He is vice-president of the Rochelle National Bank. Fraternally he is a member of the Masonic lodge and chapter, of Rochelle, and Rockford commandery, K. T., also the Independent Order of Odd Fellows, and is a striking example of the self-made American, who commands the respect of all who meet him.

The father of this gentleman, Deloss A. Baxter, was born near Ogdensburg, New York, on the 23d of December, 1826. He attended the common schools and the Canton Academy, of Canton, New York, until the age of seventeen, when he learned the harness-maker's trade, serving an apprenticeship of three years. During the winter of 1847 and '48 he clerked in a hardware store in Ogdensburg, and in the spring of 1848 came west to Cleveland, Ohio, working there and in the surrounding towns for three years, and in 1851 removing to Pawpaw, Illinois, where he opened a harness shop. In the spring of 1856 he came to Rochelle, where he entered the same line of business, and in 1898 he retired, selling out to his son, Burt B. Baxter. Mr. Baxter was married to Mary Wirick, a daughter of Jacob and Mary (McCoy) Wirick, natives of Ohio, on the 8th of November, 1854. To this union seven children have been born, here given in order of birth: Delos W., the subject of this sketch; Allison B., a resident of Chicago; Guy A., living in Texas; Bert B., his father's business successor; Blanche P., the wife of Clarence E. Gardner; Paul G., an official at the state penitentiary, at Joliet; and Mary Maud, a teacher in Rochelle. Deloss A. Baxter departed this life at Rochelle on December 11, 1898.

The grandparents of our subject were Alexander Baxter, Jr., and Philinda (Baxter) Baxter. Deloss A. Baxter was now a member of the Masonic Lodge, F. & A. M., and chapter, R. A. M. He was made a Mason in Ohio, and assisted in organizing the lodge in Rochelle, and was the last of the original charter members of the Masonic lodge in Rochelle. In politics he was a Republican, though casting his first presidental ballot for Franklin Pierce, and his popularity in the community in which he resided is illustrated by the fact that he was twice elected mayor of Rochelle, three times alderman and in 1872 was elected township collector.

CHARLES KLEIN.—No foreign element has become a more important part in our American citizenship than that furnished by Sweden. The emigrants from that land have brought with them to the new world the stability, enterprise and perseverance characteristic of their people and have fused these qualities with the progressiveness and indomitable spirit of the west. Mr. Klein is a representative of this class. He came to America in limited circumstances, hoping to benefit his financial condition, and his dreams of the future have been more than realized. He is to-day a successful dealer in grain, coal and lumber at Kings, and occupies a very prominent place in business circles in Ogle county.

Mr. Klein was born April 22, 1849, in the central part of the province of Jenkoping, Sweden, near the town of the same name, and is a son of C. P. and Johanna (Moberg) Klein. The father was a farmer and had a thorough technical as well as practical knowledge of that occupation, having been regularly educated in an agricultural college, as was required in that country, to fit him for the position he held, that of superintendent of a large agricultural property. Our subject is the seven in order of birth in a family of nine children, of whom the following came to America. Elizabeth, crossed the Atlantic with our subject and stopped first in Chicago, where they had acquaintance living. Later she was married in Rochelle to Charles Skepstedt, but is now living in Chicago. A year after their arrival Sophia came to the United States, and she is now the wife of Nels Nelson, a farmer of Flagg township, Ogle county. Five years later Franz, Augusta and Hedda also came to America. Franz is now a resident of Rockford, Illinois. Augusta makes her home with our subject. Hedda married Richard Harding, a farmer of Marion township, Ogle county, and later they removed to Lincoln county, South Dakota, where he owns and operates a farm.

During his boyhood and youth Charles Klein attended the common schools of his native land and assisted his father in his duties. At the age of twenty-one he and his sister Elizabeth sailed for the new world, and leaving her in Chicago he proceeded to Chariton, Iowa, where he had friends living, and where he was employed for one year. At the end of that time he came to Rochelle, Ogle county, Illinois, his sister having already married and located here. In 1871 he commenced working on the farm of A. F. Crawford, near Rochelle, and in the fall of that year went to Chicago, where he easily found employment, there being a demand for laborers after the great fire which destroyed much of that city. The following spring he returned to Ogle county and obtained work on the farm of W. H. King, with whom he remained for five years. During this time he attended the public schools during the winter terms and thus acquired a good knowledge of the common English branches. This was followed by a commercial and scientific course at Mt. Morris College. In 1878 he embarked in the coal and lumber business at Kings, and two years later became interested in the grain trade in partnership with W. H. King. Since 1882, however, he has been alone and does a large and profitable business in all branches. Kings has become quite a grain center and he usually ships from two hundred and fifty to three hundred car loads in course of a season.

On the 21st of June, 1879, Mr. Klein was married in Chicago to Miss Helen Oleson, who was also born in Sweden, August 27, 1851, but during her infancy was brought to this country by her parents, Daniel and Ingri Christina, who located in Lake county, Indiana, where the father owned a farm and made his home until his death. Mrs. Klein is one of a family of eight children, the others being Peter, who still owns and occupies a farm in Lake county, Indiana; Mari, who married F. Johnson and lives in Chicago; Lena, wife of John Carleson, a photographer of Rochelle; Christine, wife of J. N. Crona, who is in the United States mail service in Chicago; Hannah, wife of a Mr. Fents, of Chicago; Paul, a resident of St. Louis, and Anton, who was formerly a photographer of Rochelle, and from there removed to St. Louis, where his death occurred. Five children have been born to Mr. and Mrs. Klein, namely: Helen Pauline, who was born January 10, 1884; Carl Reuben, who was born July 24, 1886, and died October 16, 1892; Crystal Victoria, who was born December 16, 1888; Esther May, who was born March 30, 1893, and died June 22, 1893, and Reba Ruth, who was born October 30, 1894. The year previous to his marriage, Mr. Klein erected the comfortable residence in Kings which the family now occupy. Politically he is a stanch supporter of the Republican party and its principles, and takes quite an active and prominent part in public affairs. For four consecutive years he served as town clerk, and has been a member of the school board in his district for eight years. During almost his entire residence here he has been a member of the Presbyterian church of Kings, has always taken an active part in its work, serving as elder for ten years and superintendent of the Sunday-school for eight years.

THOMAS GUEST, one of the most honored and highly esteemed citizens of Ogle county, passed away at his home in Rochelle, August 5, 1886, after a life of industry and rich in those rare possessions which only a high character can give. In all the relations of life he was found true and faithful to every trust reposed in him, and when called to his rest and reward of the higher world his best monument was found in the love and respect of the community in which he lived for so many years.

Mr. Guest was born in the province of Ontario, Canada, December 28, 1820, a son of Thomas and Ann (Todd) Guest, who were natives of Ireland, where their marriage was celebrated and where some of their children were born. At an early day they emigrated to the new world and took up their residence in Canada, where the father continued to make his home until called from this life March 5, 1860. By occupation he was a farmer. Immediately after his arrival in Canada, he united with the Methodist Episcopal church and was always an active worker in the church, serving as class leader and in other official positions. In his family were eight children, four sons and four daughters, all of whom were reared and married in Canada, and remained there with the exception of our subject, and Richard is the only one now living. In order of birth they are as follows: James; Mary, the wife of Alexander Gibson, who was of Scotch origin; John; Eliza, wife of James Brownlee, who is also deceased; Thomas, our subject; Ann, wife of John Armitage, deceased; Richard and Amelia.

On the home farm in his native province, Thomas Guest was reared to manhood and his education was obtained in the common schools of the neighborhood. During his active business life he engaged in agricultural pursuits and early acquired land of his own, having at the time of his removal to Illinois two hundred acres of good land, well improved with excellent buildings. He was married in Canada May 16, 1856, to Miss Ann Pettepiece, who was born in the province of Ontario December 23, 1832, and is a daughter of Thomas and Catherine (Stokes) Pettepiece, natives of Ireland and early settlers of Canada. She is one of a family of nine children, six sons and three daughters, and herself and brother George are now the only survivors. All remained in Canada but Mrs. Guest and her brother Joseph, who also came to Illinois and died here in 1897.

Immediately after their marriage Mr. and Mrs. Guest disposed of their property in Canada, and leaving a fine home came to Ogle county, Illinois. In Flagg township he purchased a quarter section of land on section 30, on which he made his home for thirteen years. In the meantime he bought one hundred and sixty acres in Lee county, Illinois, and five hundred and twenty acres on sections 5 and 6, Dement township, near Rochelle, and on leaving his first purchase he removed to the latter place, where he resided until he retired from active life in 1882, spending his last days in ease and quiet in Rochelle.

To Mr. and Mrs. Guest were born the following children: Aaron W., born December 9, 1869, is engaged in business in Rochelle; Francis J., born July 3, 1861, is a farmer of Ogle county; George W., born September 22, 1863, is a retired merchant of Rochelle; Anna M., born September 28, 1865, lives with her mother; Naomi, born November 25, 1868, died December 30, 1868, and Elsie May, born July 15, 1872, is the wife of Peter Wagner, a jeweler of Denver, Colorado. The children were all given the benefit of good school privileges and are graduates of the high school of Rochelle, while Frank and Aaron also attended Wheaton College.

Mr. Guest always took an active and commendable interest in public affairs, especially educational matters, and for many years was a most efficient member of the school board. He was a life-long member of the Methodist Episcopal church and an earnest, consistent Christian gentleman. He was one of nature's noblemen and the world is certainly better for his having lived. As a citizen he was honorable, prompt and true to every engagement; as a man he held the honor and esteem of all classes; and as a husband and father was a model worthy of all imitation; unassuming in manner, sincere in his friendships, steadfast and unswerving in his loyalty to the right. His funeral services were conducted in the Presbyterian church of Rochelle, by Rev. M. M. Bates, the Methodist Episcopal minister, and his remains were interred in Lawn Ridge cemetery. We quote from an obituary written at the time by one who knew him well: "The highest encomium possible to be given any one can be truthfully said of Thomas Guest—'He was an honest man.'"

GEORGE W. PERKINS, the present popular mayor of Polo, is entitled to distinction as one of the most progressive and enterprising men of Ogle county, and has for many years been prominently identified with the interests of Polo. Upon the commercial activity of a community depends its prosperity and the men who are now recognized as leading citizens are those who are at the head of extensive business enterprises. He is a member of the well-known lumber firm of Perkins & Pettibone, and is a man of broad capabilities who carries foward to successful completion whatever he undertakes.

Mr. Perkins is a native of Ogle county, born in Buffalo Grove, November 11, 1850, and is a son of Rufus Perkins, whose birth occurred in New York, July 13, 1827, and whose parents were Timothy and Sarah (Vacty) Perkins. About 1838 or 1840 the father came west and took up his residence in Buffalo Grove, where he purchased a farm and operated the same until 1852. Having an attack of the "gold fever," he started for California across the plains. The Indians were very troublesome and the cattle stampeded several times, but fortunately none of the party were killed. During this trip Mr. Perkins made what he considered one of the most famous trades of his life. Vegetables were the articles of food most needed on the long journey, and he succeeded in trading an injured ox, which would have had to have been abandoned, for one onion. In the Golden state he engaged in mining with fair success and became possessed of much valuable property on the Pacific coast. After his return to Ogle county, in April, 1863, he frequently made trips to the west to look after his possessions there, crossing the plains fourteen or fifteen times. Mr. Perkins became interested in the lumber trade after his return to Ogle county, and was engaged in that business until his retirement from active life in 1875. Upright and honorable in all his dealings, he has the confidence and respect of all who know him. In politics he was a Republican. He married Miss Maria A. Saltzman, who was born in Wisconsin, February 26, 1830, and died October 8, 1891, while he passed away December 9, 1888. Our subject is the older of the two children born to them. Mary G., who was born during the sojourn of her parents in California, was married in Polo, November 2, 1876, to Charles D. Reed, a native of Buffalo township, Ogle county, and a son of Luman and Mary (Hull) Reed. They have two children, Rufus Maynard and Julia H. The maternal grandparents of our subject were Peter and Polly (Lynn) Saltzman. The grandfather, who was a soldier of the war of 1812, was born March 28, 1797, and died July 12, 1851, at Pittsburg, Pennsylvania, while his wife was born March 4, 1804, and died in Tennessee, July 10, 1870.

George W. Perkins was taken by his parents to California in 1852, but in 1857 he returned east with friends, by way of Cape Horn, and made his home with an uncle in Indiana until his parents returned to Ogle county, where he joined them. He attended school in Indiana and in Polo until he attained the age of twenty years, and began life for himself in the spring of 1870 by working in the lumber yard of Hunt & Perkins, his father being the junior member of the firm. Two years later his father purchased the interest of his partner and admitted our subject to the firm, the name being changed to Rufus Perkins & Son. In 1873 the latter took full charge and carried on operations under the style of G. W. Perkins, with branch yards at Woosung and Maryland. In 1882 the business was merged into the Minnesota Lumber Company, which at one time owned fourteen yards in different towns, and Mr. Perkins served as its secretary as long as the company was in existence. On the death of Mr. H. D. Barber, a leading member of the firm, in 1896, the affairs of the company were dissolved and our subject associated himself with Chauncey Pettibone, under the firm name of Perkins & Pettibone. They do an extensive and profitable business, which is largely foreign, shipping pine lumber principally to Liverpool, England, and Glasgow, Scotland.

On the 10th of November, 1875, in Polo, was celebrated the marriage of Mr. Perkins and Miss Mary L. Buck, who was born in Americus, Indiana, and is one of a family of six children, whose parents were Daniel and Lucy A. (Humphrey) Buck. The mother was born in Wayne county, Pennsylvania, July 10, 1833, and in early life removed to Americus, where she gave her hand in marriage to Daniel Buck, who was a native of Butler county, Ohio, who was born October 10, 1829, and died December 15, 1874. In 1856 he removed his family from Indiana to Polo, Illinois, where he was engaged in the dry goods trade. Mr. and Mrs. Perkins have two children, Bryant L., who is a graduate of the Polo schools and also the Northwestern University at Evaston, Illinois, completing the scientific course in the latter institution in 1898; and Clara, who is a pupil in the Polo schools.

Mr. Perkins is a stalwart Republican and while not a politician he takes great interest in public affairs, and has most efficiently served as mayor of Polo for four years. Never were the reins of government in more capable hands, as greater improvements have been made during his administration than ever before. A street grade has been established, a park system adopted, the city lighted by electricity, and the water works extended. Prior to his election to the office of mayor, Mr. Perkins was a member of the city council for six years, during which time the beginning of the water works was established and he was a member of the committee that had the matter in charge. The first water main was laid on Mason street for fire purposes and has since been extended until now there are six miles of mains in the city. Mr. Perkins was city treasurer two years, and school treasurer of Polo school district for fourteen years, succeeding the first treasurer, J. C. Luckey, who served in that office for twenty years. Mr. Perkins is at present a member of the board of education and under the direction of the present board there is being erected one of the finest and up to date school houses in the northern portion of Illinois. As a citizen he ever stands ready to discharge every duty devolving upon him and justly merits the esteem in which he is held

LEWIS STOCKING, for many years a leading and influential farmer in Lynnville township, was born in Ashfield, Massachusetts, February 25, 1820. His father, Herod Stocking, was born in the same county and state, May 13, 1791, and there followed the honorable occupation of a farmer. He was twice married, his first union being with Miss Lydia Ames, their marriage being solemnized January 12, 1814. She was also a native of Ashfield, Massachusetts, and was born April 14, 1796. By this union there were ten children—John A., Joseph, third; Lewis, William Chandler, William, second; Jonathan S., Henry, Horace, and Horace, second. The mother of these children died March 2, 1847, and June 29, 1848, Mr. Stocking wedded Miss Lavina Forbush.

Herod Stocking moved with his family to Cuyahoga county, Ohio, in 1832, and from there to Ogle county, Illinois, in 1839. He selected a location for his future home in what was then Monroe precinct, but now Monroe township, which continued to be his home until his death, February 21, 1884. His wife died February 2, 1865. They were both good people, highly respected, and had many friends in the country of their adoption.

The subject of this sketch spent his boyhood in his native state, and his youth in Ohio. He came with his parents to Ogle county, but soon afterward returned to Ohio, and in his twentieth year began life in earnest for himself. Previous to this, however, he had worked for stipulated monthly wages, his earnings going to his father. He received but a limited education in the schools of Massachusetts and Ohio, but in the school of experience he has obtained much valuable knowledge.

On the 10th of December, 1843, Mr. Stocking was united in marriage with Miss Mary Burroughs, of Lorane, Ohio. She was born in Alden, Erie county, New York, November 13, 1823. Two years after their marriage they came to Illinois, making their journey with ox teams, experiencing many hardships on the way. The townships had not been organized on their arrival here, and they settled in Monroe precinct, in that part, however, which is not included in the township of Lynnville. The first purchase made by Mr. Stocking was eighty acres located on section 6, for which he paid one dollar and twenty-five cents per acres. No time was lost in the improving of the place, and as time passed he added to his possessions until he is now the owner of four hundred and fifty acres, one eighty of which is on section 7. His improvements are in keeping with the times and he is rated as a No. 1 farmer.

To Mr. and Mrs. Stocking four children have been born, three sons and one daughter. The oldest, Layton C., died in infancy. Eda A. married George Yo, formerly of England, and they have four children, Bessy M., Elva, Alfred and Alice. Milton D. married Sarah Holmes, of Lynnville township, and to them two children were born, Myrtle H. and Iva R. Duane C. married Polly Smith, also of Lynnville township, but a native of England. They have two sons and two daughters, Lewis C., Hazel E., Elsie G. and Spencer D.

Charles Burroughs, the father of Mrs. Stocking, was born in New York state, July 22, 1790. He was educated in the common schools and in his youth learned the hatter's trade, which he later followed in connection with farming. He married Lucinda Cunningham, also a native of New York, born in 1796. They were the parents of eleven children, as follows: Charles C., Lucinda M., Corydon P., Gleason S., Mary L., Annie L., Lorain G., John W., Vienna, Philena C. and Philinda A. (twins). Mr. Burroughs died in 1841, and his widow in 1865. Charles Burroughs, the grandfather of Mrs. Stocking, came to this country prior to the Revolutionary war, the records going to show that he was a soldier on the side of those fighting for their independence and was a prisoner on one of the sugar ships. Herod Stocking was also a true patriot, and served as a soldier in the war of 1812. The grandfather of our subject was Abram Stocking, and his great-grandfather, named Abram, was a shipbuilder in Chatham, on the Connecticut river.

In their religious views Mr. and Mrs. Stocking are Adventists, and in his political affiliations he is a thorough Prohibitionist. He is truly a self-made man, and all that he has he has accumulated by his own industry, assisted by his good wife, for he realizes the truth of the statement of Solomon, that "A good wife is from the Lord. She shall do him good and not evil all the days of his life, and her children shall arise and call her blessed." No couple in Lynnville township are held in higher esteem.

ALFRED B. McCREA, who has been actively engaged in the grain, lumber and coal business in the village of Creston, since the fall of 1865, came to the state in 1857. He was born in Orange county, New York, April 27, 1838, and is the son of William and Abigail (Harkness) McCrea, both of whom were born in Ireland, though the former was of Scotch parentage. Soon after their marriage they set sail for the United States, and were three months on the ocean. One son, Abraham, was born on the ocean, while en route. He grew to manhood, settled in Malta, DeKalb county, where he engaged in the grain, lumber and coal business, and there died some years ago.

On his arrival in the United States, William McCrea located in Orange county, New York, but later moved to Monroe county and settled in the town of Brighton, near Rochester, where he engaged in farming. Still later he removed to Wayne county, New York, where he remained for several years. From Wayne county he joined his children in Illinois, where his death occurred, April 4, 1888. His wife passed away some years before, while the family were still living in New York.

In his native state our subject remained until the age of seventeen, and received a good education in the Macedon Academy. In the fall of 1856 he came west to Hillsdale county, Michigan, where he engaged in teaching until in March, 1857, when he went to Whiteside county, Illinois, and joined his brother Samuel H., who was in the grain business at Morrison. The latter later moved to Chicago, where he became quite a prominent figure in business and politics. For some years he served as president of the board of trade of that city, and also served a term of four years as county treasurer of Cook county.

Mr. McCrea assisted his brother in the summer seasons and taught school for three winters. In the spring of 1859 he made a trip to Pike's Peak, driving two yoke of cattle and one yoke of cows. He went into the mountains and was there about three months, but had no success in finding the yellow metal. He returned to the state with the oxen, but minus the cows. During the winter of 1859-60, he taught school, and in the spring of 1860 again went into his brother's office. In the winter of 1860-61, he was engaged in teaching in Lasalle county.

On the 17th of September, 1861, Mr. McCrea enlisted in Company C, Eighth Illinois Cavalry, commanded by Colonel Farnsworth, who was afterwards made a major-general. Mr. McCrea enlisted as a private, but was soon promoted quartermaster-sergeant. With his regiment he participated in all the engagements of the Army of the Potomac, including the seven days' fight in the wilderness, and was in the advance of the army through Maryland, participating later in the engagements at South Mountain and Antietam. After the latter engagement the Eighth Cavalry was in the advance at Fredericksburg, participating in that battle under Burnsides. They were next at Chancellorsville, and later at Gettysburg. In the winter of 1863-64, with his regiment he veteranized and received a furlough of thirty days. On rejoining the army with his regiment he went as far as the wilderness, and later was called back to assist in the defense of Washington. Still later the regiment was in the fight at Frederick, Maryland, under General Lew Wallace, and the last regular engagement in which our subject participated was at Fairfax Court House. During his entire time of service Mr. McCrea lost but little time off duty, being but ten days in the hospital on account of illness. At the close of the war the regiment was ordered west to operate against the Indians, but on reaching St. Louis it was ordered to Chicago, where it was mustered out of service.

After receiving his discharge Mr. McCrea spent about three months in Palatine, Cook county, and then located in Creston, where he engaged in the grain, lumber and coal business. Later he formed a partnership with his brother, John A., which continued twenty-seven years, since which time he has conducted the business alone. His business has been quite an extensive one, the amount of grain handled each year being very large, Creston being considered one of the best grain markets on the Northwestern road.

Mr. McCrea was married in Philadelphia November 19, 1868, to Miss Matilda L. Hunter, a native of that city, where she was reared. Three daughters came to bless their union—Jennie, Ida H. and Edith B. All have been given good educational facilities, Ida H. now taking a course in the State Normal at Normal, Illinois. Mrs. McCrea passed to her reward June 10, 1893, and was laid to rest in the Creston cemetery. She was a devoted member of the Congregational church.

Politically Mr. McCrea is a life-long Republican, his first presidential ballot being cast in 1860 for Abraham Lincoln. He has taken quite an interest in local politics, but has never sought office. He has, however, served in several official positions, being a member of the village board for several years, and one term president of the board. He was elected and served two terms as a member of the board of supervisors, making a valuable member of that body and serving on several important committees. He has been a member of the county central committee of his party, and is now chairman of the congressional committee, a position which he has held for about sixteen years. He is a member of the Congregationalist church of Creston, and has been an active worker in the Sunday-school, both as a teacher and superintendent. Fraternally he is a Master Mason. A good business man, he is thoroughly enterprising and progressive, and enjoys in a remarkable degree the confidence of those among whom so many years of his life has been spent.

WILLIAM J. METTLER, of Creston, Illinois, is one of the active and enterprising farmers of Ogle county, owning and operating two farms, the home place, which adjoins the corporate limits of the village of Creston, comprising two hundred and forty acres of fine land, which is kept under a high state of cultivation. A resident of the state since 1840, and of Ogle county since 1868, he was born in Tompkins county, New York, January 9, 1834, and came with his parents, Relph and Mary Ann (Housewert) Mettler, to Winnebago county, the family locating about six miles southeast of Rockford. His father died the following year, and the mother reared the family. Mr. Mettler remained with his mother until he was eighteen years old, in the meantime receiving his primary education in the common schools. He later attended Rock River Seminary, at Mt. Morris, two terms, which completed his school life.

In 1858 Mr. Mettler drove across the country to Texas, from which he returned the following year. He passed over the greater part of northeast Texas, and also through Missouri, Kansas, Arkansas and Louisiana, visiting at the time the city of New Orleans. On returning home he engaged in farming the old home place, remaining there until 1864, when he went to Lee county and purchased a farm of eighty acres, and remained there until 1868, when he came to Ogle county and purchased residence property in Creston. With his brother he invented a tiling machine which

WM. J. METTLER.

he manufactured and operated for four years. In 1869 he purchased his farm of one hundred and sixty acres in Linnville township. In 1884 he moved to his present place of residence, the farm originally comprising but one hundred and twenty acres of the estate of Willis S. Roberts, to which he later added a like number of acres, giving him a fine farm of two hundred and forty acres. He has remodeled the dwelling on the place, and has built one of the best barns in the township, what is well termed a model barn. It has a capacity for one hundred and fifty tons of hay, two hundred and fifty tons of silo, and some three thousand bushels of grain, with basement room for fifty-four head of cattle. The plan of the barn originated with Mr. Mettler, and he has been complimented over and over again on its convenience and perfect adaptability for the purposes intended. His farm is rented the greater part of the time, but he has given his personal attention to its cultivation to some extent, and has raised much grain. He has been a successful farmer and financier, having commenced life with but little means, and by his industry and thrift has acquired valuable property and is regarded as among the best farmers in the county.

On the 25th of February, 1865, Mr. Mettler was united in marriage with Miss Selina H. Roberts, a native of Putnam county, New York, and a daughter of Willis S. and Phœbe S. (Stevens) Roberts, the former a native of New York and the latter of Danbury, Connecticut. Her father came to Ogle county in 1865 and purchased a farm adjoining the village of Creston, where he spent the remainder of his life, dying in 1883. His wife survived him some years, dying in 1896. Both were laid to rest in the cemetery at Creston. To Mr. and Mrs. Mettler two children were born: Minnie, wife of Orson N. Phelps, station agent at DeKalb, Illinois, and Edgar Willis, who is now assisting on the home farm, but who received a good education in the schools of Creston and a Chicago business college. After leaving the business college, he held a responsible position with a bank at Englewood, Chicago, for one year, which he left to assist his father in the management of the home place.

Mr. Mettler cast his first presidential vote for John C. Fremont, and for years voted the regular party ticket, but of late he has been voting independent, voting for the man rather than the party. Fraternally he is a Master Mason, holding membership with the lodge at Creston. He is a man of superior business ability, of upright character and moral worth, and wherever known is held in high esteem. He is one of the few left who came to this section in pioneer times, and who has a vivid recollection of early events.

WILLIAM WALLACE GOULD, M. D., is one of the successful physicians of Ogle county and a prominent resident of Rochelle. He has much natural ability, but is withal a close student and believes thoroughly in the maxim "there is no excellence without labor." His devotion to the duties of his profession therefore, combined with a comprehensive understanding of the principles of the science of medicine, has made him a most successful and able practitioner, whose prominence is well deserved.

The Doctor was born in the town of Hamburg, Erie county, New York, July 16,

1826, a son of Emmons S. and Maria (Greene) Gould, in whose family were three children, namely: Emmons S., deceased; and Wellington R., who is now living in Canada, at the age of eighty-three years. The father, who was a native of Connecticut, and a sergeant in the war of 1812, died a few months before our subject was born, at about the age of fifty-five years, and the mother died at his birth. Dr. Gould was then reared by an aunt at Buffalo, New York, until about eighteen years of age, and his literary education was acquired in the public schools of that city. When his aunt married and moved to a farm, he accompanied her, and the following eight years were passed amid rural scenes, working for wages upon the farm after he attained his majority. He commenced the study of medicine with Dr. Gobel, at Worthington, Ohio, and later graduated at the Berkshire Medical College, Pittsfield, Massachusetts. He engaged in the practice of his chosen profession at Ingersoll, Canada, for three years, but in June, 1860, came to Rochelle, then known as Lane, where he was not long in building up a good practice, which he still enjoys.

In Ingersoll, Canada, Dr. Gould was married, February 22, 1853, to Miss Mary E. Chase, a native of Windsor, Vermont, whose parents died when she was an infant. She was adopted and reared by her father's uncle, Salmon P. Chase, who was one of the distinguished members of President Lincoln's cabinet. Of the five children born to the Doctor and his wife, Mary E. and Frank C. are both deceased. Josephine E. is the wife of H. D. Judson, of Aurora, Illinois, superintendent of the Chicago division of the Chicago, Burlington & Quincy railroad, and they have had four children: Bessie; Howard M.; Fred H., deceased; and William Wallace. Mary Gertrude is the wife of Dr. W. R. Franklin, of Rockford, Illinois, and they have two sons, Ralph G. and William R. Anna Chase, who completes the family, has for four years taught in a kindergarten in Chicago. All the daughters are graduates of the Rochelle high school.

Fraternally, Dr. Gould is a member of the American Institute of Homeopathy of the United States; the American Association of Orificial Surgery; the Illinois Homeopathic Medical Society; and the Northwestern Homeopathic Medical Society, while politically he is identified with the Republican party. Wherever he goes the Doctor wins friends and has the happy faculty of being able to retain them. His popularity has made him a great favorite in all circles.

JACOB I. KREBBS, M. D.—One of the most exacting of all the higher lines of occupation to which a man may lend his energies is that of the physician. A most scrupulous preliminary training is demanded, a nicety of judgment but little understood by the laity. Our subject, who is a prominent and successful physician of Polo, Illinois, is well fitted for the profession which he has chosen as a life work, and his skill and ability have won for him a lucrative practice.

Dr. Krebbs was born in Selin's Grove, Pennsylvania, July 16, 1857, and on the paternal side is of German descent, his grandfather, Jacob Krebbs, having been born in Germany and when a young man emigrated to America, settling in the Keystone state. He became quite wealthy and married a Miss Kiefer, of Pennsylvania. Their son,

Alexander Krebbs, the Doctor's father, was born in Selin's Grove, in 1825, and died in 1894. He was a member of a Pennsylvania regiment during the Civil war and after peace was restored made his home at Elkhart, Indiana, until called from this life. For twenty-eight years he was in the service of the Lake Shore railroad, returning to them after the war. Politically he was identified with the Republican party, socially affiliated with the Grand Army of the Republic and the Independent Order of Odd Fellows, and religiously was a member of the Lutheran church. The Doctor's mother, who bore the maiden name of Elizabeth Thursbey, was also a native of Selin's Grove, Pennsylvania, and died in 1862, at the age of ninety-eight years. Her father, Thomas Thursbey, was a soldier of the war of 1812, a farmer by occupation, and lived to the extreme old age of ninety-nine years. To the parents of our subject were born two children, the younger being David Newton, now a resident of Chicago.

Dr. Krebbs was only six years old when his mother died, at which time his father was at the front, valiantly fighting for the old flag and the cause it represented. His early life was mostly passed in Elkhart, Indiana, where he worked on farms during the summer months and attended school through the winter season until seventeen years of age. Coming to Eagle Point, Ogle county, Illinois, he studied medicine with Dr. McPherson one summer, and then entered the medical department of the Iowa State University at Iowa City, Iowa, but did not graduate from that institution until March, 1886. Immediately after his graduation he opened an office in Hampton, Iowa, where he engaged in practice until 1890, in which year he took a post graduate course at the Chicago Polichnic under Drs. Senn and Fenzer. He remained in Chicago until 1896 and for five years held the chair of surgery in the Physio Medical College, being lecturer and clinic surgeon. He has met with unusual success in his chosen profession and is especially successful in the line of surgery. On leaving Chicago he came to Polo, and it was not long before he succeeded in building up a large and lucrative practice which he still enjoys.

In Polo, Dr. Krebbs married Miss Effie Ormsbee, a native of that place and a daughter of C. N. and Fannie (Porter) Ormsbee. To the Doctor and his wife has been born a son, Claude Naem. In his political affiliations our subject is a Republican, and while a resident of Chicago served as a member of the board of health. He is a Royal Arch Mason and a member of the English Lutheran church. Fraternally he belongs to the Chicago Medical Society and the State Medical Society of Iowa, and in the ranks of his professional brethren he occupies an enviable position.

E L. ROSECRANCE, who resides on section 5, Monroe township, and one of the substantial farmers of Ogle county, has been a resident of the county since 1855. He was born in New York state, April 29, 1829, and is the son of John W. and Mary (Edson) Rosecrance, also natives of the same state. By occupation his father was a farmer, which vocation he followed during his entire life, having a farm of one hundred and twenty acres. He died in 1850 in his native state, his wife surviving him many years, dying at South Bend, Indiana, in 1886.

The subject of this sketch grew to manhood in his native state and was reared to farm life. His education was mostly obtained in the school of experience, that obtained in the school room being very meagre indeed. The opportunities afforded in the prairie state for the enterprising man had come to his ears, and he determined to here try his fortune. Accordingly in 1855 he came to the state and located in Stillman Valley where he resided three years. The first year he worked by the month, but the second and third years he rented and cultivated farms, the first comprising one hundred and twenty acres, and the second eighty acres. He then moved to Monroe township and purchased a farm of eighty acres, and later, in 1884, forty acres additional, giving him a fine farm of one hundred and twenty acres, all of which is under cultivation.

On the 18th of February, 1852, Mr. Rosecrance was united in marriage at Elbe, Genesee county, New York, with Miss Addie L. Norton, daughter of Lochlin and Laura (Clark) Norton. By this union two children were born. Frank E. grew to manhood and married Stella Chase, daughter of Henry and Catherine (Hanford) Chase, who were early settlers of Winnebago county. Frank E. is recognized as one of the substantial farmers of the township and is operating a farm of two hundred acres. Hattie M. married Arthur Chase, son of Henry and Catherine Chase, and they now reside in Cherry Valley township, Winnebago county, where he operates a farm of two hundred acres. After forty-five years of married life, Mrs. Rosecrance was called to her reward, her death occurring April 10, 1898. She was a loving wife and mother, a kind and obliging neighbor, and her death was deeply regretted by all who knew her.

Since removing to his present farm, Mr. Rosecrance has made many substantial improvements upon the place, erecting new barns, putting up a good windmill, setting out orchards and ornamental trees, and remodeled the house. In addition to general farming, Mr. Rosecrance has engaged in stock raising to some extent, giving special attention to raising Poland China hogs, and Hereford cattle. He generally ships his own stock to Chicago.

In politics Mr. Rosecrance is a Republican. He has served as highway commissioner nine years and school director ten years. He is a member of the Methodist Episcopal church at New Milford. A residence of more than half a century in Ogle county has brought him in contact with the best people, and wherever known he is held in high esteem.

COLONEL DAVID CHAPIN MAY.— The deserved reward of a well-spent life is an honored retirement from business, in which to enjoy the fruits of former toil. To-day after a useful and beneficial career Colonel May is quietly living at his pleasant home in Rochelle, surrounded by the comfort that earnest labor has brought him. He is a prominent citizen of Ogle county, and for many years he was actively identified with its business and agricultural interests.

The Colonel was born in Burlington, Otsego county, New York, March 8, 1815, a son of Harmon May, whose birth occurred in Windham county, Connecticut, in 1780. The paternal grandfather, Joseph May, was also a native of Connecticut, but the family was originally from Massachusetts. Harmon May followed the occupation of farming throughout life, and at an early day removed to Otsego county, New York, where he died in 1857, honored and respected by all who knew him. In politics he was a Whig and in religious faith a Presbyterian. He married Miss Sarah Monroe, who was born in Burlington, New York, in 1790, and died in 1834. Her parents were William and Deborah (Pope) Monroe, quite prominent and highly respected people of Burlington. Mr. Monroe also engaged in farming as a life work, served as a justice of the peace for many years, and as a country lawyer wrote many deeds and settled many estates for his neighbors and friends. He was from Massachusetts and was one of the pioneers of Otsego county, New York, having located there when the country was almost an unbroken wilderness, and the family learned the true meaning of the term hard times in their pioneer home. Of the seven children born to Harmon and Sarah (Monroe) May, only two are now living: David C., of this review, and Josiah, who is also living in Rochelle.

Colonel May was reared in his native township and acquired his education in a district school, where ninety pupils were often accommodated in a small room. This he attended only for two months during the winter season, walking two miles and a half to and from school. On attaining his majority he started out in life for himself and for several years engaged in farming. After his marriage he bought a small farm, but sold it a year later and purchased a small hotel in the town of Edmonston, New York, which he conducted for five years. On disposing of that property he bought another farm near the village, owning and operating the same for two years. At the end of that time he sold, and in March, 1855, we find him a resident of Rockford, Illinois, where he carried on a hotel for five years. It was at that place he received his title of "colonel," in the following manner: The editor of a Rockford paper was passing the hotel one Sunday forenoon and stopped for a friendly chat with the landlord. He accepted our subject's invitation to dinner. It was such a one as was not usually served in those early days in a western inn, and in the notice of it, in the following issue of his paper, the editor spoke of the excellent dinner to which he had been invited by "Colonel May." The title seemed to suit the jovial host and has clung to him up to the present time. On leaving Rockford he came to Rochelle, where he also engaged in the hotel business for five years on the site of the present hotel De Los. At the end of that time he disposed of the hotel and engaged in business as an agricultural implement dealer for the same length of time. For the following twenty years he lived on a small farm near the town, and engaged in raising pure blood Devonshire cattle, and also dealt in all kinds of cattle, but, in 1885, he sold the farm and returned to Rochelle, where he has since lived retired.

In Burlington, New York, November 11, 1841, Colonel May was united in marriage with Miss Rebecca Clark Staunton, and now for over fifty-seven years they have traveled life's journey together, sharing its joys and sorrows, its adversity and prosperity. Mrs. May was born in South Kingston, Rhode Island, November 12, 1820, and is a daughter of John Staunton, Jr., who was serving as sheriff of his county at the time of his death, August 9, 1822.

He married Eliza Riter Boss, a daughter of William Boss, and a native of New York state, who died at the age of forty-one years. The Colonel and his wife had one son, Henry R. May, who was born in Edmonston, New York, June 22, 1845, and was educated in the schools of Rockford and Racine College. After holding a position in a store for a time, he accepted a place with the Chicago, Burlington & Quincy railroad, and was stationed at St. Paul, Minnesota, as assistant auditor, but at the time of his death was serving as auditor and cashier of the City street railway, of St. Paul. He died December 6, 1889, mourned by all who knew him. He made many friends, as he was of a singularly amiable and friendly disposition, and was always even tempered and cordial in manner. He married Miss Ida Monroe, in Rochelle, a daughter of Woodward and Mary Ann (Wayman) Monroe, and to them were born two sons: Harry M., who graduated with honors in June, 1898, from the Illinois University at Champaign, as an electrical engineer, ranking first in a class of sixty, and is now holding a responsible position with the Union Electric Company, of Chicago, and William, who is attending the Rochelle high school.

ROBERT N. JOHNSON, whose farm lies in sections 2 and 3, Taylor township, is one of the energetic and enterprising farmers of Ogle county. He was born June 22, 1843, in Delaware, Ohio, and is the son of William and Margaret (Noe) Johnson, the former a native of Virginia and the latter of New Jersey. The paternal grandfather, Jesse Johnson, was also a native of Virginia, but removed to Ohio, with his family, about 1800, where he later died. William Johnson was a farmer and speculator, an enterprising and influential man in the state of his adoption. In his family of children, our subject was sixth in order of birth. Of the others John lives in Oklahoma; Caroline, the widow of Samuel Maceer, resides in Cunningham, Kansas; Mary Ann, who married a Mr. Henry, lives near Delaware, Ohio; Abbacinde married Thomas Doty, but is now deceased; Morgan is a business man in Chicago; Ahaz, resides in Alma, Colorado; Adam lives in Carthage, Illinois; Phebe married Liberty Walkup, and they live in Rockford; Clara died at the age of sixteen years; Clinton resides near Ashton, Illinois; while the remaining one died in infancy.

The subject of this sketch remained at home until eighteen years old, assisting in the farm work, and in attendance upon the common schools. The war for the union being in progress, he enlisted in the second battalion, eighteenth United States Infantry and served three years. During 1862 he was in the siege of Corinth, the battles of Perryville and Stone River, besides various lesser engagements. In 1863 he was in the battles of Hoover's Gap, Chickamauga and Mission Ridge. In May, June and July, 1864, he was with General Sherman in his various campaigns, and at Atlanta, Georgia, September 20, 1864, he was mustered out of service, having given full three years to his country. His record was a commendable one during the entire time.

After receiving his discharge, Mr. Johnson returned to his father's farm and continued to assist in its cultivation until the fall of 1867. On the 21st of September, of that year, he was united in marriage with Miss Sarah Stevens, daughter of Joseph and

Margaret (Sharp) Stevens, who were among the early settlers of Ogle county, her father being a native of Kentucky. By this union there have been six children, the first and second dying in infancy. William grew to manhood and married Minnie Chalmers, and they make their home in Rockford, Illinois, where he is employed as billing clerk in the freight department of the Chicago & Northwestern railway. Fred S. resides at home and assists in carrying on the home farm. The mother of these children died February 24, 1882, and September 28, 1886, Mr. Johnson married Miss Addie Bly, daughter of Isaac and Rebecca Bly, who were also numbered among the early settlers of Ogle county. By this union there is one child, Mildred.

Mr. Johnson has three hundred and nineteen acres of well improved land and is engaged in general farming. Nearly all the improvements upon the place have been made by himself. He has but lately completed a new and elegant dwelling, two stories and attic, and his barns are large and commodious, capable of sheltering many head of stock. One wind-mill is in constant use pumping water for the stock. Since 1880, Mr. Johnson has been engaged quite extensively in stock raising, which has been a valuable part of his business. All the accessories of the place are such as to prove conclusively that he thoroughly understands his life work.

Mr. Johnson has never been an aspirant for political or official honors, and he has therefore held but few public offices. For one term he served as road commissioner, and for some years was on the school board. Fraternally he is a member of the Grand Army of the Republic, uniting with that organization for the reason that he desired to mingle now and then with those with whom he suffered in field and in camp during the days of the Civil war. Politically he is a Republican, believing that party best embodies the principles for which he fought. Mrs. Johnson is a devoted member of the Methodist Episcopal church. Whether as a soldier, fighting in the defense of his country, or as a private citizen engaged in tilling the soil, every duty laid upon him he discharges faithfully and conscientiously.

CLARENCE E. GARDNER.—Foremost among the prominent citizens of Rochelle, stands the gentleman whose name heads this sketch. He is one of Illinois' native sons, having been born in Franklin township, De Kalb county, on the 19th of February, 1865, and is a son of Edward and Mary Gardner. The former was born in Lancastershire, England, and came to America with his mother at the age of twelve years, sailing from Liverpool on the "John and Lucy," which, owing to severe storms off the coast of Nova Scotia, was five weeks and two days in reaching New York harbor. Upon landing they came direct to Franklin township, where Edward grew to manhood and followed farming, having acquired three hundred and sixty acres of valuable land in that locality. In 1868 he retired from farming and took up auctioneering, having been called upon to serve in that capacity upon various occasions before leaving the farm. Later he removed to Belvidere, where he now resides. The paternal grandparents of our subject were Edward Gardner, Sr., a native of Lancastershire, England, who died three months previous to his son's birth, and Ellen Hargrave, who, a number of years after her husband's death, married Thomas Moon, who brought the family to America, reaching Franklin township in 1851.

Clarence E. Gardner, the subject of this review, attended the common and high schools of Rochelle, graduating from the latter in 1882. He attended the Evergreen Business College, of Bloomington, and after graduating, went into the drug business, which he gave up after six years to read law in the office of Hathaway & Baxter, being admitted to the bar in 1891. His father was a successful auctioneer, and his son early acquired the art. Since 1886 he has been actively engaged in this line of business and in the fall and spring sales he is much in demand, owing to his successful method of selling. In addition to his law practice, Mr. Gardner has, since 1894, been interested in the real estate business, in which he is as successful as in auctioneering. He is the owner of a fine farm adjoining the town of Rochelle, and is interested in the breeding of pure blood Jersey and short horn cattle. He is also a lover of the horse and possesses some very fine roadsters.

On the 25th of May, 1886, he was married to Alice E. Reed, sister of the present county judge, Frank S. Reed, and one son, Fred Eugene, was born to them October 7, 1887. Mrs. Gardner died January 19, 1889, with consumption, shortly after her return from Colorado.

On November 26, 1891, Mr. Gardner married Blanche P. Baxter, of Rochelle, a daughter of Delos A. and Mary (Witrick) Baxter, whose history is given in the sketch of Delos W. Baxter, of this edition. Mr. Gardner is a Republican in politics and is now serving his fourth term as city attorney. He was first elected before being admitted to the Bar, and was on the anxious seat lest he fail of admission. He passed the examinations with honors and in due season was qualified. He is a member of the Masonic lodge and chapter of Rochelle and Sycamore commandery, K. T., and also of the K. O. T. G., of Malta. He is a brilliant and eminent lawyer and an energetic and much honored citizen of Rochelle.

DR. JEROME B. SNYDER is engaged in the practice of medicine and surgery in Polo, Illinois, and has that love for and devotion to his profession which has brought to him success and won him a place among the ablest representatives of the medical fraternity in Ogle county. He was born in Pittstown, Rensselaer county, New York, February 28, 1844, a son of John G. and Elizabeth (Rollins) Snyder. The father, who was a farmer by occupation, spent his entire life in Rensselaer county, where he died at the age of seventy-seven years. In politics he was a stanch Democrat. The mother died at the age of sixty-five years. To them were born eleven children, all of whom reached years of maturity and married, but two sons and one daughter are now deceased.

In the county of his nativity, the Doctor remained until fifteen years of age and then came to Illinois, making his home with a brother in Earl, La Salle county. He continued to attend school during the winter months until seventeen, and later worked in the office of his brother, who was a prominent attorney and banker of that place, but was clerking in a store at the outbreak of the Civil war. Responding to his country's call for aid, he enlisted at Earl, in 1861, in Company I, Fourth Illinois Cavalry under Colonel Dickny, was mustered in at Ottawa, and was first sent to Cairo, Illinois, where the regiment made their headquarters for two or three months, during which they engaged some in scouting in Kentucky. Dr. Snyder participated in the battles of Fort Henry, Fort Donelson and Shiloh, was wounded in the last engagemen, and sent to the hospital, where he was discharged three months later on account of physical disabilities. Returning to Illinois, he read medicine with Dr. Hinkley, at Leland, for one year, and later attended the Chicago Medical College, continuing his reading during the summer months under the direction of Dr. D. M. Vosburg. In the spring of 1864 he was admitted to practice, and first located at Grand Detour, where he remained for five years. During the following five years he was engaged in practice at Woosung, and in 1874 came to Polo where he was not long in building up a large and lucrative practice, which he still enjoys. He has given special attention to surgery and has met with most excellent success in his chosen calling.

At Earl, Illinois, Dr. Snyder was married in 1867, to Miss Maria M. Brown, a native of that place and a daughter of Allen and Sarah (Burt) Brown. The father, who came to this state from Massachusetts, died at the age of seventy-seven years, but the mother is still living at the age of eighty-five years and continues to make her home in Earl. To the Doctor and his wife have been born five children, namely: Maria, who died in infancy; Frank, a resident of Galt, Iowa, who married Minnie Miller, and has one son, Rex; Gerald, also a resident of Galt, Iowa, who married Philo Sweet and has one son, Gerald; Leone, who is a graduate of the Polo schools and is now a student in Stemmans Musical College, Dixon; and Ina, a pupil in the Polo schools.

Since attaining his majority Dr. Snyder has been identified with the Democratic party, was a member of the city council of Polo for two years, president of the board of education seven years, and assistant supervisor while living in Woosung. He was United States examining surgeon four years under President Cleveland's adminitsration, and is a member of the Ogle County Medical Association. The place he has won in the medical profession is accorded him in recognition of his skill and ability, and the place which he occupies in the social world is a tribute to that genuine worth and true nobleness of character which are universally recognized and honored.

WILLIAM RICE, one of the earliest settlers of Ogle county, was born on the 15th of September, 1822, in Nunda township, Livingston county, New York, and is of Welsh extraction. He has lived in the west since 1837, and watched with interest the remarkable development of the country since the days of the stage coaches and log houses. When a child of six years, his parents moved from Livingston to Chataqua county, where they lived until 1832 and then removed to Geauga county, Ohio. During the fall of 1836 the family lived in Cass county, Michigan, but believing that there were broader fields for advancement farther west, they came to Illinois and took up a claim in White Rock Grove, Ogle county.

Mr. Rice has eight brothers and sisters whose names are here given in order of birth. Erastus N.; Manson, living in Iowa, Amanda, deceased; Esther, living in Ogle county; Edwin, residing at Kings, Ogle county; Mary Ann, living in White Rock township; George, residing at Oklahoma; and Mariana and Emily deceased. In 1848 Mr. Rice entered government land in company with a friend, and together they secured a quarter section in Pine Rock township, which fifty years ago was a vast expanse of waving prairie grass, but lies to-day in great fields of green and yellow grain.

In 1854 Mr. Rice was united in marriage to Mary E. Boyce, a native of Hartford, Washington county, New York, and a daughter of Benjamin Boyce, Sr., one of the honored pioneers of Ogle county. Eight children have graced this marriage. Emma, the eldest, is a teacher of music, and is attending the Chicago College of Music. Frank is living at home and has assumed the management of the farm. Benjamin and Carrie are deceased. Mattie resides at home and is engaged in teaching school. Stella and Freddie are also deceased, and Ethel is attending school at Maywood, near Chicago.

Mr. Rice has an inexhaustible fund of stories and anecdotes of pioneer days; the hauling of grain to Chicago before the era of railroads; the Driscoll troubles, etc. He has a pleasing personality and a kind and courteous manner. His home is bright, cheerful and attractive, and at once impresses strangers with its hospitality, good taste, refinement and domestic luxury. His children are bright and intellectual and his ideas of educational advantages are reflected in their attained qualifications. No other man in Ogle county stands higher in popular esteem. In business transactions he is the soul of honor, and his name is synonymous with sterling integrity and uprightness.

GILBERT B. TREAT, D. D. S.— Among those who devote their time and attention to the practice of dental surgery and have gained a leading place in the ranks of the profession is Dr. Treat, who has spent almost his entire life in Polo, Illinois, his birth occurring there December 25, 1859. His father, Lewis J. Treat, was born in Glenwood, Erie county, New York, March 31, 1834, a son of Isbon and Apphia (Thompson) Treat, both of whom attained the age of about eighty years. The grandfather owned and operated a small farm in Erie county, New York. By trade the Doctor's father was a carpenter. Before coming west he married Miss Fannie Barden, who was born near Collins Center, Erie county New York, October 3, 1831, a daughter of Gilbert and Salina (Washburn) Barden, farming people of Erie county. Her paternal grandfather was Jacob Barden, and her maternal grandparents were Rufus and Mary (Finney) Washburn. Soon after their marriage Mr. and Mrs. Treat emigrated to Illinois, locating in Polo September 10, 1855, and here the mother made her home almost continuously since. The father was selling threshing machines throughout Iowa at the outbreak of the Civil war, and while in Floyd county, that state, he enlisted in Company G, Twenty-seventh Iowa Volunteer Infantry. While conveying prisoners, —some of the Quantrell guerrillas—to places of safety, he was stabbed and killed by one of them, Shelby Cole, to whom he had loaned his blanket to keep him warm. This was one of the most dastardly murders committed during the war. Besides his widow, he left two sons: Gilbert B., of this review, and Lewis Edward, a painter by trade, who was killed June 23, 1898, by falling from a building in Polo, on which he was at work. He married Rhoda Strahh, to whom a son, Lewis Edward, Jr., was born after the father's death.

The childhood and youth of Dr. Treat were passed in Polo and Albert Lea, Minnesota, and his education was obtained in the district schools, which he attended until fifteen years of age. He commenced the study of dentistry under Dr. W. W. Krape, now of Freeport, Illinois, who was the founder of the Knights of the Globe. He remained a much longer time, however, in the office of Dr. Maidwell, and in 1879 began practice in Polo, where he has carried on operations continuously since, with the exception of the time spent at Sharon, Wisconsin, in 1884 and 1885. His skill and ability in his chosen profession are widely recognized and he enjoys a good practice.

On the 9th of June, 1892, at Mt. Morris, Ogle county, Dr. Treat was united in marriage with Miss Clara M. Good, who was born near that village, a daughter of Jacob and Elizabeth (Plum) Good, and granddaughter of John Good, all natives of Pennsylvania. The father died in 1865, and the mother passed away at her birthplace in the Keystone state, in 1873. The children born to our subject and his wife are Earl Murillo and Milbrey Elizabeth.

Dr. Treat is a pronounced Republican in political sentiment, and for several years he most creditably and satisfactorily served as fire marshal in Polo. Socially he is a member of the Independent Order of Odd Fellows. He is a man of strong artistic turn of mind and is an excellent amateur artist, though but few of his most intimate friends are aware of the fact, as he makes use of this talent solely for his own pleasure. He is also an expert taxidermist, having mounted many hundred specimens of birds and animals from this region, and with a friend made a collection that was disposed of to a museum in St. Louis for fifteen hundred dollars. Of a social, genial nature, he has become widely and favorably known, and has a host of friends throughout Ogle county.

A. D. CLARK, an enterprising farmer residing at Flagg Center, and whose farm lies in sections 16 and 17, Flagg township, was born on the farm where he now resides, January 17, 1855, and is the son of A. D. and Melinda (Biggers) Clark, both of whom were natives of Steuben county, New York, the former born October 14, 1822, and the latter August 10, 1827. He was the son of Silas D. and Rhoda (Webster) Clark, the latter being a close relative of Daniel Webster. In his youth Silas D. Clark learned the shoemaker's trade, but soon abandoned it for the life of a farmer. He came west in an early day, but becoming homesick he returned to New York, where his death occurred when past seventy years old. His wife survived him and died when past eighty years of age.

A. D. Clark, the father of our subject, spent his boyhood and youth in his native county, and at the age of twenty was united in marriage, April 26, 1843, with Miss Melinda Biggers, daughter of Clark B. and Huldah Biggers. Her father, who was a farmer in Steuben county, New York, came west in the early forties and located in Flagg township, Ogle county, and lived there for a number of years. He then moved to Winnebago county, Illinois, where his death occurred in 1878, his wife preceding him a number of years. To A. D. and Melinda Clark seven children were born: Alonzo B., a farmer living in Cowley county, Kansas; Silas D., a farmer living in Lafayette township, Ogle county; Oscar F., who died November 18, 1849, at the age of ten months; Rhoda A., now the wife of G. Reed, of Lafayette township; Amerett B., who married E. R. Cooley, of Pine Rock township; Anson D., our subject, and Frank, a farmer of Flagg township.

With his wife and one child, A. D. Clark came to Ogle county in 1845, arriving here on the 18th of September, and taking up a claim of one hundred and sixty acres of wild land, a part of the farm where our subject now resides. For the land he paid the government price of one dollar and twenty-five cents per acre. He broke the land and built a small log cabin, which for some years was not only used as the home of the family, but as a tavern and postoffice, Mr. Clark serving as postmaster for a number of years. He was a good farmer and succeeded in improving and making a valuable place of over five hundred acres, a part of which he sold to his son. At the time of his death he yet retained two hundred and fifty-seven acres. While giving his attention especially to his farm, during the civil war he dealt largely in horses, buying and selling to the general government.

In politics, A. D. Clark, Sr., was a Democrat. He was township trustee for several terms, and was the first assessor and the second township clerk of Flagg township. He also held two commissions from the governors of the state as justice of the peace. For twenty-eight years he was superintendent of the Sunday school at Flagg Center. He was a true Christian man, one having at heart the interests of his fellow men. During the later years of his life he traveled quite extensively, visiting Europe and Asia in 1868. He enjoyed his travels and it was a pleasure to listen to his narration of places visited and events connected therewith. He died on the old homestead, November 21, 1893, while his good wife passed away June 3, 1891.

The subject of this sketch grew to manhood on the old home farm, and was educated in the school at Flagg Center, which he attended during the winter months, his summers being spent in labor on the farm. He continued in school until he was twenty years old, when he rented forty acres of his father's farm, and forty acres of another man, which he proceeded to cultivate. He continued to farm rented land until 1886, when he moved to Webster county, Nebraska, where he purchased a farm of one hundred and sixty acres, and there remained until the fall of 1890, when he returned to Ogle county, where he has since continued to reside. He now owns an interest in the home place, and is engaged in general farming.

Mr. Clark was married March 18, 1884, to Miss Lucy E. Mayberry, born June 25, 1867, and daughter of Samuel and Rachel (Thornberg) Mayberry. By this union three children have been born—Pauline M., Walter D. and Howard A. The latter died in infancy, and Pauline and Walter are now attending the district school which their father attended many years before.

In politics Mr. Clark is a Democrat. While in Nebraska he served as road commissioner, and since his return has served four years as a member of the school board. Fraternally he is a member of Kyte Camp, M. W. A. Mrs. Clark is a member of the Methodist Episcopal church. Both are well known in Ogle county, where their friends are many.

PETER COOPER, who resides on section 12, about two miles north of Rochelle, is one of the early settlers of Flagg township, one who has endured all the trials incident to pioneer life, and one who, commencing life without means, without friends, or help of any kind, has by his own industry, thrift and enterprise, gained a competency, and well provided for his family in future years. He was born in Marsh county, New Jersey, August 22, 1823, and is the son of Garrett and Sarah (Smith) Cooper, both of whom were natives of the same state, the former born in 1791, and the latter in 1800. The paternal grandfather, John Cooper, was also a native of Marsh county, New Jersey, as was also his wife, Catherine. They were the parents of eleven children, of whom Garrett was third in order of birth. John Cooper was a shoemaker by trade, an occupation which he followed in early life. He later engaged in farming, in which line he continued the remainder of his life, his death taking place in his native state during the second decade of the present century. His wife survived him a number of years.

Garrett Cooper grew to manhood in Marsh county, New Jersey, and was reared to farm life, and when arriving at man's estate chose farming as his life work. He was united in marriage with Sarah Smith, daughter of Peter and Sarah Smith, both of whom were natives of New Jersey, the former born November 10, 1775. He followed farming as a means of livelihood, and continued to reside in his native state, where his death occurred January 23, 1854. His wife died November 21, 1857. They were the parents of nine children, of whom Sarah, wife of Garrett Cooper, was third in order of birth.

Garrett Cooper and wife came to Ogle county in November, 1858, and here the wife passed to her reward in October, 1861. He then returned east, where he remained about eighteen years. His children by this time had all made for themselves homes, and he was left homeless. Our subject then went east and persuaded his father to once more come to Ogle county and spend the remainder of his life with him. He did so, and the son and his family made it as pleasant as possible for the old man. He did not, however, long survive, and passed away in June, 1890. He was a good man, one who endeavored to live right with his fellow-men. In politics, he was a Jackson Democrat.

The subject of this sketch spent his boyhood and youth in his native county and state, and assisted his father in the farm work, while attending the common schools as the opportunity was afforded him. When eighteen years of age he left school and commenced life for himself. For the next five years he worked on farms, and then learned the moulder's trade in Marion, Ohio, at which he worked for about two years. Borrowing twenty-five dollars of his uncle, George Smith, in the fall of 1849 he left Ohio and came to Ogle county, having previously purchased a soldier's land warrant for one hundred and sixty acres of land, for which he gave one hundred and twenty-five dollars. With his land warrant he took up a tract comprising one hundred and seventy-two acres, paying the government for the twelve acres additional at the rate of one dollar and twenty-five cents per acre. He then returned east, where he remained until the spring of 1855, when he came back with the intention of making this his permanent home. He now boasts that on coming here he built his house, manufactured the furniture for it, and was married, all within one week.

On the 29th of May, 1855, Mr. Cooper was united in marriage with Miss Mary E. Serick, who was born in Henry county, Ohio, December 12, 1836, and a daughter of John and Mary (Miller) Serick, both natives of Pennsylvania, but of German origin. They located in Henry county, Ohio, where he engaged in farming, and there the remainder of their lives were spent. In their family were twelve children, of whom Mrs. Cooper was eleventh in order of birth. Immediately after their marriage Mr. and Mrs. Cooper moved into the house which he had built, and in which the first two years of their married life were spent. It was a car-roof shanty, 12 x 16 feet, with one window and one door. It was, however, their home, and the beginning of better things. In two years they had laid by enough to purchase a house located on another farm, for which they paid three hundred dollars. The house was removed to their farm, and in that they lived until 1868, when their present commodious house was erected. The new house, which is of brick, was erected on an eighty-acre tract adjoining his original purchase, and compares favorably with many of the more modern structures. The brick house has been the home of the family up to the present time. In the years that have passed fortune seems to have smiled on our subject. In the home place, and in the adjoining township of Dement, he has some five hundred acres of excellent land, all of which is under cultivation. He has also over a section of well improved land in Gage county, Nebraska.

To Mr. and Mrs. Cooper fourteen children were born. Mary L. married Joseph Haines, and with their children they reside in O'Brien county, Iowa. Garrett P. is a stock buyer, living in South Omaha. He married Alice Sweeney, and they have one child. Oliver is living in Rochelle. Edith A. married Fred Crandall, and is living in Woodson county, Kansas. They have four children. Alma K. is the wife of Jonathan Lynn, and they reside in Flagg township. Nettie E. died at the age of nine years. Albert C., who is living in Rochelle, where he is engaged in the butcher business, married Anna Strite and they have three children. Minnie is living at home with her father. William W. died as the result of an accident, at the age of thirteen years. Charlie is living on his father's farm. He married Elsie McDowell, and they have one child. Lucinda died when one month old. Howard is attending the Rockford Business College. Clifford died in infancy. Florence is living at home.

Mr. Cooper has done well by his children, and has given each a good start in life. In March, 1897, he gave to each of his ten children a present of eight thousand dollars, a sum that is certainly not to be despised. Notwithstanding he has passed his three score years and ten, he is yet hale and hearty, and gives personal attention to his business interests. He has been a successful farmer, running after no special fads, but content to go along in the even tenor of his way, giving his time to general farming and stock raising, looking carefully after the little details of his business. When he came to this section it was but thinly settled, the great body of the land which is now paying such golden tribute to the husbandman was untouched by the plow. The settlers' cabins were yet few and far between. He has lived to see a remarkable change, one that can scarcely be realized even by those who have not only been eye witnesses but active participants in effecting the great transformation. Scarcely an acre of untilled land is to be found in all this section, and thousands of acres which were considered worthless by reason of their swampy nature have been reclaimed and are now the most productive lands. Villages and cities have sprung up, railroads have been built, miles upon miles of telephone and telegraph wires have been strung, school houses and churches dot the prairies, and a happy and contented people are living at peace with all mankind. Our subject has not only the satisfaction of having witnessed these things, but he has the double satisfaction of knowing that the credit is due to himself and other pioneers for all that has been done.

ANDREW C. SPINK is a prosperous farmer residing on section 27, Scott township, where he owns and operates a finely improved farm of two hundred and forty acres, which is kept under the highest state of cultivation. He was born in Washington county, New York, June 10, 1840, and is the son of Robert and Julia (Warner) Spink, the former a native of Rhode Island, and the latter of Connecticut. They were the parents of three children—Andrew C., Julia and Angelina.

The paternal grandfather of our subject, Michael Spink, was also a native of Rhode Island, and followed the sea for many years as commander of a vessel, and sailed almost over the entire known world, finally retiring and purchasing a farm in Washington county, New York, where he engaged in agricultural pursuits during the remainder of his life. The maternal grandfather, Nathaniel Warner, was a soldier in the Revolutionary war.

When our subject was twelve years old his parents moved to Winnebago county, Illinois, where his father purchased a farm of eighty acres near Rockford, and in connection with farming followed the trade of a carpenter which he had learned in his youth. His death there occurred, in 1895, at the age of eighty-five years, his good wife having preceded him to their heavenly home some two years previously, having died at the age of eighty-four. They were greatly esteemed people in their western as well as in their eastern home, being excellent people who delighted in doing good as the opportunity was afforded them. Their death was sincerely mourned by a large circle of friends.

After spending his boyhood in his native state, Mr. Spink came to Illinois with his parents, and remained with them until after he attained his majority, assisting in the cultivation of the home farm and attending the district schools a portion of the time, principally during the winter months. The habits of industry acquired in youth have remained with him during his mature years, as is shown by his well cultivated fields and the excellent appearance of his farm.

On the 23d of October, 1865, Mr. Spink was united in marriage with Miss Anna Rogers, who was born in England, and who accompanied her father, John Rogers, to the United States in her childhood. By this union eight children have been born, six of whom are living, as follows: Lilly, William, Belle, May, Fred and Frank. The deceased were Angeline and Charles.

Mr. Spink was elected assessor of Scott

township in 1893, re-elected in 1895, and again in 1897, filling the position to the entire satisfaction of the tax-payers of the township, one of the hardest positions that one can be called upon to fill. He has also satisfactorily performed the duties of road commissioner, another position in which it is difficult to satisfy all the people. For some years he has been one of the directors of the Scott and Marion Townships Fire Insurance company, which is doing a good business in insuring the farmers of the two townships at a comparatively small cost. Fraternally he is a member of the Masonic order, holding membership with the blue lodge at Rockford. He is also a member of the Modern Woodmen of America, his membership being with the local camp at Davis Junction. In politics he is a Republican, being a firm believer in the principles of the party. While a citizen of the county but fifteen years, Mr. Spink is well known, especially in the northeastern part, and as a citizen he is held in high esteem.

FRED FREDERICKSON, the leading tailor of Mt. Morris, is a native of Denmark, born in Copenhagen March 20, 1872, and is a son of J. P. E. and Johanne Marie (Skjellet) Frederickson, the former born September 12, 1846, in Storskoven, Orsö, Fjerding, Dromingland, Sogn, and the latter August 4, 1850, in Agersted, Bakker, Wor, Sogn. J. P. E. Frederickson is the son of Frederick C. Jensen, Gjelstrup. The latter word is a title bestowed upon him for bravery, similar to that which might be given one in this country by congress for some brave act. It was given him for his courage in reconnoitering the defenses of the German army during the Danish-German war of 1848-51, being compelled in so doing to pass through a line of ten thousand German soldiers. In addition to the title he was given eleven thousand five hundred crowns.

Frederick C. Jensen was a poor shepherd boy, and when fourteen years old he entered the military school of Denmark, completing the course at the end of five years with the rank of second lieutenant. On account of his being poor, with no influential person to back him, he was not given a post. Rather than be honorably discharged, he re-entered the military school as a private. After about two years had passed the colonel in command of the school sent a petition to the king reciting the facts in the case, and within twenty-four hours an answer was received complimenting the young man and assuring him that something would be done for him. In the meantime he would be sent to the naval academy. Time passed, and at the age of twenty-five he graduated from the academy with the rank of second lieutenant. After graduating, the king shook hands with him and told him that he would be looked after. He was then offered the rank of first lieutenant in the army or second lieutenant in the navy. He chose the former and was sent to Randers, Synder, Jylland. His first real service, with the exception of a number of skirmishes between Denmark and Germany, was in the war of 1848-51 between Denmark and Germany. He was also actively engaged in the Danish-German war of 1864, during which time he served as acting lieutenant general. For fifty-six years he served his country in active service, including the time spent in the military school and the naval academy. He

FRED FREDERICKSON.

MRS. FANNIE FREDERICKSON.

is now living a retired life, receiving a pension from his government.

J. P. E. Frederickson is one of a family of seven children. At the age of fourteen he quit school and commenced to learn the cabinet-maker's trade, but later took up painting, and is to-day a fresco painter of superior ability. He has a large establishment in a six-story building of his own. At the age of twenty he married Johanne M. Skjellet, and they became the parents of fourteen children: Fred, F. C., Eida M. C. F. (deceased), Eida M. C. F., R. C. (deceased), C. L., Jensine, K. U. M. F., Martinus, Thorald, Elvinus, Dasinus, Inger and Johannes.

At the age of thirteen years the subject of this sketch graduated from the public school and was then apprenticed in a large tailoring establishment in Copenhagen to learn the tailor's trade. After serving an apprenticeship of five years he left Copenhagen for Tronhjem, Norway, and worked there about four months, going from there to Christiana, Norway, where he remained a short time. From Norway he went to Stockholm, Sweden, and, after traveling over that country a few months, he returned home. He next went to Hamburg, Germany, and after traveling over the principal portions of Germany he went to Calais, France, where he remained nine weeks. He then returned home and was examined for the army, but was rejected. After remaining at home for a week he determined to try his fortunes in the United States. Accordingly he took a steamer for New York, and after landing came direct to Mt. Morris and commenced work for Gregor Thompson. After working for him a short time he concluded to establish a business of his own. He has now been in business for himself about five years and has built up a good substantial trade.

Mr. Frederickson was united in marriage, September 17, 1893, with Miss Fannie Wilson, a native of Ogle county, and daughter of James M. and Margaret (Downs) Wilson, the former born in Perry county, Pennsylvania, in November, 1806, and the latter in Champaign county, Ohio, March 1, 1816. James M. Wilson was the son of William Wilson, a native of Philadelphia, Pennsylvania, and who later removed to Carlisle, Pennsylvania, and who never came west.

James M. Wilson received his education in the common schools of his native state, and at the age of eighteen quit school and commenced to learn the carpenter trade in Lancaster, Pennsylvania. After learning his trade he went to Urbana, Ohio, and there remained until 1836, working as a journeyman. He then moved to a farm in Logan county, Ohio, where he resided two years, moving from there to Clark county, Ohio, where he worked at his trade for fourteen years. He then came to Ogle county, purchased a farm in Pine Rock township, and there remained until his death, August 20, 1874. His wife survived him nine years, dying January 10, 1898, at the age of eighty-two years and ten months. They were the parents of fourteen children—Sarah J., Mary E., William O., Samuel M., Alice D., Melvina R., Adel M., Margaret, Fannie H., Elizabeth, Katherine, Harry B., Josephine and one who died in infancy. In politics, Mr. Wilson was a Republican. While residing in Clark county, Ohio, he served as deputy sheriff of the county, and was then elected sheriff. He also served one term as justice of the peace. Fraternally he was a Mason, as his father was before him

Religiously he was a Baptist. Two of his sons, William O. and Samuel M., were members of the Eighth Illinois Cavalry, and served through the Civil war. Of the fourteen children, ten are yet living.

In politics, Mr. Frederickson is a Republican, and fraternally he is a member of Elysian Lodge, No. 56, I. O. O. F., and Mt. Morris Camp, No. 4526, M. W. A. Religiously he is a Lutheran, as is also his wife. While of foreign birth, he is a true American citizen.

WILLIAM H. BARKMAN, a well-known blacksmith of Polo, Illinois, and one of its highly esteemed citizens, was born near Hagerstown, Washington county, Maryland, February 6, 1831, a son of David and Rebecca (Guyton) Barkman, who were also natives of that county, the former born in Boonsboro, in 1801, the latter in 1808. The father, who was a shoemaker by trade, came west in 1863, soon after the battle of Gettysburg, his place having been stripped of its stock and fences by the contending armies passing to and fro continuously, "leaving nothing but the house." On reaching Ogle county, he bought a farm of forty acres at Franklin Grove, where he continued to make his home until called from this life in 1875, while on a visit to our subject's in Polo. He retired from his trade on coming to this state and devoted his attention exclusively to agricultural pursuits. His father was a soldier of the war of 1812. The mother of our subject died in Ogle county in 1876. There were ten children in the family, of whom he is the third in order of birth, but only seven are now living.

William H. Barkman received a district school education, walking each day three miles to the school house. At the age of fourteen he began his business career by working for neighboring farmers, and was thus employed for four years, after which he learned the blacksmith's trade at Beaver Creek, where he worked for a few months. The spring of 1853 witnessed his arrival in Illinois, making the journey by railroad to Rockford, whence he soon drifted to Grand Detour. There he secured employment in the Andrews Plow Works, but in the fall of the same year went to Buffalo Grove, the "Old Town," where he worked for Mr. Curtis until the first of the following year. Since then he has made his home in Polo, his first employment here being with Major Aplington, who was in charge of railroad construction. He remained with that gentleman until the railroad was completed, and then entered the blacksmith shop of Mr. Frost, where he worked as a journeyman until 1857, when he bought out his employer and has since engaged in business on his own account with marked success. In 1861 he built his present shop, where the anvil has rung a merry tune for over thirty-eight years.

At Mt. Pleasant, Washington county, Maryland, Mr. Barkman was married in July, 1851, to Miss Catherine Bombarger, who was born in that county, January 1, 1830, a daughter of Moses and Catherine (Betz) Bombarger. Eight children have been born of this union: Annie, now the wife of Harry Hearst, a railroad employe in Colorado, by whom she has two children, Charles and Alice; Elhannen, a traveling salesman for a Chicago house, residing in Decatur, Illinois, who married Rena Hill, of Tama City, Iowa, and has three children, Nina, Inda and Robert, Laura Virginia, who is the widow of Reuben Wilder, and has four children, Nellie, William, Eva and Harry; Ida, wife of William Poffenbarger, a blacksmith of Polo, by whom she has one child, Goldie; William E., who is in the shop with his father; Della, widow of Edward Farringer; Alice, deceased; and Mollie, wife of William Filson, a cutter in a shoe factory in Dixon, Illinois.

Socially Mr. Barkman is an active and prominent member of the Odd Fellows lodge of Polo, has filled all its chairs, and has been a delegate to the grand lodge four or five times. The Republican party has always found in him a stanch supporter of its principles, and he has been an influential member of the board of supervisors one term and city council for several terms. He has witnessed the entire growth and development of Polo, and can well remember when this region was all wild prairie with only a railroad grade passing through the present enterprising little city. He has been an important factor in advancing its moral and material welfare and has ever been recognized as one of its valued and useful citizens. There is no one still living in Polo who was here when he located in the village, for the pioneers are fast passing away.

BARZILLA KNAPP, justice of the peace and notary public, Creston, Illinois, and the efficient collector of the township of Dement, is a well-known citizen of the county, of which he has been a resident for forty-five years, or since 1854. He was born in Danbury, Connecticut, January 2, 1822, and in the same house in which his father, Hon. James Knapp, was born. The family is of English ancestry, and were early settlers of Connecticut, the grandfather, James Knapp, Sr., being a native of the state. James Knapp, the father of our subject, was twice married, his second union being with Miss Zeruah Gregory. She was the mother of Barzilla. Her death occurred in June, 1849. James Knapp was a prominent man in his native state, and served two or more terms in the state legislature. By occupation he was a farmer and owned and operated the old homestead which was in possession of the family for many years. He died in February, 1845.

Barzilla Knapp spent his boyhood and youth in his native county and assisted his father in the cultivation of the farm. His educational advantages were good, but the knowledge acquired in school has been largely supplemented by reading and contact with his fellow men. In early life he worked in a mill and was an expert miller. He was married in Danbury, Connecticut, in October, 1841, when in his twentieth year, to Miss Ruth A. Roberts. After marriage he carried on the home farm for his father for a few years and rendered what assistance he could to his father in his declining years. His wife died in 1846, leaving two children—Charles J., now of Creston, Illinois, and Ruth A., wife of Prof. H. N. Halleck, of Vinton, Iowa. Mrs. Halleck was well educated in the Creston schools and in the high school at Rockford, Illinois. She was a teacher for a number of years prior to her marriage, and later assisted her husband for nearly twenty years. Prof. Halleck is now living retired in Vinton, Iowa, while Mrs. Halleck is engaged in the millinery business at that place.

Mr. Knapp's second union was celebrated September 17, 1847, when he was united in marriage with Miss Melvina A. Read, a native of Connecticut, and daughter of Tilly W. Read, also a native of Connecticut. After marriage, and until his removal west, Mr. Knapp engaged in farming in the summer and in teaching in winters. In 1852 he came to Illinois on a prospecting tour, after passing through the states of Indiana and Michigan. This section seemed to him more attractive than any other, and he accordingly selected a location in Ogle county, near Brodies' grove. In 1854 he moved here with his family, and at once commenced the improvement of his tract of two hundred acres. Fences had to be built, dwelling and barns erected, the prairie broke, and crops planted.

After remaining on the farm until 1862, Mr. Knapp sold out and moved to Rockford, where he engaged in the lumber business until 1868. He then sold the business and removed to Creston, where he lived retired, building up his impaired health, which had been broken down by close application to his work. In the spring of 1869 he was elected justice of the peace, and by re-election has served continuously for more than thirty years. He was not inexperienced in the duties of the office, having served in the same while residing in this county prior to going to Rockford. In 1869 he was appointed notary public and has served in that office to the present time. He served one term as supervisor of Dement township before moving to Rockford. Since his return he has served eight years as township treasurer, and is now serving his eighth year as township collector. He has represented his township on several occasions in county and judicial conventions. In every position filled he has discharged the duties devolving on him in a most satisfactory manner. Since the organization of the party he has been a thorough and consistent Republican, but in local elections he votes for the men rather than party.

Fraternally Mr. Knapp is an ancient Odd Fellow. He was a member of the Rockford lodge while residing in that city, and was one of the charter members of the lodge in Creston, and remained in full fellowship until the surrender of the charter of the lodge. His wife is a member of the Methodist Episcopal church, and although he is not a member of the church, he yet attends with his wife and assists in the maintenance of the church in Creston. As a citizen he is held in the highest esteem by all who know him, and his friends are numerous in Winnebago, De Kalb and Ogle counties.

HUGH L. GRIFFIN, an enterprising young business man of Polo, Illinois, was born in that city April 24, 1870, and the greater part of his education was obtained in its public schools, though he attended the Dixon Commercial College, where he was graduated in December, 1890. He then went west and after spending a short time at Walla Walla, Washington, he settled at Port Gamble on Puget sound, where he was in the office of a lumber firm for five years and a half. His health failing, he returned home and took charge of the livery business left by his father. He carried on the business in partnership with his mother from July, 1896, until October, 1898, when he took complete control. In the successful conduct of the business he manifests good executive ability and sound judgment, and by fair and honorable dealing he has won a liberal share of the public patronage. He has a general livery and feed stable, and is also interested in the transfer business.

Leander Griffin, father of our subject, was born at Royalton, Niagara county, New York, April 18, 1838, and came to Polo, April 25, 1861. On the 3d of the following December he joined the boys in blue as a member of Company L, Fifteenth Illinois cavalry. His company served as body guard for General Halleck at the siege of Corinth, and later was with General Grant in the same capacity. Mr. Griffin was discharged June 24, 1862, on account of physical disability and returned to Polo. He then engaged in farming until 1867, and after a very short time spent in the grocery business, he purchased a livery stable the same year, conducting the same quite successfully up to the time of his death, which occurred January 7, 1892. He was unwavering in his support of the men and measures of the Republican party, and took quite an active and prominent part in public affairs, serving as as a member of the city council and as deputy sheriff for a number of years. He was one of the directors of the Ogle County Agricultural board for a period of six years, and was always found true and faithful to every trust reposed in him.

William Griffin, the great-grandfather of our subject, was one of the defenders of the country during the war of 1812. The grandparents, James and Jane (Brazee) Griffin, came west at an early day and purchased a farm near Polo, where the former died at the age of sixty-seven years. The Griffins were of English and Dutch descent, while the Brazees were of Scotch and Dutch extraction.

On the 19th of December, 1866, Leander Griffin was united in marriage with Miss Mary C. Hawkes, who was born at Lockport, New York, May 14, 1845. Her father, Norman Hawkes, was born June 20, 1802, in Franklin county, Massachusetts, of which his parents, Zebra and Rebecca (Sexton) Hawkes, were also natives. Norman Hawkes was married in 1829 to Miss Sarah Smith, a daughter of Eleazer and Mehitable (Bartlett) Smith, and in the spring of 1844 they came to Illinois. For eighteen months they made their home in Chicago and for two and a half years lived in Dixon, but finally took up their residence in Buffalo township, Ogle county, where Mr. Hawkes and his son-in-law, Leavitt Moore, owned five hundred acres of land. He died in 1884 and his wife passed away the year previous. The children born to Mr. and Mrs. Leander Griffin were Norman H., deceased; Hugh L., our subject; Roy; and J. Leavitt.

WILLIAM QUEST, section 35, Eagle Point township, is an active and enterprising farmer, the owner of a farm of one hundred and forty-eight and a half acres of valuable land. He was born in Pittsburg, Pennsylvania, August 20, 1850, and is the son of W. C. Quest, a native of Indiana county, Pennsylvania, born June 9, 1829, and who in his youth went to Allegheny City, Pennsylvania, to learn the blacksmith trade. He was married October 9, 1848, to Miss Mary D. Hart, a native of Pennsylvania, who was left an orphan in early childhood. W. C. Quest was the son of Matthew Quest, a native of Germany, and one of three brothers who left their native land to make homes elsewhere. One of the brothers was lost at sea, and one settled in London, England, where he amassed a large fortune. Matthew Quest was a pioneer of Indiana county, but later moved to Illinois, locating in Lena, Stephenson county, where he worked at his trade of jeweler.

W. C. Quest came to Illinois with his family in 1856, and joined his father in Stephenson county, and there worked at his trade until 1856, when he came to Ogle county, locating in Eagle Point township, where he built a shop and carried on business for some years. The last years of his life were spent at the home of his son, where his death occurred April 20, 1895. His wife died in 1893, and their remains were laid to rest in the United Brethren cemetery. Of their family, six sons and three daughters are yet living. One son, Charles, died at the age of six years. Of the living, W. H. is the subject of this sketch; Samuel is engaged in farming in Eagle Point township; George is living in Jo Daviess county, Illinois; Frank is living in Hazelhurst; Henry is a farmer of Ogle county; Margaret is the wife of Lawrence Piper, of Carroll county, Illinois; Anna is the wife of Sherman Stephens, of Nora, Jo Daviess county; and Eva is the wife of Charles Tillman, of Ogle county.

W. H. Quest was nine years old when he came with his parents to Ogle county, and here his life has been spent. He had but limited school advantages in early life, and is mostly self-educated, since arriving at mature years. He usually worked on a farm in the summer months, and attended school a few weeks in winter. On the 19th of January, 1885, he was united in marriage to Miss Emma Schryver, a native of Ogle county, and daughter of Jesse Schryver, a substantial farmer of Eagle Point township, who is a brother of Erastus Schryver, whose sketch appears elsewhere in this work. By this union there are six children—Jesse A., Mary Jane, Gracie Pearl, William Walter, Ida D. and Charles H.

After his marriage, Mr. Quest rented and farmed for a few years, and in the spring of 1883 made his first purchase of land, a farm of one hundred and forty-three acres, a place which had been very much run down. He got possession and located upon the place in the spring of 1884, and at once began its improvement. He has since remodeled the house, built to and made a good barn, planted an orchard and set out shade and ornamental trees, making a very attractive place. When a young man he commenced threshing grain during the season, a business which he has kept up for thirty-three years. For the past twelve years he has owned and operated a steam thresher. He is now making a specialty of feeding cattle for the general market, and annually feeds and ships from two to four car loads, and in addition about one hundred head of hogs. In this branch of his business he has met with success. He had but little to commence life with, but that little has been well used, and he is meeting with a just reward for his industry.

Mr. Quest cast his first presidential ballot in 1872 for Gen. U. S. Grant, and has since cast his ballot for every presidential nominee of the Republican party to the present time. He has taken some interest in local politics, and has often been a delegate to the conventions of his party, where he has used his influence in securing good men for the various offices. He has always been in favor of the public schools, and believes in having good ones. He has served on the school board for nine years, and for the same length of time was clerk of the board. He is now serving his second term as commissioner of highways. While not members of any church, Mr. and Mrs. Quest attend the United Brethren church, having been reared in that faith. He is a member of Polo Camp, No. 10, M. W. A. A man of strict integrity of character, he has many friends, especially in the western part of the county, where forty years of his life has been spent.

DAVID F. HIBARGER was born at Sharpsburg, Washington county, Maryland, on the 30th of November, 1832, and is a son of David and Rachel (Barnes) Hibarger. The former was also born in Sharpsburg, December 7, 1796. He was a carpenter by trade, but on coming west he took up a claim of one hundred and sixty acres, five miles from Mount Morris, where he resided until his death, January 11, 1854. During his lifetime he was a prominent and highly respected member of the German Reformed church. His wife was born October 26, 1791, near Baltimore, Maryland, and died in Ogle county, on the 22d of October, 1866. Ten children have been born to them, here named in order of birth: Adam and Daniel, deceased; Mary, the wife of Joseph Reynolds; Catherine, who married Isaac Long; Saliel; Calvin; David, the subject of this sketch; Emily, the wife of Edward King, now deceased; Ansevilla, also deceased; and Otha R. The paternal grandfather of our subject was Adam Hibarger, a wagonmaker, whose wife lived to be eighty years of age.

David Hibarger, the subject of this review, attended the common schools of Washington county, Maryland, until the family removed to the west in 1847, one son having preceded them by two years. When our subject was twenty years of age, he learned the brickmason's trade at Mount Morris, which he followed for two years, and then took charge of the home farm for his mother, his father having previously died. About this time he was married, and for two years rented the farm from his mother, renting elsewhere the following year. In the summer of 1864 he was prospecting in Colorado, and the two years following farmed in Lincoln township, Ogle county. In 1866 he removed to Polo, Illinois, where he has since worked at his trade. He has had charge of the brickwork of most of the buildings in Polo. He helped build the Harvester shops and a number of brick residences. Mr. Hibarger has made business trips through Colorado, Iowa, Minnesota and Illinois, and in 1871 went to Chicago, where he remained eighteen months. He has also spent three summers in St. Paul, Minnesota.

On the 22d of October, 1857, at Mt. Morris, David F. Hibarger was united in marriage to Mary Catherine Waltmeyer, who was born in Smithsburg, Washington county, Maryland, April 27, 1839. She is the eldest of a family of six children, and is a daughter of Joseph and Catherine (Adams) Waltmeyer, who came west in March, 1857, and settled near Mt. Morris. The former was born in York county, Pennsylvania, September 27, 1812, and was a son of Phillip Waltmeyer, and before coming west was the proprietor of a hotel and was also constable. Upon reaching Illinois he purchased a farm with his stepfather, but sold his share and rented a farm in West Grove township, which he retained for several years, and which he gave up to purchase in Lincoln township. He lived for a time at Maryland Station, Illinois, and later at Haldane, where his death occurred in November, 1893, at the age of eighty-three years. His grandfather took an active part in the war of the Revolution. Mrs. Waltmeyer was a daughter of John and Catherine (Bentz) Adams; the former was a son of George Adams.

Mr. and Mrs. Hibarger are the parents of eight children, the eldest being Oscar, who is married and is a brickmason, living at St. Louis. Willis married Henrietta Triber and lives at Aurora, Illinois, where he is employed on structural iron work. Of their five children, three are living, namely: Eva, Ada and Vera. The third son, Oliver, is a farmer and carpenter in Brown county, Kansas, and married Anna Pulvermaher. They have two children, Carl and Wanda. Cora married Blair Seyster, also of Brown county. The fifth child, Anna, is deceased, and David is employed on a farm in Iowa. Frank is deceased, and the youngest child, Pearl, is a successful teacher, who has for five years taught in the school of Lincoln township. Mr. Hibarger is a Democrat, giving his support to that party at each election. Among his business associates he is held in the highest repute for his integrity and uprightness, and in the social circles in and about Polo he and his family are held in the highest esteem.

JOHN W. SOUTHWORTH, who is practically living a retired life in the city of Rochelle, was born April 17, 1856, in Dryden, New York, and is the son of Thomas G. and Malvina A. (Freeland) Southworth, of whom a sketch is found elsewhere in this volume. He attended the public school and the academy at Dryden until the age of eleven years, when he came with his parents to Lee county, Illinois, the family locating in Reynolds township, where his father engaged in farming for seven years, and then removed to a farm adjoining the city of Rochelle, Ogle county. In the district schools of Lee county our subject continued his studies until the removal of the family to Ogle county, when he attended the schools of Rochelle for a time. Later he went to Rockford and took a short course in Miss Alice's Business College, after which he assisted his father on the farm in Flagg township until his marriage.

On the 14th of February, 1882, Mr. Southworth was united in marriage with Miss Katherine DeCourcey, who was born in Ashton, Lee county, Illinois, May 21, 1858, and daughter of David and Norah (Doody) DeCourcey, both of whom were natives of county Limerick, Ireland. David DeCourcey came to America at the age of seventeen, with his father, James DeCourcey, and located in Ashton, Illinois. Soon after his arrival he went to work for the Chicago & Northwestern Railway, and was in the employ of the company for a period of thirty years, serving as section boss, baggage master, brakesman, fireman, agent and other positions. After leaving the railroad, he bought and sold grain for a few years, and then went to farming in Dement township, Ogle county, where he remained one year. He then went to Malta, De Kalb county, and was there ten years. His next move was to a farm in Reynolds township, Lee county, where he died January 30, 1898. David and Norah DeCourcey were the parents of eleven children—Katherine, Margaret, James, Norah, Edward, Mary, David, Helen, Elizabeth, Victoria and Celia. Mrs. DeCourcey is still living in Rochelle. To Mr. and Mrs. Southworth three children have been born. Thomas G., born July 11, 1883; Helen, born December 31, 1889; and

Ruth, born November 30, 1895. The two oldest are now attending the public schools of Rochelle.

After his marriage, Mr. Southworth located on his farm in Flagg township, and at once commenced its cultivation. On that farm he continued to reside until March, 1893, when, having built one of the finest residences in Rochelle, he moved with his family to the city. The first floor of his house is elegantly finished, the parlor and library being in birch and cherry, and the dining room in cypress. The second story, in which are the bed rooms, is finished in Georgia pine. Everything about the place shows excellent workmanship. The library room is not built for show, but is well filled with the best literature of the day.

In politics, Mr. Southworth is a Republican, having voted the ticket of that party since casting his first presidential vote for James A. Garfield. He is now serving his third term as alderman from his ward, the duties of which office he discharges with fidelity. Fraternally he is a member of Willow Camp, No. 44, M. W. A. Mr. Southworth is a member of the Catholic church. A good business man, Mr. Southworth works for the best interest of his adopted city and county, and enjoys the confidence and good will of all with whom he has been brought in contact.

PETER GOVIG, an enterprising farmer, residing on section 35, Dement township, has been a resident of Ogle county since 1867. He is a native of Norway, and was born near Stevanger, January 4, 1833, and is the son of John and Martha (Randa) Govig, both of whom were also natives of Norway, the former born December 3, 1799, and the latter in March, 1800. In early life John Govig learned the trade of a shoemaker, which he followed for some years; but later, however, he engaged in carpentering. His children having come to this country, he followed them with his wife in 1859, and spent the last years of his life with his son, Peter, where his death occurred August 27, 1883, at the age of eighty-four years. His wife died in September, 1884, and her remains were laid to rest beside those of her husband in the Norwegian church cemetery in Alto township, Lee county. They were the parents of three sons and six daughters, all of whom grew to mature years. Melvina married Thole Sawyer, and they located in LaSalle county, Illinois, where her death occurred. Dora, widow of Eber Knudson, resides in LaSalle county, Illinois. Lars is a farmer of Lee county, Illinois. Martha Jane married Nels Aske, but is now deceased. Peter is the subject of this sketch. Mrs. Melina Foss, a widow, resides with our subject. Mrs. Bertha Hill resides in DeKalb county. Mrs. Martha Hill resides in Pasadena, California. John is a resident of Ogle county.

Peter Govig grew to manhood in Norway, and in 1857 came to the United States, where he joined an older brother. He first located in LaSalle county, Illinois, and worked as a farm hand by the month for about two years. In 1859 he made a trip to Pike's Peak, starting from Leland, Illinois, April 15, with three yoke of oxen. He did not, however, stop at the Peak, but pushed on to California, arriving there in September. On his arrival he commenced chopping timber for a sawmill, but later went to mining, in which he met with little success. In the spring of 1860 he made up his mind to return east, and started toward

Carson Valley and Camp Floyd, and then on to Gregory, now Colorado City, Colorado, where he again went to mining, at which he continued three years with varying success. Leaving Colorado he went to Montana, where he spent about four years, and meeting with fair success. In 1866 he returned to Illinois with some means and purchased the farm where he now resides, consisting of three hundred and twenty acres of excellent land. With little experience in farming, he commenced work, and is now numbered with the most successful and practical farmers in the county.

Mr. Govig was married in LaSalle county, Illinois, with Miss Berthena Aske, also a native of Norway, born May 15, 1850, the marriage ceremony being celebrated September 9, 1868, and to them have been born twelve children—John, Elsie, Peter, Mary, Peter, Nellie, Nels, Mabel, Noah A., Marth, Samuel and Daniel. Of these the first Peter and Nellie are deceased.

Politically, Mr. Govig is a Republican, but he has never asked or accepted public office. He is a good citizen, however, and lends aid and support to all worthy measures for the general good of the public. He has been a resident of this county for forty-two years, and although he came here poor in this world's goods, by his industry, thrift and economy he has accumulated sufficient means to enable him to live in comfort and ease during the remainder of his life.

ROMANZO G. SHUMWAY, of Polo, is one of the leading bankers in this section of the state, and bears a wide reputation as a most capable financier and business man. While as a prosperous business man, he has given close attention to his private affairs, he has never forgotten or ignored that bond of common interest which should unite the people of every community and he has always been ready to promote progress in every line.

Our subject traces his ancestry back to Peter Shumway, who founded the family in Massachusetts as early as 1665. His son Peter was the father of Oliver Shumway, who was born October 12, 1724. The latter's son, Elijah Shumway, was born October 24, 1754, and was the father of Lewis, who was born August 18, 1776, and became the grandfather of our subject. David Shumway, the father, was born March 27, 1803, in Jamaica, Vermont, where he lived until reaching man's estate. After his marriage he removed to Ohio, and in the spring of 1836 came to Illinois, settling in Winnebago county, where he entered a tract of land at the mouth of the Kishwaukee river, near Rockford. He was a man of great energy and thrift, who succeeded in accumulating a competency and surrounded his family with all the comforts of life. He died in 1879. In early life he was a Democrat, but on the organization of the Republican party in 1856 he joined its ranks and continued to fight under its banner. In Vermont he was united in marriage with Miss Sallie Greeley, who was born in that state in 1806 and died in Illinois in 1887. Her father, Solomon Greeley, married a Miss Smith, who died young, but he lived to an advanced age and spent his last days in Illinois. To David and Sallie (Greeley) Shumway were born five children, and our subject is the eldest of the five who reached years of maturity.

On the site of the present city of Oberlin, Ohio, Romanzo G. Shumway was born February 12, 1832, and was therefore but a small child when brought by his parents to Illinois. He was reared on the home farm near Rockford and attended the local schools until twenty years of age. On attaining his majority he left the parental roof and clerked for a time in a drug store in Rockford. Later he was similarly employed in a drygoods store in Dixon, and shortly afterward embarked in the drug business on his own account at Milledgeville, with a branch store at Lanark, continuing operations along that line for sixteen or seventeen years. In November, 1871, he took up his residence in Polo and became interested in a private bank, which was shortly afterward merged into the Exchange National Bank. During the fifteen years he was connected therewith he served as either its president or vice-president. He still carries on the banking business, being interested in nine different banks in Illinois, Minnesota and Wisconsin. A man of keen discrimination and sound judgment, he has met with marked success in all his undertakings, and his good executive ability and excellent management have brought to the concerns with which he is connected a high degree of prosperity.

On the 17th of October, 1855, Mr. Shumway was united in marriage with Miss Eugenia M. Palmer, a native of Aurora, Illinois, and a daughter of Dr. W. K. and Anna (Barnum) Palmer, the former born in Lane, Canada, in 1803, the latter in 1806. Dr. W. K. Palmer was one of the pioneers of Illinois, he having practiced medicine in Carroll county for many years, moving to Aurora when there was only one white family living there. Her paternal grandparents were Azariah and Anna (Kerley) Palmer, the former a son of Azariah Palmer, Sr. Her maternal grandfather was Herman Barnum, a son of Daniel Barnum, who married a Miss Hoskins, a daughter of Asa and Elizabeth (McCarthy) Hoskins. To our subject and his wife were born three children, as follows: Clara, deceased, studied art at Evanston, Illinois, was a painter of great promise and was an especially fine colorist. Anna is the wife of W. P. Wagner, cashier of the Citizens National Bank, of Green Bay, Wisconsin, and they have two children: Perry and Eugenia. Lucia is a graduate of the Polo high school and La Salle Seminary, of Auburndale, Massachusetts.

Religiously Mr. and Mrs. Shumway are members of the Methodist Episcopal church, and socially was formerly a member of the Masonic fraternity. In his political affiliations he is a Republican, and he has been honored by his fellow citizens with a number of responsible official positions. He has served as school treasurer for fourteen years; as supervisor for four years; postmaster of Milledgeville for fourteen years; and a member of the Polo school board for six years. The duties of the offices were always most faithfully and conscientiously discharged, and his public and private life are alike above reproach. His strict integrity and honorable dealing in business commend him to the confidence of all; his pleasant manner wins him friends, and he is one of the popular and honored citizens of Polo.

JESSE F. CATER, who resides on section 11, Taylor township, is well known in Ogle and Lee counties as an active and enterprising farmer, one who endeavors to keep abreast of the times. His farm of two hundred and seventy acres is always kept under a high state of cultivation and well supplied with all modern machinery rendered necessary in this progressive age. He was born October 25, 1866, in Bureau county, Illinois, and is the son of James and Susan (Perry) Cater, both of whom were natives of Montgomery county, Ohio, where they grew to manhood and womanhood, were married, and afterwards still resided for some years. In 18— they came to Illinois and settled in Bureau county, about ten miles east of the county seat. Purchasing a farm of one hundred and thirteen acres, the father engaged in agricultural pursuits. On that farm he continued to reside during the remainder of his life, his death occurring August 8, 1868. His wife is yet living.

The subject of this sketch remained under the parental roof until twenty-two years old, helping in the work of the farm, and when practicable attended the district school. He was married September 20, 1888, in Taylor township, to Miss Laura E. Harris, who was born in the township October 16, 1866, and a daughter of Ameriah and Hannah A. (Northrup) Harris. Her father was a native of Maine, born in Turner, Oxford county, October 24, 1822, while her mother was born near Halifax, Nova Scotia, July 12, 1826. They were married August 20, 1847, at Grand Detour, Ogle county. Mr. Harris was a well educated man, and for some years engaged in teaching school, devoting his days to the school room and his evenings to the manufacture of brooms, being an expert broommaker. Saving his means, he invested in land, and at the time of his death, which occurred June 13, 1868, he was the owner of one hundred and fifty-two acres of improved land in Taylor township. His wife died August 12, 1898. For more than fifty years she was a member of the Methodist Episcopal church at Light House, and was a strong believer in the doctrines of that church. In their family were seven children, Mrs. Cater being the only one now living. John B. died at the age of seventeen years; Sumner B. when six years old; Vesta E. at two years; addie L. at two years; Louisa E. at one month; and Lucia, a twin sister of Mrs. Cater, when nearly four years old.

Mr. Cater was one of a family of eight children. Edward married Mary Belknap, and now lives in Carson, Iowa, where he is engaged in the mercantile business; Mary M. married Harry Belknap, a carpenter by trade, and they reside at Goldfield, Wright county, Iowa; William H. married Hattie Scurr, and they reside in Colfax, Iowa, where he is engaged in the mercantile business. Arvin died in infancy; Ella J. married Cyrus Hills, who is engaged in the creamery business at Lamoille, Illinois; Henry M. married Carrie Fish, and they live in Berlin township, Bureau county, Illinois, where he is engaged in farming; Katie B. married Uri Jacobs, and they also reside in Berlin township, Bureau county, where he is engaged in farming.

Mr. and Mrs. Jesse F. Cater are the parents of two children—Sumner H., born February 12, 1891, and Orville E., born December 20, 1894. The former is now a pupil in the pupil schools.

In addition to general farming, Mr. Cater devotes considerable attention to stock raising, principally well bred horses of light and heavy weight stock, and Poland China hogs. He annually buys a number of head of cattle, which he fattens for the Chicago markets. He usually attends to his own shipments. In this branch of his business he has been fairly successful. He is not a politician in the ordinary sense of the term, but gives that time to his duties of citizenship that should be given by all. The only official position held by him has been that of clerk of the school board. He is a member of the Methodist Episcopal church at Light House, his wife also being a member of the same body. In politics he is a Republican.

FRANK J. CRAWFORD, editor and proprietor of the Polo Semi-Weekly Visitor, was born in Delhi, Delaware county, New York, November 10, 1843. He is the son of William S. and Orra A. (Sweet) Crawford, the former a native of Connecticut, born September 7, 1807, and the latter born in Green county, New York, September 19, 1810. They were married November 16, 1831. In his native state, William S. Crawford was made a Mason in 1828, and the principles of the order were ever dear to him. His wife died in Delhi, Delaware county, New York, April 18, 1888, aged seventy-seven years and seven months. He is still living in his native state. The maternal grandfather, Cyrus Sweet, who was a soldier in the war of 1812, died in 1861, at the age of eighty-four years.

In his native county, our subject obtained his education in the public schools, which he attended in the winter months until he was thirteen years old. When seventeen years old he went to Franklin, New York, and commenced to learn the printer's trade, at which he continued until in August, 1862. He was now in his eighteenth year, and the war for the union had been in progress for a little more than one year. He could resist the call of his country no longer, and as a private he enlisted in Company D, One Hundred and Forty-fourth New York Volunteer Infantry, August 13, 1862, at Franklin, Delaware county. After enlisting he went into camp at Delhi, where the regiment was thoroughly drilled, and on the 8th of October, following, having received marching orders, they set out for the seat of war. At Elmira, New York, they stopped long enough to receive Enfield rifles and accouterments, and then proceeded on their journey. In February, 1863, they were brigaded with the One Hundred and Twenty-seventh, One Hundred and Forty-second, and the One Hundred and Forty-third New York Volunteers.

The first engagement in which Mr. Crawford participated was near Suffolk, Virginia, May 3, 1863. His next engagement was on John's Island, South Carolina, July 2, 1864, followed by another July 9th, at which time they were charged by the Confederates, whom they repulsed, and then fell back to their line of earthworks. The enemy soon following, again charged them, attempting to capture the two guns attached to their brigade, but were again repulsed with a loss of five to seven hundred men. Mr. Crawford was promoted to corporal April 10, 1863, also promoted to sergeant May 30, 1865. While on their way from Washington to Frederick City, Maryland, July 12, 1863, their train was run into, a portion of it wrecked, and many soldiers were injured. The regiment was later stationed on Folly Island, Seabrook, Kiowa, James and other islands in South Carolina. While there they suffered very much from sickness.

Mr. Crawford was so fortunate as to keep a diary while in the service. From this record we find that he stood guard fifteen times, was corporal of the guard one hundred and sixty times, and sergeant of the guard forty-four times. The following extract from his diary shows what a soldier's life used to be: "Sunday, July 19, 1863, marched twenty miles and crossed the Potomac river at Berlin on pontoons; Monday, marched fifteen miles; Thursday, called into line, and marched twenty miles without rations; Saturday, we marched eighteen miles." Among his most intimate comrades while in the service were Lieutenant Boyd, J. H. Cobine and Giles M. Tiffany. After serving three years, save one month, he was honorably discharged from the service at Elmira, New York, July 13, 1865.

On receiving his discharge, Mr. Crawford returned to his old home at Delhi, New York, and for a few weeks worked in a printing office at that place. For several years following he worked as a journeyman printer in various offices of the east, and in 1876 came west and located in Dixon, Illinois, where he continued to work at his trade. In May, 1877, he came to Polo and found employment in the office of the Polo Press, where he continued for nine years. He then went to St. Paul, Minnesota, where he remained one year, and then returned to Polo, and went into the clothing business in partnership with W. R. Miller, continuing in that line until 1890, when he sold his interest in the establishment and purchased the office of the Polo Semi-Weekly Visitor, since which time he has been sole editor and proprietor. Under his control, the Visitor has taken front rank among the local papers of the state. While the paper advocates the principles of the Republican party, it gives special attention to local affairs, espousing all measures tending to advance the local interests of Polo and vicinity.

On the 19th of March, 1869, Mr. Crawford was united in marriage, in Franklin, Delaware county, New York, with Miss Aggie D. Field, a native of Andes, New York, born February 4, 1851, and daughter of Henry and Aseneth (Ferguson) Field, the former born in Green county, New York, June 11, 1821, and the latter in Andes, New York, September 15, 1824. They were married December 5, 1842. Mrs. Field died August 16, 1857, while her husband is still living in the east. To Mr. and Mrs. Crawford two children were born: Lulu May, born in Delhi, Delaware county, New York, June 12, 1872, died at Walton, New York, December 17, 1874; Earl F., born in Polo, Ogle county, Illinois, October 2, 1877, is now assisting his father in his printing office.

Fraternally Mr. Crawford is a charter member of Polo post, No. 84, G. A. R., and has held office in the post continuously since its organization, a period of eighteen years. He is past commander, and for some six or eight years has been serving as adjutant of the post, a position that he still holds. He is past master of Mystic Tie lodge, No. 187, A. F. & A. M., and past high priest of Tyrian chapter, No. 61, R. A. M., of Polo, Illinois, and is a member of Dixon commandery, No. 21, K. T., also a member of the Eastern Star. Politically he is a Republican, being a stanch advocate of the principles of the party, his views being plainly expressed through the columns of his paper. From 1881 to 1885, inclusive, he served as city clerk of Polo. Before coming to Polo he was a member of the Congregationalist church, but is now a member of the Methodist Episcopal church, and one of the official members, holding the office of steward. In the work of the church he takes considerable interest. As a citizen he is held in high esteem.

JAMES TAYLOR. As a representative of the intelligent and hardy pioneers who opened up Ogle county for settlement and have since taken a conspicuous part in its development, we are pleased to place in this volume a brief sketch of the life of the gentleman whose name stands at the head of this notice. He arrived here in 1841 and for many years was actively identified with its agricultural interest, but is now living retired in the village of Byron, surrounded by many comforts and luxuries, all of which have been acquired through his own industry, perseverance and good management.

Mr. Taylor was born in Blendon township, Franklin county, Ohio, twelve miles northeast of Columbus, February 16, 1823. His father, Ambrose Taylor, was a native of New York, where he married Abigail Meade, a native of New Jersey, who lived at Meade's Bason, sixteen miles from New York city. From the Empire state they removed to Pennsylvania, and later to Ohio, settling in Franklin county, where the father developed a farm. Subsequently he became a resident of Indiana, then spent several years in Ogle county, Illinois, and finally went to Iowa, where he passed the remainder of his life.

Our subject accompanied his father on the removal of the family to Indiana and located near Lafayette, on the Wabash river. In 1841 he came to Ogle county, Illinois, where he first worked by the month during the summer season for fourteen dollars, and also cradled wheat for fifty cents an acre. In this way he secured a start in life and later purchased a team and engaged in teaming on his own account. In early life he was quite a hunter, and as deer and other wild game still abounded in this region, he had ample opportunity to indulge in that sport. Although he worked for others he continued to make his home with his father until he attained his majority and together they entered eighty acres of land in this county, but later our subject purchased his father's interest. He continued to engage in teaming for some time, hauling lead from Franklin to Galena, and in the winter of 1848, made nine trips with a sleigh to Chicago. In connection with freighting he also followed farming to some extent, broke his eighty-acre tract and erected thereon a hewed-log house, for which he purchased the shingles at St. Charles, Illinois. Later he built a good frame residence and otherwise improved his land, adding to it from time to time until he had two hundred and eighty acres in the home farm in Marion township, all valuable and well improved land. Besides this place he owns a farm of one hundred and fifty acres in Byron township, through which both railroads pass, and which is pleasantly situated a mile northwest of the village of Byron, and also has a good residence in Rockford, valued at twenty-seven hundred dollars. Renting his farm in 1890 he removed to Byron, where he purchased a nice home and has since devoted his time to looking after his investment.

In Ogle county was celebrated the marriage of Mr. Taylor and Miss Martha Conway, on December 21, 1852. She is a native of Morgan county, Ohio, and a daughter of Jesse and Nancy Conway, who removed to Lawrence county, Illinois, in 1837, and nine years later became residents of Ogle county, where they spent their remaining years. They now sleep side by side in Byron cemetery. To Mr. and Mrs. Taylor have been born five children, of whom four are now living, namely: Ambrose, a resident of California; Vinton, who died at the age of ten years; Eveline, wife of Alfred Rood, of Rockford, Illinois; Sherman, who is operating the old home farm; and Martha, wife of John Shearer, a farmer of Byron township.

Since the organization of the Republican party, Mr. Taylor has been one of its stanch supporters, voting for Fremont in 1856 and Lincoln in 1860, but he has never cared for official honors. For the success that he has achieved in life he deserves great credit, for he came to the county empty-handed, and has not only gained a comfortable competence, but has also won the respect of those he has come in contact with by his honorable, upright life.

GEORGE W. DICUS is not only one of the best known and most popular citizens of Rochelle, but is also one of the heroes of our late war with Spain, having taken an active part in the capture of Porto Rico. For eight years he has been editor of the Rochelle Register, and is now most creditably and satisfactorily serving as postmaster of that place.

Mr. Dicus was born in Marshall county, Illinois, December 18, 1860, and is a son of George W. and Hannah (Lynch) Dicus, natives of Ohio, the former born in 1814, the latter in 1816. The maternal grandfather, —— Thompson, served throughout the Revolutionary war as captain of a company from Virginia, and he died in Dayton, Ohio, in 1842. The progenitor of the Thompson family in America came from England and settled with the first colony at Jamestown in 1620. The Dicus family, however, is of German origin and was not founded in this country until 1810, when the paternal grandparents of our subject crossed the Atlantic and took up their residence in Ohio, being among the pioneers of that state. Both died during the cholera epidemic of 1818, leaving their son, George W., an orphan at the age of four years. He was adopted by George Goodrich, who in 1826 removed from Ohio to Lacon, Marshall county, Illinois, settling there before that village was established. Our subject's father was thus reared to manhood amid pioneer scenes in this state and was educated in the schools of Marshall county. During his youth he returned to Ohio, and in a small town near Columbus he learned the blacksmith's trade. Having thoroughly mastered the business, he again came to Marshall county, Illinois, at the age of twenty-one and established the first blacksmith shop there. In his early life he was very successful, but after his service in the Civil war he met with reverses in business. In August, 1862, he enlisted in the One Hundred and Fourth Illinois Volunteer Infantry and served for about two years as regimental blacksmith with the rank of sergeant. He participated in the battles of Missionary Ridge, Chickamauga and other notable engagements, and was captured by John Morgan, being imprisoned at Montgomery, Alabama, for about three months, after which he was sent to Nashville to be exchanged. In the meantime he had suffered a severe attack of brain fever. During his imprisonment all trace of him

GEO. W. DICUS.

was lost, and his wife, leaving her seven children at home, went in search of him, and for about a year served as nurse at Nashville. She was twice married, her first husband being John Riley Russell, a contractor and builder, who died of yellow fever at Port Lavaca, Texas, in 1853. By that union she had six children, one of whom, John H. Russell, was also among the boys in blue during the Rebellion, in which he served for four years and two months. He was a member of the One Hundred and Seventh Illinois Volunteer Infantry, and was only fifteen years of age at the time he took part in the battle of Chickamauga. Mrs. Dicus is a sister-in-law of Albert Ringe, of Philadelphia, who was for years the president of the Philadelphia Plate Glass Insurance Company, and was one of the capitalists who furnished the means to Dr. Gatling to prosecute the manufacture of his guns. He was at the front for some time, being with Butler while testing the guns. After the war, the father of our subject resumed blacksmithing at Wenona, where he continued in business for some years, but spent the last eight years of his life in retirement at Streator. He died while on a visit to Ottawa, Illinois, August 20, 1891. His widow is still a resident of Streator. Our subject is the second in order of birth in the family of six children born of their union and all are still living with the exception of one son who died in childhood.

George W. Dicus, of this review, completed his education in the high school of Wenona, Illinois, and at the age of fourteen years commenced learning the printer's trade under Cadet Taylor in the office of Wenona Index, though he was still attending school. On leaving there at the age of nineteen, he went to Streator, and has since worked on most of the prominent dailies throughout the United States. In 1888 he purchased the Milledgeville Free Press, and in 1891 bought the Rochelle Register, which he has since successfully published, being one of the ablest representatives of the journalistic profession in this section of the state.

Mr. Dicus has been for years active in editorial association work, being first vice-president of the Illinois Press Association for three years past, a member of the State Republican Editorial Association, and has been a delegate five times to the National Editorial Association; in 1892, at San Francisco, California; 1894, Asbury Park, New York, 1895, St. Augustine, Florida; 1897, Galveston, Texas, and 1899, Portland, Oregon.

On the 7th of June, 1877, Mr. Dicus enlisted in Company C, Tenth Battalion Illinois National Guards, under command of Colonel Parsons and was later transferred to Company C, Fourth Illinois. After coming to Rochelle, he enlisted in 1892, as second sergeant in Company M, Third Illinois National Guards, subsequently was promoted to first sergeant and November 30, 1895, was elected first lieutenant. He assisted in quelling the riots at Lamont and Chicago, and in 1880 the company of which he was then a member carried off the honors at Mobile, Alabama. When the war between Spain and the United States broke out, Mr. Dicus was mustered into the United States service at Springfield, May 7, 1898, as first lieutenant of his company, and on the 14th of May proceeded to Chickamauga Park, where he remained until July 22, when the Third Illinois was picked out of the sixty-five regiments to accompany General Brooke to Porto Rico. They were transported on the auxiliary cruiser St. Louis and arrived at Ponce July 29, 1898, and after one day spent at that place proceeded to Arroyo, a distance of forty miles, where they landed on the 1st of August under the fire of the guns of the St. Louis, Cincinnati and Gloucester bombarding the town and woods. Capturing the place they occupied it for three days, during which time they took part in a number of skirmishes with the Spaniards. On the 5th of August they advanced on Guayama, captured the town and killed a number of Spaniards without loss to themselves. On the 8th of August they supported the Fourth Ohio regiment in the Cayey mountains, driving the Spaniards out. They were already to engage in battle on the 13th when the news of peace reached them, but they remained at Porto Rico on outpost duty for some time. At the order of General Haines, Lieutenant Dicus planted the flag of truce opposite the Spanish works. On the 11th of May, he was appointed by President McKinley as ordnance officer, having full charge of the equipments, ammunition, etc. With his regiment he sailed November 3 on the transport Roumania for New York, where they arrived on the 9th, and over the Erie railroad proceeded at once to Chicago. They were mustered out January 17, 1899. Lieutenant Dicus was a gallant officer and brave soldier, who was held in high esteem by his fellow officers and had the confidence and respect of those under him.

While in Springfield, preparing to go to the front, Mr. Dicus was notified of his appointment as postmaster of Rochelle, and was sworn in at Chickamauga Park by Colonel Fred Bennitt. His wife then served as acting postmaster until February 1, 1899, when he assumed the duties of the office, which he has since so efficiently discharged. He was married on the 22d of June, 1884, to Miss Mary Louise Johnston, who was born in Lancaster county, Pennsylvania. Her father, George W. Johnston, also a native of Pennsylvania, has borne his part in the wars of this country, having served in the navy during the Seminole war and the war with Mexico, and as a member of the One Hundred and Seventy-seventh Pennsylvania Volunteer Infantry during the Civil war. He was a cousin of Albert Sidney Johnston, the great Confederate general.

Politically, Mr. Dicus is an ardent supporter of the Republican party and its principles. He is prominent in Masonic circles, being a member of Horicon Lodge, No. 244, F. & A. M.; Rochelle Chapter, No. 158, R. A. M.; Sycamore Commandery, K. T.; Medinah Temple, A. A. O. N. M. S.; and the Eastern Star. He is deservedly popular as he is affable and courteous in manner, and possesses that essential qualification to success in public life, that of making friends readily and of strengthening the ties of all friendships as time advances.

ALVIN JOINER.—There are no rules for building characters; there is no rule for achieving success. The man who can rise from the ranks to a position of eminence is he who can see and utilize the opportunities that surround his path. The essential conditions of human life are ever the same, the surroundings of individuals differ but slightly; and, when one man passes another on the highway to reach the goal of prosperity before others who perhaps started out before him, it is because he has the power to use advantages which probably encompass the whole human race. To-day among the most prominent business men in Ogle county stands Mr. Joiner, of Polo.

The Joiner family was founded in America by three brothers, one of whom settled in New England, another in the Middle states, and the third in the South, and it is from the first that our subject is descended. His grandfather, Alvin Joiner, was a native of Royalton, Windsor county, Vermont, and one of the pioneers of Ogle county, Illinois, having taken up his residence here in 1836. He was a farmer by occupation and in Oak Ridge township he bought a farm of one hundred and sixty acres. He married Hannah Van Wagoner, of New York, a cousin of Roscoe Conklin.

Charles W. Joiner, father of our subject, was born in Windsor county, Vermont, December 8, 1816, and was educated in the common schools of that state and in Middlebury College. He came west with his parents in 1836, and much of his early life was devoted to farming in Ogle county. Later he became interested in lumbering in Michigan and spent twenty-seven years in the pineries of that state, but is now living retired with our subject in Polo. Though well past his four-score years he is still active in body and mind, and is numbered among the highly esteemed citizens of the community. He married Harriet M. Waterbury, who was born in Andes, Delaware county, New York, November 26, 1815, a daughter of John Waterbury, a native of Ballston Spa, New York, who was born March 26, 1791, and moved to Delaware county in 1808. His parents were Daniel and Mary (Stephenson) Waterbury, the latter of whom was born May 20, 1765, a daughter of David Stephenson. Daniel Waterbury was a son of Captain Daniel and Anna (Bouton) Waterbury, and was a member of his father's company in the Revolutionary war, in which both served with distinction. John Waterbury, the grandfather of our subject, was married, in 1813, to Miss Phœbe B. Bradwell, a daughter of Ezra and Sarah (Beach) Bradwell. She was born in Charlton, Saratoga county, New York, May 6, 1790, and died October 24, 1860. To the parents of our subject were born two children, he being the younger. Mary W. is the wife of John S. Thompson, who is engaged in the steamboat and salt business in Michigan.

Alvin Joiner, of this review, was born near Polo, November 13, 1848, and as soon as old enough began attending the district school near the home farm. In 1857 the family removed to Port Sanilac, Michigan, where he continued his studies in the common schools, was later a student in the Royalton Academy, Vermont, and took a special course in a business college at Hillsdale, Michigan, fitting himself to assist in his father's business. He completed his education about 1869, and at the age of twenty-one was admitted to partnership in the business. They purchased large tracts of pine lands, established sawmills, and shipped large quantities of lumber to the New England states, Richmond, Virginia, and also sold much in Ohio, Indiana and Michigan. Shingles were manufactured on an extensive scale and our subject himself has bundled enough to make thirty miles of bundles placed end to end. During their business they were burned out six different times. He retired from the lumber business in the fall of 1883, and the following spring returned to Polo, where he has since made his home, he with his father having invested some of their capital in farming lands in this region. They also own tracts in Florida and Dakota and are engaged in loaning money.

In Wood county, Ohio, Mr. Joiner was married, January 14, 1874, to Miss Ida Wood, a native of that county and a daughter of Major H. L. and Jane (Kunkel) Wood, the former born in Albany county, New York, June 2, 1809, but was reared in the western part of that state by an aunt. When a young man the Major secured the contract to build the Buffalo & Niagara Falls railroad, having learned something of railroad construction while engaged in building the Baltimore & Ohio road in Maryland. He went to Toledo, Ohio, to construct a part of the Wabash & Erie canal, and while there bought a farm in Wood county, Ohio, where he made his home from 1844 until 1876. In 1847 he was commissioned major of the first brigade of Ohio militia, and in 18— was made brigadier-general of the third brigade. During the Civil war he enlisted in the Sixty-seventh Ohio Volunteer Infantry; served as quartermaster for two years, and with his regiment was present at the battles of Winchester and Fort Wagner. From 1866 until 1870 he served as a member of the state legislature, and was superintendent of the Western Reserve & Maumee road from 1871 until 1875. The following year he removed to Monroe, Michigan, where his death occurred April 23, 1886. His father, Abraham Wood, was born in Rensselaer county, New York, January 28, 1774, and died April 28, 1850. He was a farmer by occupation, and wedded Mary Stuart, a descendant of the royal family of Stuarts. The Woods were of English origin. Major Wood was married in Fremont, Ohio, March 27, 1845, to Miss Jane Kunkle, who was born in the Wyoming Valley, Pennsylvania, April 20, 1820, and died August 23, 1883. Her father, Conrad Kunkle, a miller and mill owner in the Wyoming Valley, married Hannah Luce, who was an own cousin of Louisa Chandler Moulton. His father was a native of Germany. To our subject and his wife have been born five children, namely: Jennie H., who is a graduate of the Conservatory of Music, Oberlin College, and is now engaged in teaching in Danbury, Connecticut; Alice, who is preparing for Cornell University at the Hillside Home School, Iowa county, Wisconsin, where she will graduate in 1899; Charles Henry, Alvin, Jr., and Flora Isabel, who are attending the Polo schools.

In his political views Mr. Joiner is a Republican, and in his social relations is a member of the Knights of the Globe, the Mystic Workers of the World, and the Liberal Congress of Religions. He has served as mayor of Polo for two terms, and was the first postmaster of Chase, Lake county, Michigan, which office was established for the benefit of the lumber camps in that region. He and his father laid out the town at that place, and were prominently identified with its growth and development. In business affairs he is energetic, prompt and notably reliable, and as a citizen merits and receives the confidence and high regard of all who know him.

ELIJAH H. MILLER, who is living a retired life on his farm on section 15, Dement township, has been a resident of Ogle county since 1864. He was born near Auburn, Cayuga county, New York, September

27, 1837. His father, John Miller, was also a native of the same county and state, while his grandfather, John Miller, Sr., was a native of New Jersey. The latter, who was a wheelright by trade, and also a miller, built the first mill in Oswego, New York, and for years engaged in the milling business in connection with farming. He moved to the county when it was little better than a vast wilderness, purchased a large tract of land, cleared it of its timber, and made a fine farm. While he ran the mill his sons and hired help ran the farm.

John Miller, the father of our subject, grew to manhood in Cayuga county, and there married Christiana Dills, a native of New York, and reared in Cayuga county, and daughter of Abram Dills, who was an early settler of that county. By this union there were ten children, two of whom died in childhood. Purchasing a farm near that of his father, John Miller engaged in agricultural pursuits, and there reared his family. He died there about 1862, his wife surviving him until about 1879, when she, too, passed away.

Elijah H. Miller was third in order of birth of the ten children. He grew to manhood on the old farm of his father, and in the common schools of the neighborhood received a fair education. He is, however, mostly self-educated. He was married in his native county April 19, 1857, to Miss Emma McArthur, a native of Wayne county, New York, a daughter of John and Eliza (Waldron) McArthur, both natives of Onondaga county, New York. For four years after his marriage, Mr. Miller engaged in farming in Cayuga county, and in 1861 moved to Wayne county, in the same state, where he bought a farm of fifty acres near the village of Red Creek, on which he lived for three years. He then came to Ogle county, Illinois, and located in Dement township, where he purchased a farm of one hundred acres, sixty acres of which had been broken, but on which no further improvements had been made. He bought a small and cheap house which he moved to his place, and in which the family lived for several years. Later he built an addition to the house, making of it a neat and comfortable residence. He also built two large barns and erected other outbuildings, set out fruit and ornamental trees, and otherwise improved the place. After a few years he purchased forty acres adjoining, and in 1876 bought the eighty acres on which his present residence is located, and to which he removed in 1896. Since moving to his present home he has lived a retired life, leaving the management of both farms to his sons.

Mr. and Mrs. Miller are the parents of six children, five of whom are now living. Henry E. is a farmer in Dement township. Edward D. resides in Wisconsin. Bertha C. is living at home with her parents. Calvin F. is living on the old homestead. George A. is carrying on the present home farm. One daughter, Eliza May, died at the age of three years. Henry E. married Josephine Kendall and they have five children—Winifred V., William Elijah, Emert J., Guy and Elizabeth E. Edward D. married Nellie Miles and they have two sons, Roy Harold and Ralph Edward. Calvin F. married Rose Gibson and they have two children, Alice E. and Floyd Arthur.

Politically Mr. Miller is a life-long Republican, his first presidential vote being cast for Abraham Lincoln in 1860. He has never swerved from allegiance to his party, and has voted for every candidate of his party for the presidency from that time to the present. He has served several years as township trustee, and for a number of years as member of the school board, at times being president of the board. Religiously he is a Congregationalist, holding membership with the Congregationalist church at Creston, of which body his wife is also a member. For thirty-five years they have been respected citizens of Ogle county, and in that time have made many friends and few enemies. While their financial ability was very limited on coming to the county, they have the satisfaction of knowing that they have been prospered, and have enough to enable them to live at ease, should they so desire, the remainder of their lives.

HORACE STOCKING, one of Ogle county's leading agriculturists and a prominent grain dealer of Lindenwood, has spent his entire life in the county, his birth having occurred in White Rock township, October 13, 1848, and is the son of William Stocking, whose sketch appears elsewhere in this work. He received his preliminary education in the common schools and later attended the Rockford high school. Throughout his active business life he has followed the honorable occupation of farming, and has made a specialty of the breeding of shorthorn cattle. In 1898, he purchased a half interest in the grain elevator at Lindenwood, which is now conducted under the firm name of Horace Stocking & Son, and they are also doing a large and profitable business at that place as dealers in lumber, coal, all kinds of agricultural implements, carriages, wagons, etc.

On the 22d of October, 1873, Mr. Stocking was united in marriage with Miss Alma C. Weeks, a daughter of David H. and Eliza (Shaw) Weeks, of White Rock township, and four sons have been born of this union, namely: Dexter W., Elmer D., Howard L. and George E. Mrs. Stocking's father was born in Starkville, Herkimer county, New York, March 29, 1819, was well educated in the schools of his day and early acquired an excellent knowledge of farm work in its various departments. He was married, June 15, 1851, to Miss Elizabeth Shaw, of his native land, and to them were born seven children: John, who married Emma Murphy; Ida L., wife of William Ritchie; Alma C., wife of our subject; Dayton N., who married Carrie Danforth and has four children, Ethel, Charles, Hazel and Ida; Albert, who resides in Minneapolis; Henry, a commercial traveler; and George, who died at the age of five years. Both Mr. and Mrs. Weeks are still living and now make their home in St. Lawrence, Dakota.

Politically Mr. Stocking has always affiliated with the Republican party, and for twelve years he has most capably and satisfactorily served as highway commissioner. Socially he is a member of Linden Lodge, No. 820, I. O. O. F., of Lindenwood. As a business man he is energetic, prompt and notably reliable, and as a citizen he meets every requirement, manifesting a commendable interest in everything that is calculated to promote the welfare of his community in any line.

JOSEPH O'KANE, an honored veteran of the Civil war and one of the most philanthropic and generous citizens of Ogle county, has throughout the greater part of his active business life engaged in agricultural pursuits near the city of Polo. He was born in Franklin county, Indiana, December 23, 1836, and is a son of Daniel O'Kane, a native of County Tyrone, Ireland, who was born in 1811, and died in April, 1892. When a lad of eleven years the father came with his parents to the United States, landing at New York, when they proceeded to Franklin county, Indiana. In 1839 he came to Ogle county and bought a tract of land which he operated during the summer season, while during the winter months he worked at the cooper's trade. Knowing something of medicine, he was frequently called upon to prescribe for his neighbors in early days. In connection with farming operations he also engaged in the grain business to some extent in later years. His parents both lived to be ninety years old. He married Miss Lucinda Johnson, who was born in Kentucky, in 1813, and died in August, 1868. To them were born fifteen children, of whom only seven are now living. Three make their home in Polo, namely: Joseph, our subject; Mary S., wife of George Kingery; and Aaron A., a barber and insurance agent. James, the oldest, lives in Kerney, Nebraska; John W. lives in Wahoo, Nebraska; S. Byron lives in Lincoln, Nebraska; Caroline married Charles Hadsel and lives near Wahoo, Nebraska.

The subject of this review came with his parents to Ogle county in the spring of 1839, and grew to manhood on the home farm at Elkhorn Grove, attending the district schools only through the winter months, and working hard during the summer on the farm as he was the second in order of birth in the family of fifteen. In 1859 he went to California by way of New York and the Isthmus of Panama, it being thirty days from the time he left home before he arrived in San Francisco. He first worked on a ranch in Siskiyou county for fifty dollars per month, and during most of his stay on the Pacific coast was thus employed. In the spring of 1861 he returned to Ogle county by the same route.

Feeling that his country needed his services, Mr. O'Kane enlisted September 5, 1861, in Company B, Seventh Illinois Cavalry, the first cavalry regiment in that state, and was mustered in at Springfield on the 15th of that month. They were first sent to Bird's Point, Missouri, and for some time were engaged in scouting in that state, reaching Shiloh two days after the battle at that place. Their first engagement was at Corinth, followed by Grierson's raid from Memphis to Port Hudson, during which time they were sixteen days in the saddle without rest. Mr. O'Kane was captured at Coldwater, Mississippi, November 3, 1863, and for four months each was confined at Cahaba, Alabama, Charleston and Columbia, South Carolina, and Columbus, North Carolina, being finally exchanged at Annapolis, Maryland, March 1, 1865. He suffered untold agonies during his sixteen months imprisonment and it was only those of strong will who survived. Five days' rations consisted of a quart of meal and a pint of sorghum, so that many starved to death. At one time our subject and fifteen others dug a tunnel eighty feet in length, and twelve officers and four privates made their escape from Cahaba prison, and succeeded in traveling eighty miles by night, and were within one night's journey of the Union lines when recaptured. When a man gave out the rest would not leave him and all were caught, being tracked by blood hounds. After his exchange Mr. O'Kane was mustered out on release as his regiment had veteranized during his imprisonment and he was supposed to be dead. He reached home March 18, 1865, a wreck of his former self, and spent the following summer in recuperating. During his service he had sent to his home his wages, and this his father had invested for him in eighty acres of land, which was nearly all paid for. The fall after his return he was married and began life in earnest upon his farm, which he has since successfully operated. With wheat at two dollars a bushel, he finished paying for the place and has since bought one hundred and ten acres near Polo, and one hundred and five acres of pasture land on Buffalo creek.

At the Methodist Episcopal church, in Polo, September 17, 1865, was celebrated the marriage of Mr. O'Kane and Miss Jenette Rowand, who was born in "Old Town," Buffalo Grove, Ogle county. Her father, Andrew Rowand, was born in Paisley, Scotland, in 1813, and on crossing the Atlantic in 1831, first located in Canada, but seven years later became one of the pioneers of Ogle county. At that time he could have purchased any amount of land in the present heart of Chicago for almost nothing, but would not have taken it as a gift. He was a stonemason and farmer by occupation and bought one hundred and sixty acres of land three miles from Old Town, where he departed this life December 27, 1887. In politics he was a Democrat. His father spent his entire life in Scotland on the same farm, where the family have resided for two centuries as leaseholders, as few can own land in that country. Andrew Rowand married Elizabeth Lawson, who was also born in Paisley, Scotland, in 1811, a daughter of John and Jenette (Downey) Lawson. She came to the new world in the same vessel as her future husband and they were married in Canada. To them were born six children, of whom four are still living: Jenette, wife of our subject; Maria, wife of Marion Shoemaker, of Elkhorn Grove; Andrew J., who lives on the old home farm; and Agnes, widow of William O'Kane, a brother of our subject.

Fraternally Mr. O'Kane is a member of the Grand Army of the Republic, and in politics is an ardent Republican. Both he and his wife are active and consistent members of the Methodist Episcopal church and are noted for their generosity and kindly spirit. Having no children of their own, they have at various times taken into their home nine orphans, several of whom were legally adopted. These are as follows: Mabel is now the wife of William Lyons, who is successfully conducting a laundry at Pecatonica, Illinois. James Edward O'Kane lived with them for many years, but finally went to Chicago, where he assumed the name of Foster. He married Alice Vancil, and now resides in Chicago. Among the number who have lived with Mr. and Mrs. O'Kane at times are Katie Smith, Thomas Fassett, George Garrett, and Philla Sweet, who married Gerald Snyder. Their latest charge is Jerome Kilmarton, who now makes his home with our subject. Some one from Polo found him at the stock yards in Chicago, and knowing the philanthropic character of Mr. O'Kane and his wife, and being sure that he would find a good home with them, he brought him here. Such a couple certainly deserve honorable mention in a work of this character and we take pleasure in presenting this brief sketch of their lives to our readers, knowing that it will be perused with interest by their many friends and acquaintances in Ogle county.

JOHN HARTWIG, who resides on section 27, Eagle Point township, and who owns and operates a farm of one hundred and seventy acres, has been a resident of Ogle county since August, 1857. He was born in the kingdom of Prussia, Germany, April 3, 1829, and there received a good education in his native language, his knowledge of English having been acquired since coming to the United States. In September, 1853, he was united in marriage with Miss Catherine Schmidt, also a native of Germany. Friends in the United States had duly informed them of the opportunities afforded a poor man to acquire a good living, and even wealth, and they determined to here try their fortunes. Accordingly they left Bremen in a sailing vessel, and after spending some seven weeks and two days on the broad Atlantic, during which time they encountered several severe storms, they landed at Baltimore, from which place they came direct to Polo, Ogle county, where some of their German friends were then living. From Polo they went to Eagle Grove, and for the next two years Mr. Hartwig worked for others, in the meantime accustoming himself to the changed conditions of a new country, and acquiring a knowledge of the English language. In that two years he had succeeded in saving a small sum of money, with which he purchased twenty acres of brush land and built a small log house. From the land he cut the timber for the erection of his house.

A turn had now come in the affairs of Mr. Hartwig. He was now the owner of a home of his own, and even if it was unpretentious, it was a home, and the beginning of what he hoped would be better times to him. And it was the beginning, for fortune has since smiled on them. He came here when the country was experiencing the effects of hard times, from which it required several years to recover. But he was industrious, and he had a helpful wife, and by their united efforts they have placed themselves above want. To his original twenty he later added forty acres, and from time to time made other purchases, until he has now a well-improved farm of one hundred and seventy acres. He has now a large, neat frame residence, large barn, good outbuildings, with the place well supplied with fruit and ornamental trees.

Mr. and Mrs. Hartwig have three sons and three daughters. Casper married Rachael Schreiver, and they have two children, Aggie and Edith. He is the owner of a good farm in Ogle county. Valentine yet remains at home and assists his father in carrying on the home place. Seibert married Miss Ella Post, and has one son, Robert. He is also the owner of a valuable farm in Ogle county. Elizabeth is the wife of Edward Schreyver, of Sterling, Illinois, and they have one child living, Nellie, who is married and has one child. Kate is the wife of Fred Scholl, and they have five children: Frank, John, Arthur, Mabel and Emma. They reside in Ogle county. Emma married George Webster, and they have two sons, John and Howard. They reside in Carroll county, Illinois.

Politically, Mr. Hartwig and his sons are stanch Republicans. Religiously, he and his wife were reared in the Lutheran faith, and yet adhere to the doctrines of that church, but there being no church of their choice in the neighborhood, they attend the United Brethren church, and give their means to its support. They are well-known and highly respected people, and have many friends in the county. They came here with but little means, and when the country was but comparatively new, but have lived to see the country thickly settled with an industrious and thrifty people, and their children are all well settled in life. They have no cause to complain that they chose to make for themselves a home in this favored land.

THOMAS CRILL, who is now living a retired life on his farm on section 25, Monroe township, has been a resident of Ogle county for almost half a century, and is therefore numbered among the early settlers. He is well known in the county and has always been held in high esteem. A native of New York, he was born in Steuben, Oneida county, August 16, 1819, and is the son of Henry and Betsy (Brooks) Crill, both natives of the same state. Thomas Crill, the paternal grandfather, first enlisted in the British army during the Revolutionary war, was later taken prisoner by the Colonial army, under Washington, took the oath of allegiance, joined the American army, and was with Washington until the close of the struggle, when the independence of the country was acknowledged. For his services, in later years he received a pension from the general government. By trade he was a miller and for some years operated a mill on Van Horn creek. Subsequently removing to Herkimer county he purchased a farm and engaged in tilling the soil during the remainder of his life, dying at the age of ninety-three years.

Henry Crill, our subject's father, was born in the town of Stark, Herkimer county, New York, and there grew to manhood and married Betsy Brooks. He was a farmer by occupation and in his native state owned and operated a farm of two hundred acres. With a view of bettering his condition, or rather to give his family better opportunities, he sold his place and in September, 1844, came to Ogle county and bought a squatter's claim of one hundred and sixty acres in Monroe township, but later removed to the village of Monroe Center, where he purchased a cottage and lived a retired life. His death occurred in that village at a ripe old age, and his memory is held in grateful remembrance by those who were fortunate enough to know him.

The subject of this sketch grew to manhood in his native state, where he received but a very limited education in the primitive schools, the knowledge since acquired being received in the school of experience, and by reading and observation. On the 25th of March, 1845, he was united in marriage with Miss Caroline Smith, a native of York state, and a daughter of Wolcott and Betsy Smith. By this union five children were born, two of whom died in childhood. Those arriving at mature years were: Elizabeth, who married a good, substantial farmer of Fayette county, Iowa, where they now reside; Willard, who married Pauline Heller, and who is now working four hundred acres of his father's farm; and Etta May, who married James Mead, but who died at Kirkland, Illinois, leaving four children.

In September, 1852, Mr. Crill came to Ogle county and located on sections 25 and 26, Monroe township, and for some years lived in a house not over twenty feet from where his present residence now stands. When he located in the township there was comparatively little improvement made and settlements were as yet few and far between. His own place was entirely unimproved and he broke the first sod on the farm. The changes that have since been made are wonderful, indeed. His journey to Ogle county was made by water and rail to Chicago, and from thence by teams to his stopping place. There was then no railroad in Ogle county. From the time of his settlement here he has pursued an active life, and he has been honored by his fellow citizens with a number of local offices, serving three years as assessor, three years as collector, and the same length of time as commissioner of highways. In politics he has always been a Democrat, and a stanch advocate of the principles of the party. But he has always given more time to his business interests than to politics, and he has the reputation of being one of the best farmers in his section of the county. His place is well improved and kept in excellent repairs. In addition to general farming he has given more or less attention to stock raising, especially Holstein cattle. He usually ships his own stock to the Chicago markets, thus saving the dealer's profit. His long residence in the county has brought him in contact with many people, and he has the happy faculty of making and keeping friends.

PROF. C. F. PHILBROOK, superintendent of schools, Rochelle, Illinois, is a well known educator of more than a state reputation. He was born in Shelby county, Illinois, December 9, 1859, and is the son of Flavius J. and Sarah E. (Carter) Philbrook, the former a native of Licking county, Ohio, born January 8, 1836, and the latter in Knox county, Ohio, August 31, 1838. They were married September 12, 1858, at St. Elmo, Illinois. The Philbrooks trace their ancestry back to Thomas Philbrick, or Philbrook (the name being written both ways), who was born in Lincolnshire, England, and who came from England in 1636, locating in the southern part of Maine. A part of the family later went across the line to Exeter, New Hampshire, but that part which were sea-faring men remained in Maine. Thomas Philbrook was a mariner in early life, and was master of a vessel. He settled in Watertown, Massachusetts, his home being on the corner of Belmont and Lexington streets.

Seth Philbrook, the paternal grandfather of our subject, of the seventh generation from Thomas, was born in Vinalhaven, Maine, January 5, 1795, and in 1813 moved to Ohio. He married Margaret Ward, April 2, 1818, and in 1843 moved to Illinois, locating near Vandalia, becoming one of the pioneers of that locality. He was a farmer, and the farm purchased by him on locating there is still in possession of the family. His death occurred November 10, 1861, his wife surviving him but one month. They were the parents of twelve children, of whom eleven grew to maturity, the father of our subject being tenth in order of birth.

Flavius J. Philbrook spent his boyhood and youth in Ohio, being about eighteen years old when he accompanied his parents to Vandalia, Illinois. On coming to this state he engaged in farming in summer and teaching in winter until the second year of the Civil war, when he enlisted in the One Hundred and Fifteenth regiment Illinois Volunteer Infantry, and with his regiment marched to the front. He was not destined, however, to see much service in the field, as on the day before the battle of Lookout Mountain, he was captured by the enemy, and for five hundred long and weary days was held a prisoner, being confined in various prisons, including Belle Isle, Florence, Macon, Jonesboro, Atlanta, and last, but far from being least, in the notorious Andersonville prison. His experience was not one likely to be forgotten. There must, however, be an end to all things, and he was finally exchanged, and on the 1st of July, 1865, was discharged from the service, having had but little opportunity to distinguish himself in any way, being in no regular engagement.

After his return from the army, he engaged in farming in Shelby county, in which he continued until 1870. About 1858 he was united in marriage with Miss Sarah E. Carter, by whom he had eight children, our subject being first in order of birth. Gertrude married James Otto, of Independence, Kansas, where he is engaged in the real estate and loan business. Mary Belle married John R. Hogg, a banker of Drayton, North Dakota. Cora is a teacher in the public schools of Normal, Illinois. Lowell M. is a student in the State Normal school, at Normal, Illinois. Warren R., who is married and living in Bloomington, is in the employ of the McLean County Telephone Company. Margaret died in childhood, and one died in infancy. With the desire to give his children better educational advantages than the home schools afforded, Mr. Philbrook moved to Normal, after leaving the farm in 1870. He made that city his home during the remainder of his life, his death occurring in February, 1898. His wife died in October, 1896.

The subject of this sketch commenced his school life in the public schools of his native county, and was eleven years old when he accompanied his parents to Normal. Entering the public school at that place, he was graduated from the high school at the age of seventeen. After his graduation he commenced to learn the trade of plasterer, in which he continued for three years. It was always his intention, however, to obtain a better education than that afforded by the high school, and accordingly he entered the State Normal School when twenty years old, from which he was graduated in 1888. Being unable to pursue continuously the regular course, during the intervening nine years from the time he entered until his graduation, he taught school in the country surrounding and later in the schools at Normal. For a time he was principal of the schools of Golconda, Illinois. While teaching in Normal, he served as town clerk one year, and one year was alderman.

After his graduation, Professor Philbrook took charge of the public schools of Lena, Stephenson county, Illinois, and for four years was superintendent of its schools, giving good satisfaction to the patrons of the school. He could have continued there indefinitely, having been elected by the board for the fifth year, but having received an offer from the Rochelle board of education to become the superintendent of its schools, he accepted the offer, and in the fall of 1892 moved to that city, where he has since continued to remain.

On the 29th of June, 1892, Professor Philbrook was united in marriage with Miss Maud E. Simmons, a native of Illinois, and daughter of Rev. O. J. Simmons, a Methodist minister of the Rock River conference, and the only child of her parents.

Professor Philbrook is by nature and

training an educator. He has a love for the profession of a teacher, and gives almost his undivided attention to his professional work. He is an active member of the National Teachers' Association and of the Northern Illinois Teachers' Association, and in the latter body has been railroad secretary for ten years. Religiously he is a member of the Methodist Episcopal church. Fraternally he is a member of the Sons of Veterans, Horicon Lodge, No. 512, A. F. & A. M., of Rochelle Chapter, No. 126, R. A. M., and of the Order of the Eastern Star, of Rochelle. Of the latter body his wife is also a member. He is likewise a member of the Knights of the Globe. In each of these societies he has taken an active interest.

In politics Professor Philbrook is a Republican on state and national issues. In local elections he votes independently of party. During the campaign of 1896 he was secretary of the McKinley club of Rochelle, and in each of the county conventions of his party in the past seven years he has served as secretary. In the state convention of his party he has served as a delegate, representing his county. Thoroughly posted on the various issues of the day, he makes a representative citizen in every sense of the term. He is held in great esteem, not only because of his educational ability, but because of his worth as a man.

GUILFORD McDAID.—The world instinctively pays deference to the man who has risen above his early surroundings, overcome the obstacles in his path, and reached a high position in the business world. This is a progressive age, and he who does not advance is soon left far behind. Mr. McDaid, by the improvement of the opportunities by which we are all surrounded, has steadily worked his way upward, and attained a fair degree of prosperity. He is now numbered among the leading professional men of Oregon, where he is an attorney and also police magistrate.

Mr. McDaid was born in Lawrence county, New York, April 17, 1853, and received his early education in the schools of that county, and later in the schools of Oregon and Ogle county after his parents came west in 1865. He was appointed to the naval school at Annapolis by H. C. Burchard, member of congress, where he remained one year and then resigned and returned home to read law. During the year 1884 and '5 he attended a law school at Bloomington and was admitted to the bar on June 9, 1885. At the same time he was appointed police magistrate, and the esteem in which he is held in that capacity is illustrated by the fact that, though a stanch Democrat, he has been repeatedly re-elected by a Republican community. One who knows him well says that he gives his judgment without fear or favor, and allows no friendship or sympathy to warp his mind in passing on a case. He is a member of the Presbyterian church where he is held in the highest esteem.

Mr. McDaid is the son of James McDaid, who was born in Londonderry, Ireland, in 1816, and came to America in 1832, settling on a farm in St. Lawrence county, New York. He followed farming until the breaking out of the Civil war, when he enlisted in Company A, One Hundred and Twenty-fourth New York Volunteer Infantry. He participated in the siege of Fort Sumter, and was with the army of the Potomac in the various battles of the Virginia campaign. His father, Daniel McDaid, was a farmer in Ireland, and died at the age of sixty years before James came to America. The mother of our subject, Cerena (Drake) McDaid, who was born February 10, 1814, in Prescott, Canada, is a daughter of Lyman Drake, a farmer in New York state, who died in 1840 in his sixtieth year, and his wife, Polly (Woodcock) Drake, a native of Canada. The Drakes are an old Connecticut family who moved to Canada about the time of the war of 1812.

Guilford McDaid is one of seven children, four of which are living. Frances, the eldest, makes her home with the subject of this sketch. George resides in Clinton, Iowa. The third child is the gentleman whose name heads this review. James, the fourth child, resides in Chicago. Hiram O. and Lyman, both deceased, were in the Union army during the Civil war. Jennie, also deceased, was the wife of Alfred Woodcock, of Oregon, who served as consul to Italy, also as internal revenue collector for northern Illinois. He is now a traveling land agent for the Union Pacific railroad.

ORLANDO F. CRILL, residing on section 15, Monroe township, is an active and enterprising farmer, a life-long resident of the township and one who stands high in the estimation of his fellow citizens. His farm, which consists of two hundred and fifty-seven acres of well-improved land, is always kept under a high state of cultivation. He was born in Monroe township, May 30, 1850, and is the son of John J. and Margaret (Keith) Crill, the former a native of Herkimer county, New York, born May 12, 1825, and the latter of Morgan county, Ohio, born in 1830. Henry Crill, the paternal grandfather, a native of New York, married Betsy Wilkins, and both lived and died in York state. The great-grandfather, Thomas Crill, was a native of Hesse, Darmstadt, Germany, and at an early day emigrated to America, where he passed his latter days. John J. Crill, the father, was among the honored pioneers of the county, and came to Monroe township in 1844.

On the home farm our subject grew to manhood, assisting in its cultivation and attending the district schools as the opportunity was afforded him. He remained under the parental roof until twenty-two years of age, when he began life for himself. He was united in marriage December 17, 1873, with Miss Julia Matthews, daughter of John T. and Alvira P. (Garvin) Matthews. She was born June 1, 1852, in Franklin county, New York, and when a child of six years came with her parents to New Milford, Winnebago county, Illinois, and there grew to womanhood. By this union three children have been born. Perry J., born March 27, 1877, after receiving his education in the public schools, took a course in a commercial college of Rockford, thus preparing himself for an active business career. Edna, born May 10, 1883, and Margaret, born October 24, 1885, are yet attending the home school.

When Mr. Crill removed to his present farm the sod only had been broken, but with the characteristic energy of the family he went to work to further improve the place, and has now one of the best improved farms in the township, with a good orchard and an abundance of shade and ornamental trees, substantial dwelling, good barns and other outbuildings, and the land is kept under the highest state of cultivation. He has no especial hobby in the management and cultivation of his farm, but gives his attention to general farming and stock-raising. He has met with a fair degree of success, and feels that he has no just grounds of complaint. The short-horned cattle and Poland-China hogs which he annually raises upon the place he ships to Chicago, thus realizing the entire proceeds of their sale.

Politically, Mr. Crill is a Republican, and with the Republican party he has continued to act since attaining his majority. Fraternally, he is a member of the Modern Woodmen of America, holding membership with the camp at Monroe Center. A friend of education, he has always lent his aid to the public schools. In fact, to every enterprise calculated for the public good he is ready to extend a helping hand.

GEORGE HISCOCK is a well-to-do farmer residing on section 14, Dement township, one-half mile north of the village of Creston, where he owns a fine farm of one hundred and twenty acres, and which has been his home since about 1856. He was born in England, November 23, 1830, and was but two years old when brought by his parents, John and Frances (Dare) Hiscock, to the United States. They were both natives of England, and came to this country that they might better their condition in life. John Hiscock was a shoemaker by trade, an occupation which he followed for many years. He located in Danbury, Fairfield county, Connecticut, where he reared his family, and where his death occurred when nearly eighty-three years old. His wife survived him a year or two. They were good and highly respected people.

George Hiscock grew to manhood in Fairfield county, Connecticut, being reared on a farm, and receiving his education in the common schools and in a private academy. A young man of twenty-two years he came west, in 1852, and worked on a farm in LaSalle county during the summer. In the fall of the same year he returned to his old home, and during the winter of 1852-3 was engaged in running a stationary engine. In the spring of 1853 he again came to this state, and for several seasons was engaged in breaking prairie, having seven yoke of oxen which he used for that purpose. When in Illinois for the first time he purchased the land on which he now resides, and in 1856 came to the county, and in the spring of 1857 commenced its improvement. Year by year some improvements were made, his present substantial dwelling being erected in 1873.

In 1869 Mr. Hiscock was united in marriage with Miss Emily A. Potter, who was born, reared and educated in Onondaga county, New York, and daughter of Joseph and Jane (Carpenter) Potter, the former a native of New York, and the latter of London, England. Previous to her marriage Mrs. Hiscock was for a time a teacher in the public schools. By this union four children were born. Blanche is now the wife of Charles Schofield, editor of the Marengo News, of Marengo, Illinois. Mabel is the wife of Rev. A. F. Brewster, a minister of the Methodist Episcopal church, of Arlington Heights, Illinois. Previous to her marriage she was a successful teacher in the public schools. Alice was also a teacher in the public schools. She is now the wife of Charles A. Darnell, a lawyer of

Plano, Illinois. Georgia, a graduate of the Creston schools, is yet at home.

Politically Mr. Hiscock is a Republican, and has been a life-long advocate of the principles of the Republican party. His wife is a devoted member of the Methodist Episcopal church. Both are well known, especially in the eastern part of the county, and have many friends. A residence of forty-three years has enabled Mr. Hiscock to have been an eye witness of the great progress in the way of improvement, not only of Ogle county, but of the northern part of the state as well, and in the work of its transformation he has borne his part.

HON. MILES J. BRAIDEN.—Prominent among the energetic, far-seeing and successful business men of Rochelle is the subject of this sketch. His life history most happily illustrates what may be attained by faithful and continued effort in carrying out an honest purpose. Integrity, activity and energy have been the crowning points of his success, and his connection with various business enterprises and industries have been of decided advantage to Ogle county, promoting its material welfare in no uncertain manner.

Mr. Braiden was born in Castile, Wyoming county, New York, on the west bank of Silver Lake, October 10, 1835, and on the paternal side is of Scotch descent, his grandparents, Joseph and Nancy (Gillespie) Braiden, being natives of the north of Ireland. In their family were but two children, a son and daughter, Roger and Jane. The grandfather was born about 1767 and died in 1792.

Roger Braiden, the father, was born in 1788, and arrived in New York City with his parents the same year. They first located in New York city, and in the public schools of the Empire state he was educated, while later he became a farmer near Silver Lake, New York. In that beautiful locality he was united in marriage with Miss Sophia Fletcher, a daughter of Isaac and Ruth (Pierce) Fletcher, both natives of Westfield, Massachusetts, where for many generations the family has resided. Her father was born October 26, 1763, and as a soldier of the Continental army, he took an active part in the Revolutionary war. He died in 1837 in Tazewell county, Illinois, and his wife in 1839, near Joliet, Illinois. In their family were ten children: Gardner, Joseph, Benjamin, Polly, Charlotte, Sophia, Nancy, Eliza and Sarah. Five children, three sons and two daughters, were born to the parents of our subject, namely: George E., Cinderella, Marian, Isaac G. and Miles J. The father died on the 20th of May, 1843, and five years later the mother, with her children, came to Illinois, locating first near Waukegan, but she spent her last days in Rochelle, Illinois, where she passed away October 1, 1872. The Fletcher family can trace its record in England back to the thirteenth century, and still farther back in France and Switzerland, the name originally being spelled Flechiere.

The early education of Miles J. Braiden was acquired in the public schools of his native state, and it was completed in the Waukegan Academy, after the removal of the family to this state. He began life for himself as a farmer, and carried on operations along that line in Lake county, Illinois, until 1856, when he and his mother came to Rochelle, Ogle county, where he embarked in the grocery and grain business in company with his brother-in-law, H.

M. J. BRAIDEN.

MRS. CLARA V. BRAIDEN.

Burlingim, under the firm name of H. Burlingim & Company. On account of ill health, caused by the dust from the grain, he was obliged to give up the business in 1860, after which he purchased a farm in Reynolds township, eight miles southwest of Rochelle, becoming the owner of six hundred and forty acres on sections 8 and 17. He continued to devote his time and attention to the occupation of farming until 1872, when he returned to Rochelle and purchased the Flagg farm of one hundred and forty-six acres, upon which he has platted two additions to the city. He also purchased sixty-five acres of Mills Stewart in 1868, on which he platted two additions of one hundred lots. On his return to Rochelle he began dealing in lumber, coal, ice and building stone from quarries on his own land, and in these combined interests he has been eminently successful.

Mr. Braiden has been twice married, his first wife being Julia P., a daughter of Willard P. Flagg. Four children were born of this union: May E., Nettie C., Lucy S. and Wilber F., but all died of diphtheria with the exception of Nettie C., who is now the wife of A. A. McClanahan, a prominent attorney of Chicago, and has five living children, Nettie M., Miles, Alice, Bayard and A. Braiden. For his second wife our subject married Miss Clara E. Vaile, and to them have been born three children, two sons and one daughter: Roscoe V., Bryant F. and Marian G. Mrs. Braiden was for eleven years a most successful teacher in the primary department of the public schools of Rochelle, and her grade took first prize at the state fair in 1881. Her father, Edward G. Vaile, was born in Washington county, Pennsylvania, March 2, 1827, and was married May 23, 1848, to Miss Caroline Cooper, a native of the same place. In 1854 they came to Rochelle, where he died March 30, 1897, but at the present writing, in 1899, the mother is still living. To them were born six children, one son and five daughters, as follows: Mary E., Clara E., Maria S., Anna E., Emma C. and Edward L.

Socially, Mr. Braiden is a prominent Mason, belonging to Horicon Lodge, No. 244, F. & A. M., of Rochelle; Rochelle Chapter, No. 58, R. A. M.; and Dixon Commandery, No. 21, K. T. He is an active member of the Rochelle Agricultural and Mechanical Association, of which he was president for three years. In political sentiment he is a stanch Republican, and he has ever taken prominent and influential part in public affairs. Immediately after locating in Reynolds township, he was appointed township treasurer of school funds and held that position until his return to Rochelle in 1872. He was also elected supervisor of the township and most creditably and satisfactorily filled the office for six years in the township of Reynolds and for the three last terms received every vote cast for supervisor. He also served six years as supervisor of Flagg township, Ogle county. In 1870 he was elected to the twenty-seventh general assembly of Illinois, from Lee county, and most ably represented his district in that body for one term. In 1895 he was president of the Old Settlers' Association. He has served as alderman of Rochelle for two terms, and has been a member of the school board for six years. He has discharged his various official duties with a promptness and fidelity worthy of all commendation, and all that pertains to the public welfare receives his hearty support. He is emphatically a man of enterprise, positive character, indomitable energy and liberal views, and is thoroughly identified in feeling with the growth and prosperity of his adopted county and state.

RICHARD M. KING.—Prominent among the energetic, enterprising and successful citizens of White Rock township is the subject of this sketch, whose home is on section 21. He is public-spirited and thoroughly interested in whatever tends to promote the moral, intellectual and material welfare of Ogle county.

Mr. King was born in Pelham, Hampshire county, Massachusetts, January 28, 1843, a son of John M. and Lucy (Boyington) King. The father was a native of England and on coming to this country located first in the east. Having previously learned the art of manufacturing cloth, he was employed as overseer of woolen mills at various places, among them being Lowell, Massachusetts. He established and for some time operated a mill in Georgia, but in 1846 took up his residence permanently in Ogle county, Illinois, and turned his attention to agricultural pursuits and shoemaking, which trade he learned after retiring from the manufacturing business. In this county he met with success in his undertakings and acquired about two hundred acres of valuable land. In his political views he was a strong Abolitionist and was one of the first to cast his ballot for the Free Soil party, later becoming a Republican. He was born in November, 1802, and died in the village of Kings in 1886. The mother of our subject passed away in March, 1852. Of the eight children born to them, seven reached years of maturity and six are still living. They are George W., a resident of Flagg, Ogle county; James H., who is living retired in Rockford; William H., of Kings; Charles T., of White Rock township; Isabelle J., who married Kingsbury Morehead and died in Jackson county, Iowa; John, who is a resident of Hand county, South Dakota, and has represented his district in the state senate; Richard M., our subject; and Lucy, who died in infancy.

Richard M. King was only four years old when brought by his parents to Ogle county, but he well remembers many incidents of the journey made overland. His boyhood and youth were passed upon the home farm, and he was educated in the common schools and Mt. Morris Academy. In the fall of 1863, with his brother, John M., he enlisted in Company B, Ninety-second Illinois Volunteers, which, a year later, was made a mounted infantry regiment, and was first under Colonel Atkins, brigadier commander, and Colonel Sheets, regiment commander. Our subject participated in the battle of Chickamauga, the campaign resulting in the capture of Atlanta, Sherman's march to the sea, and the Carolina campaigns. After almost three years of arduous service he was mustered out at Concord, North Carolina, June 21, 1865, and was honorably discharged on the 7th of July, at Chicago. After his return home he attended school at Mt. Morris for one term, and then engaged in teaching in district No. 1, White Rock township, now the village of King's.

On the 18th of October, 1866, Mr. King was united in marriage with Miss Lettie Dalrymple, a native of Morrow county, Ohio, and a daughter of John and Eleanor (Logan) Dalrymple, who were also born in that state, where the mother died in 1849. In 1862 the father came to Ogle county and spent his last days in White Rock township, where he passed away September 13, 1891. His children were Lettie, wife of our subject; John A., still a resident of Morrow county, Ohio; Mary E., wife of W. D. Sechler, of Rochelle; and Martha A., wife of Charles Sechler, of King's. Mr. and Mrs. King have a family of six children: Carrie, who is one of the prominent instructors of the state and is now engaged in teaching in the city schools of Chicago; Frank J., cashier of the Farmers' Bank at King's; Lula, also a teacher; Harry L., who assists his father in carrying on the home farm; Jeanie, who is attending school in Rochelle; and M. Eleanor, now at home.

After his marriage, Mr. King rented land and engaged in farming, and the following winter again taught school in White Rock township. The next year he purchased forty acres of land now in the village of King's and owned by W. H. King. This he operated in connection with rented land and the following year was able to purchase an adjoining forty acres. Since then as his financial resources have increased, he has bought more land until he now owns three hundred and seventy-five acres of as fine land as can be found in the county. In 1875 he located upon his present place, which was then owned by his father-in-law, and to its further improvement and cultivation he has since devoted his energies. After occupying the small house standing thereon for one year, he built his present residence which he has since enlarged and improved. He has ever given his attention principally to general farming and stock raising, but at different times has also been interested in other enterprises. In 1875,

after the completion of the railroad through King's, he established the lumber and coal business there which is now conducted by Mr. Klein, but he carried on the same for three years. He was the one of the prime movers in organizing the White Rock Mutual Fire Insurance Company in 1873, and served as one of its directors for ten years. In 1891 he became a fourth owner in the Farmers Bank of Kings, and a year later his son Frank bought a fourth interest and has since acted as cashier. Fraternally Mr. King is an honored member of Rochelle Post, No. 546, G. A. R., and politically is a Republican, but at local elections supports the man and principles, rather than the party. He has provided his children with liberal educations and the home circle is one of culture and refinement. He has always taken an active interest in educational matters and for nine years has most creditably served as school trustee. He is a well-informed, pleasant and genial gentleman, and is very popular, having a most extensive circle of friends and acquaintances who esteem him highly for his genuine worth.

THOMAS G. SOUTHWORTH, a well-known farmer and capitalist, residing in the city of Rochelle, although not numbered among the pioneers of Ogle county, has been a resident of it for twenty-five years. He was born in Dryden, Tompkins county, New York, November 16, 1829, and traces his ancestry back to Faber Southworth, who was born September 1, 1710, and who married Mary Seabury. Their son John, born January 4, 1743, married Elizabeth Wightman, by whom was born Thomas, who married Sally Eldridge, of Berkshire county, Massachusetts, who died April 11, 1814. Thomas Southworth died in Dryden, New York, July 27, 1863, at the age of ninety-one years. Their son, John Southworth, was born September 25, 1796, in Salisbury, Herkimer county, New York, and at the age of ten years went to Dryden, New York, where he grew to manhood and engaged in farming. He was very prosperous and became a millionaire. He was married September 9, 1819, to Nancy Ellis, a native of Tompkins county, New York, and daughter of John and Rhoda (Rathburn) Ellis. Her father, who was a very prominent man, was known in all the regions roundabout as the "King of Dryden." He was county judge for a number of years, and served his district as state senator, and also held various other local offices. John and Rhoda Ellis were the parents of five sons and five daughters. He died a very wealthy man.

To John and Nancy Southworth five children were born: Rhoda Charlotte, John Ellis, Sarah Ann, Nancy Amelia and Thomas George. The mother of these children died March 16, 1830, and John Southworth later married Betsy Jagger, and to them were born five children. John Southworth never came west to reside, although he invested largely in real estate in Illinois, which was managed for him by his son, the subject of this sketch. He died at his old home in Dryden, New York, December 2, 1877.

Thomas G. Southworth grew to manhood in Dryden, New York, and in the schools of that place received his education. At the age of eighteen he quit school and commenced work on the farm. He was married April 10, 1855, to Miss Malvina A. Freeland, who was born August 6, 1834, in Caroline, Tompkins county, New York, and daughter of John and Ruth (Lake) Freeland, who were the parents of five children—D. Wellington, Adelaide M., Malvina A., Isaac Newton and Rhoda Jane. John Freeland was a son of Robert Freeland, who was born in Armagh, in the north of Ireland, and was mixed up in the Irish rebellion, and who came to this country in 1798. In early life John Freeland engaged in teaching, but later followed farming in connection with the trade of carpenter. He died in 1854, but his wife is yet living at the age of ninety-five years. To our subject and his wife one son was born, John Willis, of whom more is said elsewhere in this volume.

After his marriage Mr. Southworth moved into the city of Dryden, and with his brother-in-law, H. W. Sears, engaged in the mercantile trade for two years, and then returned to the farm. He continued to engage in agricultural pursuits in his native county until 1867, when he concluded to come west. On coming to Illinois, he located in Reynolds township, Lee county, and there engaged in farming for seven years. He then moved to Ogle county and settled on his farm adjoining the city of Rochelle, where he lived thirteen years, since which time he has been living in his present place of residence.

Mr. Southworth is a thorough business man, and has made a success in life. He has one farm of one hundred and sixty acres in Lee county, Illinois, and has several farms in Ogle county, aggregating in all between thirteen and fourteen hundred acres of excellent farming land. He has been connected with the Rochelle National Bank as a stockholder for about fifteen years, and for ten years has been one of its efficient directors. In politics he is a thorough Republican, but he has never been a politician in the common acceptation of the term. Believing firmly in the principles of the party, he gives support to the national and state candidates, but asks no office for himself.

For thirty-two years Mr. Southworth has been identified with the farming and commercial interests of this section of the state, and through his own exertions he has attained an honorable position and marked prestige among the representative men of Ogle county, and with signal consistency it may be said, that he is the architect of his own fortunes, and one whose success amply justifies the application of the somewhat hackneyed, but most expressive title, "a self-made man." He is respected by all who know him, and he is one of the best citizens of the county.

DANIEL ETNYRE.—Ogle county has been the home and scene of labor of many men who have not only led lives that should serve as an example to those who come after them but have also been of important service to their county through various avenues of usefulness. Among them must be named Daniel Etnyre, who passed away in Oregon, October 21, 1893, after a life of industry, and rich in those rare possessions which only a high character can give.

Mr. Etnyre was born near Smithsburg, Washington county, Maryland, March 29, 1817, a son of John and Catharine (Christian) Etnyre, who were also natives of Maryland and died in Ogle county. He was reared on a farm in his native state and continued to follow agricultural pursuits there until the emigration of the family to Illinois. On reaching the Ohio river, they floated down that stream and then proceeded up the Mississippi to St. Louis, and from there came by wagon to Ogle county, reaching their destination on the 16th of June, 1839. The father bought a farm, but before much had been accomplished in the way of improvements he died, in October of the same year.

Our subject purchased land on section 4, Oregon township, and for forty-six years made that place his home while devoting the greater part of his time and attention to farming. On leaving the farm in December, 1884, he removed to the city of Oregon, where he had previously built a commodious and pleasant residence. He was unusually successful in his business career, and besides his home farm, of nearly five hundred acres, lying three-quarters of a mile from Oregon, he had over three hundred acres elsewhere in the county. He was also interested in several important business enterprises in the city. He was one of the organizers and a large stockholder of the First National Bank, of Oregon, served as its president for a number of years, and was also president of the Rock River Furniture Company.

On the 12th of January, 1843, in Oregon, Mr. Etnyre was united in marriage with Miss Mary Rice, who was born in Boonesboro, Washington county, Maryland, September 5, 1825, and came with her parents to this state in July, 1837. They drove from their old home in Maryland to Carlyle, Ohio, in three weeks, and after spending a short time at that place proceeded to Ogle county, the remainder of the journey also occupying three weeks. Her parents were Jacob and Mary (Rowland) Rice, both natives of Washington county, Maryland, and she was the tenth in order of birth in their family of twelve children. After the death of his first wife, Mr. Rice married Catherine Fink, who is now living in Mt. Morris, at the extreme old age of one hundred and two years, and is in full possession of her mental faculties.

Twelve children were born to Mr. and Mrs. Etnyre: Lauretta, born March 25, 1844, is the wife of Henry Coffman, of Pine Creek township; Mary A., born January 14, 1846, died December 25, 1846; Sarah E., born December 29, 1848, who was the wife of John B. Mix, a farmer of Oregon township, died June 29, 1888; Augusta, born January 23, 1850, died May 5, 1864; William A., born March 20, 1852, married Annie M. Lantz, and is engaged in farming in Oregon township; John J., born September 12, 1854, died March 26, 1884; Lydia C., born January 23, 1858, resides with her mother in Oregon; D. Edward, born July 9, 1859, is engaged in farming on the old homestead; A. Elizabeth, born January 3, 1861, is the wife of Samuel B. Wadsworth; Mary Emma born January 21, 1863, and Samuel L., born May 18, 1865, are both at home; and George L., born June 26, 1868, was killed by a kick from a horse September 27, 1881. Mrs. Etnyre, who is a most estimable lady and a member of the Lutheran church, still resides in Oregon.

On the organization of the Republican party, in 1856, Mr. Etnyre joined its ranks, and continued one of its stalwart supports. He served for one term as county treasurer, but never cared for political preferment. Endowed by nature with a sound judgment and an accurate, discriminating mind, he feared not that laborious attention to the details of business so necessary to achieve success, and this essential quality was ever guided by a sense of moral right which would tolerate the employment only of those means that would bear the most rigid examination by a fairness of intention that neither sought nor required disguise. It is but just and merited praise to say of Mr. Etnyre, that as a business man he ranked among the ablest; as a citizen he was honorable, prompt and true to every engagement; and as a man he held the honor and esteem of all classes.

JACOB HEWITT, who resides on section 9, Scott township, is a well-known and highly respected citizen of the township, and a resident of Ogle county since 1855. He is a native of Huntingdon county, England, and was born September 17, 1825. His parents, James and Mary (Green) Hewitt, were also natives of the same shire. They had a family of nine children, as follows: Jane, Jacob, Hannah, Elizabeth, Sarah, William, James, Daniel and Samuel.

After spending his boyhood and youth in his native land, where he received a very limited education, when twenty-five years old, our subject determined on emigrating to America where the opportunities for advancement were supposed to be much greater, and where the poor man had equal rights with the rich. Leaving home, he sailed for " the land of the free," and after a voyage of a number of days he landed at New York. After two years sojourn in various places, in 1855 he came to Ogle county, which has since continued to be his home. For two years he worked by the day at odd jobs, and having accumulated a little money he purchased sixty acres of unimproved land on section 9, and at once set about its improvement. In due time he had a well cultivated farm which he has since kept under a high state of cultivation, and which has been to himself and wife a restful place of abode.

On the 14th of February, 1855, Mr. Hewitt was united in marriage with Miss Sarah Brand, also a native of England, who came to the United States with her father, William Brand, who was born, reared and married in Huntingdon county, England. To her husband Mrs. Hewitt has been a helpmeet indeed, and their married life has been a happy one. While no children came to bless their union, they have always been happy in each other's love. Both are members of the Baptist church, in the teachings of which they have unbounded faith, and in the work of which they are greatly interested. In politics he is a Democrat.

M J. CRILL, who resides on section 14, Monroe township, is a well-known farmer and stock raiser, one who is known throughout the length and breadth of the county. He is a native of the township, born August 11, 1848, and is the son of John J. and Margaret Crill, who were married November 7, 1847, and who were numbered among the early settlers of the county, and who were the parents of three children—M. J., Orlando and Augusta. The latter married Henry Hardy, and they are now living a retired life in Rockford, Illinois.

The subject of this sketch remained under the parental roof until he was twenty-six years old, and in the common schools of the neighborhood received his education. The greater part of his education, however, was obtained in the school of experience, the lessons of which are usually well impressed upon the mind, and seldom forgotten. From the time old enough to reach the handles of the plow, he was expected to do his full share of the farm work, and whatever he did was well done. The habits of industry acquired in youth have remained with him during life, and his farm is always under a high state of cultivation and well kept in every respect.

Mr. Crill was married January 3, 1871, at Cherry Valley, Illinois, to Amelia Hondshell, a native of Winnebago county, Illinois, and daughter of Jacob and Nancy (Oh dear) Hondeshell, both of whom were natives of Pennsylvania, and who were numbered among the early settlers of Winnebago county. By this union four children were born: Nellie A. married Robert Dresser, a substantial farmer residing at Lindenwood, Illinois, where he operates a farm of one hundred and sixty acres; Maude died at the age of nine years, and Ruth Ella when ten months old, and one died in infancy.

When Mr. Crill was first married he commenced farming a tract of five hundred and ten acres of land and made a specialty of raising Percheron and Morgan horses and Shetland ponies, short horn Durham cattle, and white Chester hogs, a branch of his business in which he was quite successful. He has continued to engage in general farming, and his ability as a farmer is acknowledged by all. For three years he served as road commissioner, was twelve years a member of the school board, and for five years has been one of the constables of his township, an office which he now holds. In politics he is a Republican. Fraternally he is a Mason, a member of the Knights of Pythias and Modern Woodmen of America

GEORGE MURRAY.—Canada has furnished to the United States many bright, enterprising young men who have left the Dominion to enter the business circles of this country with its more progressive methods, livelier competition, and advancement more quickly secured. Among this number is Mr. Murray, one of the most enterprising and progressive farmers and stock breeders of Ogle county, his home being on section 17, Buffalo township.

Mr. Murray was born near Toronto, Ontario, Canada, November 15, 1850, and is a son of Thomas Murray, a native of Scotland, born in the city of Edinburg, September 26, 1818. When a young man the father came to the new world, locating in Ontario, Canada, in 1836, and there he followed the blacksmith's trade throughout the remainder of his life, dying January 17, 1866. He was married in Canada, in March, 1848, to Miss Louisa Graham, also a native of Scotland, her birth occurring in Dumfrieshire, June 28, 1826. She crossed the Atlantic with a brother and also took up her residence in Ontario. She survived her husband for thirty years, spending her last days with her son in Illinois, where she passed away January 27, 1896. She was the mother of eight children, five sons and three daughters, of whom four sons and two daughters are still living, namely: Mary, who acts as housekeeper for our subject, George, of this review; Thomas, a farmer of Holcomb, Ogle county; John, who is married and engaged in farming in Lee county, Illinois; Robert, and Mrs Margaret Copenhaver, who also resides with our subject and has two sons, George and Robert.

George Murray was reared in Ontario, Canada, and received a good common-school education, which well fitted him for life's responsible duties. As a young man he came to Illinois, in 1872, and took up his residence in Taylor township, Ogle county, where for one year he worked by the month as a farm hand. He then rented a farm, which he operated for the same length of time. Since then he has given the greater part of his time and attention to the breeding of fine stock, in partnership with his brother importing and dealing in pure-blooded Percheron, Clydesdale and French coach horses. The firm of Murray Brothers became well known among breeders and dealers in different states and they sold their horses quite extensively throughout the west, doing a large and profitable business. The partnership was dissolved in 1886, but our subject continued to engage in the business until 1893. His first purchase of land consisted of seventy-five acres in what is now Woosung township, but after residing there for three years, he sold the place and in 1881 located upon his present farm, consisting at that time of one hundred and eighty-two acres. Upon the place he has made extensive improvements, which add greatly to its value and attractive appearance, making it one of the most desirable farms of the locality. He has enlarged its boundaries so that they now contain two hundred acres of valuable land under a high state of cultivation and improved with a large, neat residence, corn cribs, granaries, barns, etc. He has also given considerable attention to the raising of Galloway cattle, and still feeds annually from one to four car loads of cattle and a car load of hogs for the market. He started out in life for himself with nothing but his own indomitable energy and through his own efforts has acquired a comfortable competence, being to-day one of the substantial men of the county.

GEORGE MURRAY.

Mr. Murray cast his first presidential vote for Grover Cleveland and continued to affiliate with the Democracy until 1896, when he supported William McKinley, the Republican candidate. For a number of years he has served as a member of the school board and has been president of the district. He is also connected with the library association and has served as one of its trustees and directors. He and his sisters hold membership in the Independent Presbyterian church of Polo, and he is also a member of the Knights of the Globe. He is held in high regard by all who know him, and he has a host of warm friends throughout the county.

THOMAS P. RUTLEDGE, deceased, was for years a well-known citizen of Ogle county, one who to know was to love and esteem. He was born February 1, 1810, in New York city, and was a son of Robert and Mary (Lurvey) Rutledge, the former a native of Ireland, born April 27, 1782, and the latter in New York state, April 14, 1783. In his youth Robert Rutledge emigrated to the United States, where he formed the acquaintance of Mary Lurvey, and in New York city they were united in marriage. From that city they emigrated to Canada, where he purchased two hundred acres of land and engaged in agricultural pursuits. There their family of ten children were born, and in that country the parents remained until 1841, when they came to Ogle county, Illinois, locating in Oregon township, Mr. Rutledge entering and purchasing six hundred and forty acres of wild land and again engaging in farming. Robert Rutledge was a benevolent, kind and free-hearted man, and his house was always open to the weary traveler. No one was turned from his door, and he was always willing to assist those in distress. The new comer from the far east was made to feel that he was welcome, and he would render any assistance in his power to help him obtain land and gain for himself a home. He was an earnest and consistent member of the Methodist Episcopal church and was an active worker in that body. His wife was also a member of that body, and both delighted in the service of the Lord's house. He was a great bible student, that book being his constant companion. His death occurred December 9, 1862, and that of his wife June 13, 1864, both passing to their reward while residing in Oregon township.

The subject of this sketch was the eldest in the family. He grew to manhood in Canada, and received such an education as the common schools of that day afforded. He was reared to farm life and made farming his life work. He was married in Toronto, Canada, February 14, 1832, to Miss Elizabeth Foster, a native of Ireland, born July 26, 1814, and daughter of Christopher and Catherine Foster, both of whom were natives of the same country. By this union thirteen children were born, seven of whom are now living. All were born in Canada. Mary died at the age of one year. Robert married Melissa Smith, and died August 18, 1894, at Storm Lake, Iowa. Foster married Caroline Hart, and they reside in Storm Lake, Iowa. Frances married J. F. Hawthorn, and they reside in Oregon township, where they are engaged in farming. John enlisted in the Seventy-fourth Illinois Volunteer Infantry, and served under General Thomas until the close of the war. He married Mrs. Lucy Goodline, but both are now deceased. William married Clara

Blood, and after her decease he married Maggie Fitch. He died at Council Bluffs, Iowa, August 3, 1891. Catherine married Edward Crewell, and they now reside in Orange, California, where he is engaged in fruit growing. Charlotte married Captain Spencer Smith, and they live near Van Horn, Benton county, Iowa, where he is engaged in farming. Thomas S. died in Rockvale township, Ogle county, at the age of sixteen years. Elizabeth married Samuel G. Walker, and they reside in Butler, Missouri. Hester A. finished her education at Mt. Morris College, and for some years was a successful teacher in Ogle county, and later in Buena Vista county, Iowa. She died July 1, 1893, at Battle Creek, Michigan. Emily is engaged in teaching in Ogle county. She is the owner of a good farm in Buena Vista county, Iowa. Edward married Fanny Riesdorf, and they reside in Browns Valley, Minnesota. He is a land owner and county surveyor.

Selling his farm in Canada in the fall of 1855, Mr. Rutledge came to Ogle county, and in the fall of that year settled in Rockvale township, where he bought a farm of three hundred acres and again engaged in farming. It did not take but a little while for him to gather around himself a host of warm-hearted friends, because he was a man of generous impulse, ever ready to do a favor. At the age of nineteen years he united with the Methodist Episcopal church and was ever afterwards one of the faithful workers in that body. A friend of education, he was one of the first to establish a school in his Canadian home, and after his removal to Ogle county he assisted in establishing one of the first schools in his neighborhood. He was a great reader and kept himself well informed on current events, and was never at a loss to express himself. A strong temperance man, he advocated the principles of total abstinence, and lived up to his professions. For about ten years prior to his death, which occurred April 7, 1879, in the city of Oregon, he was in ill health. His wife, who was also a consistent member of the Methodist Episcopal church, died in Oregon August 29, 1875, and both were laid to rest in Rock River View cemetery at that place.

VIRGIL E. REED, who resides on section 13, Nassau township, is a well known and highly respected citizen of Ogle county. He is a native of the county, born in Daysville, September 1, 1841, and is the son of Lyman and Mehitable (Clark) Reed, the former a native of Westfield, Vermont, born December 25, 1809, and the latter a native of Gilson, New Hampshire, born April 24, 1814. In 1835 the parents came west, and in the spring of 1836, settled in Daysville, where he engaged at his trade of carpentering, at which he worked for about twenty years. In the early 'fifties he built a store room and engaged in general merchandising until his death, which occurred January 8, 1866. His wife survived him many years, dying April 28, 1886.

The subject of this sketch lived with his parents until the age of twenty years, in the meantime attending the common schools of the neighborhood as the opportunity was given him. When the war for the union commenced his patriotism was aroused, and he offered his services as one of its defenders. He enlisted in Company F, Thirty-fourth Illinois Volunteer Infantry, and served nearly four years. He first enlisted for a term of three years, but at the end of two years the regiment veteranized, and with the command he enlisted "for three years or during the war." He was in all the battles and campaigns in which his regiment participated until December 31, 1862, when he was taken prisoner at the battle of Stone River, and for six months was confined in Libby prison and at Castle Thunder. He was then exchanged and returned to his regiment, which was encamped on the same battlefield where he was taken prisoner. The Thirty-fourth regiment was in active service until the close of the war, engaging in many battles and skirmishes, and was with Sherman in the march to the sea. It was also in the grand review at Washington. From the time he rejoined it Mr. Reed continued with it until the final muster out at the close of the war. His record as a soldier was a commendable one, and he has a right to look back with a just pride to the days in which as a soldier he endured trials and sufferings that cannot be realized by those who had not the same experience.

On receiving his discharge, Mr. Reed returning to his home in Daysville, but feeling the need of a better education he attended Mt. Morris Seminary for one year, and was then, April 3, 1866, united in marriage with Miss Harriet D. Carpenter, daughter of John and Louise Carpenter. She was also born in Nassau township, the date of her birth being April 8, 1844. Her parents were among the pioneers of the township, and were excellent people, well esteemed in the community. By this union there were four children. Leon yet makes his home with his parents, and is the present assessor of Nassau township. Elmer V. married Emma Carrick, daughter of John and Jane Carrick. She is a native of Ogle county, born in Nassau township. They now reside in Chicago, where he is assistant superintendent of the New York Metropolitan Life Insurance Company. Ernest C. is the superintendent of the Metropolitan Life Insurance Company, and now resides in Chicago. Oscar O. is now engaged in teaching the district school in his home neighborhood. The oldest and youngest sons are also engaged in buying and shipping stock, and assisting in carrying on the home farm.

Mr. Reed has a valuable and well-improved farm of two hundred and seventy-five acres, on which he has made some valuable improvements since the close of the Civil war. As a farmer he has been progressive, ready to adopt any improvement that appealed to his judgment. As a citizen he has always been held in high esteem. Fraternally he is a member of the Grand Army of the Republic and of the Masonic order. Always an advocate of temperance, he has done much to advance its cause.

WILLIAM J. MINNIS, a representative and highly respected farmer of Ogle county, residing on section 26, White Rock township, started out in life with nothing but his own indomitable energy, and his accumulation of this world's goods is attributable to his industry, perseverance and good management. He has won a foremost place among the leading citizens of his community, and has become the owner of four hundred acres of valuable land in White Rock township, two hundred and forty on section 26 and one hundred and sixty on section 25.

Mr. Minnis was born in February, 1831,

near Belfast, County Down, Ireland, and is a son of William and Margaret (Patterson) Minnis, also natives of that county. The father was a farmer and land owner. In the family were five children. (1) Isabella was married in County Down to Carrin Duff and later they emigrated to Canada, where both died, leaving four children, one son, William, and three daughters. One of these, Mrs. Deborah Way, with her two daughters, Eva and Flora, now makes her home with our subject and acts as his housekeeper. (2) Mary wedded Samuel Gilbraith and still resides in Ireland. (3) Lydia married Robert Wright and they came to America at the same time as our subject, locating first in Pittsburg, Pennsylvania. Later they came to Ogle county and owned a farm in Lynnville township, where he died. The sister now makes her home in Rochelle. (4) William J. is the next of the family. (5) James came to America two years after our subject, served all through the Civil war and is now living retired with his sister in Rochelle.

William J. Minnis received a common school education and remained under the parental roof until seventeen years of age. At that time his sister Lydia and her husband made arrangements to come to America, and he accompanied them on horseback to Belfast, a distance of six miles, to see them on board the vessel which they took for Liverpool, England. His sister persuaded him to go with them to Liverpool, so he sent his horse back home by a neighbor. On reaching that place he was again persuaded by her to come to America, which he did without having made any preparations, his only possessions being the clothes he wore and one pound sterling. Turning his back on home, friends and native land, he took passage with Mr. and Mrs. Wright on a sailing vessel, which, after a long and tedious voyage, landed them safely in Philadelphia. As Mr. Wright had a brother in Pittsburg, they proceeded at once to that city. Our subject's first work in the new world was at threshing rye with a flail, for which he received ten bushels of the grain and sold the same for thirty-five cents per bushel. Later he entered the employ of a farmer in Washington, Pennsylvania, for whom he worked five months for eight dollars per month, but did not receive his pay for two years. He next worked in a foundry in Pittsburg for four dollars per week, and out of that amount paid two dollars for board. Later he was employed in glass works at five dollars per week, and after five years spent at various occupations, he came west, locating first in Chicago. As he failed to find employment in that city, he accepted a position with James Garrett, an old companion and associate in Ireland, who was building wire fences for the Chicago, Burlington & Quincy railroad in Bureau county. On the completion of that task, he accompanied Mr. Garrett to his home in Ogle county.

After working here two seasons for wages, Mr. Minnis and his brother-in-law, Mr. Wright, purchased eighty acres of land in Lynnville township, which his sister now owns. For some time he made his home with them, but finally sold his interest to Mr. Wright. Having heard that his father was ill and not expected to live, he returned to Ireland in the spring of 1867, but arrived there too late to see him. He remained in his native land one year, settling up the estate, and then returned with his mother to Ogle county, Illinois. The same fall he bought one hundred and sixty acres where he now resides, and where he has continued to live with the exception of six years spent in Rochelle, during which time he rented the place. On purchasing his farm he went in debt for most of the amount, but so successful has he been that he has since been able to purchase two adjoining tracts, one of eighty and the other of one hundred and sixty acres. He now rents a portion of his land, but personally superintends the rest, and has always followed a most approved system of mixed farming and stock raising, putting considerable stock on the market each year.

While on his visit to Ireland, Mr. Minnis was married in February, 1868, to Miss Agnes Martin, a distant relative and a daughter of William and Grace (Minnis) Martin. Soon after the birth of their only child she died, February 23, 1871, at the early age of twenty-eight years, seven months and twenty-one days. Mr. Minnis has always been true to her memory and has never married again. The daughter was named Agnes for her mother, and on the 8th of October, 1895, she was united in marriage with Henry Carpenter, of Dement township.

Politically Mr. Minnis is a stanch supporter of the Republican party, but has never sought nor accepted any office with the exception of school positions. He is one of the leading members of the Methodist Episcopal church of Rochelle, has taken an active part in its work and been a member of the official board. For a quarter of a century he has belonged to Hickory Grove Lodge, No. 230, I. O. O. F., of Rochelle, and has filled all the chairs, being past grand. He has met with excellent success in life, having not only won a comfortable competence but also has the esteem and confidence of all with whom he has come in contact, either in business or social life.

JOHN SMITH, now living a retired life on his fine farm on section 4, Dement township, and which lies about six miles northeast of the city of Rochelle, has been a valued resident of Ogle county since the spring of 1859. He was born in Lincolnshire, England, May 22, 1825, and there spent his boyhood and youth, being reared to farm life. His educational advantages were very limited, but he has made the best use of the knowledge gained in youth and is now a well informed man. He remained under the parental roof until he nearly attained his majority, and then worked for others, his wages going to the support of the family. He later began work for himself, having in view his future relations in life. He was married in Lincolnshire, England, April 10, 1848, to Miss Ann Tidswell, a native of that shire, where they made their home for two years after marriage. Like all young married couples, they built for themselves many air castles and laid many plans for their future lives. They soon concluded that if their air castles were ever to turn into something more substantial, they must emigrate to the United States, where land was cheap and the opportunity was offered to every one to acquire both wealth and reputation. Accordingly, in 1850, Mr. Smith set sail for New York, where he landed in due time, and made settlement in Ontario county, and there began working by the month. Mrs. Smith joined him the following year. They remained in Ontario county for two years and then removed to Yates county, in the same state, where they remained until 1856, and then came to Illinois, locating in Winnebago county, where Mr. Smith found employment by the month with Terry Holbrook, who was residing near Rockford. For Mr. Holbrook and Mr. Allenton he worked for three years, and then moved to his present place of residence. In 1857, he made his first purchase here, consisting of eighty acres of raw land, on which there had no improvement been made. In 1858 he built on the place a small house, into which he moved with his family in 1859. They lived in that house while he was opening up his farm, and until his means warranted his building a still better one. The second one, however, was not a very pretentious affair, but it served as a home until he was able to build the present large and substantial residence, in which the family has now lived for some years. As his means increased, he added to his landed possessions until he has now about five hundred acres of as fine land as one would care to see, all of which is under cultivation. Large barns have been erected, while various outbuildings dot the place, fruit and ornamental trees have been set out, and everything in and around shows that a master mind has directed and controlled it all.

Mr. and Mrs. Smith are the parents of seven children. Lucy is the wife of George Sanders, a farmer of Flagg township. Sarah is living with her parents. George B. is married, and owns and operates a farm adjoining the old homestead. Jennie is the wife of D. F. Flowers, a carpenter by trade, but who is engaged in farming near Cortland, Nebraska. William T. is married and resides at Woodland, California. Albert E. yet remains at home. Lizzie M. is the wife of Robert Roe, of DeKalb, Illinois.

On the 10th of April, 1898, Mr. and Mrs. Smith celebrated their golden wedding, on which occasion a number of their friends and neighbors, their children and grandchildren gathered to pay their respects and to make glad the hearts of the old couple, whom they all delighted to honor. A silver tea set, and a number of other valuable presents were made to Mr. and Mrs. Smith as a reminder of the pleasant occasion.

Mr. Smith is not a politician in the current acceptance of the term, but he advocates the principles of the Republican party and votes the party ticket. With his good wife he came to the county in time to experience many of the trials and hardships of pioneer life, but he has been signally blessed in worldly goods, and can now look back to the days that are passed and smile at the hardships then endured, having the satisfaction of knowing that "all is well that ends well." He is now comfortably situated, with means to secure not only the necessities of life, but any of the luxuries that his heart might wish. In leaving the old country for the new a wise move was made.

JOHN THOMPSON, a well-known and honored citizen of Lynnville township, is the possessor of a comfortable property which now enables him to lay aside all business cares and enjoy a well-earned rest. His early life was one of toil and due success was not denied him in his chosen occupation. As a young man of twenty-one years he came to America, and with no capital started out in a strange land to overcome the difficulties and obstacles in the path to prosperity. His youthful dreams have been more than realized, and in their happy fulfillment he sees the fitting reward of his earnest toil.

Mr. Thompson is a native of the north of Ireland, born six miles from Belfast, April 19, 1823, of Scotch ancestry. His father, John Thompson, was born on the old homestead in Ireland, in 1797, and in early life married Miss Margaret Patterson, who was born May 1, 1799. Theirs was a long and happy married life of sixty-five years and they were not long separated by the hand of death, as the mother died April 4, 1885, and the father on the 2nd of the following July. In their family were nine children, namely: John, Margaret, Robert, Sarah, William, James, Rabinah, Jane Ellen and Samuel.

Our subject was educated in the schools of his native land and there remained until he attained his majority. On his emigration to the United States, in 1844, he located in Pennsylvania, where he was married, February 6, 1850, to Miss Hannah Blair, who was born in Philadelphia, January 13, 1826. In 1853 they came to Illinois and took up their residence in Ogle county, at which time the present thriving city of Rochelle contained but two log cabins. In partnership with a brother-in-law, Mr. Thompson purchased two hundred and forty acres of land in Dement township, but later he bought a farm on section 31, Lynnville township, where he now resides. He is a stone mason by trade and followed it for many years, in connection with farming, being employed by the day and also doing some contract work, but for the past ten years he has lived retired.

To Mr. and Mrs. Thompson were born nine children, four sons and five daughters, namely: Mary and William both died in infancy. Rabinah J. married Henry Blair, formerly of Pennsylvania, and of the six children born to them, four are now living: Frank, who married Nettie Sechler, of Iowa, and has two children, Elroy and an infant; and Clarence; Addie, and Elmer. Margaret, daughter of our subject, married Isaac G. Tesdor, of Flagg township, Ogle county, and they have six children: C. Edna, Fred G., Howard, Benjamin, Forest and Vance. Samuel wedded Mary E. Spaulding, of Lynnville township, and they have two children: Lawrence J. and Lizzie A. Lydia married William Burgess, of Lynnville township, and died February 1, 1895. Robert W. wedded Mary Lowey, of West Liberty, Iowa, and has two children: Robert and Ruby. Mary E. is living at home with her father. J. William married Hattie Collins, and was killed on the railroad, January 3, 1897. The wife and mother was called to her final rest August 31, 1895. She was a faithful member of the Methodist Episcopal church, to which Mr. Thompson also belongs, and of which he has been one of the trustees. In political sentiment he is an independent Republican.

CHARLES H. CANODE, editor and proprietor of the Mount Morris News, was born in Franklin county, Pennsylvania, October 24, 1872, and is the son of Arnold L. and Amelia Jane (Worley) Canode, the former a native of Washington county, Maryland, and the latter of Franklin county, Pennsylvania. They were the parents of nine children, as follows: James B., who married Flora L. Stoner, of Des Moines, Iowa, but now reside in Mount Morris; Benjamin F.; George B., a druggist of Bushnell, Illinois; Victor E., who married Miss Mae McCoy, of Mount Morris, but now make their home in Toledo, Ohio; Frederick B., who married Miss Anna Coleman, of Chicago, where they make their home; Martin Luther, living in DeKalb, Illinois; Jennie M., who married Theodore F. Haller, editor Forreston Herald; and Mary E., at home. The good mother died December 13, 1889, but the father is still living in Mount Morris, which has been his home since March 18, 1880, when he moved with his family from their Pennsylvania home. By trade he is a contractor and builder, but is now living retired. He is a member of the Lutheran church, in which faith his wife died. Fraternally he is a Mason and an Odd Fellow, and in politics a Democrat. During Governor Altgeld's administration he served as an officer in the state penitentiary at Joliet.

The subject of this sketch was but eight years old when he came with his parents to Mount Morris. In the public schools of the place he received his primary education, attending the same until he was fourteen years old, when he commenced to learn the printer's trade in the office of the Brethren Publishing Company, of Mount Morris. He later spent six years in various newspaper and job offices in Chicago, and was one of the first operators on the Thorne typesetting machine, in which he became an expert. Returning to Mount Morris he established the Mount Morris News, the first issue appearing under date May 19, 1896, and he has since been sole editor and proprietor. Under his management the paper has had a successful career, and has been doing a very satisfactory business.

On the 23d of September, 1896, Mr. Canode was united in marriage with Miss Eva M. Lutz, who was born in Melbourne, Iowa, June 25, 1875, and daughter of John M. and Sarah (Garber) Lutz, the former a native of Pennsylvania, and the latter of Illinois. They moved from State Center, Iowa, to Mount Morris in the spring of 1894. Religiously they are members of the Brethren church. They are the parents of five living children, the others being Samuel G., assistant general freight agent of the Iowa Central railroad, who married Cora B. Foreman, Marshalltown, Iowa; Dr. Ira D., a dentist of Boone, Iowa, who married Myrtle G. Praigg; Amanda G., and Viola A., at home.

Mr. and Mrs. Canode are members of the Lutheran church, and fraternally he is a member of Samuel H. Davis Lodge, No. 96, A. F. & A. M., Mount Morris, and is a charter member of Mount Morris Camp, No. 4596, M. W. A. In politics he is a Democrat.

JOSEPH F. HARLEMAN.—To a student of biography there is nothing more interesting than to examine the life history of a self-made man and to detect the elements of character which have enabled him to pass on the highway of life many of the companions of his youth who at the outset of their careers were more advantageously equipped or endowed. The subject of this review has through his own exertions attained an honorable position and marked prestige among the representative farmers of Ogle county, and is to-day the owner of a large amount of valuable land in White Rock township, his home being on section 10.

Mr. Harleman was born in Northumberland county, Pennsylvania, October 11, 1839, a son of Joshua D. and Elizabeth

JOSEPH F. HARLEMAN.

MRS. ELIZABETH HARLEMAN.

(Fogelman) Harleman, also natives of that state. The father was in early life a shoemaker, but for several years followed farming in Pennsylvania. In the fall of 1852, with his family he came to Illinois by team, our subject's thirteenth birthday occurring while en route. Locating in Marion township, Ogle county, the father purchased land and spent the remainder of his life there with the exception of a few years passed in the town of Oregon, where his wife died in June, 1878. He then returned to the farm and there passed away June 28, 1898, at the advanced age of eighty-six years and seven months. He was a quiet, unassuming man, giving his attention almost wholly to the operation of his farm, and as he met with excellent success in life, he left a good estate. In early life he was a supporter of the Democratic party, but later became an ardent Republican. In his family were four children, of whom our subject is the eldest. Mary C. is now the widow of Robert Sheadle, a resident of Rochelle. Lucy E. was the wife of Charles Hart, of Page county, Iowa, where she died. David S. now owns the old homestead in Marion township.

Mr. Harleman, of this review, was reared on the home farm and received a common school education. On starting out in life for himself he engaged in farming upon rented land in White Rock township. He was married December 29, 1864, to Miss Elizabeth Doebler, a native of Lycoming county, Pennsylvania, and a daughter of Henry and Sarah Doebler, who were also born in that state, and in 1857 removed with their family to Ogle county, Illinois, locating in White Rock township, where the father has since made his home. For the past three years he has resided with our subject. The mother is deceased, her death occurred April 11, 1888. Mrs. Harleman is the second in order of birth in a family of seven children, the others being as follows: Jacob wedded Mary Benner and resided in White Rock township, where he died, leaving five children, Harry A., John B., Ella M., Myrtle B. and Ina E. Mary S. is the wife of Marvin A. Hayner, of Janesville, Wisconsin. Ellen C. is the wife of Henry Rice, Paines Point, Ogle county. Peter B. resides on the old homestead in White Rock township. John A. is a resident of Harlan county, Nebraska. Martin L. makes his home in Ida county, Iowa. As Mr. and Mrs. Harleman have no children of their own, they have adopted Ina E., who is the youngest child of Jacob Doebler and was only a year old at the time her father's death. She has been carefully reared as their own daughter and has found a pleasant home with them.

In March, following their marriage, Mr. and Mrs. Harleman commenced housekeeping upon a rented farm on section 11, White Rock township, comprising one hundred and sixty acres of land, which he later purchased. After living there for ten years he bought an adjoining one hundred and sixty acres on section 11, and made that his home for about the same length of time. He then removed to his present farm on section 10. From time to time as his financial resources have permitted, he has bought more land and now owns nine hundred and sixty acres on sections 3, 9, 10, 11 and 15, White Rock township, having all of the land for two miles and a half south of the village of Holcomb. He has always given considerable attention to the feeding of stock and usually ships from three to five car loads of cattle annually. He now rents all of his land, with the exception of one hundred and sixty acres, which he himself operates. Like many men who have attained success, he started out with nothing, buying his first farm without a dollar of his own to pay for it, and borrowing five hundred dollars from his father to make the first payment. His success is all attributable to his industry and the good judgment he has exercised in business transactions. Politically Mr. Harleman is independent, not being bound by party ties, but voting for principle rather than party.

CHESTER KEYS WILLIAMS, deceased, who was for many years prominently identified with the agricultural and business interests of Ogle county, was born in Brimfield, Hampden county, Massachusetts, January 13, 1818, and was descended from good old colonial stock. The first of the family to come to the new world was Robert Williams, whose early home was in Norwich, England. He settled in Roxbury, Massachusetts, in 1638, and died there in 1693, at an advanced age. From him down to our subject we trace the ancestry through the following: Samuel, a native of England, 1632-1698; Samuel, 1655-1735; Ebenezer, 1690-1755; Rev. Chester, 1702-1755; Rev. Nehemiah, 1719-1800; and Ebenezer, 1777-1856. The last named, who was the father of our subject, married Eliza Whitwell, a daughter of Dr. Whitwell, a surgeon in the Revolutionary war.

Chester K. Williams attended the common schools of his native town and also the Monson Academy, and when his education was completed clerked in his father's store until twenty years of age. In October, 1838, in company with his brother-in-law, Horatio Wales, he came to Ogle county, Illinois, and in Buffalo township they purchased three hundred and twenty acres of land bordering on Buffalo Grove. Until 1851 our subject gave his time and attention to the cultivation and improvement of his land and then rented the farm and engaged in clerking in Buffalo Grove, where he also served as postmaster from 1851 until 1853. In 1855, in partnership with Drs. W. W. Burns and J. H. More, he embarked in the drug business, which they carried on together for two years, but from 1857 until 1866, our subject again followed farming. In the latter year he sold his place and removed to Polo, where he continued to make his home until called from this life, December 8, 1891.

Mr. Williams was twice married, first to Maria P. Anthony, of Avoca, New York, by whom he had four children: Lulu, Kate, Anna and Lucy, all now deceased. Lucy married Homer B. Hitt and to them was born a son, Harold Williams. On the 15th of December, 1886, Mr. Williams married Mrs. Mary McQuaid, a daughter of Charles Wheeler Samis, who was born in New York, January 21, 1861. Her grandfather, Ebenezer Samis, was a sea-faring man who died at the advanced age of ninety-three years. He was married in 1800, at the age of twenty-two or three years, to Ruth Wheeler, who died in December, 1801, and was buried in Trinity church yard, New York city. The Wheelers were an old family on Long Island, and the house in which they lived was built of bricks brought from Holland. Charles W. Samis, the only son of Ebenezer and Ruth (Wheeler) Samis, was married November 28, 1824, to Polly Bently, of Jamestown, New York, who was born October 10, 1803, and died at the age of eighty-three years. She was a member of the Presbyterian church. Her father, Uriah Bently, was a pioneer settler of western New York, where he became an extensive farmer and large land owner. Lakewood and Chautauqua Lake are on grounds formerly owned by him. Much of his property is still in the possession of the family. He was born in Rensselaer county, New York, and was married December 28, 1800, to Nancy Sweet, who died April 21, 1844, at the age of sixty-five years. Mrs. Williams was first married January 1, 1849, to William McQuaid, by whom she had three children, as follows: Charles Samis, a practicing physician, married Emma Kerr, and to them was born a son, Charles William. The Doctor died in Kansas. Amelia is the wife of George W. McCollom. William, a resident of Knob Knoster, Missouri, married Delina Andrews and they have one daughter, Mary, now the wife of James W. Silke, who is connected with the German National Bank, of St. Paul, Minnesota.

An upright and honorable man Mr. Williams had the esteem and confidence of all who knew him, and was frequently honored by his fellow townsmen with positions of trust and responsibility. Besides serving as postmaster of Buffalo Grove, he was supervisor in 1856 and 1857, and again in 1863; was mayor of Polo from 1881 until 1886, and president of the Polo Cemetery Association in 1858. He was president of the first old settlers' meeting, was also their first treasurer, and after the reorganization of the society in 1873, served as its president for two terms. He was also corresponding secretary of the Buffalo Old Settlers' Association, and in 1889 was elected president of the Ogle County Old Settlers' Association. Throughout his career of continued and far-reaching usefulness his duties were performed with the greatest care, and during a long life his personal honor and integrity were without blemish. He was a man of deep convictions, was generous and was never afraid to stand up for those principles which he believed to be right. In all the relations of life he was always found true to every trust reposed in him, and as a citizen was honored and respected by the entire community.

BARBER BROTHERS & CO., Bankers, Polo, Illinois. This business was founded in 1843 by Chanceford R. Barber and Lemuel N. Barber, brothers, under the firm name of C. & L. N. Barber. They came from near Brattleboro, Vermont, and established a store at Buffalo Grove, an early settlement in Ogle county on the old stage route, in which was carried on a general business in merchandise and produce of all kinds, and at the same time meeting the requirements of the locality in the banking line until the first exclusive banking institution of Ogle county was established at Polo in 1855 by Chanceford R. Barber and others under the firm name of Barber, Frisbee & Co.

In 1874 he formed a co-partnership for banking with Isaac H. Trumbauer, under the style of Barber & Trumbauer. Mr. Barber retained his interest in business, and was actively identified in its management until the time of his death, which occurred August 21, 1879. In 1884 Mr. Barber's widow, Mrs. Lucie H. Barber, and his two sons, Bryant H. and Henry D., purchased Mr. Trumbauer's interest and became sole proprietors of the bank, which has since been conducted under the name of Barber Brothers & Co.

The banking house of Barber Brothers & Co. conducts exclusively a general banking business, and the wealth and widely known responsibility of its proprietors give it standing among the substantial financial institutions of the state.

Henry D. Barber was born in Buffalo Grove, Illinois, March 3, 1855, a son of Chanceford R. and Lucie H. Barber, and died October 26, 1896. He was educated in the public schools of Polo and at Harvard University, receiving his business training in his father's bank where he began as a clerk when he was nineteen years old. From the formation of the present firm of Barber Brothers & Co. until his death he was actively engaged in the management of the firm's business. He took an active interest in all matters pertaining to education, and while his exacting duties prevented his acceptance of any public office he was always associated in any movement calculated to develop the highest standard of citizenship.

Mr. Barber was a man of singularly keen judgment, unimpeachable integrity and unusual attainments. His opinion was held in high esteem in prominent financial circles, and he was interested in many successful enterprises of importance. He was a deep student of finance, and his information along these lines was of remarkable range—a fact which, combined with the soundness of his judgment, caused him to be consulted as an authority by those with whom he was brought into contact in the conduct of affairs that took him into the principal business centers of the country.

Mr. Barber was married February 21, 1884, to Miss Mary J. Mix, daughter of Henry A. Mix, a pioneer and business man of Oregon. Mrs. Barber and two children, Lucie R. and Mary C., survive him. A son, Henry M., was born at Polo, November 1, 1885, died February 12, 1891.

Bryant H. Barber, of Barber Brothers & Co., Bankers, Polo, Illinois, is the son of Chanceford R. and Lucie H. Barber. He has lived at Polo since 1856, having been educated at the public schools of that city. His practical business education was received from his father with whom he was associated in the banking and other business. On the death of his father, he, with his mother and brother, Henry D. Barber, became the successors to the business founded in 1843 by Chanceford R. Barber, his father, and he is now actively engaged in the conduct of this business.

STANLEY R. PIERCE, residing on section 12, Dement township, is one of the young and enterprising farmers, stock raisers and breeders of Ogle county, who, in a few brief years, has made a reputation of which many whose years are far more may well be proud. He is a native of the county, and was born in the village of Creston, December 4, 1870. His father, Blanford K. Pierce, was born in the town of Grotten, Oneida county, New York, March 11, 1833, and there grew to manhood, receiving a good education. For some years, in his young manhood, he was engaged in teaching, both in New York and in Illinois. He was united in marriage, in Oneida county, New York, October 29, 1853, with Miss Sarah J. Potter, a native of that county and state. By this union were four sons and four daughters. Of the sons, Dr. C. A. is a veterinary surgeon residing in Elgin, where he is engaged in the practice of his profession. Dr. B. A. is also a veterinary surgeon, practicing his profession in the stock yards of Chicago. A. J. is a business man of Oketo, Kansas. Stanley R. is the subject of this sketch. Of the daughters, Florence L. is a lady of superior education, and has been a professional teacher for some years. She is now connected with the college at Albert Lee, Minnesota. Maud is residing with her parents in Chicago. Winifred is acting as housekeeper for her brother, on the old homestead. Carrie is also at home with her parents, and is now a student in the Chicago University. She was also a teacher for two years.

In 1856 Blanford R. Pierce came to Ogle county and located in the village of Creston, where he engaged in teaching, and later in the grain and stock business. He was a successful dealer in grain and stock, and continued in that line for a number of years. During this time he purchased a tract of land near Creston, and in 1877 moved to the place and commenced the life of a farmer. In addition to general farming he engaged in feeding, buying and shipping stock, and was credited with being one of the best and most successful business men of the county. As his means increased, he purchased more land, and is now the owner of four farms in Ogle county, all of which are well improved.

In 1884 Blanford R. Pierce purchased four head of pure blood polled angus cattle and began breeding the same. He kept increasing the herd from year to year, and built up a very extensive business and a reputation for the purity of his stock second to no breeder in the United States. In 1894 he turned over to his son Stanley a half interest in the business, including the management of his farm near Creston and moved to Chicago, where he purchased residence property, and is now living a retired life.

Since the retirement of the father, our subject has continued to breed and deal in pure blood polled angus cattle, and has now the largest herd of such cattle in the state, if not in the entire country, having fully one hundred head of the purest blood. He annually makes an exhibit of some of his cattle in the stock shows and fairs, and invariably carries off the best premiums. In 1893 he made an exhibit at the World's Fair, Chicago, and in the great Omaha Fair, in both of which places he received the highest awards. In 1895 and in 1896 he exhibited his cattle at the cattle show in Madison Square, New York, competing with the best herds in the whole country, and there received the highest awards, and more premiums and money than any other exhibitor.

Mr. Pierce has made the breeding of polled angus cattle a study from his youth up, and is probably as well posted on the breed as any man in the country. His success has been marvelous, his cattle bringing the highest market price at all times. In 1898 he sold one animal for the munificent sum of one thousand dollars. During the years that have passed, including those in which his father was engaged in the business, some three hundred and fifty fine, pure blood male animals have been sold from the herd, and probably twice as many heifers and cows. Together with the fine stock business, Mr. Pierce makes a business of feeding about one hundred head of steers of common stock annually for the market.

Politically, B. R. Pierce and his sons are all staunch Republicans, and give their support to the men and measures of that party. The subject of this sketch is not a politician, and gives his entire time to the management of his extensive business interests, having shown superior business ability which has given him a reputation which is not confined alone to his native county and state. He is well known as a man of upright character and worth, and has doubtless a bright future before him.

HENRY GUYER, a resident of Polo, Illinois, whose life has been one of activity and usefulness, is now living a quiet and retired life, apart from the turmoil and bustle of a busy world. He was born in Dauphin county, Pennsylvania, in May, 1830. He is a son of George and Magdaline (Tohlman) Guyer. The former was born in Wurtemberg, Germany, where he learned the miller's trade, and came to America in 1828, settling in Pennsylvania, where he plied his trade, until coming west. His death occurred in October, 1854, at the age of sixty-five years, and that of his wife in 1868. Of their ten children, six are still living, the subject of this sketch being seventh in order of birth. Two of the family are residents of Stephenson county, Illinois, one of Carroll county, in the same state, one of Iowa, and another of Kansas. The paternal grandfather of our subject was a miller, and with a fellow-workman, watched a portion of the battle of Waterloo from the roof of a mill, until a cannon ball pierced the structure, causing them to retire.

When Henry Guyer was a boy of fifteen years, he came west with his parents, on the steamer "Belle of the West," which they boarded at Pittsburg, Pennsylvania. When about seventy-five miles below Cincinnati, Ohio, the steamer took fire and was entirely destroyed. One hundred and twenty lives were lost, also the boat's freight, including household goods belonging to passengers. Our subject jumped into a small boat, followed by his parents and the rest of the family, some of whom fell into the water, but were quickly drawn up into the boat. With nothing but a board for a paddle, our subject succeeded in landing the family, and immediately returned to the scene of the disaster and rescued four girls, Blessing by name, who afterwards became warm friends of the family, frequently interchanging visits. A larger boat carried the passengers to St. Louis without remuneration, and from there they were carried to Savanna, Illinois, their transportation being furnished by a number of kind-hearted citizens of St. Louis.

On reaching Savanna, the Guyer family went directly to Haldane, Ogle county, where, for a time, they suffered severely, owing to their losses. His father struggled along and finally obtained work, which, after a time, enabled him to purchase a farm of forty acres, on which he lived until his death, in 1854. While in Haldane our subject learned blacksmithing, and shortly afterwards opened a shop in Brookville. Eight years later he moved to Pine Creek township and worked at his trade for two and a half years, and in the fall of 1860 moved to Polo, Illinois, continuing in the same line of business until 1874, when he retired, and has since lived quietly on a very comfortable income, the results of his frugality and good management.

On the 11th of January, 1855, Mr. Guyer was united in marriage to Miss Barbara Lehmen, a native of Blair county, Pennsylvania, and the youngest of eight children of John and Mary (Secrist) Lehmen, who came west on the 1st of October, 1852, the father purchasing two farms in Pine Creek township. His death occurred in 1875, at the age of seventy-seven years.

Mr. and Mrs. Guyer are the parents of eight children, five of whom are living. The eldest, John C., is a commercial traveler and makes his home in Freeport, Illinois. He married Dollie Witters, and they have two children, Ruby and Ray. The second child, Sevilla, married M. T. Myers, of Denver, Colorado, and they have three children, Clarence, Guy and Odesia. The third child of our subject, Harry L., is a traveling salesman, whose wife is deceased, and he makes his home with his parents. Addie Ann married Charles Carpenter, an attorney of Rome, Georgia, and they have one child, Ralph. Will C. is in the grocery business at Fort Dodge, Iowa.

In politics Mr. Guyer is a Republican, and takes a deep interest in all affairs of state. He is a member of the United Brethren church, and his genial manner and courtesy, and his high personal worth, have won for him a circle of friends that is limited only by his circle of acquaintances.

ALFRED MALONE, who resides on section 17, Leaf River township, is a well known citizen of the county, owning and operating a fine farm of two hundred and forty acres, a part of which lies in section 18. He is a native of the county, and was born March 8, 1851. His father, James Malone, was born in Washington county, Maryland, in March, 1817, and there grew to manhood. In 1843 he came to Ogle county and located in Pine Creek township, where he entered government land and opened up a farm. As his means increased he added to his landed possessions in that township, and there resided for thirteen years. He was married in this county, to Miss Ellen Patterson, a native of Ireland, where seven years of her life were spent, and then emigrated to Maryland with her parents, where she received her education. She is a daughter of John Patterson, who came from Maryland to Ogle county in 1843.

In 1856 James Malone bought the farm and located where our subject now resides, a farm which was opened in 1836 by Mortimer Hunt, who purchased the land from the government. Four years later, Mr. Malone moved to a farm near Leaf River, which was pre-empted by his wife's father, and there he spent the last years of his life, dying December 25, 1888. His wife survived him about ten years, dying December 3, 1898. They were the parents of three children, the others, besides our subject, being Kate, wife of James Wilson, of Leaf River township, and Mary, wife of Marcus Hess, of the same township. James Malone was a man of some prominence, serving in several offices of trust and honor, including assessor and justice of the peace, serving in the latter office a number of years.

Alfred Malone grew to manhood in Leaf River township, and when not in school, was assisting his father in farm work. His primary education was received in the Lightsville school, and at Rock River Seminary, Mt. Morris, he completed his school life. After discontinuing his studies in school, he engaged in teaching in connection with farming, teaching in all about seven winter terms, his summers being taken up with work on the farm.

On the 12th of September, 1878, Mr. Malone was united in marriage, in Mt. Morris township, with Miss Belle Cornell, a native of Ogle county, and daughter of David and Elizabeth (Hopwood) Cornell, of Maryland, who came to Illinois in 1843, being among the earliest settlers of Ogle county from the state of New York. By this union six children have been born—Kate, James, Roy, Nora, Florence and Mamie, all of whom are yet living save Roy, who died January 26, 1899.

Mr. and Mrs. Malone began their domestic life on the farm where they reside, the farm being rented for several years. He first purchased one hundred and sixty acres of the home place, and later added eighty acres, giving him a valuable farm of two hundred and forty acres, which he has under a high state of cultivation. Commencing life as he did with but little means and on a rented farm, he has certainly met with well-merited success, which is due to his own industry, assisted by his estimable wife. His farm is one of the best in Leaf River township, and he is classed among the most substantial farmers of the county, one who keeps fully up with the times.

Politically Mr. Malone is a Democrat on national issues, believing firmly in the principles of the party, but on local issues he votes independently, recognizing the man and not the party name he wears. He was elected and served as road commissioner six years, for five years was township collector, and in 1880 was elected supervisor from his township, and being re-elected, served eight consecutive years, during which time he was on a number of important committees and made a very useful member. His influence has ever been exerted in favor of good schools, and he has given of his time as a member of the school board, serving both as president and clerk of his district. A lifelong resident of the county, he has a large acquaintance in all parts of it, and wherever known he is held in the highest esteem.

GEORGE W. SWAN, a well known farmer and stock raiser of Rockvale township, was born in Chemung county, New York, in 1836, and came to Ogle county, Illinois, with his parents two years later. He is the son of Henry W. and Rachel (Westlake) Swan, the former born in Chemung county, New York, in 1799, and the latter in Newburg, Orange county, New York, September 16, 1812. While residing in the east, Henry Swan was engaged in the mercantile business, and on coming west he first engaged in the same line of business. Later he ran a grist mill and distillery, in which lines he was quite successful. He built the first log house in Byron township, and was well known as an enterprising citizen of the county. He died while yet in the prime of life, October 22, 1854. His wife survived him many years, dying May 9, 1879. They were the parents of seven children. (1) Benjamin died in infancy. (2) George W. is the subject of this sketch. (3) Annie Floyd married Henry Harding Patrick, and they had five children, as follows: Maurice Lee, born September 26, 1863, died August 22, 1889; Carrie L., born January 4, 1865, married William W. Light, June 16, 1887; Susan R., born December 11, 1870, married William VanArsdale, August 4, 1892; Henry Swan, born September 6, 1872, died April 3, 1884; Floyd Harding, born January 15, 1877. (4) Mary died when three years of age from the effects of a scald. (5) Louise, born December 14, 1845, was married June 16, 1864, to James M. Babcock, then a first lieutenant in the federal army. (6) Morris A., a farmer of Bridgewater, Dakota, was born March 22, 1848. He married Miss Fanny Kepner, and they have three children, namely: Charles James, born January 27, 1875; Floyd A., February 22, 1879; and Mary Rachel, April 25, 1887. (7) Charles E., born October 5, 1852, is a wealthy physician and banker in South Chicago, where he married Huldah Austerman. They have one child living, Nellie R., and two deceased, Louise and Charles Henry.

When Henry W. Swan first came west the country was in its primitive state. On the establishment of the land office at Dixon, his brother, James Swan, was appointed receiver, and he acted as his deputy. A band of outlaws known as the "prairie bandits" soon infested the country, giving honest people much uneasiness. Gold was required by the government in payment for land, and from time to time it was sent by stage to La Salle, and from thence to St. Louis by boat. On one occasion the stage was held up by the bandits and considerable money was taken. There were very few roads laid out, and our subject remembers well, when a mere boy, in going to Freeport over the almost trackless prairie, there being no roads until the opening of the Yellow creek brewery, three miles from the village as it then was. The country then abounded in game of all kind.

The subject of this sketch attended the subscription schools of Ogle county until he was eighteen years of age, and in 1857 took a commercial course at Rockford. He was united in marriage, January 11, 1860, with Miss Ida Louise Read, born October 23, 1841, and daughter of Hiram and Rhoda (Dewey) Read, the former born April 20, 1806, in Cornish, New Hampshire, and the latter September 30, 1803, in Oxford, New Hampshire. They were married March 26, 1837, and were early settlers of Ogle county. Hiram Read was the son of David and Hannah (Gerrold) Read, natives of Cornish, New Hampshire, who were blessed with three children—Jacob, Philip and Hiram. Mrs. Read was the daughter of Abel and Rhoda (King) Dewey, and was one of eleven children, namely: Lucy, Joanna, Timothy, Rhoda, Clara, Mary, Martha, Henry, Almisee and two who died in infancy. Her father died June 29, 1842, and her mother, May 25, 1853. The great-grandfathers of Mrs. Swan and Admiral Dewey were brothers.

Soon after his marriage, Mr. Swan, with Hiram Read, purchased land in Rockvale township, and opened up a farm. In the years that have passed, he has sown and reaped, and success has in a measure crowned his efforts. Five children came to bless his union with Miss Read. Stanley H., born July 12, 1862, died April 25, 1863. Ardelle Louise, born August 12, 1864, is the wife of Frank Canode, and they reside in Marion township. They have one child, Eva E., born August 7, 1895. Ina Lillian died when three years of age. Annie M., born January 19, 1865, married Thomas Morton, December 15, 1886, and they have four children, as follows: George A., born September 10, 1887; Harry T., February 4, 1890; Helen L., August 15, 1892; and Nellie M., March 26, 1895. Mrs. Morton died February 3, 1898. Henry W., born January 22, 1869, is residing at home and has charge of the home farm. Mary R., born November 22, 1875, married Ezra T. Stoner, March 15, 1896.

Recognizing the advantages of a good education, Mr. Swan has, in addition to the common-school course, given all his children the benefit of a high-school education in Oregon. Mary attended the Wells Training School, and a preparatory school for teachers at Oregon, and also took her teacher's examination at that place. Until her marriage, she was a successful teacher in the county.

In politics, Mr. Swan is a Republican, and although his ambitions do not run along the line of office holding, he has served for several years as school director, with great benefit to the community. His farm, on section 25, Rockvale township, is in an excellent state of cultivation, the natural result of years of good management and sound judgment. He and his wife are genial and hospitable people, and they have many friends in the county.

SAMUEL GIBSON, whose home is on section 20, White Rock township, is a representative of the farming and stock raising interests of Ogle county and is one of the prominent and influential citizens of his community. He was born in Kirkcudbrightshire, Scotland, January 4, 1828, and is a son of William and Agnes Henry Gibson, who were of pure Scotch ancestry and representatives of families who had for generations made their home in that locality. The father, who was a farmer by occupation, spent his entire life there. His children were James, William, Thomas, Robert, Alexander, John, Elizabeth, Mary Ann, Agnes and Jane.

In the county of his nativity our subject grew to manhood and received a common school education at Battle high school. On starting out in life for himself, he engaged in farming and contract work on county contracts. He was married in Scotland, in September, 1848, to Miss Margaret Adamson, a daughter of James Adamson. Our subject had a brother, John Gibson, who came to America in 1845, and located in Pine Rock township, Ogle county, Illinois. Returning to Scotland on a visit in 1860, he persuaded our subject to accompany him on the return trip. The latter had already decided to emigrate to America, and hastening his preparations for departure, they crossed the Atlantic together and proceeded at once to Ogle county. Here he purchased a farm of one hundred and sixty acres on section 20, White Rock township, and also the stock, crops, implements, etc., paying for the same fifty-five hundred dollars. Although he went in debt at that time for the greater part of the amount, he has been so successful that he is now owner of four hundred and ten acres of highly improved and well cultivated land. He is still actively engaged in farming and stock raising, feeding a number of cattle each season, and has made horse breeding an important branch of his business. He believes in the Clydesdale breed, from the fact that weight and quality combined make them ready sellers, they are more intelligent, more durable, more courageous and better action and color than the other heavy draft breeds. He has followed a wise and judicious system of mixed farming, dividing the risks and profits among varied interests rather than staking all in one enterprise.

To Mr. and Mrs. Gibson were born eleven children, six sons and five daughters, of whom six are now living, namely: Jane, wife of Harvey Haselton, of Carroll county, Iowa; Agnes, wife of William Prile, of Carroll county, Iowa; John, who is still on the home farm and operates the same in connection with his brother Robert; James, a farmer of Winnebago county, Illinois; and Samuel, a farmer of White Rock township. Those deceased are William, who married and removed to Colorado but finally returned to Ogle county, where he died in 1896, at the age of thirty-seven years; Isabella, who died in early womanhood; Mary Ann, who died at the age of four years, and Annie, who died at the age of two years. One baby boy who died in infancy. The wife and mother was called to her final rest October 8, 1881.

Since becoming an American citizen, Mr. Gibson has been a stanch supporter of the Republican principles, but has never sought political preferment, desiring rather to devote his entire time and attention to his business interests. With the exception of school trustee, he has declined all offices. In early life he united with the Presbyterian church, of which he is still a consistent and faithful member. He is one of the successful and respected citizens of his county, and the keynote to prosperity is industry, economy and perseverance, for he started out in life for himself empty-handed and the success that he has achieved is due entirely to his own well-directed efforts.

CHESTER C. HARRINGTON, now living a retired life in Lee county, Illinois, but who for years was a prominent citizen of Ogle county, was born August 22, 1813, at Sandy Hill, on the Hudson, New York, and is the son of Rev. E. Harrington, a Baptist minister, who for a number of years was located in Cayuga county, New York, but who came west in 1840, and soon after located in Burlington, Racine county, Wisconsin. His death occurred in 1842, while his good wife preceded him to her heavenly home about two years. The maternal grandfather of our subject was a soldier in the Revolutionary war.

Chester C. Harrington was educated in the schools of Cayuga county, New York, and in his youth studied surveying, and for a few years before coming west followed the profession of surveying in the east. He also for a time engaged in teaching in the schools of his native state. He came to Chicago in 1834, and in 1837 came to what was then Ogle county, but is now a part of Lee county, just across the river from Grand Detour. On first coming to the county he followed his profession as a surveyor for a time, and engaged in other work. It was, however, but a short time before he purchased a half section of land on which was a small log cabin, but on which no other improvements had been made. The lumber for his house he hauled from Chicago. On that place he has since continued to live with the exception of fourteen years spent in Grand Detour, living retired.

On the 14th of November, 1844, Mr. Harrington was united in marriage with Miss Zarina Chamberlin, a native of Genesee county, New York, born December 5, 1820, and daughter of Cyrus and Pluma (Burton) Chamberlin, both of whom were natives of Vermont, but who removed to New York at an early day. Cyrus Chamberlin followed farming in the east, but believing the prairies of the west afforded better opportunities for the enterprising man, he came west, landing in Grand Detour, July 4, 1835. He at once took up nine hundred acres of land across the river in Lee county and then returned east. In September, 1835, he was again back in this region. Soon after his return to this locality he established a saw mill which he operated in connection with his farm for many years. He finally moved to the village of Grand Detour, where he lived retired until his death, February 22, 1881, at the age of ninety-one years. He was a man of good intellectual and executive ability, and enjoyed the love and esteem of a large circle of friends. Two brothers of his wife, Oliver and Thomas Burton, served in the war of 1812, both attaining the rank of colonel.

To Mr. and Mrs. Harrington four children were born. Ingalls I. and Inez I. were twins. The former died in infancy, but the latter is yet living and makes her home in Grand Detour. She is a cultured and refined lady, with many friends wherever known. Chester Eugene is operating the old home farm in Lee county. Cyrus C. died in 1881, at the age of twenty-one years.

Mr. Harrington now makes his home with his son Chester on the old homestead, and, at the age of eighty-five years, is in full possession of all his mental faculties. He has been a very active man in the past, and quite prominent in the communities in which he has made his home. In politics he is a stanch Republican. He was always an anti-slavery man, and in the days of slavery was one of the conductors on the underground railroad and assisted in the escape of more than one slave. For a number of years he served as supervisor of Nachusa township, Lee county. He has also been assessor, collector and school director, and served in other minor official positions. He was always a strong temperance man, and was a charter member of the first temperance society formed in this section, and for years was its secretary. During the Civil war he was a member of the Union League. In religious belief he is a Baptist. For sixty-one years he has been a resident of the vicinity where he now lives, and he is well known throughout Lee and Ogle counties as a man of strict honor and integrity, and his friends are numerous in both counties.

JOHN C. PHELPS, deceased, for years occupied an enviable position among the business men of Rochelle. He was born in Lockport, Niagara county, New York, March 25, 1830, and was educated in the schools of that place. He grew to manhood in his native state and acquired a good business training. In 1855 he came to Illinois, located in Freeport, Stephenson county, and there engaged in business, in which he continued for some years. From Freeport, he removed to Rochelle, and engaged in the general merchandise business, and later became a grain dealer. He also started the First National Bank of Rochelle, and conducted it for one year, and then sold to other parties. Subsequently he purchased and sold bankrupt stock of goods, general merchandise of every description.

On the 26th of December, 1855, Mr. Phelps was united in marriage with Miss I. Frances Winchester, of Freeport, Illinois, formerly of Jersey Shore, Pennsylvania, who preceded him to Freeport one month. She is a daughter of Stephen and Nancy (Fuller) Winchester, both of whom were natives of Pennsylvania, and the parents of thirteen children, eight of whom grew to maturity—Stephen, Edmund, Elijah, William, Sarah, Mary, Alvira and I. Frances. The father, who was born in 1780, died in 1849, and his wife soon afterwards. He was also a general merchant.

To Mr. and Mrs. Phelps four children were born, one of whom died in infancy. Josephine I. married Charles Hurd, of Rochelle, by whom she had four children, two sons and two daughters—Pauline F. G. H., Helen H., Charles and Arthur H. The eldest son, Arthur Alcott, married Grace M. Countryman, youngest daughter of Harvey Countryman, of Rochelle, and they have two sons—Harvey John and Raymond Arthur. He is doing a successful business in the hardware line, and also has an interest in the Ogle County Telephone Company, of Rochelle, of which he is general manager. Fraternally he is a member of Star Lodge, No. 169, K. P., of Rochelle, and of Willow Camp, No. 44, M. W. A. The third son, John Clement, died at the age of eleven years.

John C. Phelps died at his home in Rochelle, December 16, 1896, and his remains were laid to rest in the cemetery of that city. He left not only a loving wife and family to mourn his loss, but a large circle of friends and acquaintances. He was a good man and tried to live right before his fellowmen.

GEORGE WATERBURY, a substantial farmer residing on section 10, Buffalo township, has been actively engaged in farming and stock raising in Ogle county a period of more than half a century, having become a citizen of the county in October, 1847. He was born in Beaver Kill, Sullivan county, New York, November 23, 1834. The family are of English ancestry and originally settled in Connecticut, from which state Daniel Waterbury, the grandfather of our subject, emigrated in an early day to New York, where David S. Waterbury, the father, was born. The latter grew to manhood in his native state and there married Miss Emeline Huntley, a native of Delaware county, New York, and daughter of Squire Huntley, of that county.

Daniel S. Waterbury, by trade, was a tanner and currier, which occupation he followed in early life. He also learned the carpenter trade, and was later a contractor on the Erie canal. In 1847 he came to Ogle county, coming by way of the Erie canal and the lakes to Chicago, and from thence by team to this county. He came here by the advice of some friends who had located here, and who had great confidence in the future of the county and state. On his arrival he made a permanent settlement in Buffalo township, entering a tract of land, a portion of which is comprised in the farm of our subject. The whole country was then an almost unbroken wilderness, settlers being few and far between. From the adjacent timber he secured his sleepers and joists, and from Chicago hauled the siding for his house, which was raised November 8, 1847. It was 24 x 34 feet, and a one-story structure. The farm he at once commenced to improve, and in due time had a valuable and well improved place. On that farm he spent the remainder of his life, dying soon after the commencement of the Civil war. His wife survived him many years, passing away in May, 1895.

The subject of this sketch came to this county a lad of thirteen years, and assisted his father in opening up the farm. His educational advantages were not of the best, and his school life was limited. With his parents he remained until grown to manhood, when he commenced life for himself, having purchased eighty acres of his present farm, which he set about improving. He also became interested in a threshing machine about that time, and in the years that have followed has been engaged in the business of threshing grain. He now owns an interest in a steam thresher, and was one of the first to use one in this section of the state.

In 1859 Mr. Waterbury went to Michigan, and in Sanilac county was united in marriage with Miss Anna M. Oldfield, a native of England, and daughter of Anthony Oldfield, who left England to make a home for himself and family in the United States. He first located in Cincinnati, where he was later joined by his wife and family. He subsequently removed to Michigan, where he engaged in the lumber business. While residing in Cincinnati Mrs. Waterbury received the greater part of her education. To Mr. and Mrs. Waterbury three children were born. David E. is married and now resides in Rockford, Illinois. Hattie E. is the wife of Robert C. Trollope, who is operating the Waterbury homestead. Henry R. is married and lives in Polo. David E. has two children — Ethel A. and Kenneth. Mrs. Trollope has three children, Anna E., Charles R. and Elwin B. Henry R. has one child, a daughter, Marian.

After their marriage Mr. and Mrs. Waterbury commenced their domestic life on the farm which he had already commenced to improve, and there their three children were born. In his farming operations he has met with fair success, and has now one of the best farms in Buffalo township, a township noted for its good farms. For some time Mrs. Waterbury was an invalid, and was taken by her husband to Battle Creek, Michigan, for medical treatment. Not receiving the help expected from the noted institution at that place, with the hope that a visit among her old friends and relatives in Sanilac county might do her good, she was taken there, but it was without avail. The dread disease had taken too strong a hold, and she succumbed to the inevitable, dying at her old home where her marriage occurred, and from which she left a happy bride.

Politically Mr. Waterbury is an independent, though usually supporting the Republican ticket. He is in thorough sympathy with every movement for the betterment of humanity and in the development of his adopted county he has borne his part. His residence here of fifty-two years has brought him in contact with many of the best people of the county, and wherever known he is held in the highest respect.

INDEX.

Alden, Timothy W	29
Anderson, Alexander	189
Anderson, James D.	196
Andrew, George H	33
Andrus, Leonard	317
Ayres, Charles	78
Bacon, Francis	117
Baer, Elmer E.	170
Barber Brothers	479
Barkman, William H.	418
Baxter, Delos W.	385
Beck, John	154
Bellows, Levi M.	285
Betebenner, Charles H.	130
Binkley, Alfred R.	325
Bird, William	14
Bisline, John	60
Bowers, Elias G.	74
Bowerman, Dr. Solomon B.	225
Bowman, Cornelius	93
Braden, M. J.	460
Brand, George	312
Brewster, Mortimer S.	193
Brown, Albert F.	52
Brown, S. L.	312
Bull, Matthew P.	190
Bunn, William C.	24
Burright, Milton	21
Bush, Charles	237
Buterbaugh, Edward C.	75
Buttell, Adam	103
Canning, William	59
Campbell, James	153
Campole, Charles H.	424
Carr, George W.	126
Carr, James Wesley	134
Case, Daniel	259
Cass, Aron	280
Cater, Jesse F.	427
Cheeseman, Charles F.	104
Clark, A. D	407
Clark, William M.	304
Clayton, James M.	171
Clinton, John W.	29
Coffman, Addison	303
Coffman, Henry	73
Countryman, James A.	361
Cooper, Peter	109
Crawford, Frank J	129
Crill, Orlando F	418
Crill, M. J.	461
Crul, Thomas	411
Cunningham, W. H	260
Davis, John H	149
Davis, Solomon	159
Deuth, Fred J.	289
Dicus, George W	442
Dieffenbaugh, William C	96
Dixon, Thomas	80
Dodds, Capt. William T.	112
Domer, Samuel	323
Donaldson, James	132
Donaldson, James H	111
Doughty, Benjamin	239
Drexler, George	42
Dutcher, Edward F	271
Dysinger, Rev. Holmes	286
Ellis, William	267
Etnyre, Daniel	459
Ettinger, Martin L	50
Evans, Ezra H.	37
Fisher, Charles	306
Frantz, Thomas P	384
Frederickson, Fred.	412
Frey, Martin A	321
Frint, Charles	234
Gammon, J. G.	384
Gardner, Clarence E.	403
Garman, Michael	213
Garnhart, Charles W.	250
Garnhart, George W.	40
Gibson, Samuel	186
Gould, Dr. William W.	395
Govig, Peter	425
Graehling, Henry	322
Graham, John	291
Griffin, Hugh L.	430
Guest, Thomas	388
Gugo, Solistine	301
Guyer, Henry	482
Haller, Charles M	46
Hammer, George W.	348
Hammond, William A.	349
Harleman, J. F.	452
Harrington, Chester C	487
Harrison, Alfred	242
Harner, Emanuel M.	296
Hartwig, John	413
Hastings, John S	221
Hays, Josiah A	92
Hedrick, Benjamin F.	34
Helm, John H.	246
Hettiger, George	229
Hewitt, Jacob	460
Hibarger, David F	423
Hiestand, George B	319
Hiscock, George	449
Hitt, Robert R.	1
Howe, F. W.	25
Huggans, Edmond D.	295
Johnson, C. W.	251
Johnson, Robert N.	102
Johnston, Timoleon O	243
Jones, Alvin	152
Jones, Mrs Mary I	251
Jones, Milo A.	212
Jones, George W.	296
Judson, Dr. James H	127
Kappman, Jacob	185
Kaney, August	363
Kidder, Nelson B.	203
Kindell, John F	168
King, R. M.	456
Klein, Charles	386
Knapp, Batalla	139
Knodle, Samuel	268
Knodle, Samuel	176
Korf, August J	240
Koser, John S.	101
Krebbs, Dr. Jacob I	238
Kridler, Burton D	249
Lamont, David H	308
Landers, Ziba A	20
Lawrence, Johnson	90
Lawsher, Spencer	362
Lebo, John J.	95
Lewis, Frederick H	82
Lewis, Silas W.	275
Light, John	236
Long, Andrew F.	155
McCann, Rev. John J.	436
McCrea, Alfred B.	322
McCrea, John A.	356
McDaid, Guilford	117
McGuffin, Samuel S	27
Magne, James H.	186
Mahone, Alfred	183
Marshall, Reuben S	108

INDEX

Mason, James I............ 158
Matteson, Clark K.......... 163
May, Col. D. C............. 4 0
Mendenhall, Dr. A. L....... 364
Mettler, Ira............... 380
Mettler, William J......... 394
Meyers, Henry R............ 266
Meyers, Peter R............ 64
Meyers, Peter S............ 114
Miller, Elijah H........... 438
Miller, J. H............... 244
Miller, Michael............ 11
Miller, William H.......... 241
Minnis, William J.......... 467
Moore, Amos F.............. 119
More, Rev. James H......... 383
Moring, Lewis.............. 150
Morris, Howard A........... 343
Muinix, Homer W............ 15
Mumma, Samuel P............ 344
Murray, George............. 462
Myers, James............... 430
Myers, Joseph M............ 263

Newcomer, Andrew........... 194
Newcomer, Charles.......... 287
Newcomer, Dr. David........ 137
Nettz, John R.............. 389
Nichols, John and James.... 290
Nicodemus, Cyrus........... 171
Noble, Charles B........... 354
Norton, Orlo W............. 183
Nye, John H................ 181

O'Kane, Joseph............. 149
Otto, Louis J.............. 248

Palmer, William I.......... 160
Pankhurst, Dr. James....... 66
Parks, Henry A............. 222
Peck, Franklin F........... 329
Perkins, George W.......... 389
Petrie, Lewis.............. 298
Phelps, John C............. 458
Philbrook, Prof. C. F...... 445
Phillips, John H........... 463
Pierce, Stanley R.......... 480
Preston, Noah.............. 227

Poole, George.............. 191
Powell, Samuel W........... 77
Preston, Gardner S......... 346
Price, Edward E............ 65
Price, Jacob H............. 129

Quest, William............. 421

Reed, George M............. 382
Reed, Virgil E............. 466
Revell, Wallace............ 320
Reynolds, John............. 98
Rhodes, George R........... 247
Rice, Isaac................ 370
Rice, Jacob................ 74
Rice, Joseph I............. 353
Rice, William.............. 495
Roe, Dr. Malcolm C......... 61
Rolfe, Squire.............. 135
Rosecrance, E. L........... 389
Royer, John G.............. 151
Rutledge, Thomas P......... 465

Schelling, Henry........... 309
Schneider, Charles......... 91
Schrader, Henry J.......... 175
Schrader, Henry............ 233
Schryver, Erastus W........ 224
Seibert, Benjamin D........ 311
Shafer, George W........... 46
Sharer, Henry.............. 396
Sharland, George H......... 373
Shaver, Nicholas N......... 240
Sheffield, Amos A.......... 140
Shelly, John............... 276
Shoemaker, Harvey M........ 166
Shuart, Stephen B.......... 146
Shumway, Romanzo G......... 426
Sims, Sr., Daniel.......... 177
Small, John................ 31
Smith, Francis A........... 208
Smith, George.............. 261
Smith, John................ 409
Smith, John L.............. 118
Smith, Peter............... 325
Snyder, Dr. L. F........... 54
Snyder, Dr. Jerome B....... 401
Southworth, John W......... 124

Southworth, T. G........... 457
Spalding, John F........... 277
Speaker, Noah.............. 26
Spencer, Isaac............. 187
Spink, Andrew C............ 411
Spoor, Austin W............ 314
Stabley, Rev. Andrew....... 204
Stahlhut, William.......... 81
Stauffer, Daniel H......... 316
Steffa, Jacob.............. 41
Steffa, William H.......... 331
Stires, J. Chester......... 56
Stocking, Horace........... 440
Stocking, Lewis............ 391
Stocking, William.......... 299
Stroh, Rev. N. J........... 216
Sullivan, Dennis........... 28
Swan, George W............. 484
Swank, Jacob F............. 243
Swingley, Michael N........ 70

Taylor, James.............. 431
Thomson, David............. 47
Thomas, Henry L............ 89
Thomas, Joshua............. 122
Thompson, John............. 470
Tobias, Daniel H........... 42
Treat, Dr. Gilbert B....... 406
Trumball, Asaph M.......... 44
Trump, Isaac............... 370

Waite, Judson A............ 63
Wales, Horatio............. 57
Waterbury, George.......... 489
Watts, William............. 340
Weaver, Abraham F.......... 302
West, McFarlen, J.......... 252
Williams, Chester K........ 478
Wilson, James P............ 173
Windle, George............. 116
Woodburn, James C.......... 48
Woodin, Hiram.............. 354
Wolf, Benjamin............. 279
Woodcock, John B........... 241
Wragg, Peter B............. 10

Young, Daniel W............ 228
Youngs, Ogden B............ 350

Zick, Frederick............ 84

www.ingramcontent.com/pod-product-compliance
Lightning Source LLC
Chambersburg PA
CBHW020832020526
44114CB00040B/562